"I have also been stubborn in refusing to do certain types of roles that feed into that distortion, that feed into that horrible misrepresentation [of Latinos]—the drug dealer of the month, that kind of garbage. I don't know if I wouldn't have done those roles if I had been starving, but it never quite came to it."

—Hector Elizondo, *Los Angeles Times*

"I'm Puerto Rican and that in itself seems to mean spitfire to so many people in Hollywood. It's tough enough getting roles being a woman, but being both female and Puerto Rican makes it all that much harder. I think the barriers, the stereotypes, actually are finally falling apart. I want to show that I can play several kinds of roles, not just Latinas, though I look forward to good Latina parts."

—Rita Moreno, *San Francisco Chronicle*

"This film about our people [*Stand and Deliver*] will touch the nation. It shows we can achieve anything we want. Being able to make a film like this is the finest moment of my life."

—Edward James Olmos, *Los Angeles Times*

"There's a whole new breed . . . They are just well-trained actors who just happen to be Hispanic."

—Elizabeth Peña, *Los Angeles Herald Examiner*

"I became a movie extra just to get money to eat and to lose myself as a face in the crowd. I never had that ambition to be an actor, but it was like a chain reaction. One day a director asked if I could say a line, and I did it."

—Fernando Rey, *Los Angeles Times*

"I don't want to be typed as a Latin or anything else . . . When the movies get a Latin girl they always try to make a spitfire out of her, another Lupe Velez. That's not any more typical of a Latin girl than Betty Hutton is of an American girl."

—Lina Romay, *Hollywood Studio Magazine*

"My research showed that men in that period wore bloomers, ruffles and face powder. Errol [Flynn] took one look and said, 'Not for old Dad.' So I made up my own period . . . I got an Academy Award® and he was beautifully dressed. So much for authenticity."

—Bill Tra

HISPANICS
IN HOLLYWOOD

A Celebration of 100 Years in Film and Television

LUIS REYES and PETER RUBIE

LONE EAGLE PUBLISHING COMPANY™
1024 North Orange Drive
Hollywood, California 90038
Tel: 323.308.3400 or 800.FILMBKS
A division of IFILM^{SM} Corp., www.ifilm.com

Printed in the United States of America

Cover and book design by Carla Green

Library of Congress Cataloging-in-Publication Data

Reyes, Luis.
   Hispanics in Hollywood : an encyclopedia of film and television / Luis Reyes
and Peter Rubie.
      p. cm.
   Includes bibliographical references.
   ISBN 1-58065-025-2
      1. Hispanic Americans in motion pictures—Encyclopedias. 2. Hispanic Americans
on television—Encyclopedias. 3. Hispanic American actors—Biography—Dictionaries.
I. Rubie, Peter. II. Title.

   PN1995.9.H47 R49 2000
   791.43'089'68—dc21   00-034884

Lone Eagle books may be purchased in bulk at special discounts for promotional or educational purposes. Special editions can be created to specifications. Inquiries for sales and distribution, textbook adoption, foreign language translation, editorial, and rights and permissions inquiries should be addressed to: Jeff Black, Lone Eagle Publishing Company, 1024 North Orange Drive, Hollywood, CA 90038 or send e-mail to: info@loneeagle.com

Distributed to the trade by National Book Network, 800.462.6420

Lone Eagle Publishing Company™ is a registered trademark.
IFILM^{SM} is a registered service mark.

This book is dedicated to my wife, Ronda; my son, Luis Ignacio Keonimana Reyes and my daughter, Arlinda Marie Makamae Reyes, who share the legacy of the movies; my mother, Maria, who taught me to appreciate the beauty of the performing arts in our lives; and my father, Pablo, who used to stay up late with me and watch all the Westerns on television.

—Luis Reyes

For Jack Wilkins, a fellow movie buff, brilliant guitarist, and my best friend; and in memory of Warne Marsh, jazz musician, and one of the deepest, creatively original people I ever knew.

—Peter Rubie

Contents

Acknowledgments

Special thanks and appreciation to: Sandy Varga and Bel Hernandez of *Latin Heat* Magazine for making this new edition possible; Mike Hawks; Pete Bateman; Doug Hart; Critt Davis; Leith Adams, USC/Warner Bros., Archives; Frank Rodriguez, Universal Pictures; Louis Garcia, Tri-Star Pictures; Ann Lander/Teri Avanian, Orion Pictures; Halina Krukowski, Lucasfilm Ltd.; Jess Garcia, Warner Bros.; the staff of the Academy of Motion Pictures Arts and Sciences Library and Center for Research Study; the staff of the Autry Museum of Western Heritage; Television Academy Library; Jeff Baskim; Brian Robinette, NBC; Anthony Quinn; Mel Ferrer; Ricardo Montalban; Edward James Olmos; Jesus Trevino; Pepe Serna; Alex Colon; Bart Andrews; Michael Donnelly; Jimmy Smits; Cheech Marin; Richard Dominguez; Jerry Velasco; Margaret Ward and Rodney Mitchell of SAG; and Selise Eisseman of the DGA Special Projects; Dolores Argo of HBO; Mona Lee Schilling; Bob Dickson; Lauren Rossini and Carla Green for their dedicated work on the manuscript and layout; Jeff Black for having the understanding and vision; my taskmaster, Peter Rubie; and most of all my agent, Lori Perkins, who never gave up the faith.

Foreword

As a young actress under contract to MGM Studios in the 1940s, I could not have conceived of a publication documenting the careers and artistic achievements of Latino artists—not only because Latinos were few and far between in Hollywood films, but because we seemed to be virtually invisible to the studio heads themselves. Though the road has been rough, many Latino actors have attained success in the entertainment industry and, more importantly, have earned the respect of their peers. Those who did not allow the rigidity of the system to dishearten them persevered and, in many cases, achieved great successes when afforded the opportunity.

Like many aspiring actresses, I came to Hollywood wanting nothing more than to be the next Lana Turner, but my education was to be abrupt and painful: the doors of opportunity were open to me only under strict conditions that were dictated by the studios. Like hundreds of other ethnic actors, I was relegated to playing a spate of nameless Indian maidens and Mexican spitfires. Latino contract players were afforded no options in the old studio system; we played the roles we were given, no matter how demeaning they might have been.

Even after receiving a certain amount of recognition, the struggle to be recognized as serious actors persisted. For example, after winning an Academy Award® for my work as Anita in *West Side Story*, I spent years turning down roles that were veiled versions of the same role, but without the substance that *West Side Story* possessed. Thus, I turned to theatre to practice my craft. I did everything in my power to seek out venues that were less inclined to typecasting.

It has taken too long for the entertainment industry to embrace the scope of Latino talent. Nevertheless, throughout the years, Latino actors have made many significant contributions to film and television and will undoubtedly continue to do so.

This book salutes both those who paved the way and those who broke down the barriers of stereotypes with their talent and fortitude. The time is long overdue to recognize and celebrate the Latino contribution to Hollywood.

Rita Moreno

I really believe that the motion picture industry is an ideal place where actors and actresses can play any part. To me all actors are part of a universal nation called "Actor." I am part of that nation of actors and that is how I would like to be remembered.

Anthony Quinn

Introduction

I grew up on New York City's Upper West Side in the late 1950s and early 1960s and the first Hispanic presence on television that I remember vividly is Desi Arnaz as Ricky Ricardo on *I Love Lucy*. He looked, spoke and acted—especially when he got angry and spoke Spanish—just like my Dad. Their home life resembled mine, for they lived in a tenement apartment in New York and struggled every day to make ends meet. And, though Lucy was nothing like my Latin mother, she had that universal comic humanity in her characterization to which we could all relate.

Zorro and the Cisco Kid were Hispanic, but those shows were historical: swashbucklers and Westerns. Like every other young boy, I loved cowboy films; but it was shows like *The Naked City* (1958-63) and *East Side/West Side* (1963-64), shot on location in New York, with Puerto Rican tenement dwellers played by New York Puerto Rican or Latino talent, with whom I identified.

My first movie-going memories are of seeing stars like Charlton Heston in *El Cid* (1961) and John Wayne in *The Alamo* (1960), as well as endless Jerry Lewis comedies. The only actresses I really ever liked were Susan Hayward and Marilyn Monroe, though I confess I was also drawn to the exotic and bosomy charms of Sophia Loren, Claudia Cardinale and Brigitte Bardot.

I identified with all the screen tough guys, including Kirk Douglas and Burt Lancaster (who grew up in Spanish Harlem when it wasn't Spanish), but apart from actor Gilbert Roland, who was always dashing and sly, and usually a friend to the leading man; Anthony Quinn, a towering screen presence who had a very vague ethnicity; and Ricardo Montalban, who has always somehow personified the classic Spanish don, I saw very few Latinos on screen. When Puerto Ricans Rita Moreno and Jose Ferrer became Oscar® winners, I was proud.

After seeing a film I would stand in the lobby—perhaps of the RKO Nemo on 110th Street and Broadway or the Loew's Olympia, which were just two of many movie houses that seemed to be around the corner of our third floor apartment on 109th Street—and stare at the movie posters, lobby cards, photos and banners in eager anticipation of coming attractions. Through these displays I would also relive the film I had just seen.

I didn't think about race or ethnicity as an issue until I was a teenager during the Civil Rights movement of the 1960s. By then, we had all become conscious of our own history. In my case, I began to learn about how my family had arrived in New York from Puerto Rico, and how our culture was melding with mainstream American culture, while sharing our neighborhood with the Irish, Jews and Italians.

When I entered high school I began to wonder why there were so few Hispanics in the movies and even fewer on television. I wondered why television commercials didn't feature African Americans or Hispanics; after all, I bought Nestle's chocolate and Cherrios and Pepsi just like Anglo kids. Our lives and Puerto Rican culture in general were, I thought, just as dramatic and interesting as the Italian American or Jewish American experience. To this day, there has not been one major Puerto Rican-experience film from Hollywood with a Puerto Rican director and star, though *Popi* (1969) and *I Like It Like That* (1994) come close.

Through a New York Puerto Rican youth educational and leadership program called Aspira, I was exposed to many aspects of Puerto Rican culture of which I had not been aware. Through this organization in 1972 I was able to obtain a scholarship to Elbert Covell College in Stockton, California, at the time the only bilingual (Spanish/English) college in existence in the United States. I knew Stockton because it had been the location for the television Western series *The Big Valley* (1965-69) and movies like *All the King's Men* (1949) and *High Noon* (1952). It was at school that I began to see how rich and variable Latino culture was. Half of the student body and teachers were from Latin America, making me realize that previously, I really had only been aware of Puerto Rican, Cuban and Dominican cultures.

After graduation, I went to Los Angeles and looked up the organization Nosotros, which had been founded by Ricardo Montalban and others to fight stereotypical Hispanic images and improve opportunities for Hispanics in movies and television. Here, as in New York, I found a wealth of talented artists, writers and directors who were enthusiastic and passionate about their art and considered their culture part of the American experience.

But Hollywood was only interested in the same old stereotypical images: maids, slum dwellers, drug addicts, gang members and feisty senoritas. Since then, actors like Raul Julia, Hector Elizondo, Edward James Olmos, Andy Garcia, Maria Conchita Alonso, Julie Carmen, Elizabeth Peña, Rachel Ticotin, Rosana De Soto, Jimmy Smits and more recently, Cameron Diaz, Salma Hayek, Freddie Prinze, Jr., Jennifer Lopez and Marc Anthony have risen to the forefront as the new generation of their profession who are beginning to be seen as Hispanic stars considered part of the mainstream of American culture.

Being a lifelong film buff and working in the public relations side of the film industry, I discovered a whole legacy of lesser known Hispanic talent in Hollywood. Those who had forged a place in the film industry in the early days were dying or had already passed away without ever having had their stories recorded. As the years passed, the history of Hispanics in Hollywood was in danger of being lost forever.

A ninety-three-year-old Hispanic extra player, Angela Gomez, once said, "This show business is something I've always wanted to be a part of since my youth. Times and circumstances were much more difficult then and I am grateful for the opportunity it gave me and my husband to work and provide a decent living for our family. Just as important, it was an escape, a fantasy world, like storybooks come to life in which one took part."

This book is an attempt to show the way Hollywood has depicted Hispanic Americans and Latin America, while also pointing out the contributions to Hollywood movies and television made by unsung Hispanic Americans like Angela Gomez, as well by those more famous. By way of an explicit definition, the term Hispanic American refers to all people living in the United States who can trace their background to Spain, Portugal or Latin America. The book will only deal with the history of the Hispanic American in the Hollywood film and television industry. It will not attempt to deal with the cinema of Latin America or Spain, except in terms of how they affected Hispanic American images or artists in Hollywood.

The material is based on interviews conducted specifically for this book, previously published material in magazines, newspapers and studio archives, press materials and the viewing of the films by the authors when possible.

Satir Gonzalez

Some 400 films and television shows are listed with credits, short synopses, production information pertaining to Hispanic elements and critical commentary. For inclusion, the following criteria were used:

- The film or television show stars Hispanic leading or supporting characters;
- The story takes place in Spain, Latin America, or the United States;
- It is a major Hollywood Studio or independent production;
- The film or television show deals with Hispanic subject matter.

Most of the films listed are from the sound period (post-1927) because many of the silent films are either unavailable (lost) or inaccessible.

Luis Reyes

Films / Introduction

Hispanic Americans, like many other minority groups in the United States, suffer from damaging stereotyping in motion pictures and on television. Yet while other minority groups began to get a better (or perhaps broader) portrayal in the 1990s, the Hispanic American was still cast in the old clichés.

There are few films that explore the variety of Hispanic American experience. That is, very few feature affluent, educated, middle-class, or well-to-do Latinos; gay Hispanics; Jewish or Protestant (non-Catholic) Hispanics; or non-Spanish speaking Hispanics. The diversity of Hispanic Americans and their cultures and contribution to the art and daily life of the United States has yet to be fully explored, particularly by Hollywood.

A breakthrough in reshaping a stereotyped image often comes when members of the minority group being portrayed on the screen are also prominently involved in the writing, acting and production direction of a film. Notable examples include *Zoot Suit* (1981), *Born in East L.A.* (1987), *La Bamba* (1987), *Stand and Deliver* (1988), *Hangin' with the Homeboys*

(1991), *I Like it Like That* (1994), *Desperado* (1995), *A Walk in the Clouds* (1995) and *Selena* (1997). The irony is that Hispanic Americans have been involved in the Hollywood movie making process almost from its inception but are only now beginning to affect positively how they are portrayed in the movies.

By definition, a cliché or stereotype is based on a self-evident truth, but that truth is misleading because it is one-dimensionally repetitive and, more importantly, fails to find a person's humanity. Clichés and stereotypes, in the end, are damaging because they use partial truths to give illusory weight to the racist's argument that (fill in the blanks) "all ___ are ___ because _____."

Hollywood argues that its movies (and, to a lesser extent, television) are only entertainment without any political bias, the goal of which is to give us a few hours of harmless fun. This is not only untrue—all stories have a point of view and an implicit meaning—but also disingenuously dishonest because in the course of watching this entertainment, we constantly see characters who perpetuate stereotypical racist opinions. These opinions are usually considered acceptable because "Everyone knows it's true." And how do we know it's true? Because we see examples of stereotyped "truths" in the movies or on television all the time.

More and more, Hollywood movies and television shows have become our filters for interpreting the world around us. We have become victims of the old adages "A picture is worth a thousand words" and "The camera doesn't lie." We should know better. These days, modern technology can make the camera lie with frightening conviction; even without the use of this computerized technology, the "truth" is often twisted by capturing a moment out of context and presenting it as common reality. What's more, as Hitler and Goebbels discovered, if you tell people the some lie loud enough and long enough, they start to believe it.

There is a fine line between the artistic tyranny of "political correctness" and being sensitive to perpetuating a stereotype. It could be argued that the line is best walked with an honest awareness of and a genuine attempt to portray the best in us, rather than accepting as truth stories and characters that continually reflect only the worst. Film studios, however, have not been particularly sensitive to positive minority portrayals or to a positive approach to minority storytelling. Television is not much better, especially when it comes to portrayals of Hispanic Americans and their culture and way of life.

Instead, Hollywood hides behind a bottom line, a dollar mentality that often masks a form of passive racism most people would be horrified to learn they were practicing. The insidiousness of racism is not so much the overt acts of the self-proclaimed fascist, but the moral cowardice of those who avoid speaking out against off-the-cuff offensive remarks. Accepting unchallenged, stereotyped portrayals in the movies is such a form of passive racism.

Backlot Mexico

Most film portrayals of Hispanic and Latin American characters (i.e., those living south of the Mexico-United States border or those living in the States having a Spanish heritage) by North Americans reflect the ignorance of the filmmakers and perpetuate myths that are for the most part negative. Banana republics, sleepy villages with lazy peons basking in the sun, uncivilized half-naked Indians, violent government coups spearheaded by cruel dictators, mustachioed bandits, beautiful senoritas and the idea that one Anglo is worth ten Latinos are just some of the many stereotypical images most North Americans have of Latin America, Hispanics and Hispanic Americans.

[handwritten note: put on paper.]

These negative images have not changed throughout much of the twentieth century and are alive and well in such movies as *The Alamo* (1960), *The Magnificent Seven* (1960), *Kings of the Sun* (1963), *Butch Cassidy and the Sundance Kid* (1969), *The Wild Bunch* (1969) and *The Old Gringo* (1989). *Raiders of the Lost Ark* (1981), for example, shows Indiana Jones being chased by Indians in a South American rain forest after he steals a powerful religious icon. Nick Nolte and Powers Boothe spar over drugs, the hand of Maria Conchita Alonso, and the right to be "head gringo in charge" (benevolent or otherwise) in *Extreme Prejudice* (1987), in which the bandidos are now drug traffickers.

Although Hollywood has recently rediscovered Nicaragua, El Salvador and Panama; Central and South America all seem to melt into a single, amorphous South-of-the-border culture. A great many North Americans could not even identify the names, let alone their locations on a map, of the countries south of Mexico, yet they all have an opinion about them and the people born there. As recently as 1993, in Steven Spielberg's *Jurassic Park*—which is set on an island off the coast of Costa Rica—San Jose, the capital city, in reality a bustling metropolis, is depicted as a seedy backwater port with Mexican music heard incongruously playing in the background.

[handwritten note: Movie samples of bad stereotyping]

In the past, movie-going audiences were treated to memorable images of Humphrey Bogart making his way through savage jungles while eluding bandits in his search for lost gold in Mexico (*The Treasure of the Sierra Madre* [1948]), Cesar Romero and Tyrone Power conquering the Aztecs and winning the women as well (*Captain from Castile* [19471]), Cary Grant flying mail over the Andes (*Only Angels Have Wings* [1939]) and Carmen Miranda dancing to a North American version of one type of Latin rhythm that became the stereotype for them all.

On a domestic level, the stereotypes have slowly evolved over the years from the bandido who terrorized the American West to the modern drug dealer or street gang member. Women have undergone very little change, from the jovial mamacita to the suffering mamacita, or the sexually provocative "spitfire" to the street hooker or girl gang member.

Our modern-day ideas about Hispanic Americans come primarily from Westerns and urban crime dramas, though these images have their roots in nineteenth-century yellow fiction and journalism. Newspapers, and later film and television shows, characterized all the land below the United States as one giant Mexico, and all Spanish-speaking peoples were considered somehow Mexican.

Mexico: a place to escape from American law; a place of corrupt anarchy, overwhelming poverty and cheap hedonism; a place where the American dollar can last a long time; a place where marriage and divorce are quick and easy, and dark-haired, copper-skinned beauties share will their beds for a few pesos (paradoxically, this attitude is also characteristic of the Latin Lover in films). At the same time, ". . . a piece of us expects to be murdered on holiday in Mexico, and the knife would come as no surprise," Octavio Paz commented in *Labyrinth of Solitude*. The place is dangerous and exotic, as are its people.

Mexico as an extension of the American West is an image that has been popular in the more recent adult Westerns as contemporary film-makers have focused on the closing days of the American frontier. This image has been underscored by the popularity, in the late 1960s and 1970s particularly, of the European "spaghetti Western," often filmed in areas of Italy, Spain, Israel, or Mexico that look a lot like the American Southwest.

B Westerns, produced in the 1930s and 1940s by such studios as Republic, Monogram and Columbia and starring George O'Brien, Buck Jones, John Wayne, Hopalong Cassidy, Roy Rogers and Gene Autry, had a great deal to do with creating the backlot Mexico that has passed into movie mythology, helping define stereotypical ideas of Hispanic Americans that are still with us. On the Republic Studios backlot and in most studios in Hollywood, there was a permanent standing set of a typical Mexican adobe town with a church, a plaza, a cantina and a hacienda residence. This set was used to represent Mexico and the Southwest in hundreds of films.

Writers like Ernest Hemingway created a picturesque view of exotic, tropical Cuba, and American tourists flocked there and to other South American and Caribbean countries during the Jazz Age and Prohibition. The infectious Latin rhythms of Afro-Caribbean music began to take hold in the United States with the success of bandlead-ers like Xavier Cugat, Desi Arnaz, Machito and many lesser-known musicians who influenced such great musicians as Charlie Parker, Dizzie Gillespie and Duke Ellington, as well as American composers as Cole Porter, Aaron Copeland and, later, Leonard Bernstein.

John Huston created a modern version of the romantic image of Mexico with his 1964 film of Tennessee Williams' *The Night of the Iguana*. Taylor Hackford's *Against All Odds* (1984) (a remake of 1947's *Out of the Past*) features a Mexico that serves as an exotic backdrop for murder and romance among Anglos. Oliver Stone's *Born on the Fourth of July* (1989) offers a thinly sketched shantytown Mexico that is a sex-ual haven for paraplegic Vietnam War veterans. Unfortunately, making the setting Mexico, rather than, say, Anytown, USA, exploits the audi-ence's stereotyped assumptions about Hispanics. These assumptions are so ingrained in the American consciousness and exert such a pow-erful hold over the imaginations of filmmakers the world over that they will be perpetuated in one form or another for years to come.

The Bandido and the Greaser

Long before the advent of motion pictures, many popular misconceptions and stereotypes about Hispanic Americans had been adopted. Much of this is seen in movies that deal with history. To read Carlos Fuentes' novel *The Old Gringo*, for example, and then to see how it was altered to fit not just a movie format but North American sensibilities as well, is to gain some sense of the depths of the problem, even though matters are clearly improving.

The battle of the Alamo in 1836 and the Texas War of Independence left deep-seated prejudices between Anglo Americans and Mexicans that are still reflected over 100 years later in such movies as *Man of Conquest* (1939), *The Last Command* (1955) and John Wayne's *The Alamo* (1960).

The Mexican American War of 1846 and the resulting Treaty of Guadalupe Hidalgo, which ended the hostilities in 1848, ceded 51.2 percent of Mexican territory to the United States, including the present-day states of New Mexico, Arizona and California. As a result, 100,000 former Mexican citizens suddenly found themselves second-class citizens in the United States. Spanish noblemen saw their large landholdings slowly dwindle as a result of Anglo American encroachment, facilitated by murder, deceit and legislation including California's onerous "Greaser" Law of 1855. The epithet was actually written into the text of the law, which was a series of vagrancy laws that were loosely interpreted to facilitate the detainment and/or imprisonment of Mexicans and other Spanish-speaking people.

Throughout the 1850s, groups of bandits moved about the countryside raiding and pillaging. Their actions were in part a reaction against discrimination directed at the dark-skinned minorities of the gold regions. Such things as the Greaser Law and taxes on foreigners stirred deep anti-Anglo sentiment among Latinos. Resentment of Anglo domination was deep-seated and widespread, and many of the original bandidos had at least the tacit support of the Mexican American community.

The term "greaser" has several origins and is usually negative or derogatory, referring to a non-Anglo or lower-class individual. One meaning of the term applied to Mexican laborers in the Southwest who put grease on their backs to facilitate the unloading of hides and cargo. In the dime novels of the 1880s, "greaser" usually referred to an oily, dark, swarthy villain or bandit who, more often than not, was Mexican or of mixed blood. By the 1950s, "greaser" usually applied to ethnic teenagers, considered to be juvenile delinquents, with greased hair and black leather jackets.

Nineteenth-century melodramas and the stories of popular writer Bret Harte helped shape the image of the Mexican bandit. The popularizing of the American West in the dime novels of the 1880s, written mostly by Easterners who had never been west of New Jersey, reinforced the images of bandits, beautiful senoritas and sleepy peasants in Mexican towns.

The Wild West shows of Buffalo Bill and others that toured the Eastern Seaboard compounded these images by featuring colorfully costumed Mexican vaqueros strumming their guitars and demonstrating rodeo techniques. The shows also presented them as bandits being apprehended by Texas Rangers, Buffalo Bill, or the United States Cavalry.

The era of President Teddy Roosevelt at the turn of the twentieth century, the building of the Panama Canal, the imperialistic expansion of the United States, and the concepts of "our little brown brothers" and the "yellow journalism" practiced by the Hearst and Pulitzer newspapers all helped to foster misconceptions of our neighbors to the south.

The Spanish American War of 1898, the "yellow press," lurid stories of the sinking of the battleship Maine, and stories of Teddy Roosevelt's Rough Riders charging up San Juan Hill against the Spanish enemy in Cuba solidified the idea of "Manifest Destiny," a popular doctrine expressing the destiny of the United States as continued territorial expansion.

As a result of the Spanish American War, the United States acquired Puerto Rico, the Philippines and Guam and gained temporary control of Cuba. After 1898, the island country of Cuba became a corrupt center of gambling, drugs and prostitution, controlled first by the United States government through a series of puppet dictatorships and later by organized crime. Puerto Ricans were given American citizenship in 1917, while the United States Marines were involved several times in propping up dictatorships in places such as the Dominican Republic as late as 1965.

The revolution in Mexico (1910-1917) captured the American public's imagination because it was so close to home. It gave rise to the portrayal of the bandit in the form of Francisco "Pancho" Villa, whose daring exploits became legendary on both sides of the border. The writings of American journalist John Reed described Villa as a Mexican Robin Hood and the revolution as a romantic endeavor. American ambivalence to Villa was partly brought about by Villa's attack on Columbus, New Mexico, and the punitive military expedition, led by United States General John Pershing, sent into Mexico to capture him. In 1913, President Woodrow Wilson refused to recognize the revolutionary Mexican government and sent Marines and gunboats to seize (temporarily) the Mexican port of Vera Cruz.

During this time, movies developed from peep show nickelodeons to the relatively sophisticated psychological dramas of silent film directors such as Cecil B. DeMille and D.W. Griffith, which had a powerful impact on audiences.

Bandits and sleepy Mexican towns were a standard feature in many silent Westerns, and the vicious greaser image came into being in these early silent films. *Bronco Billy and the Greaser* and *The Greaser's Revenge* (both 1914), for example, seemed to confirm the Mexican as an evil and sinister villain. In William S. Hart's *Hell's Hinges* (1916), the villain, Silk Miller, is described in the title card as "mingling the oily craftiness of a Mexican with the deadly treachery of a rattler." It was only rarely, such as in *The Mexican* (1914) starring Tom Mix, that a Mexican was treated sympathetically.

Most of the heads of the studios were Eastern European immigrants who had endured much in their homelands and in their newly adopted country and tried to integrate themselves into American society as best they could. Their films rarely reflect their own ethnic experiences. They simply bought into the American Dream and spun those fantasies and myths for millions of Americans, extending and reinforcing already established popular misconceptions.

After the revolution, the newly established Mexican government objected to the many film stereotypes by issuing an official protest in 1924, banning American films outright. Hispanic American groups in the States began expressing in their Spanish-language newspapers their opinions of negative Hollywood film portrayals.

By the end of World War I, the agricultural and industrial development of the Southwest and Midwest, coupled with the political and economic instability of the post-revolution Mexican government, resulted in the first significant migration of Mexicans into the United States. Setting a pattern that exists to the present, subsequent United States deportation policies and job opportunities (both legal and illegal) affected resident Mexican Americans, setting up a "push/pull" situation that brought millions of Mexican immigrants across the border.

Added to this was Pancho Villa's edict ordering all Spanish-born Mexicans to leave northern Mexico, which is what brought actor Gilbert Roland's family to El Paso and later California. Anthony Quinn's mother and father fought for Villa, then became disillusioned by the strife and came to the States.

The immigration of large numbers of Puerto Ricans and Cubans to the United States, on the other hand, started much later, mainly in the 1940s and 1950s, and more recently Central and South Americans have migrated to the United States via the Mexico-United States border in large numbers as a result of political turmoil in their countries.

These waves of immigration can be seen to correspond, very broadly, to portrayals of Hispanics in American films: Mexican American social problem films of the post-World War II period, the juvenile delinquent films of the late 1950s and 1960s, and more recently the drug dealer and gang stereotypes of the 1980s and 1990s.

Pioneers

The motion picture industry secured a living and a future for many Hispanic Americans by creating jobs and opportunities in the Los Angeles area. The history of Hispanics in Hollywood begins with the extra players in silent movies in the late teens and early 1920s. Extra work, along with wrangling and day labor, were the areas of moviemaking most accessible then.

Very early on, however, some Hispanics made it to the forefront of the industry. According to film historian Geoffrey Bell in *The Golden Gate and the Silver Screen* (New York: Cornwall Books, 1984), Hispanic actresses Myrtle Gonzales and Beatriz Michelena were among the first leading ladies of the silent screen, and Frank Padilla and Eustacio Montoya were two of the first silent film cinematographers. Film historian Antonio Rios-Bustamente in *Chicanos and Film* (Garland, 1992), edited by Chon Noriega, states that Myrtle Gonzales was the early film industry's "first Latina star." In 1911, she appeared in the film *Ghosts* and,

Antonio Moreno (in car)
on the set of a 1920s
silent film.

until her sudden death from influenza in 1917, received star billing in more than forty Vitagraph and Universal Pictures films. "In marked contrast to the experience of later Latinas who used their own names, Gonzalez portrayed vigorous outdoor heroines," says Rios-Bustamente.

Michelena was a star of the San Francisco musical stage at the turn of the century and appeared in her first film, *Salomy Jane*, produced by the California Motion Picture Corporation, in 1914. The next year the major trade paper *Motion Picture World* featured her on the cover with the caption, "Beatriz Micheleno, Greatest and Most Beautiful Artist Now Appearing in Motion Pictures." Between 1914 and 1919 she appeared in sixteen feature films. "The new industry's need for experienced and popular players created an opportunity for talented actors, including Latinos," concludes Rios-Bustamente, who adds, "unlike later Latino players, these early players were able to star with Spanish surnames, even prior to the Latin Lover craze which made Latinos temporarily fashionable."

Los Angeles, due to its historical antecedents, always had a large Mexican population, which became a great resource for the film studios. This population grew even more during the Mexican Revolution (1910-1917), when refugees immigrated to the United States to escape the violent turmoil across the border.

Hispanics on the East Coast, on the other hand, were relatively small in number and were virtually shut out from any kind of involvement in the early film industry that was developing there. During this early silent period their only documented involvement was as extras and laborers in films shot in Cuba and Puerto Rico. Instead, it was the European immigrant who provided the cheap labor on the East Coast. Duncan Renaldo, who later gained fame as the Cisco Kid, began as an extra at Paramount Studios in Astoria, Queens, when he first arrived in New York. He was promptly hired as an art director and artist when he re-sketched a set for a South Seas movie. The original, he told the director, was more typical of Cuba and the Caribbean.

Los Angeles became a popular spot for filmmakers because, among other things, there was plenty of sunshine and warm weather (a necessary asset in the silent days when films were made outside without lights). The area around Los Angeles also had a varied topography, including mountains, rivers, ocean beaches and deserts, that could be utilized for many different story settings. More importantly, Los Angeles was a nonunion town with a plentiful supply of inexpensive Mexican (and Asian) workers, so labor costs were half what they were back East.

Frank Quinn, Anthony Quinn's father, worked as a laborer and propman at the old Selig Studios. Many Mexican vaqueros and ranch hands were employed as cowboys and wranglers for Western movies. In general, Mexicans found work as extra players in countless movies (especially the epics) of the silent era, such as D.W. Griffith's *The Birth of a Nation* (1915) and *Intolerance* (1916); Raoul Walsh's *The Thief of Bagdad* (1924); and the Valentino vehicles *The Four Horsemen of the Apocalypse* (1921), *The Sheik* (1921) and *Blood and Sand* (1922). Mexicans portrayed Arabs, Jews, Pacific Islanders and Native Americans.

In a 1975 *TV Guide* article, Gilbert Roland wrote of his early days: "Central Casting called for Spanish and Mexican extras to report at Paramount Studios: three dollars a day and a box lunch. Over a thousand of us were hauled into trucks and driven through the narrow and dusty Cahuenga Pass to Lasky Ranch. The picture was *Blood and Sand*, the star playing the matador was Rudolph Valentino."

Angela Gomez was born in 1891 in San Bernardino, California, but her family later moved to Arizona, where she married and started a family of her own. She returned to San Bernardino in 1919 with her husband, Ralph Bauer, a Mexican of German descent. They settled in Los Angeles in 1920 around Sunset and Grand avenues, an area that was then an immigrant melting pot for Mexicans, Italians, Hawaiians, Filipinos, Jews and Chinese. In 1983, Ms. Gomez was interviewed about her life experiences as an extra player in the early days of Hollywood. All told, she appeared in over 300 motion pictures, including the original silent and the sound remake of *Blood and Sand*.

"On Temple and Diamond Street," said Gomez, "lived a man named Gamboa who was a runner for the motion picture studios. Runners were hired to gather extra players as needed in their respective ethnic areas.

"Pedro Carmona and Chris-Pin Martin (who went on to become a well-regarded character actor), who lived in the Chavez Ravine area, supplied [Hispanic] extras. The studios would call the runners and tell them they would need two or three hundred Latin types, and they proceeded to gather the people. They would congregate around "El Arbol," a big tree outside the Gamboa home. You would take your friends, relatives, whomever, for they made big pictures then. Extras would earn two or three dollars a day and a boxed lunch. A runner would get seventy-five cents a head for each extra brought in who worked."

Ms. Gomez soon placed her husband in the movies, where he also worked under the name Gomez. He started as an extra, but due to his physical abilities and a friendship with a director, he quickly became a stand-in and stuntman.

When there was no work by way of the runners, the extras would pile in someone's car or take the Red Car (a public transportation trolley) to the studios, lining up early at the studio extra casting gate. An assistant director or the director himself would come out and pick from among the crowd the types needed for the day.

This was a time before the unions and the guilds were formed. Extras were subjected to all kinds of abuses, including high employment agency fees, underpayment of wages, overwork, maltreatment, and sometimes their lives were needlessly put in danger. The Association of Motion Picture Producers formed Central Casting as a nonprofit entity in 1928. It efficiently consolidated the extra casting efforts of all the studios into one central location, which effectively ended the days of nonunion extras.

Extras would be paid additional money for unusual pieces of action or business. These would be called silent bits, a whammy, or a double whammy. Extras would compete for space within the camera range or next to the stars and would be quick to size up the situation on the set. Ms. Gomez explained, "If you were in a three shot or close to the stars or the main action, you would be used more, not only in the master shot but in close-ups or reaction shots, as in a fight scene. This way you would be employed longer and also get more money for reactions or silent bits, which were great incentives for people."

"When I was six months old Angela got my brother and me in pictures," remembers her granddaughter, veteran actress Angelina Estrada. "She raised us, and some films I remember vividly, like *Gunga Din* with Cary Grant, because they took us to the rocky and cold Sierra Lone Pine, California, location. I had to walk around barefoot and came back with the chicken pox."

Angela Gomez and her family were representative of many Hispanics who worked in the movie industry as extras. Director Luis Valdez's father worked as an extra driving a mule team and wagon in the Oklahoma land rush scene in the classic Western *Cimarron* (1931), filmed near Bakersfield, California. Hispanic extras were an integral part of the Warner Bros. classic *Casablanca* (1942), for example. Eighty-

Dolores Del Rio has her palm read by an extra player while director Raoul Walsh looks on in amusement on the set of *The Loves of Carmen.*

seven-year-old Henry Carbajal, who worked as Henry Carr, remembers he got his first taste of extra work during a weeklong night shoot at Paramount Studios and quit his job as a soda jerk at a downtown department store. "It was a cantina scene and I had a pretty girl on my lap; I made $47 for the week. At the time I was only making $18 a week as a soda jerk." Carr also recalls "working in the hot open California sun and having to wait in long lines for several hours to change into a Roman toga in a tent along with hundreds of other extras during the making of *Ben-Hur* (1926) with Ramon Novarro."

When playing themselves, however, Mexicans were still usually relegated to extra work. Male lead Mexican roles, for example, almost always went to Anglo actors wearing dark makeup and thick mustaches. Latin leading men did not come into vogue until Rudolph Valentino became a star in 1921. With the onset of the Latin Lover, personified by Valentino, a niche was created that allowed actors such as Ramon Novarro and Gilbert Roland to rise to prominence from the ranks of extras.

The Latin Lover image can be traced back to Don Juan, to the amorous exploits of nineteenth-century aristocratic Latin Americans in Europe who become popular figures in literature, and to the cultural clash between an extrovert Latin culture and a predominantly introverted Anglo-Saxon society. While there are many criticisms that may be leveled at the movie version of *The Old Gringo* (1989), its portrait of this cultural clash is well drawn and clearly seen through the characters of schoolteacher Harriet Winslow (Jane Fonda) and the Old Gringo, seventy-one-year-old Hearst newspaper journalist Ambrose Bierce (Gregory Peck). This clash is particularly pointed up by their interaction with the character of the young revolutionary general Thomas Arroyo (Jimmy Smits), who plays a variation on the Latin Lover, in particular by unleashing repressed passions in the virginal Winslow.

The Latin Lover as a screen type reached its zenith with Rudolph Valentino, who captivated audiences worldwide with his legendary silent screen portrayals during the 1920s. The phenomenon corresponded to the spirit of the times. The generation that survived and followed World War I became known as "The Lost Generation" and was typified in social customs, literature and art by F. Scott Fitzgerald, Hemingway, Gertrude Lawrence, Gertrude Stein and Dorothy Parker; accusations of loose morals, the Charleston dance, "bathtub gin" and the decade or so of prohibition that began in 1920.

Valentino's popularity allowed a number of Hispanic actors to become major stars in an attempt to duplicate his "Latin Lover" charm and success. In fact, Spaniard Antonio Moreno had established himself in Hollywood prior to Valentino's arrival, but was eclipsed by the glamorous screen icon. Soon followed Ramon Novarro, Ricardo Cortez (ironically, an Eastern European who made a career out of being identified as Latin) and Gilbert Roland, all of whom found themselves working in major motion pictures, though not necessarily in Latin roles. The Latin Lover at this time was a Mediterranean-type character, not necessarily a Hispanic American one.

With the death of Valentino in 1926, the Latin Lover as a major screen figure fell into decline, taking with it the careers of several actors who had followed in Valentino's footsteps.

Novarro, was one of the actors discovered in the wake of Valentino's popularity who managed to become a superstar during the 1930s. Born in Durango, Mexico, he fled the Mexican Revolution in 1914, going to Los Angeles with his family. Once in Los Angeles, he did odd jobs until he was discovered by a director who saw in Novarro some of the same magnetism that women all over the world loved about Valentino.

Novarro played the title role in the epic *Ben-Hur* (1926), while Gilbert Roland, another discovery who used his Latin Lover casting as a springboard to superstardom, played the young Frenchman Armand Duvalle in *Camille* (1927).

In the 1930s and 1940s, the Latin Lover types, who included Don Alvarado and John Carroll, were eclipsed by the tall, strong American hero actors, typified by Clark Gable, Gary Cooper and John Wayne.

Even so, there was still a popular Latin lover type of this period: Cesar Romero. Born in New York City of Cuban parents, Romero used a much lighter touch in his film portrayals, starring in a series of musicals with the likes of Alice Faye, Betty Grable and Carmen Miranda while under contract at 20th Century Fox.

By 1945, Metro-Goldwyn-Mayer was still promoting two major stars as Latin Lover types: Argentinean Fernando Lamas and Mexican-born Ricardo Montalban. Both Lamas and Montalban had been established stars in their home countries before coming to Hollywood, partly as a result of President Franklin Roosevelt's Good Neighbor Policy.

The idea was to exploit the Latin American movie market to replace the European film market, which, as a result of World War II, was

Ramon Novarro and Francis X. Bushman in the epic *Ben-Hur* (1926).

almost nonexistent. Montalban even starred in a 1953 movie called *Latin Lovers*, and despite some outstanding performances in movies like *Right Cross* (1950) and *Sayonara* (1957) was never totally able to escape the Latin Lover movie star image that he caricatured so well later in his career in *Sweet Charity* (1969).

The Glamour Years

The premiere of Warner Bros.' *The Jazz Singer* (1927), the first talking motion picture with synchronized sound on Vitaphone discs, ushered in a new era for motion pictures that caused major upheavals in the motion picture business.

In an April 20, 1958, *New York Times* interview with John P. Shanley, Dolores Del Rio recalled, "There was a dreadful anxiety about the talkies. I couldn't even speak English then, so I was in much worse shape than the others were." By the late 1920s, the major Hollywood production centers were concerned about the development of the new sound technology in particular because European filmmakers could now begin to make films in their respective languages. This would result in less revenue for Hollywood films in an international marketplace they had once virtually dominated. United Artists stars and owners Mary Pickford, Douglas Fairbanks and Charlie Chaplin, for example, were adored as much in Paris, France and Berlin, Germany, as in Paris, Texas, and Berlin, Massachusetts.

Dolores Del Rio's provocative appearance as the French farm maid in *What Price Glory?* (1926) had brought her wide praise and immediate fame. She achieved a fashion-plate image coupled with an elegant, exotic aura that she put to good use in several musicals and costume dramas. A 1934 contract from the Warner Bros. archives showed her to have earned $100,000 for three pictures (*Wonder Bar* [1934], *In Caliente* [1935] and *I Live for You* [1935]) in the midst of the Great Depression.

In the May 24, 1931, edition of the Los Angeles Spanish-language newspaper *La Opinion*, it was reported that Del Rio had turned down a part in *The Broken Wing* because she found the role denigrating to Mexican identity. The role was that of a "cantina girl" who jilts a "Mexican bandit" for an American airline pilot. The part eventually went to the lesser-known Lupe Velez, who began her career in silent films as Douglas Fairbanks' leading lady in *The Gaucho* (1927). She continued to play such typecast roles until she committed suicide in 1944. In between, she had a torrid romance with Gary Cooper and later married Olympic swimming champion and screen Tarzan Johnny Weissmuller. Mexican-born Raquel Torres, Rosita Moreno and Lupita Tovar also found work as exotic types in silent films as well as the new talkies. Tovar later married producer and agent Paul Kohner.

These Hispanic American stars found themselves in the midst of Hollywood social life and were photographed and pampered wherever they went, earning extraordinary sums of money. They worked opposite some of the biggest stars of the era, including Clara Bow, Norma Talmadge, Greta Garbo, Edmund Lowe, Warner Baxter and Victor McLaglen. Gilbert Roland recalled, "To be a star with United Artists [as he was] was a great thing. The studio had John Barrymore and was owned by Mary Pickford, Douglas Fairbanks and Charlie Chaplin."

Several studios, including Metro-Goldwyn-Mayer, Paramount and 20th Century Fox, decided to remake their original English-language productions in foreign-language versions for their principal overseas clients. They put a number of foreign writers, directors and actors under contract. Paramount had a studio facility in Paris that was used to produce original foreign-language productions. The Spanish-speaking market, consisting of Spain and Latin America, was a lucrative one due to its combined population, which hovered around 100 million.

With this in mind, a number of Spaniards and Latin Americans came to Hollywood in order to work in this new experiment. just as with their Anglo counterparts, much of the new talent for sound films come from the theater. Some examples were, from the Spanish theater, Martinez Sierra, Lopez Rubio, Jardiel Pioncela, Catalina Barcena and Ernesto Vilchez; from Mexico, although already established in Hollywood, Dolores Del Rio, Gilbert Roland, Rosita Moreno, Lupita Tovar and Berta Singerman; from Argentina, Carlos Gardel, Mona Maris and Barry Norton; from Brazil, Raul Roulien and Lia Tora (though they speak Portuguese in Brazil, the transition to Spanish was usually easy for Brazilian performers, who worked throughout Latin America); from Chile, Carlos Borcosque and Robert Rey; and from Cuba, Rene Cardona and Luana Alcaniz.

Two types of films were produced, Spanish-language versions of original English-speaking Hollywood productions and original Spanish-language productions.

These pictures had a curious mixture of elements that did not always gel in the final result. The Spanish versions of English-speaking films were filmed at a very fast pace. The same sets, costumes and locations were used, as were many of the same camera setups. Lines were written on chalkboards that were placed out of camera range. The director worked with an editing bench at his side in order to reproduce the same camera angles.

A controversy surfaced over which kind of Spanish would be used in the Spanish versions: the Castilian Spanish of Spain or the Spanish of Latin America, which was spoken slightly differently in each of as many as twenty countries. The films became a mishmash of varying Spanish accents, which proved confusing if not simply laughable to Spanish-speaking audiences.

However, in the case of the Spanish-speaking version of *Dracula* (1931), produced by Paul Kohner for Universal and starring Carlos Villar and Lupita Tovar, cultural and creative differences made for a version as good if not better than the Bela Lugosi English version. Simultaneously working on the same sets and using the same costumes as the English-language version, they would commence filming at seven o'clock at night, after the Lugosi production wrapped for the day, working until six the next morning.

Gilbert Roland (second from left) stars in the Spanish- and English-language versions of *Men of the North.*

Spanish-speaking roles were almost literal translations of their English equivalents. Juan de Landa played Wallace Beery's role in *El Presidio* (1930), in English, *The Big House.* Gilbert Roland had the lead role in both the English and Spanish productions of *Men of the North* (1931).

Early on, Laurel and Hardy made several Spanish-language versions of their short comedies, in which they were to find lasting success as *Flaco y Gordo (Skinny and Fat). Tiembla y Titubea (Below Zero)* (1930); *De Bote en Bote (Pardon Us)* (1931); and *Politiquerias (Chickens Come Home)* (1931) are all examples. The comedians were not bilingual; they read their lines from chalkboards placed out of camera range, speaking their lines phonetically in Spanish with the help of vocal coaches and supporting actors who were Spanish-speaking. Even the extra players in the Spanish-language versions were Latin-looking, as opposed to the English-version extras, and actress Linda Laredo appeared in most of their Spanish-speaking shorts. The foreign-language shorts were a little longer in their running time than their English-speaking counterparts. Some of the added length is padding, to take advantage of the greater rental fees that could be charged to foreign theaters. Some of this padding, however, involved a cultural propensity toward more

Spanish-language version
of Laurel and Hardy
comedy short subjects.

Photo courtesy of Critt Davis Archives.

slapstick, or "business;" more time spent in building up a gag than Anglo audiences wanted or were used to, and a greater use of supporting foreign-language players.

By 1932, this foreign-language/English-language approach was being phased out. Foreign audiences wanted many of their English films in the original language. Besides, it was cheaper and easier to dub the original English-language version, once that technique was perfected, or subtitle it, after a practical system of superimposed subtitling was developed. However, while Metro-Goldwyn-Mayer began dubbing or subtitling its movies, 20th Century Fox, Warner Bros. and Columbia Pictures continued to make original Spanish-language films well into the late 1930s.

At this time, some of the most successful Hispanic Americans in Hollywood were pioneers in behind-the-camera work. A good example was Francisco "Chico" Day, Gilbert Roland's brother. Like his famous brother, Chico began his Hollywood career as an extra. His behind-the-camera career started as a technical adviser on the Samuel Goldwyn production of *The Kid from Spain* in 1932. He advised on the bullfighting sequences and interpreted for the Spanish toreador who doubled for actor Eddie Cantor. Chico later applied for a job as an assistant director at Paramount but was turned down.

Undaunted, he got a job in the mailroom at $18 a week. That same year his knowledge of Spanish won him a job as a technical adviser on *The Last Train from Madrid* (1937), in which his brother starred. When the second assistant director (2nd AD) was promoted and given an assignment on another film, Chico was given the 2nd AD's position. When director Mitchell Leisen needed an interpreter for a film with a Mexican background, he chose Chico. Leisen made Chico 2nd AD on all his films. In *Hold Back the Dawn* (1941), much of the action takes place on the Mexican border, and Chico researched in Mexicali, Tijuana, and other towns. A border street was constructed on Paramount's backlot, and Chico had it filled with all the details he had observed.

Chico became the first Hispanic American assistant director and worked for over thirty years at Paramount Studios on such films as *The Big Broadcast of 1938* (1938), *Lady in the Dark* (1944), *Whispering Smith* (1948), *Samson and Delilah* (1949), *Streets of Laredo* (1949), *Shane* (1953) and *The Ten Commandments* (1956). He later became a unit production manager on such films as *The Magnificent Seven* (1960), *Hello Dolly!* (1969) and *Patton* (1970).

Another good example of major behind-the-scenes contributions by Hispanic Americans was the 1933 RKO production of the classic *King*

Kong. It utilized the talents of model makers Marcel and Victor Delgado, and of Mario Larrinaga, who was a background effects artist. The Delgados constructed several full-size sections of Kong for use in close-up scenes: a full-size bust of Kong with eyes that rolled, a mouth that snarled and eyebrows that moved; a full-size leg and foot, together with an all-important full-size hand, which would clutch Fay Wray in close-ups in the film. The Delgado brothers and Larrinaga were part of the creative team put together by Willis O'Brien, who was the man responsible for bringing Kong to life on screen. O'Brien evolved and perfected the technique of stop-motion animation, in which small, inanimate figures are made to move by photographing successive stages of their movement a frame at a time.

In 1934, Mexico and Mexicans were the subject of the first live-action short film, *La Cucaracha* (RKO), made in the new three-strip Technicolor process.

Eduardo Cansino (Rita Hayworth's father) and his family of Spanish dancers would quite often work for the studios by choreographing and performing Spanish and Mexican dance sequences in films. They owned and operated a dance school in Hollywood and performed in nightclubs.

Carlos Alvarado, brother of actor Don Alvarado, become an agent in Hollywood handling Hispanic talent almost exclusively, founding his own agency in 1943. Hispanic talent found it virtually impossible to find decent representation, for the talent agencies did not want performers of Latin heritage on a full-time basis. But if a studio needed a Latin actor, they would call Alvarado.

Meanwhile, Don Alvarado, also known as Don Page, went on to become an assistant director at Warner Bros., and worked on such films as *East of Eden* (1955), *Auntie Mame* (1958) and *The Old Man and the Sea* (1958).

George Herrera was one of the founders of the Screen Extras Guild, while his brother Joe at first found employment as a bodyguard for Errol Flynn in the 1940s and then, because of his association with Flynn, appeared in such Flynn films as *Objective, Burma!* (1945) and *San Antonio* (1945).

Bill Travilla won an Academy Award® for Best Costume Design for 1949 for his work on *The Adventures of Don Juan* with Errol Flynn, and later designed many of the dresses worn by Marilyn Monroe in her films. Al Ybarra, a longtime Hollywood art director, has to his credit such notable films as *The High and the Mighty* (1954) and *The Alamo* (1960).

Famed guitarist Vicente Gomez tutored many Hollywood stars when they were required to play a guitar on camera.

In a little-known interlude between his early days as an avant-garde filmmaker in pre-Franco Spain and his more mainstream but substantial participation in the fledgling Mexican film industry, the brilliant writer and director Luis Buñuel worked as a dubbing producer at Loews, dubbing films for Metro-Goldwyn-Mayer. From 1941 to 1944 he worked in the film department at the Museum of Modern Art (MoMA) in New York City, and for another year he supervised Spanish dubbing of American films at Warner Bros., in Los Angeles.

The Good Neighbor Policy

By the late 1930s and throughout the 1940s, an increasing number of Hispanic actors and actresses appeared in Latin-themed films. These were aimed at exploiting the South American film market when it became apparent to the Hollywood studios that the rumblings and then the actuality of war in Europe, beginning with the loss of Spain in 1936, would cut off the lucrative European market for American films. The Nazis in Germany seized and banned Hollywood films and applied political pressure against American movies appearing in neutral countries and countries that sympathized with the Nazis.

In 1933, the United States had signed a pact with Latin American countries ending the "gunboat diplomacy" long practiced by the United States to protect its interests in Latin America. This new pact was known as the Good Neighbor Policy; exchange programs were set up, and business ventures were encouraged.

Although Hollywood films dominated Latin America, the market had never been fully exploited. The Production Code Administration (PCA) in Hollywood regulated the content of movies, and until 1939 there was no miscegenation or intermarriage allowed on screen. The Office of Coordinator of Inter-American Affairs, the PCA and the Motion Picture Society for the Americas carefully scrutinized portrayals of Latins in Hollywood films between 1939 and 1948. Mexicans and/or Latin Americans during the period of the Good Neighbor Policy were, for screen purposes, considered Anglo, The Department of State aided Hollywood by creating the Office of the Coordinator of Inter-American Affairs (CIAA) in October 1940. The CIAA opened its Motion Picture Division almost immediately, under the directorship of John Hay Whitney. Whitney's goal was to convince Hollywood to abandon the stereotyped bloodthirsty Latin American villains in its movies and instead to produce films with Latin American themes and locales. Having achieved this, he would use the material to neutralize propaganda flowing into Argentina, Brazil and Chile from Axis wire services, features, newsreels and documentaries. Whitney created the Newsreel Section for this purpose, and by 1943, the CIAA had shipped to South America more than 200 newsreels produced in cooperation with all the studios and newsreel services. On April 26, 1942, the *New York Times* commented that while "the bulk of these 16mm films will reach influential Latin American persons through American embassies, the Latin public will see in regular Hollywood entertainment films more subject matter and scenic atmosphere of a special interest to them."

A select group of Hollywood producers went on a ten-week tour of Latin America and came back with many ideas that could be incorporated in future Hollywood productions. However, there was a problem: Hollywood movies with Latin subject matter had always been a source of controversy in Latin America because of the ignorance of the filmmakers about Latin America, its history, its people and its culture. Latin Americans would not accept films in which they were characterized absurdly; their manners, attitudes and expressions were altogether neglected; their arts and folklore, native music and dances, grotesquely deformed; their environment not even considered. More insultingly,

these "gringo fiascos" were presented as typical of the particular country being portrayed. Though successful in the States, these films were
disasters in the countries whose spirit they only half-heartedly
attempted to reproduce.

Latin American populations reacted to these Hollywood films in
many different ways. Many of the films were poorly attended or banned
outright. Some notions made official protests, and many people openly
demonstrated their disgust. In Argentina, for example, people rioted
and threw stones at the theaters showing *Argentine Nights* (1940).

While most of these Hollywood concoctions were unpopular in Latin
America, a number of films stand out for their effective use of regional
dialect, Latin themes and popular Latin American actors and musicians.

With *The Mark of Zorro* (1940), for example, 20th Century Fox
shrewdly dubbed the movie in six Spanish dialects (Mexican,
Argentinean, Chileno [Chile], Venezuelan, Cuban and the Castilian of
Spain) to match the kind of Spanish spoken in each of the principal

Orson Welles was sent by
RKO to Brazil to make a
documentary film that
would foster cultural
harmony between the
Americas. *It's All True!*
remained unfinished
when RKO had a change
in administration and
abandoned Welles and
the project.

South American nations in order to win over more completely that market. The film was a major hit in Latin America, making Tyrone Power an idol South of the border.

In 1941, Walt Disney and his staff made a goodwill trip to Latin America, and a year later hundreds of sketches, photographs and film recordings were reworked into a part-animated, part-live action travelogue called *Saludos Amigos*. The film was initially released in Latin America, where it was one of the few Hollywood films to enjoy wide acceptance and success.

Laurel and Hardy appeared to great acclaim at the Mexico City Film Festival in April 1941 as guests of President Manuel Avila Camacho. As mentioned earlier, their films continued to be very popular in Spain and Latin America.

Metro-Goldwyn-Mayer served up its own brand of Latin American flavor by hiring Xavier Cugat and his Orchestra and including them in many musicals of the day. Spanish pianist Jose Iturbi and singers Lina Romay and Carlos Ramirez were among other Latin performers featured in such Metro-Golwyn-Mayer films of the period as *Bathing Beauty* (1944), *Music for Millions* (1944) and *Holiday in Mexico* (1946).

Paramount Pictures put Arturo De Cordova under contract. De Cordova was a Mexican actor of great stature who made his debut with an important role as Augustin in *For Whom the Bell Tolls* (1943). Olga San Juan, a Brooklyn-born Puerto Rican singer, became Paramount's answer to Carmen Miranda and was featured in a few musical/comedies. In *Blue Skies* (1946), San Juan danced with Fred Astaire in the torrid "Heat Wave" number. At Universal, Maria Montez, from the Dominican Republic, had a short reign as the Queen of the Technicolor Epics. Montez played Arabian beauties and native island girls, but rarely did she play a Latina.

Down Argentine Way (1940) is notable for being the first in a series of Technicolor musicals at Fox that utilized Latin backgrounds and themes. It also introduced Carmen Miranda, the "Brazilian Bombshell," to the movies. The combination of Betty Grable, Don Ameche, Cesar Romero and Miranda proved to be unbeatable at the box office. The simple scripts placing an American in a Latin American locale were loaded with amusing situations (usually of the "fish-out-of-water" variety) and sumptuous musical numbers interspersed with stock location footage.

As a result of the American entry into World War II and the Good Neighbor Policy, Hollywood filmmakers began to seriously consider including Americans of Mexican or Spanish descent in dramatic motion pictures. The concept of the Mexican American was introduced in the action war movies produced during World War 11. After all, as many as 500,000 Hispanics served in World War II, with 53,000 from Puerto Rico alone. Twelve Hispanics were awarded the Congressional Medal of Honor; this represented one of the highest proportions of any ethnic group.

These films, based on actual wartime incidents or battles, would often revolve around plot lines utilizing an ethnically balanced platoon or squad that represented a cross section of the United States population. The typical movie squad would have a hardened veteran sergeant leading a group of men: one from Brooklyn, either Italian or Irish; one from the Midwest, one from the South, one from California, and one from Chicago. The Mexican American began to be integrated into this group in such films as *Bataan* (1943), *Bombadier* (1943), *Guadalcanal Diary* (1943) and *Battleground* (1949).

This period also saw the further development of the Hispanic American actor in Hollywood, in particular the acceptance of stars like Cesar Romero, Rita Hayworth, Anthony Quinn and Pedro Armendariz. They had no accents, were either born or raised in the United States, and portrayed ethnically diverse roles including American types. Rita Hayworth, in particular, become the epitome of the "All-American Girl" during the war years, and she married the "Boy Genius" of American film, Orson Welles.

By 1944, Hollywood's foreign market had shrunk quite drastically. Realizing that the war would soon end but that it would be quite a few years before Europe would regain any kind of economic strength, Hollywood decided it would continue to exploit the Latin American market, avoiding many past difficulties by actually filming in Latin America and utilizing some of the stars of the regional cinema.

During the war years, the Mexican cinema had developed and bloomed into an industry to rival Hollywood. In 1943, Gilbert Johnson of Atlas Theaters opened two movie houses in New York City's Times Square to show Mexican movies. These movies were reviewed by the *New York Times* and *Daily Variety* on a regular basis. Mexican films gained serious attention both in the States and internationally for their unique style and visual expression, which reflected Mexican culture and history. This was best represented in the work of director Emilio Fernandez and cameraman Gabriel Figueroa. In many ways these films were the inspiration for what, in the 1980s, become known as the Chicano cinema. Mexican movies of the period helped to give a cultural identity to many Mexicans and Mexican Americans.

Maria Candelaria (1943), starring Dolores Del Rio and Pedro Armendariz, won the grand prize at the 1946 Cannes Film Festival. That same year, *Flor Silvestre* (1943) won at Locarno, and *La Perla* (1945) won at San Sebastian in 1946. (All three films were directed and pho-tographed by Fernandez and Figueroa, respectively.)

In 1946, RKO Studios helped build Churubusco Studios in Mexico City, which became the leading state-of-the-art film production facility in Latin America. Many American films produced by RKO, set against exotic or Mexican backgrounds, utilized the Churubusco facilities.

Pedro Armendariz, one of the biggest stars in Mexican cinema, was put under contract by Mary Pickford of United Artists in 1945, and was immediately pressed into service in Hollywood films by director John Ford. Armendariz first worked with Ford in Mexico on *The Fugitive* (1947), starring Henry Fonda. Armendariz played a military officer in pursuit of a priest on the run in an anticlerical Central American coun-try. The cast also included Dolores Del Rio, Leo Carrillo, Chris-Pin Martin and Rafael Inclan. The cinematographer was Gabriel Figueroa and Emilio Fernandez was the associate producer. *The Fugitive* become the first truly Mexican American co-production, combining the best talents on both sides of the border and, in the process, crossing artistic and cultural as well as geographic boundaries.

In August 1946, Tyrone Power and Cesar Romero were sent on a goodwill tour of Latin America by 20th Century Fox, and it was a resounding success. They were mobbed wherever they went and were hosted by such dignitaries as Juan and Evita Peron.

In 1991, Cesar Romero talked about the tour: "The studio provided us with this twin engine Beechcraft which we named Saludos Amigos. Tyrone did all the flying, because he'd been a Marine pilot during the war. We flew down through Mexico, then Central America, and all of South America except for Venezuela. We hit every capital city.

"The first person we had to meet [wherever we landed] was the American ambassador, and nine times out of ten times he would arrange a meeting with the president of the country. The most amusing was when we had lunch with the Perons in Buenos Aires, Argentina.

"Evita was a very attractive lady who never stopped talking. Talk, talk, talk, all the time. The others on the trip didn't speak Spanish, so I generally acted as interpreter. Juan was a very serious, quiet man who said yes to everything Evita said.

"I was sitting next to Evita during the luncheon, and she said to me, 'Why do the people in your country call my husband a dictator? He is not a dictator, he is a patriot.' She turned to her husband and said, 'Is not that right, Juan? You're not a dictator,' and he said, 'Yes, my dear.' She told me and Tyrone [Power] over dinner, 'You're fortunate, because in America they treat movie stars right. Here they spit at them. I should know. I was an artist. Would you like to see one of my movies? I can arrange a showing at the national theater.'

"Right then and there Juan said, 'My dear Evita, I'm sure that the last thing they want to do is go to the movies.' I'm sure that if Darryl F. Zanuck had offered her a contract she would have left Juan."

The Good Neighbor Policy began to fade when the war ended in 1945. By 1948, with the approaching recovery of the European market and with a backlog of American films waiting to be seen by European audiences, Latin America began to be de-emphasized, and starting with *The Treasure of the Sierra Madre* (1948), the bandit figure and many of the old stereotypes began slowly to reappear. It became production as usual at the studios, and the tried-and-true formulas began to be recycled with some minor adjustments. Some actors were able to make the transition into better roles. Pedro Armendariz, for example, worked not only in his native Mexico but also in United States and European productions. Others, though, became bound by rigid typecasting and found it difficult to keep a diverse career going. Some, like Arturo De Cordova, who did not meet with wide audience acceptance even after starring with Joan Fontaine in the big-budget *Frenchman's Creek* (1944), left Hollywood and became big stars in the Spanish-speaking cinema, where they commanded huge salaries and were able to portray a wide variety of roles.

The Post-World War II Period

Mexican Americans who settled primarily in California and the Southwest during the Mexican Revolution had earned their United States citizenship with their own lives and the lives of their sons who had fought and in many cases died in World War II. Many Mexican Americans, however, still had memories of unjust harassment during the Zoot Suit riots in Los Angeles in the early days of the war and the racism that still prevailed back home. The nation's urban centers began teeming with new immigrants as a migration took place along the East Coast. Puerto Ricans, who are racially mixed Spanish-speaking American citizens from the Caribbean, were arriving in New York City, Newark, Boston and farther west in Chicago in search of jobs and a better way of life.

Overseas, the Marshall Plan was instituted to help Europe get back on its feet economically. In 1948 President Harry S. Truman desegregated the United States Armed Forces. In the cinema, meanwhile, the European neorealist films, growing out of the sobering nihilism of the war, began to show the physical and psychological damage the violence of war inflicts on people.

Hollywood began to reflect some of these changes. A harder-looking, pseudo documentary style of filmmaking began to emerge, and more difficult subject matter was tackled. Movies such as *The Best Years of Our Lives* (1946), *Gentleman's Agreement* (1947), *Broken Arrow* (1950), *The Men* (1950) and others dealt with such topics as war-traumatized veterans adjusting to civilian life, anti-Semitism, racial prejudice, paraplegic veterans and the plight of the American Indian.

John Huston and many of his fellow Hollywood directors, including George Stevens, Frank Capra and John Ford, were changed by the war, and this change was reflected in their postwar work.

Even the traditional heroes began to show darker, more complex sides, beginning with Bogart's Fred C. Dobbs character in Huston's *The Treasure of the Sierra Madre* (1948). Jimmy Stewart's easygoing Mr. Smith persona changed to the hard-nosed, vengeful, near antiheroes of *Winchester '73* (1950) and *Bend of the River* (1952). John Wayne showed a darker side as ruthless cattle baron Tom Dunson in *Red River* (1948). James Cagney played Cody Jarrett, a small-time gangster with a psychological mother fixation, in *White Heat* (1949).

The Treasure of the Sierra Madre (1948) signaled the end of the Good Neighbor Policy by both the reintroduction of Hispanic stereotypes and the reintroduction of location filming, largely abandoned since the silent films, utilizing real-life Mexican landscapes and people. (Another movie, *The Naked City*, made the same year in New York City, also helped popularize the location shoot, which was aided by the development during the war of lighter camera equipment.)

Because of economic advantages, technical capabilities (RKO's Churubusco Studios in Mexico City, for example), and scenic locations, many Hollywood productions were filmed in Mexico in the late 1940s and throughout the 1950s. The areas of wide desert expanse proved irresistible to Western filmmakers. Some of the films shot in Mexico include *Captain from Castile* (1947), *Blowing Wild* (1953), *Garden of Evil* (1954), *Vera Cruz* (1954), *Bandido* (1956) and *The Wonderful Country* (1959). This surge of film production in Mexico provided employment and long-term experience for Mexican and Hispanic American actors and technicians.

Several films, including *The Lady from Shanghai* (1948), *The Big Steal* (1949), *The Brave Bulls* (1951) and *The Bullfighter and the Lady* (1951), illustrated a progressive and modern image of Mexico. They featured contemporary Mexico City, Acapulco and Taxco as story backdrops.

The Western was transferred to two South American locales, Brazil for *The Americano* (1955), starring Glenn Ford; and Argentina for *Way of a Gaucho* (1952), starring Rory Calhoun.

Films made during the 1950s and early 1960s that brought a new consciousness of the Hispanic American as part of contemporary American society include *Border Incident* (1949), *The Lawless* (1950), *Right Cross* (1950), *My Man and I* (1952), *The Ring* (1952), *Salt of the Earth* (1954), *Blackboard Jungle* (1955), *Giant* (1956), *The Man from Del Rio* (1956), *Man in the Shadow* (1957), *Cry Tough* (1959) and *West Side Story* (1961).

Hispanic American veterans and older Hispanic civil rights organizations such as the League of United Latin American Citizens (LULAC) struggled for first-class citizenship through a policy of assimilation. By the 1950s, Hollywood had taken up the issues of racial injustice through "social problem" movies, though by the early 1960s and with the impact of rock 'n' roll, the industry had shifted to an almost exploitive focus on juvenile delinquents. Warner Bros., had in fact pioneered social problem films as early as the 1930s, but *Bordertown* (1935) starring Paul Muni, was one of the few sympathetic portraits of Mexican Americans made in that period.

Meanwhile, an older generation of Latino stars was passing from the screen, or becoming relegated to secondary character roles. Along with the dependable screen heroes of yesteryear like John Wayne, Clark Gable and Humphrey Bogart, a new screen hero emerged, He was young, brooding and vulnerable, and took the form of Marlon Brando, Montgomery Clift and James Dean.

The successors of Latino stars such as Cesar Romero and Dolores Del Rio—actors like Ricardo Montalban and Rita Moreno—were never able to achieve quite the same stature or access to starring roles as their predecessors.

The Señorita and the Spitfire

The stereotype of the Hispanic woman can be divided in to two categories: the virginal señorita and the loose Latin spitfire. They are extensions of their Anglo counterparts, the fair-haired, virginal Lillian Gish or Doris Day, and the vamp, a more voluptuous, sultry figure, who, in the cases of Mae West or Marilyn Monroe, is also saucily independent. In their own way, these stereotypes are as stylized within American drama as the ritualistic characters in a Japanese Noh play.

The señorita is an extension of the virgin (indeed, the word implies virginity), and has long been a staple of Hollywood Westerns and costume dramas. The sexually alluring and available spitfire (in other words, "the fallen woman") is the vamp. Both types were played alternately by such stars as Dolores Del Rio and Lupe Velez at the start of their careers and continued into and throughout the sound period.

Such characterizations caused actress Rita Cansino to toil for years in Hollywood B movies until she was cosmetically stripped of her ethnicity and became the all-American Rita Hayworth.

Maria Castenada, who achieved brief popularity when known as Movita, played a native girl in Metro-Goldwyn-Mayer's 1935 production of *Mutiny on the Bounty*. She went on to play assorted Polynesians, Indians and Mexican types for the rest of her career.

To make matters worse, these roles were often played not by Latinas, but by Anglo actresses such as Linda Darnell, who in *The Mark of Zorro* (1940) played a señorita and in *My Darling Clementine* (1946) played a Latin spitfire.

Because of Roosevelt's Good Neighbor Policy, more and more Latin actresses appeared on American screens, but they were usually limited to senorita or spitfire roles. For example, as she matured, Lupe Velez was forced into the "hot tamale" or Mexican-wildcat type in the popular *Mexican Spitfire* series at RKO. Brazilian Carmen Miranda with her dancing, cute accent and tropical fruit and banana costumes, reached the epitome of the caricature of Latin women as hip-swinging, fractured English-speaking, dizzy sex objects.

Another Hispanic actress who dominated the industry in the 1940s was Maria Montez. Born in the Dominican Republic, she starred in a series of extravagant Technicolor adventure films at Universal that exploited her undeniable sexuality and exotic beauty. However, typically, she too was limited to the roles of senorita and vamp, playing native girls and Arabian princesses.

In sum, Hispanic actresses could find plenty of work in films but only as part of a parade of hip-swinging, finger-snapping, raven-haired Marias and Rositas. There also developed the all-knowing "suffering mother" or jovial mamacita.

Such female stereotyping was not exclusive to Hispanics, however. Jane Darwell made a career out of such roles, one of her most famous portrayals being the mother in *The Grapes of Wrath* (1940), for which she won an Oscar®. Hattie McDaniel, an African American actress, usually played the mammy, housekeeper, or maid—a role which won her an Academy Award® for Best Supporting Actress in *Gone with the Wind* (1939). As McDaniel commented, "It's better to get $7,000 a week for playing a servant than $7 a week for being one" (article on Hattie McDaniel by Eleanor Traylor in *Dictionary of American Negro Biography* [New York: Norton, 1982]).

Latinas were (and still are) portrayed as subservient to men and victims of male Hispanic and Anglo violence. They often betrayed their Hispanic men (who were depicted as wicked, violent and stupid) when shown the error of their ways by the Anglo hero with whom they had fallen in love. At the film's end, the Anglo hero would ride off into the sunset with the promise that he would be back. But the audience, and the Latina, knew that once over the border, he would forget her and fall into the arms of his fair-haired Anglo girlfriend. Or, in another variation, the Latina would conveniently die.

Jennifer Jones as Pearl Chavez in *Duel in the Sun* (1946) is perhaps one of the strongest Latina characterizations ever presented in a Hollywood film. Pearl is strong willed, a fully realized multidimensional character who is a virtual life force around whom the story revolves. There were a number of Hispanic actresses who could have played the role, but ultimately, Jones won the role. Several years later, Mexican actress Katy Jurado impressed audiences with her striking features and acting ability as Helen Ramirez in *High Noon* (1952), and was later nominated for an Academy Award® as Best Supporting Actress for her role as an Indian woman in *Broken Lance* (1954), opposite Spencer Tracy.

Though they played diverse roles in their native countries, Mexican actresses, no matter how talented, were most often relegated to roles as Indian squaws, beautiful senoritas, or spitfires in Hollywood films. This was true even as late as the 1960s. For example, after leaving Hollywood and becoming Mexico's First Lady of the cinema, Dolores Del Rio returned to the States after a long absence to play Elvis Presley's Indian mother in *Flaming Star* (1960) and then played the dignified Cheyenne matriarch Spanish Woman in *Cheyenne Autumn* (1964). Most recently, Spanish actress Penelope Cruz played the role of a virginal Mexican senorita in *The Hi-Lo Country* (1998)

Actress Rita Moreno captured critical attention as Tuptim in the celebrated movie version of the Broadway musical *The King and I* (1956) and won an Oscar® as Best Supporting Actress for her portrayal of Anita in *West Side Story* (1961). An Academy Award® usually assures an actress a choice of the best roles and financial security. However, Moreno, Puerto Rican, did not work in movies for seven years after winning her Oscar® because she refused to continue accepting roles she felt were demeaning and artistically limiting. Her richly comic portrayal of Googie Gomez in *The Ritz* (1976) is a biting satire of all the roles she (and other talented Latinas) had to play early in their careers.

More recently, Mexican actress Elpidia Carrillo has become the all-purpose victimized native Latin girl in a series of major motion pictures in which she appeared opposite some of the world's most important leading men, beginning with *The Border* in 1982 starring Jack Nicholson. Elizabeth Peña played a sexually liberated, tough-talking maid in *Down and Out in Beverly Hills* (1986). Argentine actress Norma Aleandro, who first drew attention in the United States in 1985 in *The Official Story* (which won an Oscar® for Best Foreign Language Film), was nominated for an Academy Award® as Best Supporting Actress in *Gaby—A True Story* (1987), in which she played a Mexican Indian maid. Aleandro went on to other important roles in Hollywood films, as did sexy Brazilian Sonia Braga in *The Milagro Beanfield War* (1988) and *Moon over Parador* (1988). Madeleine Stowe, of Costa Rican heritage, played a very positive and modern Hispanic American woman as Maria McGuire in *Stakeout* (1987).

Luis Valdez's *La Bamba* (1987), the first major film of the Chicano cinema to achieve mainstream box office success, has made the most dramatic statement about Hispanic women.

Connie Valenzuela (Rosana De Soto) is the all-suffering noble mother who watches over her family. De Soto brought to life a character with many complexities who, as the head of her family, has to work and keep her two boys, Ritchie (Lou Diamond Phillips) and Bob (Esai Morales), in line. Connie loves and defends her sons and is there with Ritchie through his first triumphs, taking an active part in his success. When the record producer who wants to sign Ritchie assumes she is a simple Spanish woman and asks, "Habla Ingles?" she replies, "We speak business."

Rosie (Elizabeth Peña) in *La Bamba*, on the other hand, is a much darker character who starts out being the virginal senorita to Ritchie but is more attracted to his older brother, Bob. She runs off with Bob and becomes pregnant by him, becoming a victim of her own cultural upbringing in a cycle she is never likely to break.

Rosana De Soto has gone on to play a variety of characters such as Dustin Hoffman's Jewish wife in *Family Business* (1989) and a Klingon princess in *Star Trek IV: The Voyage Home* (1986).

In August 1992, a group of Hispanic American actresses in Los Angeles were outraged when it was announced that Laura San Giacomo would be cast in the role of Mexican artist Frida Kahlo in a film biography called *Frida and Diego* opposite Raul Julia as acclaimed Mexican muralist Diego Rivera. They were outraged because they had not been given the chance to audition and were effectively being blocked from access to this major leading role. When director Luis Valdez was reportedly told by the producers that a recognizable star name was required, they were harking back to the old Hollywood mind-set that prevented Hispanic actors and actresses from finding stardom or leading roles for years. But, the actresses reasoned, how big a star was Laura San Giacomo before her sensational 1989 film debut in *sex, lies and videotape?*

New Line Cinema pulled out of its financing agreement on the film, which has yet to be made, just prior to the negative publicity. Writer and director Luis Valdez issued a press release that said in part: "Art is not a question of affirmative action. It is an affirmation of one's belief in human universality. I will not be intimidated into making my vision of America coincide with whatever is politically correct at the moment. I have helped to define the Latino identity in America through my plays and films, but I will not be coerced into limiting my artistic choices in violation of basic human principles. My social objective has always been to counteract racism in the world, not reinforce it."

However, the actresses were protesting not Valdez's choice for the role, but the fact that the movie industry continues to block Latinas from even trying out for roles they are ethnically as well as technically equipped to handle. The point was their quest for equality of opportunity in the casting process, not guaranteed success.

Along with their male contemporaries such as Andy Garcia, Hector Elizondo, Jimmy Smits, Antonio Banderas and John Leguizamo, Hispanic actresses are now managing to find non-stereotypical leading roles.

Examples include Jennifer Lopez's starmaking title role in *Selena* (1997), and a succession of varied parts that led to the role of Federal

Marshall Karen Cisco in *Out of Sight* (1998); Lauren Velez's young, married, inner city Puerto Rican woman Lisette, in Darnell Martin's *I Like It Like That* (1994); Salma Hayek's sexy yet strong star turn in *Desperado* (1995), followed by the romantic comedy *Fools Rush In* (1997); Maria Conchita Alonso's immigrant Bloomingdale's shopgirl in Paul Mazursky's *Moscow On the Hudson* (1984), to the repressed housewife in Robert M. Young's *Caught* (1996); Elizabeth Peña as the sensuous Jezzie in *Jacob's Ladder* (1990), to Pilar, a widowed high school teacher in John Sayles' *Lone Star* (1996); Rachel Ticotin appeared in the role of Melina, an alien mystery woman, in the science fiction film *Total Recall* (1990) and a policewoman in *Falling Down* (1998); Madeleine Stowe played a Latin woman in *Revenge* (1990), an English woman in pre-Revolutionary war America in *The Last Of The Mohicans* (1992) and a contemporary woman in *The General's Daughter* (1999).

And let's not forget Rosie Perez's memorably feisty New York Latina in *White Men Can't Jump* (1992), who not only proves she is smart and determined enough to realize her dream, but remains true to herself even at the cost of abandoning her Anglo lover, a fascinating reversal of roles from the days when the Anglo hero rode off into the sunset, leaving his Latina dalliance in favor of the Anglo blonde who had been waiting for him to "come to his senses."

Coming of Age

North American Latino culture is not homogeneous. It is divided by nationality, class, geographical area and degrees of assimilation. The three principal Latino groups in the United States are Mexicans, Puerto Ricans and Cubans. There is also a growing population of immigrants from Spanish-speaking Caribbean islands, such as the Dominican Republic and Dominica, but they have not as yet been much recognized by Hollywood.

The coming of age of Hispanic Americans in the Hollywood motion picture industry is tied to the way Hispanic Americans have evolved as a part of American society. Their role and growing visibility in mainstream American society is being defined and reflected partly in cinematic terms. Most of the progressive work in this area has been initiated by independent filmmakers in such films as Jesus Trevino's *Raices de Sangre (Blood Roots)* (1979) and Robert M. Young's *Alambrista!* (1977) and *The Ballad of Gregorio Cortez* (1983). Other works, such as *Stand and Deliver* (1988, financed by PBS, released by Warner Bros.,) and Robert Redford's *The Milagro Beanfield War* (1988, initiated by producer Moctesuma Esparza and financed and distributed by Universal), and *My Family* (1995) have come to fruition through a curious mixture of both independent and studio financing.

Considering the abundance of American films dealing with war, most, unfortunately, have overlooked the participation of the Hispanic American. Even in the Vietnam era the only exceptions are Oliver Stone's *Platoon* (1986), which had minor Hispanic characters in platoon members Rhah (Francesco Quinn) and Rodriguez (Chris Castillejo); Stanley Kubrick's *Full Metal Jacket* (1987), which featured one Hispanic

Anthony Quinn, Gilbert Roland and Ricardo Montalban at Nosotros Awards, 1980.

Photo courtesy of Satir Gonzalez

Marine recruit (Sal Lopez); and Sidney I. Furie's *The Boys in Company C* (1978), which featured a Hispanic Marine drill instructor played by Santos Morales, although none of the recruits were Hispanic. The reality is that thirteen Hispanics won Congressional Medals of Honor for service in Vietnam.

Taylor Hackford's *An Officer and a Gentleman* (1982), a romantic service drama about elite Air Force pilots starring Richard Gere and Debra Winger, featured a multiethnic cast including Tony Plana as a recruit named De La Serra. His character represented a minor breakthrough in that he was depicted as an intelligent, mainstream American rather than as a dim-witted working-class migrant worker, artisan or a violent gang member.

As the 1960s progressed, the civil rights movement, led by African Americans, also encouraged other disenfranchised or ignored groups, such as women and Hispanic Americans, to recognize their own unsatisfactory condition. A rediscovery and reexamination of America's heritage began to take place as seen through the eyes of groups who had been either left out of the history books or relegated to a minor, often stereotyped role. Colleges and universities established African

American, Chicano and Puerto Rican studies programs that filtered down to the high school level.

Out of this period of political unrest and great social movements came funding for public television and education-related programs, many of which were specifically designed to meet the needs of ethnic minorities. Young Hispanic Americans with an interest in the arts, education and communication were able to use their talents to explore social consciousness. Forms of self-expression and awareness manifested themselves through street-culture murals that popped up in barrios across the country, while *centro culturales* (cultural centers) began to be formed along with theater groups like El Teatro Campesino, El Teatro de la Esperanza, and the Puerto Rican Traveling Theatre. Public television stations allowed aspiring filmmakers access to 16mm cameras and equipment, and they set about recording the events of the day as they affected their communities, producing documentaries about Hispanic American life in the United States.

In 1969, Nosotros (the Spanish word for "we, the people"), a Hispanic actors' organization, was formed in Hollywood by Ricardo Montalban, Richard Hernandez, Anthony Quinn, Gilbert Roland, Val DeVargas, Rudolfo Hoyos, Jr., Carlos Rivas, Tony DeMarco and Henry Darrow.

The organization is dedicated to improving the image of Hispanic Americans and Spanish-speaking peoples in general in film, television, theater and radio. The group also seeks to improve opportunities for Hispanic performing artists through training and workshops. At great personal cost to their careers, these few individuals, led by Ricardo Montalban, confronted studio heads, network heads, producers and writers and urged them to reevaluate the problems of stereotypical depictions of Hispanics. These meetings and discussions come to a head when the "Frito Bandito" television commercials began to be broadcast in 1970.

The advertising for a popular brand of corn chips featured a stereotypical sombrero-ed and mustachioed cartoon bandit as a corn chip thief. The commercials were so offensive that various Mexican American communities and their leaders rallied around Nosotros and forced the advertiser to abandon the campaign. As Nosotros president Ricardo Montalban commented in an interview, "Why couldn't the cartoon have been the Frito Amigo, who gave the chips away instead of the negative image of the bandido who steals?"

The controversy focused national attention on the preponderance of negative, stereotypical images of Hispanics in the media. Hispanic American children had too few role models and were being fed numerous negative images without any positive Hispanic images to balance them. Furthermore, the negative stereotyping of Hispanics was being reinforced in Anglo children, condemning yet another generation to perpetuate a growing problem.

Hispanic actors found themselves in a dilemma: by accepting negative roles in order to work, they were sacrificing personal dignity and artistic growth; but if they protested too loudly, producers could blacklist them. Nevertheless, through Nosotros and community-based groups, pressure was applied to the entertainment industry, and small yet significant changes began to take place.

By the 1970s, the acclaimed work of Spanish filmmaker Luis Buñuel and the cinema of Castro's Cuba like *Lucia* (shot in 1969, but not released in the United States until 1972), directed by Humberto Solos, and *Memories of Underdevelopment* (1968, released in the States in 1973), directed by Tomas Gutierrez Alea, were penetrating the American progressive moviegoing consciousness, especially on college campuses and the art house circuit. Such films had a profound influence, inspiring a new generation of Hispanic American filmmakers.

This new generation has ushered in Chicano cinema, which it is necessary to define. A Chicano is a Mexican American whose consciousness was born out of the civil rights movement of the 1960s and who is aware of his or her dual heritage. To qualify as true Chicano cinema, a movie should

- concern itself with Mexican American subject matter;
- express a Mexican American viewpoint on life in the United States;
- contain principal characters who are Mexican American;
- have creative forces (director, writer, producer) who are predominantly Mexican American;
- and/or be a film that speaks from a personal and unique vision that stems from a political base.

As of 2000, Chicano cinema is just over twenty-one years old and it has had a slow, somewhat isolated development. Chicano cinema owes much of its existence to organizations like the Corporation for Public Broadcasting and the private investors, grants, funding sources and community supported public television that have acted as the economic and creative genesis for many of these independent works. *Raices de Sangre* (1979), *Zoot Suit* (1981), *Sequin* (1982), *The Ballad of Gregorio Cortez* (1983), *El Norte* (1983), *Born in East L.A.* (1987), *La Bamba* (1987), *Stand and Deliver* (1988), *Break of Dawn* (1989), *American Me* (1992), *My Family* (1995), *Desperado* (1995) and *Selena* (1998) would all be considered Chicano cinema. All of these titles, along with *El Super* (1979), *Crossover Dreams* (1985), *Hangin' with the Homeboys* (1991) and *Star Maps* (1997) would also be considered Hispanic American cinema. Hispanic American cinema subscribes to the same basic criteria as Chicano cinema, but the term Hispanic American is an umbrella title that includes Chicano, Cuban, Puerto Rican and all other Hispanic groups living in the United States.

These films signify a difference in the way Hollywood looks at Hispanic Americans. As filmmakers, Hispanic Americans are creating and defining their own images rather than allowing themselves to be defined by someone else. *Stand and Deliver, Born in East L.A., La Bamba, My Family* and *Selena* all share the common theme of the reaffirmation of the promise of the American Dream.

Latin themed films, on the other hand, are films produced in Hollywood with Latin characters or situations (set in or out of the United States, but whose stories are generally told through Anglo protagonists. The 1980s and 90s saw a number of these films produced, and they usually fell into the conventional genres of gang films, border stories, Westerns and war-torn banana republic stories. In Latin themed films, there is usually no Hispanic involvement in the key creative filmmaking positions. Examples of recent Latin themed films are *Under Fire* (1983), *Havana* (1990), *The Mambo Kings* (1992), *Bound By Honor* (1993) and *Clear and Present Danger* (1994)

Gregory Nava's *El Norte* (1984) won an Academy Award® nomination for its screenplay, and Luis Valdez's *La Bamba* in 1987 became a worldwide hit, but it wasn't until Alfonso Arau's 1994 independent Mexican production of *Like Water For Chocolate*, that the Hispanic American film movement really made an impact. The film captivated American audiences, as well as audiences worldwide, making it the highest grossing independent foreign film in the United States up to that time.

1995 is the year that Hispanic American filmmakers finally took center stage in Hollywood with three films that created a momentum that is still being felt today and leading us into the next century: Alfonso Arau's *A Walk in The Clouds*, Robert Rodriquez's *Desperado* and Gregory Nava's *My Family*.

These films brought Hispanic American talent, both in front of and behind the camera, greater recognition from Hollywood. Arau's *A Walk in the Clouds* was 20th Century Fox's most profitable film of 1995. The romantic fantasy changed the central characters from Italian to Mexican American and the clash between the Latin and Anglo cultures was a focus point of the story. The international cast, led by Keanu Reeves, Giancarlo Gianni and Anthony Quinn, made for a rich film experience. Wunderkind Robert Rodriquez remade his $7,000 dollar film *El Mariachi* (1992), into a big budget action film for Columbia Pictures. The result was *Desperado* (1995), starring Antonio Banderas. Rodriquez cast the beautiful and talented actress Salma Hayek as the female lead and the film led to her stardom.

Gregory Nava's critically acclaimed multi-generational drama, *My Family*, showcased an ensemble cast of Latino actors giving them roles where they could demonstrate their talent with flesh and blood characters. Jimmy Smits received wide acclaim for his role as the troubled single father, as did Esai Morales as the son caught between two worlds. The film's significance lies in its artistically presented Latino American immigrant story from a Hispanic American point of view. It also marked the feature film debut of future star Jennifer Lopez. This led to her collaboration with Nava two years later when he cast her in the title role of the young Tejana singing sensation in *Selena*. The film grossed $38 million dollars at the domestic United States box office, largely from Hispanic audiences.

There are of course, Hispanic directors working in Hollywood on projects without a Latin cultural link, such as Mexican Luis Mandoki who directed *White Palace* (1990) with Susan Sarandon, *When a Man Loves a Woman* (1994) with Meg Ryan and Andy Garcia, and *Message in a Bottle* (1999) with Kevin Costner, Paul Newman and Robin Wright Penn. Mexican Alfonso Cuaron received critical notice for his sensitive direction of *The Little Princess* (1995), which led to his directing *Great Expectations* (1997); and Peruvian Luis Llosa directed the action adventure films *Sniper* (1993) and the snake thriller *Anaconda* (1997). Guillermo Navarro was the director of photography for Quentin

Tarantino's *Jackie Brown* (1997) and the box office hit *Stuart Little* (1999); and Rodrigo Garcia directed *Things You Can Tell Just by Looking at Her* (2000), starring Cameron Diaz. Gregory Nava directed the African American musical biography *Why Do Fools Fall in Love?* (1998) for Warner Bros., and British-born Latino Sam Mendes directed the highly acclaimed and Oscar®-winning film, *American Beauty* (1999).

Titanic (1997), the most successful movie of all time, was filmed largely in Baja, California at studios built by 20th Century Fox. Both Mexican and American craftsmen and technicians were involved in the production and the majority of the passengers on the ill-fated ship were Mexican extra players. David Valdes, longtime production associate of Clint Eastwood, branched out on his own after producing the Oscar®-winning *Unforgiven*. He has since produced the special effects thriller *Turbulence* (1997) and the Oscar® nominated Tom Hanks film, *The Green Mile* (1999).

Jennifer Lopez, Salma Hayek and Cameron Diaz have emerged as female stars and sex symbols. In 1996, Lopez became the first Latina actress to be paid $1 million dollars for her role in *Selena*. By the end of 1999, Lopez was earning nearly $8 million dollars a film. In an *US magazine* interview of April 1997, Lopez stated "I want to be *the* Latina in American cinema. We need somebody to be a star for the times, If its me, that's fine: but if it's not, I just hope it's somebody really soon. Doing Latino roles is important, but so is being considered for roles that are non-Latino." She further explained, "Because then you're just being seen as an actress who has the ability to bring people into the theater, which is what's important in Hollywood." Salma Hayek's first romantic comedy *Fools Rush In* earned $28 million dollars at the American box office, with a significant portion of ticket sales from Latino moviegoers. Hayek also co-starred in the hit film *Wild Wild West* (1999) opposite Will Smith and Kevin Kline. Diaz made her film debut as a sexy lounge singer in *The Mask* (1994) opposite Jim Carrey, and confirmed her stardom in the quirky hit comedy *There's Something About Mary* (1998).

Freddie Prinze Jr., son of the late Hispanic comedian, has also emerged as a movie star in the late 1990s, especially among the young adult moviegoers in such films as *She's All That* (1999)and *I Know What You Did Last Summer* (1997). Spanish-born Antonio Banderas can be considered an international box office movie star from his roles in *Evita* (1996) and *The Mask of Zorro* (1998).

As the century turns, Latino culture in the United States is rapidly becoming part of the mainstream. Nearly all of the successful actors and directors as well as a significant number of singers and musicians (such as Ricky Martin, Jennifer Lopez, Marc Anthony, Carlos Santana, Christina Aguilera and the late Selena) were born and reared in the United States and are responding to the influences of a multi-cultural environment and creating music and art that appeals in growing numbers to both Hispanic and non-Hispanics alike.

In 1999, *New York* magazine featured Jennifer Lopez on the cover, and for that issue changed its name to *Nueva York* in recognition of the city's Hispanic population and its influence on the city's cultural and economic lifestyle. Lopez's career move from actress to top pop recording star with a number one record and album, "On The 6," whose title is derived from the number of the subway train she would ride from her home in the Bronx into Manhattan, shows the cross-over impact that Latin themed arts are beginning to have on non-Hispanic Americans.

The political and economic strength of the Hispanic American community is only now starting to be recognized as a major force in American society and the entertainment industry is slowly beginning to reflect those concerns in films and television.

Salsa has now surpassed ketchup as the number one selling condiment in the United States. By the year 2009 Latinos will pass African Americans as the largest minority group in the United States. According to the Motion Picture Association of America, Latinos accounted for 15 percent of all movie ticket sales in the United States in 1998. By the year 2010, Latino buying power is expected to be $1 trillion.

There are many different voices of expression that encompass the breath and complexity of the Latino community in the United States. Though films do not have the responsibility, they do have the capability to educate and provoke thought as well as to entertain. With the new developing technologies (videocassettes, DVD, cable television, digital computer imaging and computer generated imagery) images created on film and video tape will be with us long after their creators are gone.

So it is appropriate, as we move into the new millennium, one of its first major success stories is that of Cuban-born Eduardo Lopez, co-producer and co-director of the phenomenally successful *The Blair Witch Project* (1999). Via the Internet, Lopez, along with his partners, changed the way movies are marketed and proved that audiences would line up to see a feature length video in theatres. Lopez's spectacular and innovative success may well show the way for how movies will be made, marketed and distributed in the future.

A new generation of Hispanic American filmmakers is following the footprints of the many Hispanics in Hollywood who paved the way by overcoming the still existing obstacles of ignorance and racism. These talented new artists are producing an entertaining world cinema, a unique form of storytelling that will paint the changing face of America in light and shadow as we enter into the twenty first century, marking almost one hundred years of Hispanic participation in Hollywood.

Films / Alphabetical Listing

Aaron Loves Angela (1975 Columbia)
D: Gordon Parks Jr.
S: Gerald Sanford
P: Robert J. Anderson
Cast: Kevin Hooks, Irene Cara

A Romeo and Juliet love story set in New York City starring engaging young performers and a happy ending despite the obstacles. An African American boy from Harlem falls in love with a Puerto Rican girl from Spanish Harlem.

Irene Cara went on to star in the film *Fame* (1980) and sing the title song, which became a pop hit and won an Academy Award®.

Jose Feliciano scored the music.

The Addams Family (1991 Paramount)
D: Barry Sonnefeld
S: Caroline Thompson and Larry Wilson
P: Scott Rudin
Cast: Raul Julia, Anjelica Huston, Christopher Lloyd

Based on the 1300 darkly humorous cartoons drawn by Charles Addams that have been published in *The New Yorker* Magazine since the 1930s. This extended family of freaks and misfits caught the imagination of the American public when sixty-four half hour films were produced as a series for ABC television in 1964-1966, with John Astin playing the role of Gomez.

This film is a curious entry because it was a major studio produced hit film with the leading male character named Gomez played by actor Raul Julia in a flamboyant style. Gomez is an exotic romantic swashbuckler with his slicked back hair, near pencil-thin mustache and trademark cigars. He fences with his accountant, wears sumptuous satin and velvet smoking jackets and is wildly in love with his wife, Morticia, and his family. Gomez backflips through windows, dances and likes to stage massive train wrecks with his toy locomotives. He tends to fly through life blinded by his own enthusiasm, which at times gets him in trouble. "Raul Julia plays Gomez as a Chivalrous Caballero," Patricia Dobson, *Screen International* (11/21/91).

The plot concerns Gomez's yearning for the homecoming of his long lost brother, Fester and the arrival of someone who is a dead ringer for and claims to be Uncle Fester.

Adventure (1946 Metro-Goldwyn-Mayer)
D: Victor Fleming
S: Frederick Hazlitt Brennan and Vincent Lawrence
P: Sam Zimbalist
Cast: Clark Gable, Greer Garson, Thomas Mitchell, Lina Romay,
    Tito Renaldo

The story of a romance between a rough-and-ready merchant seaman and a librarian. The first ten minutes of the film takes place in a port on the seacoast of Chile where Gable has a brief romance with a native girl named Maria, played by Lina Romay, whom he leaves behind. Romay sings a couple of Spanish tunes.

The Adventurers (1970 Paramount)
D: Lewis Gilbert
S: Lewis Gilbert and Michael Hastings, based on the novel by
    Harold Robbins
P: Lewis Gilbert
Cast: Bekim Fehmiu, Ernest Borgnine, Olivia de Havilland,
    Fernando Rey

A melodramatic potboiler that subscribes to the "banana republic in violent turmoil" stereotype. A Latin-American ambassador's son (Yugoslavian actor Bekim Fehmiu), who is a jet setting playboy eventually returns to his native land to take revenge on the corrupt government official who raped and murdered his mother.

Hispanics and Latins are noticeably absent except for Fernando Rey and thousands of Columbian extras, where part of the film was shot. Brazilian Laurindo Almeida scored the music.

The Adventures of Don Juan (1949 Warner Brothers)
D: Vincent Sherman
S: George Oppenheimer and Barry Kurnitz
P: Jerry Wald
Cast: Errol Flynn, Viveca Lindfors, Robert Douglas, Romney Brent

Flynn comfortably essayed the role of the famous Latin Lover, Don Juan, in this fun and amusing Technicolor swashbuckler.

The movie was made with the usual Warner Bros., attention to accuracy and detail in costumes, sets and props, though many were borrowed from the studio's previous historical outings.

Art Director Edward Careere designed one master set for the palace in Madrid at Warner Bros., studios in Burbank with a floor area of 26,600 sq. feet. The mobile wall units were shifted to form backgrounds for twenty-two different sections of the palace.

The film won an Academy Award® for Best Costume design in 1949. The Oscar® was shared by Leah Rhodes, Marjorie Best and a young Latino designer named Bill Travilla.

Concerned more with politics than tender passions, the film is about how Don Juan (Flynn) saves Queen Margaret (Lindfors) and the King

(Brent) from the treachery of the evil Duke De Lorca (Douglas) in 17th century Spain.

Don Juan has been the hero of many literary works, and is supposedly modeled on the life of Don Juan Tenorio of Seville. Famous versions of his life include Gellez's *El Burlador de Sevilla*, Moliere's *Le Festin de Pierre*, and Mozart's opera *Don Giovanni*. Cornielle, Dumas, Browning and Shaw have also contributed their own chronicles of his life.

The basic story involves a Don Juan who seduces the daughter of the commander of Seville and kills her father in a duel. Then while visiting the statue of the victim he is seized by it and dragged off to hell.

Don Juan was previously filmed with great success in 1926 by Warner Bros., starring John Barrymore. The Flynn version met with mild success in the United States, but did tremendous business overseas especially in Europe and South America. Neither version is true to its origins, but rather, they are swashbuckling vehicles created by screenwriters to showcase what their stars did best.

Affair in Havana (1957 Allied Artists)

D: Laslo Benedek
S: Burton Lane and Maurice Zimm
P: Richard Goldstone
Cast: John Cassavetes, Sara Shane, Raymond Burr, Sergio Peña, Lilia Lazo, Celia Cruz, Jose Antonio Rivero

A young musician, Nick (Cassavetes), has an affair with Lorna (Shane), the wife of a paralyzed Cuban plantation owner, Mallabee (Burr, before his other wheelchair-bound role as the title character in television's *Ironside* [1967-75]). Mallabee is drowned by a manservant (Peña) who has long been infatuated with Lorna and the manservant's wife (Lazo) proceeds to avenge Mallabee by knifing Lorna. Nick returns to his piano playing.

This dreary melodramatic film relies on the scenic beauty of Cuba and its Afro Cuban music, which is highlighted in a fiesta sequence featuring some of Cuba's best musical talents of the time, including famed singer Celia Cruz in one of her first film appearances. The film was produced by Dudley Pictures of Cuba as the first in a series of planned English language films jointly financed through an agreement with the Agricultural and Industrial development bank of Cuba (BANFAIC) which set up a $1 million revolving fund. Produced and filmed entirely on location in and around Havana and the resort town of Varadero.

Against All Odds (1979 Columbia)

D: Taylor Hackford
S: Eric Hughes, based on a story by Hackford and Hughes
P: Taylor Hackford
Cast: Jeff Bridges, Rachel Ward, James Woods, Richard Widmark

A ruthless power struggle in Los Angeles provides the background for this contemporary drama, which is based on the 1947 RKO film noir *Out*

Against All Odds, directed by Taylor Hackford, stars Jeff Bridges and Rachel Ward as Gringos caught in an exotic, dangerous Mexico.

of the Past in which a gangster hires a private eye to find a beautiful woman. Central to this story of love and murder is an intriguing love triangle comprised of an ex-football player, Terry (Bridges); a femme fatale, Jesse (Ward); and a night club owner, Jack (Woods). Jesse leaves Los Angeles to escape Jack, who then sends Terry after her.

Much of the movie is devoted to Terry's pursuit of Jesse—who is hiding out on a gorgeous island off the coast of Mexico. They become lovers and travel around majestic ruins, beaches and jungles where they make love until violent forces pull them back to Los Angeles. The film offered a tourist's romantic view of Mexico as a playground for gringos but there are no Hispanic leading or supporting characters in this story. The Mexican government would not allow a violent murder scene to be shot in one of the ruins, so the scene was eventually filmed on the studio lot in a reconstruction of the interior of the ruins.

Alambrista! (1978 Independent)

D: Robert M. Young
S: Robert M.Young
P: Robert M. Young
Cast: Domingo Ambriz, Trinidad Silva, Edward James Olmos

Alambrista! (Wirejumper) provides a gritty and realistic look at the lonely and frightening encounters of Roberto, an illegal Mexican farmworker in the United States

The film won the Palme D'or Award at Cannes for Best First Feature and the San Sebastian Film Festival, Gran Concha de Oro Award. It played numerous film festivals around the United States, though it had been commissioned as part of the "Visions," Public Broadcasting service series, and had previously aired on public television in 1977.

It is a small and beautifully made film with many touching and amusing scenes illustrating the human cost of illegal immigration, such as having to buy forged green cards, picking crops only to be run off by the INS just before payday and coping with the fears and loneliness of being in a foreign country.

Actor Domingo Ambriz as Roberto gives a performance dependent on body language and facial expressions to communicate what he is going through that is brilliantly realized. Trinidad Silva as a farmworker gives a Chaplin-esque lesson to Roberto on how to act like a gringo.

In the last scene of the movie, a Mexican woman in the process of being deported by American authorities at a border crossing gives birth to a baby while still on the American side, She shouts hysterically,

"He was born on American soil! He will need no papers," as Roberto watches from a bus that is returning him to Mexico.

Alambrista! had a limited United States art house release in 1979. The project had its origins while Young was filming a documentary in Arizona on migrant farm workers and their children.

The Alamo (1960 United Artists)

D: John Wayne
S: Edward James Grant
P: John Wayne
Cast: John Wayne, Richard Widmark, Laurence Harvey, Frankie Avalon, Linda Cristal, Richard Boone, Carlos Arruza

It took John Wayne over twelve years to bring his epic movie, *The Alamo*, to the screen. The movie centers around the historical conflict in March, 1836 between 180 Texas settlers and the Mexican general Santa Anna's army. Against this historical canvas are woven the personal stories of the Alamo defenders, highlighted by the conflict over command between Jim Bowie (Widmark) and Colonel Travis (Harvey). Wayne starred as Davy Crockett and directed and produced the film.

In 1951 Wayne received script approval for an Alamo movie from the Mexican government and permission to shoot in Mexico from the Mexican craft unions. However, the script for the final 1959 production, filmed in the United States, was vastly different from the original script developed while Wayne was under contract to Republic Pictures. He parted company with Republic Pictures when the studio passed on making the Alamo movie, and in 1952 Republic president Herbert J. Yates rushed into production with *The Last Command*, utilizing major elements from the original 1951 script.

Beginning in 1951, Wayne and Alfred Ybarra, art director for his company, (first called Wayne-Fellows, then Batjac), searched for locations in Peru, Panama and Mexico but could find no financing for the project despite Wayne's box office prominence, because of the film's projected high production costs. It eventually cost $12 million to make.

In 1957, Happy Shahan's ranch in Brackettville, Texas, was chosen as a location. Financing was finally arranged with United Artists and several independent Texas businessmen.

Ybarra's set recreation San Antonio and the Alamo mission combined authenticity, practicality, dramatic invention and imagination. It took over a year to construct and eventually sprawled over 400 acres.

Filming took place from September through December of 1959. The cinematography of William H. Clothier captured strikingly beautiful images while the action sequences are some of the most exciting ever put on film.

Edward James Grant's script avoided the complexities of the real historical situation, however, and became a simplistic patriotic overture. While the script features Tejano historical figures such as Juan Seguin, portrayed by Joseph Calleia, they are not developed characters. Surprisingly, though Santa Anna and his army are never personalized, they are treated as a dignified and gallant enemy. At one point in the film one of the Alamo defenders says, "It sure is the prettiest army I ever did see," while another replies, "Don't be fooled, they've been putting down rebellions for over two years and have marched over a thousand miles."

Over 1,500 Mexican extras were used to represent Santa Anna's army, townspeople and some Alamo defenders.

Spanish bullfighter Carlos Arruza portrayed Lieutenant Reyes, messenger for General Santa Anna. Linda Cristal, an Argentine born actress, played a variation of the traditional Mexican señorita in her role as Flaca (Spanish for skinny, though that is an unfair description of her), Crockett's love interest.

Flaca is landed, widowed, beautiful and educated and it is ironic (because she is Mexican), that she becomes the one chosen by Crockett to help spread the word about the Alamo and the fight for freedom against tyranny.

Richard Widmark, Linda Cristal, Laurence Harvey and producer/director/star John Wayne on the set of *The Alamo*.

Wayne's love of the Mexican people is illustrated by Crockett's benevolent—if somewhat patronizing—attitude toward the señorita and her young boy. In an introductory scene, Crockett helps her avoid an unwanted suitor and insists that the boy be given a tip for carrying the luggage despite the fact that Crockett carries both the luggage and the boy up the stairs under each arm.

In a letter reproduced in the *Hollywood Citizen News* dated November 11, 1960, Wayne wrote, "Because of my close friendship with many wonderful Mexicans and my honest love for the people of our neighbor country . . . I knew that a great piece of drama could be told about this incident without in any way disparaging Mexico. Ours is a picture of heroics and within its chapters we have shown not only the bravery of its defenders but also of its attackers."

There are touching scenes of the Mexicans removing their dead from the battlefield and Santa Anna permitting a survivor, Mrs. Dickinson, and her children to depart safely after all the Alamo defenders have been killed.

It's worth noting, though, that the long held myths of United States foreign policy "Manifest Destiny," with regard to Latin America in particular, and the idea that it takes many Mexicans to equal or best one Yankee, had their origins in the Alamo legend. Both are faithfully rendered in the movie at a time when the Cold War was at its height and American involvement in Vietnam was just beginning.

In 1960, the Mexican government banned *The Alamo*, but this seems in no way to have hurt Wayne and his relationship with the Mexican government or film industry, which continued to support his filmmaking activities. Many of his later films were made in Durango, Mexico.

Alive (1993 Touchstone)
D: Frank Marshall
S: John Patrick Shanley
P: Robert Watts and Kathleen Kennedy
Cast: Vincent Spano, Ethan Hawke, Michael DeLorenzo

Based on the true story of the Uruguayan rugby team whose plane crashed in the snow-covered Andes Mountains between Argentina and Chile in 1972. Of the twenty-seven who survived the crash, only sixteen made it off the mountain. The men were forced to resort to eating the dead in order to stay alive for the seventy-two days spent trying to get off the remote mountain.

Alvarez Kelly (1966 Columbia)
D: Edward Dmytryk
S: Franklin Coen and Elliott Arnold
P: Sol C. Siegel
Cast: William Holden, Richard Widmark, Janice Rule

In 1864, a group of American drovers and Mexican vaqueros, led by the Irish Mexican Alvarez Kelly (Holden), bring a herd of 2,500 cattle from Mexico to Virgina. Their purpose is to feed Union Army forces during the Civil War, but they are intercepted by Confederate Army troops. This is an average Western, and features Pepe Callahan, Roberto Contreras and Pedro Regas.

American Me (1992 Universal)
D: Edward James Olmos
S: Desmond Nakano and Floyd Mutrux.
P: Sean Daniel, Robert M. Young, Edward James Olmos
Cast: Edward James Olmos, William Forsythe, Pepe Serna,
     Evelina Fernandez, Sal Lopez, Danny De La Paz, Vira Montes

A brutal, relentless, unflinching and grimly honest look at thirty years in the life of an Hispanic American family living in East Los Angeles, following one of its members, Santana (Olmos) from his teenage years to adulthood and the vicious cycle of violence and imprisonment that consumes his soul.

Olmos not only stars and produces but makes a forceful theatrical feature film directorial debut with this harrowing documentary-like drama. *American Me* is a powerful, richly textured film that is both satisfying and disturbing.

Santana becomes a ruthless crime lord whose power over life and death flows from his prison cell and extends to the streets. The movie is structured like a memoir with Santana narrating his life as he contemplates old photographs while waiting for his shocking but inevitable death.

We meet Santana's ill-fated parents on the night of the 1943 Los Angeles Zoot Suit riots. American soldiers and sailors, fueled by racism and war hysteria, attack and brutally beat Santana's Zoot Suited father Pedro (Lopez), and rape his mother, Esperanza (Montes).

American Me then follows Santana and his two friends, J.D. and Mundo (Panchito Gomez, Steve Wilcox and Richard Coca as the youths), on their long journey through life, beginning with their first stay at Juvenile Hall (the result of a show of machismo in which they cross a rival gang's turf and are forced to break into a restaurant to escape the gang's wrath) and the first of many murders that lead them to the maximum security cells at Folsom Prison.

Fifteen years later the boys are grown men and still in prison (now played by Olmos, Forsythe and Serna). Santana shrewdly gains power when he organizes prisoners under racial lines in order to control illegal inmate activities both in and out of prison. Three years later he is released from prison and finds himself ill at ease in the outside world. In truth, he is trying to pick up his life from where it was cut off at the age of fifteen.

There are no visible rewards for the criminal in this film, no money is ever seen and Santana returns to live in the impoverished barrio neighborhood where he grew up. In fact, it is his friend Mundo (which means "world" in Spanish) who causes Santana's demise.

Santana slowly begins to find his humanity as he tentatively develops a relationship with Julie (Fernandez), a single mother he meets at a fiesta. Ironically, it is this late but welcome effort to change and do

Edward James Olmos—
director, producer and
star of *American Me.*

something positive with his life that proves Santana's downfall. Julie comes to represent the only glimmer of hope in the community as she tries to turn her life around by going back to school, but the boys in the neighborhood are involved in the same cycle of violence and drugs that first entrapped Santana, and the cycle will not be broken. She is the only one to dare tell him the truth. "You're nothing but a dope dealer," she tells him. "Your business kills kids."

The film failed to win over a larger segment of the audience. Its characters and situation are not sympathetically portrayed and the grim, violent nature of the piece kept audiences away—except for the Chicano Community and Olmos' fans, primarily in California and the Southwest, who showed up at the box office to the tune of 15 million dollars.

Olmos dreamed of making *American Me* for eighteen years, ever since he read the original script by Mutrux in 1974 when he played a bit part in Mutrux's *Aloha Bobby and Rose* (1975). *American Me* has a long history; at one point it was going to be filmed with Al Pacino, as a more romanticized traditional prison drama. Pacino went on to play an Hispanic crime lord in *Scarface* (1983) and *American Me* languished.

Edward James Olmos, the bit player, reached stardom over a ten year period beginning with his role in 1978 as El Pachuco in the acclaimed hit play *Zoot Suit* and the sullen no-nonsense Lieutenant Castillo in the television series *Miami Vice* (1984-89), culminating in his 1988 Oscar®-nominated performance as the quirky math teacher Jaime Escalante in *Stand and Deliver.*

As the years went by, the script to *American Me* grew more relevant as the problem of gang violence escalated. "A segment of our nation's youth is growing up in a self perpetuating lifestyle spent in and out of prison, resulting in violent crime, drugs and certain death," said Olmos. "*American Me* [was] made with the hope that the lives of some of the children will be redirected toward more positive goals."

The movie represents the largest gathering of Hispanic American talent in Hollywood, beginning with Olmos as star, director and producer; Reynaldo Villalobos as director of photography; Joe Aubel, production designer; Sylvia Vega Vasquez, costume designer; Bob Morrones, casting director and Richard Espinoza as first assistant director. Among the ensemble cast are fine performances by Pepe Serna as Mundo, Evelina Fernandez as Julie, Sal Lopez as the father who carries unresolved pain and resentment and Danny De la Paz as Puppet, a gang member who is torn between his loyalty to the crime syndicate and his love for the younger brother, Little Puppet, (Villarreal) whom he must kill.

The filming locations included Folsom Prison, Chino Men's Institution, Los Angeles County Juvenile Hall and areas of East Los Angeles. The Mercado, an outdoor market, brought Olmos back to a location that is on the doorstep of his boyhood home. The backlot of Universal Studios, Hollywood is where the New York Street set was redesigned and redressed to stand in for downtown Los Angeles circa 1943 in an elaborate recreation of the city's notorious Zoot Suit Riots seen in the opening sequence of the film.

John Anderson in *Newsday* said, "*American Me* is about death, not only of men but of dreams. A Chicano *Godfather,* it is about the violence men do and why they do it; how a criminal enterprise, born out of the need to protect one's own, grows beyond control: how once noble intentions are perverted by power and brings friends and brothers to betray each other."

David Elliot of the *San Diego Union* commented, "Olmos has star power. His pitted face glows with macho presence, lit well by Reynaldo Villalobos, and his tense aura of command is both creepy and sexy. He's like a deadlier, Mayan-faced Bogart."

In the *New York Times* Janet Maslin said, however, "Violent as it is, *American Me* is seldom dramatic enough to bring its material to life."

The Americano (1955 RKO Radio Pictures)

D: William Castle
S: Guy Trosper, from an original story by Leslie T. White.
P: Robert Stillman
Cast: Glenn Ford, Abbe Lane, Ursula Theiss, Frank Lovejoy, Cesar
    Romero, Rudolfo Hoyos Jr., Salvador Baquez

An American cowboy (Ford), is asked to deliver some Brahma bulls to a powerful rancher (Lovejoy) in Brazil. During his adventure Ford encounters rough terrain, bandidos and discovers a land-hungry rancher as well as some lovely ladies.

Cesar Romero turned in a colorful performance as a bandit leader. This is an average Western with a switch in locale and a good cast and Technicolor location footage.

Shooting began in 1953 with Glenn Ford, Cesar Romero and Sarita Montiel. The cast and crew arrived in Brazil but a combination of bad weather and customs red tape made it nearly impossible to film there. By the time the weather cleared up and the equipment was finally released, star Ford's contract had run out.

Director William Castle shot what footage he could and returned to Hollywood. The production resumed a year later when Ford was again available, but the rest of the film was shot at RKO and at a ranch in Riverside, California. Sarita Montiel could not return to the film and was replaced by Abbe Lane.

Anaconda (1997 Columbia)

D: Luis Llosa
S: Hans Bauer and Jim Cash and Jack Epps Jr.
P: Verna Harrah, Leonard Rabinowitz and Carol Little
Cast: Eric Stoltz, Jennifer Lopez, Jon Voight, Ice Cube

A documentary film crew enters the Amazon armed with cameras, sound equipment and the optimism of the uninitiated. They embark on a river expedition to find the legendary and undocumented Shirisharma Indians, their boat piloted by the colorful Mateo (Castellanos). Along the way, they encounter Sarone (Voight) stranded on a deserted boat. A charismatic loner who has lived by his wits in the jungle for years, Sarone engenders their friendship, if not their complete trust. Nevertheless, his professional knowledge of the elusive Shirishama tribe entices them. They follow him down the river, despite their misgivings. But Sarone has his own motives for driving the crew deeper into the river. He is on his own dark quest to track a lethal forty-foot Anaconda snake, a predator so vicious that it has become legend, and he will sacrifice everything and anyone to find this adversary. The expedition becomes a jungle nightmare as Sarone's obsession leads them directly into the jaws of the Anaconda, and they must use every primal resource to stay alive.

Filmed in Brazil and at the Los Angeles County Arboretum.

And Now Miguel (1966 Universal)

D: James B. Clark

S: Ted Sherdeman and Jane Klove, based on the award-winning novel by Joseph Krumgold.

P: Robert B. Radnitz

Cast: Pat Cardi, Michael Ansara, Pilar Del Rey, Guy Stockwell, Clu Gulager

The story of a ten-year-old boy, Miguel (Cardi), coming of age in the American Southwest, and filmed on location on a 23,000 acre ranch of one-time sheep grazing land in the Chama River Valley of New Mexico near the small town of Abiqui.

For generations, the Chavez family has been one of successful sheepherders living near the Sangre de Cristo mountains in the high plateau country of north central New Mexico. Young Miguel has a burning desire is to gain stature in his father Blas' (Ansara) eyes so he may accompany him to the mountains in the summertime with the herd. Miguel's father believes Miguel is too young to do a man's work. An itinerant sheepherder (Gulager) gives Miguel a chance to show what he can do. Miguel proves his courage and resourcefulness in the face of emergency when he has a chance encounter with a deadly snake and protects the herd from a pack of coyotes.

Ansara (a Lebanese-American) as the father, personifies strength and dignity and received especially good notices for his work in the film. Solid performances and outstanding Technicolor photography highlight this simple story that focused on the Spanish Indian peoples of the American Southwest. The award-winning book and the film reveal sensitively, if somewhat idealistically, a little-known part of American life and culture to young movie going audiences.

Robert Radnitz made a name for himself producing family films such as *A Dog of Flanders* (1959), *Misty* (1961) and *Island of the Blue Dolphins* (1964). Radnitz's 1972 production of *Sounder*, a Depression-era story about a family of African American sharecroppers in the American South, won four Academy Award® nominations, including one for Best Picture.

... and the Earth Did Not Swallow Him (Kino International 1995)

D: Severo Perez

S: Severo Perez, based on the novel *... Y No Se Lo Trago La Tierra* by Tomas Rivera

P: Paul Espinoza

Cast: Jose Acala, Danny Valdez, Rose Portillo, Marco Rodriguez, Lupe Ontiveros, Evelyn Guerrero, Sam Vlahos, Art Bonilla, Sal Lopez

Like many boys coming of age in 1952, Marcos Gonzales is trying to find his place in the world. He is having trouble in school, his brother is a soldier in the Korean War and his family is struggling to earn a decent living. But unlike other boys, Marco's journey of self discovery takes place amid a backdrop of prejudice and injustice while his family follows the crops from Texas to Minnesota as migrant farmworkers.

Released to American art house theaters, this film won numerous awards at film festivals around the world. Adapted by writer and director Severo Perez, the film is based on the 1971 novel of the same name by the late write and educator Thomas Rivera. The film was part of the prestigious *American Playhouse* series on PBS.

" . . . is as sincere and earnest as the Mexican American family it depicts with love and respect. Although the film, which is based on the classic Chicano novel, could use more of a sense of style and pace, it is nevertheless and affecting experience, beautifully photographed and illuminating . . ." Kevin Thomas, in the *Los Angeles Times* (5/5/1995).

The Appaloosa (1966 Universal)

D: Sidney J.Furie
S: James Bridges and Roland Kibee
P: Alan Miller
Cast: Marlon Brando, Anjanette Comer, John Saxon, Emilio Fernandez, Miriam Colon, Rafael Campos

An intense, but laborious, dramatic Western starring Marlon Brando as Matt Fletcher, a gringo saddle tramp who is determined to settle down and breed Appaloosa horses. He is thwarted in this desire when a magnificent Appaloosa stallion he plans to use as a stud is stolen from him by a Mexican bandit named Chuy Medina (Saxon).

He sets off across the Texas border to retrieve his horse from the bandit's stronghold in the Mexican village of Cocatlan. Medina subjects the gringo to indignities and tests of strengths highlighted by an arm wrestling game in which a scorpion's sting is a dangerous outcome for the arm that gives out first. Matt retrieves the horse and heads back across the border with Medina in pursuit. In a climatic gun battle on a snow covered mountain Matt kills Medina. He and the horse ride off into the sunset.

Director Furie fills the screen with tables littered with tequila bottles, extreme close-ups of the bandits, moody landscapes, interiors and sweaty faces. The film is full of stereotypes, from Mexican bandits to noble peasant farmers and the fiery young señorita.

There are similarities to Brando's own self-directed Western, *One Eyed Jacks* (1960), in particular the theme of a loner on the trail of revenge. The latter film's romantic and civilized view of Monterey and its citizenry, along with the strong portrayals from Katy Jurado and Pilar Pellicer as mother and daughter, give way to a more hellish fantasy of Mexico in *The Appaloosa*; perhaps a film ultimately more suited to the talents of a director like Sam Peckinpah. The Mexican bandit in *One Eyed Jacks* is Rio's (Brando) friend and companion, not the greaser Medina is made to be. Both characters Matt and Rio are subjected to suffering and indignities before they can reclaim what is theirs.

Trini is the archetypal fiery señorita played by Anjanette Comer who had only two previous film acting assignments prior to this film, a role in *Quick Before It Melts* (1964) and *The Loved One* (1965).

Ironically, Emilio "El Indio" Fernandez, who plays one of the bandits—beginning a series of portrayals in Hollywood films of despicable

Mexican bandits and ruffians—was the director of some classic Mexican films creating beautifully stirring images of Mexico.

Appointment in Honduras (1953 RKO Radio Pictures)
D: Benedict Bogeaus
S: Karen De Wolf, based on a story by Mario Silveira and Jack Cornall
P: Benedict Bogeaus
Cast: Glenn Ford, Ann Sheridan, Zachary Scott, Rodolfo Acosta

This film, set in 1910, is an escapist entertainment consisting mainly of a grueling trek through the Central American jungles.

Jim Corbett (Ford) is bringing money to the deposed president of Honduras and his loyal followers. When the ship's captain refuses to dock at Honduras, passenger Corbett frees a group of criminals bound for Nicaragua, enlisting their aid in the takeover of the ship. Led by Reyes (Acosta), they grab a lifeboat forcing two other passengers, Harry and Sylvia Sheppard (Scott and Sheridan) to accompany them as hostages, and the couple is made to accompany the troop through the jungle. Harry Sheppard successfully tries to worsen discord between Corbett and the bandit Reyes. Besides each other, Corbett and Reyes also have to contend with assorted jungle menaces such as tiger fish, alligators, snakes and torrential rain. Eventually a showdown between Corbett and Reyes occurs with Corbett the victor. Harry is also killed and Sylvia and Corbett ride off together into the Central American sunset.

The cast also features Ric Roman, Rico Alaniz, Julian Rivero, Pepe Hern, Henry Escalante and Victor Ottero.

Argentine Love (1924 Paramount)
D: Allan Dwan
S: John Russell, adapted from the story by Vicente Blasco Ibanez
P: Allan Dwan
Cast: Bebe Daniels, Ricardo Cortez, James Rennie, Mark Gonzales, Aurelio Garcia

Juan Martin (Cortez) a refined local Argentinean strong man, awaits the homecoming of his betrothed Consuelo (Daniels). She, however, falls in loves with an American engineer Phillip Sears (Rennie) who is building a bridge in her native Argentina. The film is a very typical melodrama.

Argentine Nights (1940 Universal)
D: Albert S. Rogell
S: Arthur T. Horman, Ray Golden and Sid Kuller, story by J. Robert Bren and Gladys Atwater
P: Ken Goldsmith
Cast: The Ritz Brothers, The Andrews Sisters, George Reeves, Constance Moore.

A lightweight musical comedy about three unemployed female American singers who run off to Argentina on a cruise ship with their managers in search of new opportunities.

Argentine Nights met a good reception with audiences in the United States but in South America, particularly in Buenos Aires, the film caused riots and people stoned the theaters showing the film. These Hollywood productions were presented as "typical" of their countries, but Latin Americans would not accept films in which the characterizations of their countries and countrymen were totally absurd.

The film made fun of the conventional Latin American stereotypes as seen in most American movies but the Latins did not see it that way. The Andrews Sisters sing a song called "Rumboogie," a combination of the rumba and boogie woogie and the "Brooklynonga," a Brooklyn synonym for a Gaucho conga line. The only problem is that the rumba is not from Argentina, but from Cuba, as is the conga. Both have Afro-Caribbean influences that are not part of the Argentina musical history.

Hollywood was alarmed by the official government outcries. The United States Department of State sought to aid Hollywood by creating the office of the Coordinator of Inter-American Affairs (CIAA), which opened a motion picture division headed by John Hay Whitney. The CIAA advised Hollywood to take more care in its productions set in Latin America if it wanted to successfully win over the Latin American markets. Even with the activation of this office, the studios paid only lip service to accuracy for the most part.

The Argentine government sent a counsel member to advise on the film's accuracy. Initially welcomed by the studios, he said he was later ignored once production had begun. When shown still photographs from the film, he remarked, "In the first place, the rumba is unknown in Argentina. It is a Cuban folk dance. Furthermore the costume is one that used to be worn by women in Cuban houses of prostitution and even they don't wear them anymore."

Actor George Reeves, who later became famous as television's Superman during the 1950s, here plays Eduardo, a wealthy Argentine polo player and Latin Lover.

Around the World in Eighty Days (1956 United Artists)
D: Michael Anderson
S: James Poe, John Farrow and S.J. Perelman from Jules Verne's novel
P: Michael Todd
Cast: David Niven, Cantinflas, Shirley MacLaine

A journey around the world in 1872, undertaken by Phileas Fogg (Niven) and Passpartout (Cantinflas), his faithful servant, on a bet wagered by members of London's prestigious Reform Club. In the course of their race against time, Fogg and his servant experience all sorts of wild adventures. The film introduced Mexico's superb comedian Cantinflas to an international audience in his first English speaking film, casting him as Niven's French manservant, Passpartout. Cantinflas used his well known Spanish clown characterization, and no mention was made of his ethnicity.

Winner of five Academy Awards® including Best Picture and based on a novel by Jules Verne, the film was a tremendous hit and broke worldwide movie attendance records up to that time. A grand entertainment made with the international film market in mind, it was filmed in seven countries, two United States locations and the backlots of five major Hollywood studios. The cast featured fifty international stars in cameo roles. Latin stars included Gilbert Roland, Cesar Romero, Jose Greco and Luis Miguel Dominguin. The production was conceived, produced and supervised by the tireless and creative genius, millionaire showman Mike Todd. He died in a plane crash soon after winning his Oscar® for Best Picture.

Assassins (1995 Warner Bros.)
D: Richard Donner
S: Andy Wachowski and Larry Wachowski and Brian Helgeland
P: Richard Donner, Joel Silver, Bruce A. Evans, Raynold Gideon,
   Andrew Lazar, Jim Van Wyck
Cast: Sylvester Stallone, Antonio Banderas, Julianne Moore

An action thriller about a veteran hitman, Robert Rath (Stallone), who wants to retire and a younger, more ambitious assassin, Miguel Bain (Banderas), who wants him dead.
The final segment of the film was shot in Old San Juan, Puerto Rico.

At Play in the Fields of the Lord (1991 Universal)
D: Hector Babenco
S: Jean Claude Carriere and Hector Babenco, based on the novel by
   Peter Mathesson
P: Saul Zaentz
Cast: Tom Berenger, John Lithgow, Daryl Hannah, Aidan Quinn,
   Tom Waits, Kathy Bates, Stenio Garcia

A family of Protestant Christian missionaries (Quinn and Bates) arrive in the Amazon jungle to work under the supervision of the missionary director and his wife (Lithgow and Hannah). Their task is to reactivate a disused Catholic mission in the heart of the jungle and convert the local natives before the Brazilian Army moves in and drives the natives off their land in a more brutal fashion. Meanwhile, an American Indian pilot (Berenger) resolves to find his roots and parachutes from his plane. Stripping himself naked—quite literally—he walks into the natives' village and is mistaken for a god.

The jungle, however, is far from the Eden it seems to be and begins to take its toll on the outsiders. Instead of "civilizing" the jungle and its inhabitants, the jungle and its inhabitants start to change the outsiders, causing them to lose the thin veneer of civilization they brought with them, which they shed as easily as Berenger's Indian shed his clothes.

The meddling of both the missionaries and Berenger lead to disaster for the Indians and the outsiders. Terrific performances are given by Quinn and Bates in a generally well acted and beautifully photographed piece that is perhaps a little too long in the end.

Stenio Garcia plays the police chief in the village where Lithgow is based, who is all set to illegally bomb the Amazon Indians out of their homes if Lithow and Quinn cannot convert the them and convince them move peacefully.

Back to Bataan (1945 RKO Radio Pictures)

D: Edward Dmytryk
S: Ben Barzman and Richard Landau
P: Robert Fellows
Cast: John Wayne, Anthony Quinn, Fely Franquelli

In this patriotic World War II action film Anthony Quinn co-stars as Filipino guerrilla leader Captain Andres Bonifacio, grandson of the legendary Filipino patriot. With American Colonel Madden (Wayne), he helps to fight the Japanese enemy in the Philippine Islands in anticipation of General MacArthur's return. Hollywood recognized the culture and background of the Filipino people and for once a clearly Spanish-surnamed hero played by a Hispanic American actor figures in a leading role.

The Bad and the Beautiful (1952 Metro-Goldwyn-Mayer)

D: Vicente Minnelli
S: John Houseman
P: Charles Schnee
Cast: Kirk Douglas, Lana Turner, Dick Powell, Gilbert Roland,
Gloria Grahame

Jonathan Shields (Douglas) is a deceased and unlamented producer whose legacy is a deathbed letter to three of his protégés reminding them that, for all his sins, they owe their careers to his genius.

Gilbert Roland plays Victor "Gaucho" Ribera, an easygoing Latin Lover movie star. Shields used him to help a screenwriter (Powell) with his unbearable Southern wife (Grahame) by arranging for Ribera to take her on a plane ride with a disastrous outcome.

Roland's appearance—playing a character associated with his own real-life career as a Latin Lover type—acknowledged some of the contributions made by Hispanics to Hollywood's legendary past, even in these limited roles.

The film won five Academy Awards®, including Best Supporting Actress (Grahame) and Best Screenplay (Schnee).

Bad Boys (1983 Universal)

D: Rick Rosenthal
S: Richard Dilello
P: Robert Solo
Cast: Sean Penn, Reni Santoni, Jim Moody, Eric Gurry, Esai Morales

A gritty tale full of ethnic stereotypes and predictable situations. While fleeing a robbery in a stolen car, a youthful hoodlum, Mick (Penn) causes the death of his best friend and the eight-year-old brother of a Hispanic gang leader, Paco (Morales). For his crime, Mick is sent to juvenile detention center where he is placed in a life-or-death situation among other young felons. Paco, who has vowed to revenge for his brother's death, is later sent to the same institution when he is convicted of raping Mick's girlfriend. The eventual violent confrontation between Paco and Mick settles the score.

Esai Morales plays Paco as a hot-tempered Latin thug with few apparent redeeming qualities. Reni Santoni plays Ramon Herrera, a youth counselor who takes an interest in Mick. In an interesting twist on the traditional role of the Anglo saving the Hispanic, here it is the Hispanic who saves the Anglo.

The Bad Man (1930 First National)
D: Clarence Badger
S: Howard Estabrook (English version), Baltazar Fernandez Cue
 (Spanish version); based on the play by Porter Emerson Browne
Cast: Walter Huston (English version), Antonio Moreno (Spanish version)

The story of outlaw bandit Pancho Lopez; his exploits and eventual death at the hands of a Texas Ranger.

With the advent of sound, in an attempt to reach non-English speaking countries, a number of Hollywood studios began filming foreign language versions simultaneously with their domestic films. The films would share sets and scripts, but were made with completely different casts.

The English version of this film, with Walter Huston in the lead, was shot in twenty-four days for the cost of $253,561.45. Huston earned $5,000 per week. The Spanish version was shot in eighteen days at a cost of $73,027.94, with an entirely Spanish-speaking cast headed by Antonio Moreno, who earned $2,000 per week. Baltazar Fernandez Cue was hired to write the Spanish version of the script for $10,000; he eliminated some of the derogatory elements that were inherent to the English version. Huston played Pancho as a vicious greaser; Moreno portrayed him as a devil-may-care character, which he enhanced with his own charismatic personality.

Badge 373 (1973 Paramount)
D: Howard W. Koch
S: Pete Hamill
P: Howard W. Koch
Cast: Robert Duvall, Verna Bloom, Felipe Luciano, Luis Avalos Chico
 Martinez, Marina Durell, Henry Darrow

This was a sequel of sorts to *The French Connection* (1971) in that it follows the further exploits of real-life New York City cop Eddie Egan, who, as the character of Popeye Doyle, had become a big sensation.

As written by Egan, the original story took place with Castro and Batista but the film shifted the locale to New York's Puerto Rican community and a radical liberation group (this was probably done to keep the budget down—period films are much more expensive to make).

Columnist and author Pete Hamill wrote the script that moves through the seamy, oppressed Puerto Rican world of New York City. Doyle (Duvall) discovers that his dead partner knew of the plans of a cultured Puerto Rican gangster, Sweet William (Darrow), to sell stolen guns to radicals, allowing them to mount a rebellion on the island.

Richard Cuskelly in the *Los Angeles Herald Examiner* of August 3, 1973, summed up the movie: "Puerto Ricans are portrayed as either animalistic, violence-prone thugs, or as foolish and also violence-prone would-be revolutionaries. The police aren't treated much better unless we're supposed to admire their unnecessary manhandling of suspected criminals and unabashed racism."

Real life Puerto Rican activist Felipe Luciano, a member of the then-radical group The Young Lords, played a character like himself with fierce intensity, but the Puerto Rican community turned on him when the film was released, calling him a hypocrite. Luciano had agreed to do the film for the opportunity to present a speech on Puerto Rican independence, but the speech—as shot in a rally at the Central Park bandshell—was lost in the intercutting of a chase sequence.

Representatives from various New York-based Puerto Rican groups demanded that Paramount withdraw the film, publicly apologize and increase Puerto Rican technicians in the production end of the business. The protesters claimed that the film portrayed all Puerto Ricans as prostitutes, thieves or bomb throwing radicals. The one Puerto Rican police officer in the movie, played by Chico Martinez, turns out to be crooked and is humiliated by Duvall in front of his family.

The head gangster, Sweet William, is a Puerto Rican Harvard graduate who makes every effort to let you know it by quoting famous poets. Puerto Rican actor Henry Darrow had made a name for himself on television as the lovable rogue son of a Mexican land baron on the successful series *The High Chaparral* (1967-71), and it was disappointing to see him in such a role. Marina Durell (as Rita Garcia) appears as a junkie prostitute who is murdered for what she knows. Luis Avalos (as Chico) plays a junkie Egan brutalizes into falling off a roof. Salsa musician Johnny Pacheco and his music are featured in the film.

The Ballad of Gregorio Cortez (1982 Embassy Pictures)

D: Robert M. Young

S: Victor Villasenor, based on the novel, *With His Pistol in His Hand*, written by Americo Paredes

P: Michael Hausman

Cast: Edward James Olmos, Tom Bower, Pepe Serna, Rosana DeSoto, James Gammon

The true story, set in 1901 Texas, of a legendary Mexican cowboy who, in self-defense, shoots and kills an Anglo sheriff when a poor translation from English to Spanish results in a tragic misunderstanding. Cortez is not a typical Hollywood hero, but is presented as an ordinary human being, who draws on his own resourcefulness, commonsense, and extraordinary horsemanship to outwit and outride the formidable posse set out after him, though he is captured in the end.

Robert M. Young's work on this project reflects the same sensitivity and humanity he brought to *Alambrista!* (1977) Young says of his work, "All my stories are about people to whom life gives a raw deal. But they are not losers. They have dignity and they find out who they are."

When he was approached for his participation, actor Edward James Olmos was the one to suggest Young be brought in as a director; based on his respect for Young's previous work. Olmos, who masterfully portrays Cortez, states, *"The Ballad of Gregorio Cortez* is a film about humanity. It never tries to polarize the audience. Just as the shooting evolves out of cultural and linguistic misunderstanding, in other encounters between Anglos and Cortez who have the same language barrier, they unite through their common humanity." In one scene Cortez's hunger overcomes his suspicion, fear and curiosity when a lonely Anglo cowboy offers him food. Olmos' silent gratitude is as memorable as his look of total defeat and despair when he discovers his wife and children have been jailed.

The film was produced under the auspices of the National Council of La Raza, PBS, CPB, and Moctezuma Esparza. Though it takes place in Texas, it was filmed in New Mexico on a $1.3 million budget. The production captured a strong feeling of authenticity and turn of the century western ambiance. The striking visual images were by cameraman Reynaldo Villalobos. Robert M. Young and Olmos wrote the *Rashomon*-like screenplay (but did not receive credit) with Victor Villasenor based on the Americo Parades novel *With a Pistol in His Hand*.

Olmos calls Cortez the first Hispanic American hero figure based on a true person and actual events ever in American cinema. "Films like this are meant to enhance the image of Hispanics and especially Chicanos. But at the same time they have a universal appeal that makes them important to American society as a whole."

The film aired on PBS television as part of the *American Playhouse* series. Because PBS reaches a limited audience and Olmos wanted to take it out to the general public, he obtained rights to the movie and started screening it theatrically in movie houses first in Los Angeles then across the country free of charge. He also screened it at theaters and community halls with 35mm film equipment. Through persistence and hard work, which resulted in wide exposure and a rave review from leading *Los Angeles Times* film critic Charles Champlin, the film was soon picked up for distribution by Embassy Pictures in a limited theatrical release.

Bananas (1971 United Artists)

D: Woody Allen
S: Woody Allen and Mickey Rose
P: Jack Grossberg
Cast: Woody Allen, Louise Lasser, Carlos Montalban, Jacobo Morales, Miguel Suarez, Rene Enriquez

This is one of Woody Allen's first outings as a director, and the resulting film is a wild, satirical and funny treatment of Latin American politics and culture and American policies at home and abroad.

The film opens with the new dictator of the banana republic of San Marcos island, General Vargas (Montalban), promising to shut down the newspapers, train his soldiers and fight off a new band of rebels.

Woody Allen is Fielding Millish, a mousy young products tester living in New York who falls in love with a radical college student, Nancy (Lasser). She believes he doesn't have leadership qualities and breaks off the affair. Disillusioned, he quits his job and heads off to the island of San Marcos.

Upon his arrival, Fielding becomes the unexpected object of an assassination plot. The dictator plans to have Fielding murdered, and to blame the killing on the rebels. The dictator believes that the American government, outraged over the murder of one of its citizens, will send in American armed forces to quell the rebels and back the ruling dictator. His assassination does not go as planned, however, and Fielding winds up with the real rebel forces in their mountain hideout. He is taken in by the rebels and meets their leader, Esposito (who resembles Cuba's Castro), played by Jacobo Morales.

Fielding quickly becomes a rebel and reluctantly exerts the very leadership qualities he was told he lacked. He defeats the dictator and the rebel leader, and eventually becomes president of San Marcos. Fielding turns to the United States for aid for the island, which is in dire economic shape. He travels to New York in disguise where the FBI uncovers his ruse. He meets up with Nancy again, but now she awed by his incarnation as the president of San Marcos. Fielding reveals his true identity to her and they eventually fall in love and marry. The FBI drops their case against Fielding.

The movie is brilliantly realized by Allen who shot the San Marcos sequences in Puerto Rico using many Hispanic actors, which brought a sense of realism and naturalism to the proceedings. The film cleverly combines quick-witted humor with classic slapstick comedy. Rooted in American sixties-era counter culture and politics, the film may seem a little dated in some situations and very contemporary in others.

Victor Junco, Rudolfo Acosta and Gilbert Roland in *Bandido*.

Bandido (1957 United Artists)

D: Richard Fleischer
S: Earl Felton
P: Robert L. Jacks
Cast: Robert Mitchum, Gilbert Roland, Zachary Scott, Ursula Thiess, Rudolfo Acosta, Victor Junco, Alfonso Sanches Tello

In 1916, an Anglo gunslinger (Mitchum) who sells his services for adventure and hard cash, drifts into Mexico with his weapons hoping to take advantage of reports of an impending revolution. He meets a local rebel bandido (Roland) and helps him win several battles.

Mitchum is the gringo hero who sees Mexico as a land of adventure and who brings his superior technology in the form of weapons to help the rebel bandits. Filmed on location in Mexico, the film offers plenty of action in a tongue-in-cheek style. Mitchum and Roland are both excellent in their respective roles.

Raquel Welch portrays Maria Stoner, a young Mexican widow, in *Bandolero!*

Bandolero! (1967 Twentieth Century Fox)

D: Andrew V. McLaglen
S: James Lee Barrett
P: Robert L. Jacks.
Cast: James Stewart, Dean Martin, Raquel Welch, George Kennedy, Perry Lopez, Rudy Diaz

This action adventure film is set in Texas and Mexico in the post-Civil War period. Raquel Welch portrays Maria, a young Mexican girl widowed by Dee's (Martin) band during a bank holdup and taken hostage in their escape. When she is kidnapped she shows her strong character by standing up to the outlaws.

The film perpetuates the worst Mexican stereotypes as a posse chases outlaws into a Mexico of endless barren desert landscapes peopled by bandidos whose only purpose in life is to kill gringos.

In the middle of a climatic skirmish, the Mexican bandit Munoz (Diaz) spots Maria, drops everything and runs toward her; he rips her blouse and his hand disappears up her skirt. The greaser image is flagrant and offensive, portraying the Mexican as someone of uncontrollable bursts of violence and lust. On the other hand, the Anglo outlaws are not much better, even with our so-called heroes (Stewart and Martin) keeping them in check. Welch's Maria is a woman with a past, a former prostitute, who is not out of place with her outlaw captors.

Barbarosa (1982 Universal)

D: Fred Schepisi
S: Wiliam Wittliff
P: Paul N. Lazarus III
Cast: Willie Nelson, Gary Busey, Gilbert Roland, Isela Vega, Danny De La Paz, Alma Martinez

Willie Nelson stars as Barbarosa ("red beard" in Spanish), a notorious outlaw whose name is both feared and hated by residents of a Mexican village. He is married to Josephina (Vega) but her father, Don Braulio (Roland), despises him—so much so that he has given his sons the mission of killing Barbarosa. Undaunted, Barbarosa creeps into the village by night to see his wife, while by day he outruns and out-foxes his would-be assassins. When Barbarosa meets Karl (Busey), a naive farmhand also on the run for an accidental killing, he decides to teach him the tricks of the trade.

This is a brilliantly realized Western with an extraordinary visual quality in which Mexicans are seen as noble ranchers, bandidos and superstitious, stalwart peons. Roland, in his last theatrical feature film appearance, is excellent as the patriarch Don Braulio. Willie Nelson is adequate but is the weakest link in the film. Mexican actress Isela Vega contributes a strong portrayal as Jospehina. De La Paz is convincing as the youthful son who goes after Barbarosa.

The Barefoot Contessa (1954 United Artists)

D: Joseph L. Mankiewicz
S: Joseph L. Mankiewicz
P: Joseph L. Mankiewicz
Cast: Ava Gardner, Humphrey Bogart, Warren Stevens, Edmond O'Brien, Rossano Brazzi

Three American movie executives (Stevens, Bogart and O'Brien) discover an extraordinary Spanish dancer, Maria Vargas (Gardner), in Spain. They bring her to Hollywood, "launch" her as a star and rename her Maria d'Amata.

The producer, Kirk (Stevens) is a dictatorial sexist bigot who is infatuated with her. She despises him and finds herself at ease among truck drivers, gypsies and handsome young men. On a trip to Rome, she encounters an older Italian count (Brazzi) whom she marries. Her discovery on the wedding night that her new husband is impotent triggers the contessa's tragic end.

Francois Truffaut called *The Barefoot Contessa*, "The most beautiful portrait of a woman ever filmed, in the person of Ava Gardner." Top stars, a good adult story and resourceful direction are all skillfully blended into a beautiful production filmed in Italy and Spain. The film is said to be based loosely on the lives of Rita Hayworth and Sophia Loren, and Ava Gardner is captivating in the lead role. The mystique of the exotic, sexual and beautiful Latina was certainly exploited in this film. Humphrey Bogart was never better as her friend and director Harry Dawes, while Edmond O'Brien won an Ac⁻ demy Award® for his role as press agent Oscar Muldoon.

Bataan (1943 Metro-Goldwyn-Mayer)

D: Tay Garnett
S: Robert Andrews
P: Irving Starr
Cast: Robert Taylor, Thomas Mitchell, George Murphy, Robert Walker, Desi Arnaz

The story of the American and Filipino troops who hopelessly defended Manila during the Japanese invasions in the first days of World War II.

Desi Arnaz portrays Private Ramirez, a Mexican American from California's Salinas Valley. Indeed, many of the real life Bataan defenders were Mexican Americans from New Mexico; the soldiers who surrendered faced the infamous "Bataan Death March." This was one of the first films to recognize Mexican Americans as part of the armed forces during World War II and thus as part of the American society. Representative cross sections of the United States were a popular mainstay in World War II films of the era, and quickly became a cliche.

Battle Cry (1954 Warner Brothers)

D: Raoul Walsh
S: Leon Uris, based on his novel
P: Henry Blanke
Cast: Van Heflin, Tab Hunter, Aldo Ray, Anne Francis, Dorothy Malone, James Whitmore, Fess Parker, Victor Millan, Eduardo Noriega, Perry Lopez

Raoul Walsh directed *Battle Cry* as a broad, exciting picture of American Marines in action and as a series of touching stories of men and their relationships with the women in their lives. The film follows them through camp training, romances and problems, then takes them to the bitter, bloody battles of the South Pacific theater of World War II.

Battle Cry was filmed on the island of Vieques, Puerto Rico, where the United States armed services maintain a base, with the film crew receiving the assistance and full cooperation of the United States Navy and the Marines. Battle scenes recreated the invasions of Guadalcanal, Tarawa and Saipan. The cast roughed it like Marines, living in tents on the island location.

Three of the prominently featured soldiers were Hispanic, including the larcenous Spanish Joe Gomez (Lopez), Pedro (Millan) and the Indian marine named Crazy Horse (Noriega).

Actor Victor Millan said that the role of Pedro was more substantial in Leon Uris' original novel. In the book, Pedro was a silver star war hero who had to deal with a redneck Texan in his platoon. There was a scene in the film in a bar in which Pedro relates his feelings to the platoon sergeant (Whitmore), and tries to make friendly overtures to another redneck, Speedy (Parker). Speedy rejects his offer of friendship and throws beer on Pedro, causing a fight. The scene was cut from the final film because the Marine Corps. insisted there was no racial prejudice in the Corps. Warner Bros., which relied heavily on the assistance of the Marines, bowed to pressure and cut the scene.

Aldo Ray, Victor Millan, James Whitmore, Fess Parker and Bill Campbell (head down on table) in a scene that was cut from *Battle Cry* because the Marines demanded it be removed from the film, citing that there was "no racial prejudice in U.S. Marine Corps."

Photo courtesy of Victor Millan.

Battleground (1949 Metro-Goldwyn-Mayer)

D: William Wellman
S: Robert Pirosh
P: Dore Schary
Cast: John Hodiak, Van Johnson, Ricardo Montalban, George Murphy,
    Marshall Thompson, Leon Ames, James Whitmore, Don Taylor

William Wellman powerfully directs this story of American GIs during World War II's Battle of the Bulge. It was also a big commercial hit. Ricardo Montalban plays Rodrigues, a Mexican American enlisted man, recognizing the valiant efforts and sacrifices made by Mexican Americans during the war.

From a commercial standpoint, the studio was building up Montalban as a star. Montalban had made a number of films in Mexico prior to his arrival at MGM, and his name had an exploitable marquee value, while carrying a vestige of the Good Neighbor policy. From a public relations standpoint, it was reassuring to see American citizens of Latin origin fighting for freedom in an American-made World War II film. Actual World War II veterans were employed as extras to play themselves.

The Beast of Hollow Mountain (1956 United Artists)

D: Edward Nassour and Ismael Rodriquez
S: Robert Hill, based on a story by Willis O'Brien
P: William Nassour, Edward Nassour
Cast: Guy Madison, Carlos Rivas, Patricia Medina, Mario Navarro

Guy Madison is partnered with Carlos Rivas on a Mexican ranch in this science fiction Western filmed in Mexico.

A wealthy rancher develops a dislike for Madison when his fiancée demonstrates an interest in the Anglo. The love story and the cattle rustling soon take a back seat when they are all menaced by a prehistoric Tyrannosaurus Rex who lives in the mountains near the ranch.

Behold a Pale Horse (1968 Columbia)

D: Fred Zinnemann
S: J.P. Miller
P: Fred Zinnemann
Cast: Gregory Peck, Anthony Quinn, Omar Sharif

This is a post-Spanish Civil War story in which Peck plays Manuel Artiguez, a Loyalist hero who is now a bandit in exile. His implacable enemy is police Chief Vinolas (Quinn) of the Guardia Civil who has sworn for twenty years to capture Artiguez dead or alive.

At his dying mother's request, Artiguez leaves the safety of his retreat on the French side of the Pyrenees to return to his native village in Spain.

The film was made in southern France, because a film in which a member of Franco's Guardia Civil is the villain would never have been allowed to be filmed in Spain while Franco was in power. While some might argue that Peck is miscast as a Spaniard, he manages to bring an air of tired integrity to his portrayal of a man whose burning passions as a guerrilla leader fighting Franco's fascists during the Spanish Civil

War have been transformed into the hollow emotions of a common-place bandido. However, It is Quinn's excellent portrayal of the obsessive police chief that stands out. Omar Sharif as a village priest with divided loyalties is also very effective. Unfortunately, the story never has any real dramatic tension and never captured general audience interest.

The Believers (1987 Orion)
D: John Schlesinger
S: Mark Frost
P: John Schlesinger
Cast: Martin Sheen, Robert Loggia, Jimmy Smits

After his wife's death, Cal Jamison (Sheen) arrives in New York to start a new life with his young son. Hired by the NYPD to help out stressed out cops, he's asked by Lieutenant McTaggert (Loggia) to treat a young detective (Smits) who is acting as strange as the series of ritualistic child murders he is investigating. Jamison is soon plunged into a frightening world of a strange black magic cult.

The film deals with the Caribbean religion of Santeria, portraying it as a mysterious dark magic practiced by superstitious, bloodthirsty, and simpleminded African Americans and Puerto Ricans in the city of New York. The stereotype of the Anglo saving poor minorities from themselves is prevalent in this film.

Ben-Hur (1925 Metro-Goldwyn-Mayer/United Artists)
D: Frank Niblo
S: Bess Meredyth, Carey Wilson, June Mathis, adapted from the novel by Lew Wallace
P: Charles B. Dillingham, Abraham L. Erlanger, Louis B. Mayer and Florenz Ziegfeld, Jr.
Cast: Ramon Novarro, Francis X. Bushman, Betty Bronson, May McAvoy

Ramon Novarro stars as the lead of this epic film about a man unfairly imprisoned who devotes his life to revenge. With a proclaimed cast of more than 125,000, location shoots in Italy and the death of a stuntman during the chariot race, the film was plagued by delays and political tension and cost a (then) record $4,000,000.

Beyond the Limit (1983 Paramount)
D: John Mackenzie
S: Christopher Hampton, based on the novel *The Honorary Consul* by Graham Greene
P: Norma Heyman
Cast: Michael Caine, Richard Gere, Elpidia Carillo, Bob Hoskins, A Martinez, Joaquin DeAlmeida

Filmed in Mexico, this is an adaptation of Graham Greene's novel *The Honorary Consul,* in which Gere plays a Paraguayan doctor in an Argentina-Paraguay bordertown who gets caught up in the kidnapping of an alcoholic British Consul (Caine). He also falls in love with the consul's wife, a native former hooker played by Elpidia Carillo. *Beyond the Limit* holds similarities with Huston's 1984 film adaptation of Lowry's *Under the Volcano*. Both deal with an alcoholic British consul in a Latin American country, a love triangle and the death of the consul as a result of political unrest.

The Big Boodle (1957 United Artists)
D: Richard Wilson
S: Jo Eisnger, based on the novel by Robert Sylvester
P: Lewis F. Blumberg
Cast: Errol Flynn, Pedro Armendariz, Carlos Rivas, Rossana Rory,
  Gia Scala, Sandro Giglio

This film is a solid melodrama about the search by the Havana police for $3 million in counterfeit pesos and the plates that made them. Flynn stars as a casino blackjack dealer who finds himself involved in the intrigue when a glamorous blonde passes him a 500-peso note, and he suddenly finds himself caught between the police and the gang of counterfeiters.

Filmed against the backgrounds of Batista's (pre-Castro) Havana, the film features an exciting chase and gun battle along the walls of a sixteenth-century Spanish fortress. Flynn is good in his role as a world-weary American blackjack dealer, as is Pedro Armendariz as the police chief and Carlos Rivas as one of the heavies. Cuban actors featured include Guillermo Alvarez Guedes, Carlos Mas, Rogelio Hernandez, and Velia Martinez.

The Big Country (1958 United Artists)
D: William Wyler
S: James R. Webb, Sy Bartlett and Robert Wilder
P: William Wyler and Gregory Peck
Cast: Gregory Peck, Charlton Heston, Carol Baker, Jean Simmons,
  Charles Bickford, Burl Ives, Chuck Connors, Alfonso Bedoya

A big-budget, entertaining Western with a visual scope to match the big-name cast and sprawling epic storyline. James McKay (Peck) is a retired sailor from Baltimore who comes out West to San Rafael to marry Pat Terrill (Baker), the pampered daughter of cattle rancher Major Terrill (Bickford). McKay finds himself caught in the middle of a local feud between the Major and his nemesis, a neighboring rancher named Hannassey (Ives) and his family.

Bedoya has a featured role as Ramon Guttierrez, a Mexican wrangler on the Terrill spread who has been with the family for a long time. Amused by the antics of McKay, Ramon quickly comes to respect his gentle, nonviolent way of proving himself. Terrill berates Ramon and calls him an idiot for letting McKay ride out alone in the expansive ranch country. The audience and Ramon both know that McKay has a compass and knows exactly where he is going and that the true idiot is Terrill. Mexicans are also seen in traditional roles as house servants and ranch hands. The Spanish heritage of the Southwest is acknowledged when the schoolteacher (Simmons) tells McKay that the land was originally a present from the king of Spain to her great-grandfather.

The Big Fix (1978 Universal)
D: Jeremy Paul Kagan
S: Roger L. Simon, based on his novel
P: Carl Borack and Richard Dreyfuss
Cast: Richard Dreyfuss, Susan Anspach, Bonnie Bedelia, Ofelia Medina

Moses Wine (Dreyfuss), a private detective who has left his radical campus ideals behind him at Berkeley and who can barely make a living, is asked by a one-time campus activist (Anspach) to investigate an attempt to discredit a gubernatorial candidate. Ofelia Medina co-stars as a sensitive and intelligent Chicana student movement leader.

The Big Steal (1949 RKO Radio Pictures)
D: Don Siegel
S: Geoffrey Homes and Gerald Drayson Adams, based on a story by Richard Wormser
P: Jack J. Gross
Cast: Robert Mitchum, Jane Greer, Patric Knowles, William Bendix, Ramon Novarro, Don Alvarado, Pascual Garcia Peña

The story of a thief who has stolen a United States Army payroll and is being pursued across Mexico, from the port of Vera Cruz through the surrounding villages.

This is a first-rate thriller that owes much to its atmospheric Mexican locations.

Blackboard Jungle (1955 Metro-Goldwyn-Mayer)
D: Richard Brooks
S: Richard Brooks, based on the novel by Evan Hunter
P: Pandro S. Berman
Cast: Glenn Ford, Anne Francis, Louis Calhern, Sidney Poitier, Vic Morrow, Richard Kiley, Paul Mazursky, Rafael Campos

Richard Dadier (Ford) is a struggling young teacher assigned to a tough inner-city American high school. He faces a school whose staff is made up mostly of indifferent teachers and whose racially mixed student body is dominated by a group of juvenile delinquents with no respect for education or authority.

Although his pregnant wife (Francis) urges him to get out, Dadier withstands the students' taunts and is able to reach some of them. He faces a showdown with the head of a group of toughs (Morrow) in the classroom. Dadier overcomes him by sheer brute strength with the assistance of Miller (Poitier), one of the students he has been trying to reach. As both the writer and director, Brooks displayed strong direction showing the anguish and pain of urban American educational institutions of the mid-1950s.

The Puerto Rican as part of the American scene was introduced to films through the character of Pete Morales, one of Dadier's students, played by Dominican actor Rafael Campos in his feature film debut.

The film ushered in a whole new era for a generation of young Americans with its use of rock 'n' roll on the film's soundtrack, featuring "Rock Around the Clock," by Bill Haley and the Comets.

A tremendous hit at the box office, the film became a center of controversy over its unflattering portrayal of American youth and the American inner-city school system.

Blackboard Jungle began what became a cinematic convention of having an Anglo schoolteacher help the poor inner-city minority kids to better their lives through education, perseverance and acceptance of middle-class American values. In these earlier outings minority meant not only African Americans and Hispanics but also poor European immigrants.

Many of the young actors portraying the high school students went on to respectable careers in Hollywood. Sidney Poitier became Hollywood's first Oscar®-winning African American leading man. Campos went on to become a well-established character actor. Paul Mazursky has become one of Hollywood's most important writers and directors. Jameel Farah (Jamie Farr) years later found fame as Klinger on television's hit series, *M*A*S*H* (1972-83), as did Vic Morrow on the long-running series *Combat* (1962-67).

Blame It on Rio (1984 Twentieth Century Fox)
D: Stanley Donen
S: Charles Peters and Larry Gelbart
P: Stanley Donen
Cast: Michael Caine, Joe Bologna, Valerie Harper, Demi Moore

A comedy about a coffee executive whose teenage daughter has a romantic fling with his best friend, turning their vacation in exotic Rio de Janeiro upside-down. Americans' passions are unleashed in the more primal atmosphere of Rio through their exposure to native rituals and music. Reynaldo Villalobos' lush cinematography captures the colors of Rio and Brazil.

Blockade (1938 United Artists)
D: William Dieterie
S: John Howard Lawson
P: Walter Wanget
Cast: Madeleine Carroll, Henry Fonda, Leo Carrillo, Lupita Tovar, Carlos de Valdez

Arriving in Spain after a year of travel, a young English woman (Carroll) finds that her father and his associate have been fomenting civil war in Spain. Marco (Fando), whom the young woman has met and fallen in love with, becomes a soldier when war breaks out. After killing her father in a pistol duel, Marco follows her every movement because he suspects her of being a spy. After a series of dramatic events, she is instrumental in saving a city from starvation and destruction, and exposes the real warmongers.

This muddled film stirred controversy at the time of its release because it was set during the then-contemporary Spanish Civil War. Conservative, isolationist, Depression-era America saw it as an appeal for the Spanish Loyalist cause; some saw it as Marxist propaganda, and the Catholic church managed to ban the film in many American cities and towns.

The producers took precautions not to name the Spanish region specifically, and the viewer cannot be quite sure which side the hero is fighting for.

De Valdez plays Major Del Rio, Lupita Tovar plays a palm reader and Carrillo plays Luis.

Blondie Goes Latin (1941 Columbia)

D: Frank R. Strayer
S: Richard Flournoy and Karen De Wolf, based on a story by
   Quinn Martin
P: Robert Sparks
Cast: Penny Singleton, Arthur Lake, Larry Simms, Irving Bacon,
   Ruth Terry, Tito Guizar

Chic Young's famous syndicated comic strip about an all-American, middle-class family made its way to the movies in the form of a long and popular series at Columbia starring Penny Singleton as Blondie. The eighth entry in the series had a half-dozen songs in a plot that found the Bumsteads at sea on a trip to South America with Dagwood's ailing boss.

Blondie never actually sets foot in a Latin country in this story, but the film has plenty of atmosphere, including Guizar as a South American romancing Blondie. Five musical numbers, dances by Singleton and singing by Ruth Terry and Guizar enhance the entertainment value.

Blood and Sand (1922 Paramount)

D: Fred Niblo
S: June Mathis, based on the novel *Sangre y Arena*
   by Vicente Blasco Ibanez
P: Famous Players—Lasky
Cast: Rudolph Valentino, Lila Lee, Nita Naldi

One of the great silent films, this is the story of an awkward small-town boy, Juan Gallardo, who becomes Spain's greatest matador. He marries his childhood sweetheart, Carmen, but soon falls under the spell of the alluring and aristocratic Doña Sol, who draws him into a reckless affair and humiliates his wife. Remorseful at having betrayed Carmen, the anguished Juan faces death in his dangerous profession.

Every care was taken to make *Blood and Sand* a special film; it was when Valentino's first film for Paramount following three films at Metro, where he was never under contract.

June Mathis, who had scripted *The Four Horsemen of the Apocalypse* (1921), was hired to do the adaptation. Costumes and bullfighting equipment were imported from Spain and Mexico. A retired matador coached Valentino in the art of the corrida as did a young extra named Luis Alonzo, who later found fame as Gilbert Roland. Valentino immersed himself in the character and the role was a perfect vehicle for his talents.

"With a seemingly authentic Spanish background, a cast of people who both look and act like Spaniards, and a director capable of painting his pictures with veracity, *Blood and Sand* at The Rivoli this week could not fail to be entertaining," *New York Times* (8/7/22).

Blood and Sand (1941 Twentieth Century Fox)

D: Rouben Mamoulian
S: Jo Swerling, based on the novel *Sangre y Arena*
   by Vicente Blasco Ibanez
P: Darryl F. Zanuck
Cast: Tyrone Power, Linda Darnell, Rita Hayworth, Alla Nazimova,
   J. Carroll Naish, Anthony Quinn

Tyrone Power stars as Juan Gallardo, the ragged urchin who becomes Spain's greatest matador and succumbs to the adulation of the mob and the temptations of an international socialite. Hayworth appears as the statuesque but cold-hearted Doña Sol. Linda Darnell is Carmen, Gallardo's sweetheart, who remains faithful to him until death. Quinn plays Gallardo's rival in the arena, Manolo, and Naish appears as Garabato, a matador who ends up as a beggar.

For Power, the role was his second as a Spaniard, and he turned in a believable performance as the young bullfighter. Quinn found himself in the most demanding and showiest role of his career up to that time. As a rival of Gallardo's, both for the affection of Doña Sol and the cheers of the arena mob, he plays in a score of passionate love scenes, paces through beautiful cape-work in the ring and does a sensational dance with Doña Sol. The young Quinn demonstrated range and ability in a fully realized role, a departure from the stock characters he had been playing and to which he would return.

The film made a certifiable star out of Hayworth in her sultry performance as Doña Sol. According to a studio press item, Hayworth, to save herself embarrassment, began learning to speak Spanish during the filming. Although of Spanish blood, she was born and raised in the United States. Darnell spoke a little Spanish and was in Mexico with her mother and a family friend who also spoke Spanish.

The film marked the fourth romantic screen teaming of Power and Darnell, similar to the pairing of Errol Flynn and Olivia de Havilland at Warner Bros.

The film isn't entirely satisfactory as forceful drama, but it is gorgeous to look at. Director Rouben Mamoulian attempted three innovations in this version of *Blood and Sand*. He painted the picture instead of merely photographing it; he used as little dialogue as possible, letting the action tell his story; and he insisted that the studio sign Gomez, the famous Spanish composer and guitarist, to write and record authentic Gypsy songs in the true flamenco style.

Mamoulian set about "painting" the Blasco Ibanez story by drawing on the coloring and composition of the famous Spanish masters for the spirit of his scenes. He went to Murillo for the browns and sepias that dominate the early romance between Gallardo and Carmen; to Sorolla, the great master of light and shadows, for the filming of market scenes; to El Greco, famed for his religious paintings, for Gallardo's death in a chapel with Carmen by his side. During Gallardo's struggles for fame, the director drew on Goya, noted for his studies of the lower classes. When Dona Sol, an aristocrat by birth, enters the picture, the style of Velazquez provides the motif for the sets.

The director had two of Hollywood's best color cinematographers, Ernest Palmer and Ray Rennahan, to help him achieve his desired look for the film. For their cinematography and mastery of the three-strip Technicolor process, they were won the Academy Award® for Best Cinematography. Mamoulian used spray guns and several chests of bright cloth for his palettes. He would draw on his chests to put a blue ribbon in Linda's hair to accentuate a feeling of serenity or drape a brown shawl around Gallardo's mother to intensify her despair. At the time, cloth usually photographed flatly, so the spray guns were used in order to accentuate an oil texture such as characterizes many of the old master paintings. The film builds dramatically with color, opening with subdued shades and progressing through brighter and brighter hues until the red climax in the arena.

Though the story takes place in Spain, it was filmed in Mexico and in Hollywood. (With Spain coming out of a civil war and Europe engulfed in World War II, a location trip was out of the question.) A troupe of 300 went to Mexico City for four weeks, spending most of the time in the Plaza de Toros, where crowds of more than 30,000 people gathered to watch the filming, and in turn be shot as extras.

The studio signed Armillita, then one of the world's greatest bull-fighters, to act as a technical advisor and double for Power in the bull-ring. Budd Boetticher, a casting director and a bullfighter in his own right, who had become enamored of the sport on a trip to Mexico years earlier, also acted as technical advisor. Quick to learn, Power sufficiently (for film) mastered the very intricate and difficult cape passes of a matador.

Blood In . . . Blood Out . . . (1993 Buena Vista)
See *Bound by Honor*.

Blood and Wine (1997 Twentieth Century Fox)
D: Bob Rafelson
S: Nick Villiers and Alison Cross
P: Jeremy Thomas
Cast: Jack Nicholson, Judy Davis, Jennifer Lopez, Michael Caine, Stephen Dorff

With the help of a con man (Caine), Alex (Nicholson) plans to steal a diamond necklace so he can leave his wife (Davis) and run off with his Cuban mistress (Lopez). During a fight with his wife, Alex is knocked unconscious and she unknowingly takes off with the jewels before he has a chance to fence them. In the meantime, Alex's stepson falls for Gabrielle—not knowing she is his stepfather's mistress.

Blowing Wild (1953 Warner Bros.)

D: Hugo Fregonese
S: Philip Yordan
P: Milton Sperling
Cast: Gary Cooper, Barbara Stanwyck, Ruth Roman, Anthony Quinn

An old-fashioned melodrama set in the early 1930s, when Americans sought sudden wealth in Mexico's oil fields.

Jeff Dawson (Cooper) and his partner are discouraged from their oil claim by Mexican bandits and head to Mexico City. There they meet Paco Conway (Quinn), whose wife, Marina (Stanwyck), had been in love with Dawson years before. All four decide to return to the oil fields. Dawson spurns Marina's advances, and, in a fury, she pushes Paco into an oil well pump. In turn, raiding bandits kill Marina and blow up the oil works, which makes for the action climax of the film.

The actors are much better than their material. In 1952, both Quinn and Cooper, Oscar®-nominated for other films, found themselves unable to attend the award ceremonies because they filming on location near Cuernavaca, Mexico. Quinn won the Academy Award® for Best Supporting Actor for his work in *Viva Zapata!* and Cooper won as Best Actor for his performance in *High Noon*.

Blue (1968 Paramount)

D: Silvio Narizzano
S: Ronald M. Cohen and Meade Roberts, based on a story by Cohen
P: Judd Bernard and Irwin Winkler
Cast: Terence Stamp, Joanna Petter, Ricardo Montalban

An American, played by the British actor Terence Stamp, is raised by Mexicans in the Old West. Resented by his adoptive brothers, he violently conflicts with their bandit chief father (Montalban). He learns to trust only when a bullet wound forces him to depend on a woman. Stamp is convincing neither as an American nor as a Mexican, and the film is not much better.

Bombardier (1943 RKO Radio Pictures)

D: Richard Wallace
S: John Twist, based on a story by Twist and Martin Rackin
P: Robert Fellows
Cast: Pat O'Brien, Randolph Scott, Eddie Albert, Robert Ryan,
    Richard Martin

American bombardiers train for combat duty at the outbreak of World War II. Martin plays Chito Rafferty, an Irish Mexican, one of the bombsight trainees. Martin later developed this character as a sidekick to Tim Holt in a series of Westerns made by RKO.

Elpidia Carrillo and Jack
Nicholson in *The Border*.

The Border (1983 Universal)

D: Tony Richardson
S: Deric Washburn, Walon Green and
 David Freeman
P: Edgar Bronfman, Jr.
Cast: Jack Nicholson, Valerie Perrine,
 Warren Oates, Harvey Keitel,
 Elpidia Carrillo, Mike Gomez

The story of a border patrolman (Nicholson) who refuses to go along with the corruption and complacency of his fellow officers when he gets emotionally involved with a beautiful illegal immigrant woman (Carrillo) whose baby has been kidnapped by a drug-smuggling ring. He comes to her aid at the expense of exposing his fellow patrolmen.

This is a traditional Western in the guise of a contemporary action drama. Gomez plays a sleazy, mousy greaser type. This violent film was shot on location in El Paso, Texas, and features a strong portrayal by Nicholson and an interesting American film debut for Carrillo as the exotic Guatemalan madonna he rescues.

Border Incident (1949 Metro-Goldwyn-Mayer)

D: Anthony Mann
S: John C. Higgins, based on a story by Higgins and
 George Zuckerman
P: Nicholas Nayfack
Cast: George Murphy, Ricardo Montalban, Howard da Silva

Pablo Rodriguez (Montalban) and Jack Bearnes (Murphy) are secret agents of the Mexican and United States governments who volunteer to uncover the methods of a band of crooks who are smuggling truckloads of undocumented Mexican nationals across the border to work as field laborers in California's Imperial Valley.

Rodriguez disguises himself as a worker, or bracero, and buys transportation from the crooks, while Bearnes poses as a man wanted by the law in the United States who has work permits to sell. Bearnes' true identity is discovered, and he is tortured and brutally murdered. Rodriguez is saved from a horrible death only by the timely arrival of the Border Patrol.

The film shows the abuse and suffering of the workers, who have no legal redress and who are cheated, robbed and killed. After working in the fields they are dumped in a desert they call the Canyon of Death, a morass of quicksand that swallows its victims.

The pairing of Montalban and Murphy as equal representatives of their governments provides human interest in the background of the story. These were new roles for both actors, both of whom were previously were associated with musicals.

The stark documentary look of the film was unusual for glossy MGM. The film was relegated to the bottom half of a double bill at theaters, where it played as a B film, but the reviews were uniformly good. The cast also included Alfonso Bedoya, Teresa Celli and José Torvay.

Border River (1954 Universal)

D: George Sherman
S: William Sackheim and Louis Stevens, based on a story by Stevens
P: Albert J. Cohen
Cast: Joel McCrea, Pedro Armendariz, Yvonne De Carlo, Alfonso Bedoya

With the South's plight growing more desperate in the closing days of the Civil War, a Confederate major (McCrea) and a band of cohorts steal $2 million in gold bullion from a Union mint. The major crosses the Rio Grande and, in the anything-goes-for-cash town of Zona Libre, seeks to make a deal for ammunition and supplies for the rebel army. During the course of events he has to deal with a renegade Mexican general (Armendariz) and his girlfriend (De Carlo).

This is a good Technicolor action Western with the usual bandido stereotypes, but at least this time out they are wearing uniforms and have major roles to play. Armendariz is effective as the cruel and sinister general. Bedoya scores as one of the general's aides. The name of the town, Zona Libre (free zone), suggests the North American bordertown fantasy of a Mexican village. There are plenty of Hispanics cast in this one, including Felipe Turich, Nacho Galindo, George J. Lewis, Martin Garralaga, Salvador Baguez, Pilar Del Rey, Orlando Beltran, Zarco Carreno, Estelita Zarco and Jack Del Rio.

Borderline (1950 Universal)

D: William A. Seiter
S: Devery Freeman
P: Milton H. Bren and William A. Seiter
Cast: Fred MacMurray, Claire Trevor, Nacho Galindo, José Torvay, Pepe Hern

A female Los Angeles Police Officer (Trevor) and a United States Treasury agent (MacMurray) are sent to Mexico to uncover a nest of dope smugglers and bring them back to the United States. This routine B thriller has some interesting Mexican scenery.

Borderline (1980 American Film Distribution)

D: Jerrold Freedman
S: Steve Kline and Jerrold Freedman
P: James Nelson
Cast: Charles Bronson, Bruno Kirby, Ed Harris, Michael Lerner, Bert Remsen, Karmin Murcelo, Enrique Castillo, James Victor, Panchito Gomez

A contemporary melodrama that depicts the plight of illegal Mexican aliens and the problems encountered by the United States Border Patrol.

A veteran Border Patrol officer, Jeb Maynard (Bronson), is on the trail of the people responsible for his longtime partner's death along the United States-Mexico border. The murderer is a former Vietnam vet (Harris), who is part of an illegal-alien smuggling ring headed by a corporate mogul (Lerner) and operated by a rancher (Remsen).

A clue leads Maynard to Elena (Murcelo), an illegal worker employed as a maid in the California town of La Jolla, whose young son (Gomez) was shot alongside the border patrolman. She bravely leads Maynard, disguised as an illegal, back to Tijuana through northern Mexico and onto the smugglers' route.

They look at a traffic jam of cars awaiting entry into the States, only to hear howls of pain emanating from under the hood of a Mercedes-Benz. The Anglo woman at the steering wheel rushes to the hood and unlatches it, and a Mexican woman emerges screaming from radiator burns. As she is carted off by the United States officials for attempting illegal entry, Elena observes, "So they let the gringa go and next week she'll be back to smuggle a new maid."

A young New York agent (Kirby), sent out to assist the Border Patrol, is horrified when he investigates some shantytowns while in pursuit of the killers. He is unable to arrest the immigrants because, he realizes, "How can you bust people for trying to better themselves?" These are the real and honest moments in a film that is essentially a mediocre modern-day revenge tale, in which the illegal alien has no face, no history, no motivation. These immigrant masses, huddled in trucks beneath flats of tomatoes, seem to have no other reason for coming across than to give the Border Patrol something to do. The filmmakers use them as bodies, as nonentities.

Bordertown (1935 Warner Bros.)

D: Archie Mayo
S: Laird Doyle and Wallace Smith, from an adaptation by Robert Lord, based on a novel by Carroll Graham
P: Robert Lord
EP: Jack L. Warner
Cast: Paul Muni, Bette Davis, Margaret Lindsay, Eugene Pallette, Soledad Jimenez

Bordertown began shooting September 17, 1934, on a tight, four-week schedule. The opening sequences were shot on a roped-off Olvera Street in downtown Los Angeles. Paul Muni plays Mexican American self-made lawyer Johnny Ramierez from the Los Angeles barrio in this socially oriented melodrama. Indignation at patronizing treatment causes him to strike a member of the law bar's fraternity. He runs off to a bordertown, where he becomes the manager of a nightclub. In the end, a murder, the madness of Davis and the death of his dream girl as she attempts to flee from him convince Ramierez that his place is with his people.

In his review in the *New York Herald Examiner* (11/24/35), Richard Watts, Jr., said, "Upon occasion it seems to hint that Americans of Mexican parentage should keep their place and not try to mingle with

Paul Muni as the Mexican American lawyer Johnny Ramierez plays opposite the flirtatious Bette Davis in *Bordertown*.

their superiors. Chiefly, though, its more race conscious moments have a way of looking with proper disapproval on California snobbishness, which, the work tells you, has fine words and cruel treatment for Mexican immigrants who attempt to achieve success in the sacred practice of the law."

Born in East L. A. (1987 Universal)

D: Cheech Marin
S: Cheech Marin
P: Peter MacGregor-Scott
Cast: Cheech Marin, Daniel Stern, Jan-Michael Vincent, Daniel Valdez, Paul Rodriguez, Kamala Lopez, Lupe Ontiveros, Tony Plana

Based on a hit video and song Cheech and Chong had produced a year earlier, inspired by the Bruce Springsteen song "Born in the USA," and a newspaper account of a young Mexican American who had been illegally deported to Mexico.

Cheech decided to go without Chong and explore his own charismatic comic persona in an insightful, comic and satirical look at what it means to be an American of dual heritage in contemporary America.

Rudy (Marin) is a Chicano living in Los Angeles who is mistakenly arrested during an immigration raid and deported to Mexico. The bulk of the film revolves around Rudy's attempts to prove his identity and citizenship and return to the United States. In the process he rediscovers who he truly is and some basic truths surrounding the dual nature of being Hispanic in the United States. The film reveals an important emerging artist at work in a somewhat uneven comedy. There are some very funny and touching scenes that show Marin at his best—Rudy trying to show illegals how to be Chicanos, a border crossing featuring hundreds of undocumented workers crossing in broad daylight to the tune of Neil Diamond's "Coming to America," and Rudy trying to prove his citizenship to disbelieving American immigration authorities. The irony is that Rudy does not even speak Spanish. Rodriguez is featured as a recently arrived illegal cousin who visits the family in East Los Angeles and finds no one home.

Boulevard Nights (1979 Warner Bros.)
D: Michael Pressman
S: Desmond Nakano
P: Bill Benenson
EP: Tony Bill
Cast: Richard Yniguez, Danny De La Paz, Marta DuBois, Betty Carvalho

This film was a trendsetter for the 1980s with its dark, dismal and disturbing view of gang life in the barrio of Los Angeles. Yniguez as Raymond and De La Paz (making his screen debut) as Chuco star as brothers involved in gang activities, and Marta Du Bois is Raymond's girl, Shady. Raymond, as the older brother who has long since abandoned gang life, promises his mother (Carvalho) that he will take care of Chuco and keep him away from gangs.

The stylistic, innovative lighting and camera work, coupled with sensitive performances from a largely Latino cast filmed on actual East Los Angeles locations, give *Boulevard Nights* an uncompromising realism. Director Michael Pressman and Executive Producer Tony Bill deserve credit for their work, but ultimately the film proved too bleak for most audiences. The Chicano community in the Southwestern United States protested against the unflattering and violent portrayal of a portion of its community. Japanese American and first-time screenwriter Desmond Nakano wrote the script, which was optioned by Bill when Nakano was still studying at UCLA under the tutelage of Paul Schrader. Tony Bill at the time stated, "What makes *Boulevard Nights* special is that it is not an exploitation film but rather the story of two brothers and their family ties, told realistically and with humanity. It is also the first film of its kind with an all Latino cast. We've broken some new ground."

Bound by Honor [aka: *Blood In . . . Blood Out . . .*] (1993 Buena Vista)

D: Taylor Hackford
S: Jimmy Santiago Baca, Jeremy Iacone, Floyd Mutrux
P: Taylor Hackford and Jerry Gershwin
Cast: Benjamin Bratt, Jesse Borrego, Enrique Castillo, Damian Chapa

This is a twelve-year saga that follows the lives of three cousins from East Los Angeles. One is a gifted painter who turns to narcotics after a brutal beating Another is a short-tempered boxer who becomes an undercover cop in his old neighborhood. The third is a half-Chicano gang member who goes to San Quentin and gets caught up in an inter-racial prison gang war.

The story is a variation on themes and ideas first explored in Edward James Olmos' *American Me* (1992) and shares a writer, Floyd Mutrux. The films were in production at the same time (the summer of 1991) and were filmed in many of the same East Los Angeles locations. Olmos filmed at Folsom Prison, and Hackford filmed at San Quentin. Hackford's saga is the more ambitious in terms of story and character (Hackford envisioned two epic films); running almost three hours it went into general release as *Bound by Honor*, though it was known under its original shooting title: *Blood In . . . Blood Out . . .* , up until the month before national release. The film opened and was test marketed in various smaller markets around the country under its original title and was reviewed by *The Hollywood Reporter* as such. The original title was restored for the video release in early 1994.

Branded (1950 Paramount)

D: Rudolph Mate
S: Cyril Hume and Sydney Boehm
P: Mel Epstein
Cast: Alan Ladd, Mona Freeman, Charles Bickford, Robert Keith,
　　　Joseph Calleia, Peter Hansen, Felipe Turich, Joe Dominguez,
　　　Salvador Baguez

Choya (Ladd), a wandering gunfighter in Texas and Mexico during the 1890s, poses as the long-lost son of a rancher (Bickford) as part of a con-spiracy to steal the man's land. However, once Choya meets Bickford's daughter (Freeman) and finds himself accepted by the family, he changes his mind and refuses to go through with the swindle. Subsequently, Choya learns that the real son (Hansen) is alive in Mexico. He goes after the man and succeeds in bringing him home. In so doing he antagonizes the Mexican bandit, Mateo Rubriz (Calleia), who has adopted the real heir. After a chase and a battle, all-around reconciliations are effected.

This is an entertaining Technicolor Western that includes an unusu-al portrayal by Calleia as a cultured Mexican bandit with a possessive devotion to his adopted son.

The Bravados (1958 Twentieth Century Fox)

D: Henry King
S: Philip Yordan, based on the novel by Frank O'Rourke
P: Henry B. Swope, Jr.
Cast: Gregory Peck, Joan Collins, Henry Silva, Lee Van Cleef,
Ada Carrasco

Jim Douglass (Peck) rides into a small bordertown and chases four escaped outlaws into Mexico because he believes they are responsible for the rape and murder of his wife. One by one he guns the men down, and the last man (Silva) confesses to him that they had nothing to do with the murder. Douglass, now remorseful about killing innocent men, suspects his ranch neighbor and returns home to confront him. This strong Western features Peck in fine form and Silva in a sympathetic portrayal as a Mexican Indian outlaw.

The Brave Bulls (1951 Columbia)

D: Robert Rossen
S: John Bright, based on the novel by Tom Lea
P: Robert Rossen
Cast: Mel Ferrer, Anthony Quinn, Miroslava, Eugene Iglesias

Mel Ferrer is Luis Bello, a young Mexican peasant who rises to prominence as a matador. He begins to doubt his own abilities, and thus loses his courage, after he enters into a passionate romance with a high-toned tramp (Miroslava) who double-crosses him with his rough-hewn manager (Quinn) and then dies in a tragic car crash.

Filming on location in Mexico City, Rossen achieved the strong sense of Mexican culture and life in modern-day Mexico City that was also present in the novel.

Quinn is excellent as the rough manager. Ferrer, as the matador, gives a convincing performance. The Yugoslavian-born, Mexican-raised actress Miroslava committed suicide soon after the film was completed. Iglesias, a Puerto Rican born actor, plays Bello's young bullfighter brother.

The details of bullfighting and the action in the bullring were captured in great detail, though the production code at the time would not allow the killing of the bulls to be shown. The cinematographers were Floyd Crosby and James Wong Howe.

The Brave One (1956 RKO Radio Pictures)

D: Irving Rapper
S: Harry S. Franklin and Merrill G. White, based on the story by
Dalton Trumbo (as Robert Rich)
P: Maurice and Frank King
Cast: Michel Ray, Rudolfo Hoyos Jr., Elsa Cardenas, Carlos Navarro

The Brave One remains the King brothers' most prestigious and highly regarded achievement. Starting from scratch in the 1940s, the three brothers (Frank, Maurice and Herman), made a quickie exploitation film, Paper Bullets (1941), which was a modest box office success. They

Rudolfo Hoyos, Jr. and Elsa Cardenas play father and sister to Michel Ray (center) in *The Brave One*, a story of a boy's love for his pet.

continued to produce, specializing in exploitation-type pictures, each successive film boasting a slightly bigger budget. Among their tremendously successful films are *Dillinger* (1945), *Mutiny* (1952), *Southside 1-1000* (1950), *Drums in the Deep South* (1951), *The Ring* (1952) and *Carnival Story* (1954).

The Brave One was their first film in Technicolor and Cinemascope with stereophonic sound. The original story was entitled "The Boy and the Bull," and was to have been directed by Kurt Neumann. Irving Rapper, the director of some of Warner Bros.' human drama stories (*Now, Voyager* [1942] and *The Corn Is Green* [1945] among them), wound up directing the picture, and in an interview with Charles Higham expressed his fondness for the film: "One picture of mine wasn't compromised: *The Brave One*. They all said, 'What do you see in it?' And I said, 'It's simple, it reads like a fairy tale, it cost $430,000 to make and grossed $8.5 million.'"

The extensive search by the King brothers to find the right star for the film ended when they saw an English picture called *The Divided Heart* (1954), featuring a young boy called Michel Ray. After a screen test, the twelve-year-old was cast in the lead role.

The film deals with the fierce love of a Mexican boy for his pet. The animal happens to be a prize-fighting bull nurtured from birth to full-grown magnificence by the youngster, who vehemently refuses to permit the killing of his lifelong companion in the bullring.

Jack Cardiff, Academy Award®-winning cinematographer for *The Red Shoes* (1948), photographed the film on location in Mexico City and surrounding areas. The Mexican government gave the film company special permission to film scenes at historic Chapultepec Castle and other locations, including the vast Plaza de Mexico bullring in Mexico City. Celebrated matador Fermin Rivera played himself in the climactic arena sequences.

Of 150 speaking parts, 148 Latin roles were cast in Mexico. Michel Ray is of French-German parentage and a naturalized British citizen. Mexican-born but United States-raised Rudolfo Hoyos Jr., plays the father. Hoyos had been featured in a number of Hollywood films including *The Fighter* (1952), *Second Chance* (1953), *The Americano* (1955) and *Timetable* (1956). Mexican actress Cardenas plays the boy's sister. An established actress in Mexico, Cardenas was signed by a Hollywood talent scout for a major role in Warner Bros.' *Giant* (1956), based on her work in *The Brave One*.

The film won an Academy Award® for Best Motion Picture Story in 1956, at which time it was discovered that there was no writer named Robert Rich. At the time, there was considerable suspicion that black-listed writer Dalton Trumbo was the author, and he admitted it publicly two years later when the Academy repealed the blacklist ruling. In May 1975, Trumbo was given his belated Oscar® by Academy president Walter Mirisch, about a year before the acclaimed screenwriter died.

Brazil (1944 Republic Pictures) [aka: *Stars and Guitars* (1951)]
D: Joseph Santley
S: Frank Gill Jr., and Laura Kerr, based on a story by Richard English
P: Robert North
Cast: Tito Guizar, Virginia Bruce, Veloz and Yolanda, Frank Puglia, Fortunio Bonanova, Aurora Miranda

A young Brazilian composer attempts to capture the heart of an American woman who has written a book called *Why Marry a Latin?* She finds herself the victim of her own book when she travels to Brazil to write her second book.

This pleasant musical comedy is dominated by Tito Guizar, who is an engaging personality and sings quite a few songs. Ary Barroso, the distinguished Brazilian composer and author of the song "Brazil," wrote the musical score for the film. Roy Rogers makes an appearance singing "Hands Across the Border," by Hoagy Carmichael. Aurora Miranda is seen briefly as a dancer, and Veloz and Yolanda do a specialty dance number. *Brazil* was filmed at Republic Studios in Hollywood with background scenes filmed by a second unit on location in Brazil. The film was re-edited and re-released in 1951 as *Stars and Guitars*.

Break of Dawn (1989 Platform Releasing)

D: Isaac Artenstein

S: Isaac Artenstein

P: Jude Eberhard

Cast: Oscar Chavez, Maria Rojo, Pepe Serna, Tony Plana, Socorro Valdez

The true story of Pedro Gonzalez, the first Spanish-language radio and recording star on the West Coast of the United States, who in 1934 was sent to San Quentin Prison on fabricated charges.

The film documents Gonzalez's rise in popularity during the Golden Age of Radio with his original and romantic ballads and his daily commentary on radio station KMPC in Los Angeles. Gonzalez's rise and success occur during the Depression, when nearly half a million people of Mexican descent were deported to Mexico.

He becomes an outspoken critic of the unjust scapegoating of Mexicans in a stagnant United States economy. Gonzalez refuses to heed the warnings of the authorities and is framed on rape charges by a fearful and power-hungry district attorney. Gonzalez is convicted and sent to San Quentin. The film culminates with his wife, Maria, organizing the Mexican community in the United States to free her husband and clear his name.

Break of Dawn was written and directed by Isaac Artenstein, a Mexican of Jewish ancestry who resides in San Diego. It was produced by his longtime associate Jude Eberhard, and the project had its beginnings in a documentary on the life of Gonzalez, *Ballad of an Unsung Hero*, which aired nationally on PBS and won numerous awards, including an Emmy.

Break of Dawn was shown at the 1989 United States Film Festival and represented the United States at the 1989 Moscow Film Festival. The bilingual film was released in art houses and English-language theaters in the Southwest for limited runs. Critical response to the film was respectful but lukewarm, charging that the script lacked depth and was not clear as to the events. It was filmed on a budget of less than $1 million in and around San Diego, doubling for 1930s Los Angeles. Artenstein and Eberhard were able to raise the money for the modestly budgeted feature from private investors largely because of the success of other independent features such as *Heartland* (1979) and *El Norte* (1984). "The restrictions of a small independent feature like this have one big advantage, complete creative responsibility," remarked Artenstein.

The cast was headed by noted Mexican folksinger Oscar Chavez as Pedro J. Gonzalez and Maria Rojo as his wife. Chavez as Gonzalez had the singing voice but lacked charisma and strong acting ability. Serna turned in one of his dependable supporting portrayals as a relative. Plana was excellent as an ambitious police official. The film offers an alternative view, another voice in documenting a piece of Hispanic American history, though it cannot overcome a first-time director's script and limited budget.

Breakout (1975 Columbia)

D: Tom Gries
S: Howard B. Kreitsek, Marc Norman, and Elliot Baker
P: Robert Chartoff and Irwin Winkler
Cast: Charles Bronson, Robert Duvall, Randy Quaid, Alejandro Rey,
Jill Ireland, John Huston, Emilio Fernandez

This is a standard action film in which American aviator Nick Colton (Bronson) is hired to engineer a daring helicopter rescue from a Mexican prison yard. The prisoner being rescued is an American citizen, Jay Wagner (Duvall), who has been framed by his father-in-law (Huston).

The Bridge of San Luis Rey (1929 Metro-Goldwyn-Mayer)

D: Charles Brabin
S: Alice Duer Miller, Ruth Cummings, and Marian Ainslee, based on
the novel by Thornton Wilder
Cast: Lily Damita, Ernest Torrence, Raquel Torres, Don Alvarado,
Duncan Renaldo

Based on the classic Thornton Wilder novel, the film is set in Peru and explores how the five victims of a bridge collapse happen to be there at the same time.

The Bridge of San Luis Rey (1944 United Artists)

D: Rowland V. Lee
S: Herman Weissman and Howard Estabrook, based on the novel by
Thornton Wilder
P: Benedict Bogeaus
Cast: Lynn Bari, Alla Nazimova, Louis Calhern, Akim Tamiroff,
Francis Lederer, Donald Woods

A remake of Wilder's moody story about five people meeting their doom on a rickety bridge.

The Bright Shawl (1923 First National)

D: John S. Richardson
S: Edmund Goulding, based on a 1922 novel by Joseph Hergesheimer
P: Charles H. Duell
Cast: Richard Barthelmess, Dorothy Gish, Mary Astor,
Edward G. Robinson, George Humbert, William Powell

Romance and adventure in the 1850s, when Cuba sought its independence from Spain. A wealthy New Yorker accompanies a Cuban friend to Cuba and is thrust into dangerous adventures and two romances. This silent drama was filmed on location in Cuba.

Bring Me the Head of Alfredo Garcia (1974 United Artists)

D: Sam Peckinpah
S: Sam Peckinpah and Gordon Dawson, based on a story by
   Frank Kowalski
P: Martin Baum
Cast: Warren Oates, Isela Vega, Gig Young, Emilio Fernandez

A down-and-out gringo soldier of fortune (Oates) becomes entangled in a web of murder and deceit when a wealthy Mexican (Fernandez) patron offers a $10,000 reward for the head of a young hustler who has made his daughter pregnant. The film opens beautifully and ambiguously with the father's confrontation of his wayward daughter in what appears to be nineteenth-century Mexico; then the film unexpectedly cuts to modern limousines roaring out of hacienda gates and jets taking off from airports.

This ugly, ultra-violent film is full of Mexican stereotypes and harsh Mexican scenery. Isela Vega, an attractive Mexican actress, plays a whore companion who gives the film's lead (Oates) a venereal disease and is raped by a biker.

The Mexican government co-produced this film, and apparently the stereotypes did not bother them, as in reality many of the character types were frequently featured in Mexican films of the period. The film met with a cool reception at United States box offices.

The Buddy Holly Story (1978 Columbia)

D: Steve Rash
S: Robert Gittler, based on the book by John Coldrosen
P: Fred Bauer
Cast: Gary Busey, Maria Richwine, Charles
   Martin Smith, Don Stroud, Gloria Irrizary

Maria Richwine portrays Buddy Holly's wife in *The Buddy Holly Story*. Gary Busey stars in the title role.

The story of Texas-born rock 'n' roll legend Buddy Holly, who, at the beginning of his rise to fame in 1959, died in a tragic plane crash. This superior film was produced as a heartwarming, sentimental bio-pic, which found favor with critics and audiences alike. All the actors played their own music, and Busey sang Holly's songs. The music was recorded live during the shooting of the scenes, which helped to capture the energy of early rock 'n' roll.

The film sensitively handles Holly's courtship and marriage to a Puerto Rican girl from New York, Maria Elena (Richwine), who worked at the record company for which he recorded.

Busey earned an Academy Award® nomination as Best Actor for his performance. The Colombian-born, United States-raised Maria Richwine played a variation of the traditional señorita in her film debut. Unfortunately, her career never quite took off the way it should have. She was stymied for a time, after an altercation with the film's influential casting director, Joyce Selznick. Since then she has been featured in a number of low budget films and guest shots on television. Irrizary played Maria Elena's aunt.

Teen rock 'n' roll icons the Big Bopper and Ritchie Valens were also killed in the plane crash. Valens, who is a minor figure in this film, is played by Gilbert Melgar. Valens was later immortalized in the film *La Bamba* almost ten years later, in 1987.

The Bullfighter and the Lady (1951 Republic Pictures)

D: Budd Boetticher
S: James Edward Grant, based on a story by Budd Boetticher and
    Ray Nazarro
P: John Wayne
Cast: Robert Stack, Joy Page, Gilbert Roland, Virginia Grey,
    John Hubbard, Rodolfo Acosta, Katy Jurado

The story of an American, Chuck Regan (Stack), vacationing in Mexico with two friends (Grey and Hubbard). He falls in love with a Mexican girl, Anita de la Vega (Page), and, to impress her, he persuades a matador, Manolo Estrada (Roland), to instruct him on the use of the cape and sword. When the matador dies in the ring saving Regan's life, Regan must vindicate his honor and exhibit courage in the face of a hostile crowd.

Like his hero, director Boetticher had studied bullfighting in Mexico as a young man. Earlier in his film career, he had been the technical advisor for the bullfight sequences in Rouben Mamoulian's *Blood and Sand* (1941). After *The Bullfighter and the Lady* he went on to make *The Magnificent Matador* (1955) and *Arruza* (1972). *The Bullfighter and the Lady* has a great feeling for the land and can be compared favorably to Robert Rossen's *The Brave Bulls*, which came out the same year.

Produced by John Wayne for Republic, it was originally to star Wayne, who felt himself too big physically to play a matador believably and therefore gave the role to Robert Stack. Eight of Mexico's leading matadors appear in the film as themselves, and two of them, the Briones brothers, also double for Stack and Roland in the bullfighting scenes. Jurado played Chelo, wife of the matador. It was filmed entirely in Mexico over seven weeks on a $400,000 budget.

The project lent itself to bilingual treatment, and Boetticher believes he succeeded in obtaining complete linguistic realism. English and Spanish are used by the characters, without sacrificing coherence, exactly as they would use them in actuality. Boetticher had to emasculate the great Latin fiesta at its three climaxes—the impact of the *toro* and the *pic*, the insertion of the *banderillas* and the final sword thrust—to mollify the Society for the Prevention of Cruelty to Animals.

The film was originally released in an 87-minute version and edited by director John Ford, who admired Boetticher's work and thought the editing would improve the film's chances of commercial success. In 1987 the UCLA Film Archive restored the film to its original 124-minute length with the assistance of Boetticher.

Roland received excellent notices for his portrayal of the aging bull-fighter: "The most exciting performance in a collection of good ones is that of Gilbert Roland, who plays the popular matador, the teacher of Stack," Darr Smith, *Los Angeles Daily News* (4/26/51).

"Without overplaying, [Roland] gives his matador character color and vigor, bravery without bravado, and dignity. Katy Jurado, as Roland's wife, is another who makes a very strong impression," *Variety* (5/2/51).

The Bullfighters (1945 Twentieth Century Fox)
D: Malcolm St. Clair
S: W. Scott Darling
P: William Girard
Cast: Stan Laurel, Oliver Hardy

Laurel and Hardy in Mexico as private detectives in search of a lady criminal.

Butch Cassidy and the Sundance Kid (1969 Twentieth Century Fox)
D: George Roy Hill
S: William Goldman
P: Paul Monash and John Foreman
Cast: Paul Newman, Robert Redford, Katharine Ross, José Torvay

The story of turn-of-the-century outlaws Butch Cassidy (Newman) and the Sundance Kid (Redford). This clever, well-acted Western depends a great deal on the offbeat casting and striking chemistry of its two stars. In this buddy picture, the relationship of the two characters is explored through numerous adventurous—and sometimes funny—escapades.

Robbing banks and being chased by the law throughout the American Southwest, the pair decide to go to Bolivia in order to escape the American authorities and start a new life. Upon their arrival they quickly discover that the pickings are meager and the territory and language present insurmountable problems. The two are besieged by a band of bandidos led by Torvay, whom they are forced to kill. Butch and the Kid meet their deaths in a gun battle with 200 Bolivian soldiers. While the climax echoes the "truth" of the end of the two anti-heroes in real life, it can be argued that the ending continues the time-honored North American film tradition of needing an army of Latinos kill two gringos.

The Bolivian scenes were actually shot in Taxco and Cuernavaca, Mexico. It was reported that when director George Roy Hill was informed that the Bolivia of the film looked nothing like the Bolivia of real life, he replied, "Well, it does now."

Bye, Bye Birdie (1963 Columbia)
D: George Sidney
S: Irving Brecher, based on the stage play by Michael Stewart,
   Charles Strouse, and Lee Adams
P: Fred Kohlmar
Cast: Janet Leigh, Dick Van Dyke, Ann-Margret, Maureen Stapleton

A film version of the hit 1960 Broadway musical, in which Chita Rivera originated the role of Rosie. Conrad Birdie, rock 'n' roll idol, is about to be drafted into the United States Army, which spells doom for Albert Peterson (Van Dyke), a bankrupt songwriter who has written the title tune for the singer's new movie. Now there will be no movie, no title tune, no royalties. Adding to Albert's woes is a possessive mother, Mae (Stapleton), intent on breaking up his romance with Rosie DeLeon (Leigh). Rosie schemes to have Albert write a special farewell song for Birdie in an effort to make Albert rich and pry him away from Mama. A small-town U.S.A. television extravaganza results when Birdie visits the hometown of a fan and complications ensue.

In an offbeat casting venture, blonde star Janet Leigh was given a black wig and asked to sing and dance as Rosie DeLeon, the Spanish secretary.

California (1946 Paramount)
D: John Farrow
S: Frank Butler and Theodore Strauss, based on a story by
   Boris Ingster
P: Seton I. Miller
Cast: Ray Milland, Barbara Stanwyck, Anthony Quinn

Set in nineteenth-century California, Ray Milland stars as a cowboy who meets a lady gambler (Stanwyck) and gets involved in foiling an attempt by a former slave trader who wants to establish California as a separate empire.

In this loosely historically based film, Quinn is featured as Don Luis Rivera y Hernandez, who is asked to support the attempt to usurp power while the Anglo settlers are deciding on California statehood.

California Conquest (1952 Columbia)
D: Lew Landers
S: Robert E. Kent
P: Sam Katzman
Cast: Cornel Wilde, Teresa Wright, Alfonso Bedoya, Eugene Iglesias,
   Tito Renaldo, Rico Alaniz, Alex Montoya

A melodramatic film with historical overtones and an emphasis on action. Young Arturo Bordega (Wilde) is the leader of a group of well-to-do Spanish Californians who, tired of Mexican rule and fearing British, French and Russian claims on their homeland, are hoping for peace and freedom under United States rule. Bordega disguises himself as a peon in order to evade capture and gain entrance to a Russian fortress. Wright is an American girl whose father has been slain by the Russians.

The film is representative of the McCarthy-era Cold War paranoia that permeated America in the 1950s, in that the heavies turn out to be Russians. Wilde, who had played suave Latinos previously, was excellent as the California don. Bedoya contributed his patented bandit portrayal to good effect.

The Californian [aka: *The Gentleman from California*] (1937 Twentieth Century Fox)
D: Gus Meins
S: Gilbert Wright, based on a story by Harold Bell Wright, adapted by Gordon Newell
P: Sol Lesser
Cast: Ricardo Cortez, Katherine DeMille, Marjorie Weaver

The story of Ramon Escobar (Cortez), an early California patriot. The film's plot revolves around a Robin Hood theme, and the villains are early American settlers from back east who, by force and connivance, steal the rich landholdings from the dons.

Of B movie quality with no originality, the film is dull and cliched despite its potentially provocative themes.

Cannery Row (1982 Metro-Goldwyn-Mayer/United Artists)
D: David S. Ward
S: David S. Ward, based on novels by John Steinbeck
P: Michael Phillips
Cast: Nick Nolte, Debra Winger, Santos Morales, Rosana De Soto

The script by David S. Ward (who had previously won an Academy Award® for his script of *The Sting* [1973], and who later scripted *The Milagro Beanfield War* [1988]) is based on John Steinbeck's *Cannery Row* and its sequel, *Sweet Thursday*. Set in a boisterous waterfront haven for derelicts, dreamers and nonconformists, the film focuses on the love affair between an ex-baseball star, Doc (Nolte), and a feisty prostitute, Suzy (Winger). The couple triumph over harsh realities with their compassion and good humor. The film got off to a shaky start when Raquel Welch, who was to play Suzy, was replaced by Debra Winger after several days of filming. The final film received mixed reviews and a poor box office response.

Captain from Castile (1947 Twentieth Century Fox)
D: Henry King
S: Lamar Trotti, based on the novel by Samuel Shellabarger
P: Lamar Trotti
Cast: Tyrone Power, Jean Peters, Lee J. Cobb, Cesar Romero, Thomas Gomez, John Sutton, Antonio Moreno

The first and only major Hollywood film to date about the conquest of Mexico actually filmed in Mexico. *Captain from Castile* is a sumptuously romantic, entertaining film produced at the pinnacle of Hollywood's Golden Age. Any resemblance to history in this account of the conquest of the Aztecs is a swashbuckling, Technicolor coincidence. The story is a partial telling of the Spanish Inquisition and the conquest in 1519 from a Spanish point of view. Only the first part of Shellabarger's massive and popular novel was filmed.

Pedro De Vargas (Power) is a young Spanish nobleman who flees to the New World when his family is persecuted by the Inquisition, headed by the brutal and arrogant Diego De Silva (Sutton). While still in Spain, Pedro forgets his vows to a Spanish lady and instead finds romance with the beautiful peasant girl Catana Perez (Peters, in her movie debut), whom he befriends. Catana becomes consumed by a burning love for Pedro, helps him escape from Spain, and follows him to the New World.

Pedro joins Hernando Cortez (Romero) and his expedition at Hispanola in the exploration of and the conquest of the Aztec nation. Aided by a brave but alcoholic and guilt-ridden soldier of fortune, Juan Garcia (Cobb), Pedro rises to power in Cortez's army. Amidst innumerable hardships, inspired by his love for Catana and driven by his hatred of De Silva, Pedro covers himself with glory yet is unable to wreak his revenge. Finally, justice comes to the fanatic Inquisitor, but from an entirely unsuspected source.

Jean Peters was given the star buildup in her first role after winning a talent contest. Romero played Cortez, giving a strong performance, which he considered his favorite. He was chosen for the role during a visit to Darryl Zanuck's home when friend Tyrone Power suggested him for the part and Zanuck agreed.

This was the third and final time Power played a Spaniard. He was a big star in Mexico from his previous Spanish outings in *The Mark of Zorro* (1940) and *Blood and Sand* (1941) and he was mobbed wherever he went in Mexico. Before commencing work on *Captain from Castile*, Power made a personal appearance tour of South America with Romero using their own aircraft, *Saludos Amigos*. As a former United States Marine pilot, Power flew the plane himself.

Silent screen veteran Moreno plays Power's father, Don Francisco. Stella Inda, a prominent Mexico City stage and screen actress, portrays Dona Marina, the Indian girl who was the interpreter for Cortez and who aided him immensely in his conquest. Dolly Arriaga plays Pedro's sister who dies a victim of the Inquisition. Jay Silverheels, a Native American actor (later famous as Tonto, the Lone Ranger's 1950s television sidekick), plays the Aztec nobleman Coatl, who is taken as a slave to Spain and escapes back to the New World.

The Mexican government approved the script and cooperated with the film company, which employed many Mexican film technicians.

Filming on a $3.5 million budget on a 106-day shooting schedule beginning November 15, 1946, the company did not return to the States until March 1, 1947. In the almost four months spent filming in Mexico, three major locations were utilized: Morelia for six weeks, in which the interiors of 300-year-old homes were used to represent Spain; Uruapan for five weeks; and Acapulco for four. The company returned to Los

Cesar Romero as Cortez is pleased with Dona Marina (Stella Inda) and with what he sees of the representatives of Montezuma's Aztec Empire in *Captain from Castile*. Jay Silverheels (rear right) portrays Coatl. (Unidentified man in headdress.)

Angeles for an additional thirty days of filming interiors at the Fox studio, where twenty sets were erected.

A special train of eight railroad cars was sent to Mexico City from Los Angeles. One car contained some 5,000 Aztec lances, 6,000 Indian shields and 400 crossbows. Another car carried lighting and grip equipment as well as refrigerator units to protect the Technicolor film from the heat and humidity of the remote locations. Also included were wardrobe for extras as well as costumes for the leading and supporting players. The Mexico City Museum cooperated with the Twentieth Century Fox research department for details of culture and time period.

Four thousand extras in Mexico, including Tarascan Indians, were employed to portray Aztecs and Spaniards for the final sequences of the film. An Aztec temple, forty feet high and twenty feet long, surrounded by a village of forty huts, was built inland from Acapulco in Uruapan with the then-active volcano Parícutin in the background.

Mexican artists were hired to re-create on the walls inside the temple chambers murals that were exact copies of the ones preserved in the museum in Mexico City.

James Basevi, an art director on the film, recalled one intentional error in an interview with Virginia Wright in the *Daily News* (4/30/47): "Every student of history knows that Cortez landed on the East Coast of Mexico, but in the movie we have him landing on the West Coast. We had two reasons for the shift. The locations were enough of an undertaking without the added complications of transporting actors and equipment all the way across Mexico. Then, weather is uncertain on the East Coast at the time of the year we wanted to shoot. There is very little difference in the tropical foliage. Both locations have coconut palms. More fortunate for our purposes, the coastal contours at Acapulco are such that the sun actually rises over the water. We photographed a sunrise and nobody would be able to tell we shot the other ocean."

One of the film's highlights is a rousing, now-classic musical score by Alfred Newman. The "March Conquest," which serves as the film's finale, is one of the most stirring compositions for the screen and is still popular with college and high school marching bands.

Captain from Castile has an irritating ending because the film ends before Cortez establishes diplomatic relations with Montezuma and before the ensuing clash of cultures. It ends with the conquistadors being led by Aztec messengers into the Valley of Mexico in a triumphant march into the sunset with a voice-over by Fray Bartolome de las Casas (Gomez) expressing hopes that the Spaniards are less interested in gold than in opening up a great new world to Old World civilization.

Captain Thunder (1931 Warner Bros.)

D: Alan Crosland

S: Original story by Hal Davitt and Pierre Couderc; adaptation by Gordon Rigby; dialogue by William K. Web

P: Warner Bros.

Cast: Victor Varconi, Fay Wray, Charles Judels, Robert Elliott, Don Alvarado

Captain Thunder (Varconi), a Mexican Robin Hood, always keeps his word to friend or foe. He has fun when Commandant Ruiz dispatches soldiers to capture him for a 50,000 peso reward. Thunder sends them back, bound and gagged on horses. Fay Wray plays Inez Dominguez. The Italian Varconi's accent is not quite Spanish in this early sound film.

Captains Courageous (1937 Metro-Goldwyn-Mayer)

D: Victor Fleming
S: John Lee Mahin, Marc Connelly, and Dale Van Evers, based on the
   novel by Rudyard Kipling
P: Louis D. Lighton
Cast: Spencer Tracy, Freddie Bartholomew, Lionel Barrymore

Based on Rudyard Kipling's classic nineteenth-century story of the developing friendship between a spoiled rich boy and a simple Portuguese fisherman named Manuel.

Spencer Tracy, of Irish descent and born near Milwaukee, Wisconsin, plays a Portuguese fisherman. Although his attempts at an accent are inconsistent, he projects sincerity, understanding, an infectious good humor and a joy for life that melt the boy's prejudice.

Tracy was at first reluctant to tackle the part, for he did not want to have his hair curled or to attempt a dialect role, but in the end he won the 1937 Academy Award® for Best Actor for his performance.

Carlito's Way (1993 Universal)

D: Brian De Palma
S: David Koepp, based on the novels by Edwin Torres
P: Martin Bregman, Willi Baer, and Michael S. Bregman
Cast: Al Pacino, Sean Penn, Penelope Ann Miller, John Leguizamo,
   Luis Guzman, Viggo Mortensen, Jorje Porcel, Jaime Sanchez,
   John Ortiz, Al Israel

Al Pacino reteams with *Scarface* filmmakers Brian De Palma and Martin Bregman to star as Carlito Brigante, a once-notorious Puerto Rican gangster who, after winning his release from prison, tries desperately to retire from his life of crime. Although he dreams of settling down in the Bahamas, the treachery of old friends and rivals inevitably forces him onto a path of self-destruction.

The film is full of the Hispanic/Puerto Rican stereotype as the violent, inarticulate, poverty-stricken urban dweller who deals in drugs. There are no positive Puerto Rican characters, and the script meanders all over the place. There are no Hispanic women in the film except as sex object salsa dance queens who hang out at an after-hours club. There is no character development that reflects Carlito's ethnic background, and whatever there is of Spanish Harlem life is painted in very broad, superficial strokes. He has an Anglo dream girl, Gail (Miller), who is not all she makes herself out to be and who does not acknowledge Carlito's ethnicity, calling him Charley instead of Carlito. Rather than go to Puerto Rico, Carlito wants to retire to the Bahamas and open a car rental agency, as if the character is rejecting his roots. The filmmakers had a chance to make an interesting film about the New York-Puerto Rican experience but instead made a crime saga devoid of a genuine ethnic or sociological point of view. Leguizamo as Benny Blanco from the Bronx makes an impression but is essentially wasted in a small role. Guzman as Carlito's thickheaded bodyguard Pachanga gives a good performance grounded in reality. Mortensen gives a chilling and heartfelt performance as Lalin, a wheelchair-bound former crony of Carlito. Sanchez plays a waiter at the club.

Carnival in Costa Rica (1947 Twentieth Century Fox)
D: Gregory Ratoff
S: John Larkin, Samuel Hoffenstein, and Elizabeth Reinhardt
P: William A. Bacher
Cast: Cesar Romero, Vera-Ellen, Celeste Holm, Dick Haymes,
    J. Carroll Naish, Pedro de Cordoba

A pleasant and diverting musical comedy about two well-to-do families who have betrothed their children (Romero and Vera-Ellen) without
taking the couple's wishes into consideration. He is in love with an
American nightclub singer (Holm), and she is in love with a young
American visitor (Haymes). The fathers (Naish and de Cordoba) are left
to straighten out the situation. Full of music and songs, the picture was
filmed on the Fox backlot and studio. A film crew was sent to Costa Rica
without the cast to gather background footage of the country for insertion in the film.

Casualties of War (1989 Columbia)
D: Brian De Palma
S: David Rabe, based on the book by Daniel Lang
P: Art Linson and Fred Caruso
Cast: Michael J. Fox, Sean Penn, John Leguizamo

American soldiers during the Vietnam conflict on a long-range recon-
naissance mission abduct, brutally rape and then murder a South
Vietnamese village girl. A battle of wills ensues between the rookie
Eriksson (Fox) and the deranged squad leader, Sergeant Maserve
(Penn), over the incident. Leguizamo plays Diaz, the newest member of
the squad, whose allegiance vacillates between Eriksson and Maserve.

Cat Chaser (1990 Vestran)
D: Abel Fentara
S: Jim Borrelli and Alan Sharp, based on the novel by Elmore Leonard
P: Peter S. Davis and William Panzer
Cast: Peter Weller, Kelly McGillis, Tomas Milian, Juan Fernandez,
    Frederic Forrest, Charles Durning, Victor Rivers

An overly complex caper movie about a former Marine, George Moran
(Weller), who was involved in the American invasion of Santo Domingo
(now the Dominican Republic) during the 1960s. He returns to the
island to search for the woman who taunted him with the name "Cat
Chaser," but who had saved his life when he was captured by the guerrillas. His journey finds him in an affair with Mary DeBoya (McGillis),
who happens to be married to Andres DeBoya (Milian), the former head
of the Santo Domingo secret police now living in Miami. There is a subplot about Nolan Tyner (Forrest) and Jiggs (Durning) trying to steal
Andres DeBoya's money.

Catlow [aka: Maverick Gold] (1971 Metro-Goldwyn-Mayer)

D: Sam Wanamaker
S: Scot Finch and J.J. Griffith, based on the novel by Louis L'Amour
P: Euan Lloyd
Cast: Yul Brynner, Richard Crenna, Daliah Lavi

A tongue-in-cheek Western about Catlow (Brynner), a cattle rustler pursued by a longtime friend and lawman (Crenna). Catlow gets involved in Mexico with a Mexican spitfire (Lavi) and the lawman finds romance with the aristocratic Mexican woman, Christina, while eluding Indians and Mexican cavalry.

This fair-to-amusing Western with stereotyped characterizations all the way around was filmed in Spain, standing in for a Texas-Mexico border area.

Cha-Cha-Cha Boom (1956 Columbia)

D: Fred F. Sears
S: James B. Gordon and Benjamin H. Kline
P: Sam Katzman
Cast: Steve Dunn, Alix Talton

This low-budget film was designed to capitalize on the cha-cha and mambo dance crazes that spread across the United States in the mid-1950s. A disc jockey attempts to sign new talent from Cuba for his own recording company. The plot is really just a contrivance to string together a number of musical acts.

The only value the movie has today is its musical and visual record of the legendary Perez Prado, the Mary Kaye Trio, Helen Grayco and the bands of Luis Acaraz and Manny Lopez. Comic actor José Gonzalez-Gonzalez provided the comedy relief. Director Fred Sears also helmed the first rock 'n' roll movie, *Rock Around the Clock*, the same year.

Charlie Chan in Panama (1940 Twentieth Century Fox)

D: Norman Foster
S: John Larkin and Lester Ziffren, based on the character created by Earl Derr Biggers
P: Sol M. Wurtzel
Cast: Sidney Toler, Jean Rogers, Lionel Atwill, Chris-Pin Martin

Charlie Chan (Toler) works for the American government to thwart a plot to destroy the American naval fleet as it passes through the Panama Canal on its way to the Pacific.

Charlie Chan in Rio (1941 Twentieth Century Fox)

D: Harry Lachman
S: Samuel G. Engel and Lester Ziffren, based on the character created by Earl Derr Biggers
P: Sol M. Wurtzel
Cast: Sidney Toler, Mary Beth Hughes, Cobina Wright, Jr.

In Rio de Janeiro, Chan (Toler) works with the local police to solve a pair of murders. The locale allowed for music and romance in doses unusual for a Chan picture, but in line with the studio's first attempts at the Good Neighbor Policy. This is a reworking of *The Black Camel* (1931), an early Charlie Chan film starring Warner Oland. Hamilton MacFadden, who directed *The Black Camel*, appears in this movie as Bill Kellogg.

Charro! (1969 National General)
D: Charles Marquis Warren
S: Charles Marquis Warren, based on a story by Frederic Louis Fox
P: Harry Caplan and Charles Marquis Warren
Cast: Elvis Presley, Ina Balin, Victor French

A tedious, melodramatic Western in which an outlaw and his henchmen steal from the Mexicans a gold-and-silver-adorned victory cannon that had fired the last shot against the emperor Maximilian.

Former outlaw Jesse Wade (Presley) is branded and falsely accused of being the cannon-stealing culprit. Soon soldiers on both sides of the border are hunting down Wade. He must prove his innocence and protect a bordertown from being ravaged by the outlaw gang.

Ina Balin is Tracy, a saloon keeper with whom Wade renews a friendship. Balin's character could be Mexican based on her appearance and the location of the story, but she plays the role without an accent. The bearded Presley, who plays it straight, is named Jesse Wade, yet is called Charro, the name for a Mexican cowboy. Presley's dark looks suggest he could be a Mexican or a "half-breed," like the characters he had played in *Flaming Star* (1960) and *Stay Away, Joe* (1968). Tony Young plays Lieutenant Rivera and James Almanzar plays Sheriff Ramsey.

Che! (1969 Twentieth Century Fox)
D: Richard Fleischer
S: Michael Wilson and Sy Bartlett, based on a story by Bartlett and David Karp
P: Sy Bartlett.
Cast: Omar Sharif, Jack Palance, Cesare Danova, Robert Loggia, Woody Strode, Perry Lopez, Rudy Diaz, Barbara Luna, Frank Silvera, Sarita Vara

Soon after the death of controversial Latin American revolutionary Dr. Ernesto "Che" Guevara, Twentieth Century-Fox chief Darryl F. Zanuck sent a request to Richard D. Zanuck, executive vice president in charge of production, to explore the possibility of producing a biographical film about the famous guerrilla fighter. Producer Sy Bartlett was assigned to the project because of his long record of association with Latin American people and their countries and because of his knowledge of the Spanish language. Bartlett then interviewed more than 100 people, traveled thousands of miles, and used his contacts through governmental and military sources in the United States and Latin America to gather his material. Two months after Che's death and some forty-five days after he had started his extensive research program, Bartlett turned in two voluminous reports that became the basis for the screenplay, written by Bartlett and Michael Wilson.

The film covers the period from Che's landing with Castro in Cuba through the successful revolution that swept the Batista regime from power and on to the futile guerrilla campaigns on the rugged Andean slopes. It concludes with his death in Bolivia at the hands of Bolivian soldiers.

Omar Sharif, who had appeared in English-speaking films since *Lawrence of Arabia* (1962), *Doctor Zhivago* (1965) and *Funny Girl* (1968), was cast as Guevara. With beard and mustache, he bears an uncanny resemblance to Che. Jack Palance plays Fidel Castro. Luna is Nurse Anita Marquez, who aids in doctoring guerrillas, Cuban peasants and army soldiers alike. Near the end of the film, Silvera appears as an old goatherd who tells Che and an officer that he has no interest in what either of them pretend to offer. The film also features Sarita Vara, Perry Lopez and Rudy Diaz in small roles.

Che! was filmed in Puerto Rico, subbing for Cuba, and in Hollywood with the Fox Ranch as Bolivia. Many actors from Puerto Rico were cast in small roles.

This middle-of-the-road film, which does not delve deeply into its subject matter and presents its story in a haphazard flashback narrative style.

Cheyenne Autumn (1964 Warner Bros.)

D: John Ford
S: James R. Webb, based on the novel by Mari Sandoz
P: Bernard Smith
Cast: Richard Widmark, Carroll Baker, Gilbert Roland,
    Ricardo Montalban, Dolores Del Rio, Sal Mineo, Karl Malden

The long trek of the Cheyenne nation forced off their lands by the United States government in 1876 afforded the opportunity for three of Hollywood's legendary Hispanic American actors (Roland, Del Rio and Montalban) to work together in starring roles for the only time. Curiously, they played Native Americans, under the direction of John Ford.

These kinds of roles have often previously gone to Hispanic or other ethnic players for limited, one-dimensional characterizations (e.g., Henry Brandon as Chief Scar in *The Searchers* [1956]). These three actors, however, brought enormous weight, dignity and presence to a movie that affords an unusually epic and sympathetic view of Native Americans.

Roland plays Chief Dull Knife, who takes his people on a trek back to their homeland rather than face starvation and humiliation on a reservation. Montalban plays Little Wolf, whose desire is to lead his people in a fight to the death with the white man. Del Rio plays Spanish Woman.

Roland, Del Rio and director Ford had begun their careers in the silents and understood intuitively what was needed before the cameras. Montalban had proven himself a serious actor, not just a Latin Lover type. After a successful career in Mexico, Del Rio had returned to Hollywood four years earlier to play Elvis Presley's Native American mother in *Flaming Star* (1960). Del Rio had maintained a close relationship with Ford since her early days in Hollywood and had worked with him previously in *The Fugitive* (1948).

In *Life* magazine (11/27/64), Richard Oulahan in his review said that "[though Del Rio] may be the handsomest woman of the 20th century in this 3 1/2 hour Trojan horse opera, she seldom gets a chance to show her acting skill. All she is allowed to do is look noble or sad while the camera gazes fondly at her classic face from any angle."

Perhaps for Ford these icons of both the silent and sound cinema represented a symbolic acknowledgment of a passing of the Hollywood he had helped to create, both on screen and off. This passing of a way of life paralleled the experience of the Native Americans in the film.

Italian American Sal Mineo, then Hollywood's all-purpose ethnic teenager, was cast as a Native American along with another screen veteran, Victor Jory, as an old medicine man. The film's sympathies clearly lie with the Native Americans, but you never really get to know them as individual human beings. Much too much screen time is devoted to the white cavalry officer (Widmark), well-intentioned and scheming Anglos and the bureaucratic red tape of Washington's policies. As with any Ford film, *Cheyenne Autumn* has some masterful moments highlighted by William H. Clothier's cinematography.

The Children of Sanchez (1978 Lone Star International.)

D: Hall Bartlett
S: Cesare Zavattini and Hall Bartlett, based on the book by
   Oscar Lewis
P: Hall Bartlett
Cast: Anthony Quinn, Dolores Del Rio, Lupita Ferrer, Katy Jurado

After many years of trying to produce a feature film from the classic 1961 book about Oscar and Ruth Lewis' experiences living with Jesus Sanchez and his family in a Mexico City slum, Hall Bartlett was able to overcome Mexican government objections to its negative depiction of Mexican urban life. Unfortunately, the result was this bleak, disjointed, depressing film that Bartlett produced, wrote and directed.

The talented cast of Latino performers could not overcome the script and the directorial weaknesses. Gabriel Figueroa's color lighting was inappropriate for this story of slum life. The film featured all the typical Latin stereotypes, without depth or understanding. Quinn's performance is the strongest element in the film, but even he can't overcome the movie's shortcomings despite the fact that for many years Quinn had also longed to do a film of this story. *The Children of Sanchez* was a co-production with the Mexican government. Popular jazz artist Chuck Mangione scored the film, and the theme from the movie became a popular seller and more widely known than the movie itself. The film had an extremely limited United States release through a small distribution company, Lone Star International, that quickly folded.

"Earnest but flawed attempt to flesh out Oscar Lewis' book," *Variety* (9/20/78). "*The Children of Sanchez* is a heartbreaker, but not in the sense it was intended to be. The sadness, which ends up not much short of heartbreak, is that so monumentally important a work has been so abysmally translated into a movie. It is amateurish, stiff, uncinematic and unmoving," Charles Champlin, *Los Angeles Times* (9/22/78).

Chinatown (1974 Paramount)

D: Roman Polanski
S: Robert Towne
P: Robert Evans
Cast: Jack Nicholson, Faye Dunaway, John Huston, Perry Lopez

Lopez plays a Mexican American police detective, Lieutenant Luis Escobar, friend to Nicholson's detective character, Jake Gittes, in this classic mystery thriller. Lopez's role was a major one in an important motion picture, which found favor with critics and audiences alike. It was unusual to find a Mexican American detective as a positive law enforcement figure, free of stereotypical restraints, in a film set in 1930s Los Angeles. More unusual was that the role was actually played by a Hispanic. Lopez, a screen veteran, seized the opportunity and gave a memorable and well-rounded portrayal opposite Nicholson.

Sixteen years later he re-created the role in the long-awaited but disappointing sequel, *The Two Jakes* (1990), written and directed by and starring Jack Nicholson. The story continues ten years later, but the character of Escobar, now a captain, lacks the vitality and the importance he had in the original film. The film does explain Escobar's loss of a leg due to a war injury, acknowledging the valiant sacrifices made by Mexican Americans in World War II.

Christopher Columbus (1949 Universal)

D: David MacDonald
S: Sydney and Muriel Box and Cyril Roberts
P: A. Frank Bundy
Cast: Fredric March, Florence Eldridge, Francis L. Sullivan

A sumptuous, handsome Technicolor production with March as a Columbus without much vitality in a weak script. The ocean voyage ship exteriors were photographed in the studio against painted backdrops.

"Often heavy handed, lumbering and far too prosaic in setting forth its story. The Anglo-Saxon approach to fervid Latin emotions is inept," Edwin Schallert, *Los Angeles Times* (11/9/49).

Christopher Columbus: The Discovery (1992 Warner Bros.)

D: John Glen
S: Mario Puzo, John Briley, and Cory Bates
P: Ilya Salkind
Cast: Marlon Brando, Tom Selleck, Rachel Ward, George Corraface

The sweeping, lightweight, one-dimensional saga of a man who challenged the limits of his own universe and became the world's most influential explorer. The evil Spanish Inquisitor Torquemada, played by Marlon Brando, is softened, and the only Hispanic in the cast, Benecio

Del Toro, plays a dastardly villain. Rachel Ward plays Queen Isabella, and Tom Selleck plays the role of King Ferdinand. Filmed on location in Spain and in the West Indies, this film presents history as you might expect from the makers of *Superman* (1978). Plenty of bare-breasted Indian women are on display at Columbus' landing in the New World. The unrealistic and unlikely image of the engine of the Spanish Inquisition, Torquemada, waving good-bye to Columbus from the dock probably best sums up this movie's "dedication" to historical accuracy. The motto of this movie is clearly "Never let the facts interfere with a good story."

Cisco Pike (1971 Columbia)
D: B.W.L. Norton
S: B.W.L. Norton
P: Gerald Ayres
Cast: Kris Kristofferson, Karen Black, Gene Hackman, Antonio Fargas

A dramatic film debut of Kris Kristofferson as Cisco Pike, a former folk rock composer and an ex-con who is being blackmailed by a corrupt narcotics detective (Hackman) into dealing drugs. Fargas has a small role as a dope dealer.

Nothing in the film indicates the lead character to be Hispanic except for his first name.

City Across the River (1949 Universal)
D: Maxwell Shane
S: Maxwell Shane, Dennis Cooper, and Irving Shulman, based on a
   novel by Shulman
P: Maxwell Shane
Cast: Stephen McNally, Richard Benedict, Luis Van Rooten, Peter
   Fernandez, Anthony (Tony) Curtis, Thelma Ritter, Richard Jaeckel

Adapted from Irving Shulman's novel *The Amboy Dukes* about juvenile delinquency and youth gangs in a Brooklyn slum, *City Across the River* is quite possibly the first so-called youth gang film. The nineteen-year-old Peter Fernandez, of Irish-Cuban descent and with ten years of stage and radio experience, plays a Polish youth, Frankie Cusack. Frankie, because he lives in slum conditions and is neglected by parents who both work, joins a gang of tough Brooklyn boys calling themselves The Amboy Dukes (after Amboy Street).

Violent and somewhat simplistic, *City Across the River* has a semi-documentary tone: much of it was shot on location and it features many young unknown actors, with the unusual casting turn of a Hispanic, Fernandez, playing a Polish character.

Though he played the central character here, Fernandez apparently made no other films. Several years later Anthony Curtis would emerge a full-fledged star under the name of Tony Curtis. Richard Benedict went on to become a successful television director and Richard Jaeckel became an accomplished supporting player.

Clear and Present Danger (1994 Paramount)
D: Phillip Noyce
S: Donald Stewart, Steven Zaillian and John Milius
P: Mace Neufeld and Robert Rehme
Cast: Harrison Ford, Willem Dafoe, James Earl Jones, Anne Archer,
    Joaquim de Almeida, Miguel Sandoval, Benjamin Bratt,
    Raymond Cruz, Jorje Luke, Belita Moreno.

The third film to be adapted from John Clancy's best-selling Jack Ryan novels, following the global success of *The Hunt for Red October* and *Patriot Games*. Jack Ryan (Ford) is promoted from analyst to Deputy Director of the CIA and finds himself thrust into one of America's most dangerous conflicts—the war on drugs. He discovers a link between a Colombian drug cartel and an influential friend of the President of the United States, leading Ryan from Washington D.C.'s corridors of power to the jungles of Colombia and the streets of Bogota. Surrounded by deceptive alliances, an American covert operation team and the complex hierarchy of the cartel, Ryan is not sure who the true enemy is.

Mexico doubled for Colombia and the film was shot in Cuernavaca, Mexico City, Xalapa, Coatepec and La Concepcion, Mexico.

The Cockeyed World (1929 Fox)
D: Raoul Walsh
S: Raoul Walsh and William K. Wells
P: William Fox
Cast: Edmund Lowe, Victor McLaglen, Lily Damira

Originally released in both sound and silent versions. The characters of Captain Flagg and Sergeant Quirk originally appeared in Laurence Stallings and Maxwell Anderson's play and subsequent hit film version *What Price Glory?* (1926).

The Cockeyed World centers on the adventures of two bawdy United States Marines which take them from Russia to Brooklyn to Nicaragua. Lily Damira is Mariana, a Nicaraguan woman of easy virtue, which indicates the way Latin women are viewed in the film— as easily available sexual creatures. One Marine even refers to a woman as "the lay of the land."

Code of Silence (1985 Orion)
D: Andy Davis
S: Michael Butler, Dennis Shryack, and Mike Gray
P: Raymond Wagner
Cast: Chuck Norris, Henry Silva, Mike Genovese, Ran Henriquez

In Chicago, the daughter of an underworld don is kidnapped and used as a pawn in an escalating drug war between the dangerous South American Camacha family and the Luna organized crime family. Detective Sergeant Eddie Cusack (Norris) must settle the situation, which also involves a detective who is responsible for the shooting of a Hispanic teenager. Silva plays Luis Camacha, head of the Camacha family.

Colors (1988 Orion)

D: Dennis Hopper
S: Michael Schiller and Richard Dilello
P: Robert Solo
Cast: Robert Duvall, Sean Penn, Maria Conchita Alonso, Trinidad Silva, Rudy Ramos

Bob Hodges (Duvall) and Danny "Pacman" McGavin (Penn) are two Los Angeles policemen fighting African American and Mexican American street gang violence. Hodges is a twenty-year veteran cop who is about to retire and trying to teach the ropes to his know-it-all rookie partner, McGavin. Finally the younger cop learns his lesson, but too late to save his partner.

Colors is a highly emotionally charged film that offers nothing new except some style, music and two seasoned leading actors. Chicanos and African Americans are seen as street gang members with little subtlety or depth except for the character of Frog, played by Silva. There are a few minority policemen, but they are relegated to the background. The film comes off to some as a block-and-white racist statement, feeding off the fears of the white American middle class toward inner-city minorities.

It is more complex than that, however. It is perhaps more accurate to say that the film falls prey to its intent to trace the development of a racist cop (Penn). The efforts of his older partner (Duvall) and girlfriend (Alonso) to save him from himself are not enough to salvage the movie.

In one telling scene, Penn, who has had an ongoing affair with a Mexican American girl (Alonso), discovers her all painted up as a street gang girl when he is called to the scene of a party where a drive-by shooting has occurred. He is almost visibly sickened when he realizes she has apparently been making love to an African American man.

The viewpoint of Penn's character made the harsh, almost stereotyped presentation of minorities as violent gang members inevitable. It is interesting to compare *Colors* to Edward James Olmos' *American Me* (1992) or to the much more obviously stereotyped *Badge 373* (1973).

To the film's credit, through the death of his partner, "Pacman" does appear to learn his lesson.

Trinidad Silva (right) as gang member Frog meets Hodges (Robert Duval) in order to discuss upcoming gang activities in *Colors*.

The Comancheros (1961 Twentieth Century Fox)

D: Michael Curtiz
S: James Edward Grant and Clair Huffaker, based on the novel by
    Paul I. Wellman
P: George Sherman
Cast: John Wayne, Stuart Whitman, Ina Balin, Nehemiah Persoff,
    Lee Marvin

A rough-and-tumble, larger-than-life oater filled with rowdy Western types. The story is set in 1860s Texas when renegade Anglos, Native Americans and Mexicans were selling whiskey and arms along the Texas-Mexico border.

John Wayne is a Texas Ranger on the trail of a gentleman gambler (Whitman) wanted for a murder in Louisiana. A set of circumstances leads them to the Comancheros' secret encampment, where in order to stay alive, they form an uneasy alliance. They are spared an unkind fate by the Comanchero chieftain's young daughter (Ina Balin), who has an interest in the gambler and whose betrayal of her father eventually leads to his demise.

The trio make their escape from the encampment, holding the Comanchero chieftain hostage, and they are saved by a detachment of Texas Rangers who arrive just in the nick of time. Nehemiah Persoff gives an interesting performance as the educated, wheelchair-bound Comanchero chieftain. Some Hispanic American history is interjected into the Comanchero stronghold when a Native American called Iron Shirt is shown wearing a Spanish conquistador breastplate. It is explained that his grandfather fought the Spaniards in what was then Mexico. Michael Ansara plays Amelung, a Mexican bandit. *The Comancheros* was the last film directed by master director Michael Curtiz (*Captain Blood* [1935], *Casablanca* [1942], *Mildred Pierce* [1945]).

Commando (1985 Twentieth Century Fox)

D: Mark Lester
S: Steven De Souza
P: Joel Silver
Cast: Arnold Schwarzenegger, Rae Dawn Chong, Dan Hedaya

A retired special operations officer, Matrix (Schwarzenegger), is forced to return to the fictional country of Val Verde by a dictator he helped depose when his daughter is kidnapped by the revenge-seeking ousted dictator. The dictator wants Matrix to undertake one last mission—to kill the democratically elected President Velasquez so General Arius (Hedaya) can take over. Schwarzenegger is a one-man American killing machine running around a Latin American country overrun by dictators and gun-toting Latin thugs trying to keep down a helpless, freedom-loving populace.

Compromising Positions (1985 Paramount)
D: Frank Perry
S: Susan Isaacs, based on her novel
P: Frank Perry
Cast: Susan Sarandon, Raul Julia, Joe Mantegna, Judith Ivey

This film is the story of Judith Singer (Sarandon), a former newspaper reporter whose long-dormant writer's instinct is triggered by the murder of her dentist. Detective David Suarez (Julia) is the divorced law officer in charge of the investigation, which brings him unexpectedly into a love relationship with Singer.

It is refreshing and fairly new to see a non-stereotypical Hispanic American law officer in this essentially upper-middle-class white suburban tale. Suarez's growing attraction to Singer is balanced by his respect for her investigative skills. Julia turns in a good performance.

Copacabana (1947 United Artists)
D: Alfred E. Green
S: Laslo Vadnay, Allen Boretz, and Howard Harris, based on a story by
   Vadnay
P: Sam Coslow
Cast: Groucho Marx, Carmen Miranda, Steve Cochran

Groucho, without the other Marx Brothers, in a low-budget, mostly unfunny musical comedy that has little to do with the famed legendary New York nightclub of the title. Lionel Devereaux (Groucho) is Carmen Novarro's (Miranda's) agent. In his desperation to book his sole client in a nightclub, Devereaux convinces the Copa manager (Cochran) that he has another client available for a second booking. Novarro auditions for and lands both jobs, forcing her to take up the guise of a blonde French chanteuse as well as her usual Brazilian bombshell self.

A Covenant with Death (1966 Warner Bros.)
D: Lamont Johnson
S: Larry Marcus and Saul Levitt, based on a novel by Stephen Becker
P: William Conrad
Cast: George Maharis, Laura Devon, Katy Jurado, Earl Holliman,
   Arthur O'Connell, Sidney Blackmet, Wende Wagner,
   Emilio Fernandez, Gene Hackman

Hypocrisy, sex, murder and racism form the background of this story, which takes place in a small Southwestern town in the 1920s. An innocent man (Holliman), accused of murdering his wife, is sentenced to hang. Amid a frenzy of protests, he leaps from the gallows, accidentally causing the hangman's death. The sentenced man is returned to his cell, and then another man confesses to the first killing. Will justice be served in the death of the hangman?

Maharis is Ben Lewis, a young Mexican American judge who finds himself on trial before the community when he is faced with this taxing and unprecedented legal predicament. He has philosophical differences with an older judge and altercations with a district attorney who wanted Lewis' appointment and bitterly resents Lewis because of his inexperience and mixed ancestry. Meanwhile, Lewis is juggling romances with a Swedish woman (Devon) and a Mexican woman (Wagner).

A Covenant with Death is frequently interesting but never achieves the high-tension drama or excitement its subject matter promises. It is frequently slow, and there is much dialogue that does not advance the storyline. The film plays like a 1930s Warner Bros. social melodrama reminiscent of actor Paul Muni's *Bordertown* (1935), without the conviction or social punch. There are various similarities to *Bordertown* in that both protagonists, Paul Muni's Johnny and Maharis' Ben Lewis, are caught between two worlds, the Anglo and the Mexican. Both are lawyers and both have Anglo love interests. The endings are similar: Muni loses the Anglo girl and returns to the barrio; Maharis loses the Anglo girl and marries the Mexican girl in a symbolic return to his own kind.

Maharis is adequate in the role of the young judge. A Greek American, he was a popular star of the *Route 66* (1960-64) television series of a few years earlier. Jurado plays Eulalia, his domineering, cigar-smoking Mexican mother. Fernandez plays Ignacio, his hearty uncle. The film was shot on location in Santa Fe, New Mexico, and at Warner Bros. studios.

Cowboy (1958 Columbia)

D: Delmer Doves
S: Edmund H. North
P: Julian Blaustein
Cast: Glenn Ford, Jack Lemmon, Anna Kashfi, Dick York,
     Victor Mendoza, Eugene Iglesias

The story of a Chicago hotel clerk, Frank Harris (Lemmon), who decides to become a cowboy and joins cattleman Tom Reece (Ford) and his crew on a trek across the Southwest into Mexico. After on arduous journey of several weeks in which Harris learns the ways of a cowboy, the outfit crosses the Rio Grande and arrives at the Vidal Ranch to purchase cattle from a wealthy Mexican land baron, with whose lovely daughter, Maria (Kashfi), Harris had struck up a romance in Chicago. While Reece bargains for Vidal's cattle, Harris seeks out Maria and learns to his dismay that she has married Manuel (Iglesias) to satisfy the wishes of her family. During the Fiesta of San Margarita, characterized by violence, at nearby Guadalupe, the gringos win respect for their marksmanship and Reece's daring in which he bests Manuel in the dangerous "Game of the Bulls," a form of bullfighting. One of the cowboys gets himself in trouble chasing Mexican women. His fellow cowpokes refuse to come to his aid when he is apprehended by four tough Mexican hombres.

The Cowboys (1972 Warner Bros.)

D: Mark Rydell

S: Irving Ravetch, Harriet Frank, Jr., and William Dale Jennings, based on a novel by Jennings

P: Mark Rydell

Cast: John Wayne, Roscoe Lee Browne, Bruce Dern, A Martinez

A cattle rancher (Wayne) is forced to recruit eleven teenaged boys to help him on a cattle drive when his own men desert him upon hearing of a local gold strike. On the way, the trail becomes a rite of passage to manhood for the boys. They are left on their own when the rancher is murdered by a gang of bandits before their eyes. The boys decide to avenge his death and retrieve the cattle.

The film was popular, but controversy ensued due to its ending, which finds the boys shooting down the rancher's murderers in a spree of violence.

Martinez plays Cimarron, a young Mexican American cowboy (fulfilling the stereotype, he is hot tempered and carries a knife) who joins Wayne and proves himself. The film also toplined an African American trail cook played by Roscoe Lee Browne. These were obvious signs of the liberal social changes taking place in the late 1960s and 1970s, offering the inclusion of African American and other minority characters in a more accurate historical context, from which previously they had been omitted.

Cradle Will Rock (1999 Buena Vista)

D: Tim Robbins

S: Tim Robbins

P: Jon Kilik, Lydia Dean Pilcher, Tim Robbins

Cast: Hank Azaria, Rubén Blades, John Cusack, Cary Elwes, Angus MacFadyn

Based on a series of actual events, the film is a tapestry of different interwoven stories. Nelson Rockefeller (Cusack) commissions Mexican artist Diego Rivera (Blades) to paint the lobby of Rockefeller Center with a giant mural—later destroyed by Rockefeller because of its pro-Leninist and anti-capitalist sentiments. Meanwhile, Orson Welles (MacFadyn) is trying to stage a play about a steel strike while the Federal Theater Project frets about industrial unrest and the threat of communism in 1930s New York.

Creature from the Black Lagoon (1954 Universal)

D: Jack Arnold

S: Harry Essex, Arthur Ross

P: William Alland

Cast: Richard Carlson, Julia Adams, Richard Denning, Antonio Moreno, Nestor Paiva

Paleontologists in the Amazon stumble on to a prehistoric creature lurking in the dreaded Black Lagoon. The humanoid creature is lured into the open out of his fascination for the female member of the expedition. The title creature has remained one of the most indelible images from the 1950s Universal horror films. The film was so successful it spawned two sequels, *Revenge of the Creature* (1955) and *The Creature Walks among Us* (1956).

Filmed at Universal studios, the Los Angeles County arboretum and in Florida.

Crisis (1950 Metro-Goldwyn-Mayer)

D: Richard Brooks
S: Richard Brooks, based on the story "The Doubters" by George Tabori
P: Arthur Freed
Cast: Cary Grant, José Ferrer, Paula Raymond, Signe Hasso, Antonio Moreno, Gilbert Roland, Ramon Novarro, Pedro de Cordoba, Vicente Gomez, Martin Garralaga; Rudolfo Hoyos, Jr.; Roque Ybarra, Felipe Turich, Soledad Jimenez, José Dominguez

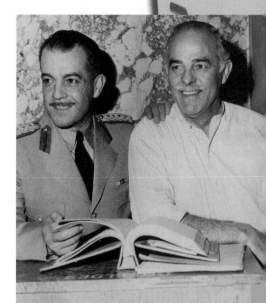

An American surgeon (Grant) on his honeymoon in a fictional South American country must perform on emergency brain operation on ruling dictator Raoul Farrago (Ferrer) in order to save his life.

The fictional Latin American country in this gripping but talky story seems to be more of a Peron-like Argentina than the traditional banana republic.

Writer and director Brooks (in his debut movie) had the idea of bringing together in supporting roles such former silent screen matinee idols as Moreno, Novarro and Roland. He also had the Spanish-speaking characters converse in their own language when they were alone and in English when they weren't.

One-time matinee idols Ramon Novarro and Antonio Moreno appear together in *Crisis*. Here they are rehearsing for their next scene.

Crossover Dreams (1985 Independent)

D: Leon Ichaso
S: Leon Ichaso, Manuel Arce, and Rubén Blades
P: Manuel Arce
Cast: Rubén Blades, Elizabeth Peña, Shawn Elliott, Frank Robles

The rise and fall of a Salsa singer, Rudy Veloz (Blades), who yearns to hit it big in the Anglo pop music business. This is an old-fashioned morality tale with a contemporary New York Latin perspective. Rudy betrays his heritage by chasing success in the American record business. He signs with a big producer, compromises his music (working with Anglo musicians) and loses his devoted Latin girlfriend (for an Anglo party girl).

"It is not only their talent and intelligence that makes the work of Mr. Ichaso and Mr. Arce so special, it's also their particular experiences as émigrés (from Cuba) which enables them to interpret, for better or worse, aspects of our culture that have become invisible to the rest of us," Vincent Canby, *New York Times* (9/1/85).

Cry Tough (1959 United Artists)

D: Paul Stanley
S: Harry Kleiner, based on the novel *Children of the Dark* by
Irving Shulman
P: Harry Kleiner
Cast: John Saxon, Linda Cristal, Perry Lopez, Joseph Calleia,
Barbara Luna, Miguel Estrada

(Saxon) is a Puerto Rican youth determined to break out of the Spanish Harlem barrio. Fresh out of prison after serving a year for armed robbery, he tries to resist efforts to have him rejoin his old street gong. Fate turns against him when he gets involved with Sarita (Cristal), a Cuban dancehall hostess who is picked up by immigration authorities for being in the country illegally. The gang chief provides Estrada with money for the girl's bail provided that he rejoins the gang. Estrada double-crosses the gang, and the girl walks out on him when he cannot provide her with the lifestyle she wants. Distraught, he asks the gang leader's forgiveness and again pursues a life of crime, which ends in tragedy.

This is the first Hollywood film that used the problems of second-generation Puerto Ricans in New York as a backdrop for a juvenile delinquency gang movie. It was filmed on the backlot New York street of MGM studios.

Producer and screenwriter Harry Kleiner spent several weeks researching the story in New York's Spanish Harlem, where he amassed 400 pages of notes before returning to Hollywood to put the screenplay together. In a *Los Angeles Examiner* interview with Neil Rau (10/12/58), Kleiner remarked, "I roamed the streets of the district every free moment I had, but most of the time I spent with two secretaries interviewing hundreds of people from the neighborhood on every level of life."

The resulting screenplay and film did not do justice to the research, however. Saxon gave value to his performance as did Cristal, Lopez and Luna. Brazilian Laurindo Almeida provided the musical score. "What starts out a promising picture about poor Puerto Ricans in New York and the obviously circumscribed endeavors of one young fellow 'to belong' ends up as a routine gangster melodrama . . . More's the pity, because this whole matter of the environment and economic patterns in which the masses of Puerto Ricans live in this city, and the motivations that agitate their minds, cry for illumination and enlightened sympathy," Bosley Crowther, *New York Times* (9/17/59).

"There is no obvious evidence that anybody concerned with making *Cry Tough* bothered to

Linda Cristal and John Saxon in *Cry Tough*.

look behind the headlines to understand or feel the background of New York's West Side or to catch the idiom or quality of the Puerto Ricans with which it makes such a point of dealing," Paul V. Beckley, *New York Herald Tribune* (9/17/59).

Cuba (1979 United Artists)

D: Richard Lester
S: Charles Wood
P: Arlene Sellers and Alex Winitsky
Cast: Sean Connery, Brooke Adams, Martin Balsam, Hector Elizondo, Danny De La Paz, Lonette McKee, Louisa Moritz, Alejandro Rey, Chris Sarandon

In Havana on the eve of Castro's revolution, Major Robert Dapes (Connery), a British mercenary, is brought in by the Batista government to squash the guerrillas hiding out in the Sierra Madre.

Fifteen years earlier, Dapes had an affair with Alexandra Pulido (Adams), an American woman who is now married to a weak-willed Cuban tobacco factory owner, Juan Pulido (Sarandon). Dapes and Alexandra Pulido are reunited. He finds himself still in love with her as he grows increasingly aware of the corruption and brutality of the regime and of the enormous discrepancy between Cuba's wealthy and poor.

De La Paz is Julio, a Fidelista who runs guns for the revolutionaries out of the Pulido cigar factory and is sworn to revenge against Pulido for the rape of his sister. Elizondo is Ramirez, a Cuban Army officer who is assigned to maintain vigilance over Dapes but who understands what is happening to his country. The film has many points of similarity with *Havana* (1990) as they were written around the same time but produced ten years apart. Filmed in Spain.

Cuban Love Song (1931 Metro-Goldwyn-Mayer)

D: W.S. Van Dyke
S: John Lynch, John Colton, Gilbert Emery, Robert E. Hopkins, and Paul Harvey Fox, based on a story by Gardner Sullivan and Bess Meredyth
P: Metro Pictures
Cast: Lawrence Tibbett, Lupe Velez, Jimmy Durante

A typical musical of the 1930s, set in turn-of-the-century Cuba and involving the romance of Terry (Tibbett), a United States Marine, with Nenita (Velez), a Havana peanut vendor. Filmed on soundstages and on the backlot at MGM, the film creates a Cuba of the popular imagination.

World War I interrupts the romance, but after the war Terry returns to the States and marries his American sweetheart. When he returns to Cuba, the former Marine discovers that Nenita has died but left him a son born out of wedlock, whom he takes back to the States.

Cuban Pete (1946 Universal)

D: Jean Yarbrough
S: Robert Presnell, Sr., and M. Coates Webster, based on a story by
   Bernard Feins
P: Howard Welsch and Will Cowen
Cast: Desi Arnaz

An advertising executive attempts to lure a Cuban band onto an American radio program. The film was a low-budget romantic musical comedy produced to play as the bottom half of a double bill.

Dance with Me (1998 Columbia)

D: Randa Haines
S: Daryl Matthews
P: Lauren C. Weissman, Shinya Egawa and Randa Haines
Cast: Vanessa L. Williams, Chayanne, Kris Kristofferson,
   Jane Krakowski, William Marquez

A brokenhearted former dance champion (Williams), working as an instructor at a faded Houston dance studio, struggles to revive her career. Miles away in Cuba, an enterprising young man, Rafael Infante (Chayanne), leaves for Texas equally determined to make his dreams a reality. Fate brings this unlikely twosome together in *Dance with Me*, where their passions ignite beneath a glittering world spotlight at a national dance competition.

Filmed in Los Angeles, Las Vegas, the Dominican Republic and Houston.

Deal of the Century (1983 Warner Bros.)

D: William Friedkin
S: Paul Brickman
P: Bud Yorkin
Cast: Chevy Chase, Sigourney Weaver, Gregory Hines, Vince Edwards,
   William Marquez, Pepe Serna, Tony Plana, Loyda Ramos,
   Eduardo Ricard, Wallace Shawn, Richard Libertini, Alex Colon

Eddie Muntz (Chase), a second-hand arms dealer, is selling weapons to local rebels somewhere in Central America, where he gets involved with the widow of an arms dealer. Back in the States, when an expensive war plane begins to act like a lemon, a representative of the military-industrial complex recruits Muntz to unload the plane on a Latin American dictator, General Arturo Cordosa (Marquez), and his country.

The movie can't make up its mind whether it's a satire or a farce, and as a result it is an obnoxious and offensive mishmash. Expert production design creates a most believable Central American atmosphere in an opening sequence filmed on downtown Los Angeles' Olvera Street.

"We begin to notice how Friedkin was taking cheap shots at all Latins. San Miguel is merely an updated version of Al Capp's El Ignoranto, with chickens in the presidential palace and 'La Cucaracha' on the soundtrack. All these Latins on the screen give the characters a certain authenticity, but their roles as preening colonels, menacing Indian soldiers and raggedy-assed rebels are ethnic caricatures like the bespectacled, bucktoothed Japanese of old war movies or the whole ignominious roster of Hollywood shuffling Negroes," Enrique Fernandez, *Village Voice* (11/15/83).

Death of a Gunfighter (1969 Universal)

D: Alan Smithee
S: Joseph Calvelli, based on the novel by Lewis B. Patten
P: Richard E. Lyons
Cast: Richard Widmark, Lena Horne, John Saxon

Marshal Frank Patch (Widmark) is a man past his time whom the citizens of the town consider an embarrassment and a relic of the past. Patch and his kind of law and order are viewed as a detriment to the community and as standing in the way of big business interests. When they ask him to resign, he refuses and becomes the target of a death plot by the people of the town. Tough, shrewd county sheriff Lou Trinidad (Saxon), a Mexican whom Patch once had to force his town to accept, is now charged with bringing in the man to whom he owes the most. Not wanting to take sides, he leaves on the next train.

The citizens of the town are shown to be vehemently anti-Mexican, referring to Trinidad as a "greaseball." Lena Horne is Claire Quintana, the marshal's faithful mistress and the local madam. Quintana is supposedly a Mexican woman, although she is played by a very fair African American actress. Horne makes no obvious attempt at a clichéd Mexican spitfire portrayal. This slow-moving story with potentially interesting but muddled themes was directed by Robert Totten (first half) and Don Siegel (second half) and credited to the fictitious Smithee.

Death of an Angel (1986 Twentieth Century Fox)

D: Petru Popescu
S: Petru Popescu
P: Peter Burrell
Cast: Bonnie Bedelia, Nick Mancuso, Pamela Ludwig, Alex Colon,
    Abel Franco, Irma Garcia

Grace Mackenzie (Bedelia), an ordained Episcopal minister with a wheelchair-bound daughter, comes home to discover both her daughter and her Mexican housekeeper are missing. A mysterious stranger in a white suit (Colon) takes her to her daughter, who is with a religious faith healer named Angel (Mancuso), whom Grace comes to believe is a fake. His following is largely comprised of infirm and disabled Mexican peasants. Don Tarjetas (Franco), a big, bad, Mexican rancher who smuggles undocumented aliens across the border, believes Angel is turning against him. This is a dull and incomprehensible film.

Defiance (1980 American International Pictures)

D: John Flynn
S: Thomas Michael Donnelly, based on a story by Donnelly and
   Mark Tulin
P: William S. Gilmore, Jr., and Jerry Bruckheimer
Cast: Jan-Michael Vincent, Theresa Saldana, Rudy Ramos,
   Santos Morales, Ismael "East" Carlo

Merchant seaman Tommy (Vincent) moves into a Lower East Side New
York City neighborhood that is being terrorized by Puerto Rican gang
members. He is threatened by the gang and decides to fight them
head-on, inspiring the neighborhood people to reclaim their neighborhood. In stereotypical fashion, the Anglo protagonist comes to save the
poor minorities from themselves.

Salma Hayek and
Antonio Banderas star
in *Desperado*, Robert
Rodriguez's multimillion
dollar remake of his
seven thousand dollar
film *El Mariachi*.

Delta Force 2: Operation Stranglehold (1990 Metro-Goldwyn-Mayer)

D: Aaron Norris
S: Lee Reynolds
P: Yoram Globus and Christopher Pearce
Cast: Chuck Norris, Billy Drago, Begonia Plaza, Héctor Mercado

Colonel McCoy (Norris) is the leader of an American assault squad sent
into a Latin American country to apprehend Ramon Cota (Drago), an
underworld drug czar who wreaks terror from his jungle fortress. He is
helped by Quiquina (Plaza), a beautiful native woman who becomes a
victim of Cota's cruelty. The film features a typical paternalistic, jingo-
istic Anglo-American in Latin America saving the helpless natives from
an international, homegrown drug czar. It was filmed in the
Philippines.

Desperado (1995 Columbia)

D: Robert Rodriquez
S: Robert Rodriquez
P: Bill Borden
Cast: Antonio Banderas, Salma Hayek, Joaquin de Almeida,
   Steve Buscemi, Cheech Marin, Danny Trejo, Mike Moroff

Banderas is the Mariachi with no name. This time the Mariachi plunges
headfirst into the dark border underworld when he follows a trail of
blood to the last of the infamous Mexican drug lords, Bucho (de
Almeida), for an action-packed, bullet-ridden showdown. With the help
of his best friend and a beautiful bookstore owner (Hayek), the
Mariachi tracks Bucho, takes on his army of desperados and leaves a
trail of blood of his own. This film is a big budget remake of Rodriguez's
El Mariachi (1992), made with flair, technical expertise and world class
actors.
   Filmed in Cuidad Acuna, Mexico.

The Devil Is a Woman (1935 Paramount)

D: Josef Von Sternberg
S: John Dos Passos and Sam Winston (as S. K. Winston), based on the
   novel *La Femme et le Pantin* by Pierre Louÿs
P: Adolph Zukor
Cast: Marlene Dietrich, Lionel Atwill, Cesar Romero, Don Alvarado

Set against the backdrop of the nineteenth-century Spanish Revolution, this is the story of Concha Perez (Dietrich) and the men she ruins. Romero, in one of his first major film roles, is effective in a part largely requiring a handsome appearance. The movie was not well received by audiences, and Franco's Fascist Spanish government protested the film on the grounds that it made fun of the Guardia Civil and threatened to ban all of Paramount's films in Spain if the film was not withdrawn. Paramount capitulated and the film was eventually withdrawn from worldwide distribution.

Dime with a Halo (1963 Metro-Goldwyn-Mayer)

D: Boris Sagal
S: Laslo Vadney and Hans Wilhelm
P: Laslo Vadney and Hans Wilhelm
Cast: Barbara Luna, Roger Mobley, Paul Langton; Manuel Padilla, Jr.;
   Rafael Lopez, Tina Menard, Robert Carricart

An offbeat and endearing low-budget comedic melodrama about five street urchins in Tijuana, Mexico, who take a dime from a church collection box to help buy a ticket in the big pool at the Caliente race track. They win a fortune, but because of their age, they can not cash in the ticket. This leads to adventures and misadventures until the story reaches its unusual climax. Luna plays Juanita, the orphaned American sister of one of the five, who, in an attempt to keep her brother (Mobley) with her, moves to Tijuana and becomes an entertainer in a small nightclub.

Luna, who is of Filipino descent, started her career on Broadway as a child actress in *South Pacific*. She attracted attention in her role as the blind nurse who marries Frank Sinatra in *The Devil at 4 O'clock* (1961) and in *Five Weeks in a Balloon* (1962). Rafael Lopez, the sixteen-year-old leader of the boys in this film, was born in Mexico City and started his career as a child dancer with Perez Prado's Orchestra. He came to the United States at age eleven and appeared in the feature film *The Young Savages* (1961) as well as many television shows. Manuel Padilla, Jr., was a seven-year-old discovery who went on to work in several motion pictures as a child, including *The Young and the Brave* (1963), and co-starred on the *Tarzan* (1966-69) television series starring Ron Ely. Robert Carricart, Tina Menard and Raymond Sanchez were also featured in supporting roles.

The Dirty Dozen (1967 Metro-Goldwyn-Mayer)
D: Robert Aldrich
S: Nunnally Johnson and Lukas Heller, based on the novel by
   E.M. Nathanson
P: Kenneth Hyman
Cast: Lee Marvin, Robert Ryan, Ernest Borgnine, Jim Brown,
   John Cassavetes, Charles Bronson, Clint Walker, Trini López

Singer Trini López was one of The Dirty Dozen in this World War II action movie that has a touch of 1960s social consciousness. The stellar cast included Lopez as Mexican American Pedro Jimenez and Jim Brown as African American soldier Robert Jefferson, two of the twelve condemned men led by Colonel Reisman (Marvin) on a suicide mission behind enemy lines on the eve of D-Day. The film was very popular with audiences but was described as "entertaining as a blow torch" by the *New York Times*.

The Disappearance of Garcia Lorca (1997 Columbia)
D: Marcos Zurinaga
S: Marcos Zurinaga, Juan Antonio Ramos and Neil Cohen
P: Enrique Cerezo
Cast: Esai Morales, Edward James Olmos, Andy Garcia, Jeroen Krabbe,
   Giancarlo Giannini, Miguel Ferrer

As Civil War brews across Spain in 1936, teenagers Ricardo Fernandez and Jorje Aguiorre are wrapped up in the poetry and plays of their idol, the Grenadine poet Federico Garcia Lorca (Garcia). They attend the tumultuous premiere of Lorca's expressionistic play, *Yerma*, in Madrid, where Ricardo experiences the thrill of meeting Lorca backstage. "Don't forget me," the poet tells him.

In 1954 Puerto Rico, Ricardo (Morales), now thirty-one, is a journalist working in San Juan. But Ricardo is obsessed by the traumatic events that occurred eighteen years earlier at the outset of the Spanish Civil War, and one in particular haunts him: the mysterious murder of his beloved Lorca. Knowing he will never be at peace with himself until he identifies Lorca's killer, Ricardo decides—against his father's wishes—to return to Spain. But Franco's Spain is a country keen to bury its immediate past. Moreover, Spain is still rife with enemies of the poet, such as the shadowy Ceteno (Ferrer). Ricardo defies Ceteno's warnings, threats, beatings and imprisonment in his dogged determination to confront the true culprit. When uncovered, the killer's identity is a shock for which even Ricardo is ill prepared.

A muddled and unexciting script mars the beautiful photography and production design. Morales has never been better in a role that is a departure from his typical roles as an angry young man.

Filmed on location in Spain, Puerto Rico and Los Angeles.

Down and Out in Beverly Hills (1986 Touchstone)

D: Paul Mazursky

S: Paul Mazursky and Leon Capetanos, based on the play *Boudu Sauvé des Eaux* by Rene Fauchois

P: Paul Mazursky

Cast: Richard Dreyfuss, Bette Midler, Nick Nolte, Elizabeth Peña

This is a loose remake of Jean Renoir's *Boudu Saved from Drowning* (1932). Jerry Baskin (Nolte) is a homeless bum who wanders Beverly Hills for food and shelter and then decides to end his life by drowning himself in a swimming pool at the Whiteman's (Dreyfuss and Midler) home. He is saved by Mr. Whiteman. Baskin's subsequent presence in the household changes and disrupts their lives. Peña plays the sexy, smart-mouthed Hispanic maid, Carmen, who is made politically aware by Jerry. The actress had to relearn a Spanish accent for the role. "After thousands of dollars trying to get rid of my Spanish accent and having acquired a New York accent, I had to go back to my original way of speaking," recalls Peña, who attracted attention in the role.

Down Argentine Way (1940 Twentieth Century Fox)

D: Irving Cummings

S: Darrell Ware and Karl Tunberg, based on a story by Rian James and Ralph Spence

P: Darryl F. Zanuck

Cast: Don Ameche, Betty Grable, Carmen Miranda, J. Carroll Naish, Chris-Pin Martin

Notable for being the first in a series of popular Technicolor musicals at Fox, starring Betty Grable and Don Ameche, and for introducing Miranda, the "Brazilian Bombshell," to film audiences. The film was also an attempt by Fox to increase business in Latin and South America.

Horse-loving American heiress Grable falls for rich Argentine horse breeder Don Ameche. Ameche's proud father (Henry Stephenson) is still bitter over losing a girl to Grable's father when they were both students in Paris long ago. The picture was filmed almost entirely on Twentieth Century-Fox soundstages. A special crew flew to Buenos Aires without the principals to get the necessary exterior and atmosphere shots. Another crew flew from Hollywood to New York to spend five weeks photographing Miranda and recording the songs she sings in the picture. She is the only cast member to appear in the picture without having set foot in Hollywood. The unusual arrangement was made because Miranda was under contract to a New York nightclub and found it impossible to come to Hollywood.

Musical songs and splendid travelogue color photography made the film popular with stateside audiences, but in Argentina it found disfavor. Someone must have confused Buenos Aires with Cuba, since the music sounds more like the Cuban rumba than the Argentinean tango.

Duck, You Sucker! [aka: *A Fistful of Dynamite; A Fistful of Revolution*] (1972 United Artists)

D: Sergio Leone
S: Luciano Vincenzoni, Sergio Donati, and Sergio Leone, based on a
   story by Leone
P: Fulvio Morsella
Cast: Rod Steiger, James Coburn

The story is set in 1913 Mexico and concerns a rascally Mexican peon, Juan Miranda (Steiger), who is unwillingly goaded into heroism in his people's revolution by Sean Mallory (Coburn), an Irish man haunted by the ghosts of his own people's revolution. Together they join forces to rob a bank. This was Steiger's first screen appearance as a Mexican. Steiger recalls, "It was unlike anything I've ever done before. I've never played a Mexican although I've worked with just about every other type of accent and nationality."

In a revealing interview with *Take One Magazine* (January-February 1972), Leone is quoted as saying about the film, "The Mexican Revolution in the film is only a symbol and not the Mexican Revolution ... It's a real myth. To avoid misunderstanding, I rejected the romance of the sombrero, preferring to deal with the theme of friendship which is so dear to me." There is plenty of action in the usual Leone style.

Duel in the Sun (1946 Selznick International)

D: King Vidor
S: Oliver H.P. Garrett and David O. Selznick, based on the novel by
   Niven Busch
P: David O. Selznick
Cast: Jennifer Jones, Gregory Peck, Joseph Cotten, Herbert Marshall,
   Lillian Gish, Lionel Barrymore, Walter Huston

Passion and furor swirl in this lurid tale of a young woman and the renegade son of an empire builder. The film has much to offer, including florid acting, spectacular action sequences and superb color photography.

Pearl Chavez (Jones) is left orphaned when her Confederate father, Scott Chavez (Marshall), is sentenced to hang for murdering his Indian wife and her lover. Before he hangs, he arranges to ship his daughter off to the household of the cousin he should have married.

Pearl goes to live with Texas Senator McCanles (Charles Bickford) and his family. The senator resents her Indian heritage, as well as the fact that Laura Belle (Gish), his wife, was once in love with Pearl's father. Further complicating matters, Pearl is attracted to both of the Senator's sons: the charming Jess (Cotten), who is banished for contesting his father's opposition to the railroad, and Lewton (Peck), whose virile arrogance eventually overwhelms her. Lewton guns down her fiancé on the eve of the wedding and escapes into exile. Pearl accepts an invitation from Lewton to join him at his hideout, where the two engage in a shoot-out that results in both their deaths.

Selznick, who produced *Gone with the Wind*, was determined to outdo himself with this epic Western tale, showcasing the talents of his

Jennifer Jones as Pearl Chavez co-stars with Joseph Cotten as Jess in *Duel in the Sun*.

wife, actress Jennifer Jones, who had won an Academy Award® as Best Actress for her role in *The Song of Bernadette* (1943).

It is unusual that a Spanish-surnamed female character had the leading role in a Western motion picture in which she is a virtual life force. Pearl Chavez may be the most liberated, free-spirited Hispanic American female ever portrayed on film. Chavez belongs to the school of heel-clicking spitfires; the critical difference being that this film revolves around her.

Though she is referred to as a "half-breed," her Confederate gambler father is described in the program notes as a "renegade ne'er do well, ill fated son of Creole ancestry," so we can suppose he had some Spanish and French blood with a name like Chavez.

A prologue involving Pearl's mother and father in a spectacular bordertown café scene is quite moving. Pearl dances to the music of the Mexican hat dance outside a presidio, while inside her Indian mother is dancing a very different kind of dance, the Orizaba. It is generally considered a Mexican native fertility dance and, as used in the film, a sexual act. Tilly Losch, who had played the dancing girl in *The Garden of Allah* (1936), did much the same thing in her portrayal of the mother, only in a more flamboyantly sexual manner. Scott Chavez's gambling companions taunt him over his wife's infidelity, and he proceeds to shoot her and her lover. This prologue sets up the premise and themes of the movie.

"Like her father, Pearl inevitably will die for her acts of violence but in her sacrifice she will have insured the survival of the only happy couple in the film, Jess and Helen. Pearl makes the moral decision to protect them from Lewton by destroying both Lewton and herself. It is this decision to function as a protector that makes Pearl, in the most essential sense, the Western hero of *Duel in the Sun*. She is placed in the classic position of defending a civilized society too weak to stand up for itself from the lawless savage (Lewton)." (*Cinema Texas Program Notes*, Vol. 10, No. 2, March 2, 1976)

Though panned by the critics, *Duel in the Sun* was a popular success, eventually grossing $17 million at the nation's box offices. It was the most expensive film of its day, made at a cost of $6 million, and shot over a year's time in Hollywood and on locations near Phoenix and Tucson, Arizona.

Jones received an Academy Award® nomination as Best Actress for her role. Lillian Gish as Laura Belle was nominated as Best Supporting Actress.

"The audience eventually learns (thanks to the Johnston office) that illicit love doesn't really pay in the long run but for about 134 minutes it has appeared to be loads of fun," *Time* (3/17/47).

Eating Raoul (1982 Twentieth Century Fox International Classics)

D: Paul Bartel
S: Richard Blackburn and Paul Bartel
P: Anne Kimmel
Cast: Paul Bartel, Mary Woronov, Robert Beltran

A middle-class couple, disgusted with the violence of city life, dreams of opening a suburban restaurant, but they are beset by financial woes. They think their prayers have been answered when they accidentally kill a would-be rapist "swinger" neighbor with a swat to the head with a frying pan and his fat wallet falls to the floor.

In a local newspaper, they advertise for swingers and successively do them in. It looks as if they will soon be working in suburbia until a Latino burglar named Raoul discovers their bulging trash bags. Raoul turns a profit by selling the jewelry and clothes of the victims and, being one hot number, becomes the wife's lover. When Raoul's tricks become too much for the couple, they are forced to make their first big dish a Latin stew, its main ingredient being Raoul.

Paul Bartel describes his movie this way: "[It] touches on many things, the perversion of middle class values, the resurgence of

Nixonism, Latin machismo versus WASP fastidiousness, film noir. *Eating Raoul* is a title with several meanings, one of which is that the Paul and Marys of this world can figuratively (or even literally) eat the Raouls of this world whenever it suits them. I don't mean to imply that Raoul deserves to be eaten, in fact he is probably the most sympathetic character in the story for all his peccadilloes. He's so forthright, so full of life. It's just that in our society, the Paul and Marys are the kickers and he's usually the kicked. Paul and Mary share an aversion to sex and provide a haven for each other until the snake comes in, in the form of the hot Latin sexuality of Raoul."

Although the film is meant as a spoof and a dark cartoon, Raoul (Beltran), a cocksure, leather-jacketed Latin stud, opportunistic thief and hustler, reinforces negative stereotypes. In truth, however, the Anglos come out of this movie looking just as shallow and vampire-like. The difference here is that the Anglos seem to be satirized and the Hispanic stereotyped. The film, in limited art house release and in film festivals, met with enthusiastic audiences and critical reaction and has become a cult film with a huge following.

El Cid (1961 Allied Artists)
D; Anthony Mann
S: Philip Yardan and Frederic M. Frank
P: Samuel Branston and Anthony Mann
Cast: Charlton Heston, Sophia Loren, Hurd Hatfield, Gary Raymond, Herbert Lom

An epic and sweeping saga of romance and adventure filmed on location against authentic backgrounds of Spain's breathtaking countryside and ancient castles and featuring an international cast. Charlton Heston stars as the eleventh-century Spanish hero Rodrigo Diaz de Bivar, better known as El Cid, who devotes his life to driving the Moors out of Spain.

The fabled Christian liberator of the Spanish nation was in fact a professional soldier who once hired himself out to a local Muslim leader to fight his fellow Christians. Even after reconciling with his Christian king, he pursued his own course, taking the territories he conquered for his own. Poets, writers, monks and historians through the centuries have contributed to the myth of El Cid as national hero.

Heston was the logical choice for the role of El Cid after his success in such epic costume dramas as *The Ten Commandments* (1956) and his Academy Award®-winning role in *Ben-Hur* (1959). Sophia Loren, the most popular international actress of the time, was cast as his wife, Jimena, which also helped in the complicated international financing agreements for the production of the film.

Producer Samuel Branston took advantage of inexpensive labor and production costs in Spain. His success caused a boom in foreign film production in Spain during the 1960s and 1970s, creating a cottage industry that afforded a very poor country necessary capital and an international filmmaking experience on a grandiose scale that has served it well ever since.

Spaniard José Lopez Rodero was an assistant director on the film, which featured thousands of Spanish extras and many Spanish actors in small roles. Directed by Anthony Mann and handsomely photographed by Milton Krasner, *El Cid* was a tremendous international success.

El Condor (1970 Carthay Continental/National General)
D: John Guillermin
S: Larry Cohen and Steven Carabatsos, based on a story by Carabatsos
P: Andre de Toth
Cast: Jim Brown, Marianna Hill, Lee Van Cleef, Patrick O'Neal

Two fortune hunters, Luke (Brown) and Jaroo (Van Cleef), plan to steal a cache of gold stored in a Mexican fort and commanded by a powerful Mexican general (O'Neal) following the American Civil War.

Filmed in Spain, this mindless Western is chock full of sex and violence, an unreal melange of Apaches, convicts, sleepy Mexican villages and Juaristas (followers of Indian Zapotec leader Benito Juarez during French occupation of Mexico). A whole army battalion rapes a town's female inhabitants as the two fortune hunters wait patiently on a hill, moving in to shoot the soldiers while they are copulating. At the fort, a Mexican woman (Hill) distracts the soldiers so the fortune hunters can gain entrance unnoticed.

The film subscribes to a fantasy Mexico, where the women are sex objects and the men are violent. This is not a new idea, but it is taken to an extreme under the influence of Italian filmmakers in the era of the "spaghetti Western." It also mirrors social changes of the late 1960s in America by having Jim Brown, an African American, co-star with Van Cleef, an Anglo, as the so-called antiheroes, reflecting their established international box office popularity in the action market.

El Mariachi (1993 Columbia)
D: Robert Rodriguez
S: Robert Rodriguez
P: Robert Rodriguez and Carlos Gallardo
Cast: Carlos Gallardo, Consuelo Gomez, Peter Marquardt

This is Rodriguez's remarkable $ 7,000 debut film, made as a twenty-four-year-old writer and director. An impressive, effective entertainment breakthrough in mainstream Hispanic American filmmaking in the United States, *El Mariachi* is true to its Mexican setting and characters, without being preachy or constrictive. This is a genre piece of Hollywood B moviemaking that is visually fun. The adventure is set in a Mexican bordertown and concerns a lone musician who dreams of being a respected Mariachi singer like his father and grandfather before him. He enters a small town at the same time as a hit man. They both wear black and carry similar guitar cases, except that the Mariachi's contains his beloved guitar and the hit man's contains his weapon. The Mariachi falls in love with a beautiful bar owner who takes him in after he is accidentally confused with the hit man. The Mariachi

Writer, director, producer and cameraman Robert Rodriguez gives direction to Carlos Gallardo in *El Mariachi*.

finds himself ushered into a violent underworld, and is forced to battle the evil that lurks around him. There are strange story twists, and the gringo is the bad guy here. The supermacho hit man guzzles beer and sleeps with three machine-gun-toting women at the same time.

To finance part of the film, Rodriguez checked himself into a medical research program, which afforded him the time to write the script while he earned $3,000. He borrowed a 16mm non-synchronized camera and a tape recorder and shot the film in the Mexican bordertown of Ciudad Acufia, near Del Rio, Texas, where his lead actor grew up and had access to several locations. He used nonprofessional actors and rarely shot more than one take. He transferred the film to videotape and edited on videotape using two VCRs. On a trip to Los Angeles he sent an edited tape to an agent whose name he had seen in *Premiere* magazine. The agent was impressed with the work and secured a development deal for Rodriguez at Columbia Pictures, which released the film after visually enhancing it up to 35mm and improving the soundtrack. In January 1993 *El Mariachi* won the Audience Award at the Sundance Film Festival.

El Norte (1983 Cinecom-Island Alive)

D: Gregory Nava
S: Gregory Nava and Anna Thomas
P: Anna Thomas
Cast: Zaide Silvia Gutiérrez, David Villalpando, Ernesto Gómez Cruz, Trinidad Silva, Abel Franco, Lupe Ontiveros, Tony Plana, Enrique Castillo

El Norte is Spanish for "the North," but it means more than that to sister and brother Rosa (Gutierrez) and Enrique (Villalpando), two Indians from Guatemala. To them it means "the United States," a mythical paradise where even the poor have private toilets and every person has the right to earn a decent wage. The story traces the plight of the two Guatemalan refugees as they strive to enter the United States illegally to seek a better life.

After their mother is taken prisoner and their father is killed by government troops, Rosa and Enrique are forced to leave their village to avoid a similar fate. Posing as Mexicans, they make a cruel odyssey from Guatemala's pastoral highlands to Tijuana's infested shanty-towns and finally to Los Angeles. They enter the United States by crawling through a rat-infested sewage tunnel, a circumstance with tragic consequences.

El Norte explores the ignorance, poverty and exploitation of the poor in overpopulated and underdeveloped as well as developed countries. Director Nava thoroughly immerses the viewer in the world of Latin immigrants and their individual experiences in this country. Upon arriving in downtown Los Angeles, Rosa asks in bewilderment, "Where are all the gringos?" All she sees around her is a sea of Latin faces. Nacha, a woman she has befriended, tells her, "The gringos don't like to live with us, they live in a separate area far away."

This powerful drama has a style of photography that approaches modern Latin American literature's fascination with magical realism. The imagery juxtaposes a dreamlike world and reality. Rosa, sitting in her adobe hut with its open cooking fire as she pages through an old *Good Housekeeping* magazine and marvels at the modern kitchens. Enrique on his first day as a busboy in an upscale restaurant stares at the patrons and their dinners. Busboys eat croissants instead of tortillas. Rosa washes clothes by hand in a swimming pool at a Beverly Hills home when she can't figure out how to use the washing machine. Their tiny run-down room in Los Angeles is a far cry from what they saw in *Good Housekeep*ing, but it nonetheless has a private toilet and electricity.

Director Nava is of Mexican Basque ancestry, grew up in San Diego, and attended UCLA Film School. He talked about the long struggle to get the film made, "We kept hearing, again and again, that we should make Americans the main characters, that we would never get the film financed otherwise. We have nothing against films like *Missing* or *Under Fire*, but we wanted to make a film where Latin American people were the protagonists. We wanted the film to be true to their customs, their way of life, and we wanted the characters to speak in their own language."

Working with a limited budget, Nava and crew went to Chiapas in southern Mexico. Nava recalls, "We took a professional 35mm crew and a lot of complicated equipment into areas that were difficult to reach and film in. We shot in places where no one ever shot before and probably no one will shoot again ... like the sacred burial ground of Romerillo." They also shot in the state of Morelos near Mexico City, Tijuana, San Diego and Los Angeles.

The film, funded by the *American Playhouse* series, aired on PBS, but received theatrical distribution prior to its airing. Primarily playing the art-house circuit in the States, the film received good reviews and was a modest financial success. Nava and Thomas had the distinction of having their screenplay nominated for an Oscar® for Best Original Screenplay by the Academy of Motion Picture Arts and Sciences. The film is in Spanish with English subtitles.

David Villalpando and
Zaide Silvia Gutierrez
in *El Norte*.

"What makes it unique, especially to American audiences so used to hearing about the influx of illegal aliens and the problems they cause in the Southwest, is its humane explanation of the plight of these people from their point of view," Mawlynn Uricchio, *Pittsburgh Post-Gazette* (2/24/84).

"A small, personal independently made film with the sweep of *El Norte*, with solid, sympathetic performances by unknown actors and a visual style of astonishing vibrancy must be regarded as a remarkable accomplishment," Janet Maslin, *New York Times* (1/11/84).

"What gives this film substance is the manner in which the characters are developed. They become real people and down to earth friends to one another as well as to those of us who put ourselves in their shoes. We like them, care about them and that means we become genuinely engrossed in their situations," Bob Polunsky, *San Antonio Express News* (3/16/84).

El Super (1979 Max Mambru Films Ltd.)

D: Leon Ichaso and Orlando Jiménez-Leal
S: Leon Ichaso and Manuel Arce, based on a play by Ivan Acosta
P: Manuel Arce and Leon Ichaso
Cast: Raymundo Hidalgo-Gato, Zully Montero, Reynaldo Medina, Elizabeth Peña

In Spanish, with English subtitles, this is the first film to depict the American experience of Cuban refugees, written, produced and directed by Cuban refugees and released to warm critical praise. Heading the cast of Cuban and Puerto Rican actors are Raymundo Hidalgo-Gato as the "el super" of the title and Zully Montero, Reynaldo Medina, Elizabeth Peña and Efrain Lopez Neri.

Filmed in New York City on a low budget ($250,000), *El Super* is the story of Roberto (Raymundo Hidalgo-Gato), a Cuban exile who is a superintendent of a large tenement building on Manhattan's Upper West Side. Roberto is fed up with his life in New York's harsh, cold environment, where he tends the boiler to provide heat for the tenants, makes minor repairs and plays dominoes with his friends. He faces the challenges and dreams of most immigrants in America today and hopes to return to Cuba someday but sees life in Miami as a more attainable alternative. He has also to contend with his wife, Aurelia (Montero), and their teenage daughter, Aurelita (Peña), who are assimilating into the American lifestyle with ease.

Filmed with insight, intelligence and humor, this was the first feature to be co-directed by Ichaso and Jiménez-Leal. The motion picture was based on the play by Ivan Acosta, which was originally produced by the Cuban Cultural Center in New York City.

El Super is not a political film, though it does deal with working-class people who fled Castro's Cuba. Several political statements are made while the superintendents are sitting around talking and playing dominoes, when thoughts of returning to Cuba and the like emerge as natural conversation rather than heavy-handed statements.

El Super represented a labor of love for the filmmakers. Ichaso spent ten years making commercials before filming this first feature. It took a year to complete, though only three weeks were spent shooting and two months editing. Money was hard to come by and came from private investors while payments and salaries were deferred. *El Super* was a critical and financial success, playing in limited art house release and in film festivals throughout the United States. "When you can laugh at the tragedy of being displaced . . . you're saved," said Ichaso, who hoped this film would give audiences insight into Cubans adjusting to life in the United States.

"This topic, long overdue for film treatment, is explored with insight and gentle humor in *El Super*, an engaging new movie made by Cuban exiles," Candice Russell, *Miami Herald* (2/4/79).

"*El Super* is not just for Cuban viewing, it is for everybody. Anglos will learn more about their Cuban friends in 90 minutes with *El Super* than they can learn in seminars, lectures or inter-community programs," Bill van Maurern, *Miami News* (2/2/79).

The Emerald Forest (1985 Embassy)
D: John Boorman
S: Rospo Pallenberg
P: John Boorman
Cast: Powers Boothe, Meg Foster, Charley Boorman, Dira Pass

Powers Boothe is Bill Markham, an engineer helping civilization conquer the world's last frontier, the Brazilian Amazon, through the construction of the Trans-Amazonian highway. Charley Boatman is Markham's young son, who disappears one day at the jungle's edge. Markham returns to the Amazon year after year in the hope of finding his lost son. Ten years later, Markham finds the boy, now a Brazilian Indian warrior, whom he must help survive. Director John Boorman's brilliant visualization breathes life, danger and mysticism into this captivating, beautifully photographed adventure, based on a true story. Terrific music score by Junior Hamrich.

Evita (1996 Buena Vista)

D: Alan Parker
S: Alan Parker and Oliver Stone
P: Robert Stigwood, Alan Parker and Andrew G. Vajna
Cast: Madonna, Antonio Banderas, Jonathan Pryce, Jimmy Nail

Alan Parker's film, based on the highly acclaimed international musical stage production of *Evita* by Sir Andrew Lloyd Webber, with lyrics by Tim Rice, chronicles the brief but brilliant career of Eva Peron (Madonna). Recounted by an everyday local character Che (Banderas), Evita traces her rise from humble beginnings to the top of Buenos Aires society. Fiercely ambitious, Eva first becomes a radio soap opera actress. With her marriage to Juan Domingo Peron (Pryce), the impending President of Argentina, Evita—as she became known—became a figure of wealth, power, adulation and scorn. Both desperately loved (by the *descamisados*, or working poor) and passionately hated, Evita's brief tenure at the pinnacle of power left an indelible impression on her country and history. Six weeks of location filming in Argentina began on February 8, 1996, but not before Director Alan Parker and Madonna met with the President of Argentina to request access to the famed Casa Rosada balcony, where the actual Eva Peron stood to look down upon thousands of her adoring fans.

A well-mounted, handsome, innovative and cinematic production. Madonna is excellent as Evita and Antonio Banderas displays a singing voice and passion as Che.

Extreme Prejudice (1987 TriStar)

D: Walter Hill
S: Deric Washburn and Harry Kleiner, based on a story by John Milius and Fred Rexer
P: Buzz Feitshans
Cast: Nick Nolte, Powers Boothe, Maria Conchita Alonso,
William Forsythe, Luis Contreras, Rick Garcia, Carlos Cervantes

Two friends, one a Texas Ranger (Nolte), the other a drug dealer (Boothe), on opposite sides of the law and the border are in love with the same woman, who happens to be a Mexican cantina singer. Alonso is the Latin spitfire torn between the two men, who are both Anglo. This updated, violent Western features all the clichés and stereotypes. The bandidos are well played, though they fall more into the category of the vicious greaser of the silent era.

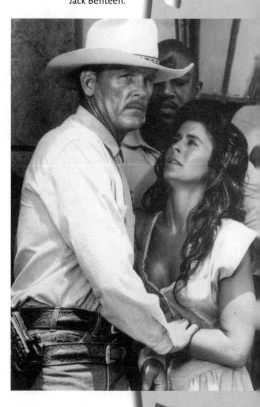

In *Extreme Prejudice*, Maria Conchita Alonso portrays Sarita, a Mexican cantina singer torn between the love of two men on opposite sides of the law and the border. Nick Nolte portrays Jack Benteen.

The Fabulous Señorita (1952 Republic Pictures)
D: R.G. Springsteen
S: Charles E. Roberts and Jack Townley, based on a story by
Charles R. Marion and Townley
P: Sidney Picker
Cast: Estelita, Robert Clarke, Nestor Paiva, Marvin Kaplan,
Rita Moreno, Tito Renaldo, Martin Garralaga, Nita del Rey

An amusing romantic comedy about Cuban businessman José Rodriguez's (Paiva's) two daughters, Estelita (Estelita) and Manuela (Moreno), who are sent to school in the United States. Manuela uses the opportunity to get married, and Estelita tries to cover for her by playing two roles, while at the same time falling for a young college professor (Clarke).

The Falcon and the Snowman (1985 Orion)
D: John Schlesinger
S: Steven Zaillian
P: Gabriel Katzka and John Schlesinger
Cast: Sean Penn, Timothy Hutton

Based on the nonfiction account by Robert Lindsay, and largely filmed in Mexico City, this is the true story of an unstable young American idealist, Christopher Boyce (Hutton), disillusioned by the CIA's covert intervention in foreign lands, who decides to punish his country by selling secrets to Soviet agents. He achieves this through a dope-smuggling friend, Lee (Penn), who has escaped American authorities by running away to Mexico.

With Lee as his go-between, Boyce manages to contact the Russian Embassy in Mexico and pulls off a number of deals until the Mexican police arrest and brutally interrogate him before giving him up to American authorities.

Mexican police are seen as efficient but brutal in an interrogation sequence that had to be filmed in the United States because the Mexican government objected to the negative image it presented of its police force.

The Falcon in Mexico (1944 RKO Radio Pictures)
D: William Berke
S: Gerald Geraghty and George Warthing Yates, based on a character
created by Michael Arlen
P: Maurice Geraghty
Cast: Tom Conway, Cecilia Callejo, Nestor Paiva, Mona Maris,
Fernando Alvarado, George J. Lewis, Julian Rivero, Pedro de Cordoba

The suave amateur sleuth of the screen, the Falcon, untangles a murder mystery South of the border. It involves a dead artist's paintings and the attempts of the beautiful Mexican woman who posed for the paintings to recover them, which result in a gallery owner's death. The trail leads the Falcon from New York City to Mexico City and to the artist's daughter. Since the film shows effective work by Mexican police and the criminal is an American, the Hays Office gave the film a special commendation as one designed to cement Good Neighbor standing between the United States and Mexico.

Fatal Beauty (1987 Metro-Goldwyn-Mayer)
D: Tom Holland
S: Hilary Henkin and Dean Riesner, based on a story by Bill Svanoe
P: Leonard Kroll
Cast: Whoopi Goldberg, Rubén Blades, Sam Elliott

A disappointing and predictable melodrama laced with action and sophomoric humor as police detectives Rizzoli (Goldberg) and Carl Jimenez (Blades) search for those making and selling the lethal drug called "Fatal Beauty."

The film features the usual assortment of Hispanic and African American drug dealers and bad guys, somewhat balanced with the multiethnic casting of the leads.

Fearless (1993 Warner Bros.)
D: Peter Weir
S: Rafael Iglesias, based on his novel
P: Paula Weinstein and Mark Rosenberg
Cast: Jeff Bridges, Isabella Rossellini, Rosie Perez, Tom Hulce,
   Benicio Del Toro

The story of a man, Max (Bridges), whose perspective on life undergoes a dramatic change after he survives an airplane crash. Perez plays Carla Rodrigo, a woman whose baby died in the air crash. For this role, Perez was nominated for an Academy Award® as Best Supporting Actress.

A Few Good Men (1992 Columbia)
D: Rob Reiner
S: Aaron Sorkin, based on his play
P: David Brown, Rob Reiner, and Andrew Scheiman
Cast: Tom Cruise, Jack Nicholson, Demi Moore, Michael DeLorenzo

On the United States naval base at Guantanamo Bay in Cuba, two young Marines are accused of murdering PFC William T. Santiago, a member of their platoon, during an unconventional disciplinary action known as a "Code Red." Naval lawyer Kaffee (Cruise) is determined to unravel the mystery behind the death and bring those responsible to justice.

This critically acclaimed film, based on a Broadway play, revolves around the death of a Hispanic United States Marine, but ethnicity and race are not the real issues. Because the Marines are in Cuba where the enemies are Latin and the murder victim is Latin, he is seen as the "enemy." Santiago's life is therefore marginalized. (This issue of racism is somewhat diffused, however, because one of the defendants is African American.) Although Michael DeLorenzo, who plays Santiago, is seen only briefly at the beginning of the film, his Hispanic presence is felt every time his name is mentioned in this highly charged courtroom drama.

Fiesta [aka: *Gaiety*] (1941 United Artists)
D: Leroy Prinz
S: Cortland Fitzsimmons
P: Hal Roach
Cast: Anne Ayars, Jorje Negrete, Armida, Antonio Moreno

A Mexican rancher's daughter returns home from Mexico City for her approaching marriage, although she is engaged to another man. This Technicolor musical is stage bound and is peopled with stereotyped characters. One in a series of 50-minute B movies produced by Hal Roach for United Artists, the movie marks the only Hollywood film appearance of Mexican singing film star Jorje Negrete, who is billed as George Negrete. Armida ably and comically sings a song called "Never Trust a Jumping Bean." Also featured are Nick Moro, Carlos Valadez, José Arias and his Mexican dancers, and The Guadalajara Trio.

Fiesta (1947 Metro-Goldwyn-Mayer)
D: Richard Thorpe
S: George Bruce and Lester Cole
P: Jack Cummings
Cast: Ricardo Montalban, Esther Williams, Cyd Charisse, Mary Astor,
    Fortunio Bonanova, Alex Montoya, Nacho Galindo, Carlos Ramirez

Filmed in Mexico. Featuring gorgeous scenery, music, and charming singing and dancing, this film introduced a new screen personality to American audiences, Ricardo Montalban. He danced so ably with Cyd Charisse on film that many thought him a professional dancer.

Though born in Mexico, Montalban spent his teen years in Los Angeles. After a brief stint on Broadway, he returned to Mexico and starred in over twenty Mexican films before being put under contract to MGM.

The plot concerns a lady matador, Maria Morales (Williams), and her twin brother, Mario (Montalban).

The Mexican locations were Pueblo and Telacala. Aaron Copland's composition "El Salon Mexico" was used in the film, renamed "Fantasia Mexican" and adapted and orchestrated by Johnny Green. The movie also featured Ramirez, who appeared and sang in a number of MGM musicals of the era.

The Fighter [aka: The First Time] (1952 United Artists)
D: Herbert Kline
S: Aben Kandel and Herbert Kline, based on "The Mexican" by
    Jack London
P: Alex Gottlieb
Cast: Richard Conte, Lee J. Cobb, Frank Silvera, Rudolfo Hoyos, Jr.,
    Margaret Padilla, Paul Fierro, Rico Alaniz

Set in 1910, this film concerns a Mexican fisherman who becomes a prizefighter in El Paso to provide funds for a revolutionary movement South of the border.

After his family is massacred by the Federales, Felipe Rivera (Conte) travels to the United States and pledges to fight against the Diaz regime. He swims across the Rio Grande to El Paso and joins the Madera forces in exile. Felipe earns money by sparring with prizefighters and then turns the money over to his fellow exiles. He wins a main event against a formidable boxer and uses the $5,000 purse to buy badly needed rifles for the Madera cause.

In this competently made B film, Richard Conte gives a strong performance supported by such actors as Lee J. Cobb as a Mexican revolutionary leader. The film utilizes some documentary footage of the village of Janitzio on Pftzcuaro Island in the Pueblo area shot by Herbert Kline for his film, *The Forgotten Village* (1941).

The Firebrand (1962 Twentieth Century Fox)
D: Maury Dexter
S: Harry Spalding
P: Maury Dexter
Cast: Valentin De Vargas, Kent Taylor

Mexican Robin Hood Joaquin Murieta (De Vargas) robs the gold-crazed American settlers in Old California. A determined California Ranger, Major Tim Bancroft (Taylor), kills another man, lops off his head and starts rumors that it is the head of Joaquin. He charges admission to see it in order to draw Murieta into the open. Joaquin has a showdown with the Major, then rides off into the sunset. This dismal low-budget film is below the level even of a B Western, but it has the distinction of having a Hispanic in the lead role.

Fires Within (1992 Metro-Goldwyn-Mayer/Pathé)
D: Gillian Armstrong
S: Cynthia Cidre and Peter Barsocchini
P: Wallis Nicita and Lauren Lloyd
Cast: Jimmy Smits, Greta Scacchi, Vincent D'Onofrio, Bri Hathaway

A family is separated in Cuba by Fidel Castro's oppressive government. The husband, Nestor (Smits), is imprisoned for life for his writings about the injustice and inhumanity of the revolution he once fervently believed in. He insists that his wife, Isabel (Scacchi), and their infant daughter escape to Miami, Florida.

Nearly dying at sea, they are rescued by Sam (D'Onofrio), an American fisherman. He and Isabel meet again in Miami several years later and fall in love. Looking after Isabel and the now seven-year-old Maribel (Hathaway), Sam is convinced that he and Isabel will eventually marry.

Eight years following Isabel's escape from Cuba, Nestor is unexpectedly released from prison and arrives in Miami to reclaim his family, unaware that he will force his wife to choose between him and the man she has grown to depend on and in whom she has invested her future.

This romantic drama about Cuban exiles in America was filmed on location in Miami and co-written by Cuban-born, Miami-raised screenwriter Cynthia Cidre.

Firewalker (1986 Cannon)
D: J. Lee Thompson
S: Robert Gosnell, based on a story by Gosnell, Jeffrey Rosenbaum and Norman Aladjem
P: Menahem Golan and Yoram Globus
Cast: Chuck Norris, Louis Gossett, Jr., Melody Anderson

Americans in exotic Mexico are featured in this escapist adventure film. After ten years of life-threatening, money-losing schemes and expeditions, fortune hunters Max Donigan (Norris) and Leo Porter (Gossett) are about to call it quits. Then a beautiful young woman (Anderson) appears with a map to the long-lost gold hoards of the ancient Aztecs. Dollar signs in their eyes, the trio embarks on a journey to Guatemala, where they battle heartless mercenaries and the Aztec medicine man El Coyote (Will Sampson). Zaide Silvia Gutierrez is featured as an Indian girl.

The First Texan (1956 Allied Artists)
D: Byron Haskin
S: Daniel B. Ullman
P: Walter Mirisch
Cast: Joel McCrea, Felicia Farr, Wallace Ford, Jeff Morrow, Rudolfo Hoyos, Jr.

The story of Sam Houston (McCrea) and the independence movement led by resolute Mexicans and Americans determined to free themselves from oppressive Mexican rule and the events leading up to the battle of San Jacinto. Houston's army wins decisively against superior Mexican forces, capturing General Santa Anna and eventually winning independence for Texas.

Hoyos portrays Cos; David Silva is General Santa Anna; Frank Puglia is Pepe; and Salvador Baguez is Veramendi. The film also features Maurice Jura as Pablo, Nestor Paiva as a priest and George J. Lewis as a Mexican doctor.

The First Time
See *The Fighter.*

A Fistful of Dollars (1964 United Artists)
D: Sergio Leone
S: Sergio Leone and Duccio Tessari
P: Arrigo Columbo and Giorgio Papi
Cast: Clint Eastwood, John Wells, Marianne Koch, Antonio Prieto, José Calvo

The international cult phenomenon that launched the film careers of Italian writer, director and producer Sergio Leone, composer Ennio Morricone, and little-known American television actor Clint Eastwood. A Western remake of Kurosawa's *Yojimbo* (1961), this film created the genre of "spaghetti Westerns." Both films are adaptations of Dashiell Hammett's novel *Red Harvest*.

Eastwood is the "Man with No Name," a greedy, amoral drifter of a gunfighter who arrives in a hellhole of a frontier community where two gangs of bandits are vying for power. John Wells plays Ramon Rojo, the bandit and the leader of one of the gangs.

It is a Western taken to the extreme with unremitting violence, gritty realism and, at times, tongue-in-cheek antics. Leone used breathtaking panoramas as well as extreme close-ups of the quivering lips and darting eyes of the international cast just before a memorable climactic shoot-out. Mexican bandidos, sleepy villages and beautiful señoritas inhabit this Western (much of which was shot in Spain and Italy). Ennio Morricone's haunting and quirky musical score became a well-known signature theme.

A Fistful of Dynamite [aka: A Fistful of Revolution]
See *Duck, You Sucker!*

Flying Down to Rio (1933 RKO Radio Pictures)
D: Thornton Freeland
S: Cyril Hume, H.W. Hanemann, and Erwin Gelsey, based on a play by Anne Caldwell from an original story by Brock
P: Lou Brock
Cast: Gene Raymond, Dolores Del Rio, Fred Astaire, Ginger Rogers, Raul Roulien

Dolores Del Rio and Fred Astaire dance to "Orchids in the Moonlight" in *Flying Down to Rio.*

This musical comedy stars Del Rio and Raymond, but it was a new dance team that stole the film, Astaire and Rogers in their screen debut.

Del Rio plays a beautiful Brazilian woman engaged to a wealthy man, played by Roulien. Into her life comes aerialist and songwriter Roger Bond (Raymond), and complications ensue.

One of the great production numbers featured an aerial ballet in which scores of chorus girls anchored to the wings of old bi-planes dance and remove their clothes to the delight of the inhabitants of Rio de Janeiro below.

Del Rio actually danced with Fred Astaire before Rogers in the film, but in the "Carioca" number, Astaire and Rogers emerged as one of the screen's greatest dance teams. The film was shot entirely on sound-stages at RKO Studios in Hollywood, which re-created the look of Rio as an escapist postcard fantasy for a Depression-era America.

Fools Rush In (1997 Columbia)
D: Andy Tennant
S: Katherine Reback, based on a story by Joan Taylor and Reback
P: Doug Draizin
Cast: Matthew Perry, Salma Hayek, Tomas Milian, Carlos Gomez, Anne Betancourt

A romantic comedy of fated lovers. Alex (Perry) is a young real estate executive from the East Coast who has a one night stand with a Mexican photographer Isabel Fuentes (Hayek) that results in an unexpected pregnancy. They marry in haste and the two eventually fall in love, though a series of misunderstandings threaten to destroy their potential happiness. Love and cross-cultural stereotypes abound on both sides—from Isabel's huge Hispanic family to Alex's uptight WASP family. Isabel is the classic Latin spitfire, displaying uninhibited dancing as she cooks in the kitchen and screaming at Alex in Spanish when she gets angry. When Alex meets her parents, it's at a family backyard party with at least 100 guests and Mariachis. This was Hayek's first leading role in a major studio film and she shines with great comic talent and loveliness.

For a Few Dollars More (1965 United Artists)
D: Sergio Leone
S: Sergio Leone and Luciano Vincenzoni
P: Alberto Grimaldi
Cast: Clint Eastwood, Lee Van Cleef, Gian Marie Volonte

Eastwood, the "Man with No Name," and Van Cleef as Colonel Mortimer, an aging bounty hunter, form an uneasy alliance in quest of the reward money offered for the bandit El Indio (Gian Marie Volonte) and his band of desperados. During the climactic shoot-out it is revealed that Colonel Mortimer's reason for hunting El Indio is not the reward money but vengeance for the murder of a family member.

This was the second film in the successful "Man with No Name" series, a "spaghetti Western" trilogy that also included *A Fistful of Dollars* (1964) and *The Good, the Bad, and the Ugly* (1967).

For Whom the Bell Tolls
(1943 Paramount)

D: Sam Wood
S: Dudley Nichols, based on the novel by
   Ernest Hemingway
P: Sam Wood
Cast: Gary Cooper, Ingrid Bergman, Akim
   Tamiroff, Fortunio Bonanova, Katina
   Paxinou, Arturo De Cordova, Joseph Calleia,
   Duncan Renaldo, Pedro de Cordoba

Left to right: Arturo
De Cordova, Gary Cooper,
Ingrid Bergman
and Katina Paxinou
in a scene from *For
Whom the Bell Tolls*.

Many films have been adapted from Hemingway's stories and novels, including *A Farewell to Arms* (1932 and 1957) and *The Old Man and the Sea* (1958). Paramount bought the film rights to Hemingway's controversial best-seller *For Whom the Bell Tolls* shortly after its publication in 1940. The film version of *For Whom the Bell Tolls* made its debut in 1943 after three years of prerelease publicity which was second only to the publicity buildup for *Gone with the Wind*.

It is the story of an American university professor turned explosives expert on the side of the Loyalists in the 1936 Spanish Civil War. The demolition of a strategic bridge and the love of Robert Jordan (Cooper) for a lovely Spanish girl, Maria (Bergman), were the main dramatic thrusts of the movie.

Cooper was Hemingway's and the public's choice for the role of Robert Jordan. The movie script let go of the political overtones of the Spanish Civil War, thus robbing the film of its timely power and sense of a specific place and time. The modern viewer is never quite sure for whom and what the characters are fighting.

The film is overly long yet entertaining and distinguished by good acting and beautiful camera work. It features a terrific supporting cast, including Calleia as El Sordo, a guerrilla fighter; Tamiroffas Pablo; Paxinou (winner of the Best Supporting Actress Oscar®) as Pilar, Pablo's woman; and De Cordova as Agustin. A young Yvonne De Carlo plays a dancer in a café sequence. In smaller supporting roles are Bonanova as Fernando, Renaldo as Lieutenant Berendo, de Cordoba as Colonel Miranda, Frank Puglia as Captain Gomez and Martin Garralaga as Captain Mora. Trini Varela, Alberto Morin, Pedro Regas, Soledad Jimenez and Tito Renaldo play bit parts.

Location scenes were filmed in the Sierra Nevada near Tuolumne, California. William Cameron Menzies was the production designer (he served in a similar capacity on *Gone with the Wind*). Ray Rennahan was the color cinematographer.

"It is a great picture without political significance. We are not for or against anybody," stated Adolph Zukor, head of Paramount Studios. "Love story set against a brutal backdrop" is how director Sam Wood described the movie.

Forever Darling (1956 Metro-Goldwyn-Mayer)
D: Alexander Hall
S: Helen Deutsch
P: Desi Arnaz
Cast: Lucille Ball, Desi Arnaz, James Mason, Louis Calhern

Lucy and Desi play Susan and Larry Vega, a couple who experience difficulty in their marriage. Larry's job as a chemist keeps him burning the midnight oil, so Susan spends time with friends whom Larry finds distasteful.

Soon the couple find themselves growing steadily apart. But when Susan's guardian angel (Mason) appears, he encourages her to try to put the romance back in her marriage. She decides to accompany Larry on a camping trip, but after a sleepless night and disastrous morning, Susan and Larry are really on the rocks. Just when it seems that the couple will part ways, a few surprises send them traveling down the road to marital bliss.

Produced by Desi and Lucy's production company, Desilu, the film presented a modern Hispanic American married couple as the leads. In their first theatrical feature film outing, *The Long, Long Trailer* (1954), they presented themselves as a nondescript, presumably Italian American couple. By the time of *Forever Darling*, however, following their success in television, it was not necessary to disguise Desi's Latin heritage.

Fort Apache, The Bronx (1981 Twentieth Century Fox)
D: Daniel Petrie
S: Heywood Could
P: Martin Richards and Tom Florella
Cast: Paul Newman, Ken Wahl, Edward Asner, Pain Crier, Rachel Ticotin, Gloria Irrizary

A veteran Irish American cop, Murphy (Newman), teaches a young rookie cop, Corelli (Wahl), about life on the harsh streets of New York City's crime- and poverty-ridden South Bronx. The film is very similar to *Colors* (1988), which is set in the urban sprawl of East Los Angeles.

During a riot, a cop throws a young Hispanic boy from a rooftop to his death. Feeling justified in his actions, the cop causes a crisis of conscience in fellow policeman Murphy, who has witnessed the murder. Murphy exposes what happened and causes a rift among his fellow officers.

Since *Fort Apache, The Bronx* predates *Colors* by seven years, it is interesting to note the plot similarities. In both movies, the police station stands as an outpost of law, order and Anglo European civilization against the "savages" (meaning Hispanics and African Americans). In *Fort Apache*, Murphy falls for a Puerto Rican nurse (Ticotin) who betrays his trust by turning out to be a heroin addict and overdosing. In *Colors*, the rookie cop falls for a Chicana (Maria Conchita Alonso) who works at a burger stand and who betrays him by sleeping with an African American gang member.

African Americans and Puerto Ricans are seen as prostitutes, junkies and lowlifes. There are no positive African American or Puerto Rican characters in the film. The white cops protect society from inner-city minorities.

During production, the film met with protests from a coalition of African American and Puerto Rican South Bronx residents. Protesters cited the exaggerated violence in the script, the lack of positive Spanish-surnamed or African American characters, and the film's failure to explain how racial bias and poverty entrap many residents of the South Bronx. The producers declined to make changes in the script.

Playwright Miguel Pinera (*Short Eyes*) plays a junkie with stinging veracity. Tito Goya and Gloria Irrizary are also featured.

A nurse, Rachel Ticotin, is comforted by a compassionate cop, played by Paul Newman. The two are involved in a bittersweet romance in this powerful account of an embattled police precinct in a devastated, violent neighborhood in *Fort Apache, The Bronx*.

The Four Horsemen of the Apocalypse (1921 Metro)

D: Rex Ingram
S: June Mathis, based on the novel by Vicente Blasco Ibanez
P: Rex Ingram for Metro Pictures
Cast: Rudolph Valentino, Alice Terry, Pomeroy Cannon

Silent. Rudolph Valentino became a star when he danced the tango in a seedy Buenos Aires cabaret in the role of Julio Desnoyers, a young South American in Paris on the eve of World War I.

Filmgoers remember Valentino dressed as a gaucho, boldly interrupting a couple on the dance floor and claiming the woman (Beatrice Dominguez) for a tango, and the mystical note on which the film ends.

Madariaga (Cannon), a wealthy old cattle owner of Argentina who despises his German son-in-law, lavishes all his affections on Julio. After Madariaga's death, the estate is divided, and the family disperses to Europe, the von Hartrotts to Germany and the Desnoyers to France. Julio buys a castle on the Marne and opens a studio, where he entertains, paints pictures and soon falls desperately in love with Marguerite Laurier (Terry), the youthful wife of a jurist. World War I breaks out, and Marguerite joins the Red Cross, while her husband enlists. Finding her husband wounded and blinded in action, Marguerite resists the attentions of Julio. Spurred on by the words of a stranger who invokes the symbols of the Four Horsemen of the Apocalypse—war, conquest, famine and death—Julio enlists. After distinguishing himself for bravery in the French Army, he is killed in an exchange with his cousin, an officer in the German Army.

The Four Horsemen of the Apocalypse
(1962 Metro-Goldwyn-Mayer)
D: Vincent Minnelli

S: Robert Ardrey and John Gay, based on the novel by
   Vicente Blasco Ibanez

P: Julian Blaustein

Cast: Glenn Ford, Yvette Mimieux, Lee J. Cobb, Paul Henreid

In an attempt to duplicate the success of forty years earlier, this costly and important production for MGM was both a critical and commercial failure. Comparison with the famed silent version starring Rudolph Valentino could not have been helpful, but they were two entirely different films similar only in superficial terms. Nevertheless, silent director Ingram's approach to the story was considerably less imaginative than Minnelli's, who had the benefit of all the technical advancements made in photography, directing and acting techniques since the original was shot. Glenn Ford played Julio in a characterization totally different from Valentino's.

The story was updated to World War II and centers around Julio in Paris and his efforts as a French Resistance fighter. Filming took place on location in France and at MGM Studios.

1492: Conquest of Paradise (1992 Paramount)
D: Ridley Scott

S: Roselyne Bosch

P: Ridley Scott and Alain Goldman

Cast: Gérard Depardieu, Armand Assante, Sigourney Weaver

A handsomely photographed and visually striking but dull and disjointed production. Depardieu is a lumbering, heavily French-accented English-speaking Italian Columbus. A lot of attention is paid to historical accuracy, however, though the four voyages are condensed into two.

Freebie and the Bean (1974 Warner Bros.)
D: Richard Rush

S: Robert Kaufman, based on a story by Floyd Mutrux

P: Richard Rush

Cast: James Caan, Alan Arkin

An action comedy film starring James Caan as Freebie Waters and Alan Arkin as Benito "Bean" Vasquez, a pair of plainclothes cops in San Francisco tracking down a numbers racketeer. The "Bean" is a Mexican American who puts up with the ethnic slurs of his partner and friend Freebie, including being called a "spick" and "wetback."

This supposedly comic bantering between the two makes up much of the humor of the film, which also includes broad car chases and crashes. Against this, however, is the contemporary characterization by Arkin of a Mexican American policeman as a positive, if new, kind of hero figure. Valerie Harper (later of television's "Rhoda" fame) plays Arkin's Hispanic wife, whom he suspects of infidelity.

From Dusk Till Dawn (1996 Miramax)

D: Robert Rodriquez

S: Quentin Tarantino

P: Gianni Nunnari and Meir Teper

Cast: Harvey Keitel, George Clooney, Quentin Tarantino,
Juliette Lewis, Cheech Marin, Fred Williamson, Salma Hayek,
Mike Moroff, Danny Trejo

The notorious Gecko brothers (Clooney and Tarantino), are a pair of thieves making their getaway across the border into Mexico who pick the wrong place for a pit-stop. The Titty Twister is a biker bar whose staff turns into vampires and feed on the clients after dark. This genre bending horror thriller combines the chase action drama with a vampire horror thriller. It has elements of Aztec culture and mythology thrown in as the fictional basis for the vampirism, since the bar sits on the remnants of a lost Aztec temple. A relative newcomer in this film, Salma Hayek plays Satanico Pandemonium, a seductive snake dancer in Aztec regalia. Cheech Marin plays multiple roles.

The Fugitive (1947 RKO Radio Pictures)

D: John Ford

S: Dudley Nichols, based on the novel *The Power and the Glory* by
Graham Greene

P: Merian C. Cooper and John Ford

Cast: Henry Fonda, Dolores Del Rio, Pedro Armendariz, Leo Carrillo,
J. Carroll Naish, Fortunio Bonanova, Miguel Inclan, Chris-Pin Martin,
José Torvay

Fonda plays the lone surviving priest in a fictional Latin American country that has become a police state with a severely anticlerical stance. Del Rio plays the beautiful Magdalena figure Indian woman who helps the priest and is the cast-off mistress of the pursuing police lieutenant (Armendariz).

Filmed in Mexico, *The Fugitive* is truly the first Mexican American co-production in terms of bringing together the best and most celebrated filmmaking talents of both countries, director John Ford, associate producer Emilio Fernandez, cinematographer Gabriel Figueroa, actors Henry Fonda, Pedro Armendariz and Dolores Del Rio. Mel Ferrer was an assistant to director Ford. Figueroa's cinematography captured images of Latin America in its churches, its countryside and its people. A cast of mostly Latin actors was gathered from both Mexico and the United States. Armendariz gives a stunning performance as an Indian who is hard on his own people, with a demonstrable antipathy toward the Catholic religion.

Elvis Presley sang (in Spanish) in the Mexican romp *Fun in Acapulco*.

Fun in Acapulco (1963 Paramount)

D: Richard Thorpe
S: Allan Weiss
P: Hal Wallis
Cast: Elvis Presley, Ursula Andress, Elsa Cardenas, Alejandro Rey, Robert Carricart

The soft, lush and inviting backgrounds of Acapulco frame the setting of Presley's romp in Mexico, complete with the King singing in Spanish and diving off the high cliffs of La Quebrada into the ocean surf.

This light tale concerns a young man with a psychological problem as well as a romantic one. Having been a trapeze artist, Mike Windgren (Presley) is terrified of heights due to his failure years before to catch his partner, whose death he blames on himself. A local shoeshine boy with a head for business, Raoul Almeido (Larry Domasin), happens to overhear Mike's singing and appoints himself his manager.

He gets Mike a job as a part-time singer and lifeguard at a swank hotel. Mike soon becomes romantically involved with Margarita

Dauphine (Andress), the daughter of a European immigrant, and Dolores Gomez (Cardenas), a lady bullfighter. Another lifeguard and high-dive specialist, Moreno (Rey), becomes jealous of Mike's attention to Margarita. Eventually, Mike overcomes his fear of heights. Alberto Morin is featured as the hotel manager and Robert Carricart plays Jose.

The film was shot largely on Paramount Studios soundstages, with a second-unit crew shooting all the Acapulco exteriors on location with doubles standing in for the stars. All the attention and publicity surrounding an Elvis Presley picture certainly helped to create a fun image of the Mexican resort for youths all over the world, who would later, as adults, want to make Acapulco a vacation travel destination.

Fun with Dick and Jane (1977 Columbia)
D: Ted Kotcheff
S: David Giler, Jerry Belson, and Mordecai Richler
P: Hank Bart and Max Palevsky
Cast: George Segal, Jane Fonda, Ed McMahon, Dick Gautier

An upwardly mobile young couple's dreams come crashing down when the husband loses his job. Their attempts to deal with the situation and the desperate lengths to which they go to maintain their upper-middle-class lifestyle are the basis of this comedy. Desperate for work, college-educated aerospace engineer Dick (Segal) turns for help to the Chicano janitor who used to clean his office. Stand-up comedian Hank Garcia plays Raoul Esteban, the janitor who becomes Segal's streetwise counsel on such matters as unemployment insurance and food stamps.

The Furies (1950 Paramount)
D: Anthony Mann
S: Charles Schnee, based on the novel by Niven Busch
P: Hal B. Wallis
Cast: Barbara Stanwyck, Walter Huston, Wendell Corey,
    Gilbert Roland, Thomas Gomez, Blanche Yurka, Movita

T.C. Jeffords (Huston), pioneer cattle baron, is the larger-than-life figure who finally meets his match in his own daughter. Vance (Stanwyck) is the strong-willed woman who upsets her father by choosing Rip Darrow (Corey), a sworn enemy, as her boyfriend.

T.C. chooses a San Francisco widow as his new wife, and Vance in a rage attacks her. T.C. goes off on a rampage and hangs Juan Herrera (Roland), Vance's childhood sweetheart and sometime lover. This incident sets up Jeffords' own death at the finale at the hands of Herrera's avenging mother (Yurka). Gomez plays the ranch foreman El Tigre, and Movita Castenada plays Chiquita. Pepe Hern and Joe Dominguez are also featured.

This well-acted Western was the first in a series of melodramas directed by Anthony Mann.

Gaby—A True Story (1987 TriStar)

D: Luis Mandoki
S: Martin Salinas and Michael James Love, based on a story developed
   by Mandoki from events narrated to him by Gabriela Brimmer
P: Pinchas Perry and Luis Mandoki
Cast: Liv Ullmann, Norma Aleandro, Robert Loggia, Rachel Levin,
   Lawrence Monason, Robert Beltran, Tony Goldwyn, Danny De La Paz

The true story of a young woman with cerebral palsy who becomes a professional writer. The movie is drawn from the 1979 autobiography of Gaby Brimmer, the daughter of Jewish refugees in Mexico City. Gaby had the good fortune to be raised by an extremely understanding nurse, Florencia, who became her friend and companion.

Aleandro plays Florencia, who, according to director Luis Mandoki, "represents the heart and soul of the Mexican people." Mandoki waited five years to get the production made the way he wished it to be. It is a modern-day look at life in Mexico. Aleandro as the Indian maid in an Anglo European household in Mexico gives evidence of a racist legacy in Mexico in which Eurocentric values are nurtured at the expense of mother Mexico. Florencia serves almost the same function as did the African American mammy/nurse in such films as *Gone with the Wind*. Aleandro received an Academy Award® nomination for Best Supporting Actress.

Filmed on location in Cuernavaca, Mexico, it was an international co-production with the Mexican government.

"Norma Aleandro, the fine Argentine actress, gives a quietly complex performance as the withdrawn servant who simply took charge of the child Gaby one night—and never left," Julie Salamon, *Wall Street Journal* (10/2/87).

"A superb performance by Norma Aleandro, the Argentine actress who . . . is a real standout, and . . . contributes greatly to the film's verisimilitude," Janet Maslin, *New York Times* (10/30/87).

"Luis Mandoki's treatment is blunt, outspoken and full of strong emotions. He receives immeasurable help from a sublime casting stroke that pairs two powerhouse actresses," Deborah Kunk, *Los Angeles Herald* (11/13/87).

Gaiety
See *Fiesta* (1941).

Gang
See *Walk Proud*.

The Gang's All Here (1943 Twentieth Century Fox)

D: Busby Berkeley
S: Walter Bullock, based on a story by Nancy Winter, George Root Jr.,
    and Tom Bridges
P: William LeBaron
Cast: Alice Faye, Phil Baker, Carmen Miranda, Benny Goodman

A soldier goes off to war and leaves behind two young women who both believe they are engaged to him. One of them (Faye) is a chorus girl at a New York nightclub where Dorita (Miranda) is the star. Miranda steals every scene she is in. Miranda's version of the song and production number "The Lady in the Tutti Frutti Hat" has Mae West-type comic sexual overtones that are difficult to ignore when sixty chorus girls are prancing about with giant phallic bananas. It was Busby Berkeley's first color film and a high point in his career as a choreographer and director. Dancer Tony DeMarco, an Italian American, is also featured.

Garden of Evil (1954 Twentieth Century Fox)

D: Henry Hathaway
S: Frank Fenton, based on a story by Fred Freiberger and
    William Tunberg
P: Charles Brackett
Cast: Gary Cooper, Richard Widmark, Susan Hayward, Cameron
    Mitchell, Rita Moreno, Hugh Marlowe, Victor Manuel Mendoza

Three American adventurers (Cooper, Widmark and Mitchell) and one Mexican (Mendoza) in a Mexican port agree to help a beautiful American woman (Hayward) rescue her husband (Marlowe), who is trapped in a gold mine deep in the wilds of Mexico. They rescue the husband but have to battle Indians on the way back. The movie was filmed on location in Mexico in CinemaScope and Technicolor.

The Mexican character comes off as courageous but dumb. For example, when Widmark asks Mendoza to cut the cards in a card game, he literally does so, using a machete. Moreno plays a seductive dancing cantina girl in the opening sequence.

The Gaucho (1928 United Artists)

D: F. Richard Jones
S: Lotta Woods, based on a story by Elton Thomas [Fairbanks]
P: Douglas Fairbanks
Cast: Douglas Fairbanks, Lupe Velez

In Argentina, the Gaucho (Fairbanks) fights against the evil usurper Ruiz (Gustave van Seyfferitz) in the town of Milagros.

Velez made her major film debut in *The Gaucho* as the female lead. She replaced Dolores Del Rio, who had been previously announced for the role but who had to drop out due to personal problems. Lupe got excellent notices, and the film made her a star. She matches Fairbanks in athletic prowess, acting and humor.

In the *Los Angeles Record* (4/12/27), columnist Dan Thomas quoted Fairbanks' views on film production, shared by most of his colleagues at that time: "In this picture I will be a gaucho, a South American cowboy. There will be no time element in the story, which might have taken place any time during the last century. Naturally it will be colorful, showing the South Americans as we think of them rather than as they are." He continued, "A film depicting the southern continent as it actually is today would be very uninteresting. We have to show the gauchos in colorful costumes and romantic village settings in order to make them interesting. This is what we call movie license."

The Gay Defender (1927 Paramount)
D: Gregory La Cava
S: Lay Harris, Sam Mintz, and Kenneth Raisbeck
P: Adolph Zukor and Jesse L. Lasky
Cast: Richard Dix

Fictionalized silent film biography of the legendary California bandit Joaquin Murieta. Some location scenes were filmed near Mission San Juan Capistrano in Southern California's Orange County.

"Dix has sideburns and a mustache, but it's still a tough job for him to look Spanish. He ought to remain on this side of the border. Other than that neither Mexico nor Spain will have anything to squawk about because the villain is an American. *Gay Defender* is just a Western and not a good one," *Variety* (12/28/ 27).

Leo Carrillo, Ida Lupino and Nino Martini pose for a picture in their costumes from *The Gay Desperado*.

The Gay Desperado (1936 United Artists)
D: Rouben Mamoulian
S: Wallace Smith, based on a story by Leo Birinski
P: Mary Pickford and Jesse L. Lasky
Cast: Nino Martini, Leo Carrillo, Ida Lupino, Allan Garcia, Chris-Pin Martin

A musical comedy based on a popular Broadway show that spoofed the Western and gangster genres. It served as a film vehicle for then-popular Italian Metropolitan Opera singer Nino Martini.

The plot follows a Mexican bandit (Carrillo) who kidnaps Martini because he likes his singing and an American heiress (Lupino) in order to extract a ransom. Carrillo got the best notices for his wild, fun interpretation of a bandit. He even does a takeoff of gangster portrayals by James Cagney and George Raft.

The Gay Señorita (1946 Columbia)

D: Arthur Dreifuss
S: Edward Eliscu
P: Jay Gorney
Cast: Jinx Falkenburg, Steve Cochran, Thurston Hall, Marguerita Sylva, Jim Bannon

The story revolves around the efforts of big businessman J.J. Frontess (Hall) to take over a historic city district and convert the area into a huge warehouse. Its Mexican American population, descended from those early Californians who founded the city on that very spot, refuse to sell. Dona Maria de Sandoval (Sylva) dreams of the time when Sandoval Lane can be rebuilt and stand as a monument to the spirit of the early Mexican pioneers.

J.J. lets his nephew Phil (Bannon) try his hand at acquiring the properties. The usual romantic complications arise when Phil falls for Elena (Falkenburg), daughter of Dona Maria, and turns against his uncle. He meets old friend Tim O'Brian (Cochran), now a bandleader who works under the name Tim Obrion. While J.J. is on a business trip, Phil uses company money to completely rebuild Sandoval Lane. Surprised and upset at what he sees upon his return, J.J., treated with nothing but kindness by the local citizenry, relents and decides to build the warehouse somewhere else.

This modest-budget musical offering sheds light on and acknowledges the history and contributions of Mexican Americans in the Southwest and their pride in that accomplishment. It could be called one of the first Chicano consciousness movies because of its theme of people banding together to save the remnants of their cultural heritage. Based on the actual efforts of citizens to save historic Olvera Street in downtown Los Angeles, The Gay Señorita features numerous Hispanic actors and performers including Corinna Maura, Isabelita, Luisita Triana, Lola Montes, Nina Bara and Leander de Cordova.

The Ghost Breakers (1940 Paramount)

D: George Marshall
S: Walter De Leon
P: Arthur Hornblow, Jr.
Cast: Bob Hope, Paulette Goddard, Pedro de Cordoba, Anthony Quinn

Larry Lawrence (Hope) is a breezy radio columnist who innocently becomes involved in a murder. Mary Carter (Goddard) saves him from the police and helps him escape in a trunk to a ship sailing for Cuba. They get romantically involved during the trip, and when Mary discovers she has inherited a spooky island castle called Castillo Maldito in Cuba, Larry offers to help her rid the castle of evil spirits.

Bob Hope and Paulette Goddard had been teamed previously in the popular The Cat and the Canary (1939). The comedy thriller The Ghost Breakers helped establish Bob Hope as a top film comedian at Paramount. A young Quinn played two roles as Cuban twin brothers, Ramon and Francisco Maderos. Willie Best plays the eye-popping African American sidekick.

The action takes place mainly in the haunted castle on an island off the coast of Cuba and in Paramount's reconstruction of the castle on two huge soundstages. The film was based on a play by Paul Dickey and Charles W. Goddard. There were two previous silent film versions, one in 1914 and the other in 1922, starring Wallace Reid.

Giant (1956 Warner Bros.)

D: George Stevens
S: Fred Guiol and Ivan Moffat, based on the novel by Edna Ferber
P: George Stevens and Henry Ginsberg
Cast: Rock Hudson, Elizabeth Taylor, James Dean, Dennis Hopper, Elsa Cardenas, Victor Millan, Pilar Del Rey, Felipe Turich, Tina Menard, Natividad Vacio, Maurice Jara

A multigenerational saga based on the novel by Edna Ferber that tells the story of a ranch dynasty as it encounters the sweeping changes brought on by the twentieth century. This was Dean's last movie, and Stevens won an Oscar® for Best Director.

Henry Ginsberg commented in a 1973 interview in *Condo-News* (Palm Beach, Florida) that it was tough at first to get the book made into a film. "*Giant* was a forerunner of the black and white situation of today. It dealt with, in some parts, the attitudes of the Texans towards the Mexicans. The industry may have been scared off at first by the inherent social issues."

The Benedicts are a cattle dynasty, and the head of the family, Bick Benedict (Hudson, in one of his best performances), chooses a wife from Virginia. She brings a subversive influence into the extraordinary house set in the middle of the Texas plains. Wife Leslie, played by Elizabeth Taylor, finds it strange that, among other things, Mexican servants and their children should be allowed to die because a "white doctor cannot possibly attend to those people."

Years later, during a big reception at the Benedict ranch, Reata, Jordy Benedict III (Hopper) announces that he has married Juana (Cardenas), a beautiful Mexican girl. Bick is outraged at the idea of a Mexican being Mrs. Jordan Benedict III. Before a banquet for the opening of a new hotel, Juana is refused service at a beauty salon and is not allowed to enter the banquet hall with Jordan and their baby.

The climax of the film finds Bick accompanying his family to a burger joint, where the owner scowls at the fact that Bick has entered with Juana and the baby. Shortly thereafter, some Mexican workers enter the café and are ordered out by the owner. Bick intercedes and becomes involved in a fight. He loses the fight, but gains respect for having defended the Mexicans.

Based on a best-selling book, *Giant* was a major Hollywood production with a well-respected director and an all-star cast. The film proved big at the box office but received mixed critical notices.

Marfa, Texas, was headquarters for the location shooting. The Mexican village was constructed in the town of Valentine, forty miles from Marfa.

Elsa Cardenas portrays Juana (center), a beautiful Mexican girl who marries the son (Dennis Hopper, in trench coat) of a wealthy Anglo rancher in *Giant*.

The film features a number of Mexican American actors including Victor Millan as Angel Obregon; Pilar Del Rey as Mrs. Obregon; Felipe Turich as Gomez, head of the Mexican village; Maurice Jara as Dr. Guerra; and Tina Menard as Lupe. Menard was also responsible for casting the many Mexican American extras used in the film, both on location and at the studio. Sal Mineo plays Angel Obregon III, the son of one of the Benedicts' ranch hands. He was saved during an illness as a baby at the intervention of Leslie Benedict. Angel later dies a hero in World War II.

The importance of *Giant* to Hispanic Americans is that it was the first major film to expose the racism that Mexican Americans suffered in the Southwest. It highlighted the problem of racism in general in the United States to audiences on the national and international levels. The problem was presented in a sympathetic liberal light in which the Mexicans were not the main players. The ending of the film, with its fusing of the Anglo and Mexican through intermarriage and the birth of their baby, signaled hope for a better future through integration and understanding. The film's importance as a catalyst for discussion in the media, however, was overshadowed by the death of its young star, James Dean, prior to the film's release.

Gilda (1946 Columbia)

D: Charles Vidor
S: Marion Parsonnet, based on an adaptation by Jo Eisinger of
E.A. Ellington's original story
P: Virginia Van Upp
Cast: Glenn Ford, Rita Hayworth, George Macready, Joseph Calleia

From the moment she appears on screen, hair disheveled and cascading down her naked shoulders, Hayworth, as Gilda, exudes an almost explosive sexual electricity that brings together her best qualities as a star. The image of Gilda is the one that Hayworth has come to be most identified with over the years.

The plot has something to do with entrepreneur Ballin Mundson's (Macready's) efforts to establish a tungsten cartel involved with the atomic bomb.

Johnny Farrell (Ford), from the gutter, makes it to the top in Buenos Aires' posh casinos working for Ballin. Johnny meets Gilda, whom he knew previously. She is now married to Ballin, and a love/hate relationship develops between Johnny and Gilda, which Ballin soon notes.

Gilda turned out to be durably profitable for Columbia and was reissued twice with international success before being made available to television. Another Hayworth-Ford teaming, *Affair in Trinidad* (1952), a similar film, made even more money at the box office. *Gilda* was filmed at Columbia Studios in Hollywood.

"When things get trite and far fetched, somehow, at the drop of a shoulder strap, there is always Rita Hayworth to excite the moviegoer," *Variety* (3/20/46).

"Has its setting in that hot spot, The Argentine. It is always a hot spot in the movies, because it can be thick with secret agents, soft spoken Latin Lotharios and tango tunes, and *Gilda* makes the most of this," Edwin Schallert, *Los Angeles Times* (4/27/46).

The Girl from Mexico (1939 RKO Radio Pictures)

D: Leslie Goodwins
S: Lionel Houser and Joseph A. Fields
P: Cliff Reid
Cast: Lupe Velez

A madcap comedy starring Velez as Carmelita, a fiery Latin nightclub entertainer in New York City.

Girl of the Rio (1932 RKO Radio Pictures)

D: Herbert Brenon
S: Elizabeth Meehan, based on the Willard Mack play *The Dove*
P: Herbert Brenon
Cast: Dolores Del Rio, Leo Carrillo, Norman Foster

The egotistical, wealthy and politically influential Don José (Carrillo) makes unwelcome advances to cantina dancer Dolores (Del Rio), whose sweetheart, Johnny (Foster), runs a gambling operation in a Mexican bordertown. When Don José frames Johnny on a murder charge,

Dolores is forced to offer herself to Don José in order to save her lover. The banned Mexican government the film because of the negative storyline and Carrillo's despicable portrayal. The story had been filmed before in a Sicilian island setting in a 1928 silent version with Norma Shearer. Norman Foster later became a noted director in Mexico and the United States.

Gloria (1980 Columbia)
D: John Cassavetes
S: John Cassavetes
P: John Cassavetes
Cast: Gena Rowlands, John Adames, Buck Henry, Julie Carmen

A mobster's ex-mistress Gloria (Rowlands), tries to protect a six-year-old Puerto Rican boy, Phil Dawn (Adames) who is the sole survivor of the gangland execution of his family. At first reluctantly, Gloria becomes the fierce protector of a child her mobster cronies want to eliminate because he possesses a diary of illegal business transactions that his father, a mob accountant, had kept. This gripping, if somewhat melodramatic, action movie follows the developing relationship between tough-as-nails woman and a smart-mouthed kid as they run for their lives. Under Cassavetes' direction, the production walks the line between serious melodrama and tongue-in-cheek humor.

Julie Carmen plays Jeri Dawn, the young wife of Jack Dawn (Henry), a mousy former Mafia accountant who squeals to the FBI. New York-based casting director Vic Ramos did the casting, and the saxophone playing over the opening scenes is by Tony Ortega. Adames is the New York-born son of parents from the Dominican Republic.

Gloria received the Golden Lion Award for Best Picture at the Venice Film Festival. Rowlands was named Best Actress for her role by the Italian Network Commentators, who also honored Julie Carmen as Best Supporting Actress and Basilio Franchina as Best Supporting Actor.

Goldfinger (1964 United Artists)
D: Guy Hamilton
S: Richard Maibaum and Paul Dehn
P: Harry Saltzman and Albert R. Broccoli
Cast: Sean Connery, Gert Frobe, Honor Blackman, Shirley Eaton, Harold Sakata, Naja Regin

The third film in the popular James Bond adventure series full of villains, gadgetry, sex, humor and action, *Goldfinger* was the first of the blockbuster Bond films. The furor with which moviegoers greeted the film was unprecedented.

The five-minute pre-credit opening sequence is racy, violent, sexist and brutal. In it, Bond (Connery) emerges from the sea to wreak havoc on a drug-dealing revolutionary called Ramirez by blowing up his South American compound. After his mission is accomplished, Bond enters the smoke-filled interior of a local nightclub, where he meets his contact. Dancer Bonita (Regin) sets Bond up for a fall: as she steps out of her hot bath to give him a warm, sexy welcome, Bond spies an approaching South American heavy reflected in the girl's eyes. Bond soon dispatches his assailant in a crackling flurry of sparks and steam.

The Good, the Bad, and the Ugly (1967 United Artists)

D: Sergio Leone
S: Sergio Leone and Luciano Vincenzoni, based on a story by Age-Scarpelli, Vincenzoni, and Leone
P: Alberto Grimaldi
Cast: Clint Eastwood, Lee Van Cleef, Eli Wallach

Eli Wallach turns in a scene-stealing, hammy, outrageous performance as Mexican bandit Tuco the Terrible in this quintessential "spaghetti Western." The third and final "Man with No Name" adventure, this became an international hit and helped rocket Clint Eastwood to stardom. Lee Van Cleef lends his evil black clad presence as the sadistic Angel Eyes. This unholy trio's lethal pursuit of $200,000 in gold bullion forms the core of this action-filled tale that covers the period of the American Civil War.

Green Mansions (1959 Metro-Goldwyn-Mayer)

D: Mel Ferrer
S: Dorothy Kingsley, based on the novel by W. H. Hudson
P: Edmund Grainger
Cast: Audrey Hepburn, Anthony Perkins, Lee J. Cobb, Henry Silva, Sessue Hayakawa

This immortal romance of the savage wilderness is the story of Rima (Hepburn), the bird girl, who is found in the Venezuelan jungles by the political refugee Abel (Perkins). The superstitious natives want to kill Rima, whom they consider an evil spirit because she is able to communicate with nature. The girl is finally destroyed by the Indians, who kill her in a fire when she is trapped atop a huge hollow tree.

MGM and director Ferrer went on a 25,000-mile location trip through Venezuela, Colombia and British Guiana (now known as Belize) for some exterior filming. Famed Brazilian composer Heitor Villa-Lobos scored special music for the film.

Guadalcanal Diary (1943 Twentieth Century Fox)

D: Lewis Seiler
S: Lamor Trotti and Jerry Cady, based on the novel by Richard Tregaskis
P: Bryan Fay
Cast: Preston Foster, William Bendix, Lloyd Nolan, Anthony Quinn

A factual account of a group of United States Marines from varied backgrounds fighting the Japanese forces landing in the Solomon Islands during a bloody World War II battle. Quinn was prominently featured as Soose (short for Jesus), a Mexican American Marine private, who is the lone survivor of a dangerous patrol.

Guns for San Sebastian (1968 Metro-Goldwyn-Mayer)
D: Henri Verneuil
S: James R. Webb, based on the novel *A Wall for San Sebastian* by
William Barby Flaherty
P: Jacques Bar
Cast: Anthony Quinn, Charles Bronson, Anjanette Comer, Sam Jaffe,
Silvia Pinal, Jorge Russek, Pedro Armendariz, Jr.

Written by a Jesuit priest, Flaherty based his story on Father Keno, who
established missions in Sonora and Arizona in the late 1700s. Quinn
plays Leon Alastray, a rebel outcast and thief who is mistaken by desert
villagers for a man of the cloth when he wears a dead priest's clothes.
Alastray helps the villagers rebuild their church and village and staves
off vicious Yaqui Indian attacks. In the process he restores the faith of
the villagers and of himself. This violent action Western, filmed in
Durango, Mexico and at Churubusco Studios in Mexico City, was an
American, French, Mexican and Italian co-production.

Guns of the Magnificent Seven (1969 United Artists)
D: Paul Wendkos
S: Herman Hoffman
P: Vincent M. Fennelly
Cast: George Kennedy, James Whitmore, Reni Santoni, Frank Silvera,
Bernie Casey, Fernando Rey

George Kennedy takes over the Yul Brynner role of Chris, the strong,
silent gunfighter and leader of men, in this second sequel to *The
Magnificent Seven* (1960). Persuaded by a fervent young Mexican revolutionary (Santoni) to help free his noble leader (Rey) from a Mexican
prison, Chris recruits a team of the deadliest men in the West, experts
with gun, knife, rope and explosives. Little Tony Davis plays Emiliano
Zapata as a child. The picture was filmed in Spain.

Hangin' with the Homeboys (1991 New Line Cinema)
D: Joseph B. Vasquez
S: Joseph B. Vasquez
P: Richard Brick
Cast: John Leguizamo, Doug E. Doug, Mario Joyner, Nestor Serrano

Four young men from the South Bronx, two African American and two
Puerto Rican, head for Manhattan on a Friday night. They crash a party
and a car, go after women, get nabbed jumping subway turnstiles,
squeeze into a single booth to watch a peep show in Times Square, and
discover a few truths about life and themselves along the way.

The writing is sharp and the characters sure, brought alive by a
young cast of actors. Writer and director Vasquez manages to unpre-
tentiously show contemporary New York City life through a lighthearted
ed boys' night out. In the process, we discover the various social pressures the characters are under and how these shape their point-of-
view. The Latino insists his name is "Vinny" and rejects his heritage
because he finds discrimination too difficult to deal with. The African

American character challenges people with, "it's because I'm black" every time he doesn't get his own way. This is a well-made movie by a talented writer and director.

The Harder They Fall (1956 Columbia)
D: Mark Robson
S: Philip Yordan, based on the novel by Budd Schulberg
P: Philip Yordan
Cast: Humphrey Bogart, Rod Steiger, Jan Sterling, Mike Lane,
    Carlos Montalban

The Harder They Fall is a study of corruption within the fight game. The film has an unyielding harshness in exposing a machine of deceit in which each individual has a place and in which the fighter himself is more spectacle than man.

The syndicate secures a hulking figure from Argentina, Toro Moreno, who is manipulated by a gambling promoter (Steiger) and sports columnist-turned-press agent named Willis (Bogart). The duped Toro Moreno is not the principal character (although he is an effectively realized presence as played by the imposing and somber Mike Lane). The pitifully inadequate Toro is built into a contender for the heavyweight championship. Bout after bout is fixed until the final fight, which cannot be fixed. However, because of the big buildup the syndicate has given the South American wonderman, they are counting on a big take from the bets placed on his adversary. The fight becomes one of the messiest ever when the innocent Toro, who does not lack courage or pride, takes a terrible beating. While Toro is lying battered in the hospital, Willis tries to collect Toro's share of the million-dollar purse. He is informed that after expenses, Toro's share is exactly forty-nine dollars.

Havana (1990 Universal)
D: Sydney Pollack
S: Judith Rascoe and David Rayfiel
P: Sydney Pollack and Richard Roth
Cast: Robert Redford, Lena Olin, Raul Julia, Tomas Milian, Alan Arkin,
    Tony Plana

A love triangle story, reminiscent of *Casablanca*, between cynical gambler Jack Weil (Redford), impassioned freedom fighter "Bobby" Duran (Olin), and her well-born revolutionist doctor husband Arturo (Julia) on the eve of the Cuban Revolution.

Jack, in Havana in 1959 for the biggest card game of his life, finds himself falling in love and finding his true self. Bobby and Jack first meet en route to Cuba. Later, she is arrested and sought out by Weil, who buys her release from prison. Believing her husband dead, she returns to the rebels, and Weil goes after her, risking his life in rebel territory. Returning to Havana, he discovers Duran is alive and tells her. He buys Duran's release, and Bobby goes to him, leaving Weil. An epilogue set four years later has Weil on the beach in Miami still thinking of the woman he loved and lost in Havana.

Pollack moves his story along, cutting between casinos and torture chambers, strippers and shootings and garish neon flashing lights and nightclubs. There is no real feeling of impending doom or acknowledgment of what Fidel and the Cuban Revolution mean, except in expository speeches. The main character has an apolitical attitude, the rebels are unseen for the most part, and politics are generally avoided. The film features large lavish set pieces, gorgeously lit by cinematographer Owen Roizman, but it loses steam in the second half with its anticlimactic resolution.

Mark Rydell as Meyer Lansky, head of the organized crime syndicate, sums up the American position on Cuba and Batista. "We invented Havana and we can goddamn well move it someplace else if he can't control it."

Robert Redford plays the world-weary Jack effectively, and Olin is excellent as the Swedish-born American wife of the revolutionary Duran, well played by Julia. Cuban-born actor Milian does a nice job as secret policeman Colonel Menocan. Plana as alcoholic journalist Felix Ramos does as well as can be expected with an inadequate role.

Due to the existing trade embargo, the movie was filmed in Santo Domingo in the Dominican Republic, the second-largest island in the Caribbean (after Cuba itself). The main exterior set of Havana's famous wide boulevard, El Prado, was constructed on the Dominican Air Force base. This quarter-mile-long street, surrounded by facades representing casinos, restaurants and hotels, was one of the largest and most comprehensive sets constructed in contemporary cinema.

Both *Havana* and *Casablanca* share the same basic story, though this film is depressing and its lack of political stance is disappointing. In *Havana*, Swedish actress Olin plays a role similar to Swedish actress Ingrid Bergman's in *Casablanca*. *Havana* is, in an obvious way, a tribute to the movies of the past, in which American protagonists find love and adventure in exotic locales. *Havana* also has similarities to another film, *Cuba*, starring Sean Connery. Both were written in the late 1970s, but *Havana* took much longer to reach the screen.

Raul Julia and Lena Olin star as Arturo and Roberta "Bobby" Duran in *Havana*.

Heartbreak Ridge (1986 Warner Bros.)

D: Clint Eastwood
S: Jim Carabatsos
P: Clint Eastwood
Cast: Clint Eastwood, Marsha Mason, Everett McGill, Moses Gunn, Eileen Heckart, Mario Van Peebles, Ramon Franco

Gunnery Sergeant Tom Highway (Eastwood) is a Marine veteran of Korea and Vietnam. He rejoins his old unit, now featuring the usual assortment of sloppy recruits (African American, Hispanic, Italian). He earns their hatred, and ultimately, their respect as he whips them into an efficient fighting force in time for the liberation of the Caribbean island of Grenada. Two of the recruits are Hispanic: Aponte (Franco) is a distant, brooding individual with family problems. Quinones (Mike Gomez) is a competitive lifer with a discipline problem. One telling sequence has Aponte coming face to face with a dead Cuban soldier whom he realizes looks just like him.

Heartbreaker (1983 Emerson/Monorex)

D: Frank Zuniga
S: Vincente Gutierrez
P: Chris D. Nebe and Chris Anders
Cast: Fernando Allende, Dawn Dunlap, Peter Gonzales Falcon, Miguel Ferrer, Pepe Serna

This silly, low-budget film with no style is reminiscent of the drive-in movies of the late 1950s and 1960s that Roger Corman made for American International Pictures.

Beto (Allende), the handsome, twenty-five-year-old president of a low-rider customized car club, falls in love with an Anglo girl from outside the area. Beto has his share of troubles from Hector (Gonzales Falcon), with whom he has an ongoing rivalry that dates back to when they were children. Hector tries to undermine everything Beto achieves. The film features positive Latin characters free of the barrio gang stereotype trappings.

"Conflict in the script, written by former Samuel Goldwyn Writing Award winner Vincente Gutierrez, develops much too slowly and fails, given the chance, to really render any social insights to life in a Latin-dominated community beyond belonging to a car club," *Daily Variety* (5/6/83).

Heat (1987 New Century-Vista)

D: R.M. Richards
S: William Goldman, based on his novel
P: Keith Rotman and George Pappas
Cast: Burt Reynolds, Karen Young, Peter MacNicol

In Las Vegas, Nick Escalante (Reynolds), known as "Mex," is a professional bodyguard who is fiercely loyal to his friends. When a mobster's son savagely beats an old girlfriend of Escalante's, the incident ignites a violent series of events that pit him against the mob and culminate in a vicious cat-and-mouse climax. Burt Reynolds makes a believable Mexican American, which is the only redeeming feature of this ugly and violent story.

Hell to Eternity (1960 Allied Artists)

D: Phil Karlson
S: Ted Sherdeman and Walter Roeber Schmidt, based on a story by
    Gil Doud
P: Irving H. Levin
Cast: Jeffrey Hunter, David Janssen, Sessue Hayakawa, George Takei,
    Tsuru Aoki

The true story of United States Marine war hero Guy Gabaldon, a Mexican American orphan from East Los Angeles who was adopted by a Japanese American family prior to World War II. His knowledge of the Japanese language and culture, coupled with his fighting ability, constituted a huge asset during the crucial battle of Saipan in the Pacific theater of war. The real-life Gabaldon faced a crisis of conscience when his Japanese American family was forcibly interned in a stateside prison camp during the war.

This was the first dramatic feature film to show the stateside internment of Japanese Americans under Executive Order 366 during World War II. The film presents sensitive story elements and plenty of battle action, though from watching the movie you would never have known that Gabaldon was Mexican American. All-American, blue-eyed Jeffrey Hunter played Gabaldon, which in retrospect is not that unusual since Hunter also played Native Americans and "half-breeds" in several films. The movie never explores Gabaldon's own racial identity, only his adoptive Japanese American family. East Los Angeles looked like any Depression-era neighborhood as seen in the movies, when, in fact, at that time East Los Angeles was a very ethnically mixed area. Gabaldon is one of the few true-life Mexican American hero figures portrayed on screen.

Hellfighters (1968 Universal)

D: Andrew V. McLaglen
S: Clair Huffaker
P: Robert Arthur
Cast: John Wayne, Jim Hutton, Katharine Ross, Vera Miles,
    Alberto Morin, Pedro Gonzalez-Gonzalez

An American oil-well firefighting movie, loosely inspired by the exploits of "Red" Adair, which climaxes with an oil fire in Venezuelan oil fields under attack by rebels.

Herbie Goes Bananas (1980 Buena Vista)
D: Vincent McEveety
S: Don Tait, based on characters created by Gordon Buford
P: Ron Miller
Cast: Cloris Leachman, Charles Martin Smith, John Vernon, Joaquin Garay III

The fourth film in the Herbie the Love Bug (Volkswagen) car series, which was popular with young audiences in the late 1960s and 1970s. Herbie sets sail for Rio de Janeiro's Grande Premio auto racing competition with his two new owners. En route they get sidetracked by a smuggling syndicate, pestered by a pint-sized Mexican pickpocket and bullied by a raging bull. The movie was filmed in Puerto Vallarta and Guadalajara, Mexico, with background shots filmed in the Panama Canal Zone. Other Latin cast members from the United States include Ruben Moreno, Tina Menard, Jorge Moreno, Dante D'Andre, Alma Beltran and Bert Santos.

The Hi-Lo Country (1998 Polygram)
D: Stephen Frears
S: Walon Green
P: Barbara DeFina, Martin Scorsese, Eric Fellner, Tim Beavan
Cast: Woody Harrelson, Billy Crudup, Patricia Arquette, Enrique Castillo, Penelope Cruz, Jacob Vargas, Katy Jurado

Two good friends in post World War II Texas fall in love with the same married woman, and complications and consequences ensue for all of them.

The film is a touching and effective elegy to the Western way of life and the people who lived it. Enrique Castillo is excellent as Levi, the ranch foreman. Penelope Cruz makes an impressive American film debut as Josepha. Katy Jurado has a brief cameo as a fortuneteller. Mexican American cultural blending is an intrinsic part of this Texas tale.

High Noon (1952 United Artists)
D: Fred Zinnemann
S: Carl Foreman
P: Stanley Kramer
Cast: Gary Cooper, Grace Kelly, Katy Jurado, Lloyd Bridges, Ian MacDonald

Mexican actress Jurado made an impression on audiences with her striking features and acting ability in High Noon as Helen Ramirez, the owner of the town saloon and general store. Helen is unmarried and is looked down upon by the rest of the town for her ethnic origins as well as her illicit past. She was once involved with Marshal Will Kane (Cooper) and Miller (Macdonald), an ex-con who has recently been released from prison, and is now out to get Kane. Kane is left alone to fight Miller and his gang when none of the townspeople are willing to help him stand up to this threat to their community.

Lloyd Bridges, Katy Jurado,
Gary Cooper and Grace
Kelly, the stars of the
legendary Western
High Noon.

Helen is one of the strongest and most complex Mexican American female character ever portrayed on film. Although she is relatively wealthy, she still endures the prejudiced attitudes of her town. She tells the puritan Grace Kelly to fight for her man, advice she herself did not follow as, Kane, once her lover, is no longer hers. Jurado won praise for her work.

In a 1992 interview, Jurado said that producer Stanley Kramer had seen her in *The Bullfighter and the Lady* (1951) and asked her to come to Hollywood for a screen test. Jurado politely refused, telling Kramer she was an established actress in Mexico with five years of film work to her credit. If Kramer wanted to see how well she could act, all he had to do was go to downtown Los Angeles and catch one of her Mexican films. He did, and she got the part.

Jurado knew little English and learned her lines phonetically. She had actor friend Antonio Moreno translate the script for her on her arrival in Los Angeles, and he told her it was a fabulous part, though it called for someone slightly older than the twenty-five-year-old actress. Jurado won the New York Film Critics Award for Best Supporting Actress. Academy Awards® went to Gary Cooper as Best Actor, Elmo Williams and Henry Gerstad for Best Film Editing, Dmitri Tiomkin and Ned Washington for the theme song, "Do Not Forsake Me, Oh My

Darlin'," and Tiomkin for Best Score. It was filmed at the Columbia Ranch in Burbank and near Sonora, California.

A High Wind in Jamaica (1965 Twentieth Century Fox)
D: Alexander Mackendrick
S: Stanley Mann, Ronald Harwood, and Denis Cannan, based on the novel by Richard Hughes
P: John Croyden
Cast: Anthony Quinn, James Coburn, Lila Kedrova

Quinn stars as pirate Juan Chavez in a tale about a family of British youngsters kidnapped by Caribbean pirates in the 1870s.

Hold Back the Dawn (1941 Paramount)
D: Mitchell Leisen
S: Billy Wilder and Charles Brackett, based on a story by Ketti Frings
P: Arthur Hornblow, Jr.
Cast: Charles Boyer, Olivia de Havilland, Paulette Goddard, Nestor Paiva

European refugees are stuck in a Mexican bordertown awaiting permission to enter the United States just prior to American entry into World War II. One refugee, a suave Romanian dancer, Iscovescu (Boyer), desperate to enter the United States, takes the advice of his former dance partner (Goddard) and decides to marry his way into the States. He meets a naive American schoolteacher (de Havilland) on a field trip with her students in Mexico, and the ensuing complications brought on by the affair make up most of the drama.

This was Paramount's most honored film of the year, receiving Academy Award® nominations for Best Picture, Best Actress, Best Screenplay, Best Cinematography and Best Score. Every effort was made to show Mexico in its best light. The Mexican border patrolmen were shown to be uniformed, neat and clean-shaven. A Mexican street facade resembling a bordertown was constructed on the Paramount lot.

Holiday for Lovers (1959 Twentieth Century Fox)
D: Henry Levin
S: Luther Davis, based on the play by Ronald Alexander
P: David Weisbart
Cast: Clifton Webb, Jane Wyman, Jill St. John, Nico Minardos, José Greco, Nestor Amaral and his Orchestra

A Boston psychiatrist (Webb) and his wife (Wyman) take their daughters on a trip to South America and find that most of their time is spent keeping the attractive young daughters away from men. The film takes them to Rio de Janeiro and Sao Paulo, Brazil, and Lima, Peru, with stock footage in CinemaScope. A very late entry for the Good Neighbor Policy, the film has the feel of a 1940s script that got shelved.

A young actor by the name of Henry Delgado, later known as Henry Darrow (of television's *The High Chaparral* fame), made his film debut in a small role as a bus driver.

Holiday in Mexico (1946 Metro-Goldwyn-Mayer)

D: George Sidney
S: Isabel Lennart, based on a story by William Kozlenko
P: Joe Pasternak
Cast: Walter Pidgeon, José Iturbi, Jane Powell, Ilona Massey,
   Xavier Cugat

A slight musical offering with a little something for everyone, from opera to boogie woogie, with Iturbi and Cugat.

The daughter (Powell) of an American ambassador (Pidgeon) in Mexico is planning a garden party to which Cugat and his Orchestra are invited along with a soloist (Massey), a Hungarian who is an old flame of the ambassador's. The girl also imagines herself in love with Iturbi, who plays himself.

Powell sings and romps her way through the film, shot in Hollywood at MGM Studios. Iturbi plays classics and jazz on elaborately photographed pianos.

"The likeliest Mexicans who appear in Holiday in Mexico are the impassioned maraca shakers in Cugat's band. Non-Mexican accents abound, however, Iturbi (Spanish), Massey (Hungarian), Roddy McDowall (English), Pidgeon (Canadian) and Powell (American). The Technicolor film itself speaks in MGM's expensive accents. It is lavish, intensely musical and occasionally funny," *Life* (9/9/46).

Hombre (1967 Twentieth Century Fox)

D: Martin Ritt
S: Irving Ravetch and Harriet Frank, Jr., based on the novel by
   Elmore Leonard
P: Martin Ritt and Irving Ravetch
Cast: Paul Newman, Diane Cilento, Fredric March, Richard Boone,
   Frank Silvera, Martin Balsam

John Russell (Newman), a white man raised by Apache Indians, finds himself on a stagecoach journey when the coach is suddenly held up by outlaws. The very passengers who shunned him because of his Indian appearance soon find they need him to protect them from the bandits.

The ensuing interrelationships among passengers and outlaws make up the crux of this superbly acted adult Western featuring an all-star cast. James Wong Howe's harsh photography of the Arizona desert location adds to the stark feel of the story.

Silvera comes over strongly as a humorous but deadly Mexican outlaw.

Hour of the Gun (1967 United Artists)

D: John Sturges
S: Edward Anhalt
P: John Sturges
Cast: James Garner, Jason Robards, Jr., Robert Ryan, Jorge Russek

Opening with the 1880s shootout at the O.K. Corral in Tombstone, Arizona, the movie goes on to relate what happens to the surviving participants, centering on Wyatt Earp (Garner). Earp finally tracks down Ike Clanton (Ryan) in Mexico, where he has returned to cattle rustling. In a small village, Earp kills Clanton. Shot on locations throughout northern Mexico, including Torreón and San Miguel de Allende, the Arizona Territory of the 1880s was re-created by famed art director Alfred C. Ybarra. Mexican actor Jorge Russek plays Latigo, one of Clanton's henchmen.

House of the Spirits (1993 Miramax)

D: Bille August
S: Bille August, based on the novel by Isabel Allende
P: Bernd Eichinger, Edwin Leicht, Dieter Meyer, Mark Rosenberg, Paula Weinstein
Cast: Meryl Streep, Jeremy Irons, Glenn Close, Winona Ryder, Antonio Banderas, Vanessa Redgrave, Maria Conchita Alonso, Miriam Colon

Filmed in Portugal and Denmark, this multi-generational saga follows the fortunes of the powerful Trueba family, and is set in South America just prior to World War II. Ambitious Esteban (Irons) marries the clair-voyant Clara (Streep), exploits the peasants on his property and becomes a conservative senator. Their rebellious daughter, Blanca (Ryder), falls for the rabble-rousing peasant, Pedro (Banderas), as the country undergoes a bloody revolution. The magical realism of the novel by Allende is lost in the soap-opera-style histrionics. Anglos play upper class Latinos and Latinos play the over-sexed lower class characters.

Human Cargo (1936 Twentieth Century Fox)

D: Allan Dwan
S: Jefferson Parker and Doris Malloy, based on the novel *I Will Be Faithful* by Kathleen Shepard
P: Sol M. Wurtzel
Cast: Brian Donlevy, Claire Trevor, Rita Cansino [Hayworth]

A melodrama about rival newspaper reporters (Donlevy and Trevor) exposing a smuggling ring that transports illegal aliens into the United States from Canada and then blackmails them. The film also highlights Rita Cansino (soon to become Rita Hayworth) as Carmen, a Mexican dancer who is blackmailed by the smugglers and eventually killed.

I Like It Like That (1994 Columbia)

D: Darnell Martin
S: Darnell Martin
P: Ann Carli and Lane Janger
Cast: Lauren Velez, Jon Seda, Rita Moreno, Jesse Borrego, Lisa Vidal

A romantic comedy and drama about a young Puerto Rican couple try-ing to raise their children, set against the vibrant, colorful and passion-ate street life of the Bronx. Chino (Seda) is a hardworking and devoted father, yet he can barely support his family on his salary as a bicycle

Lauren Velez and Jon Seda
star in *I Like It Like That*,
a story set in the Bronx
about love, family and a
young woman's coming
of age.

messenger. When his wife, Lisette (Velez), threatens to get a job so she can buy a new stereo, Chino impulsively joins in some neighborhood looting during a blackout so he can bring home the stereo she wants so much. However, he gets caught and is thrown in jail. From his cell, Chino orders Lisette to take the last of the cash and play the numbers in order to make bail, but Lisette resists. Instead of gambling with the money, she decides to find a job and take charge of her life. She takes the last of the family's cash and uses it for subway fare downtown to look for work. Through a series of misadventures, she actually manages to get hired as an assistant to an executive at a Latino record label. All well and good, but even as Lisette struggles to earn the money to free her husband and make a place for herself in the larger world, she finds that the reaction at home is not always what she expected.

Excellent natural performances from the cast and spirited fresh direction from Darnell Martin, who utilized the New York inner city locations to best results to enhance her story.

Dolores Del Rio as the Spanish dancer Rita Gomez in *In Caliente*.

In Caliente (1935 Warner Bros.)

D: Lloyd Bacon
S: Jerry Wald and Julius Epstein, based on the story "Caliente" by Ralph Black and Warren Duff
P: First National
Cast: Dolores Del Rio, Pat O'Brien, Leo Carrillo

Larry MacArthur (O'Brien) is a magazine editor whose review infuriates "La Espanita," a Spanish dancer named Rita Gomez (Del Rio).When he is sent on assignment to Agua Caliente, he falls in love with the dancer whose performance he had so unmercifully panned. In the process of exacting her revenge, Rita falls in love with him.

This lightweight musical comedy is a commercial endorsement for the popular-with-the-Hollywood-crowd Mexican resort and casino across the border from San Diego. Del Rio looked ravishing in her gowns and dresses. Carrillo lent solid support, while Soledad Jimenez played a maid, Martin Garralaga, a waiter; and Chris-Pin Martin, the leader of a Mexican quartet. Judy Canova had a bit as a Mexican hillbilly, and the film also showcased the Sally and Tony Marco dance team. Busby Berkeley arranged the dance numbers.

In Old Arizona

See "Zorro & the Cisco Kid" listings.

Incendiary Blonde (1945 Paramount)

D: George Marshall
S: Claude Binyon and Frank Butler
P: Joseph Sistroms
Cast: Betty Hutton, Arturo De Cordova

Based on the life of Texas Guinan (Hutton), a famous nightclub entertainer of the 1920s. Texas is the star of a rodeo show who falls in love with an Irish Mexican, Bill Romero Kilgannon (De Cordova), who is the married owner of the show. He becomes the love of her life, and their lives become entwined again years later when she finds stardom on Broadway and in Hollywood and he becomes a gangster. American audiences and theater owners objected to Kilgannon's character being changed to an Irish Mexican in order to accommodate the actor playing the role, De Cordova. The actual Kilgannon character was Irish, and notwithstanding the Good Neighbor Policy, it was considered objectionable to have a Mexican making on-screen love to an Anglo woman, particularly in the state of Texas.

The In-Laws (1979 Warner Bros.)

D: Arthur Hiller
S: Andrew Bergman
P: Arthur Hiller and William Sackheim
Cast: Alan Arkin, Peter Falk, Richard Libertini

The daughter of a New York Jewish dentist is about to marry the son of a man who claims to be in the CIA. The two prospective fathers-in-law (Arkin and Falk) meet. The CIA man gets the dentist involved in a series of incredible misadventures that send them on a bullet-riddled chase from Manhattan to a South American banana republic. Richard Libertini is General Garcia, the nutty dictator of the fictional capital Tijada. Upon their arrival the fathers-in-low are welcomed by one of Tijada's leading statesmen, who is gunned down as he steps across the tarmac to greet them. Thus, this unpredictable and otherwise enjoyable comedy is marred by stereotyped Latin images. The Latin scenes were filmed in Cuernavaca, Mexico.

Internal Affairs (1990 Paramount)

D: Mike Figgis
S: Henry Bean
P: Frank Mancuso, Jr.
Cast: Richard Gere, Andy Garcia, Nancy Travis, Laurie Metcalf

Raymond Avila (Garcia) is a detective who has been promoted to the Internal Affairs Division of the Los Angeles County Police. While researching a misconduct case, Avila becomes convinced that a respected street cop named Dennis Peck (Gere, playing well against type) is involved in a complicated web of criminal activities. When Avila begins to investigate him, Peck retaliates by drawing Avila's wife, Kathleen (Travis), into what becomes an intense psychological struggle between the two men.

This is a landmark film in that it shows a Hispanic American leading character, Avila (as played by the Cuban American Garcia), in a perceptive, complex portrayal, free from stereotypes, as an integral part of American society. In the role of a law enforcement officer, Garcia offered a positive role model, and the role proved to be a major step in his own rise to stardom. The film also features one of Richard Gere's best performances to date.

Jack (1996 Buena Vista)

D: Francis Ford Coppola
S: James DeMonaco and Gary Nadeau
P: Fred Fuch & Ricardo Mestres, Francis Ford Coppola
Cast: Robin Williams, Jennifer Lopez

Jack Powell (Williams) is a ten-year-old boy in contemporary Northern California born with a condition that makes him grow and age at four times the normal rate. He looks middle-aged when his protective parents decide to allow him to attend public grade school. The comedy comes from Jack's encounters with his fifth grade class. Jennifer Lopez plays his teacher, Ms. Marquez, in this sweet and delicate tale about life.

Jivaro (1954 Paramount)

D: Edward Ludwig

S: Winston Miller, based on a story by David Duncan

P: William H. Pine and William C. Thomas

Cast: Fernando Lamas, Rita Moreno, Pascual Garcia Peña, Nestor Paiva

Lamas is well cast as a rugged trader and Amazon riverboat captain who goes in search of lost missionaries and treasure seekers in the treacherous Jivaro Indian country. Pascual Peña plays Lamas' Indian assistant, and Rita Moreno plays a native girl.

In a scene from *Joe Kidd*, Rita Sanchez (Stella Garcia) is disillusioned to discover that Luis Chama (John Saxon) refuses to disarm his men and return to a small town to face a prejudiced judge.

Joe Kidd (1972 Universal)

D: John Sturges

S: Elmore Leonard

P: Sidney Beckerman

Cast: Clint Eastwood, Robert Duvall,
    John Saxon, Stella Garcia, Joaquin Martinez

In New Mexico at the turn of the century, a loner, Joe Kidd (Eastwood), is hired by an American landowner, Harlan (Duvall), to lead a party of gunmen against rebel Luis Chama (Saxon), a Mexican American trying to save the original Spanish land grants handed to his people. The loner soon changes sides and joins Chama's forces in a climactic gun battle, in which the Mexicans eventually win. Kidd forces Chama to surrender and face a fair trial, leaving his fate in the hands of the Anglos. Pepe Hern has a supporting role as a priest.

"It forthrightly depicts injustices to Mexican-Americans, which strikes a note of contemporary awareness without seeming to strain for it," Kevin Thomas, *Los Angeles Times* (7/19/72).

Juarez (1939 Warner Bros.)

D: William Dieterle

S: Aeneas MacKenzie, Wolfgang Reinhardt,
    and John Huston, based on the novel
    The Phantom Crown by Bertita Harding
    and the play *Juarez & Maximilian* by
    Franz Werfel

P: Hal B. Wallis and Henry Blanke

Cast: Paul Muni, Bette Davis, Brian Aherne,
    John Garfield, Claude Rains, Gilbert Roland,
    Joseph Calleia, Pedro de Cordoba, Martin
    Garralaga, Manny Diaz

In the fall of 1937, Jack L. Warner and Hal B. Wallis began an intensive search for popular actor Paul Muni's next starring vehicle. Writer Wolfgang Reinhardt suggested that Wallis consider the story of

Hundreds of Mexican American extras listen to the "Mexican Abraham Lincoln" (played by Paul Muni) in *Juarez*.

Mexico's legendary liberal president, Benito Pablo Juarez. Reinhardt felt that Juarez's struggle against the Habsburg monarchy backed by French emperor Napoleon III would make exciting and topical screen fare. Muni liked the idea and agreed to do the film. He felt that the parallel world situation at the time (the recently ended Spanish Civil War and impending World War II) would make the film timely and hoped that the film might influence people against dictatorships no matter how benevolent. The studio research department assembled as complete a bibliography as possible on Juarez and the abortive reign of Maximilian and Carlotta.

Considered one of Hollywood's best Latin American films of the period, *Juarez* is a reverential treatment of its subject. In reality, however, it was two films in one—the story of Juarez and the story of Maximilian and Carlotta von Habsburg. The film ultimately suffered from this duality. Performances were good all around, except for John Garfield as

Porfirio Diaz, whose New York accent kept getting in the way. Muni as Juarez was an incredible re-creation of the man as drawn from books and pictures. Considered the Mexican Abraham Lincoln, Juarez reportedly admired Lincoln, who was then President of the United States and in the midst of his country's Civil War.

The film was popular everywhere except Mexico. When Juarez went into production, it was reported that the technical adviser pointed out that the Porfirio Diaz character was historically incorrect. His advice was ignored. In the eyes of Mexicans, Hollywood was doing something as wrong as placing Abraham Lincoln at the Battle of Bunker Hill.

The film went into production in September 1938 with a budget of $1,750,000 and a cast of 1,186. Art director Anton Grot and his assistant Leo Kuder drew 3,643 sketches of sets, from which the construction department built 54, the largest being an 11-acre re-creation of Mexico at the Warner Ranch in Calabasas, California.

Muni, along with Wallis and director William Dieterle, went on a six-week tour of Mexico prior to filming. They delved into every possible area of Juarez's life and times, steeping themselves in the atmosphere of the country. Muni wanted to know how Juarez looked, walked and talked and wanted to learn any mannerisms that were particularly noticeable. Returning to the studio, they went through a series of makeup tests with different rubber masks in an attempt to make Muni resemble Juarez. It was agreed that it would be most believable to let Muni play with a minimum of structural change. Perc Westmore, head of Warner's makeup department, accentuated Muni's bone structure, made his jaws appear wider, squared his forehead and gave him an Indian nose. He had to be darker than anyone else in the picture, since the film was in black-and-white, so they used a dark reddish-brown makeup highlighted by yellow. More than 3,500 extras were used in total during the eighty days of actual production. Roland plays Colonel Lopez, Calleia plays Urad, de Cordoba plays Palacio and Diaz plays Pepe.

Just the Ticket (1999 Metro-Goldwyn-Mayer)
D: Richard Wenk
S: Richard Wenk
P: Andy Garcia
Cast: Andy Garcia, Andie MacDowell

Longtime New York con man Gary (Garcia) is the king of hustle, a god among scam artists and a loser in life. The only thing he has going for him is his girlfriend Linda (MacDowell), a stunning chef-in-the-making with a soft spot for underdogs. Accepted into a Parisian cooking school, Linda decides it is time to leave Gary because she sees no future with a career ticket scalper. Seeking advice from a man of the cloth, Gary is told—for a couple of Knick's tickets—to trust in God. Just as he is about to give up on the face value of faith, he learns that the Pope is to visit Yankee Stadium. Gary sees this as his sign to score big, get off the street and win Linda's heart. But a competitive rival has beaten Gary to the punch, buying all the tickets in order to muscle him out. Now Gary must hustle like never before to nab some Papal tickets before he loses

Linda and remains a hustler forever. Filmed on location in New York and with a soundtrack that utilizes music by Cuban musician and composer Israel "Cachao" Lopez.

Key Witness (1960 Metro-Goldwyn-Mayer)

D: Phil Karlson
S: Alfred Brenner and Sidney Michaels, based on the novel by
   Frank Kane
P: Kathryn Hereford
Cast: Jeffrey Hunter, Pat Crowley, Dennis Hopper, Corey Allen,
   Frank Silvera

A suburbanite, Fred Morrow (Hunter), stops in an East Los Angeles bar to make a phone call. He witnesses a brutal stabbing and discovers that none of the other witnesses are willing to testify. Regardless of the consequences, Morrow decides to appear in court, but it is not long before he regrets his decision. The alleged assailant, "Cowboy" (Hopper), and his gang begin to terrorize Morrow and his family.

Silvera plays Mexican American Detective Rafael Torno. The highlight of the film is a night chase on foot in which Torno corners "Cowboy" on a freeway.

This film presents gang life superficially, in a way typical of the 1950s juvenile delinquent movies, with switchblades, sports cars, dope and sex. The gang members are multiethnic.

The Kid from Spain (1932 United Artists)

D: Leo McCarey
S: William Anthony McGuire, Bert Kalmar, and Harry Ruby
P: Samuel Goldwyn
Cast: Eddie Cantor, Lyda Roberti, Robert Young, J. Carroll Naish,
   Paul Porcasi, Julian Rivero

Eddie (Cantor) and his Mexican pal Ricardo (Young) are expelled from college. They inadvertently get mixed up in a stateside bank robbery, which forces Eddie to go South of the border as an innocent fugitive from American law. He impersonates Don Sebastian II, son of a famous bullfighting family, and complications arise.

The movie is a dated musical comedy based on the true story of Sydney Franklin, a pop-eyed Jewish boy from Brooklyn who became one of the world's greatest bullfighters. Many funny scenes include a bullfight in which Eddie is chased all over the arena. Francisco "Chico" Day, later a famed assistant director, worked on the film as an interpreter for the Mexican bullfighter brought from Mexico City to double Cantor. Frank Leyva handled all the Mexican extras during shooting in Hollywood.

Actor Robert Young, who plays Ricardo, later found greater fame on television, starring in the 1950s in the long-running *Father Knows Best* series and in the 1970s in the *Marcus Welby, M.D.* series.

Why it is called *The Kid from Spain* when the story takes place in Mexico is anyone's guess.

Kings of the Sun (1963 United Artists)

D: J. Lee Thompson
S: Elliott Arnold and James R. Webb, based on a story by Arnold
P: Lewis J. Rachmil
Cast: Yul Brynner, George Chakiris, Richard Basehart,
     Shirley Anne Field, Armando Silvestre

This film offers a superficial treatment of the potentially fascinating subject of the ancient Mayan civilization at a point of crisis.

Fierce warriors from the north menace ancient Mayan tribes of Mexico. Invaders kill the Mayan king, and his young son, Balam (Chakiris), becomes the new Mayan ruler. The Mayans are forced to flee to the coast, where they commandeer boats owned by fishermen and sail to what is now North America, where they settle and start to build a new civilization. Black Eagle (Brynner), chief of a local tribe of Indians who resent the "invasion," decides to attack these people, but the Mayans capture him. Balam spares Black Eagle's life, and they decide to live in harmony. When the Mayan high priest (Basehart) attempts to prepare Black Eagle as a sacrifice to the Mayan gods, Balam refuses, and the high priest sacrifices himself. Later, another group of Indians attack the Mayans and Black Eagle is killed.

Brynner is excellent as the Indian chief, but Chakiris, Field, Basehart and Leo V. Gordon as Mayans stretch credibility, especially when you put them alongside authentic Mexican Indian extras. The only Mexican with a major role was actor Armando Silvestre, who plays a heavy.

Art director Alfred Ybarra and his assistant, Lynn Sparhawk, along with construction coordinator Bill Maldonado designed and built Mayan cities, fishing villages, Mayan homes and other sets, including pyramids and ruins of the Mayan civilization.

Several major outdoor locations were used for the filming. Shooting began in Chichén Itza in Yucatan, where the ruins of the pyramids still stand. The Mexican government gave special permission to the film company to shoot among the actual pyramids and ruins. The company later moved to Mazatlan. All interior sequences were filmed on soundstages at Churubusco Studios in Mexico City. One hundred fifty Mexican film technicians and a total of 5,000 Mexican extras were employed during the filming.

Kinjite: Forbidden Subjects (1989 Cannon)

D: J. Lee Thompson
S: Harold Nebenzal
P: Pancho Kohner
Cast: Charles Bronson, Perry Lopez, Juan Fernandez

Veteran Los Angeles cop Crowe (Bronson) and his partner Rios (Lopez) attempt to catch a sinister pimp (Fernandez) who has kidnapped the daughter of a Los Angeles-based Japanese businessman in this violent police drama.

Kiss Me a Killer (1990 Concorde)

D: Marcus De Leon
S: Marcus De Leon
P: Catherine Ryan
Cast: Robert Beltran, Julie Carmen

A young Latina woman (Carmen), married to an Anglo nightclub owner, finds passion and freedom with a mysterious and handsome young musician (Beltran) who comes to work at the club. They soon plot to kill her husband and become entangled in a web of murder and deceit. The film marked a promising beginning for writer and director De Leon. Beltran and Carmen exude the appropriate sexual steam in this low-budget barrio version of *The Postman Always Rings Twice*.

Kiss of Fire (1955 Universal)

D: Joseph M. Newman
S: Franklin Coen and Richard Collins
P: Samuel Marx
Cast: Jack Palance, Barbara Rush, Rex Reason, Martha Hyer

This film is an uneven mixture of period swashbuckler and Western. A Spanish nobleman known as El Tigre (Palance) is engaged to lead a royal party from Santa Fe, New Mexico, to Monterey, California. A ship awaits to take the heir apparent to the Spanish throne, Princess Lucia (Rush), to Spain when it is learned that Charles V is on his deathbed. Spanish hirelings and Indians try to stop the party before they reach their destination, and the princess finds true love with El Tigre and renounces the throne. Jack Palance is miscast in a role better suited to Errol Flynn or Cornel Wilde. Soundstage night exteriors clash with outdoor exteriors, and water is never a problem for these people theoretically crossing desert landscapes.

Kiss of the Spider Woman (1985 Island)

D: Hector Babenco
S: Leonard Schrader, based on the novel by Manuel Puig
P: David Weisman
Cast: William Hurt, Raul Julia, Sonia Braga

The film is described by director Hector Babenco in the *Los Angeles Times* (11/23/83) as "a story about . . . the slowly growing friendship between two men of totally different emotional, cultural and social backgrounds. The South American prison cell they share is the boxing ring where they resolve their conflicts before arriving at a stage of mutual affection."

This was the first Brazilian-made film to star American actors. The film stars Hurt as Molina, a homosexual convicted on morals charges, and Julia as Valentin, a highly disciplined and intellectual political prisoner. Molina lives in a fantasy world of glamour movies and romantic screen heroes and heroines that at first disgusts Valentin, then later hypnotizes him.

Director Hector Babenco (center) helps William Hurt (left) and Raul Julia (right) prepare a scene from *Kiss of the Spider Woman*.

Little by little the two men form a bond of friendship and love. The two actors dominate the film, but Brazilian actress Braga is notable in not one but three roles. She is the captivating Spider Woman of the title and a French chanteuse, both of whom are part of Molina's fantasy, as well as Valentin's girlfriend.

Kiss of the Spider Woman was a tremendous worldwide success and reaped enormous box office and critical raves in the United States. William Hurt won the Academy Award® as Best Actor.

"*The Kiss of the Spider Woman* succeeds on a deep emotional level and as spellbinding entertainment as well," Sheila Benson, *Los Angeles Times* (8/23/85).

"[There aren't] sufficient clues in the previous film careers of the director, Hector Babenco (the highly praised *Pixote*) and the two stars, William Hurt and Raul Julia, to anticipate the stature of the work they do here. *Kiss of the Spider Woman* is a brilliant achievement for all of them, staged with the perfect control and fierce originality that makes it one of the best films in a long time," Janet Maslin, *New York Times* (7/26/85).

"Filmed in Brazil (in English), directed by the Argentine born Hector Babenco from a script by the American Leonard Schrader and a novel by Argentine Manuel Puig . . . This time the artistic melting pot bubbled to perfection," Richard Schickel, *Time* (8/5/85).

The Kissing Bandit (1948 Metro-Goldwyn-Mayer)

D: Laslo Benedek
S: Isabel Lennart and John Briard Harding
P: Joe Pasternak
Cast: Frank Sinatra, Kathryn Grayson, J. Carroll Naish, Vicente Gomez, Alberto Morin, Julian Rivero, Ricardo Montalban, José Dominguez

This movie chronicles the efforts of Ricardo (Sinatra), just returned to California from learning the hotel trade in Boston, to step into his father's romantic boots. Before he was killed, dad was known as "The Kissing Bandit" because he kissed every female he held up. A specialty dance number directed by Stanley Donen called the "Dance of Fury" featured Ricardo Montalban, Cyd Charisse and Ann Miller. Vicente Gomez played Mexican guitar tunes. This muddled spoof of Zorro, adventure and musical comedy plots is not helped by uneven direction.

La Bamba (1987 Columbia)

D: Luis Valdez
S: Luis Valdez
P: Taylor Hackford and Bill Borden
AP: Daniel Valdez
Cast: Lou Diamond Phillips, Esai Morales, Rosana De Soto,
    Elizabeth Peña, Daniel Valdez

La Bamba was the brainchild of Daniel Valdez, the brother of writer/director Luis Valdez, who had wanted to make a musical biography of the late Chicano rock 'n' roll star Ritchie Valens for over ten years. With the success of the theatrical musical *Zoot Suit* and with a film version of it being readied at Universal, Valdez approached Universal Studios in 1981 but found no interest. The studio felt that *The Buddy Holly Story* (1978) had gone over similar ground and had not been enough of a box office success, though it did win critical acclaim and an Oscar® nomination for its star, Gary Busey.

Ritchie Valens, whose real name was Ricardo Valenzuela, was born and raised in Pacoima, California, in the San Fernando Valley. His meteoric rise as a rock 'n' roll star lasted only eight months. He recorded three hit records before his death at the age of seventeen in the same 1959 plane crash that also killed Buddy Holly and disc jockey J.P. Richardson (known as The Big Bopper). Valens had been overshadowed by Holly, and his life was shrouded in mystery. "I went and tried to research this guy and couldn't get anything, zero. I only had a hint he was Latin," recalls Valdez in press notes for the movie's release.

Undaunted, Daniel tracked down the Valens family and convinced them of his artistic intentions. He secured a five-year option on the Valens story and began to search for avenues of production. Meanwhile, he enlisted the aid of his brother Luis, who wrote a screenplay. The project was brought to Taylor Hackford, the writer and director of such hit films as *The Idolmaker* (1980), *An Officer and a Gentleman* (1982) and *Against All Odds* (1984). The Valdez brothers had followed Hackford's career since his early documentary work at PBS television station KCET in Los Angeles.

Hackford had started a production company called New Visions that was to produce modest-budget features, and *La Bamba*, as the Ritchie Valens script was now called, was put into development. The film went into production in the summer of 1986 with Luis Valdez as writer and director, and Daniel as associate producer. It was filmed on location in and around Los Angeles on a $6.5 million budget with a 45-day shooting schedule. The opening farm worker labor camp scenes were filmed near Hollister, California.

An intense talent search was launched to find the right young actor to play Ritchie Valens. When casting director June Lowry returned from a search of Texas and the Southwest, she thought she had found the ideal actor to play Ritchie's brother Bob. Lou Diamond Phillips was flown to California, but the more he auditioned with other actors, the clearer it became that they had found the man for the starring role instead. Phillips recalls in press notes, "I was a nobody from Texas. The

Luis Valdez directs Lou Diamond Phillips in his starring role as Ritchie Valens in *La Bamba*.

entire time I was auditioning, I thought I would walk away with a good attitude and my head held high, and even though I wouldn't get the role it would pay off down the line. I just couldn't comprehend that I was to land this one."

A reverse situation occurred when it came time to cast the role of Ritchie's brother Bob. Morales, who was initially considered for Ritchie, was quickly found to be the right actor to play Bob. "Bob was the dark side of Ritchie," says Morales in press notes. "He didn't know how to fight his own feelings of resentment toward his brother's success."

The final script had at its core the turbulent relationship between Ritchie and his brother Bob during Ritchie's eight-month rise to stardom. Luis recalls in press notes, "In writing the screenplay I stayed close to a reality I know . . . capturing . . . certain images that . . . were a part of Valens' life as much as they were a part of mine." He continued, "We all understand love/hate relationships between two brothers and the difficulties of a single mother trying to raise her children."

La Bamba became a smash success during the summer of 1987, earning $60 million and favorable critical response. Valens' hit song was re-recorded for the movie by the popular Mexican American group Los Lobos, who made the song "La Bamba" an even greater hit for Valens in death than it ever was when he was alive.

Valdez remarked on his work, "I like to think that there's a core that's constant . . . I'm not just a Mexican farm worker. I'm an American with roots in Mayan culture. I can resonate and unlock some of the mysteries of this land which reside in all of us."

La Cucaracha (1934 RKO Radio Pictures)
D: Lloyd Corrigan
S: Jack Wagner and John Twist
P: Kenneth MacGowan
Cast: Don Alvarado, Steffi Duna, Paul Porcasi

In 1934, Mexico and Mexicans were the subject of this film, the first live-action short film made in the three-strip Technicolor process. The 20-minute short showcased dancers and extras in a cantina alive with music and colors swirling to the song "La Cucaracha."

RKO brought to Hollywood Robert Edmond Jones, the famous stage designer, whose use of color lighting had revolutionized Broadway in the 1920s. Jones felt that color, used properly, could affect the emotional and psychological content of a film, and in *La Cucaracha*, he utilized all manner of stylized devices to heighten the dramatic and comedic aspects of the story.

The storyline revolves around a cantina girl, played by Steffi Duna, and her problems with her dancer lover, played by Alvarado. Porcasi plays a Mexico City impresario.

The jealousy, the quarreling, and the comedy are skillfully blended in this truly colorful romantic fantasy of Mexico and Mexicans.

The film was an immediate success with critics and the public, receiving more attention than most of the features it played with. It won an Academy Award® for Best Comedy Short in 1934.

Lambada (1989 Warner Bros.)
D: Joel Silberg
S: Sheldon Renan and Joel Silberg
P: Peter Shepard
Cast: J. Eddie Peck, Melora Hardin, Adolfo "Shabba Doo" Quinones

An East Los Angeles teacher spends his days motivating students and his nights at a nightclub where he engages in lambada dancing.

Lambada—The Forbidden Dance (1990 Columbia)
D: Greydon Clark
S: Albert Goldman
P: Marc Fisher
Cast: Laura Martinez Herring

A quickly produced youth-oriented movie designed to take advantage of the short-lived Brazilian lambada dance craze that began in Europe and found temporary favor with Hispanic populations in the United States. The film starred Laura Martinez Herring, a former Miss USA. The plot, such as it was, concerned a young Brazilian Indian girl sent by her tribe to the United States to try to save the Amazon rain forest. The film distorted the fact that lambada had its origins among the Afro-Carribean people of Brazil and not among the Indians—another case of Hollywood misrepresenting a Latin American culture and its people through convenient filmic conventions and dramatic license.

The Lash (1931 Warner Bros.)

D: Frank Lloyd
S: Bradley King, based on the story "Adios" by Lanier Bartlett
P: Warner Bros.
Cast: Richard Barthelmess, James Rennie, Mary Astor

A young Spanish nobleman, Don Francisco Delfina (Barthelmess), in 1848 Baja California, is duped out of his cattle by a swindling American land commissioner and becomes a desperado, assuming the sobriquet of "El Puma." He fights the Americanos, who are cheating and stealing to obtain Spanish/Mexican lands through crooked land commissioners. In the end, "El Puma" disbands his followers and crosses the border into Mexico, where he makes his new home. This is another variation on the Robin Hood, Zorro and Joaquin Murieta legends in which, for once, the Americanos are not placed in a very good light. This is an average Western highlighted by panoramic scenery and good action sequences.

The Last Command (1955 Republic Pictures)

D: Frank Lloyd
S: Warren Duff
P: Herbert J. Yates
Cast: Sterling Hayden, Anna Maria Alberghetti, Richard Carlson,
    Arthur Hunnicutt, Ernest Borgnine, J. Carroll Naish

Jim Bowie (Hayden) is a personal friend of Santa Anna (Naish) until the latter's despotic actions lead Bowie to the siege of the Alamo. Bowie is torn between his love of Mexico and his United States citizenry during the fight for Texas independence. Italian singer Anna Maria Alberghetti portrays Consuela, the daughter of a Spanish born Texas landowner.

Naish depicts General Santa Anna as a three-dimensional character who insists on calling Bowie "Jimmy." The film is slow to build to its climax but is interesting in its characterizations and point of view.

The Last Command, like *The Alamo* (1960), utilizes the racial imagery of the Anglo versus the Mexican less than prior films made on the subject. World War II and the Good Neighbor Policy kept blatant negative stereotypes of Latin Americans in check for a while.

Filmed on location in Texas and at Republic Studios in Hollywood, the film includes many Hispanic actors in featured roles, including Vincent Padula, Argentina Brunetti, Alex Montoya, Pepe Hern, Rico Alaniz, George Novarro, Fernando Alvarado, Abel Fernandez, Tom Hernandez and Alberto Morin.

The Last of the Fast Guns (1958 Universal)

D: George Sherman
S: David P. Harmon
P: Howard Christie
Cast: Jock Mahoney, Gilbert Roland, Linda Cristal, Lorne Greene,
Carl Benton Reid

An average oater gorgeously photographed in Cuernavaca, Mexico, made by Hollywood and Mexico's top craftsmen.

In the 1880s, gunfighter Brad Ellison (played by former stuntman Jock Mahoney) accepts an offer from wealthy John Forbes (Reid) to locate his brother, who disappeared into Mexico thirty years before. In the course of his search, Ellison learns that the brother is now a well-respected local priest.

Nineteen of the twenty-eight speaking roles went to Mexican actors and actresses. Argentina-born actress Cristal made her American film debut and was signed by Universal to an exclusive long-term contract. Many of Mexico's finest English-speaking actors were recruited to play supporting roles. Prominent among them were Eduardo Noriega, who also played featured roles in such American productions as *Serenade* (1956), *The Beast of Hollow Mountain* (1956) and *The Sun Also Rises* (1957); roly-poly George Trevino, who is known to television fans as Desi Arnaz's comical Cuban uncle in the *I Love Lucy* series; Francisco Reyguera, a film veteran whose career dates back to Mack Sennett comedies; and pretty Gilda Fontana, an American actress who transferred her career from Hollywood to Mexico. Roland, a veteran actor since silent films, plays a double-dealing ranch foreman.

Last Plane Out (1983 Shapiro-Glickenhaus)

D: David Nelson
S: Ernest Tidyman
P: Jack Cox and David Nelson
Cast: Jan-Michael Vincent, Julie Carmen, Mary Crosby, Lloyd Batista

A routine and uninspired treatment of an American journalist in Nicaragua during the end of the Somoza regime. This film is filled with negative stereotypes—from cute kids who run a taxi service in a war-torn country to a rebel leader Nicaraguan woman, Maria Cardena (Carmen), who falls for the journalist. Similar material has been handled better in films like *Under Fire* (1983) and *Salvador* (1986).

Based on the real-life experiences of conservative journalist Jack Cox (played by Vincent), the movie is politically slanted to the right. Cox gets to talk to both Somoza and the rebels, and the rebels put a price on Cox's head because of his pro-Somoza government pieces and alleged connection to the CIA. As the Sandinistas close in on the capital, Cox and his television crew find themselves struggling to reach the airport to catch the last plane out before the rebels succeed in killing them. The movie was filmed in southern Florida.

Last Rites (1988 Metro-Goldwyn-Mayer/United Artists)
D: Don P. Bellisario
S: Don P. Bellisario
P: Don P. Bellisario and Patrick McCormick
Cast: Tom Berenger, Daphne Zuniga

A Mexican woman named Angela (Zuniga) witnesses the murder of a mobster in an elegant New York hotel. She escapes, and eventually comes under the protection of a streetwise New York priest, Father Michael Pace (Berenger). His task of protecting her is complicated by their erotic attraction to each other and the fact that the murderer is Father Pace's sister and the victim is his brother-in-law. He finally takes her to Mexico to rid her of her pursuers.

The Last Train from Madrid (1937 Paramount)
D: James Hogan
S: Louis Stevens and Robert Wyler, based on a story by
   Paul Harvey Fox and Elsie Fox
P: George M. Arthur
Cast: Dorothy Lamour, Lew Ayres, Gilbert Roland, Anthony Quinn

It was inevitable that Hollywood would seize upon the powerful drama of the Spanish Civil War. However, *The Last Train from Madrid*, like *For Whom the Bell Tolls* (1943), is devoid of any political stance and becomes instead a simple Grand Hotel-type of melodrama in which the lives of different people intersect when they all try to leave on the last train from Madrid to Valencia.

The film marked the first major role for Quinn and his only teaming with Roland, of whom he said at the time he was "in awe." Lamour, who made her screen debut in the title role in *The Jungle Princess* (1936), was cast in her first serious dramatic role. Her exotic beauty and charm led to her playing Latinas several times in her long career. She had previously worked with Quinn in *Swing High, Swing Low* (1937), in which he played a Panamanian, with all his dialogue spoken in Spanish.

It is the story of ten people thrown together for twelve feverish hours. The movie goes from the time it is announced that a train will leave the war-stricken Spanish capital to the hour when the train steams out for Valencia and safety. During those hours the passengers live a lifetime of emotions, bringing out the best and worst in them. Quinn is Captain Ricardo Alvarez, an army officer who manages to get passes for his sweetheart Carmelita Castillo (Lamour) and his pal Eduardo (Roland). The cast also includes Lew Ayres as Bill Dexter, an American reporter who finds the love he has been seeking in the flaming city; Olympia Bradno as Maria, a member of the Spanish women's battalion; Karen Morley as an adventuress; and Frank Leyva.

It was filmed at Paramount Studios in Hollywood with the use of hundreds of Latin-looking extras. Francisco "Chico" Day worked as a second assistant director on this, his first film in that capacity.

Latin Lovers (1953 Metro-Goldwyn-Mayer)

D: Mervyn LeRoy
S: Isabel Lennart
P: Joe Pasternak
Cast: Ricardo Montalban, Lana Turner, Joaquin Garay, Rita Moreno

An embarrassing musical featuring a suave Montalban as a Latin Lover in Rio de Janeiro involved with a rich American (Turner) who wants to live it up. Montalban dances with Moreno in one scene.

Latino (1985 Cinecom)

D: Haskell Wexler
S: Haskell Wexler
P: Benjamin Berg
Cast: Robert Beltran, Tony Plana, Annette Cardona

Sixteen years after he made *Medium Cool* (1969), a "faction" about the violent 1968 Democratic National Convention in Chicago, Haskell Wexler returned as a feature film director with *Latino*, an overtly left-wing melodrama about the United States-backed Contras fighting the Sandinista government in Nicaragua.

Eddie Guerrero (Beltran), a Chicano Green Beret from East Los Angeles, is sent by the United States Army to Honduras to train CIA-sponsored Contra counterrevolutionaries. Through Eddie's eyes, Wexler tells the story of one man's awakening to the quagmire of self-destruction that can develop when a soldier believes in "my country right or wrong" without questioning the morality of his actions.

Eddie falls in love with a Nicaraguan woman (Cardana) living in Honduras, and is thus forced to face the ethical questions raised by his participation in the undeclared war his government is waging.

While naively idealizing the Sandinista movement in a way reminiscent of Sergei Eisenstein's early Soviet movies such as *The Battleship Potemkin* (1925), the film nevertheless raises thorny questions about covert American foreign policy, particularly in Latin America. It also brings up the cultural conflict of a Chicano soldier's struggle with self-identity when he is ordered to fight people who look like him, speak Spanish like him and eat tortillas just like his mother makes back home.

Latino was filmed on a budget of $4 million on location in Honduras in February 1984. Lucas Films provided post-production facilities. The film had an extremely limited release in the States because it could not find a major distributor.

"There's a potency and fiber about *Latino* that you have to admire, [and] at its best it has moments of beauty, of power. But the simple minded pro-war action movie it wants to recall and deflate may have left too big a strain on its style," Michael Wilmington, *Los Angeles Times* (11/13/85).

"Although doubtlessly not intended as such, Latino comes off distressingly like a left wing [version of John Wayne's] *The Green Berets*," *Variety* (5/15/85).

Lalo Rios (left) portrays a young Latino falsely accused of attacking a policeman (Ian MacDonald) in *The Lawless*.

The Lawless (1950 Paramount)

D: Joseph Losey
S: Geoffrey Homes, based on his [Daniel Mainwaring's] book
P: William H. Pine and William C. Thomas
Cast: Macdonald Carey, Lalo Rios, Gail Russell, Argentina Brunetti, Felipe Turich, Pedro de Cordoba

In an agricultural northern California community with a sizable Mexican American population working as farm labor, a hysterical manhunt begins for a nineteen-year-old Latino (Rios) accused of attacking a policeman at a dance.

Frightened by his actions, the youth flees in an ice cream truck and steals a car at a roadside café before he is captured. A series of events leads to the young man being charged with crimes he did not commit, and the press, reflecting the sentiments of the Anglo townspeople, sensationalizes and distorts the facts even further. Only the editor of the local paper will stand up for the young Mexican, and as a result the angry farm workers turn on him. Though they wreck his publishing plant, he manages to save the youth from a lynching.

Russell plays Sunny Garcia, the youth's lawyer, and Brunetti and Turich play the boy's parents.

The film received generally good reviews and made a nice profit for Paramount and producers Pine and Thomas. It was filmed in eighteen days in Marysville and Grass Valley, California, and at Paramount Studios at a cost of $385,000.

In the October 1950 issue of *Holiday* magazine, William Pine said of the film, "I [just] couldn't get the right Mexican girl for the lead. So we got Gail Russell who isn't Mexican but . . . has dark hair and . . . knows how to work." (By this he meant that she was used to working at the fast pace of B pictures.) Director Losey discovered Rios working as a housepainter in Los Angeles.

"It is the first picture to be made about discrimination against Mexican-Americans," said screenwriter Homes, in a *New York Times* story (3/5/50). "I laid the story in the farm country north of Sacramento where a great number of migratory workers, at least a third of them Mexican or Mexican American, are employed during the various fruit harvests."

The Lawless was considered a B picture. The reviewers cited the film for its subject matter and Rios' performance. It was two years before Rios, who had never acted prior to making the movie, got another chance at a major role, in the King brothers' *The Ring* (1952). That both films deal with the issues of Mexican Americans, were filmed on low budgets, and share the same starring actor make them fine companion pieces. Along with such movies as *A Medal for Benny* (1945), they are among the American cinema's first statements on the condition of the Hispanic American in American society. The success of *Gentleman's Agreement* (1947), *Home of the Brave* (1949) and other films dealing with ethnic or racial prejudice in America made this film possible.

That Sunny Garcia was a Latina lawyer in a small town was a progressive step for the time and marks one of the first modern Chicana images on the screen.

The Left-Handed Gun (1958 Warner Bros.)

D: Arthur Penn
S: Leslie Stevens, based on the teleplay *The Death of Billy the Kid* by
    Gore Vidal
P: Fred Coe
Cast: Paul Newman, Lita Milan, John Dehner, Hurd Hatfield,
    Martin Garralaga, Nestor Paiva, Tina Menard

Memorable for Paul Newman's intense portrayal of the legendary Western outlaw Billy the Kid, the film interestingly combining elements of action and psychology.

Billy resembles a juvenile delinquent who has violent, uncontrollable rages in this story of an unbalanced youth whose lust for revenge is born of the killing of his benefactor, an English cattleman, during a range war. Running from the law, he takes sanctuary in a small Mexican town, where he meets and falls in love with a Mexican girl, Celsa, played by Lita Milan, an actress of Hungarian-Polish ancestry. When he returns home, he finds a second father figure in lawman Pat Garrett (Dehner), who is eventually forced to kill the Kid.

The movie was filmed on a low budget in black and white by Warner Bros. at its standing Mexican set (built for *Juarez* [1939]) at the Warner Ranch in Calabasas and the Janss Ranch near Thousand Oaks, California. It was the first film for famed director Arthur Penn (*Bonnie and Clyde* [1967]). Hispanic cast members in featured roles include Nestor Paiva, Martin Garralaga, Tina Menard and Frank Leyva.

The Leopard Man (1943 RKO Radio Pictures)
D: Jacques Tourneur
S: Ardei Wray and Edward Dein, based on the novel *Black Alibi* by Cornell Woolrich
P: Val Lewton
Cast: Dennis O'Keefe, Margo, Richard Martin, Eliso Gamboa, Joe Dominguez

New Mexico background for an uneven but interesting and ambitious mystery thriller shot entirely at RKO Studios. A New Mexico nightclub uses a tame leopard for a publicity stunt, which backfires when the leopard escapes and presumably kills a girl. Margo plays Clo-Clo, a Spanish dancer. The religious penitent parade at the end is as weird a procession as anything ever seen on film.

Let's Get Harry (1987 TriStar)
D: Alan Smithee [Stuart Rosenberg]
S: Charles Robert Carner, based on a story by Mark Feldberg and Samuel Fuller
P: Daniel H. Blatt and Robert Singer
Cast: Mark Harmon, Robert Duvall, Gary Busey, Elpidia Carrillo, Gregory Sierra

A group of small-town American blue-collar workers finds out that their best friend, Harry, a pipeline worker, has been kidnapped by terrorists and drug runners in South America and decides to do something about it.

They demand action from Washington and when thwarted by an uncaring bureaucracy, they hire a mercenary to lead them on a renegade recovery mission. Inexperienced, naive and brash, they soon find themselves face to face with real bullets.

This barely competent action flick saw limited United States theatrical release. Stereotypes include Latin bad guy drug dealers and terrorists, double-crossers, and violent, corrupt police and army officials. It was filmed in Mexico (subbing for Colombia) with Elpidia Carrillo, Gregory Sierra and Guillermo Rios, who plays drug kingpin Ochobar. Director Stuart Rosenberg had his name removed from the credits.

Licence to Kill (1989 Metro-Goldwyn-Mayer/United Artists)

D: John Glen

S: Michael G. Wilson and Richard Maibaum, based on the characters created by Ian Fleming

P: Albert R. Broccoli and Michael G. Wilson

Cast: Timothy Dalton, Robert Davi, Carey Lowell, Talisa Soto, Pedro Armendariz, Jr.

James Bond (Dalton) is in Florida for his old friend Felix Leiter's (David Hedison's) marriage. On the eve of the wedding, Bond and Felix capture South America's most ruthless drug lord, Franz Sanchez (Davi). But after a $2 million bribe, Sanchez is a free man and exacts revenge by murdering Felix and his new bride.

The usually cool Bond is enraged, but Her Majesty's government doesn't approve of secret agents with personal vendettas. When Bond refuses to obey, his Licence to Kill is revoked and he heads to a fictional South American country in search of Sanchez. Puerto Rican model-turned-actress Soto is one of the celebrated Bond girls. Filmed in Mexico with all the usual big-budget James Bond action, beautiful women and thrilling stunts and car chases, it is surprisingly free of Hispanic stereotypes, except for the drug lord.

A Life in the Balance (1955 Twentieth Century Fox)

D: Harry Horner

S: Robert Presnell, Jr., and Leo Townsend, based on a story by Georges Simenon

P: Leonard Goldstein

Cast: Ricardo Montalban, Anne Bancroft, Lee Marvin, José Perez, Rodolfo Acosta, José Torvay

Ricardo Montalban, Jose Perez and Anne Bancroft in *A Life in the Balance*.

A murder mystery filmed in Mexico City, *A Life in the Balance* is unusual in that it offers a very modern and non-stereotypical view of life in Mexico City with Mexican leading characters.

A young boy (Perez) tracks down a psychopathic killer (Marvin) in order to prove the innocence of his musician father, who has been arrested for the murder of a woman who lives in their building. Well paced and well done, it gave Ricardo Montalban an escape from the Latin Lover portrayals with which he had become saddled.

The film features a young Anne Bancroft as Montalban's lover in one of a series of ethnic portrayals early in her career. Acosta, usually cast as a heavy in American films, portrays the police detective. Puerto Rican Perez went on to work on the Broadway stage and, as an adult, in many film and television shows.

The Life of Villa (1914 Mutual Film Corp.) [aka: *A Tragedy in the Life of General Villa* (1915)]

D: Raoul Walsh
P: D.W. Griffith

Silent. In 1914, Pancho Villa sold the movie rights for the revolution he was fighting in Mexico for his own personal gain. Though he could not read or write, Villa understood the power of the moving pictures he saw in El Paso.

Journalists and photographers from around the world came to Mexico to meet Villa and cover the colorful hero of the revolution. In January 1914 in a hotel room in Juarez, Mexico, Villa met with Frank M. Thayer, a representative of the Los Angeles-based Mutual Film Corporation headed by D.W. Griffith, and signed a contract for $25,000 in gold and 50 percent of the profits. (Griffith felt that the story of this celebrated figure who made headlines in all the American newspapers would be surefire film material.) In a stunning piece of early "photo-op" thinking, the major contract stipulation was that the general would have to fight all his battles during the day so that they could be photographed using the slow film stocks of the period!

Young director and actor Walsh directed the film troupe, which included famed cameraman L.M. Burrud. After many months of personal tribulations and adverse shooting conditions, all at the mercy of the whims of General Villa, they returned to Hollywood exhausted. Finding most of the footage unusable as a narrative, cohesive whole, Griffith ordered a script written. Additional footage was shot with actors and dozens of extras at a ranch in the nearby San Fernando Valley with Walsh playing Villa, complete with sombrero, six-guns and a sinister moustache.

Released in 1915 as *A Tragedy in the Life of General Villa*, the film was never a hit, but it did play in enough theaters to recoup the investment. Some of the actual Villa footage made it into the final film.

Life with Mikey (1993 Buena Vista)

D: James Lapine
S: Marc Lawrence
P: Ted Schwartz
Cast: Michael J. Fox, Christina Vidal, Nathan Lane, Rubén Blades

Michael Chapman (Fox), a former child star turned agent, discovers a tough-talking homeless ten-year-old street kid, Angie Vega (Vidal), whom he catches picking his pocket. She turns out to be a natural in front of the camera, so he decides to represent her and to take her into his home. Angie is later reunited with her father, played by Blades.

Like Water for Chocolate (1993 Miramax)

D: Alfonso Arau
S: Laura Esquivel, based on her novel
P: Alfonso Arau
Cast: Lumi Cavazos, Marco Leonardi, Regina Torne, Yareli Arizmendi, Mario Ivan Martinez

The story takes place in Rio Grande, Mexico beginning in the year 1895 and jumps fifteen years later to 1910. Tita (Cavazos) is the youngest daughter of Maria Elena (Torne) and by tradition is required to take care of her in her dotage. When Pedro (Leonardi) asks for Tita's hand, Mama refuses and talks him into marrying Rosuara (Arizmendi), Tita's sister. He agrees because doing so will keep him close to Tita, who is never to be allowed to marry. Tita makes the wedding cake and some of her tears fall into the batter with a most unusual consequence for the wedding guests. Soon, Mama orders the newlyweds to San Antonio. Tita's misery and longing are translated into the food she cooks with the recipes she collects in a magical book. When she cooks for Pedro, their passion is overwhelming. When she is angry at her relatives, her food creates indigestion. Although it takes many years, Tita's destiny with Pedro survives her tyrannical mother, the birth of Pedro's daughter and even a competing suitor.

The novel remained on the *New York Times* bestseller list for more than a year. At the time, *Like Water for Chocolate,* with a box office take of more than $21 million, broke all American theatrical earning records for a foreign language film.

The Littlest Outlaw (1955 Buena Vista)
D: Roberto Gavaldon
S: Bill Walsh, based on a story by Lansburgh
P: Larry Lansburgh
Cast: Pedro Armendariz, Andres Velasquez, Joseph Calleia,
    Rodolfo Acosta, José Torvay

Armendariz stars in this Walt Disney production about a little boy who runs away with his horse rather than see it killed.

Andres Velasquez plays the youngster, Little Pablito. The cast also includes Rodolfo Acosta and Joseph Calleia. It was filmed in English and Spanish on location in and around San Miguel de Allende, Mexico.

Director Roberto Gavaldon was one of the leading directors in Mexico from the 1940s until the early 1960s. He was responsible for such classics of the Golden Age of Mexican Cinema as *The Count of Monte Cristo* (1941), *La Barraca* (1944), *La Otra* (1946), *La Rosa Bianca* (1961) and *Macaria* (1959). His other English-language films include *The Adventures of Casanova* (1948) and *Beyond All Limits* (1957).

Lone Star (1996 Sony Pictures Classics)
D: John Sayles
S: John Sayles
P: Paul Miller and Maggie Renzi
Cast: Matthew McConaughey, Chris Cooper, Kris Kristofferson,
    Elizabeth Peña, Miriam Colon, Joe Morton, Tony Plana,
    Frances McDormand, Richard Coca

John Sayles' hugely ambitious tracing of the complex ways in which past and present, love and hate, rumor and reality intertwine to form the ragged social and political fabric of bordertown life in the

Southwestern United States. Sheriff Deeds (Chris Cooper) begins to investigate the discovery of a skull and a lawman's badge in the desert just outside the Tex-Mex bordertown of Frontera. He believes it is the remains of ruthless bigoted Sheriff Charley Wade (Kristofferson). He thinks it might have been murder and he suspects the man who murdered Wade was the sheriff who replaced him, Sam's own father. It may of course be connected with the racial tensions that have always divided Frontera's population of Anglos, Hispanics and African Americans. Deeds' own teenage romance with Pilar Cruz (Peña)—now a teacher with a troubled son of her own—was put to an end by his father. The past also weighs heavily on Pilar's mother (Colon) who wants to distance herself from her Mexican roots. *Lone Star* is less about solving the mystery of who shot the sheriff than about the relationship between belief and knowledge among multiple points of view of the many characters who figure prominently in the story.

Lone Wolf McQuade (1983 Orion)
D: Steve Carver
S: B.J. Nelson, based on a story by H. Kaye Dyal and Nelson
P: Yoram Ben-Ami and Steve Carver
Cast: Chuck Norris, David Carradine, Barbara Carrera, Robert Beltran, Jorge Cevera, Jr.

McQuade (Norris) is a renegade Texas Ranger who is assigned a Mexican American rookie partner (Beltran) by his superiors. They become embroiled in stopping a crime spree led by Rawley (Carradine).

This typical Chuck Norris vehicle is a violent and well-made action film combining a contemporary Western with martial arts. Beltran is good as the rookie partner in a role free of stereotypical action or dialogue. Carrera is a strong presence as the villain's Native American girlfriend who falls for McQuade.

Losin' It (1983 Embassy)
D: Curtis Hanson
S: B.W.L. Norton
P: Bryan Gindoff and Hannah Hempstead
Cast: Tom Cruise, Jackie Earle Haley, John Stockwell, Shelley Long, Henry Darrow, Enrique Castillo, Santos Morales

In 1963, four American teenagers head South of the border to Tijuana for fun, sex and excitement. One boy, Dave (Haley), leads his friends in search of the boisterous nightlife, and another brings his red Chevy convertible in hopes of having his car cheaply reupholstered. Instead, the car falls prey to the eye of a local police chief. Shelley Long plays Kathy, an American housewife in search of a Mexican divorce.

The film is every Southwest American kid's fantasy of what happens during a wild weekend in a Mexican bordertown. Included in this fantasy is every conceivable Mexican border stereotype, including corrupt police officials, prostitutes, saloon barkers, pimps, switchblade-wielding toughs and cynical taxi drivers. "You come to Mexico to do things you wouldn't do in your own country," points out one of the Mexicans to the boys.

The Loves of Carmen (1948 Columbia)

D: Charles Vidor
S: Helen Deutsch
P: Charles Vidor
Cast: Rita Hayworth, Glenn Ford, Ron Randell, Victor Jory, Luther Adler, Arnold Moss, Natividad Vacio, Rosa Turich

Hayworth is the ultimate spitfire heroine in Prosper Mérimée's famous story of passion and death. Carmen (Hayworth) convinces Don José (Ford) to desert his duties, kill her husband in a fight for her love and take over the leadership of a gang of mountain-dwelling outlaws.

Hayworth made the film in Technicolor and at a cost of $2.5 million for her own Beckworth Productions. She tried to ensure box office success by re-teaming with *Gilda* (1946) star, Glenn Ford and director Charles Vidor. Ford was miscast as Don José as he was never able to make audiences believe he was a Spaniard. He himself referred to it as "a Rembrandt of miscasting, with me as a Spanish Gypsy" at a Directors Guild of America tribute to Richard Brooks in 1991.

Hayworth replaced Bizet's music with that of a contemporary composer. Her father, Eduardo Cansino, assisted Robert Sidney in choreographing the dance numbers, which replaced the ballet of the opera. The movie was filmed on location in Lone Pine, California, and at Columbia Studios, locations which did not correspond with Seville and the surrounding Spanish countryside. Despite a lukewarm critical reception, *The Loves of Carmen* was able to achieve commercial success.

Luminarias (2000 New Latin Pictures)

D: Jose Luis Valenzuela
S: Evelina Fernandez
P: Sal Lopez
Cast: Evelina Fernandez, Scott Bakula, Marta DuBois, Angela Moya, Dyana Ortelli, Seidy Lopez, Robert Beltran, Pepe Serna, Lupe Ontiveros, Cheech Marin

Luminarias is the name of a hilltop restaurant in East Los Angeles where four Latinas meet regularly to share their life adventures and a few tequilas. *Daily Variety* called the film a "sleek spirited romantic comedy" that is "warm, funny and consistently entertaining."

Independently produced and made on a shoestring budget, the film deals with a unique female perspective (that of Mexican American women from East Los Angeles) through the experiences of several mature Latina women. The characters grapple with the changing roles of men and women in an American society that is inevitably moving to a multi-cultural and multi-ethnic society.

Machete (1958 United Artists)
D: Kurt Neumann
S: Carroll Young and Kurt Neumann
P: Kurt Neumann
Cast: Mari Blanchard, Albert Dekker, Juano Hernandez, Carlos Rivas, Lee Van Cleef, Ruth Cains

A standard melodrama about a middle-aged plantation owner in Puerto Rico, Don Luis Montoya (Dekker), whose young bride, Jean (Blanchard), very quickly tries to seduce Carlos (Rivas), the foreman, whom Montoya has raised since childhood. Miguel (Van Cleef) is a troublemaking cousin who has his own designs on the plantation. Miguel sets fire to the plantation but is killed, while Carlos saves Montoya's life. Jean perishes in the fire, but Carlos is consoled by his true love, Rita (Cains). The most notable aspect of the production is that it was filmed entirely on location in Puerto Rico.

Mackenna's Gold (1969 Columbia)
D: J. Lee Thompson
S: Carl Foreman, based on the novel by Will Henry
P: Carl Foreman
Cast: Gregory Peck, Omar Sharif, Lee J. Cobb, Telly Savalas, Camilla Sparv, Eduardo Ciannelli, Julie Newmar, Rudy Diaz

An overproduced, cliché-ridden big-budget Western starring Gregory Peck as a drifter who is given a map to the secret location of lost gold in the Canon del Oro by a dying Indian in the desert. Omar Sharif plays Peck's Mexican bandit adversary, Colorado, and Keenan Wynn plays Sanchez, Colorado's second in command. The film features Rudy Diaz and Pepe Callahan as outlaws.

The Magnificent Fraud (1939 Paramount)
D: Robert Florey
S: Gilbert Gabriel and Walter Ferris, based on a play by Charles G. Booth
P: Harlan Thompson
Cast: Akim Tamiroff, Lloyd Nolan, Patricia Morison, Steffi Duna

A dramatic actor impersonates the drunken dictator of a fictional South American country until a large American loan can be completed. Akim Tamiroff plays the dual roles of actor Jules LaCroix and President Alvarado. The film never reaches the comic potential of the premise. Paul Mazursky remade this comedy spoof more successfully five decades later as Moon over Parador (1988).

The Magnificent Matador (1955 Twentieth Century Fox)
D: Budd Boetticher
S: Charles Lang, based on a story by Boetticher
P: Edward L. Alperson
Cast: Anthony Quinn, Maureen O'Hara, Thomas Gomez, Manuel Rojas

The Magnificent Matador captures the pageantry and heroic excitement of the bullring in this love story set in Mexico. In a Technicolor framework of haciendas, mountains and plateaus, matador Quinn, an idol of the arena, superstitiously deserts the bullring because of an ill omen. Pursued by a rich American (O'Hara), he finally proves his fear is not for himself but for a younger bullfighter, his illegitimate son Rafael, played by Manuel Rojas. In a stirring climax, father and son enter the bullring in turn, proudly displaying their skill and bravery.

"Anthony Quinn as the Matador hero...is, as always, a capable and convincing player ... Mexico, in fact and film, is a beautiful country, and *Matador* does it justice," Jesse Zunser, *Cue Magazine* (5/28/55).

The Magnificent Seven (1960 United Artists)

D: John Sturges
S: William Roberts
P: John Sturges
Cast: Yul Brynner, Steve McQueen, Eli Wallach, James Coburn,
    Charles Bronson, Horst Buchholz, Robert Vaughn, Brad Dexter

In the Kurosawa film *The Seven Samurai* (1954), upon which this movie was based, the villagers and bandits are all Japanese. In the American version, six of the seven professional killers were to be American gunmen who are recruited by village elders to help the villagers rid themselves of marauding Mexican bandidos, a notable difference to which even the Mexican government took exception. They pointed out that Mexican gunfighters were perfectly capable of helping the villagers rid themselves of Mexican bandidos.

Anxious to make the film on a budget, director Sturges made two of the seven gunmen Mexican (Bronson and Buchholz), and the Mexican government okayed the script.

Nevertheless, Americans in Mexico killing Mexicans is a critical but subtle difference that carries cultural and political implications of implied superiority, marring what is otherwise a landmark Western.

Many of the original film's characters and situations are retained in William Roberts' screenplay. The Seven Samurai (i.e., the Magnificent Seven) are out-of-work gunmen and fugitives in a bordertown. Each of the gunmen is individualized: Chris (Brynner) is the leader. Vin (McQueen) is restless and seeks action and employment. Harry (Dexter) is seeking a fortune. Britt (Coburn) is an opportunist who tests his skills to their limit. O'Reilly (Bronson) who is half Mexican Indian, is a wanderer who sympathizes with his people. Lee (Vaughn) is a fugitive gunman who is looking for asylum and an escape from failing ability. Finally, Chico (Buchholz) is the young Mexican who denies his heritage in order to gain prestige by joining the group. Calvera, the Mexican bandit leader, is played with hammy exuberance by Eli Wallach. Four of the seven die in the savage fighting.

Future Hollywood cameraman John Alonzo played one of the bandidos as did actor Lorry Duran. Juan Martin de Hayos, Elsa Monteros and Mexican American actor Natividad Vacio played featured parts as villagers. Francisco "Chico" Day was the unit production manager on the

Yul Brynner as Chris (center), a hired gunman, confronts a gang of Mexican bandidos in *The Magnificent Seven*.

film, which employed 150 Mexican film technicians and hundreds of Mexican extras.

The Magnificent Seven was filmed near Tepotzlan, Mexico, and became one of the first so-called international Westerns. The casting of Yul Brynner, among others, in a Western, a genre with which he was not generally associated, was innovative. Brynner makes a perfect samurai gunfighter, a role he later repeats in the movie *Westworld* (1973). His black outfit, previously associated with villains, was perfectly in tune with the antihero movies that were to follow in the 1960s and early 1970s.

With the exception of Brynner, who was already well known, the film's relatively little-known main players went on to become stars (with the possible exception of Dexter). Elmer Bernstein wrote the popular and now classic musical score.

The film also started a 1960s preoccupation with the displacement of the men who tamed the West as civilization took over. This theme continued in such movies as *The Man Who Shot Liberty Valance* (1962), *The Wild Bunch* (1969) and *Butch Cassidy and the Sundance Kid* (1969).

The Magnificent Seven spawned three sequels, each using a variation of the same basic plot (*Return of the Seven* [1966], *Guns of the Magnificent Seven* [1969] and *The Magnificent Seven Ride* [1972]).

The Magnificent Seven Ride (1972 United Artists)

D: George McGowan
S: Arthur Rowe
P: William A. Calihan
Cast: Lee Van Cleef, Luke Askew, Pedro Armendariz, Jr., Rodolfo Acosta

Notable for managing to rip off two films at the same time and still failing: *The Dirty Dozen* (1967) and the original *The Magnificent Seven* (1960). Lee Van Cleef is Chris, the Bulletproof. Acosta took his turn as the bandit chieftain and Armendariz is one of the seven, who are now convicts.

Major Dundee (1965 Columbia)

D: Sam Peckinpah
S: Harry Julian Fink, Oscar Saul, and Sam Peckinpah, based on a story by Fink
P: Jerry Bresler
Cast: Charlton Heston, Richard Harris, Senta Berger, James Coburn, Mario Adorf

Union Army Major Dundee (Heston) forms an uneasy alliance with Confederate prisoners of war led by Captain Tyreen (Harris) in order to ride into Mexico and track down a renegade Apache chief and his band of followers, despite not having any authority in Mexico.

During their pursuit, Union and Confederate soldiers must overcome their hatred, suspicion and fear of each other to band together to fight Apaches and Maxilmilian's French occupation troops. Freeing a Mexican village from French troops adds to the responsibilities of Dundee, who must protect various Mexicans and Teresa Santiago (Berger), the beautiful Austrian-born widow of a Mexican doctor. Dundee and Tyreen soon find themselves in competition for her favors.

A seriously wounded Dundee finds solace in the bottle and whores when he loses his confidence. He regains it in time for a final confrontation with the Apaches and French soldiers before heading back across the border.

Peckinpah directed and co-wrote this strong, rousing Western, which was filmed in and around Durango, Mexico, though he later disowned the film, which was truncated and recut by others. Mario Adorf plays a soldier in the Union Army.

Antonio Banderas and
Armand Assante blare
out hot Latin rhythms
as the Castillo brothers
in 1950s New York in
The Mambo Kings.

The Mambo Kings (1992 Warner Bros.)

D: Arne Glimcher
S: Cynthia Cidre, based on a novel by Oscar Hijuelos
P: Arne Glimcher and Arnon Milchan
Cast: Armand Assante, Antonio Banderas, Cathy Moriarty,
    Maruschka Detmers, Talisa Soto, Tito Puente, Desi Arnaz, Jr.

The film version of Oscar Hijuelos' Pulitzer Prize-winning novel *The Mambo Kings Play Songs of Love* (1989) about two musician brothers, Nestor and Cesar Castillo, from Havana, Cuba, who come to New York during the Latin mambo dance craze of the 1950s.

The story lost much of its subtle cultural atmosphere and character nuance in its transition to the screen and is more like a typical musician's rise-and-fall-type movie of the 1930s.

Working in a meat processing plant during the day, the brothers try to make their mark on the Latin dance club circuit of New York, and after some success, they run up against the Cuban gangsters who control the nightclubs. The fact that these Cuban gangsters are African American and would never have been allowed in the clubs, except as musicians, let alone been in control, is completely ignored.

The brothers are offered a contract for a long run at a preferred nightclub but refuse the offer, thus upsetting the gangsters, who put out the word. No one else will hire the boys. However, they are given a temporary reprieve when Desi Arnaz (Arnaz, Jr.) catches their act, and later offers them a guest appearance on his *I Love Lucy* television show. Nestor (Banderas), who pines for his lost love in Cuba, does not share his brother's burning determination to "make it" unless it is on their own terms. He just wants to play music. As a result, he sells out to the gangsters without Cesar's (Assante's) knowledge, regrets his decision, and ultimately pays for his sins with his life.

Armand Assante overplays his character of the older brother, Cesar, who wants to be his own man. Antonio Banderas, however, is a quiet surprise as the brooding younger brother, Nestor.

The musical numbers are truncated, and the sense of what the music means to the people and the personalities involved is never fully explored. The women in the brothers' lives and their interactions get very short shrift. Tito Puente, the original Mambo King, appears as himself.

Director Arne Glimcher, a wealthy New York art dealer, is not a director, and this film puts the lie to the idea that anyone can direct a movie. The film is driven by its music, its colorful and stylized art direction, and by the cinematography by Michael Ballhaus.

Nevertheless, with all its flaws, the movie does somewhat introduce mainstream America to the reality of Hispanic Americans. Hispanics are seen as an established, historical presence in American society. This reality was ignored for many years and has only recently been touched upon by much better movies such as *Zoot Suit* (1981) or the far superior *Stand and Deliver* (1988) and *La Bamba* (1987). These portrayals counterbalance the stereotypical view that all Hispanic men are knife-wielding drug dealers and that their women are hip-swinging hookers.

The *I Love Lucy* re-creation was cleverly staged, intercutting film footage of the original show with shots of Lucille Ball and new footage with Arnaz, Jr., and the Castillos in the skit. Desi Arnaz, Jr., however, is but a pale imitation of his father.

The Man Behind the Gun (1953 Warner Bros.)

D: Felix Feist
S: John Twist, based on a story by Robert Buckner
P: Robert Sisk
Cast: Randolph Scott, Patrice Wymore, Lina Romay, Robert Cabal, Alan Hale, Jr.

Scott is a major in the Union Army sent in disguise to prevent armed insurrection and the setting up of a separate state by pro-slavery elements in California of the 1850s. Romay is effective as Chona Degnon, the proprietress of the Palacio saloon and gambling den. Romay sings two songs, "La Paloma" and "Adios Mi Amor."

Cabal makes a brief but memorable appearance as the boy, Joaquin Murieta.

The Man from Del Rio (1956 United Artists)

D: Harry Horner
S: Richard Carr
P: Robert L. Jacks
Cast: Anthony Quinn, Katy Jurado, Peter Whitney

An unusual, modest-budget Western starring Quinn. Significant for the fact that it features a Mexican American sheriff and a Latina, Jurado, as Estella, a nurse to the town doctor.

In order to rid itself of some outlaws, a frontier town swallows its prejudice and makes drifter Dave Robles (Quinn) sheriff. He expects to be accepted by the town when he takes the dangerous job as sheriff but discovers that he has been hired as a gunman and will not be acknowledged as a man.

Man in the Shadow (1957 Universal)

D: Jack Arnold
S: Gene L. Coon
P: Albert Zugsmith
Cast: Jeff Chandler, Orson Welles, Martin Garralaga

A contemporary but routine Western drama in which Chandler plays a sheriff in an agricultural community who investigates the death of a Mexican laborer on a powerful rancher's land despite his and the townspeople's objections. In the end, the murderer is discovered to be the ranch foreman.

Man of Conquest (1939 Republic Pictures)
D: George Nicholls
S: Wells Root; E.E. Paramor, Jr.; and Jan Fortune, based on an original
   story by Harold Shumate and Root
P: Sol C. Siegel
Cast: Richard Dix, Joan Fontaine

The rousing story of Sam Houston—from his start in Tennessee politics under Andrew Jackson to his election as governor, his journey to Arkansas, his adoption by the Cherokee Indians, and finally his part in the Texas Wars for Independence. No Hispanics appear in major roles in this one except for Pedro de Cordoba as an old Indian. Plenty of Mexican extras were recruited near Stockton, California, and the Salt Springs Reservoir, where much of the film was shot.

Man of La Mancha (1972 United Artists)
D: Arthur Hiller
S: Dale Wasserman
P: Arthur Hiller
Cast: Peter O'Toole, Sophia Loren, James Coco

An overblown, big-budget screen version of the hit Broadway musical based on Cervantes' *Don Quixote*. The film was made largely on studio sets in Italy. There are no Hispanics in the cast.

It stars Peter O'Toole in the dual role of Cervantes and Don Quixote, Sophia Loren as Aldonza and James Coco as Sancho Panza. The singing voices of O'Toole and Loren were dubbed.

Maracaibo (1958 Paramount)
D: Cornel Wilde
S: Ted Sherdeman
P: Cornel Wilde
Cast: Cornel Wilde, Jean Wallace, Abbe Lane, Francis Lederer,
   Michael Landon

Set in the oil fields of Lake Maracaibo and Caracas, the capital of Venezuela, where producer, director and star Cornel Wilde shot most of the film on location. Vic Scott (Wilde), an American vacationing in Venezuela and romantically interested in novelist Laura Kingsley (Wallace), is called upon to extinguish a treacherous offshore oil well fire on Lake Maracaibo. The land belongs to a wealthy deaf mute, Miguel Orlando (Lederer), who is engaged to a former girlfriend of Scott, Elena (Lane). The rugged American finally extinguishes the fire in a spectacular sequence, but Orlando's close friend and interpreter, Lago (Landon), is killed by accident.

Wilde went on to produce and direct such films as the romantic *Lancelot and Guinevere* (1963), the critically acclaimed *The Naked Prey* (1965), the antiwar drama *Beach Red* (1967) and the post-Jaws shark adventure *Shark's Treasure* (1975). Michael Landon went on to find stardom on television's long-running *Bonanza* series soon after this.

Maria Candelaria [aka: Portrait of Maria] (1946 Metro-Goldwyn-Mayer)

D: Emilio Fernandez
S: Emilio Fernandez and Mauricio Magdaleno
P: Agustin J. Fink
Cast: Dolores Del Rio, Pedro Armendariz

Though filmed in 1943, *Maria Candelaria* wasn't picked up for release by MGM International until 1946. It had little United States box office success, though it did well internationally. Originally shot in Spanish, the movie was dubbed into English.

Del Rio became a top star in Mexico soon after returning home from Hollywood. Del Rio's Maria was a perfect piece of film acting, and she found Fernandez to be a director who helped her realize her potential to the full for the first time.

Maria is a simple and deeply spiritual peasant girl who lives in beautiful and isolated Lake Xochimilco. Her fellow villagers, who mistrust and fear her innate goodness, stone her to death. Mario and Lorenzo (Armendariz), her Indian lover, represent innocence corrupted and destroyed by civilization.

Gabriel Figueroa's brilliant black-and-white photography brought out the spirituality of Del Rio's beauty in a way no Hollywood film had ever done. Though playing a young girl, Del Rio was almost forty years old at the time.

With this, her second Mexican film (the first being *Flor Silvestre* [1943]), Del Rio, her co-star Armendariz, director Fernandez, and cameraman Figueroa established themselves as the "big four" of the Mexican film industry.

Maria Candelaria was the first Mexican film to make an impact in Europe after World War II. It won the Grand Prize at the Cannes Film Festival in 1947 and helped initiate what is now called the Golden Age of Mexican Cinema.

Fernandez's films were immediately seen as uniquely Mexican, both in style and subject matter. Mexico's colorful folklore, expansive landscapes, coastlines, dramatic skies, vibrant cloud patterns and the ethereal presence and passionate Indian beauty of the actors were fully realized under Fernandez's direction and Figueroa's masterful cinematography.

The Mark of Zorro (1940 Twentieth Century Fox)
See "Zorro & The Cisco Kid" listings.

The Mask of Zorro (1998 TriStar)
See "Zorro & The Cisco Kid" listings.

Masquerade in Mexico (1945 Paramount)

D: Mitchell Leisen

S: Karl Tunberg, based on a story by Edwin Justus Mayer and Franz Spencer

P: Karl Tunberg

Cast: Dorothy Lamour, Arturo De Cordova, Patric Knowles, Ann Dvorak, Martin Garralaga, The Guadalajara Trio

As part of a jewel theft scheme, American nightclub singer Angel O'Reilly (Lamour) impersonates a Spanish countess in Mexico. An entertainer in a Mexico City nightclub, she is then engaged by banker Thomas Grant (Knowles) to divert the attention of matador Manolo Segovia (De Cordova) from the banker's wife (Dvorak) to herself.

A pleasant and entertaining romantic musical shot at Paramount Studios in Hollywood. Lamour recalled in a *Saturday Evening Post* (1/18/47) interview, "Even the atmosphere of the set helped make *Masquerade in Mexico* a delight. I had never been South of the border, but had often dreamed of such a trip. The atmosphere of our neighbor nation was simulated so convincingly on the set that working there was like being in Mexico."

Lamour sings songs from a garlanded gondola on a simulated Lake Xochimilco, and a gigantic ballet is performed in a rural Mexican hacienda. This is clearly the Mexico of the popular American romantic imagination, and it is delivered with good dancing and singing, amid lavish settings and costumes.

Arturo De Cordova headed the Latin cast members as the warm-hearted matador who falls madly in love with Lamour. Other Latin cast members include Martin Garralaga, Enrique Valadez, Rita Lupino, Elisa Gamboa, Ray Beltran, Roque Ybarra, Juan Torena, Felipe Turich, Pepito Perez, Leon Lombardo, Primo Lopez (Cushion Boy), Rodolfo Hayos (Sr. and Jr.), Julian Rivero and Frank Leyva.

The Master Gunfighter (1975 Billy Jack Enterprises)

D: Frank [Tom] Laughlin

S: Harold Lapland

P: Philip Parslow

Cast: Tom Laughlin, Ron O'Neal, Barbara Carrera, Hector Elias, Victor Campos

Set in California during the 1850s, this film deals with the conflicts between native Spanish Californians and encroaching American land grabbers.

In order to fight off efforts by the Americans to foreclose on their land, Spanish Californians need gold. When members of an Indian village that has been enslaved by the Spanish try to convey some illegally obtained gold to the Americans, one of the leaders of the haciendas, Paulo (O'Neal), has the Indians slaughtered so they cannot reveal the source of their wealth. Finley (Laughlin) objects to the slaughter and leaves for Mexico. He returns for a fight with Paulo when he hears that Paulo has plans to massacre another village.

A stylized Western, it is a cross between a Kung Fu epic and a "spaghetti Western." Its star had an unprecedented box office success *Billy Jack* (1971), in which he played the title role. One of the best things about the movie is the creative casting. Paulo is played by Ron O'Neal, an African American actor who had gained popularity in 1972 with *Superfly*. Fashion model-turned-actress Carrera made her film debut as Eula, an elegant Spanish noblewoman who marries Finley. GeoAnn Sosa plays Chorika, a young Indian woman who is the sole survivor of a massacre. Victor Campos is Maltese and Hector Elias is Juan, two henchmen. The film was shot on location in Big Sur and Malibu, California.

Maverick Gold
See *Catlow*.

A Medal for Benny (1945 Paramount)
D: Irving Pichel
S: Frank Butler and Jack Wagner, based on a story by John Steinbeck and Wagner
P: Paul Jones
Cast: J. Carroll Naish, Arturo De Cordova, Dorothy Lamour, Mikhail Rasumny, Frank McHugh, Rosita Moreno, Charles Dingle, Nestor Paiva, Fernando Alvarado, Pepito Perez, Martin Garralaga, Julian Rivero

Based on a twenty-page story idea by John Steinbeck and Jack Wagner, *A Medal for Benny* was the first Hollywood motion picture to deal somewhat sensitively with the problems of Mexican Americans living in the United States, recognizing them as part of the American scene. The film illustrates the effects of racism and poverty in a subtle, inoffensive way that audiences of the time could accept.

Though he never appears in the film, Benny's presence is always felt. He is the lovable renegade of the paisano colony who is ordered out of town by the police. He disappears for a year. We later learn that Benny has died on a Pacific battlefield in World War II. He is posthumously awarded the Congressional Medal of Honor.

The town fathers go crazy with civic pride, as do the members of the Chamber of Commerce. A general, along with reporters and newsreel cameramen, soon arrives and the town becomes the center of national attention. The town fathers cannot find Benny's family to receive the medal. The entourage is horrified to realize too late that Benny's last name, which is Martin, is pronounced "Marteen" and that Benny comes from the other side of the tracks.

When the dignitaries first visit Benny's father, he thinks they are trying to evict him for nonpayment of rent. When he finally realizes what is going on, he proudly receives his son's medal.

One of the finest and most versatile character actors in the business, Naish received an Academy Award® nomination as Best Supporting Actor for his portrayal of Benny's Mexican American father. De Cordova is excellent as the young fisherman, Joe Morales, who vies for the affection

J. Carroll Naish (left) and
Arturo De Cordova (right)
in *A Medal for Benny*.

of the dead hero's girlfriend, Lolita Sierra, believably played by Dorothy
Lamour. Along with De Cordova, the cast features many Mexican
American actors in principal roles and as extras.

During World War II, Hispanic soldiers won more Congressional
Medals of Honor (12) than any other minority group in the United
States armed forces.

Medicine Man (1992 Buena Vista)

D: John McTiernan
S: Tom Schulman and Sally Robinson
P: Andrew Vajna and Donna Dubrow
Cast: Sean Connery, Lorraine Bracco

Deep in the Amazon rainforest, a brilliant but eccentric research scientist, Dr. Campbell (Connery), is on the verge of astonishing the world
with a major medical breakthrough, a cancer cure, but he has lost the
formula and must now reinvent the elusive serum. The corporation
sponsoring his research sends another biochemist, Dr. Crane (Bracco),
to investigate the reclusive Campbell. They become caught up in a race
against time to find the antidote before the coming destruction of

their section of the rainforest to make way for a highway. Though it takes place in the Amazon, it was filmed in the jungles of Catemaco, Mexico, with some additional second-unit work in Brazil.

Although a great idea, the film was woefully lackluster in its direction and script, despite the efforts of Connery and Bracco to make it work, and suffers from one of the worst, most artificial and unbelievable upbeat endings in years.

Mexican Hayride (1948 Universal)
D: Charles T. Barton
S: Oscar Brodney and John Grant
P: Robert Arthur
Cast: Bud Abbott, Lou Costello, Virginia Grey, Luba Malina,
    Pedro de Cordoba

An uninspired, but mildly amusing film. Abbott and Costello romp through Universal's backlot Mexican street with Costello as the fall guy for a group of con men with a fake mining operation in Mexico.

Joe Bascam (Costello), an American fugitive from justice, goes to Mexico to get Harry Lambert (Abbott) to confess. Joe is being pursued by two American detectives, and his old girlfriend Mary (Grey) is now a bullfighter working under the name of Montana in Mexico. Montana is about to throw a hat to a group of American tourists when she sees Joe, and in a rage she throws the hat at him. Because he catches the hat, Joe becomes the "Amigo Americana" and tours Mexico as an honored guest to symbolize Mexican American goodwill. Harry and his accomplice Dagmar (Malina), a Mexican spitfire type, use Joe's fame to put over another phony deal. The action culminates in a bullfight, with Joe making a very unlikely matador.

One of the highlights is Costello dancing a samba with a bull with the aid of trick photography. Costello also assumes a variety of disguises including a female tortilla vendor and a mariachi performer. Hispanic actors Chris-Pin Martin, Argentina Brunetti, Julian Rivero, Roque Ybarra, Felipe Turich and Alex Montoya, among others, have supporting roles in the film.

Mexican Spitfire (1939 RKO Radio Pictures)
D: Leslie Goodwins
S: Joseph A. Fields and Charles E. Roberts, based on a story by Fields
P: Cliff Reid
Cast: Lupe Velez, Leon Errol

Velez's career was revitalized in the B movie *Mexican Spitfire* series. In the first film in the series, made at RKO in 1939, a follow-up to *The Girl from Mexico* (1939), Velez introduced the character Carmelita, an exaggerated comedic stereotype of a Mexican woman living and dealing with life in the United States. Leon Errol co-starred in a dual role as Uncle Matt and Lord Basil. They made a very popular comic teaming, which was not originally planned as such. This was the second film in the series.

Mexican Spitfire at Sea (1942 RKO Radio Pictures)
D: Leslie Goodwins
S: Jerry Cady and Charles E. Roberts
P: Cliff Reid
Cast: Lupe Velez, Leon Errol

The "Mexican Spitfire" (Velez) gets herself and Uncle Matt (Errol) involved in all kinds of madcap situations on an ocean liner bound for Hawaii.

Mexican Spitfire Out West (1940 RKO Radio Pictures)
D: Leslie Goodwins
S: Charles E. Roberts and Jack Townley, based on a story by Roberts
P: Cliff Reid
Cast: Lupe Velez, Leon Errol

Carmelita's (Velez's) craving for more attention from her husband (Donald Woods) leads her to threaten divorce and run off to Reno, with Uncle Matt (Errol) in tow.

Mexican Spitfire Sees a Ghost (1942 RKO Radio Pictures)
D: Leslie Goodwins
S: Charles E. Roberts and Monte Brice
P: Cliff Reid
Cast: Lupe Velez, Leon Errol

The "Mexican Spitfire" finds herself in a haunted house that turns out to be the secret hideout of enemy agents making nitroglycerin.

Mexican Spitfire's Baby (1941 RKO Radio Pictures)
D: Leslie Goodwins
S: Jerry Cady, Charles E. Roberts, and James Casey, based on a story by Roberts
P: Cliff Reid
Cast: Lupe Velez, Leon Errol

Uncle Matt (Errol) imports a French war orphan (who turns out to be a voluptuous young woman) in an attempt to calm the discord between his nephew (Charles "Buddy" Rogers) and his explosive niece (Velez).

Mexican Spitfire's Blessed Event (1943 RKO Radio Pictures)
D: Leslie Goodwins
S: Charles E. Roberts and Dane Lussier, based on a story by Roberts
P: Bert Gilroy
Cast: Lupe Velez, Leon Errol

A garbled telegram indicates the birth of a baby to the "Mexican Spitfire," which prompts Lord Epping (Errol) to award a big business contract to the baby's father. In truth, the baby is really a baby ocelot and Carmelita (Velez) borrows a real baby in order to fool Lord Epping and help keep her husband's contract. This was the final film in the *Mexican Spitfire* series. A year after completion of the film, Velez found herself pregnant after a failed affair and committed suicide.

Mexican Spitfire's Elephant (1942 RKO Radio Pictures)

D: Leslie Goodwins
S: Charles E. Roberts, based on a story by Goodwins and Roberts
P: Bert Gilroy
Cast: Lupe Velez, Leon Errol

This film has a nutty plot about a smuggled toy elephant being used as a hiding place for a valuable gem.

Mexicana (1945 Republic Pictures)

D: Alfred Santell
S: Frank Gill, Jr.
P: Alfred Santell
Cast: Tito Guizar, Leo Carrillo, Constance Moore, Estelita Rodriguez

This is the story of the love-hate relationship between Mexican crooner "Pepe" Villarreal (Guizar) and American New York musical comedy star Alison Calvert (Moore) in Mexico City. It was reissued in 1951 as *Beyond the Border*.

"The Hollywood version of the Good Neighbor Policy continues to portray Latin America in the standard plot and surreal satin and gloss of the routine studio musical," John T. McManus, *PM Exclusive* (10/18/45).

The Milagro Beanfield War (1988 Universal)

D: Robert Redford
S: David S. Ward, based on a novel by John Nichols
P: Moctesuma Esparza
Cast: Chick Vennera, Julie Carmen, Christopher Walken, Rubén Blades, Sonia Braga, Carlos Riquelme, Natividad Vacio, Alberto Marin, Robert Carricart, Freddy Fender

A contemporary tale about a man named Joe Mondragon (Vennera), a New Mexico handyman who illegally irrigates his parched bean field using water that has been earmarked for an upscale development. This tiny act snowballs, setting in motion a chain of events that has overwhelming consequences for both Joe and the people of his town.

The Milagro Beanfield War was based on the 1974 novel, written by John Nichols. Producer Moctesuma Esparza acquired the rights to the novel in 1979 and Robert Redford expressed interest in making a film version (his second directorial effort) after his Academy Award®-winning *Ordinary People* (1980).

"One of the things Bob and I talked about when we got together," says Esparza, in press notes on the movie's release, "was the importance of treating this with integrity, to try and open up opportunities for Hispanics."

Their approach extended behind the camera as well as in front of it. Many talented Chicanos got important production team jobs, including art director Joe Aubel, production manager David Wisnievitz, and construction coordinator Bill Maldonado.

The cast highlights some of the leading talents in the Latino acting community, including Chick Vennera as Joe Mondragon, Blades as Sheriff Bernabe Montoya, Braga as Ruby Archuleta, and Carmen as Joe's wife, Nancy. Mexican comic actor Riquelme plays his first and only major role in an English-language production as Amarante.

Filming began in Las Truchas, New Mexico, in early August 1986 and finished in late November.

The film attempted to portray on the screen the Latin American literary tradition of "Magical Realism." In any event, however, it became an uneven blend of fantasy and reality and presented Hispanics as cute and slightly inept. Joe Mondragon was not presented with a strong enough characterization to ground the movie. Vennera as Mondragon did not suggest a salt-of-the-earth type of individual, coming off instead as weak and indecisive. His New York accent also got in the way of his believability as a New Mexico farmer. Braga was uncomfortable as Ruby Archuleta. Carlos Riquelme almost stole the film with his portrayal of Amarante, the old man.

The film was much anticipated due to Redford's helming of the project along with David Ward's (*The Sting*) screenplay. It was hoped that it would be a watershed film for Hispanics in the film industry the way Steven Spielberg's *The Color Purple* (1985) was for African Americans. The latter film was instrumental in launching the careers of Whoopi Goldberg, Oprah Winfrey and Danny Glover. This did not happen with *The Milagro Beanfield War*, though Blades and Braga have gone on to successful Hollywood acting careers. The film received generally favorable reviews, but met with a lukewarm reception at the box office.

Mi Vida Loca (1993 Sony Pictures Classics)
D: Allison Anders
S: Allison Anders
P: Colin Callender, Carl Colpaert, Daniel Hassid
Cast: Angel Aviles, Seidy Lopez, Jacob Vargas, Monica Lutton, Christina Solis, Magali Alvarado, Salma Hayek, Panchito Gomez, Jesse Borrego

Mousie (Lopez) and Sad Girl (Aviles) are childhood best friends in their Echo Park neighborhood of Los Angeles. But when Sad Girl becomes pregnant by Mousie's boyfriend, a drug dealer named Ernesto, the two become bitter enemies. While their dispute escalates toward violence, the violent street life of drugs and gangs also impacts their lives.

Allison Anders' well done stylistic street life drama shows gang life from the women's point of view. The girls empower themselves in a world where their boyfriends are usually dead or in prison by the time they are in their twenties. The young women are left to fend for themselves, usually with their children. Anders gets natural and realistic performances from the young cast. Salma Hayek appears in her American feature film debut as a character named Gata.

A Million to Juan (1994 Samuel Goldwyn)

D: Paul Rodriquez

S: Francisca Matos, Robert Grasmere, based on a story by Mark Twain

P: Steven Paul

Cast: Paul Rodriquez, Bert Rosario, Pepe Serna, Jonathan Hernandez, Edward James Olmos, Cheech Marin, Liz Torres, Tony Plana

Juan Lopez (Rodriquez) is a Mexican immigrant without a green card who sells oranges by the freeways of Los Angeles and is struggling to get along with his son when a chance encounter with a mysterious wealthy man makes him a millionaire. The money proceeds to change Lopez and those around him. This low budget comedy is loosely based on the Mark Twain short story "The Million Pound Bank Note." Completing the film for a mere $165,000, Rodriquez called in favors from his friends and fellow actors for his directorial debut with this small and successful comedy.

Filmed in and around Los Angeles.

Gilbert Roland as Hugo Da Silva, a man who believes the children of Fatima when they say they have seen a vision of the Virgin Mary in *The Miracle of Our Lady of Fatima*.

The Miracle of Our Lady of Fatima (1952 Warner Bros.)

D: John Brahm

S: Cran Wilbur and James O'Hanlon

P: Bryan Foy

Cast: Gilbert Roland, Angela Clark, Frank Silvera

A reverent, affectionate, literate and elaborate film of the true story of three small children who reported that they saw a vision of the Virgin Mary in a field near the village of Fatima, Portugal, in 1917.

Roland plays Hugo Da Silva, a disbeliever and a rascal who once was an aristocrat and follower of the church. He has a wry sense of humor, and he believes the children.

Fatima has become one of the greatest shrines in Christendom since the three children reported the apparition. The Virgin reportedly predicted the end of World War I and the beginning of World War II, and countless miracles and cures have been reported over the years. The project was filmed at the Warner Bros. Studios and at the Warner Bros. Ranch permanent Mexican village, with some alterations to make it pass for Portugal.

Missing (1982 Universal)
D: Constantin Costa-Gavras
S: Donald Stewart and Constantin Costa-Gavras
P: Edward Lewis and Constantin Costa-Gavras
Cast: Jack Lemmon, Sissy Spacek

In his first American film, Greek director Costa-Gavras—known for political thrillers such as *State of Siege* (1973) and *Z* (1969)—tells the real-life story of Charles Horman, an American journalist who disappeared along with 2,500 Chileans during the 1973 coup in Chile. Horman was part of a band of Americans who were essentially trying to avoid the Vietnam War and other domestic turmoil, who moved to Chile to work for social reform and became trapped in the midst of a coup.

Sissy Spacek and Jack Lemmon portray Horman's wife and father, who battle the Chilean government and a complacent United States State Department (which led the protests and stirred controversy when the film was released) for word about the missing man. The American diplomats pretend to be helping but seem to know all along that the Chilean military authorities have already murdered young Horman.

Though the movie is based on actual events, Chile and Allende are never mentioned, in much the same way that the Greek colonels are never specifically mentioned in *Z*. This is a very European-style American movie eschewing brash challenge in favor of subversive whispers. Costa-Gavras chillingly captured the oppressive atmosphere and intense terror of a social system in upheaval through understated documentary-like texture and poetic imagery. For example, a frightened white horse is seen racing through the embattled streets at sunrise followed by an armed troop carrier; impersonal helicopters are shown holding captured victims in their searchlights before machine guns cut the victims down and the killing becomes so overwhelming they must use a soccer stadium to retain prisoners and house the corpses. Although it reinforced the image of Latin America as a place of violent social upheaval, the film dealt very effectively with historic truth and managed to steer away from blatant stereotypes. It was filmed in studios in Mexico City, Acapulco and Churubusco.

However, in the February 17, 1982, edition of the *New Republic*, reviewer Stanley Kauffmann commented, "[While] Costa-Gavras wanted to make a film attacking United States interference in Chile, using the Horman story as his focus . . . that intent got watered down . . . It never comes close to excitement. Whatever your views on the anti-Allende coup, it's boring to watch a film obviously on the subject in which Allende is never named and which carefully avoids having any view."

The Mission (1986 Warner Bros.)
D: Roland Joffé
S: Robert Bolt
P: Fernando Ghia and David Puttnam
Cast: Robert De Niro, Jeremy Irons, Monirak Sisowath, Asuncion
    Ontiveros, Ray McAnally, Ronald Pickup, Cherie Lunghi, Liam Neeson

The story of the power struggle between church, in particular the Jesuit order, and state in colonial South America, *The Mission* dramatizes a period of colonization never before treated on film and about which very little has been written. The screenplay is by Robert Bolt (*Lawrence of Arabia* [1962] and *A Man for All Seasons* [1966]). Mendoza (De Niro), is a Spanish mercenary and slave trader who kills his brother (a cameo appearance by Aidan Quinn) and then renounces his former life and decides to enter the priesthood to atone for his past misdeeds. The other protagonist is a Jesuit priest, Father Gabriel (Irons), with whom Mendoza tries to protect the Guarani Indians (though the church has forbidden such actions).

The film was shot entirely on location; in Argentina at the monumental Iguassú Falls; in Colombia in the sixteenth-century walled city of Cartagena and the jungle near Santa Marta. Director Roland Joffé used some 350 Waunana Indians from the Chaco region of Colombia, who were housed in a specially built village close to the location. In addition to salary, a trust fund for health and education was set up for them by the film's producers. Monirak Sisowath, a Cambodian who appeared in *The Killing Fields* (1984), plays Ibaye, a Guarani Indian who becomes a Jesuit priest. Asuncion Ontiveros, who was born in Argentina and who is an Indian rights activist, also has a major role.

Joffé stated in press notes at the movie's release, "It's about South America, but it's about people. It's about choice, about power, about redemption, a luminous story on many levels."

The Mission won the Palme d'Or prize at the Cannes Film Festival and was nominated for seven Academy Awards® including Best Picture of 1986, but won only a single Oscar®, for Best Cinematography (Chris Menges).

Reviews for the film were mixed and widely divergent, but generally agreed about the majesty of the scenery and the earnestness and ambition of the themes presented. Irons and De Niro are very good, though De Niro's Mendoza is not quite believably Spanish.

Mr. Majestyk (1974 United Artists)
D: Richard Fleischer
S: Elmore Leonard
P: Walter Mirisch
Cast: Charles Bronson, Linda Cristal, Alejandro Rey

A Colorado melon farmer named Mr. Majestyk (Bronson), an ex-Vietnam vet, hunts down and kills the Mafia gang that has been terrorizing the Mexican American farm workers. Leonard's script, however, delivers a better-than-average revenge movie that has its lighter moments.

With a name like Mr. Majestyk, we're not quite certain if Bronson is Mexican American or just the "Immigrant Everyman" with its echoes of Eastern European immigrants of days gone by. This ambiguity suggests that Latin immigrants are no different from the Poles and Italians of the turn of the century, and treated as badly. Bronson does look the part of the Latin farm worker, and seems to sympathize with the farm workers' plight. This is a typical Charles Bronson violent action movie with a bit of social relevance. Cristal plays a Chicana activist who works with the farm workers, a potentially interesting character that is given short shrift once the macho action gets going. Rey is a friendly farm worker who gets his legs crushed for siding with Bronson.

Money Train (1995 Columbia)
D: Joseph Ruben
S: Doug Richardson and David Loughery, based on a story by Richardson
P: Doug Claybourne and Michael Steele, Jon Peters, Neil Canton
Cast: Wesley Snipes, Woody Harrelson, Jennifer Lopez, Robert Blake

Two New York City transit cops decide to rob the money train, a subway car that collects all the cash accrued from the transit system each day. To further complicate matters, they are also foster brothers and both in love with their new partner, Grace Santiago (Lopez).

Moon over Parador (1988 Universal)
D: Paul Mazursky
S: Leon Capetanos and Paul Mazursky, based on a story by Charles Booth
P: Paul Mazursky
Cast: Richard Dreyfuss, Raul Julia, Sonia Braga, Fernando Rey, Charo

This sophisticated and humorous farce is reminiscent of Anthony Hope's novel *The Prisoner of Zenda* and Mark Twain's novel *The Prince and the Pauper*.

On location in the fictional Latin American country of Parador, a struggling New York actor is kidnapped and forced to impersonate the country's late dictator, with funny and unexpected consequences.

Richard Dreyfuss plays Jack Noah, who gets the role of his life when Parador's fascist strongman drinks himself to death the day before the elections. The chief of police (Julia) then forces Noah to assume the role of president. Noah's confidence grows with each speech and with personal support from the dead leader's sultry mistress (Braga), a champion of Parador's downtrodden masses. But when guerrilla fighters strike, Noah wonders if it might be time to move on to a new role.

This film somewhat subscribes to the tired notion of an American being needed to save a Latin American country from itself. The movie was filmed in Brazil.

Murieta (1965 Warner Bros.)
D: George Sherman
S: James O'Hanlon, based on a story by O'Hanlon
P: José Sainz de Vicuna
Cast: Jeffrey Hunter

Set during the 1849 California Gold Rush, Jeffrey Hunter plays the legendary Mexican bandit Joaquin Murieta, who seeks revenge when his young wife is killed by three racist American miners. Murieta swears vengeance and sets out to find the killers. Made in Spain against desert backgrounds (though the story actually took place in the foothills of the High Sierras of California), it has the trappings of a "spaghetti Western." Slow moving and ponderous, there is nothing special or out of the ordinary in its execution.

Music of the Heart (1999 Miramax)
D: Wes Craven
S: Pamela Gray
P: Marianne Maddalena, Walter Scheuer, Allan Miller and
    Susan Kaplan
Cast: Meryl Streep, Angela Bassett, Gloria Estefan, Aidan Quinn

The true story of an East Harlem schoolteacher who fights to save her school's music program. Meryl Streep stars as Roberta Guaspari, the passionate school teacher determined to make music a part of every child's education. Popular singer Gloria Estefan makes her motion picture acting debut in a small role as Isabel Vasquez, one of the parents who support Guaspari's program. Estefan also sings the movie's title theme song "Music of My Heart," on the soundtrack. New York's East Harlem is shown with restraint as any low income urban neighborhood.

My Darling Clementine (1946 Twentieth Century Fox)
D: John Ford
S: Samuel G. Engel and Winston Miller, based on a story by
    Sam Hellman from the novel *Wyatt Earp, Frontier Marshall* by
    Stuart N. Lake
P: Samuel G. Engel
Cast: Henry Fonda, Victor Mature,
    Walter Brennan, Linda Darnell

My Darling Clementine centers on the true story of the Earp brothers, the Clanton gang, Doc Holliday and the famous gunfight at the O.K. Corral in Tombstone, Arizona, in the 1880s.

The Wyatt Earp-Doc Holliday partnership in the Earp-Clanton feud had been a popular subject for Westerns since the mid-1930s. (Cesar Romero played Wyatt Earp in *Frontier Marshall* in 1939, also for Fox.)

Director John Ford chose to emphasize the polarity between good and evil, adding the fictional women Chihuahua and Clementine, the archetypal dark and fair women of American fiction. He also portrayed the Earps as heroes, when both the Earps and Clantons were probably equally corrupt in real life.

Chihuahua (Darnell), a Mexican prostitute, is petulant, scheming, dishonest and unfaithful.

Linda Darnell (left) as Chihuahua, a Mexican prostitute, and Victor Mature (right) as Doc Holliday, in John Ford's *My Darling Clementine*.

She dies at the end of the film in typical Hollywood code justice. This is the third film in which Darnell plays a Latina.

When Earp (Fonda) first takes the job as marshal of Tombstone, she tells him, "This is Doc Holiday's town." As the plot develops, Tombstone becomes Earp's town. Chihuahua dotes on Doc (Mature) and gets jealous when Doc's ex-fiancée from the East, Clementine (Cathy Downs), arrives in town. Clementine meets Earp, and he becomes smitten with her. Things turn serious when Wyatt notices Chihuahua wearing a medallion that belonged to his murdered brother, Jim. After she confesses that Billy Clanton (John Ireland) gave it to her, Clanton shoots her. She dies a few hours later, and Doc Holliday then sides with the Earps in their battle with the Clantons at the O.K. Corral. All the Clantons die, as does Doc. The town moves away from outlaws like the Clantons and social misfits like Chihuahua and Doc Holliday to ordinary folks and civilization in the form of Earp and Clementine.

This was Ford's first film after serving in World War II, and also the first in which he exhibits doubts as to the nature of heroism and the American version of the history of the Old West.

My Family (1995 New Line Cinema)
D: Gregory Nava
S: Gregory Nava and Anna Thomas
P: Anna Thomas
Cast: Jimmy Smits, Esai Morales, Eduardo Lopez Rojas, Jenny Gago, Elpidia Carrillo, Lupe Ontiveros, Jacob Vargas, Jennifer Lopez, Maria Canals, Leon Singer, Enrique Castillo, Michael DeLorenzo, Jonathan Hernandez, Constance Marie, Edward James Olmos, Benito Martinez, Bel Hernandez,

Jose Sanchez (Rojas) is one of millions of immigrants who have come to Los Angeles in search of the American Dream. Ultimately, he finds the American Dream in his own family. *My Family* chronicles the divergent forces that affect the Sanchez family in a sweeping but intimate multi-generational saga, set against the turbulent social changes which transformed Los Angeles from a dusty pueblo settlement into one of America's leading cities. *My Family* depicts the joys and hardships of the Sanchez family during three momentous eras in American life—the twenties, the fifties and the eighties—as intimately recounted by their son Paco, an aspiring writer, played by Edward James Olmos.

Jimmy Smits plays Jimmy Sanchez, a troubled single father, and Esai Morales plays Chucho Sanchez, the wild rebellious son caught between two ways of life. Toni, as played by Constance Marie, is the social activist daughter. Elpidia Carrillo plays Isabel, a Salvadoran immigrant who slowly wins Jimmy's love and affection. Jennifer Lopez makes a memorable film debut as the young Maria.

Gregory Nava turns his script into an ambitious and stylistic film that is sentimental yet angry, focusing on one family over a sprawling canvas, and he is generally successful on all levels. Nava has assembled

one of the finest Latino acting ensembles ever and gives them the opportunity to play three dimensional characters and display talents that have too often gone unappreciated. Francis Ford Coppola wanted to get involved with a Latino project and Tom Luddy at American Zoetrope brought the script to Coppola's attention.

The film was shot in East Los Angeles and surrounding areas.

Gregory Nava's multi-generational drama, *My Family*, stars (clockwise from upper left) Constance Marie, Elpidia Carrillo, Jimmy Smits, Enrique Castillo, Lupe Ontiveros, Eduardo Lopez Rojas, Jenny Gago and Edward James Olmos.

My Man and I (1952 Metro-Goldwyn-Mayer)

D: William Wellman
S: John Fante and Jack Leonard
P: Stephen Ames
Cast: Ricardo Montalban, Claire Trevor, Wendell Corey, Shelley Winters, José Torvay, Jack Elam, Pascual Garcia Peña

Ricardo Montalban plays Chu Chu, a Mexican American farm worker in California who has just become a citizen and whose prized possession is a letter from the President congratulating him on his achievement. He spends his money not on drink (as so many of his compatriots are pictured doing) but on encyclopedias.

He takes a farm job with Mexican-hating Ansel Ames (Corey). Mrs. Ames (Trevor), a sultry and neglected woman, makes advances toward Chu Chu, which he rebuffs. He is in love with a suicidal taxi dancer named Nancy (Winters). Upon completion of the job, Ames pays him with a bad check, and Chu Chu tries unsuccessfully to collect. In the struggle, Ames is accidentally wounded with his own gun and coerces his wife to testify that Chu Chu shot him.

Chu Chu is convicted, but his friends force the Ameses to confess their perjury. Chu Chu is cleared of the charges and reunited with his true love, Nancy.

Torvay, Jack Elam and Pascual Garcia Peña lend fun to the script as Chu Chu's buddies, at one point using his volumes of encyclopedias to sit on during a poker game.

The fact that Chu Chu believes in the American system and that his friends take matters into their own hands by psychologically pressing the Ameses refreshingly demonstrates an assertive role for the Mexican American. The subject of integration is introduced through Chu Chu's love for Nancy, but the suggestion is that it is possible only with a lower class Anglo, which Nancy seems to represent. Superior acting saves a script that is fairly mediocre, despite its clear echoes of John Steinbeck's fiction.

Mystery Street (1950 Metro-Goldwyn-Mayer)

D: John Sturges
S: Sydney Boehm and Richard Brooks, based on an unpublished story by Leonard Spigelgass
P: Frank E. Taylor
Cast: Ricardo Montalban, Sally Forrest, Elsa Lanchester

Montalban is Pete Moralas, a Portuguese-American detective for the Boston Police, investigating the murder of a well-to-do amateur prostitute known to socialize with members Cape Cod high society. Moralas gets involved with the case because the body of the dead girl is found in the Portuguese section of the town in which he works. The thrust of the film is the demonstration of scientific techniques as applied to crime detection through the pioneering work of the Harvard University Department of Forensic Medicine. It was filmed partly in and around Boston. It is a refreshing change-of-pace mystery with Montalban as a

Latin investigating Boston's wealthy elite. His character, while out of his element, is neither patronized nor condescended to.

The Naked Dawn (1955 Universal)
D: Edgar G. Ulmer
S: Nina and Herman Schneider
P: James Q. Radford
Cast: Arthur Kennedy, Betta St. John, Eugene Iglesias

This film explores the corrosive effect the prospect of easy money has on a Mexican farmer (Iglesias) and his wife (St. John).

Santiago (Kennedy) hires the farmer to help him collect on the money from a freight train holdup, thus putting temptation in the way of the indigent farmer. Previously satisfied with his modest lot, the farmer now plans Kennedy's death in order to obtain the ill-gotten loot.

The film plays like a mixture of *The Pearl* (1948) and *The Treasure of the Sierra Madre* (1948) with strong performances in a very downbeat story that lacks the emotional and artistic punch of its predecessors.

The Naked Jungle (1954 Paramount)
D: Byron Haskin
S: Ranald MacDougall and Philip Yardan, based on the story "Leiningen Versus the Ants" by Carl Stephenson
P: George Pal
Cast: Charlton Heston, Eleanor Parker, William Conrad

A drama about a mail order bride (Parker) arriving at a South American plantation run by a lonely American (Heston). Despite conflicts, they must pull together when an army of killer ants threatens to destroy everything in its path, including the plantation. Heston refers to having civilized the Indians by taking them out of the jungle, giving them jobs, and developing the land, though he acknowledges their strength and intelligence as descendants of the Mayas.

The Naked Maja (1959 United Artists)
D: Henry Koster and Mario Russo
S: Georgia Prosperi and Norman Carwin, based on a story by Oscar Saul and Talbot Jennings
P: Goffredo Lombardo
Cast: Anthony Franciosa, Ava Gardner

The story of the tempestuous love affair between famous Spanish painter Goya (Franciosa) and the Duchess of Alba (Gardner). His painting of the noblewoman in the nude scandalized eighteenth-century Spain.

This was an American-Italian co-production and filmed in Spain. Gardner and Franciosa are fine in their roles, and though the film is uninvolving and slow moving, it is spectacularly photographed.

Nancy Goes to Rio (1949 Metro-Goldwyn-Mayer)
D: Robert Z. Leonard
S: Sidney Sheldon, based on a story by Jane Hall, Frederick Kohner, and Ralph Block
P: Joe Pasternak
Cast: Ann Sothern, Jane Powell, Xavier Cugat, Carmen Miranda, Barry Sullivan, Fortunio Bonanova

A mother (Sothern) and daughter (Powell), both actresses, are unwilling competitors for the same part in a Rio theatrical production and for the same man (Sullivan). There is a glaring error on a painted studio backdrop: the Corcovado and Sugarloaf Mountain, two of Rio's most famous sights, are joined together even though they are geographically separate.

To this fluffy musical comedy filmed at MGM Studios, Miranda adds a musical bright spot.

The Navy Comes Through (1942 RKO Radio Pictures)
D: A. Edward Sutherland
S: Roy Chanslor and Aeneas MacKenzie
P: Islin Aurtes
Cast: Pat O'Brien, George Murphy, Jackie Cooper, Desi Arnaz

The story of a naval gun crew aboard a freighter in the Atlantic during World War II. Arnaz plays Tarriba, a Cuban enlistee who hopes to do what he can to serve America.

The Night of the Iguana (1964 Metro-Goldwyn-Mayer)
D: John Huston
S: Anthony Veiller and John Huston, based on the play by Tennessee Williams
P: Ray Stark
Cast: Richard Burton, Deborah Kerr, Ava Gardner

Huston created a modern and adult rendering of the romantic image of Mexico with his version of Tennessee Williams' *The Night of the Iguana.*

The film paints Mexico as an exotic land of unbridled passions, steamy sex, exotic tropical vistas, friendly natives and a refuge in a primal setting from the problems of civilized white society.

The story is of a defrocked American minister (Burton) who conducts tours for lonely women out of a run-down Mexican hotel. Complex psychological interactions form the basis of the drama. Ava Gardner is the sexy, boozy hotel owner who has two Mexican maraca-playing muscle boys at her sexual beck and call.

The publicity surrounding the off-screen and on-screen antics of Huston, Williams, Burton (and his then-wife Elizabeth Taylor) and Gardner in the Ray Stark production fueled the imaginations of a generation of moviegoers.

The Night of the Iguana

Director John Huston and cinematographer Gabriel Figueroa provide a romantic and visually stunning image of Mexico in *The Night of the Iguana*, with Richard Burton as a defrocked minister and Ava Gardner (center) as a voluptuous innkeeper who has two Mexican maraca boys at her beck and call.

Puerto Vallarta and Mismaloya beach became synonymous with an adult romantic Mexico, which turned the location from a tiny fishing village to a much sought-after world-class vacation destination. It was filmed largely with a Mexican crew with Gabriel Figueroa as the cinematographer.

In a 1984 interview, Huston revealed his feelings about Mexico. "I never wanted to make a travelogue of clichés about Mexico. Usually Americans see only one aspect of Mexico, the tourism. Mexico is a country with so many faces, and only through living there and going around can you get to know everything about its heart, or hearts I should say." He continued, "There's a savage face to Mexico, and another, benign and gentle, a deep humanity."

Notorious (1946 RKO Radio Pictures)

D: Alfred Hitchcock
S: Ben Hecht, based on a theme by Hitchcock
P: Alfred Hitchcock
Cast: Cary Grant, Ingrid Bergman, Claude Rains, Antonio Moreno, Luis Serrano, Tina Menard

Brazil is the setting, but this is not a film about rumbas, congas, or tropical romance. T.R. Devlin (Grant) is an American agent who enlists a Nazi's daughter, Alicia Huberman (Bergman), for an espionage mission in Rio de Janeiro. The plan is for her to infiltrate a Nazi spy ring operating out of Brazil by marrying its leader (Rains) in order to betray him to the OSS.

This melodramatic love story features Hitchcock's stylish grace of execution and mastery of film form. Moreno plays Señor Ortiza and Luis Serrano plays Dr. Silva. Menard plays a maid.

Old Gringo (1989 Columbia)

D: Luis Puenzo
S: Luis Puenzo and Aida Batnik, based on the novel *El Gringo Viejo* by Carlos Fuentes
P: Lois Bonfiglio
Cast: Jane Fonda, Gregory Peck, Jimmy Smits, Pedro Armendariz, Jr.

Directed by Puenzo (director of *The Official Story*, 1985's Academy Award® winner for Best Foreign Language Film), *Old Gringo* is a curious film, directed and written by an Argentinean (Puenzo), based on a novel by Mexican novelist Carlos Fuentes. Jane Fonda starred in and produced the film.

It is the story set in Mexico during the height of the Mexican Revolution of a romantic triangle between the aging writer Ambrose Bierce (Peck), a spinster schoolteacher (Fonda), and one of Pancho Villa's young generals (Smits).

It is based loosely on the last days of turn-of-the-century writer and newspaperman Ambrose Bierce, the "Old Gringo" of the title, who crossed the border into Mexico not long after the Mexican Revolution erupted in 1910 and was never heard from again. *Old Gringo* would probably never have been made had Jane Fonda not been captivated by the fictional character of Harriet Winslow. She is a prim and proper Washington schoolteacher who goes to Mexico as a tutor for the children of a rich *hacendado* and finds herself in the middle of a revolution while falling in love with the illiterate peasant General Arroyo.

Old Gringo was budgeted at $25 million and required hundreds of extras, period costumes, horses and wranglers. It was filmed on soundstages at Churubusco Studios in Mexico City and at a hacienda just north of the city and in the cities of Zacatecas and Torreón.

The Old Gringo, as played by Gregory Peck, seeks the peace of death; while Harriet Winslow (Fonda) seeks the challenge of a new life. General Arroyo (Smits) represents vitality and virility, and Harriet is interested in the sexuality and mystique of the Latin male. As a general, however, he is indecisive and ineffectual in leading his people. Luna, his woman, does not even attempt to take her man back from the Winslow character. Mexicans are shown as brutal and barbaric (savage, unwashed and uneducated), while the Americans are noble, loyal and sensitive. Mexican women appear most often as whores. While *Old Gringo* has a historical sweep and epic grandeur that are true to the spirit of the way the revolution caught the imagination of the American public, certainly there is more to Mexican culture than peasant revolutionaries, corridas, eating tortillas and giving in to passion, even in time of war and chaos.

Harriet Winslow's request to have the body of Ambrose Bierce, the Old Gringo, results in the death of Arroyo. In the film, American authorities find Villa (Armendariz) quickly and exert pressure on him in the midst of the revolution to return the body of the American. In fact, the United States government sent General Pershing and an army of cavalry to find Villa, and after six months of riding all over northern Mexico, the expedition returned to the States exhausted and empty-handed.

Gregory Peck, Jane Fonda and Jimmy Smits (right), who portrays a young Mexican general, are involved in a romantic triangle in *Old Gringo*, an epic adventure story of passion and power set against the backdrop of the Mexican Revolution.

The Old Man and the Sea (1958 Warner Bros.)

D: John Sturges
S: Peter Viertel
P: Leland Hayward
Cast: Spencer Tracy, Felipe Pazos, Harry Bellaver

This film is based on the novel by Ernest Hemingway, which won the Pulitzer Prize for fiction in 1952. Spencer Tracy stars as Santiago, an old Cuban fisherman. Tracy, of Irish descent, had previously played a Portuguese in *Captains Courageous* (1937) and a Mexican American in *Tortilla Flat* (1942).

An old Cuban sailor, Santiago is reduced in his old age to making a living as a fisherman. For eighty-four days he has had no luck and has lived on the charity of a small boy (Pazos) who idolizes him. Seeking to defy this string of bad luck, the old man ventures far from coastal waters and hooks a great marlin. He pits his failing strength against his deep-sea antagonist. In his lonely vigil he feels a kinship with the vastness of the ocean and its creatures. When the climax comes, he is strong enough to pull in the marlin, which is longer than his boat and harpoon. With the prized fish lashed to his frail craft he sets sail for home. But sharks repeatedly attack the carcass. In a nightmare struggle he loses his knife and harpoon but beats off the sharks. Weary and exhausted, he beaches his craft with nothing to show for his exertions but the bare spine and useless tail. He gains a brief moment of fame, for his fellows exclaim after seeing the remains, "There never was such a fish."

Spencer Tracy as Santiago, an old Cuban fisherman, befriends a young boy, played by Felipe Pazos, in *The Old Man and the Sea*.

The film began production in 1956 with Fred Zinnemann as director near Cojimar, Cuba, the setting of the original story. Tracy arrived five weeks prior to shooting to get in shape and to get his face tanned and properly weather beaten. A young eleven-year-old Cuban boy with no prior acting experience, Felipe Pazos, won the role of the young boy after an extensive search by Zinnemann. Hemingway went with a second-unit camera crew to Talara, Peru, attempting to catch the largest marlin fish he could grab. The footage would be utilized in the final film.

Due to differences of opinion with producer Hayward and star Tracy, Zinnemann left the project and was replaced by John Sturges. The production was beset by problems and much of the filming took place in a water tank at Warner Bros. Studios. It lasted a total of six and a half months, including four months with Tracy and a crew of 100 in Cuba. An additional two weeks of filming two miles off the Kona Coast of Hawaii with Tracy and a crew of fifty were required to get the final exterior scenes for proper sea and sky effects.

Faithful to Hemingway to a fault, the film is perhaps the most literal word-forward rendition of a written story ever filmed. It is essentially a one-character drama with voice-over narration and dialogue by Tracy. The camera stays with Tracy on the boat throughout his ordeal and personal triumph.

The universal story of man against the elements and his kinship with nature was difficult to transfer to film when most of the action is the inner thoughts of a man alone in a boat for days battling a fish. Critics were torn over the approach to the film, while most praised Tracy's acting efforts, they felt, good as he was, that he could not carry the film by himself. The film won an Oscar® for its musical score by Dmitri Tiomkin and garnered Academy Award® nominations for Tracy as Best Actor of 1958 and for James Wong Howe's cinematography.

Felipe Pazos was not invited to the Washington, D.C., premiere of the film in 1958, which was hosted by then Cuban ambassador Don Arroyo. Felipe's father had played a big role with Fidel Castro's revolutionaries before fleeing to the United States just a few months prior to the premiere. Arroyo represented the Batista regime and therefore, politically, the boy could not be allowed to attend.

One-Eyed Jacks (1961 Paramount)

D: Marlon Brando

S: Guy Trosper and Calder Willingham, based on the novel
The Authentic Death of Hendry Jones by Charles Neider

P: Frank Rosenberg

Cast: Marlon Brando, Karl Malden, Pina Pellicer, Katy Jurado,
Ben Johnson, Larry Duran, Miriam Colon, Rodolfo Acosta,
Margarita Cordova

One of two bank robbers on the run in Mexico is deserted by his accomplice and spends five years in a Mexican prison. When he finally escapes with another prisoner, Johnny Rio (Brando) and his new accomplice, Modesto (Duran), join up with two other bandits and set out for California to rob a small-town bank. In Monterey, California, the four meet up with Rio's original partner in crime, Dad Longworth (Malden), who is now a respectable sheriff married to a Mexican woman, Maria (Jurado), with a stepdaughter Louisa (Pellicer). Rio strikes up a romance with Louisa as a way of getting to her stepfather. Later, Rio's group carries out the bank robbery without Rio. Longworth captures the innocent Rio and intends to execute him. Maria tells Longworth that Louisa is pregnant by Rio. Longworth lashes out at his wife, saying, "Is this the thanks I get for taking you out of the bean fields?"

The meaning of the film's title has to do with two sides of man's nature, one visible, the other (like the unseen reverse side of the one-eyed jack in a deck of cards) remaining in shadow. For the good man, the shadow side is evil.

This unusual revenge Western, though overlong and somewhat slow, is highlighted by in-depth characterizations and beautiful color cinematography. Brando points up the richness of the Mexican American culture of Monterey through the strong female characters played by Jurado and Pellicer. Larry Duran as Modesto, Rios' bandit friend, is allowed to be a human being instead of a stereotype. Lush romantic use is made of the Monterey location seascapes and the fiesta atmosphere. In the Mexico sequence Brando shows us a señorita and a whore (Colon), but as real characters, not stereotypes. Felipe Turich and Nacho Galindo have minor supporting roles in the film.

One from the Heart (1982 Zoetrope/Columbia)

D: Francis Ford Coppola

S: Francis Ford Coppola and Armyan Bernstein, based on a story by
Bernstein

P: Fred Roos, Gary Frederickson, and Armyan Bernstein

Cast: Frederic Forrest, Teri Garr, Raul Julia, Nastassja Kinski

This is a fantasy musical acted out on a stylized studio set of Las Vegas with all the aplomb and dash that one would expect from a Coppola movie paying homage to the history of Latin-influenced Hollywood films. Raul Julia as a Latin Lover type acknowledged the images and the fantasies that Hollywood created and that helped to shape our collective images.

During the course of a single day, husband and wife Hank (Forrest) and Frannie (Garr) have a tiff and take up with chance romantic partners, although they still love each other. Hank takes up with Leila (Kinski) and Frannie takes up with Ray (Julia), a tuxedoed Latin singer and piano player who turns out to be a waiter. At one point Frannie and Roy do the tango on a Hollywood South Seas island set. Later, they nuzzle while "The Carioca" (which Fred Astaire and Ginger Rogers danced in *Flying Down to Rio* [1933]) plays on the record player.

One Good Cop (1991 Buena Vista)
D: Heywood Gould
S: Heywood Gould
P: Laurence Mark
Cast: Michael Keaton, Rene Russo, Kevin Conway, Benjamin Bratt, Tony Plana, Rachel Ticotin, Anthony LaPaglia

In this story of a moral dilemma, dedicated police detective Artie Lewis (Keaton) must choose between taking his revenge on the thugs who are indirectly responsible for his partner Diroma's (LaPaglia) death and looking after Diroma's three young daughters, who are left in the care of Lewis and his wife. Putting the possible adoption of the children in jeopardy, Lewis, with the help of a streetwise undercover cop named Grace (Ticotin), who has managed to work her way into the drug lord's inner circle, sees a chance to steal a fortune from Latin drug lord Beniamino (Plano). The drug lord was one of those indirectly responsible for Diroma's death.

What should have been a much more interesting film is given the typical Hollywood "dumbing down" treatment, turning a possibly interesting moral dilemma into a morally questionable, violence-driven, cliched cops-and-robbers movie about Latino drug dealers. These images, however, are offset by Hispanic police officers Felix (Bratt) and Grace (Ticotin).

100 Rifles (1969 Twentieth Century Fox)
D: Tom Gries
S: Clair Huffaker and Tom Gries, based on the novel *The Californio* by Robert MacLead
P: Marvin Schwartz
Cast: Raquel Welch, Jim Brown, Burt Reynolds, Fernando Lamas

An American lawman (Brown) crosses the border into Mexico in pursuit of Mexican outlaw Yaqui Joe (Reynolds), who has stolen rifles in order to arm the Indians against a Mexican general (Lamas) who is bent on annihilating them. Both are captured by the general and saved by a rebel Indian woman (Welch). They join forces in order to do away with the general. In the ensuing battle the Indian woman dies but the general and his forces are defeated. The lawman returns to the United States, and Yaqui Joe finds something he can believe in among the Indians.

Welch and Reynolds make believable Latins, Welch being of Bolivian background and Reynolds of part Native American heritage. Reynolds almost steals the film with his tough but fun bandido characterization, giving audiences a preview of the easygoing charm he would put to good use in his later starring films. The movie was filmed in Spain.

Burt Reynolds, Raquel Welch and Jim Brown engage in a shoot-out with a Mexican general (portrayed by Fernando Lamas, not shown) in *100 Rifles*.

187 (1997 Warner Bros.)

D: Kevin Reynolds
S: Scott Yagemann
P: Bruce Davey and Steve McEveety
Cast: Samuel L. Jackson, Kelly Rowan, Clifton Gonzalez Gonzalez, John Heard

Trevor Garfield (Jackson), an enlightened man and science teacher in an inner city New York school is menaced by an angry student who stabs him in the back. After spending more than a year in the hospital, Garfield moves to Los Angeles for a fresh start and takes a job as a substitute teacher. The school is terrorized by Latino gang members who taunt Garfield to the breaking point, forcing him to take matters into his own hands. Clifton Gonzalez Gonzalez received attention and critical raves for his role as Cesar, a antagonistic gang leader.

This controversial and simplistic film dehumanizes African-American and Latino youth and codifies the look of all Latino students—forcing them into the monolithic image of a modern gang-banger or tagger, with a tattooed and pierced body, shaved head, baggy pants and no respect for themselves, teachers, parents or community.

One Way Street (1950 Universal)

D: Hugo Fregonese
S: Lawrence Kimble, based on his story "Death on a Side Street"
P: Leonard Goldstein
Cast: James Mason, Marta Toren, Dan Duryea, Rodolfo Acosta, Margarito Luna, Tito Renaldo, George J. Lewis, Robert Espinoza, José Dominguez, Julia Montoya

A Los Angeles doctor (Mason) steals $200,000 from a gangster and his girlfriend (Toren). He flees to Mexico, and en route his plane is forced down near a small village, where he hides out. He begins to find himself while treating the natives and restoring their health. He lives with the fear of the inevitable day when the gangsters will find him.

This routine crime melodrama, with an able cast and good direction by Fregonese, who contrasted the dignity of the villagers with the ruthlessness of the gangsters, was filmed partly on location in Mexico.

Only Angels Have Wings (1938 Columbia)

D: Howard Hawks
S: Jules Furthman, based on a story by Hawks
P: Howard Hawks
Cast: Cary Grant, Jean Arthur, Rita Hayworth, Melissa Sierra, Richard Barthelmess, Noah Beery, Jr.

Set in Barranca, Peru, the film tells the story of a group of mail-plane pilots in love with danger who battle storms and hardships to fly cargo over the Andes.

Geoff Carter (Grant) is the owner of the airplane firm, driving his fliers to undertake almost suicidal trips in decrepit planes in order to ensure a government subsidy that will put his business on a secure financial footing. Bonnie Lee (Arthur), a show-girl who falls in love with Geoff and leaves her job to be with him, is attracted by his courage but repelled by his ruthlessness. Carter initially ignores her but gradually reveals the vulnerable side of his character. Judith (Hayworth) is Carter's old flame; after years of toiling in B films, this role gave her the opportunity to make an impression. Melissa Sierra is Lily, a native girl who loves the young pilot, Joe (Beery).

Typical Hollywood banana republic set for *Only Angels Have Wings*, a story about mail pilots who fly cargo over the Andes Mountains in Peru.

Only Once in a Lifetime (1978 Movie Time Films)

D: Alejandro Grattan
S: Alejandro Grattan
P: Moctesuma Esparza
Cast: Miguel Robelo, Sheree North, Socorro Swan, Estrellita Lopez

Moctesuma Esparza produced this film about Dominguez (Robelo), a Chicano artist living in a Los Angeles barrio who has lost his desire to live. Dominguez is haunted by the memory of his dead wife and, though talented, limits his own artistic success by refusing to paint in a style that will attract buyers. He begins to be transformed when he meets a Chicano schoolteacher who helps him embrace life again.

In this technically proficient film, the sensitive realism of the barrio culture of the time is felt throughout. Esparza recalled that "[making the film] was a satisfactory artistic experience, but on economic disaster. We previewed the film and got a warm reception from audiences and critics, but when we released it, nobody paid to see it."

Grattan is a Texas filmmaker, and Robelo has acted in theater and television. *Only Once in a Lifetime* is one of the first feature films written, produced, directed and cast by Spanish-surnamed people in Hollywood. The film is considered a Chicano film and was made on a $500,000 budget.

Our Man in Havana (1960 Columbia)

D: Sir Carol Reed
S: Graham Greene, based on his novel of the same name
P: Sir Carol Reed
Cast: Alec Guinness, Maureen O'Hara, Ernie Kovacs, Ralph Richardson, Noel Coward

A comedic satire set in the period before the Castro Revolution involves a British vacuum cleaner salesman (Guinness) turned British agent in Havana. A fictional spy ring with hilarious beginnings takes on a dramatic aspect when Guinness' so-called phony agents begin to be killed by real agents in the Cuban capital. The film was critically acclaimed, but its sophisticated humor did not connect with American audiences, from whom the film met with a poor box office reception.

Reed wanted to film in Cuba, but the overthrow of Batista in January 1959 left the possibility of filming there seriously in doubt. Amazingly, less than four months later, on April 13, 1959, cameras began rolling on the film after assurances from the new Cuban government under Castro that everything would go well. There was an advance agreement with Cuban labor unions that provided for thirty-seven Cuban technicians to work on the film, an additional twenty-one persons to be employed in some facet of production, and over 1,000 paid extras. During the filming, American comic genius Ernie Kovacs, playing a Batista general, narrowly escaped death when he wandered off the set in uniform and was confronted by an armed Castro policeman, ready to shoot him, believing him to be a Batista supporter. After filming for five weeks in Cuba, the production moved on to London.

Out of Sight (1998 Universal)
D: Steven Soderbergh
S: Scott Frank, based on the novel by Elmore Leonard
P: Danny De Vito, Michael Shamberg, Stacey Sher
Cast: George Clooney, Jennifer Lopez, Dennis Farina, Ving Rhames, Don Cheadle, Nancy Allen, Albert Brooks

Considered one of the best films of 1998 by nationally respected film critics and audiences, Out of Sight is a sly action comedy with a romantic twist. Clooney stars as a handsome and charming bank robber who escapes from prison, only to meet his match in a tough-as-nails Federal Marshall Karen Cisco, played by Jennifer Lopez. Out of Sight contains fast moving action, easygoing comedy, incisive and droll ensemble performances; the steamy chemistry of Clooney, in his wiliest, most complex role to date, and Lopez, who projects a charismatic mix of fire, allure and sensuality.

The Outrage (1964 Metro-Goldwyn-Mayer)
D: Martin Ritt
S: Michael Kanin
P: A. Ronald Lubin
Cast: Paul Newman, Claire Bloom, Laurence Harvey, Howard da Silva

An indifferent remake Kurosawa's Rashomon, but with an Old West setting and an improbable blue-eyed all-American Paul Newman as the darkened-up Mexican bandit Juan Carrasco. The story concerns the murder and rape of stagecoach passengers by a Mexican bandit as told from the points of view of the survivors.

"Paul Newman emerges as a sort of junior grade Leo Carrillo, spitting and spewing and wallowing in dialect and playing the villain, the lecher, the social outcast, the lover and the coward to the hilt for his own very private edification," Judith Crist, New York Herald Tribune (10/8/64).

"Mr. Newman . . . steams his way through the role of the supposed villain with notable effect," New York Telegraph (10/8/64).

The Ox-Bow Incident (1943 Twentieth Century Fox)

D: William Wellman
S: Lamar Trotti, based on the novel by Walter Van Tilburg Clark
P: Lamar Trotti
Cast: Henry Fonda, Dana Andrews, Mary Beth Hughes,
Anthony Quinn, Francis Ford, Chris-Pin Martin

The story of three drifters (Andrews, Quinn and Ford) who are summarily tried and hanged for cattle rustling and murder. The film is a searing indictment of lynch-mob frontier justice and is considered by many to be one of the finest Westerns ever made. In the end it is discovered that the hanged men did not commit the crime.

Quinn, billed as simply "Mexican," is lynched with his companions. At first he attempts to pass himself off as an ignorant Mexican, fulfilling the mob's stereotypical expectations with a series of "No sabe" answers to the campfire interrogation. When he finally drops the ruse, he reveals himself as an articulate, intelligent, tough-talking hombre. The film was made at the insistence of star Henry Fonda but proved too downbeat for audiences during World War II.

Panama Hattie (1942 Metro-Goldwyn-Mayer)

D: Norman Z. McLeod
S: Jack McGowan and Wilkie Mahoney, based on the play by
Herbert Fields, B.G. De Sylva and Cole Porter
P: Arthur Freed
Cast: Ann Sothern, Red Skelton, Dan Dailey, Jr., Lena Horne

A showgirl in Panama (Sothern) helps to capture Nazi agents. The film introduced Lena Horne in a musical number.

Panama Sal (1957 Republic Pictures)

D: William Withey
S: Arnold Belgard
P: Edward J. White
Cast: Elena Verdugo, Edward Kemmer, Carlos Rivas, José Gonzalez-
Gonzalez

A wealthy American and his two buddies crash land a plane in Panama, where they find a sensational calypso singer at a nightclub whom they believe they can turn into a star back in the States.

This mildly amusing but conventional grade B romantic musical comedy was one of the last Republic productions. It was a disappointing film return for Elena Verdugo after her success on television in the popular long-running series *Meet Millie* (1952-56).

Pan-Americana (1945 RKO Radio Pictures)
D: John H. Auer
S: Lawrence Kimble, based on a story by Frederick Kohner and Auer
P: John H. Auer
Cast: Phillip Terry, Audrey Long, Robert Benchley, Eve Arden,
    Alma Beltran, Julian Rivero

This film was constructed to showcase the talents of various Latin American performers via a storyline about of a group of American journalists who head South of the border to research a feature story. Along the way they stop off in such countries as Cuba, Mexico and Brazil just long enough for a musical number in each. The film is important in that it provides a permanent film record of many Latin performers of the period at their musical best, such as Miguelito Valdes, Isabelita, Chuy Castillion, the Padilla Sisters, Chuy Reyes and his Orchestra, and Nestor Amaral and his Samba Band. Beltran plays Miss Guatemala.

Pancho Villa (1972 Scotia Int.)
D: Eugenio Martin
S: Julian Halevy
P: Bernard Gordon
Cast: Telly Savalas, Clint Walker, Anne Francis, Chuck Connors

Savalas makes an improbable bald Pancho Villa in this badly made fictional recounting of the raid on Columbus, New Mexico, by Villa. Filmed in Spain.

Passion (1954 RKO Radio Pictures)
D: Allan Dwan
S: Beatrice Dresher, Joseph Leytes and Howard Estabrook, based on a
    story by Dresher, Leytes and Miguel Padilla
P: Benedict Bogeaus
Cast: Cornel Wilde, Yvonne De Carlo, Rodolfo Acosta, Alex Montoya,
    Rosa Turich

Juan Obregon (Wilde) is a young rancher who seeks vengeance when Mexicans murder his wife and friends in the dispute over land rights. De Carlo plays a dual role as the murdered wife, Tanya, and her younger sister, Rosa. This routine Western in an early California setting is highlighted by location photography in the California Sierras.

Pat Garrett and Billy the Kid (1973 Metro-Goldwyn-Mayer)
D: Sam Peckinpah
S: Rudy Wurlitzer
P: Gordon Carroll
Cast: James Coburn, Kris Kristofferson, Jason Robards, R.G. Armstrong,
    Slim Pickens, Katy Jurado, Emilio Fernandez

In 1880s New Mexico, Pat Garrett (Coburn), now a sheriff, warns young Billy the Kid (Kristofferson) that he must do his duty and capture Billy in spite of their former friendship. When Billy escapes, Garrett catches up with Billy and is forced to kill him.

Peckinpah's special talent for blending violence and a poetic vision of the Old West is very much in evidence in this, his last Western. In killing Billy, Garrett not only seems to signal the end of the fierce idealism that had characterized the 1960s but the 1880s as well. Garrett, in effect, also seals his own fate at the hands of the corporate types who hired him.

Jurado is the wife of an old sheriff (Pickens) who goes to her husband's aid, shotgun in hand, to rid a hornet's nest of outlaws at Garrett's request. She weeps as her husband, who has been shot during the outlaw confrontation, dies while he sits on a rock in the sunset. Fernandez plays a Mexican rancher who is attacked and left for dead by a rival gang of outlaws.

Billy's gang is seen with a group of Mexican prostitutes. Maria, Billy's Mexican girlfriend, is played by Kris Kristofferson's then-wife, Rita Coolidge. There are no virginal señoritas in Peckinpah's vision. Jorge Russek plays a nontraditional Mexican outlaw called Silva who wears a Stetson instead of a sombrero. Though the story takes place in New Mexico, it was filmed in Durango, Mexico.

The Pawnbroker (1965 Allied Artists)

D: Sidney Lumet
S: David Friedkin and Morton Fine, based on the novel by Edmund Lewis Wallant
P: Roger Lewis and Philip Langner
Cast: Rod Steiger, Geraldine Fitzgerald, Jaime Sanchez, Brock Peters

A classic character study, Sol Nazerman (Steiger) is a Jewish man who owns and operates a pawnshop amid the urban squalor of New York's Spanish Harlem. The characters inhabiting his shop and the area in which he works have a sense of reality rarely equaled in a mainstream movie. This was achieved in part by filming the movie in Spanish Harlem on and around 116th Street and Park Avenue as well as utilizing local actors. There is no sense of Hollywood here.

Nazerman's relationship with his young Puerto Rican apprentice, Jesus (Sanchez), evolves slowly as Jesus comes to understand the pawnbroker's struggle to survive the horrors of a Nazi concentration camp. The youth looks up to the pawnbroker as his teacher. "Teach me about gold, boss," he says to him, despite Nazerman's negative attitude toward everyone. Jesus gives up his own life to save the man who, in a moment of despair, told

Jaime Sanchez (left) as Jesus, a young Puerto Rican apprentice to Sol Nazerman (played by Rod Steiger), wants to learn all he can about his boss's Spanish Harlem pawnshop in *The Pawnbroker*.

him, "You mean nothing to me." The pawnbroker, who has cut himself off from all emotions, realizes too late his love for his assistant.

The Pearl (1948 RKO Radio Pictures)

D: Emilio Fernandez

S: John Steinbeck, Emilio Fernandez, and Jack Wagner, based on the story by John Steinbeck. Spanish adaptation by Emilio Fernandez and Mauricio Magdaleno

P: Oscar Dancingers

Cast: Pedro Armendariz, Maria Elena Marques, Alfonso Bedoya, Fernando Wagner

A struggling pearl diver, Kino (Armendariz), unable to support his family and needing money to pay for medical care for his baby Coyotito,

Cinematographer Gabriel Figueroa (left), stars Maria Elena Marquez and Pedro Armendariz, and director Emilio Fernandez (right), pose for a picture on the set of *The Pearl*.

finds the most magnificent pearl anyone has ever seen. The beauty and power of the jewel soon becomes a curse that threatens to destroy him, his wife, Juana (Marques), and their way of life.

Stunning night photography by the master cinematographer Gabriel Figueroa and Acapulco seascapes support the social and personal drama.

With John Steinbeck's active support, *The Pearl* was written for the screen and filmed in 1945, prior to the novel's publication in the States. The legend of Kino is based on an ancient Mexican legend. RKO shared financial responsibility for the $400,000 budget with RKO's Churubusco Studios and the Mexican government. Filmed in English and Spanish simultaneously, it grossed $2 million in its initial United States release. *The Pearl* won the International Prize at San Sebastian.

The Penitent (1988 New Century Vista Film Co.)

D: Cliff Osmond
S: Cliff Osmond
P: Michael Fitzgerald
Cast: Raul Julio, Armand Assante, Rona Freed, Julie Carmen

A melodramatic romantic triangle film set in a small present-day New Mexico town. The town is ruled by a Catholic sect of Flagellants who re-create the passion play, actually crucifying the participant playing Christ. This interesting but uneven story features high-powered performances from the leading performers. Though the story takes place in New Mexico, it was filmed in Mexico.

Pepe (1960 Columbia)

D: George Sidney
S: Dorothy Kingsley and Claude Binyon, based on a story by Leonard
    Spigelgass and Sonya Levien, from the play *Broadway Magic* by
    Ladislas Bush-Fekete
P: George Sidney
Cast: Cantinflas, Shirley Jones, Dan Dailey, Carlos Montalban

After his tremendous international success in *Around the World in 80 Days* (1956), Cantinflas chose this three-hour star-studded extravaganza as a way to introduce himself to the American public as a star in his own right, with the box office insurance of Hollywood notables in cameo roles.

Cantinflas plays a groom named Pepe, who has taken care of a white stallion for years in Mexico. One day, Pepe finds the stallion sold to an American movie director (Dailey), so Pepe travels to the States to be with his horse.

The film, shot against Mexican backgrounds and Los Angeles, offered little, though a highlight was the tequila dance number with Debbie Reynolds and an animated sequence in which the real Cantinflas fights with a cartoon bull.

The Perez Family (1994 Samuel Goldwyn)

D: Mira Nair
S: Robin Swicord
P: Michael Nozik and Lydia Dean Pilcher
Cast: Marisa Tomei, Alfred Molina, Chazz Palminteri, Anjelica Huston,
    Trini Alvarado, Celia Cruz

Set against the vibrant colors and rhythms of Miami's Little Havana, *The Perez Family* follows the lives of a group of Cuban immigrants who discover that the family has become strangers and strangers have became a family. After being released from twenty years in a Cuban jail, Juan Raul Perez (Molina), goes to Miami in hopes of reuniting with his wife Carmela (Huston) and now-grown daughter, Teres (Alvarado). On the boat over, he meets Dottie Perez (Tomei) a voluptuous free-spirit who dreams of rock 'n' roll and John Wayne. Upon their arrival in the United States, an immigration official erroneously lists Juan and Dottie as "Married." Meanwhile, anticipation turns into disappointment for Carmela, who thinks Juan is not among the final Mariel refugees.

The film was the subject of protest from Hispanic civil rights groups in the United States because Hispanic actors were not cast in leading roles and the director and writer were non-Hispanic.

The Pest (1997 TriStar)

D: Paul Miller
S: David Bar Katz, John Leguizamo, based on the story "The Most
    Dangerous Game" by Richard Connell
P: Sid Sheinberg, Jonathan Shienberg and Bill Sheinberg
Cast: John Lequizamo, Jeffrey Jones, Edoardo Ballerini,
    Freddy Rodriquez, Tammy Townsend, Aries Spears

John Leguizamo, whose inventive comedy has garnered numerous awards and legions of fans, stars as Pestario "Pest" Vargas, a chameleon-like Miami con artist able to transform himself from a fast-talking Chinese delivery boy to an unorthodox Rabbi in the blink of an eye. The Pest needs every face he can conjure up once he attracts the attention of Gustav Shank (Jones), the crazy German who is hunting him for his head, and the mobsters who want the $50,000 The Pest owes them. The film is a chase, a hunt, a party and a riot all around Miami's colorful South Beach district.

Philadelphia (1993 TriStar)

D: Jonathan Demme
S: Ran Nyswaner
P: Edward Saxon and Jonathan Demme
Cast: Tom Hanks, Denzel Washington, Antonio Banderas

A courtroom drama about a young lawyer, Andrew Beckett (Hanks), who is fired from a prestigious law firm when it is revealed he has AIDS. Determined to defend his professional reputation, Andrew hires a personal injury attorney (Washington) to represent him as he sues his former firm for wrongful termination. Banderas plays Miguel Alvares,

Andrew's life partner and lover. It is the first major Hollywood film to present a humanistic portrayal of a gay Hispanic character.

Picking Up the Pieces (2000 Independent Distribution)
D: Alfonso Arau
S: Bill Wilson
P: Alfonso Arau, Paul Sandberg, Mimi Polk Gitlin
Cast: Woody Allen, Sharon Stone, Angelica Aragon, Enrique Castillo, Maria Grazia Cucinotta, Danny De La Paz, Lupe Ontiveros, Cheech Marin, Pepe Serna, Dyana Ortelli, Jackie Guerra, Fran Drescher, Tony Plana, Lou Diamond Phillips, Jon Huertas

Woody Allen stars as a kosher butcher who murders his wife (Stone) in a fit of rage when confronted with her infidelity. While on his way into Mexico to bury the body, he loses the corpse's hand. When a blind woman literally stumbles upon it and her sight is restored, the residents of a small town see it as a miracle of sorts, while the town fathers try to concoct a scheme to benefit the town—and themselves—economically.

Pirates of Monterey (1947 Universal)
D: Alfred Werker
S: Sam Hellman and Margaret Buell Wilder, based on a story by Edward T. Lowe and Bradford Ropes
P: Paul Malvern
Cast: Maria Montez, Rod Cameron, Philip Reed, Gilbert Roland, George J. Lewis

A Technicolor action adventure Western about the Spanish Loyalist attempt to overthrow the Mexican regime just prior to California's entry into the United States, with the sultry Montez as Marguerita, a Spanish señorita. An American captain in 1840s California brings a shipment of new rifles to the Mexican presidio at Monterey in order to stop a possible attack by Spanish pirates. Roland plays Major De Roja, commander of the garrison but a rebel leader in cahoots with the pirates. Chris-Pin Martin has a bit part in the film as a caretta man.

Play It to the Bone (2000 Buena Vista)
D: Ron Shelton
S: Ron Shelton
P: Stephen Chin
Cast: Woody Harrelson, Antonio Banderas, Lolita Davidovich, Lucy Liu, Tom Sizemore, Robert Wagner

Best friends and professional boxing rivals Vince Boudreau (Harrelson) and Cesar Dominguez (Banderas), both of whom haven't worked in years, get the chance of a lifetime: an assignment to work together in Las Vegas. Their race to get to Vegas for the big showdown is complicated by two women they fall for.

Plunder of the Sun (1953 Warner Bros.)

D: John Farrow
S: Jonathan Latimer, based on the novel by David Dodge
P: Robert Fellows
Cast: Glenn Ford, Diana Lynn, Patricia Medina, Sean McClory,
Eduardo Noriega, Julio Villareal, Margarita Luna, Juan Garcia

A routine adventure drama highlighted by location filming in Oaxaca amid the ancient ruins and a cast of Mexican supporting actors. American Al Colby (Ford) finds himself broke and stranded in Cuba, where he is hired by Ana Luz (Medina) to deliver a harmless-appearing packet to Oaxaca, Mexico. Ford's path is crossed by Julie Barnes (Lynn) and Jefferson (McClory). Colby discovers that the package contains three sheets of old parchment covered with odd-looking writing, which can lead him to the secret wealth of the ancient Aztecs. With the help of Navarro (Villareal), to translate the manuscript, he strikes out with Ana Luz to solve the mystery of the Zapotec treasure.

According to director John Farrow in a Warner Bros. press item of the time, "The Mexican government is very pleased with our script because this will be the first picture ever made about Mexico and with Mexicans, where Americans are the villains and the Mexicans the heroes."

The Wayne-Fellows company, owned by actor John Wayne, produced the film for Warner Bros. Wayne also produced *Hondo* (1953) in Mexico the same year. Al Ybarra was the art director.

The Plunderers (1960 Allied Artists)

D: Joseph Pevney
S: Bob Barbash
P: Joseph Pevney
Cast: Jeff Chandler, John Saxon

Four teenage saddle tramps ride into a small, lonely Western town and cause a disturbance. Sam (Chandler), an embittered Civil War veteran who has lost the use of his arm, is riled into action by the hoodlums.

Juvenile delinquency is the theme of this downbeat Western. One of the teenagers, a Mexican named Rondo and played by Saxon, is only interested in the girl of the town. When he threatens to kill Sam with a knife, the girl shoots him.

Popi (1969 United Artists)

D: Arthur Hiller
S: Tina and Lester Pine
P: Herbert B. Leonard
Cast: Alan Arkin, Rita Moreno, Miguel Alejandro, Ruben E. Figueroa,
Antonia Rey, Gladys Velez, Santos Morales, Rene Enriquez

A touching and funny story of a Puerto Rican widower, Abraham Rodriguez (Arkin), and his elaborate effort to rescue his sons from the dangers of New York barrio life. His plan is to put them in on open boat off the coast of Miami in the hopes of their getting a new, state-assisted beginning. As refugees from Castro's Cuba, they would be considered small heroes. Their daring actions would be well publicized and would lead to a probable adoption by someone who could provide all the material advantages Abraham cannot. In the end, his plan works all too well, but everyone realizes that love is more important than any material wealth, and father and sons are reunited.

Popi (meaning "father" in Puerto Rican Spanish) was a modest commercial success. It offered a rare glimpse into Puerto Rican life in New York and introduced to the screen two young actors who were discovered for the film, Ruben Figueroa and Miguel Alejandro.

Alan Arkin as Abraham touched all the right dramatic and comedic moments, but came up with a bizarre Puerto Rican accent that had never been heard before. Moreno was featured as Lupe, a neighbor who is interested in Abraham and the kids.

The film departed from the Hollywood norm by presenting dignified Hispanic characters trying to overcome their harsh living situations in a humanistic manner. It also raised questions about how this country treats its Hispanic minorities. Refugees from Castro's Cuba receive more support when they arrive in the United States than Puerto Rican American citizens.

Abraham (Alan Arkin), a widower, orders his sons, Junior (Miguel Alejandro, rear) and Luis (Ruben Figueroa) to get into a skiff and take it out into the Gulf Stream in hopes that they may be rescued and then adopted by someone better able to care for them in *Popi*.

Portrait of Maria

See *Maria Candelaria*.

Posse (1993 Gramercy)
D: Mario Van Peebles
S: Sy Richardson and Dario Scardapone
P: Preston Holmes and Jim Steele
Cast: Mario Van Peebles, Tone Loc, Billy Zane, Charles Lane, Blair Underwood

The story of a group of African American soldiers in the United States Army fighting in Cuba during the 1898 Spanish-American War. Disillusioned with the racism and corruption of their commanding officer and having survived a suicide mission in which they best the Spanish soldiers, the "posse" finds a cache of gold and desert. They return to the States to an African American township called Freemanville, where they are forced to turn outlaw in order to protect themselves. The first twenty minutes of the film take place in Cuba.

Director and star Mario Van Peebles makes a stylized, outrageously violent attempt to bring into focus the participation of African Americans in the history of the Old West.

The Possession of Joel Delaney (1972 Paramount)
D: Waris Hussein
S: Matt Robinson and Grimes Grice, based on the novel by
   Ramona Stewart
P: Martin Poll
Cast: Shirley MacLaine, Perry King, Miriam Colon,
   Edmundo Rivera Alvarez

The spirit of Tonio Perez, a seventeen-year-old Puerto Rican murderer, invades the body of his best friend, Joel, who is living in Tonio's now-vacant apartment.

Joel is transformed into the ultimate Puerto Rican stereotype, complete with slicked-back hair, bad accent, black leather jacket and switchblade. Norah (MacLaine), Joel's sister, who lives on the swank Upper East Side, can't understand why her brother wants to live with "those people." Joel continues Tonio's killing spree by first killing his girlfriend, then his psychiatrist, and attempting to murder his sister before a policeman's bullet finally stops him. But then the spirit of Tonio enters Norah's body, and the audience is left to ponder the possibilities.

Secondary roles are played by Colon as Norah's maid and Edmundo Rivera Alvarez as the conductor of a seance.

Gary Giddins in the *Hollywood Reporter* (5/17/72) summed up the film best: "The most remarkable thing about the film is that it is wildly anti-Puerto Rican, and in a country where xenophobia is often confused with patriotism, this cannot be passed over lightly. The inhabitants of the dreadful secretive barrios are always referred to as 'They' and 'They' are all believers in witchcraft."

Il Postino/The Postman (1994 Miramax)
D: Michael Radford
S: Anna Pavignano, Michael Radford, Furio Scarpelli,
   Giacomo Scarpelli, Massimo Troisi
P: Mario and Vittorio Cecchi Gori, Gaetano Daniele
Cast: Massimo Troisi, Maria Grazia Cucinotta, Philippe Noiret

The film is a humorous and moving tale of a simple postman whose eyes are opened to a world of entirely new possibilities when he finds himself delivering letters to one of the most romantic poets of the twentieth century. The film was inspired by an incident in the life of renowned Chilean poet and diplomat, Pablo Neruda (Noiret), who was forced into exile from his native country in 1952 and granted sanctuary by the Italian government on a remote, beautiful island off the coast of Naples.

Mario (Troisi) is a shy and bumbling postman who has no chance with Beatrice (Cucinotta), the sexiest woman in town, until the world famous Chilean poet gives him the right words. Mario earnestness gains the aloof poet's confidence and an improbable but touching friendship develops between Neruda and Mario.

The film won Academy Award® nominations for Best Film, Best Direction, Best Actor and Best Screenplay adaptation, the film went on to win the Oscar® for Best Original Dramatic score for its composer Luis Bacalov.

Predator (1987 Twentieth Century Fox)
D: John McTiernan
S: Jim Thomas and John Thomas
P: Lawrence Gordon, Joel Silver, and John Davis
Cast: Arnold Schwarzenegger, Carl Weathers, Elpidia Carrillo

Dutch (Schwarzenegger) leads a group of covert military troops on a mission to rescue American hostages held by guerrillas in a Central American jungle. In the jungle they encounter a strange alien being who hunts armed humans for sport.

Exciting and unexpected, this is a well-made science fiction thriller. It is spoiled by a minor subplot of standard Reagan-era Contra politics, in which Americans put Latin guerrillas in their place.

The multiethnic United States fighting force features Carl Weathers as Dillon; Sonny Landham as Billy, a Native American; Richard Chaves as Pancho; and Bill Duke as Mac. Elpidia Carrillo appears in the role of Anna, a young native guerrilla operative. *Predator* was filmed near Puerto Vallarta, Mexico.

Predator 2 (1990 Twentieth Century Fox)
D: Stephen Hopkins
S: James Thomas and John Thomas
P: Joel Silver, Lawrence Gordon, and John Davis
Cast: Danny Glover, Gary Busey, Maria Conchita Alonso, Rubén Blades

Set in 1997 in Los Angeles, outgunned cops face hordes of Jamaican, Colombian and other assorted drug dealers and criminal gangs who rule the streets. Suddenly something terrible and inexplicable begins to happen as, one by one, the gang leaders are killed by a mysterious and terrifying adversary who strikes with unbridled ferocity and cunning supernatural power. Harrigan (Glover) sets out to bring to justice those responsible for these brutal murders until he realizes that he and his squad are no longer the pursuers. The Predator is "on safari" in the streets of the city and has begun to hunt and kill the police, who have become his next big game.

The ethnically diverse cast is headed by Danny Glover as Detective Harrigan, Blades as his partner, and childhood friend Danny Archuleta and Alonso as Detective Leona Cantrell.

Price of Glory (2000 New Line Cinema)
D: Carlos Avila
S: Phil Berger
P: Moctesuma Esparza and Robert Katz
Cast: Jimmy Smits, Jon Seda, Clifton Collins, Jr., Maria Del Mar,
    Sal Lopez, Paul Rodriquez

Arturo Ortega (Smits) is a failed boxer who raises his three sons to become champions in the ring and the ensuing problems his obsession causes within the family on their quest for the championship.

The Pride and the Passion (1957 United Artists)
D: Stanley Kramer
S: Edward and Edna Anhalt, based on the novel *The Gun* by C.S. Forester
P: Stanley Kramer
Cast: Cary Grant, Sophia Loren, Frank Sinatra

During the Napoleonic Wars, Captain Anthony Trumbull (Grant), a British naval officer, is sent to Spain to retrieve a huge cannon, abandoned by the Spanish Army, so that the British can use it against Napoleon's army. Miguel (Sinatra), a Spanish guerrilla leader, wants to use the gun to attack a French garrison at Avila. Juana (Loren) is the beautiful camp follower. They move the gun across the Spanish countryside at a huge cost in human life in order to attack the city.

This spectacle has high-powered, somewhat miscast stars and a weak script that cannot sustain interest for its two-hour-plus running time. It was shot on location in Spain.

The Private Life of Don Juan (1934 United Artists)
D: Alexander Korda
S: Frederick Lonsdale, Lajos Biros, and Arthur Wimperis, based on the
    play by Henri Bataille
P: Alexander Korda
Cast: Douglas Fairbanks, Merle Oberon

Don Juan has retired to a quiet life in a Spanish village. Annoyed by the many books and plays about him, he returns to Seville for one last amorous adventure, but no one believes him to be Don Juan. An aging Douglas Fairbanks, in his last starring film, was not well received.

The Professionals (1966 Columbia)
D: Richard Brooks
S: Richard Brooks, based on the novel *A Mule for the Marquesa* by
    Frank O'Rourke
P: Richard Brooks
Cast: Burt Lancaster, Lee Marvin, Robert Ryan, Jack Palance,
    Woody Strode, Claudia Cardinale, Ralph Bellamy

During the Mexican Revolution of 1917, a group of American mercenaries (Lancaster, Marvin, Ryan and Strode) are hired to rescue an American businessman's (Bellamy's) Mexican wife (Cardinale), who has been kidnapped by a Mexican revolutionary, Raza (Palance).

Jack Palance and Maria Gomez as Chiquita (and an unidentified man), in *The Professionals*.

One of the mercenaries questions their purpose: "What are Americans doing in a Mexican Revolution anyway?" Another answers, "Maybe there's only one revolution. The good guys against the bad guys. The only question is, which one are we?"

The film is full of images of mustachioed, scratching bandidos fiercely mowing down *rurales* (Mexican local police) and gringos besting the Mexicans. The image of Mexican women in this film is of the voluptuous, sexy spitfire type. As it turns out, good wife Cardinale is the childhood sweetheart of Palance's Mexican revolutionary and fled with him willingly. This rousing, well-written and directed Western by Brooks features an all-star cast with some nice twists. Among the many Hispanic performers featured are Maria Gomez as Chiquita, Carlos Romero, José Chavez, Rafael Bertrand, Daniel Nunez, Roberto Contreras, Dave Cadiente, Dolores Corral, Primo Lopez and Tony Mirelez. It was filmed near Las Vegas, Nevada.

Pure Luck (1991 Universal)

D: Nadia Tass
S: Herschel Weingrod and Timothy Harris
P: Lance Hool and Sean Daniel
Cast: Martin Short, Danny Glover, Pedro Armendariz, Jr.

An accident-prone accountant, Eugene Proctor (Short), is sent on a mission to find a missing—and equally accident-prone—heiress. His partner is detective Ray Campanella (Glover), who does not at first believe in bad luck. This comedic adventure was filmed in Acapulco and is a terribly weak version of the much funnier and more successful French original, *La Chévre* (1981), starring Gérard Depardieu and Pierre Richard, which has the same Mexican setting.

Q [aka: *The Winged Serpent*] (1982 United Film Distribution)

D: Larry Cohen
S: Larry Cohen
P: Larry Cohen
Cast: David Carradine, Richard Roundtree, Michael Moriarty

A giant serpent-like bird monster, the spirit of the Aztec god Quetzalcoatl, comes to life in modern times. The bird comes to roost on a turret of the Chrysler Building in New York City, where it swoops down on its victims. Its lair is finally discovered, and there is a climactic attack with helicopters and planes. A poor man's flying *King Kong* (1933), *Q* is merely a stupid horror movie with some decent performances.

Q & A (1990 TriStar)

D: Sidney Lumet
S: Sidney Lumet, based on the novel by Edwin Torres
P: Arnon Milchan and Burt Harris
Cast: Nick Nolte, Timothy Hutton, Armand Assante, Jenny Lumet,
   Luis Guzman, Charles Dutton, Gloria Irrizary

In New York, a young district attorney named Riley (Hutton) is assigned to investigate the shooting of a Puerto Rican youth by the bigoted Irish cop Brennan (Nolte). He slowly uncovers within the police department a wide-reaching conspiracy involving the underworld and his own former lover, Nancy Bosch (Lumet), who is now the wife of a Puerto Rican dope dealer, Bobby Texador (Assante).

Director Sidney Lumet traveled this territory before in *Prince of the City* (1981), also an examination of the corruption and racism in the New York City Police Department and city politics.

Q & A is based on a book by New York Puerto Rican judge Edwin Torres. This vivid examination of the New York City Police Department and the justice system crackles with a reality that only an exacting filmmaker like Lumet could capture on film. It is a tough and fascinating—if in the end slightly flawed—film, filled with unpleasant characters. Nolte's performance is a character study of a racist old-line cop. Hutton's character is an innocent who comes from a police family and has been a street cop for several years but is amazingly naive about the system. As an older lawyer friend tells him, "You suffer from the same disease I had: I thought I could make a difference."

Assante makes a believable Puerto Rican as Bobby Texador, who is streetwise and cunning, yet wants to get out of the life and do right by Nancy, whom he loves. Assante also manages to bring some dignity to a role that might otherwise have been a caricature, equaling his Mafia counterparts. Guzman brought an air of levity and reality to his role as Detective Valentin, making him a memorable and rounded character. Racist banter goes on at the station not only between Valentin and Chappy (Dutton) but among the other officers as well. In this microcosm of minorities and ethnic groups vying for power in New York, the criminals and the law enforcement officials are mirror images of each other in their corruption.

Jenny Lumet is excellent and Paul Calderon gives a good performance as a homosexual informant. Irrizary plays Nancy's mother. Rubén Blades composed the score.

R.P.M. (1970 Columbia)
D: Stanley Kramer
S: Erich Segal
P: Stanley Kramer
Cast: Anthony Quinn, Ann-Margret

Quinn is "Paco" Perez, a fifty-three-year-old Puerto Rican sociology professor who was raised in New York's Spanish Harlem (which wasn't yet Spanish when he would have been there as a growing boy). Because of his rapport with students, he is appointed acting president of the university to facilitate negotiations with a group of militant students who have taken over a campus building. Eventually, however, he has to call in the police.

The inevitable violent clash between students and police occurs, and Perez questions his own values and moral stance. Inez Pedroza plays a Chicana student named Estella. This was one of a number of films based on campus unrest in the United States during the late 1960s. Quinn gives a good portrayal of a swinging sociology professor, who drives a motorcycle, wears no tie and has a young co-ed as his mistress every semester (Ann-Margret, in this case).

Raices de Sangre (1979 Azteca)
D: Jesus Trevino
S: Jesus Trevino
P: CONACINE and Jesus Trevino
Cast: Richard Yniguez, Roxanna Bonilla-Gianini, Pepe Serna,
    Ernesto Gomez Cruz

The first Hispanic American, or Chicano, theatrical feature film, *Raices de Sangre* (Blood Roots) was written, produced and directed by Jesus Salvador Trevino. Trevino had been active as an award-winning television producer and documentary filmmaker for Los Angeles public television station KCET since 1969. On an educational trip to Mexico,

Trevino interested then-President of Mexico Luis Echevarria Alvarez in making a film dramatizing the problems of Chicanos in the United States. The president had expressed an interest in the subject matter at a prior meeting with Trevino and other artists.

At the time, the Mexican film industry was controlled by the government and headed by the president's sister. The film was produced by the Corporación Nacional Cinematografica (CONACINE) in Mexico and became the first film to involve the combined talents of Chicano actors and filmmakers and Mexican actors and filmmakers.

The story takes place in one of the *maquilladorres*, the labor-intensive factories located in bordertowns all along the United States-Mexico border, and depicts the struggles of Mexican and Chicano workers on both sides of the border to create an international labor union. A complex, multi-layered film, *Raices de Sangre* also deals with illegal aliens, drug trafficking and Chicano pride.

The story centers on Carlos Rivera (Yniguez), a young lawyer fresh out of Harvard Law School who has established a practice in San Francisco. Back on the border to work for the community action group Barrios Unidos over a summer, Rivera is reluctantly drawn into the workers' struggle.

Yniguez stars in a cast that includes Roxanna Bonilla-Gianini as Lupe Carillo, a beautiful Chicana activist who slowly becomes Carlos' love interest. She is politically aware, self-sufficient and dedicated to the people of the barrio. She teaches Carlos about having to participate in all kinds of work for the cause, even making photocopies. She does not fall into the typical screen conventions of the dedicated secretary or camp follower but is one of the best representations and positive role models of a modern Mexican American woman. Also in the cast are Serna as an ill-fated labor organizer and Gomez Cruz as a worker trying for a better life.

The film was shot in Spanish in 1976, and was released in Spanish-language theaters in the States and at art houses in an English-subtitled version in 1979. An original theme song was written for the film by actor/composer Daniel Valdez. *Raices de Sangre* received good reviews and did extremely well at the box office in Spanish-language theaters.

Trevino remarked, "I was intrigued by the chance to write and direct the film in Mexico not only because of what it represented in terms of my own artistic growth, but also because of its importance within the context of the Latino experience . . . I think it's quite significant that the first major motion picture on the Chicano and Latino experience was initiated by the Mexican film industry, and that it sought to explain much of the mutually shared reality of Mexicans to a United States audience."

The Raiders (1952 Universal)
D: Lesley Selander
S: Polly James and Lillie Hayward
P: William Alland
Cast: Richard Conte, Viveca Lindfors, Barbara Britton, William Bishop, Richard Martin, George J. Lewis

The story is set during California's Gold Rush days and early statehood. Jan Morrell (Conte) is a prospector whose claim is stolen and whose wife and brother are killed by outlaws working for a villainous land baron. Morrell, out for revenge, joins a group of California citizens who have lost their property. They are led by Felipe Ortega (Martin), a former wealthy landowner. Viveca Lindfors plays a California señorita, the daughter of a dispossessed landowner. There is plenty of action and gunplay in this Technicolor Western. Martin does well in a supporting role in his first film away from RKO, where he played Chito Rafferty, Tim Holt's sidekick, in a number of RKO B Westerns.

Raiders of the Lost Ark (1981 Paramount)
D: Steven Spielberg
S: Lawrence Kasdan, based on a story by George Lucas and
    Philip Kaufman
P: Frank Marshall
Cast: Harrison Ford, Karen Allen

In the prologue to this hit film, Indiana Jones (Ford), an adventurous American archaeologist, is chased by half-naked Indians in a South American rain forest after he steals a gold idol from a booby-trapped hidden temple.

The prologue establishes, for a new generation of moviegoers, the old racist caricatures of South America. The themes of Americans in search of hidden treasure and adventure in exotic locales are clearly evident in the Saturday matinee serials to which the Indiana Jones films were paying homage. The scenes were actually shot on location on the island of Kauai in Hawaii.

Raiders of the Seven Seas (1953 United Artists)
D: Sidney Salkow
S: Sidney Salkow and John O'Dea
P: Sidney Salkow
Cast: John Payne, Donna Reed, Gerald Mohr

Led by Barbarossa (Payne), buccaneers capture a Spanish galleon and a countess (Reed), with whom Barbarossa falls in love. Complications lead to an attack on the Spanish garrison at Havana harbor, Cuba.

Ramona (1916 State Rights Distribution)
D: Donald Crisp
S: Lloyd Brown, based on the novel by Helen Hunt Jackson
P: W.H. Clune
Cast: Adda Gleason, Monroe Salisbury, Victor Vallejo, Inez Gomez,
    Joe De La Cruz, Arthur Tovares

Silent. A massive film production for its time, directed by Crisp, a member of D.W. Griffith's troupe. Presented in seven reels, the film is divided into three parts, accompanied by a specially arranged musical score played live by a symphony orchestra.

Ramona (1928 United Artists)
D: Edwin Carewe
S: Finis Fox, based on the novel by Helen Hunt Jackson
P: Edwin Carewe
Cast: Dolores Del Rio, Warner Baxter

Silent. Del Rio plays the raven-haired half-Indian girl who elopes with an Indian chief (Baxter) against the wishes of her stern guardian, a wealthy Spanish sheep rancher. Carewe, who discovered Del Rio, directed her in this popular-with-audiences, time-tested story, filmed in Southern California locations.

Ramona (1936 Twentieth Century Fox)
D: Henry King
S: Lamar Trotti, based on the novel by Helen Hunt Jackson
P: Sol M. Wurtzel
Cast: Loretta Young, Don Ameche, Kent Taylor, Pedro de Cordoba,
    J. Carroll Naish

Romantic Old California is the setting of the tragic romance about the love of the beautiful "half-breed" Ramona (Young) and the Indian youth Allesandro (Ameche).

The story had been filmed twice before, in 1916 and 1928. Gilbert Roland and Rita Hayworth were originally scheduled to star in this version, but when Fox consolidated with Century Pictures, Young and Ameche were signed for the roles. Supporting players included Katherine DeMille as the jealous Margarita, Kent Taylor as an understanding *hacendado*, Pauline Frederick as his sternly aristocratic mother, Jane Darwell as a sympathetic settler from Tennessee, and Victor Kilian as a padre.

While filming on location in Mesa Grande near San Diego, California, Loretta Young saved the life of two-year-old Ramon Lugo. Young and the child were acting in a scene beneath a gauze netting used for photographic effects. When the netting caught fire due to the hot Technicolor lights, Young, narrowly escaping injury herself, quickly removed the baby from its cradle. This was one of the first films to use the early two-strip Technicolor process.

Red River (1948 United Artists)
D: Howard Hawks
S: Borden Chase and Charles Schnee, based on the novel *The Chisholm Trail* by Chase
P: Howard Hawks
Cast: John Wayne, Montgomery Clift

In the opening sequence of *Red River*, Tom Dunson (Wayne) shoots one of Don Diego's outriders to prove that the grazing land north of the Rio Grande now belongs to him, effectively illustrating the Manifest Destiny concept.

Red Sky at Morning (1971 Universal)

D: James Goldstone

S: Marguerite Roberts, based on the novel by Richard Bradford

P: Hal B. Wallis

Cast: Richard Thomas, Richard Crenna, Claire Bloom, Victoria Racimo, Pepe Serna, Mario Aniov, Gregory Sierra, Harry Guardino, Alma Beltran, Desi Arnaz, Jr.

Frank Arnold (Crenna) goes off to fight in World War II from a Gulf Coast port and relocates his wife, Ann (Bloom), and family to the small town of Sagrado, New Mexico. The focus is on Josh Arnold's (Thomas') exposure to multiracial contemporaries in a school where whites are the minorities. Desi Arnaz, Jr., plays the role of Steenie Moreno, son of the town's Spanish American doctor and his Greek wife, who befriends Josh and guides him through the intricacies of the New Mexico social milieu, especially as it applies to Anglos, Indians and Mexicans.

Characters are strictly formula types, including Nehemiah Persoff and Beltran as faithful servants, and Spanish American gang toughs like Serna as Chango Lopez, the toughest of them all, and Mario Aniov as the cunning and dangerous Lindo Velarde. Racimo is Viola Lopez, the tragic schoolgirl. The sturdy sheriff is played by Sierra. It was filmed in New Mexico.

Del Zamora (right) and Eddie Velez (left) as brothers Lagarto and Napa Rodriguez in *Repo Man.*

Repo Man (1984 Universal)

D: Alex Cox

S: Alex Cox

P: Jonathan Wacks and Peter McCarthy

Cast: Emilio Estevez, Harry Dean Stanton, Fox Harris, Eddie Velez, Del Zamora

This film became an unexpected cult favorite. Otto (Estevez), a young Los Angeles punker, becomes the protégé of Bud (Stanton), a crusty car re-possessor. Otto soon comes to challenge his mentor for a $20,000 repo prize, a '64 Chevy Malibu driven by J. Frank Parnell (Harris), a lobotomized nuclear scientist. The Malibu is being pursued madly by ruthless government agents, UFO followers and the infamous Rodriguez brothers, Lagarto (Zamora) and Nap (Velez). In the trunk is an unthinkable object that could change the course of civilization overnight. Then, of course, there is the climax with a "close encounter of the third kind."

Requiem for a Heavyweight (1962 Columbia)

D: Ralph Nelson
S: Rod Serling, based on his television play
P: David Susskind
Cast: Anthony Quinn, Mickey Rooney, Jackie Gleason

Quinn plays an old heavyweight fighter, Mountain Rivera, whose winning streak has run out after seventeen years in the ring. His career has left him mentally dim and threatened with blindness. His manager, Maish Rennick (Gleason), is no worse than the other low-lifes of his profession and might have preferred to see his man get some sort of peace and quiet in retirement. But Rennick has become deeply involved with strong-arm gamblers and is forced to try to squeeze some dollars out of his derelict hulk of a boxer to get himself out of a gambling debt.

Rivera was an Irish boxer in the television drama, but the role was changed to a Mexican American for the film version. Quinn drew on his own youth, when he boxed just to bring money in, and modeled the character, including his voice, partly on the great old boxer Primo Camera. This is one of Quinn's greatest and most memorable portrayals.

In a letter in *Life* magazine (2/22/63), director Ralph Nelson said, "I differed with Anthony Quinn over his interpretation of the role. As written, the hero was a lonely, sensitive human being, a prizefighter who had worked out his hostilities in the ring. Quinn was afraid gentleness would reflect upon his image of masculinity, so [he] chose to play Sonny Liston [a well-known heavyweight boxer of the time] instead. I believe Palance's concept [Jack Palance starred as the boxer in the original television version] was truer to the role and fulfilled the concept of the script more effectively than Quinn's attempts to dominate it."

Return of the Seven (1966 United Artists)

D: Burt Kennedy
S: Larry Cohen
P: Ted Richmond
Cast: Yul Brynner, Robert Fuller, Julian Mateos, Warren Oates,
   Claude Akins, Emilio Fernandez, Rodolfo Acosta, Fernando Rey

Yul Brynner, as the gunfighter Chris, was the only actor to reprise his role from the original *Magnificent Seven*. This movie was directed by veteran Western master Burt Kennedy, with Spain doubling for Mexico. Mexican actors Fernandez, as the *hacendado* chieftain, and Acosta, as his aide, bring authority and authenticity to their roles. Rey plays a priest. Castilian accents are noticeable in most of the Spanish actors playing Mexicans.

Revenge (1990 Columbia)

D: Tony Scott
S: Jim Harrison and Jeffrey Fiskin, based on a story by Jim Harrison
P: Hunt Lowry and Stanley Rubin
Cast: Kevin Costner, Anthony Quinn, Madeleine Stowe, Tomas Milian,
   Joaquin Martinez

Revenge is a lurid, violent tale with spectacular Mexican location footage. A retired United States pilot, Cochran (Costner), falls in love with the young Miryea (Stowe), wife of Tiburon Mendez (Quinn), a powerbroker with ties to the Mexican crime syndicate and an old friend of Cochran's.

Quinn turns in a strong performance but unfortunately, he is about twenty-five years too old to make the relationship between himself and Costner believable. Based on a short story by cult novelist Jim Harrison, the film perpetuated the stereotypes of Mexican men as violent and menacing, Mexican women as whores and peasants as people with a grudge against their patrons. We have seen this all before in Western dramas where the hero is left for dead and is found by noble peasants who nurse him back to health. He then returns to seek revenge against those who wronged him. Good casting provided roles for Milian, Martinez, Miguel Ferrer, John Leguizamo, Sally Kirkland, Joe Santos and James Gammon. *Revenge* was filmed in Mexico on fifty separate locations on a twelve-week schedule and features some of the country's most scenic areas including Durango, Puerto Vallarta, Cuernavaca and Mexico City.

The Reward (1965 Twentieth Century Fox)

D: Serge Bourguignon
S: Serge Bourguignon and Oscar Milland, based on the novel by
    Michael Barrett
P: Aaron Rosenberg
Cast: Max von Sydow, Yvette Mimieux, Gilbert Roland,
    Emilio Fernandez, Henry Silva, Rodolfo Acosta, Julian Rivero,
    Efrem Zimbalist, Jr.

An offbeat and highly stylized contemporary Western about an odd assortment of men seeking the $50,000 reward for the capture of an escaped American fugitive in a small Mexican desert town. Roland portrays an aristocratic police captain, and Fernandez portrays a brutal and cunning police sergeant in a small Mexican village. About a third of the film is spoken in Spanish, with English subtitles. Filmed in and around Old Tucson, Arizona, and Death Valley, this was the first and only American film by French director Serge Bourguignon, who directed *Sundays and Cybele*, which won the 1962 Academy Award® for Best Foreign Language Film. A promising story that backfires on itself, *The Reward* was a dismal failure at the box office.

Ride, Vaquero! (1953 Metro-Goldwyn-Mayer)

D: John Farrow
S: Frank Fenton
P: Stephen Ames
Cast: Robert Taylor, Ava Gardner, Howard Keel, Anthony Quinn,
    Movita Castenada, Joe Dominguez

As Anglo settlers move in, outlaw José Esqueda (Quinn) and his gang's power over their frontier territory is threatened. Opposing him and his violent ways are settlers led by King Cameron (Keel), a rancher, and his wife, Cordelia (Gardner). Esqueda sends his half-brother Rio (Taylor) to scare them off. Rio is captured by the settlers and becomes drawn to Cordelia. Esqueda decides to take matters into his own hands, murders the town's sheriff, and has his men pillage the town. He almost kills Cameron, but Rio intervenes. Rio and Esqueda face each other in a gunfight, and they both die. Castenada has a small role as a hussy.

This violent, downbeat Western features Taylor in an uncharacteristic role as a vicious killer and bad guy. Quinn turns in an outrageous and vivid portrayal, almost as if he had set out to outdo Alfonso Bedoya in Mexican banditry portrayals. He broke all the rules with this vicious flesh-and-blood center-stage greaser portrayal. His gang is made up of Mexicans and Anglos.

Ride the Pink Horse (1947 Universal)
D: Robert Montgomery
S: Ben Hecht and Charles Lederer, based on the novel by
   Dorothy B. Hughes
P: Joan Harrison
Cast: Robert Montgomery, Wanda Hendrix, Thomas Gomez,
   Rita Conde, Iris Flores, Tito Renaldo, Martin Garralaga, Maria Cortez

Half the characters in this film are American gangsters, amateur and professional, who engage in an undercover but vicious fight for certain stakes at "San Pablo." The other half are inhabitants of San Pablo's predominantly Mexican community, and both they and the town itself reflect a certain realism of Hispanic New Mexico life. Gomez is Pancho, a immense man with a proverbial heart of gold who runs a merry-go-round. Wanda Hendrix is Pila, a naive but purposeful Indian girl who follows Robert Montgomery after he buys her a ride on the carousel. Julian Rivero has a small role as a Mexican man. San Pablo is a composite of the Mexican districts of Santa Fe, Taos and Albuquerque, New Mexico. Location scenes were filmed at Santa Fe's Hotel La Fonda and at the famous Fred Harvey winter resort, as well as at Santa Fe's cemetery and its business district.

Pasquale Martinez, a real-life carousel operator from Taos, came to be known in Hollywood as the only wrangler (livestock handler) of wooden horses on record. A retired United States Forestry Service employee, he had a six-week paid vacation to Hollywood because the Lions Club of Taos would not allow their carousel to be shipped from Taos to Hollywood unless Martinez went along to oversee its care.

Right Cross (1950 Metro-Goldwyn-Mayer)
D: John Sturges
S: Charles Schnee
P: Armand Deutsch
Cast: Ricardo Montalban, June Allyson, Dick Powell

Johnny Monterez (Montalban) is a Mexican boxer with a chip on his shoulder against gringos. While his prejudice is not the result of any

Johnny Monterez
(Ricardo Montalban,
right) is a Mexican
boxer in *Right Cross*, also
starring (left to right)
Art Aragon, Dick Powell
and June Allyson. (The
man in the hat is an
unidentified player).

direct bigotry on the part of anyone in the film, we do learn that it is due to the racial consciousness he developed growing up in Los Angeles.

He becomes United States middleweight champion and falls in love with Pat O'Malley (Allyson) and ultimately develops a more tolerant attitude toward Anglos. The action builds to a solid ring fight in which Monterez, contrary to usual film formula, goes down in defeat. He comes to realize that Pat loves him as a person and that the championship has nothing to do with it. Monterez at the fadeout wins Pat away from newspaperman Rick Gavery (Powell).

The promise of a happy life together through Anglo-Mexican integration was an important message for post-World War II audiences, especially when the girl was the all-American June Allyson.

The experience of the war led to a shift in values and perceptions of freedoms and civil rights in the United States. Hollywood filmmakers began to tackle more serious subjects, such as anti-Semitism and racial prejudice, in such films as *Gentleman's Agreement* (1947), *Home of the Brave* (1949) and *Pinky* (1949). The production code regarding miscegenation on screen began to loosen up. Also, as a result of the Good Neighbor Policy, Latin Americans had come to be considered as Anglos. In the case of this film, the protagonist is specifically an economically disadvantaged Mexican from the Los Angeles barrio. The theme of racial prejudice is rather safely brought out as a psychological problem rather than as a conflict with other characters that needs resolution.

The Ring (1952 United Artists)

D: Kurt Neumann
S: Irving Shulman, based on his novel
P: Maurice, Herman, and Frank King
Cast: Lalo Rios, Gerald Mohr, Rita Moreno, Martin Garralaga,
     Pepe Hern, Victor Millan, Tony Martinez

The Ring, starring Rios, deals with the social and economic pressures of 1952 Los Angeles that drive a disadvantaged Mexican American youth into the world of boxing.

The film was shot in the Boyle Heights section of East Los Angeles, where the producers, the King brothers, were raised. The Kings first produced "soundies," the forerunner of today's music videos. Soundies, short films that featured popular singers and orchestras, were designed to promote a song and talent. They were shown in specially constructed viewing boxes in record stores. Successful in this venture, the Kings went on to produce a number of low-budget pictures, one of which was *The Ring*.

The film's storyline illustrates racial discrimination in scenes that include: tourists gazing at "those lazy Mexicans," Mexican boys being turned down for service by a waitress in a Beverly Hills restaurant and a young couple being refused entry at a skating rink because it isn't "Mexican Night."

The Ring also recognizes the Mexican American as part of the American urban experience rather than presenting the more common rural depictions. It can also be said that the character played by Rios is a symbol of the Chicano Movement, which came into being in the 1960s and dealt specifically with Mexican Americans, their rights, history and image within the American cultural context.

Both *The Ring* and *The Lawless* (1950), centering as they do on Mexican Americans, one urban, one rural, were filmed on low budgets and share the same leading actor (Rios), making them companion pieces among the American cinema's first statements on the Mexican American and/or Chicano consciousness.

Rio Bravo (1959 Warner Bros.)

D: Howard Hawks
S: Jules Furthman and Leigh Brackett, based on a story by
   Barbara Hawks McCampbell
P: Howard Hawks
Cast: John Wayne, Dean Martin, Ricky Nelson, Angie Dickinson,
   Walter Brennan, John Russell, Claude Akins, Ward Bond,
   Pedro Gonzalez-Gonzalez, Estelita Rodriguez

John T. Chance (Wayne), sheriff of a Texas bordertown, has to keep a jailed killer in and his cohorts—who have surrounded the town—out, but he doesn't do it alone. During the course of these very human events, he is saved or protected by an assortment of misfit characters. His colleagues include: a reformed drunk, Dude (Martin); a gimp-legged old geezer, Stumpy (Brennan); a dance hall girl with a past (Dickinson); and a lone young gunfighter, Colorado (Nelson). The unlikely heroes are aided by Carlos (Gonzalez-Gonzalez), a Mexican, and his wife, Consuela (Rodriguez), who own and run the town hotel. It was filmed on location in Old Tucson, Arizona.

Rio Conchos (1964 Twentieth Century Fox)

D: Gordon Douglas
S: Joseph Landon and Clair Huffaker, based on the novel *Guns of the
   Rio Conchos* by Huffaker
P: David Weisbart
Cast: Richard Boone, Stuart Whitman, Jim Brown, Tony Franciosa,
   Rodolfo Acosta

A stereotypically violent, illogical and action-packed Western in which four unsavory men head through Indian country in search of 2,000 rifles stolen from the United States Cavalry. One of the four is Rodriguez, a Mexican bandit played by Franciosa. Vito Scotti is featured as an older Mexican bandit with a mouthful of bad teeth. Acosta plays an Indian chief named Bloodshirt. Wende Wagner plays an Indian girl. It was filmed on location in Moab, Utah.

"En route they brawl and bicker, drink and debauch in a rugged Old West that appears to be crawling with bandidos, prostitutes and sadistic savages," *Time* (10/ 20/64).

Rio Rita (1929 RKO Radio Pictures)

D: Luther Reed
S: Luther Reed and Russell Mack, based on the musical by Guy Bolton
   and Fred Thompson
P: William LeBaron
Cast: Bert Wheeler, Robert Woolsey, Bebe Daniels, John Boles,
   Dorothy Lee, Don Alvarado, Georges Renavent

Rio Rita was an immensely popular 1927 Broadway musical that was made into an equally popular early sound musical film. The story concerns a Texas Ranger in an American bordertown who is after a notorious Mexican bandit, El Kinkajou. The show mixed romance, intrigue, music and comedy. Daniels and Boles star while Alvarado is featured in a major supporting role. Renavent plays the bandit. The film and play relied more on the romantic dime novels and the conventions of the Broadway musical than on any reality or authenticity concerning the Southwest or Mexico. The film was remade by MGM in 1942 as a musical vehicle for Abbott and Costello.

Rio Rita (1942 Metro-Goldwyn-Mayer)

D: S. Sylvan Simon
S: Richard Connell, Gladys Lehman, and John Grant
P: Pandro S. Berman
Cast: Bud Abbott, Lou Costello

Abbott and Costello were borrowed from Universal to star in this musical remake.

The "boys" get fired from their job at a pet shop and decide to make their way to New York by hiding in the trunk of a car with New York license plates. Unfortunately, the driver, dreamy singer Ricardo Montera (John Carroll), is headed for a fiesta in a tiny southwest Texas town called Vista del Rio. After a long and exhausting ride, Bud and Lou find themselves mixed up in shenanigans involving Nazi spies, secret codes, old flames and music. Julian Rivero has a small role as a Mexican gentleman.

The Ritz (1976 Warner Bros.)

D: Richard Lester
S: Terrence McNally, based on his play
P: Denis O'Dell
Cast: Rita Moreno, Jack Weston

Moreno won a Tony Award for her Broadway portrayal of Googie Gomez in Terrence McNally's zany comedy play *The Ritz*, which was written with her in mind. She re-created the role in the film version.

In a homosexual bathhouse in New York, Gomez is the star entertainer, a Puerto Rican waiting for her big break who mistakenly believes Jack Weston (also recreating his Broadway role), who is hiding out from a murderous relative, is a Broadway producer. Jerry Stiller and Kaye Ballard also star.

"By playing Googie, I am thumbing my nose at all those Hollywood writers responsible for such lines like, 'You Yankee peeg, you rape my sister. I keel you!'" said Moreno in press notes for the film. *The Ritz*, for Moreno, was something of a rebirth. "*West Side Story*, my last big vehicle, was fifteen years ago," she said in 1977. Moreno said of her *Ritz* role, "Googie is the essence of all the Latin Spitfires I've ever played in bad movies. She would tear out the eye of the Cyclops for the chance of hitting the big time. She is absolutely untalented and the only one in the film who comes out all right.

"In many ways, she's a bit like me. She perseveres—so do I. And Googie wasn't that difficult to get at, because she's based on a number of Latin women I've known. The accent comes from my mother."

The Road to Rio (1947 Paramount)

D: Norman Z. McLeod
S: Edmund Beloin and Jack Rose
P: Daniel Dare
Cast: Bob Hope, Bing Crosby, Dorothy Lamour, Nestor Paiva

Musicians Barton (Hope) and Sweeney (Crosby) accidentally set fire to a carnival where they are working. In an attempt to escape arson charges, the two stow away on a luxury liner bound for Rio. During the voyage the "boys" befriend a beautiful and mysterious young woman, Lucia De Andrade (Lamour), bound home for a marriage she does not want. Several days later they arrive in Rio and go searching for night-club work. To improve their chances they befriend three talented but goofy Brazilian musicians (The Wiere Brothers) and are immediately hired by a nightclub owner (Paiva) who thinks they are all Americans.

Barton and Sweeney try to teach the Brazilian musicians American slang but to no avail, and they are quickly found out and fired. The boys learn that Lucia's wedding is about to take place and they attend the affair disguised as a Caribbean pirate (Crosby) and a Carmen Miranda-like "Gootchy-gootchy" dancer (Hope), entertaining the guests by doing a hilarious Latin American routine. Abandoning their disguises, Hope and Crosby manage to obtain certain papers that enable Lucia to escape her unpleasant fate.

With a relatively traditional musical comedy format, this film bristles with clever dialogue, situations and songs. The opening titles are presented in animation where the names of the three principal players literally dance across the screen while a lively Latin American band plays the ever-popular samba song "Brasilia."

The Robin Hood of El Dorado (1936 Metro-Goldwyn-Mayer)

D: William Wellman
S: William Wellman, Melvin Levy, and Joseph Calleia, based on the novel by Walter Noble Burns
P: John W. Considine, Jr.
Cast: Warner Baxter, Margo, Soledad Jimenez, Bruce Cabot, Ann Loring, J. Carroll Naish, George Regas, Carlos de Valdez, Nick De Ruiz, Carlotta Monti

The film's central character is the legendary California bandit Joaquin Murieta.

Murieta was a Mexican from Sonora who was attracted to the gold fields of California in the late 1840s. Many of the Mexican miners were subjected to racist attacks by Anglo Americans. In the early 1850s, Murieta gathered together a band of men and began a series of raids, which the Mexicans regarded as justifiable retaliation. He is thought to have been captured by California Rangers in 1853, but his legend still had him alive well into the 1870s. He became a romantic revolutionary symbol for the Chicano movement of the 1960s and 1970s as a Mexican who fought against Anglo oppression and stood up for his rights in his own land.

Murieta here is a sympathetic avenger of his people. He suffers at the hands of American settlers, enduring the mistreatment of his blind mother and beloved bride, the loss of his land and finally his public whipping while his brother is hanged. Warner Baxter plays Murieta in his Cisco Kid acting mode. The movie was filmed near Sonora, California.

Romancing the Stone (1984 Twentieth Century Fox)

D: Robert Zemeckis
S: Diane Thomas
P: Michael Douglas
Cast: Michael Douglas, Kathleen Turner, Danny De Vito, Alfonso Arau, Manuel Ojeda

Joan Wilder (Turner) is a homebody writer of romantic adventure tales who leads a very quiet life in Manhattan. When her sister is kidnapped in South America, Joan breaks out of her safe life and goes after her. Jack Colton (Douglas) is a rugged jungle hunter who reluctantly comes to her aid. Together they battle the dangers of the wild and the ferocious men who stand between them and a successful mission. The movie is filled with all the customary stereotypes, both Anglo and Latin, for this kind of tale. Manuel Ojeda is a corrupt local detective and Arau is a dope dealer who befriends our heroine and just happens to be one of her biggest fans.

This fast-paced and witty spoof of the adventure genre takes place in the jungles of Colombia, but it was filmed in Mexico in such locales as Vera Cruz, Jalapa and Mexico City.

Roosters (1993 Astra Cinema)

D: Robert M. Young
S: Milcha Sanchez-Scott
P: Norman I. Cohen, Susan Block-Reiner, Kevin Reidy
Cast: Edward James Olmos, Maria Conchita Alonso, Sonia Braga, Danny Nucci

Gallo Morales (Olmos) is returning home after serving seven years in prison. Anxiously awaiting are his wife (Braga), his twenty-year-old rebellious son Hector (Nucci), his neglected adolescent daughter Angela and his sexy sister (Alonso). Gallo is a noted breeder of fighting cocks, which for him represents machismo and power, but it is Hector who owns a potentially prize-winning bird, precipatating some explosive family dynamics.

Slow and didactic, the film fails to live up to its intial promise.

Romero (1989 Four Seasons Entertainment)

D: John Duigan
S: John Sacret Young
P: Ellwood E. Kieser
Cast: Raul Julia, Richard Jordan, Tony Plana, Ana Alicia, Eddie Velez

This is the story of the assassination of Catholic archbishop Oscar Romero (Julia) in El Salvador in 1980 during the bloody political conflict in that country. Julia gives a moving performance of a man who grows into the responsibility of his appointed position of archbishop. The events around him lead him to speak in favor of human rights against the policies of the regime. The assassination of this gentle, once silent, but ultimately outspoken man of god as he celebrated mass indelibly etched in the world's eyes the human tragedy of El Salvador.

During a press conference to promote the film, Julia stated, "One of the most important things about this film is that it is a true story about a Latin American character that takes place in Latin America. It is not about gringos in South America where Latins are background or supporting players." The Australian director John Duigan said, "I've always been fascinated with the politics of Central America, and I was familiar with the story of Oscar Romero. When I was offered the screenplay to direct, I found it a compelling piece of writing on a very important subject."

Jordan portrays firebrand priest Rutilio Grande, a man whose own passionate efforts to aid his suffering flock would also mark him for death. Alicia portrays a beautiful Salvadoran aristocrat whose husband, the minister of agriculture, mysteriously disappears.

Filmed on location, with Cuernavaca, Mexico, doubling for El Salvador, Romero represents the first mainstream theatrical feature ever produced by the Catholic Church. Romero received fairly wide distribution in the United States but managed to collect only $3 million at the nation's box offices. Critics, who were respectful but divided over the film, generally praised Julia's performance.

Rooftops (1989 New Century Vista)

D: Robert Wise
S: Terence Brennan
P: Howard W. Koch, Jr.
Cast: Troy Beyer, Alexis Cruz, Eddie Velez, Jason Gedrick, Luis Guzman, Jay M. Boryea, Rafael Baez

In the streets of New York's "Alphabet City," the seamy section of Manhattan's Lower East Side, a group of multiethnic kids, with no family to depend on, create their own unique living spaces on the rooftops of abandoned tenement buildings. Squeak (Cruz), the artful dodger of the group, is famous for his colorful neighborhood murals. Then menacing drug dealer Lobo (Velez), his henchmen, Willie (Boryea) and Raphael (Baez), and his beautiful cousin, Elena (Beyer), move into the neighborhood and wreak havoc on the lives of the rooftop dwellers.

Director Robert Wise tried to recapture the dance and excitement of his own *West Side Story* of nearly thirty years earlier but failed to do so with this thin material.

Rose of the Rancho (1936 Paramount)
D: Marion Gering
S: Frank Partos, Charles Brackett, Arthur Sheekman, Nat Perrin,
   Harlan Thompson, and Brian Hooker, based on the play by
   Richard Walton Tully and David Belasco
P: William LeBaron
Cast: Gladys Swarthout, John Boles, Willie Howard, Don Alvarado,
   Charles Bickford, H.B. Warner, Pedro de Cordoba

This movie, based on Richard Walton Tully and David Belasco's 1906 play, was filmed previously in 1914 by the Lasky Company and Cecil B. DeMille. In Old California, the queen of the fiesta moonlights as a masked bandit with a United States government agent in pursuit. The leads are fine, and plenty of operatic-style songs are included. Broadway comedy star Willie Howard appears as a Jewish cowboy.

Rosita (1923 United Artists)
D: Ernst Lubitsch
S: Edward Knoblock
P: Mary Pickford Co.
Cast: Mary Pickford, Holbrook Blinn, George Walsh

Silent. The king of Spain falls in love with Rosita, a Spanish street singer who in turn loves Don Diego, a penniless nobleman.

The Royal Hunt of the Sun (1969 National General)
D: Irving Lerner
S: Philip Yordan, based on the play by Peter Shaffer
P: Eugene Frenke and Philip Yordan
Cast: Christopher Plummer, Robert Shaw

Originally produced in 1964 by England's National Theatre, Peter Shaffer's The Royal Hunt of the Sun achieved considerable success in a subsequent Broadway staging and would seem to offer splendid possibilities to an imaginative filmmaker. Certainly, the conquest of Peru and the confrontation between Francisco Pizarro and Atahualpa, the Inca sovereign and Sun God, provide epic scope and characters of impressive strength. And there is philosophical drama in the rape of the centuries old Inca nation by conquest-hungry, gold-obsessed Spanish Christian soldiers.

Yet, despite such promising material, this production, filmed in Spain and Peru, lacks impact and intelligence. The subject cries out for a visual expansion that the film never provides. The Royal Hunt of the Sun is infected by an oppressive, studio-bound claustrophobic screenplay. Yordan's most serious mistake, however, was in creating a superstitious, virtually barbaric Indian populace in place of the original play's concept of a sophisticated agrarian society that could shame the Spaniards. Without this sense of a powerful Inca nation awaiting both its sovereign's ransom and the opportunity for revenge, Pizarro's crucial dilemma over Atahualpa lacks reality, and the film's conclusion becomes gratuitous.

Christopher Plummer gives a Shakespearean, theatrical interpretation to the godlike Atahualpa, and Robert Shaw is good as Pizarro.

"The film is no more than an echo of J. Lee Thompson's *Kings of the Sun*. Its journey to Peru for authenticity yielding little more on screen values than Sam Katzman's old sex and sand quickies for Columbia," *Hollywood Reporter* (10/16/69).

"Christopher Plummer . . . wheezes, whispers, whines, struts, sings and uses an accent that sounds sometimes like Charlie Chan and sometimes like Gonzalez-Gonzalez," Vincent Canby, *New York Times* (10/7/69).

Rumba (1935 Paramount)

D: Marion Gering
S: Howard Green, Harry Ruskin, and Frank Partos, based on a story by
   Guy Endore and Seena Owen
P: William LeBaron
Cast: George Raft, Carole Lombard, Margo

This film is a light musical melodrama. Carmelita (Margo) and her dancing partner Joe Martin (Raft) dance the rumba in Cuba, where they win a lottery. An heiress (Lombard) has her designs on Joe. A New York dance engagement, where they will introduce the rumba, is threatened by gangsters. Carmelita refuses to dance with Joe. The heiress takes her place, and Carmelita loses Joe.

Run for the Sun (1956 United Artists)

D: Roy Boulting
S: Dudley Nichols and Roy Boulting, based on the story "The Most
   Dangerous Game" by Richard Connell
P: Harry Tatelman
Cast: Richard Widmark, Trevor Howard, Jane Greer, Peter Van Eyck,
   Carlos Henning, Juan Garcia

Conventional adventure story about a journalist in the jungles of Mexico meeting up with an ex-Nazi and forced to run for his life. This film features several Hispanic actors in small roles. One of many screen adaptations of Richard Connell's story "The Most Dangerous Game," this one was filmed in Mexico, near Acapulco and Cuernavaca.

Salsa (1988 Cannon)

D: Boaz Davidson
S: Boaz Davidson, Tomas Benitez, and Shepard Goldman
P: Menahem Golan
Cast: Robby Rosa, Rodney Harvey, Magali Alvarado, Moon Orona,
   Miranda Garrison, Angela Alvarado, Loyda Ramos

This film is a low budget Hispanic American version of *Saturday Night Fever* (1977), and the first to feature a Puerto Rican youth in a leading role.

A young man, Rico (Rosa), aspires to be king of the salsa dancers in a competition at the La Luna club in Los Angeles. If he wins, he will go to the finals at the festival of San Juan in Puerto Rico.

Rico is a brown-skinned Puerto Rican, not an Anglo actor made up to look brown- or light-skinned Hispanic. A cross-cultural relationship occurs between his best friend, Ken (Harvey), and Rico's sister, Rita (Alvarado). Race is not used as a factor here.

Rico works in a car repair shop and lives in a clean, lower-middle-class house with his single working mother (Ramos) and his sister. The film is devoid of stereotypical ghetto trappings, and Rico is not alienated from United States culture. He is sure of himself and his Latin identity. The first scenes of the film well delineate this as Rico dances at his repair shop to a song titled "Mucho Money," with the American flag draped overhead.

He is tempted by an older woman, La Luna (Garrison), the owner of the club and a former Salsa Queen, who wants him to be her dance partner, thus virtually assuring a victory and another chance to regain her glory. Conflicts arise over his sister's growing affection for Ken and with his own girlfriend Vicki (Angela Alvarado). In the end he wins the dance contest and returns to his girlfriend, and Rita and Ken get together.

Rosa as Rico does well in the dance sequences and acquits himself nicely as an actor. (Rosa is a former member of the pop group Menudo.) What the film lacks in its drama and story it makes up for in style and in the exuberance of the young performers. Kenny Ortega choreographed and staged the dance sequences imaginatively, though they look a lot like television soft-drink commercials, while Rosa's moves are reminiscent of Michael Jackson's. Celia Cruz, Tito Puente and Willie Colon make cameo appearances.

Salt of the Earth (1954 Independent Productions Distributors)

D: Herbert Biberman
S: Michael Wilson
P: Paul Jarrico
Cast: Juan Chacon, Rosaura Revueltas, Will Geer, Frank Talavera, Melvin Williams, Clinton Jencks, Virginia Jencks

This is perhaps the most outstanding attempt to bring to the screen an honesty in the way Hispanic Americans are portrayed. The story behind the making of *Salt of the Earth* has been well documented in several books and one film documentary, so we'll only briefly summarize the origins here.

The film is based on an actual zinc miners' strike in New Mexico in the early 1950s and centers on the changing relationship and roles of a Mexican American worker and his wife through the progression of the strike.

The leading roles were played by Rosaura Revueltas, an actress from Mexico, and Juan Chacon, an actual zinc miner and union president. Blending professional actors with striking union members and their families, director Biberman rendered a blunt but honest critique of racial and economic inequality in America.

During production in New Mexico the film ran into trouble with threats and disruptions on the set from outsiders. Post-production on *Salt of the Earth* was completed under clandestine circumstances in Hollywood due to the Red Scare and Communist witch hunt.

Producer Paul Jarrico heard about the actual zinc miners' strike during a visit to New Mexico. He had recently formed an independent production company to develop progressive movies. Along with screenwriter Michael Wilson, who had just won an Academy Award® for *A Place in the Sun* (1951), and director Herbert Biberman, Jarrico decided to tell this story as a fictionalized real-life drama.

Jarrico took a draft of his screenplay to the International Union of Mine, Mill, and Smelter Workers for their script approval. In the original script, the character Ramon Quintero, the married union leader, has an affair with the wife of a miner who is off fighting in Korea. The union felt that this reinforced the Latin Lover stereotype, and it was stricken from the script. Another scene showed the wife at a party using her dress to wipe some spilled beer. That scene was deleted as well, for it was felt to be demeaning.

Despite many difficulties in production and post-production, the film was completed and was shown in limited independent release (no studio or distributor would touch the film because of its creators' alleged Communist affiliations). The projectionists' union refused to run the movie, and pressure from studios and Hollywood executives made it impossible for the film to achieve wide release. Newspapers even refused to run ads for the movie. *Salt of the Earth* was denounced as subversive and subsequently blacklisted because it was sponsored by the International Union of Mine, Mill and Smelter Workers (which had been expelled from the CIO in 1950 for alleged Communist-dominated leadership). However, movie houses in the more progressive major cities like New York, San Francisco and Los Angeles did show the film.

Biberman, one of the "Hollywood Ten," was convicted of contempt of Congress in 1950 when he was called before the House Un-American Activities Committee and refused to answer questions about his political affiliations. He served six months in jail. Paul Jarrico refused to deny or confirm Communist affiliations at the same hearings. Wilson clashed with the Committee and was blacklisted but managed to work by writing scripts under an assumed name.

In the years since, *Salt of the Earth* has become a cult classic and has been recognized as a pioneer film of women's liberation and the Mexican American civil rights movements. That it went so far against the grain of conventional movies of the time in the harsh political climate of the McCarthy era was monumental. Even by contemporary standards, *Salt of the Earth* would be considered a daring and unconventional movie.

The heart of the movie is its harsh and powerful portrayal of human dignity in a social setting through the relationship of Esperanza and Ramon Quintera. Their struggle, personal growth and role reversals in the face of the strike gave new dimensions to the portrayal and image of Mexican Americans in the United States.

Sadly, the film's ultimate effect on the industry was negligible because of its limited release, lack of star power and controversial nature. Without the controversy it probably would have wound up a B movie on the second half of a double bill, much like *The Lawless* (1952) or *The Ring* (1952).

Similarly, Billy Wilder's major Paramount film *The Big Carnival* (1951), originally titled *Ace in the Hole*, a cynical look at a newspaper reporter during an actual news tragedy, was also based on a true-life event. It met with an indifferent response, though it starred Kirk Douglas, who was a major star at the time.

Saludos Amigos (1942 Buena Vista)

D: Bill Roberts, Jack Kinney, Hamilton Luske, and Wilfred Jackson
S: Homer Brightman, Ralph Wright, Roy Williams, Harry Reeves,
   Dick Hueruer, and Joe Grant
P: Walt Disney
Cast: Aloysio Oliveira (narrator and Joe Carioca), Clarence Nash
   (Donald Duck), Pinto Colvig (Goofy)

John Hay Whitney, the head of the Motion Picture Division for the Office of the Coordinator of Inter-American Affairs (CIAA) asked Walt Disney to make a goodwill tour of Latin America. The Disney films and characters were popular in South America, and CIAA officials were worried about the possible growth of pro-Axis sentiment there. Disney initially declined the offer but accepted after Whitney offered to underwrite $70,000 in tour expenses and advance up to $50,000 apiece for up to five films based on the tour. Disney, accompanied by an entourage of artists, animators and film technicians, left for Latin America in August 1941, visiting Brazil, Argentina, Bolivia and Chile.

Disney originally planned to make as many as twelve cartoons about Latin America and release them in packages of four. *Saludos Amigos* was the first installment, consisting of four films loosely strung together by travel footage of the Disney tour.

In "Lake Titicaca," Donald Duck plays a tourist who runs into trouble with a balky llama. In a variation of the 1930 Watty Piper story "The Little Engine That Could," "Pedro" is about a little mail plane struggling to fly over the Chilean Andes. Goofy wreaks some very funny havoc on the Pampas in "El Gaucho Goofy," and Donald returns to learn the samba from Joe Carioca, a jaunty parrot, in "Aquarela do Brazil" (Watercolor of Brazil).

Gilberto Souto, Alberto Soria and Edmundo Santos were credited as foreign supervision associates. Backgrounds for "El Gaucho Goofy" were inspired by F. Molina Campos. *Saludos Amigos* opened to an enthusiastic response in Latin America and the States, and is generally regarded as a rough draft for the subsequent and more ambitious *The Three Caballeros* (1944).

Salvador (1986 Hemdale)

D: Oliver Stone
S: Oliver Stone and Richard Boyle
P: Gerald Green and Oliver Stone
Cast: James Woods, James Belushi, Michael Murphy, Elpidia Carrillo, Tony Plana, Juan Fernandez

In 1980, two Americans, one the down-at-heels photojournalist Richard Boyle (Woods), the other the drug-crazed disc jockey Dr. Rock (Belushi), travel to war torn El Salvador in Central America. Both are forever changed by their experiences.

The movie flings the viewer right into the events, and is unflinching in its depiction of the very human consequences of violent political action. Directing his second film on a low budget during a rigorous seven-week schedule in Mexico, Stone was in frequent contention during production with the Mexican censors, who accused Stone of giving Mexico and Central America a negative image.

"The censor said we were making all of Latin America look like a pig sty, which of course is the reality of the situation," explained Stone in the *Los Angeles Times* (12/1/86). "So if I put in a ton of rubbish on the street, she [the censor] would take out half of it. Even when we asked for one thousand extras as dead bodies, she'd only let us use five hundred."

The film is based on the true story of Richard Boyle, a photojournalist who has covered wars in Vietnam, the Middle East, Northern Ireland and Central America. Boyle gave a clue to his perceptions in the *Los Angeles Herald Examiner* (4/11/86): "Before the War, La Libertad used to be a great surfer hangout. I was into surfing. They'd come from all over the world. Good beer, beautiful women, cheap rent. What more do you want in life? I love the people in El Salvador. It's tragic that they're slaughtering each other." He continued, "None of this movie is fiction. Everything that happens is historically real."

This is clearly a North American view of the events, and many of the Latin women are made out to be sexual creatures easily available for the pleasure of men, both Anglo and Hispanic. It is perhaps, at least, a reflection of the limited opportunities poor women have in oppressive, male-oriented cultures. The well-to-do Latinas are not presented this way. Cruel

James Woods portrays photojournalist Richard Boyle in *Salvador*, the story of violent political turmoil in El Salvador.

militaristic leaders, peasants struggling to survive and opportunistic Americans are just some of the images presented. That the facts this time enforce the stereotypes is unfortunate. The film attempts fairly successfully to skewer covert efforts at American imperialism in Latin America. The film criticizes those that, aided by poverty and cynical, engage in brutal power plays at the expense of their country.

Actor Belushi states in press notes on the movie's release, "My character is ignorant of Central American issues of which I feel most of the American general public is likewise, so I feel like I'm a touchstone for the audience at the beginning of the movie. My character discovers El Salvador as the audience does."

Plana as the clever but brutal Major Max gives a chilling performance, as does Fernandez as Lieutenant Smiling Death. Elpidia Carrillo does some fine work as the native girl Maria. James Woods was nominated for an Academy Award® for his bravura and intensely multi-leveled performance as Boyle. The film moves at a frenetic pace with scenes of great power, such as whole towns being strafed and bombed, and the murder of Archbishop Romero (José Carlos Ruiz) during the celebration of mass.

One of the most shocking images depicting political atrocities is the sequence at El Playon. Hundreds of corpses lie at a huge garbage dump as relatives search for missing loved ones who have been abducted from their homes and killed by death squads.

Boyle is slowly brought into events through his relationship with the native girl Maria. He finally abandons all hope of justice and fair play from a United States system that he has stubbornly supported, despite previous confrontations in El Salvador. His frustration builds as he deals with bigoted and politically cynical State Department officials and CIA "advisors" trying to maintain the brutal status quo for fear of a left-wing victory. The change in Boyle's attitude is completed when, after a harrowing journey to freedom and safety in the United States, Maria is taken off the bus near Las Vegas, Nevada, by United States Immigration authorities and forcibly repatriated to El Salvador, where she will face almost certain torture and death.

Hemdale put *Salvador* into limited release when all the major distributors turned the film down because of its political content. Eventually, it was released before Stone's popular Academy Award®-winning Vietnam War drama *Platoon* (1986).

Salvador earned two Oscar® nominations, one for Woods and one for Best Original Screenplay for Boyle and Stone.

The Sandlot (1993 Twentieth Century Fox)
D: David Mickey Evans
S: David Mickey Evans and Robert Gunter
P: Dale de la Torre and William S. Gilmore
Cast: Tom Guiry, Mike Vitar, Patrick Renna

A coming-of-age story about an awkward twelve-year-old boy, Scott Smalls (Guiry), who moves to a San Fernando Valley, California, suburb in 1962 and tries to fit in with a loosely knit neighborhood baseball team made up of local misfits. The team leader is the athletically gifted Benny "the Jet" Rodriguez (Vitar). He befriends Smalls and instructs him in the game. Smalls learns to make new friends and conquer his own fears. Benny is Hispanic American and is presented without stereotypical cultural trappings within the cross-cultural context of the other kids. He is a leader, and at the end of the film it is revealed that he grows up to be a major league baseball player. He fulfills his promise as part of the American Dream.

Santiago (1956 Warner Bros.)

D: Gordon Douglas
S: Martin Rackin and John Twist, based on Rackin's novel
  The Great Courage
P: Martin Rackin
Cast: Alan Ladd, Lloyd Nolan, Rossanna Podesta, Francisco Ruiz, Rico Alaniz

Rival gunrunners Cash Adams (Ladd) and Clay Pike (Nolan), en route by steamer to Cuba prior to the Spanish-American War of 1898, try to deliver guns to the people of Cuba. The Cubans are involved in a violent struggle to win independence from Spain. On board the ship they meet Dona Isabella (Podesta), who is returning from a trip to the States to raise money for her people's fight. The guns must be lugged overland, and Adams and Pike encounter Spanish troops in the jungle. They break through the Spanish blockade only to discover that the Cubans have suffered a costly defeat. Pike wants to turn around and sell the guns to the Spaniards, but Cash, now in love with Isabella, is determined his Cuban friends will have them.

The action is kept going by director Gordon Douglas, and some crackling dialogue between Nolan and Ladd makes for fun entertainment.

Saturday Night Fever (1977 Paramount)

D: John Badham
S: Norman Wexler
P: Robert Stigwood
Cast: John Travolta, Karen Lynn Gorney

Tony Manero (Travolta) is an Italian American working-class youth in Brooklyn, New York, with a dead-end job whose energies focus on a disco championship at the neighborhood disco club, 2001. The marginal Latin substory elements include a Puerto Rican couple who lose the disco championship to Tony and his girl. In another scene Tony and his friends drive their car into a Puerto Rican gang's turf, resulting in a fight that the Puerto Ricans lose.

Scandalous John (1971 Buena Vista)

D: Robert Butler
S: Bill Walsh and Don Da Gradi
P: Bill Walsh
Cast: Brian Keith, Alfonso Arau

A touching contemporary Western comedy with a *Don Quixote* theme. A seventy-nine-year-old rancher, John McCanless (Keith), tilting against the windmill of progress, drives his last remaining cattle to market in an effort to save his ranch from developers. He sets off accompanied by Paco Martinez (Arau), his Mexican hired hand.

Scarface (1981 Universal)

D: Brian De Palma
S: Oliver Stone, based on the 1932 film script by Ben Hecht
P: Martin Bregman and Peter Saphier
Cast: Al Pacino, Steven Bauer, Miriam Colon, Mary Elizabeth
Mastrantonio, Robert Loggia, Pepe Serna, Michelle Pfeiffer, Victor
Campos, Roberto Contreras, Victor Millan, Santos Morales

Brian De Palma directed this remake of the original 1932 gangster epic *Scarface* (directed by Howard Hawks and starring Paul Muni). De Palma updated to the story to a Cuban American setting in 1980s Miami with the drug trade, instead of Prohibition's liquor, as the basis for Tony Montana's (Pacino) rise to power in the criminal underworld.

Pacino convincingly plays the ruthless and charming Cuban refugee who quickly learns his way around Miami. Through force of personality and a progression of criminal acts, he finds himself at the top of the criminal hierarchy. In an inspired classic finale, hundreds of Colombian hitmen pursue the cocaine-addicted Montana through his Florida mansion as he blasts away at them with an automatic weapon until he is felled and killed. Pacino spent time studying with Cubans in order to get the speech patterns and mannerisms right.

The predominantly Hispanic cast introduced Bauer as Montana's best friend and included Colon as his mother, Pepe Serna as his doomed refugee buddy who meets his demise at the end of a chainsaw, Angel Salazar as another friend of Montana's, and Arnaldo Santana as Ernie. Mary Elizabeth Mastrantonio is Montana's sister, of whom he is very protective. The film was directed in grand style and tone by De Palma from a script by Oliver Stone.

Scarface provided the entertainment world with a new screen villain and Hispanic stereotype, the drug lord or kingpin. Previously, Hispanics had been seen as the victims of drugs, small-time hoodlums, or street dealers. Hispanics were now in control of the drug trade and every bit as clever and ruthless as their Italian Mafia screen counterparts.

Miami was re-created in an exaggerated art deco style similar to that of Michael Mann's later hit television show *Miami Vice* (1984-89), and reintroduced as a new city of overheated ambiance and color, Cuban dominated and peopled with Caribbean and South American types. Previous cinematic incarnations had pictured the city as a retirement beach resort community for middle-class Americans.

Tony (Al Pacino), his
mother (Miriam Colon,
standing) and his sister,
Gina (Mary Elizabeth
Mastrantonio) in
Scarface.

The film was a tremendous box office hit but critics were divided over the film's excessive foul language, violence and depiction of drugs. It should be pointed out, too, that De Palma and Stone take almost three hours to achieve what Hawks did in ninety minutes.

Second Chance (1953 RKO Radio Pictures)
D: Rudolph Mate
S: Oscar Millard, Sydney Boehm, and D.M. Marshman, Jr., based on a
   story by Marshman
P: Sam Wiesenthal
Cast: Robert Mitchum, Linda Darnell, Jack Palance, Rudolfo Hoyos, Jr.,
   Fortunio Bonanova, Abel Fernandez, Martin Garralaga

A South-of-the-border melodrama in which Russ Lambert (Mitchum), an American prizefighter, barnstorms through Mexico trying to assuage the guilt he feels for killing a man in the ring. There he meets Clare Shepard (Darnell), a gangster's moll, who is being stalked by a hit man (Palance) sent to kill her before a Senate crime committee can find her to testify against her ex-boyfriend.

The high point of the film is a fight atop a funicular railway between two Andean peaks (despite the fact that the film takes place in Mexico). Part of the film was shot in Cuernavaca and Taxco, Mexico. Cast members include Hoyos, Salvador Baguez, Maurice Jara, Bonanova, Fernandez, Garralaga, José Dominguez, Tony Martinez and Tina Menard.

Secret of the Incas (1954 Paramount)

D: Jerry Hopper
S: Ranald MacDougall and Sydney Boehm, based on the story "Legend of the Incas" by Boehm
P: Mel Epstein
Cast: Charlton Heston, Robert Young, Thomas Mitchell, Yma Sumac [Amy Camus]

A routine action film highlighted by Technicolor and location photography in Machu Picchu, Peru. Two American soldiers of fortune are on the trail of the Inca Sunburst jewels. The film features Yma Sumac, Peruvian songbird of the Andes, in her film debut.

Martin Garralaga, Rudolfo Hoyos, Rosa Rey and Carlos Rivero, among other Hispanic actors, have minor roles in the film.

Serenade (1956 Warner Bros.)

D: Anthony Mann
S: Ivan Goff, Ben Roberts, and John Twist, based on the novel by James M. Cain
P: Henry Blanke
Cast: Mario Lanza, Joan Fontaine, Sarita Montiel, Joseph Calleia

Lanza's comeback film after four years away from the cameras since 1952's Because You're Mine. Lanza, as Damon Vincente, is a potent personality with a rich singing voice that makes up for any acting inadequacies.

This is the tale of a California vineyard worker's rise to operatic eminence and the two women from different worlds, one Anglo, the other Mexican, who love him. Kendall Hale (Fontaine) is the wealthy society patroness who jilts him when something better comes along, and Juana Montes (Montiel) is the Mexican señorita who weds him at the finale. Mexican location scenes were filmed in San Miguel de Allende.

Serenade is based on the James M. Cain novel, extensively watered down in its adaptation for the movies. The novel dealt with male homosexuality, impotence and prostitution in the shantytowns of Mexico.

The film shared more parallels with Blood and Sand (1922 and 1941) than with its original source. The hero, a simple man with a superb voice, is brought to the heights of success and then abandoned by a sensuous, sensation-hungry female aristocrat (Doña Sol in Blood and Sand). This proves to be more than he can handle. His breakdown is cured by the love of a good woman (Carmen Espinosa in Blood and Sand).

Hispanic actor Martin Garralaga plays Romero, a minor role, and José Torvay is a mariachi bandleader.

Seven Cities of Gold (1955 Twentieth Century Fox)
D: Robert D. Webb
S: Richard L. Breen, John C. Higgins, and Joseph Petracca, based on a novel by Isabelle Gibson Ziegler
P: Robert D. Webb and Barbara McLean
Cast: Richard Egan, Anthony Quinn, Michael Rennie, Jeffrey Hunter, Rita Moreno, Eduardo Noriega, Victor Juncos, Miguel Inclan, Carlos Musquiz, Pedro Galvan

Quinn plays the hardened Spanish military explorer Gaspar de Portola, who, along with Father Junipero Serra (Rennie), explored northern Mexico and helped establish the missions of California in 1769.

Following many difficulties in hostile lands, the expedition arrives at the present site of San Diego, California. Portola sets up a garrison and leaves it in the care of Lieutenant José Mendoza (Egan) before continuing northward in search of the mythical Seven Cities of Cibola, where the streets are reportedly paved with gold.

Hostile Indians harass the settlement, but an understanding is reached when Serra saves the life of one of the chiefs. Mendoza seduces Ula (Moreno), a pretty Indian girl and sister of the chief. Portola returns, expecting a supply ship at the bay. Mendoza rejects Ula's proposal of marriage. Ashamed of herself and unable to return to her people with honor, Ula commits suicide by leaping from a cliff. Her brother, seeking revenge for his sister's death, demands that Mendoza be turned over to him. Portola and Serra refuse, but Mendoza finally surrenders himself to the Indians in order not to further endanger the garrison. The Indians cut out Mendoza's heart, and Serra brings back the body. The supply ship finally arrives and allows for the establishment of a mission at San Diego.

This film would have been more accurately called The Father Serra Story or San Diego. The title Seven Cities of Gold led audiences to expect an action spectacle about conquistadors in search of ill-gotten treasures from ancient Indian civilizations. Instead, audiences got this bare (production-wise) story that focuses on the standard Indians-versus-settlers conflicts.

It did address on a superficial level certain truths about the interactions and cross-purposes among the Catholic church, Spanish explorers and Native Americans in the New World. Quinn, as Portola, comes off best because of his Latin quality. Rennie, as Father Serra, although very British, supplies the dignity and authority the character demands. Egan comes off as hopelessly American. Moreno is quite good as Ula, yet she was already growing tired of these native-girls-with-bare-feet depictions, that comprised more than half of her film roles.

Filmed on location in Mexico around the rugged deserts of Guadalajara and the beaches of Manzanillo, the production involved some of the top motion picture talent in Mexico, both in front of and behind the camera. Rene Cardana, Mexican film producer and director, served as co-director, while Sanchez Tello and Jaime Contreras were assistant directors, Jorje Stahl, whose father was one of the pioneers of the Mexican film industry, worked as camera operator. Among the cast were Eduardo Noriega, Fernando Wagner, Lucila Nieto, José Torvay, Carlos Musquiz, Pedro Galvan, Yerye Beirute, John Cusick and Eduardo Pilega.

Selena (1997 Warner Bros.)

D: Gregory Nava
S: Gregory Nava
P: Moctesuma Esparza, Bob Katz
Cast: Jennifer Lopez, Edward James Olmos, Constance Marie, Jacob Vargas, Jackie Guerra, Lupe Ontiveros, Sal Lopez, Panchito Gomez, Richard Coca

Jennifer Lopez stars in the title role in the film charting the meteoric rise of Selena and the entire Quintanilla family as they came to live the American dream. *Selena* follows the rise of a true life hero from the suburbs of South Texas to become the brightest star ever to emerge from the regional music scene known as "Tejano" that integrates the traditions of polka, rock, R&B, pop and traditional Latin influences. Just as Selena was on the cusp of crossover success, her ascent was cut short when she was murdered at the age of twenty-three. Starring as the younger version of Selena is newcomer Becky Lee Meza, a ten-year-old Texan native chosen from thousands of hopefuls who auditioned for the chance to portray their inspirational heroine. Edward James Olmos stars as Selena's father, Abraham Quintanilla, Jr., a farmer who nurtures his family's ambitions against enormous odds. Jon Seda stars as Chris Perez, a rebellious guitarist who joins the family's band and is captivated by Selena, eventually becoming her husband. Constance Marie plays the family's devoted mother, Marcela. Jacob Vargas appears as Selena's brother Abie and her sister Suzette, is portrayed by Jackie Guerra.

Selena was filmed entirely on location in Selena's own home state of Texas, often at the very sites where the actual story happened. San Antonio served as the primary home for the company. It was there that the filmmakers staged the centerpiece sequence of the film: Selena's record breaking performance at the Houston Astrodome with over 35,000 extras in attendance. Additional locations included Poteet, Texas and Corpus Christi.

The film plays like an elongated episode of television's *The Partridge Family* in a Latin vein. The script does offer insights into duality of Mexican American heritage and identity. This was the star-making leading role for Jennifer Lopez, who captured the look, essence and appeal of the young Tejana singing sensation. Edward James Olmos does fine work as Abraham Quintanilla, as does Constance Marie as the mother. The excellent cast shines under Nava's direction.

Short Eyes [aka: The Slammer] (1977 Film League)

D: Robert M. Young
S: Miguel Pinera, based on his play
P: Lewis Harris
Cast: Bruce Davison, José Perez, Tito Goya, Miguel Pinero

A searing and grueling slice-of-life prison drama that was actually filmed in the New York correctional institution known as "The Tombs." The Obie Award-winning play was written by Pinera, who also wrote the screenplay, based on his five-year experience as an inmate at Sing Sing Prison.

A child molester is brought into the cell block, where passions run high, not only among the African American and Puerto Rican inmates but also among the guards. Juan, played by Perez, is a rational and compassionate Puerto Rican inmate. Tito Goya plays Cupcakes, and Shawn Elliott plays a cynical Puerto Rican. Mexican American singer Freddy Fender makes a cameo appearance as an inmate.

A Show of Force (1990 Paramount)

D: Bruno Barreto
S: John Strong
P: John Strong
Cast: Amy Irving, Robert Duvall, Erik Estrada, Andy Garcia,
    Lou Diamond Phillips

This film is a misrepresentation of an actual incident that was uncovered by three Puerto Rican journalists who implicated the local police and the United States government in the murder of several radical students. The film combines the journalists into one Anglo female reporter who is the widow of a Puerto Rican activist (which conveniently provides her with a Hispanic last name).

Reporter Kate Melendez (Irving) tries to get to the bottom of the killing of two militant students by police at a remote broadcast tower in Cerro Maravilla, Puerto Rico. The island is presented as a cross between Miami and a Latin American country and features a tyrannical governor surrounded by villainous police officials. Howard (Duvall), the television station news manager, doesn't seem to care about Melendez's story. Her father, a seemingly bigoted naval officer, tells her, "My biggest mistake was sending you to college. I had you leave Puerto Rico and what do you do, you come back with a Puerto Rican; not just any Puerto Rican, a radical leftist one." And she retorts, "He was a lawyer with a cause."

The problems of Puerto Rico and Puerto Ricans are seen here as internal ones, with Anglo-Americans not caring about whether justice is served, even though Puerto Ricans are also United States citizens.

There is no suspense in the film, which does not create any sympathy for the victims or involve the viewer in this miscarriage of justice or its implications. The causes of the dissatisfaction of these radicals and the politics are never explored. The final cop-out of the film is to place responsibility on an individual, not the system. Melendez seems to be the only one who has a nice family life or home. Puerto Ricans' homes and living conditions are represented as if Puerto Rico were a Third World country.

An interesting performance is given by Lou Diamond Phillips, and a fine cameo is provided by Andy Garcia as an opposition party lawyer. Another cameo features Erik Estrada as a police officer with a conscience. The movie was filmed entirely in Puerto Rico.

Sierra Baron (1958 Twentieth Century Fox)
D: James B. Clark
S: Houston Brach
P: Plato A. Skouras
Cast: Brian Keith, Rick Jason

A routine Western shot in Mexico by Alex Phillips. Encroaching Americans are threatening a Spanish clan's land grants in California.

The Slammer
See *Short Eyes*.

Sniper (1993 TriStar)
D: Luis Llosa
S: Michael Frost Beckner and Crash Leyland
P: Robert L. Rosen
Cast: Tom Berenger, Billy Zane

A United States Marine sniper and an observer go on a mission into the jungles of Panama to take out a powerful rebel guerrilla leader and his financier, a Colombian drug lord. Filmed in Australia (doubling for Panama) by Peruvian filmmaker Luis Llosa in his American directorial debut.

Sol Madrid (1968 Metro-Goldwyn-Mayer)
D: Brian G. Hutton
S: David Karp, based on the novel *Fruit of the Poppy* by Robert Wilder
P: Hall Bartlett
Cast: David McCallum, Stella Stevens, Ricardo Montalban, Rip Torn, Perry Lopez, Abel Franco, Joe Dominguez

Sol Madrid (McCallum), an undercover narcotics agent, is assigned the task of tracking down a gangster who is on the run from his Mafia cohorts. In the course of the investigation, Sol comes across one of the main sources of heroin supply from Mexico to the States. Events are played out against sunny Acapulco, Mexico, locations. Montalban plays Jalisco, a charismatic double-crossing Mexican agent.

Sombrero (1953 Metro-Goldwyn-Mayer)

D: Norman Foster

S: Norman Foster and Josefina Niggli, based on Niggli's novel *A Mexican Village*

P: Jack Cummings

Cast: Ricardo Montalban, Pier Angeli, Vittorio Gassman, Cyd Charisse, Yvonne De Carlo, Rick Jason, José Greco, Alfonso Bedoya

A blending of three love stories based on Josefina Niggli's novel *A Mexican Village*, published in 1945. Born and raised in Monterey, Mexico, Niggli resided in North Carolina at the time of production. The book consisted of ten short stories, but only three were used in *Sombrero*. The film features three Latin leading men—Montalban, Gassman (the Italian neorealist film idol in his American film debut), and newcomer Jason; and three leading ladies: Angeli, De Carlo and Charisse—who performs a sensuous dance before an ancient Aztec idol. Spanish dancer Greco plays a matador in his film debut.

Ricardo Montalban and Pier Angeli in *Sombrero*, a film combining three stories of love and romance in Mexico.

This well-intentioned and handsomely produced, but caricatured, episodic musical was filmed in Technicolor largely on location in Tepotzlan and Tetecala, Mexico, in the state of Morelos near Cuernavaca. Producer Cummings had filmed in Puebla, Mexico, six years previously on *Fiesta* (1947) for MGM. Foster was a top-flight director in Mexico City, where he lived for seven years before returning to Hollywood. The Mexican-born Montalban had become a star in Mexico under Foster's direction before coming to Hollywood. Rosaura Revueltas (*Salt of the Earth*) is featured as Tia Magdalena, and Bedoya is Don Inocente. Alma Beltran and Pilar Del Rey have minor roles in the film.

"*Sombrero* is another of those musicals which are bright, gaudy and meaningless. All the fancy trappings . . . can't compensate for lack of conviction in plot," *Hollywood Citizen News* (4/14/53).

Sorcerer (1977 Universal/Paramount)

D: William Friedkin

S: Walon Green

P: William Friedkin

Cast: Roy Scheider, Ramon Bieri

The story of four men, each of whom has had to flee his native country, who end up in a poverty-stricken village in South America where they work on American oil pipelines. When an oil well some 200 miles from the village explodes, they are hired to drive six cases of nitroglycerin across treacherous mountains and jungle roads. In return they are promised $10,000 each and legal residence in the country without police harassment. Based on Georges Arnaud's novel *The Wages of Fear* and on the critically acclaimed 1955 French film of the same name, directed by Clouzot. Friedkin's film, though well made, met with indifference at the box office. It was filmed in central Mexico and the Dominican Republic.

The Specialist (1994 Warner Bros.)
D: Luis Llosa
S: Alexandra Seros
P: Jerry Weintraub
Cast: Sylvester Stallone, Rod Steiger, Sharon Stone, James Woods, Eric Roberts

May Munro's (Stone) parents were killed by Cuban gangsters, led by father and son Joe (Steiger) and Tomas (Roberts) Leon. She decides that ex-CIA bomb specialist Ray Quick (Stallone) is the man to help her exact her revenge.

This is a formulaic action film that did surprising little business at the box office, given the caliber of the two leads.

Speedy Gonzalez (1955 Warner Bros.)
This cartoon short starred Speedy Gonzalez, a Mexican cartoon character created in 1953 at Warner Bros. Speedy Gonzalez won an Academy Award® in 1955. The voice of Speedy Gonzalez was created and done by the versatile Mel Blanc. Billed as "the fastest and smartest mouse in all of Meheeco!" Speedy proved a popular addition to the Warner Bros. Looney Tunes characters that included Bugs Bunny, Porky Pig and Daffy Duck.

Stand and Deliver (1988 Warner Bros.)
D: Ramon Menendez
S: Ramon Menendez and Tom Musca
P: Edward James Olmos, Ramon Menendez, and Tom Musca
Cast: Edward James Olmos, Lou Diamond Phillips, Rosana De Soto, Carmen Argenziano, Virginia Paris, Andy Garcia

Stand and Deliver is based on the true story of mathematics teacher Jaime Escalante and his success with a group of underachieving East Los Angeles students at Garfield High School.

In 1982, eighteen of his students took the Advanced Placement Test in calculus. The exam, which qualifies students for college credit, is so demanding that less than 2 percent of all high school students in the United States even attempt it. Through diligence and determination, all of Escalante's students received passing grades, six with perfect scores.

However, the initial triumph was short lived. After carefully examining the test papers, the Educational Testing Service concluded there was such a distinct pattern of incorrect answers among the Garfield students that they must have cheated. Their scores were invalidated and, despite the protests of Escalante, the students were given a choice: accept the Testing Service's verdict or retest. They chose to retest and again passed.

In *Stand and Deliver*, Edward James Olmos (back, left) portrays high school teacher Jaime Escalante and Lou Diamond Phillips (far right) is Angel, a school troublemaker with a secret desire to improve himself. Among Escalante's students are (back, left to right) Ingrid Oliu, Will Gotay, Lydia Nicole; (front, left to right) Vanessa Marquez, Patrick Baca, Karla Montana and Mark Eliot.

The controversial story was not lost on filmmakers Ramon Menendez and Tom Musca, who co-wrote the screenplay and produced the film with Olmos. They first learned of the story from a *Los Angeles Times* article. "The idea of being truly innocent and having to prove it seemed like an intriguing premise for a film," recalled Musca. "There was an enormous probability that the students' scores would never have been questioned had they not all come from Garfield High with predominantly Hispanic surnames. In other words, there was the distinct possibility of institutional racism."

After a discouraging response from the studios, Menendez and Musca turned to a prior relationship with Lindsay Law, the executive producer of the *American Playhouse* series. Menendez and Musca sent a synopsis of the Escalante story to Law, whose reaction was positive. Besides *American Playhouse*, Musca received funding from organizations such as Arco, the National Science Foundation, the Corporation for Public Broadcasting, and the Ford Foundation.

When it came time to find an actor to portray Jaime Escalante, Menendez and Musca contacted Olmos, who was excited not only about the prospect of portraying Escalante, but also about joining them in a production capacity. "The concept of false accusation was a theme I had dealt with in my earlier film roles, both in *Zoot Suit* (1981) as well as in *The Ballad of Gregorio Cortez* (1983)." Once committed, Olmos began preparations for the part of the Bolivian-born schoolteacher by studying the man. "Jaime and I spent extensive time together," recalled the actor. Olmos spent eighteen hours a day for a month at the instructor's side. The actor concentrated on Escalante's physical characteristics. He had his hair thinned to resemble the teacher's pate and gained forty pounds. Olmos reasoned, "Jaime's appearance, even his mannerisms, have a lot to do with the way his kids treat him. So I could not see myself playing the role in peak condition."

Lou Diamond Phillips, still relatively unknown since *La Bamba* (1987) had not yet been released, joined the cast as Angel, a youth who has to choose between education and the lure of street gang life.

Stand and Deliver was shot in and around East Los Angeles and on the actual Garfield High School site on a shoestring budget (by current standards) of $1 million, over a period of six weeks. After being screened by all the major studios, the film was picked up for theatrical distribution by Warner Bros. prior to its airing on PBS.

The movie struck a responsive chord with the American moviegoing public as well as with film critics, educators and politicians, in what it had to say about the state of American education and the difference one teacher can make in the lives of students. At a time in American life when there is concern over the quality of education and the plight of teachers and students, the film was hailed for its inspirational message.

The critics also hailed Olmos' sensitive portrayal of the math teacher. He was nominated for a Golden Globe Award and an Academy Award® for Best Actor of 1988. The film introduced a number of young Hispanic performers to the screen and showcased the talents of many established performers such as De Soto, Paris, Argenziano and Garcia.

Stand and Deliver departs from the usual Hollywood formula of an Anglo teacher helping disadvantaged minority youth. Usually, minority teachers are relegated to the background of the story and are presented as ineffectual at best. This was demonstrated as early as *Blackboard Jungle* (1955) and as recently as *The Principal* (1987). *Stand and Deliver*, however, paved the way for another film about a minority teacher, in a predominantly African American New Jersey inner-city school, *Lean on Me* (1989), a much less effective movie, which starred Morgan Freeman as real-life controversial African American principal Joe Clark.

The creative forces behind *Stand and Deliver*, Menendez and Olmos, are Hispanic. Even though Menendez is Cuban and Olmos is Mexican

American, *Stand and Deliver* is regarded as a Chicano film because of the overwhelming presence and involvement of Olmos, who helped to shape the final film as star and producer and helped to clarify its poignant subject matter.

Star Maps (1997 Twentieth Century Fox)

D: Miguel Arteta

S: Miguel Arteta

P: Matthew Greenfield

Cast: Efrain Figueroa, Lysa Flores, Douglas Spain, Martha Velez, Herbert Siguenza

A Latino father (Figueroa) with a stable of male prostitutes pimps his own son, Carlos (Spain), and his mistress on Hollywood's Sunset Boulevard under the cover of selling maps to the movie stars homes.

Arteta used Latino culture symbols throughout, including Cantinflas, stereotypes of the maternal, self sacrificing Latina, the fiery Latina and the Latin Lover, as well as magical realism. The film tries to be dramatic and funny with the subject matter. This is a delicate balancing act that does not always work, but it is a worthwhile film attempt.

Stars and Guitars

See *Brazil*.

Steal Big, Steal Little (1994 Savoy Pictures)

D: Andrew Davis

S: Andrew Davis

P: Andrew Davis and Fred Caruso

Cast: Andy Garcia, Alan Arkin, Rachel Ticotin, William Marquez, Holland Taylor, Joe Pantoliano

Action comedy that pits brothers and their allies in a comic battle of good versus evil to control a sprawling California ranch inheritance in the Santa Barbara mountains. Identical twin brothers Ruben Martinez and Robby Martin (Andy Garcia in a dual role) orphaned at an early age, have been raised by a wealthy and flamboyant woman (Taylor). Ruben and Robby have grown up constantly trying to outdo one another. Ruben has come to love the land and enjoys the simple life of a ranch hand. Robby, on the other hand, has become a social climber, more in love with money and what it can buy than with the history of his adopted home and his Latino heritage. This is an old-fashioned comedy drama, reminiscent of the 1930s. Garcia turns in a wonderful performance in the dual role of the twin brothers.

The Substitute (1996 Orion)
D: Robert Mandel
S: Roy Frumkes, Ricco Simonelli and Alan Ormsby
P: Jim Steele and Morrie Eisenman
Cast: Tom Berenger, Ernie Hudson, Diane Venora, Glenn Plummer, Marc Anthony, Raymond Cruz

A racially mixed high school in Miami, where violence and disdain for authority are rampant, comes to a head when former Vietnam veteran and covert operative Shale (Berenger) brings his own brand of higher learning as a substitute teacher. Back in Miami to visit his high school teacher girlfriend (Venora) he saves her life when a gang leader exacts his revenge for her interfering with his "business." Shale decides to substitute teach, and in the process discovers that the high school is not only a major drug depot but its principal is in just as deep as the Latino gangs. Marc Anthony plays a despicable youth gang leader.

Summer and Smoke (1961 Paramount)
D: Peter Glenville
S: James Poe and Meade Roberts, based on the play by Tennessee Williams
P: Hal Wallis
Cast: Laurence Harvey, Geraldine Page, Rita Moreno, Thomas Gomez, Pepe Hern

Set in a Southern town in 1916, this is a typically torrid Tennessee Williams tale of Alma (Page), the inhibited daughter of a minister, and John (Harvey), the boy next door and hell-bent son of the town's respected doctor.

Although intrigued by Alma's shy fumbling toward love, John takes up with Rosa (Moreno), the earthy daughter of a gambling casino owner (Gomez). Rosa's father accidentally kills John's father after a drunken party. After his father's death, John reforms but refuses Alma's love in favor of the attentions of an adoring teenager. Alma is left alone to find love with whomever comes her way.

The Sun Also Rises (1957 Twentieth Century Fox)
D: Henry King
S: Peter Viertel, based on the novel by Ernest Hemingway
P: Darryl F. Zanuck
Cast: Tyrone Power, Errol Flynn, Ava Gardner, Mel Ferrer, Eddie Albert

Set in Europe during the 1920s just following the end of World War I, The Sun Also Rises covers a few weeks in the lives and loves of a "Lost Generation" of people who lived as though they might die at any time.

Based on the novel by Ernest Hemingway (published in 1926), the film version concentrated on the tragic tale of the lives and loves of Jake Barnes (Power) and Lady Brett Ashley (Gardner). Traveling with friends from Paris to the bullfights in Spain, they meet Mike Campbell (Flynn). They become entangled with a bullfighter, Pedro Romero, played by then-unknown Robert Evans (who forsook an acting career to become a major producer).

This film is a well-acted, visually sweeping Technicolor production, despite actors a little too old for the roles in the novel. Censorship restrictions and a Hollywood-imposed happy ending marred the work's original intent.

Although the San Fermin fiesta in Pamplona, Spain, was filmed in its entirety, Pamplona had to be doubled by Morelia, Mexico, for the scenes with the principal actors because of the weather. Shooting also took place in Spain, France and California. Morelia was last used as a filming location by Fox in 1946 for its production of *Captain from Castile* (1947), also directed by Henry King and starring Tyrone Power.

Ernest Hemingway told the *London Sunday Dispatch*, as reported in *Time* magazine (12/2/57), "I saw Darryl Zanuck's splashy Cook's tour of Europe's lost-generation bistros, bullfights and more bistros. It's all pretty disappointing and that's being gracious. You're meant to be in Spain and all you see walking around are nothing but Mexicans. Pretty silly."

Surviving Picasso (1996 Warner Bros.)
D: James Ivory
S: Arianna Stassinopoulos Huffington and Ruth Prawer Jhabvala
P: Ismail Merchant
Cast: Anthony Hopkins, Natascha McElhone, Julianne Moore

An unglamorous look at the personal life of famed Spanish artist Pablo Picasso and his affair with a woman forty years his junior. Hopkins plays Picasso without effecting a Spanish accent.

The Super (1991 Twentieth Century Fox)
D: Rod Daniel
S: Sam Simon
P: Charles A. Gordon
Cast: Joe Pesci, Vincent Gardenia, Madelyn Smith Osborne,
    Rubén Blades

A dramatic comedy about a slumlord named Louie Kritski (Pesci), who is ordered by a judge to live in one of his own decrepit tenements in New York City as punishment for deliberately ignoring building code violations. While living in the tenement, he gets to know its inhabitants and experiences their terrible living conditions. Blades plays Marlon, a crafty street hustler who keeps dreaming up new ways to scam Kritski, while gradually teaching him to feel compassion for his tenants. Other Hispanics featured in the cast are Steve Rodriguez, Eileen Galindo, Marina Durrell, Olga Merediz, Chris Herrera and Juan Manual Aguero.

Sweet Charity (1969 Universal)

D: Bob Fosse
S: Peter Stone, based on the play by Neil Simon, Cy Coleman, and Dorothy Fields, adapted from the screenplay *Notti di Cabiria* by Federico Fellini, Tullio Ponelli, and Ennio Flaiano
P: Robert Arthur
Cast: Shirley MacLaine, Chita Rivera, Ricardo Montalban, Sammy Davis, Jr.

The first screen appearance of famed Broadway actress and dancer Chita Rivera, who created on stage many roles played by other actresses in the later film versions, including Anita (Rita Moreno) in *West Side Story* and Rosie (Janet Leigh) in *Bye, Bye Birdie*.

Rivera plays one of Charity's best girlfriends and demonstrates her unique singing and dancing ability to great effect. Montalban gives a splendid caricature performance of a Latin Lover leading man in this musical directed by Bob Fosse (making his feature film directorial debut).

Taggart (1964 Universal)

D: R.G. Springsteen
S: Robert Creighton Williams, based on a novel by Louis L'Amour
P: Gordon Kay
Cast: Tony Young, Dan Duryea, David Carradine, Elsa Cardenas

One of the last of Universal's modest-budget color programmers, which gave way to television movies. *Taggart* was based on a novel by famed Western writer Louis L'Amour. The slaughter of a homestead family and the revenge sought by the surviving son, Taggart, is the thrust of the story. After obtaining revenge Taggart finds himself with a price on his own head. He vies for the love of a vivacious and treacherous Mexican, Consuela (Cardenos), and a blonde "nice girl." The blonde Anglo wins his love.

Tampico (1944 Twentieth Century Fox)

D: Lothar Mendes
S: Kenneth Gamet, Fred Niblo, Jr., and Richard Macaulay, based on an original story by Ladislas Fodor
P: Robert Bassler
Cast: Edward G. Robinson, Lynn Bari, Victor McLaglen, Marc Lawrence, Mona Maris

The story of a tanker captain who loses his ship to a Nazi submarine's torpedo shortly after the vessel has left the Mexican port of Tampico. He seeks to avenge himself by discovering which of several persons who knew of his departure from port leaked the information to the enemy. The story becomes one of conflict and romance between the captain (Robinson) and a rescued passenger (Bari), and of the wartime espionage in the gulf city of Tampico. Antonio Moreno appears in a small role as a justice of the peace. Chris-Pin Martin, Nestor Paiva and Martin Garralaga also have small roles. Grace Poggi, a Spanish Italian and California born dancer, plays the dancer in a café sequence. Mexican musicians and composers Gilbert Ysais and Noel Desilva perform in the wedding sequence.

Tarzan and the Great River (1967 Paramount)

D: Robert Day
S: Bob Barbash
P: Sy Weintraub
Cast: Mike Henry, Manuel Padilla, Jr., Rafer Johnson

A Tarzan adventure set in South America along the Amazon River.

Terror in a Texas Town (1958 United Artists)

D: Joseph H. Lewis
S: Ben L. Perry [Dalton Trumbo]
P: Frank N. Seltzer
Cast: Sterling Hayden, Sebastian Cabot, Victor Millan, Ann Varela

Ed McNeil (Cabot), a Texas land baron, intimidates local farmers into giving up their land because, as the resident Mexican José Mirada (Millan) explains, "The ground, she is filled with oil." George Hansen (Hayden), a Swedish American sailor, returns to his father's home in Texas and finds that his dad has been murdered. Upon his arrival, George is beaten up by McNeil's henchmen and is found and nursed back to health by Mirada, who tells Hansen the truth about his father's murder, which Mirada witnessed. Mirada is also killed. Hansen faces down the henchmen with a whaling harpoon.

A poor man's combination of *High Noon* and *Bad Day at Black Rock*, *Terror in a Texas Town* was filmed in ten days for $80,000 and was written by blacklisted writer Dalton Trumbo. It has become a cult B movie favorite on campus and in art house theaters.

"Outdoor drama that examines fear and its consequences on men. Well made within modest framework," *Film Daily* (8/25/58).

That Night in Rio (1941 Twentieth Century Fox)

D: Irving Cummings
S: George Seaton, Bess Meredyth, Hal Long, Samuel Hoffenstein, and Jessie Ernst, based on a play by Rudolph Lothar and Hans Adler
P: Fred Kohlmar
Cast: Alice Faye, Don Ameche, Carmen Miranda, J. Carroll Naish, Maria Montez

Ameche plays two roles in this Technicolor musical comedy—Larry Martin, an American entertainer in Rio at the Café Samba, and Baron Duarte, a notorious Brazilian rake. Miranda plays an entertainer called Carmen in this, her second American film, in which she not only sings and dances but also acts. She firmly established her persona with rapid-fire dialogue, punctuated by her inspired brand of broken English, wearing a variation of the Bahian-style costume of her native Brazil. The "Chica, Chica, Boom, Chica" opening production number was spectacularly staged by Hermes Pan.

No real attempt was made to depict Rio accurately except for some painted scenic backdrops. Through Miranda's personal intervention, a young Spanish dancer, a sloe-eyed Montez, was given one of the key dance spots as Inez in the picture. The film features Miranda's orchestra, Banda de Lua. Also featured are Frank Puglia as Pedro, Fortunio Bonanova as Pereira the headwaiter, Alberto Morin as Eca the pilot, and the Flores Brothers, who also made musical contributions to *Down Argentine Way* (1940). Mack Gordon and Harry Warren, who wrote the music and lyrics but who had never been to South America, wrote some Spanish lyrics, not realizing that Portuguese is the language of Brazil. With the help of the Brazilian technical adviser, the song was translated from the Spanish "Buenas Noches" to the Portuguese "Boa Noite." The Brazilian embassy in Washington gave the film's script and music its approval.

They Met in Argentina (1941 RKO Radio Pictures)
D: Leslie Goodwins and Jack Hively
S: Jerry Cady, based on a story by Brock and Harold Daniels
P: Lou Brock
Cast: Maureen O'Hara, James Ellison, Alberto Vila, Buddy Ebsen, Robert Barrat, Joseph Buloff, Diosa Costello, Victoria Cordova, Antonio Moreno, Fortunio Bonanova

Behind-the-scenes RKO power Nelson Rockefeller, holding the title of "Coordinator of Commercial and Cultural Relations Between the American Republics," was determined to see RKO join in the trend to produce films with Latin American themes and settings. Lou Brock, producer of the hit *Flying Down to Rio* (1933), was brought in to supervise the first of three productions. The result, *They Met in Argentina*, was a major flop in every way.

It started with the script, set against an Argentine background, in which the conflict is between a young man who doesn't want to fall in love and a young girl who is used to having her own way. Maureen O'Hara was miscast as a señorita. The songs and score by Rodgers and Hart never seemed to click. Spanish-speaking audiences were offended by the whole exercise, and United States audiences were uninterested.

¡Three Amigos! (1986 Orion)
D: John Landis
S: Steve Martin, Lorne Michaels, and Randy Newman
P: George Folsey, Jr., and Lorne Michaels
Cast: Steve Martin, Chevy Chase, Martin Short, Patrice Martinez, Alfonso Arau, Tony Plana, Jorge Cevera, Loyda Ramos, Joe Mantegna, Santos Morales

This comedy spoof is set in Mexico in 1916. The poor village of Santa Poco is being terrorized and despoiled by the notorious bandit chieftain El Guapo (Arau), his henchman Jefe (Plana), and their gang of ferocious outlaws. Carmen (Martinez), a beautiful young woman from the village, sends a desperate plea for help (Santos Morales is the telegrapher) to three men whom she has seen fighting oppression and conquering evil-those dashing stars of the silent screen, The Three Amigos!

On screen, Lucky Day (Martin), Dusty Bottoms (Chase) and Ned Nederlander (Short) are fearless romantic heroes. In real life they're innocent, bumbling guys sweetly sheltered by the luxuries of stardom. Those luxuries are suddenly stripped away when the fast-talking Lucky demands a new contract from movie mogul Harry Flugleman (Mantegna). Instead, Flugleman fires the trio.

The cable from Carmen comes just in time. Assuming they've been asked to make a personal appearance—at a whopping fee of 100,000 pesos—the trio takes off for Santa Poco. Once in the village, our heroes think the bandits are fellow actors and put on a performance that dumbfounds the outlaws. But Lucky, Dusty and Ned soon discover that the bullets and bandits are real, and so is their chance to become true heroes. When El Guapo attacks Santa Poco and kidnaps Carmen, the Amigos cross the desert and infiltrate his fortress. They rescue Carmen and narrowly escape in a biplane. Then they rally the people of Santa Poco to fight for their freedom. After all, they are The Three Amigos!

A mildly amusing spoof of many Westerns, in particular, *The Magnificent Seven*, the film is played entirely for laughs, and the actors have a field day in their bandido roles, brandishing their guns, flashing smiles with missing teeth, and sporting scars, hairpieces and several days' growth on their faces. Alfonso Arau actually had a similar serious bad guy role in Peckinpah's *The Wild Bunch* (1969).

All the stereotypes are present, both Anglo and Hispanic. The three Anglo amigos are a not-too-bright lot who resemble the 1930s series Western stars The Three Mesquiteers and a number of Western characterizations. The virginal señorita (Martinez), the Latin spitfire (Ramos), the noble peasant villager (Abel Franco) and the bandit leader (Arau) are all here. The more familiar the viewer is with film history and Westerns in particular, the more enjoyable the film is, as the targets of its spoofing become obvious.

The Three Caballeros (1944 RKO Radio Pictures)

D: Norman Ferguson, Clyde Geronimi, Jack Kinney, Bill Roberts, and
   Harold Young
S: Homer Brightman, Ernest Terrazzas, Ted Sears, Bill Peet,
   Ralph Wright, Elmer Plymmer, Roy Williams, William Cottrell,
   Del Connell, and James Bodrero
P: Norman Ferguson
Cast: Aurora Miranda, Dora Luz, Carmen Molina, Nestor Amaral, and
   the voices of Sterling Holloway, Clarence Nash (Donald Duck),
   José Oliveira (Joe Carioca), Joaquin Garay (Panchito)

Captivating music and a spectacular blend of animation and live action create a dazzling South-of-the-border adventure. In this classic Disney feature, Donald Duck celebrates his birthday with his friends Joe Carioca, the Brazilian parrot, and a Mexican rooster named Panchito.

Donald opens a wondrous collection of gifts that evolve into musical journeys with a Latin American beat. The cartoon characters visit beautiful locations and interact with such human performers as Aurora Miranda of Brazil and Carmen Molina and Dora Luz of Mexico. The segments include a magical serape ride and the animated tales of "The Cold Blooded Penguin," "Baia," and "The Flying Gauchito."

This was one of the most successful American films to play in Latin America during the 1940s.

Three Godfathers (1948 Metro-Goldwyn-Mayer)

D: John Ford
S: Laurence Stallings and Frank Nugent, based on the story by
Peter B. Kyne
P: John Ford and Merian C. Cooper
Cast: John Wayne, Pedro Armendariz, Harry Carey, Jr.

While running from the law, three bandits (Wayne, Armendariz, Carey) come upon a dying woman who is about to give birth in the desert. Two of the bandits die trying to get the newborn child to town and safety.

This offbeat Western, with biblical parallels to the three wise men's journey to Jerusalem, is highlighted by the performances of the three leads and stunning color photography. The story was filmed before: twice as *The Three Godfathers* (in 1916 and 1936), as *Marked Men* (in 1919) and as *Hell's Heroes* (in 1929), but this is the only version in which one of the bandits is portrayed as a Mexican.

In *Three Godfathers*, Pedro Armendariz (center) portrays one of three bandits who care for a child when the mother dies in a desert wagon shortly after childbirth. John Wayne (left) and Harry Carey, Jr. (right) portray the other two bandits.

Armendariz is most able as the bilingual bandit Pete, who admits to the dying woman, after he has delivered her baby, that his actual name is Pedro Incarnacion Yrango y Roca Fuerte. Hightower (Wayne) keeps riding Pete about his speaking Spanish around the baby. "Cut out that Mex lingo around the kid, will you, Pete, first thing you know he'll be talking it. We got to raise him with good all-American habla, like his Ma." Pete is noticeably hurt and continues to speak Spanish.

Pete suffers a broken leg during the desert trek; knowing he cannot go on, he takes his own life with a pistol. This is an eerie foreshadowing of Armendariz's own death fifteen years later when he shot himself with a pistol after he found out he had terminal cancer.

Ironically, at the end of the film, Hightower, the only surviving member of the trio, speaks his last words to the baby in Spanish, "Adios, compañero," before he is taken off to jail.

"Armendariz has done much better in the past, but only because his material has always been better. Here he's too close to being a caricature of a Mexican," Darr Smith, *Los Angeles Daily News* (2/9/49).

On the other hand, Edwin Schallert in the *Los Angeles Times* (2/9/49) said, "Armendariz combines comedy with effectiveness and discretion."

The Thrill of Brazil (1946 Columbia)

D: S. Sylvan Simon
S: Allen Rivkin, Harry Clork, and Devery Freeman
P: Sidney Biddell
Cast: Evelyn Keyes, Keenan Wynn, Ann Miller, Allyn Joslyn, Tito Guizar, Veloz and Yolanda, Enric Madriguera and his Orchestra

Steve Farraugh (Wynn) is the manager and producer of a revue which is trying-out at Hotel Carioca, in Rio, before going to Broadway. Linda Lorens (Miller) is his star. She is in love with him, but he is still in love with his ex-wife, Vickie Dean (Keyes), a famous director. At the same time, singer Guizar (playing himself) loves Linda, but she doesn't return his love. Vickie arrives in Rio with a prospective new husband to get Steve to sign the final divorce papers. Steve has already signed them once, but he has a habit of using disappearing ink. In the end, all is resolved when Vickie admits that she really loves Steve and came to Rio just to see him. Robert Conte, Nino Bellini, Martin Garralaga, Manuel Paris, Joe Dominguez and Alex Montoya are featured.

The Tijuana Story (1957 Columbia)

D: Leslie Kardos
S: Lou Morheim
P: Sam Katzman
Cast: Rodolfo Acosta, Robert Blake, James Darren, Joy Stoner

The assassination of real-life newspaperman Manuel Acosta Mesa in Tijuana inspired this weak teenage exploitation drama. Robert Blake plays the newspaperman's son, who, in the course of the screenplay, brings the leaders of a narcotics ring to justice after his crusading father falls victim to them. The best thing about the movie is Acosta as Acosta Mesa; unfortunately, he is given too little screen time.

Tin Cup (1996 Warner Bros.)

D: Ron Shelton
S: John Norville and Ron Shelton
P: Gary Foster, Ron Shelton and David Lester
Cast: Kevin Costner, Rene Russo, Cheech Marin, Don Johnson

Costner plays Roy "Tin Cup" McAvoy, a driving range pro and golf hustler from West Texas whose legendary golf skills are matched only by his self destructive nature and lowlife charm. His comfortable life of failure, spent on the driving range with his best friend and caddy, Romeo Posar (Marin), is turned upside down when he's smitten by a woman (Russo) who comes in for golf lessons. He then sets out to qualify for the U.S. Open, competing with his longtime rival, successful tour pro David Simms (Johnson), to prove to himself (and his lady love) that he is capable of heroic achievements.

Too Many Girls (1940 RKO Radio Pictures)
D: George Abbott
S: John Twist, based on the stage play by George Marrion, Jr.
P: Harry E. Edington
Cast: Lucille Ball, Ann Miller, Eddie Bracken, Desi Arnaz

A sexy (for its time) college football musical with a Latin twist, which was a success on the Broadway stage and was transferred to film by its stage director, George Abbott, with uneven results. Desi Arnaz, in his film debut, re-created his Broadway stage role as Manuelito, a Latin football player. While making the film, Desi met and fell in love with his soon-to-be-wife, Lucille Ball.

Topaz (1969 Universal)
D: Alfred Hitchcock
S: Samuel Taylor, based on the novel by Leon Uris
P: Alfred Hitchcock
Cast: Frederick Stafford, Dany Robin, John Forsythe, Karin Dor, John Vernon, Roberto Contreras, Carlos Rivas

This Hitchcock thriller about Russian agents infiltrating the French government and betraying French security has a major subplot concerning missiles in Castro's Cuba. Juanita (Dor), a heroine of the Cuban Revolution and the mistress of French spy Devereaux (Stafford), is sent to Cuba to find evidence of Russian missiles for the United States government. John Vernon is Cuban revolutionary Rico Parra, who, though he is in love with her, must kill Juanita when he finds out she has betrayed the revolution. Rivas plays Hernandez, a Cuban soldier, and Contreras plays Munoz.

The laser disc release of the film includes two alternate endings that Hitchcock shot but decided not to use.

The Torch (1950 Eagle-Lion)
D: Emilio Fernandez
S: Adapted by Bert Granet, Inigo de Martino Noriega, and Emilio Fernandez
P: Bert Granet
Cast: Pedro Armendariz, Paulette Goddard, Gilbert Roland

A Mexican revolutionary general falls in love with the daughter of a leading citizen of a town that he takes over. Their courtship is a series of violent comic arguments, played against a background of firing squads, religious fervor and a deadly flu epidemic. *The Torch* is a remake of a Spanish-language film made in Mexico in 1946 under the title *Enamorada*. Both films have the same leading man (Armendariz), director (Fernandez) and cameraman (Gabriel Figueroa). The only critical difference is that the Spanish-language version stars Maria Felix, and the English-language one, Paulette Goddard. There are minor variations in editing and the supporting players, and one scene was rewritten. Goddard had a Hollywood-style narration added at the beginning of the film.

Goddard saw the original film on a trip to Mexico in 1947 and decided she wanted to do an English-language version and play the Maria Felix role. The film was shot a year later in the same Mexican location, the town of Cholula. Azteca Films, the Mexican national film distributor in the United States, released an English-subtitled version of the original a month after the English-language version was released. Director Fernandez later said it was a mistake to remake the film in another language. The rhythms are different and so are the circumstances that breathe life into a particular film; it is hard enough to make a film work once, let alone try to duplicate its success in other circumstances.

Torrid Zone (1940 Warner Bros.)

D: William Keighley
S: Jerry Wald and Richard Macauley
P: Mark Hellinger
Cast: James Cagney, Ann Sheridan, Pat O'Brien, George Tobias

An original comedic drama set on a Central American banana plantation and involving a love triangle among plantation boss Nick Butler (Cagney), manager Steve Case (O'Brien), and American showgirl Lee Donly (Sheridan). A local thug, Rosario (Tobias), recruits a band of marauders from among the plantation workers, and Butler leads a posse against the insurrectionists. Hispanics in small roles include Paul Porcasi, Frank Puglia, George Humbert, Elvira Sanchez, George Regas, Joe Dominguez and Manuel Lopez.

Tortilla Flat (1942 Metro-Goldwyn-Mayer)

D: Victor Fleming
S: John Lee Mahin and Benjamin Glaser, based on the novel by
　　John Steinbeck
P: Sam Zimbalist
Cast: Spencer Tracy, John Garfield, Hedy Lamarr, Akim Tamiroff,
　　Sheldon Leonard

Based on John Steinbeck's novel, set in the years after World War I, about Mexican farmers and fishermen who live in carefree poverty near Monterey, California.

Danny's (Garfield) inheritance of two houses brings him instant respectability and estranges him from Pilon (Tracy) and his other friends. Danny and Pilon vie for the affections of the Portuguese girl Dolores (Lamarr) and become enemies. But when one of Danny's houses burns down and he is hurt in a fight, Pilon comes to his aid, and all ends happily. Hispanic actors Roque Ybarra as Alfredo and Tito Renaldo as a boy have minor roles in the film. Mercedes Ruffino plays Mrs. Morales, the amorous widow. Nina Campana plays Señora Cortez, the mother of a brood of children.

Not an easy tale to translate into a motion picture, it might have emerged as a leering study of vagrancy. Luckily, what emerged through the direction of Victor Fleming (*Gone with the Wind* [1939]) was a sensitive, if sentimental, character study.

A poignantly funny scene involves a health department doctor asking the Mexican children, who seem healthy, what they eat. They naturally reply, "Tortillas and beans" to his every question. He exclaims in disbelief, "Don't you eat anything else?" The children reply, "What else is there?"

Touch and Go (1986 TriStar)
D: Robert Mandel
S: Alan Ormsby, Bob Sand, and Harry Colomby
P: Stephen Friedman
Cast: Michael Keaton, Maria Conchita Alonso, Ajay Naidu

A dramatic comedy about the romance between a professional hockey player, Bobby Barbato (Keaton), and a single Latina mother, Denise De Leon (Alonso), whose little street-savvy son, Louis, is played by Naidu.

Touch of Evil (1958 Universal)
D: Orson Welles and (uncredited) Harry Keller
S: Orson Welles, based on the novel Badge of Evil by Whit Masterson
P: Albert Zugsmith
Cast: Charlton Heston, Orson Welles, Janet Leigh, Joseph Calleia, Marlene Dietrich, Akim Tamiroff, Val De Vargas, Victor Millan, Lalo Rios

In the small and seedy town of Los Robles, situated on the United States-Mexican border, an inquest into the murder of prominent local politician Rudy Linneker develops into a war of wits between a ruthless American police captain, Hank Quinlan (Welles), and a top-ranking Mexican narcotics officer, Vargas (Heston). Though officially honeymooning with his wife, Susan (Leigh), Vargas finds himself increasingly embroiled in the criminal investigation.

Vargas is mistrustful of Quinlan's motives in arresting the suspect, Sanchez (Millan), who is the Mexican lover of Linneker's daughter, Marcia (Joanna Moore). Vargas becomes convinced that Quinlan is attempting to frame an innocent man.

Quinlan's service to justice has degenerated into a personal vendetta against Mexican Americans due to his wife's murder (for which no one was convicted due to lack of evidence) many years before.

Vargas previously has been working on exposing the Grandi gang, a pack of Mexican drug dealers headed by Joe Grandi (Tamiroff) who are active in Los Robles, and he becomes equally engaged in exposing the venal and unprincipled Quinlan. Vargas is beleaguered by an uncaring or positively antagonistic populace. He is affected by the understated problem of being a Mexican in a racist society. He describes the bombing incident that killed Linneker as being bad for "us," ambiguously referring to both his country and his wife. Since the bomb was planted in Mexico, but went off in the United States, his jurisdiction is in question, making him an outside observer. At one point, Vargas is framed against a billboard that reads: "Welcome Stranger to Picturesque Los Robles, Paris on the Border." As a Mexican he represents an alternate

Orson Welles (left) as corrupt cop Quinlan and Charlton Heston (right) as Mexican narcotics officer Vargas are at odds over a murder investigation in *Touch of Evil*. Victor Millan (center) portrays Sanchez, the Mexican lover of the murdered politician's daughter. Joseph Calleia (background) portrays Menzies, a lifelong friend of Quinlan's.

system of justice, and on the American side he has no authority. By the time his wife has been abducted by the Grandi gang, who intend to frame Vargas through his wife, he is acting as a husband, not as a police officer.

Menzies (Calleia), who is of Mexican heritage, is a lifelong friend of Quinlan's. He is the peon to this gringo master until Vargas crosses the border and frees Menzies from Quinlan's grip. Vargas helps Menzies find his own identity by helping him realize that Quinlan has been circumventing the law for years, abetted by Menzies, who has supported him out of friendship and fear. Menzies saves Vargas' life by killing Quinlan. Menzies loses his own life in the process, but not until he has found "salvation" through self-identity.

The film was directed by Welles at the insistence of star Charlton Heston. Heston's customary heroic look was toned down, he was given a darker complexion, a curl to his blackened hair, and a trim mustache. The famous, nearly four-minute tracking shot that runs under the credits is more than just a magnificent virtuoso effect; it brilliantly sets up what is to follow. It presents the milieu, the central characters and the action that drives the plot, all with remarkable economy. It was filmed in Venice, California, on Main Street, which was transformed with the help of art directors into a bordertown. Universal took the film away from Welles and recut it. Some thirty years later the film was restored to its original length and is now considered a classic; one critic described it as perhaps the greatest B movie ever made.

Trackdown (1976 United Artists)
D: Richard T. Heffron
S: Paul Edward
P: Bernard Schwartz
Cast: Jim Mitchum, Karen Lamm, Ann Archer, Erik Estrada

The subject of teen runaways and inner city crime are both exploited to the fullest in this blatantly racist story. A young Anglo rancher is bent on revenge for the brutalization of his runaway sister, who has been beaten and raped by a Chicano gang in East Los Angeles and then sold into prostitution. She becomes a high-class call girl and is murdered by a sadistic client. Estrada plays Chucho, a sensitive gang member who falls for the girl and ends up helping her brother. Gilbert De la Peña and Rafael Lopez also play gang members.

Villa supporter Juan (Gilbert Roland, right) faces off with American soldier of fortune Tom Bryan (Rory Calhoun, left) in *The Treasure of Pancho Villa*.

A Tragedy in the Life of General Villa
See *The Life of Villa*.

The Treasure of Pancho Villa (1955 RKO Radio Pictures)
D: George Sherman
S: Niven Busch, based on the story by
   J. Robert Bren and Gladys Atwater
P: Edmund Grainger
Cast: Rory Calhoun, Shelley Winters,
   Gilbert Roland, Joseph Calleia, Carlos
   Mosquiz, Tony Carvajal, Pasquel Peña

An American soldier of fortune, Tom Bryan (Calhoun), decides he would rather steal gold for himself than for the Mexican Revolution. He is hampered by dedicated Villa supporters Juan (Roland) and Ruth (Winters), who became a loyal supporter when her father was killed by Federales troops.

  Filmed on location in Mexico, the movie is full of explosive action. Though Pancho Villa's name is in the title, he never appears in the film.

Treasure of the Golden Condor (1952 Twentieth Century Fox)
D: Delmer Daves
S: Delmer Daves
P: Jules Buck
Cast: Cornel Wilde, Constance Smith

This Technicolor swashbuckler is set among eighteenth-century French nobility. A young man, Jean Paul (Wilde), is deprived of his royal inheritance by an unscrupulous uncle who has made him a virtual bonded servant. Jean Paul meets a man who is in possession of a map to a fabulous Mayan treasure. Jean Paul takes off with him and his beautiful daughter to Guatemala to get the treasure. After it is found, he returns to France to reclaim his possessions. He then returns to Guatemala to join his friend and the daughter, with whom he has fallen in love.

This is a remake of the 1942 film *Son of Fury* with the locale switched from the Pacific to Central America. The background scenes filmed in Guatemala with the principal players showcase ancient Mayan ruins and the city of Antigua.

The Treasure of the Sierra Madre (1948 Warner Bros.)
D: John Huston
S: John Huston, based on the novel by B. Traven
P: Henry Blanke
Cast: Humphrey Bogart, Walter Huston, Bruce Bennett, Tim Holt,
    Alfonso Bedoya, Bobby Blake, A. Soto Rangel, Manuel Donde,
    José Torvay, Margarito Luna, Jacqueline Dalya

This movie signaled the end of the Good Neighbor Policy with its reintroduction of the Mexican bandit while at the same time using Mexican landscapes and people. Mexicans in the film are depicted as either bloodthirsty bandits or as innocent, primitive natives.
Based on the novel by B. Traven, it is a story of a clash between three down-on-their-luck Americans (Bogart, Huston, Holt) in Tampico, Mexico, who make a last desperate attempt to find gold in the rugged Sierra Madres, where few white men have ever been. Hounded by Indians, a fortune-hunting Texan (Bennett), and cold-blooded bandidos, they must finally confront the most dangerous adversary of all: themselves.

Mexican actor Bedoya created a permanent niche for himself in movie history as the bandit Gold Hat, with the following memorable line: "Badges, we don't need no stinkin' badges." Gold Hat is a dumb bandido who mistakes gold for sand and throws it away, machetes Dobbs (Bogart) to death, and is easily caught by the Federales (Mexican police), who make him dig his own grave before they shoot him. Also featured in minor roles are Julian Rivero as a barber and Martin Garralaga as a railroad conductor.

The film was not a box office success, but today it is considered a classic. Huston wanted to shoot on the actual locations to bring to life this harsh story, of which the country is as much a part as are the leading characters. Other filming took place at Warner Bros. Studios in

Burbank and in the mountains near Bakersfield, California. The reviews particularly noted the realism Huston achieved by filming on location and praised Bedoya's characterization. The film won three Academy Awards® for the father-and-son team of Walter and John Huston—Walter for Best Supporting Actor and John for Best Director and Best Screenplay.

"John Huston's handling of the Indians is especially effective. Whether bandits, courteous mountain natives or townspeople, they have a compelling kind of dignity tempered by humor. A few among them address the Americans in pidgin English, but for the most part they speak their native tongue. A pleasant relief from the customary use of phony dialects," Virginia Wright, syndicated columnist (1/48).

"If there were no other reason to laud *The Treasure of the Sierra Madre* we'd find words of praise for the manner in which it presented the native people of Mexico in their contact with its Americans in the story," Lloyd Sloan, *Hollywood Citizen News* (1/15/48).

Alfonso Bedoya (left) as the Mexican bandit Gold Hat in *The Treasure of the Sierra Madre*, also starring Humphrey Bogart (right).

"In the background, John Huston has utilized richly Indian faces that were available in rural districts of Mexico. It is a measure of the difference between two of America's greatest directors that when they both sought Mexican villains, one, John Ford, used the Hollywood actor J. Carroll Naish [in *The Fugitive*] very effectively, while the other, John Huston, has exercised sheer genius in his choice of that particular Mexican for the role. The two parts have much in common, actually Naish is as good as it is possible for an actor to be, but the man John Huston uses, Alfonso Bedoya, is better than that. He is tremendous and very simple," Archer Winston, *New York Post* (1/26/48).

Trial (1955 Metro-Goldwyn-Mayer)

D: Mark Robson
S: Don Mankiewicz, based on his novel
P: Charles Schnee
Cast: Glenn Ford, Arthur Kennedy, Katy Jurado, Rafael Campos, Juano Hernandez

This is a high-powered, well-intentioned screen drama, full of the anti-Communist hysteria of McCarthyism. It manages to make its point about racism and bigotry in small-town America, while at the same time demonstrating an underlying and unswerving faith in American justice.

David Blake (Ford) comes to the town of San Juno to gain courtroom experience. His first case, in association with Barney Castle (Kennedy), involves a young Mexican (Campos) who has been charged with the murder of a Anglo girl (who, it is eventually revealed, was a victim of rheumatic fever, and who died of a heart attack). Bigots in the town attempt to lynch the youth but are turned back by the arguments presented. Castle seeks to raise funds for the defense and does so in a flamboyant manner, following the Communist line and turning obscure victims of local injustice into symbols. As the trial progresses, Blake does everything in his power to save the youth from hanging, legally, and is successful. However, the prosecution's final courtroom address leads him to realize he's been duped by Castle and the Communists, who have used the case to further their own cause.

Campos as the defendant and Jurado as his mother give believable performances in the young-Mexican-boy-in-trouble and the suffering mamacita tradition. Puerto Rican actor Hernandez, in an offbeat and provocative decision in keeping with the tone of the film, is cast as the African American judge who presides over the case. To see an African American judge in a 1955 film was, as in real life, extremely rare. Hernandez brings dignity and strength to the role, and is given sufficient screen time to create a three-dimensional character.

Tropic Holiday (1938 Paramount)
D: Theodore Reed
S: Arthur Hornbow, Jr.
P: Arthur Hornblow, Jr.
Cast: Dorothy Lamour, Ray Milland, Martha Raye, Tito Guizar

A musical comedy set in Mexico about a local beauty romanced by a visiting scriptwriter. The title was originally *Ensenada*, but the studio changed it to capitalize on Lamour's tropical image. Augustin Lara wrote six numbers for the film, and José Fernandez, a Latin dance director, worked with dance director Leroy Prinz.

Tropic Zone (1953 Paramount)
D: Lewis R. Foster
S: Lewis R. Foster, based on the novel *Gentleman of the Jungle* by Tom Gill
P: William H. Pine and William C. Thomas
Cast: Ronald Reagan, Rhonda Fleming, Argentina Brunetti, Rico Alaniz, Maurice Jara, Pilar Del Rey, Estelita

An dramatic adventure film shot in Technicolor and set in the fictional Central American town of Puerto Barrancas, where an American man and woman are fighting to survive in a locale dominated by crooked politicians and a ruthless dictator. Estelita sings and dances in the role of a café entertainer. The story elements are cliched and stereotypical.

12 Angry Men (1957 United Artists)
D: Sidney Lumet
S: Reginald Rose, based on his teleplay
P: Henry Fonda and Reginald Rose
Cast: Henry Fonda, Lee J. Cobb, Jack Klugman, John Savoca

Reginald Rose wrote this script originally for television's *Playhouse 90*. There are no Hispanics in this offbeat courtroom drama, which focuses almost exclusively on the jury room deliberations. The subject of the trial, however, is a nineteen-year-old Puerto Rican who purportedly killed his father with a switchblade. The film version indicates that the young man (Savoca) is a slum dweller. One of the jurors reveals himself as a prejudiced man who hates the "them" that the defendant represents. The script was inspired by a real manslaughter case in which Reginald Rose was a juror.

Two Mules for Sister Sara (1970 Universal)
D: Don Siegel
S: Albert Maltz, based on a story by Budd Boetticher
P: Martin Rackin and Carroll Case
Cast: Clint Eastwood, Shirley MacLaine, Alberto Morin, Armando Silvestre

A popular Western starring Clint Eastwood in a variation of the "Man with No Name" characterization that had made him a superstar three years earlier. An American gunfighter, Hogan (Eastwood), rescues a nun, Sister Sara (MacLaine), from being raped by French troops in 1860s Mexico. The nun decides to tag along with Hogan, who is joining a band of Juaristas fighting against the French occupation of Mexico. A romance develops, and Hogan discovers Sister Sara is really a prostitute. José Torvay, among other Hispanics, has a small role in the film.

It was adapted from an original story by writer and director Budd Boetticher, who had hoped to direct it with John Wayne and Mexican actress Silvia Pinal. Boetticher sold the rights to the story years later, and Elizabeth Taylor was cast opposite Eastwood. Shortly before production was to begin, she dropped out and MacLaine replaced her.

It was filmed on location by cinematographer Gabriel Figueroa who demonstrates his usual skill in shooting grand Mexican landscapes. The opening credit sequence features Eastwood riding through the rugged terrain of northern Mexico at dawn. While the credits appear, the camera cuts back and forth between Eastwood and the animals inhabiting the desert. The assault on the garrison, beginning with a religious procession through the streets by the townsfolk at night, is spectacularly staged and lighted. Eastwood liked Figueroa's work so much he used him to photograph his next film, *Kelly's Heroes* (1970), in Yugoslavia.

Tycoon (1947 RKO Radio Pictures)

D: Richard Wallace
S: Borden Chase and John Twist, based on the novel by C.E. Scoggins
P: Stephen Ames
Cast: John Wayne, Sir Cedric Hardwicke, Laraine Day, Anthony Quinn, Fernando Alvarado, Martin Garralaga, Judith Anderson

The storyline of this film involves the feud between an obsessive engineer (Wayne) who is attempting to build a railroad through the Andes Mountains and his employer (Hardwicke), who objects to his methods and his romance with his daughter (Day).

Quinn plays an ill-defined character named Enrique "Ricky" Vargas, an engineer and troubleshooter. This overlong but action-filled story features Englishman Hardwicke, American Day, and Australian Judith Anderson playing South Americans.

It was filmed in Lone Pine, California, with the Sierra Nevadas subbing for the Andes. A complete side of a mountain was built for the film in order to simulate mine shafts and tunnels in the mountainsides, while an entire Andean village—complete with llamas—was constructed on fourteen acres. Hundreds of Hispanic extras and supporting players were used. Some of the featured players include Argentina Brunetti, Fernando Alvarado, Martin Garralaga, Frank Leyva, Joe Dominguez, Alberto Morin and Nacho Galindo.

U-Turn (1997 Columbia)

D: Oliver Stone
S: John Ridley, based on his novel
P: Clayton Townsend and Dan Halsted
Cast: Sean Penn, Billy Bob Thornton, Jon Voight, Jennifer Lopez, Powers Boothe, Nick Nolte, Joaquin Phoenix, Claire Danes

On his way to Las Vegas, a small time hustler and gambler Bobby Cooper's (Penn) car breaks down and he lands in a desert mining town and finds himself slipping into an abyss where the seemingly normal greets the bizarre and treacherous. When Bobby meets up with the beautiful Grace Mckenna (Lopez) and her powerful husband Jake (Nolte), the original goal of simply getting out of town vanishes in the face of pure survival. Grace and Jack suck Bobby into a deadly game of lust, madness and money. Both offer him a way out, kill one for the other. Somewhere on this road things have just gone from bad to worse.

The Undefeated (1969 Twentieth Century Fox)

D: Andrew V. McLaglen
S: James Lee Barrett, based on a story by Stanley L. Hough
P: Robert L. Jacks
Cast: John Wayne, Rock Hudson, Tony Aguilar, Pedro Armendariz, Jr., Carlos Rivas

A Confederate colonel (Hudson) sets fire to his plantation house at the end of the Civil War rather than let it fall into the hands of Northern carpetbaggers. He, his family and a group of followers set off for Mexico with to make a new home for themselves. They are saved from attacks by Mexican bandits by a former Union colonel (Wayne), who has decided to drive his herd of 3,000 horses into Mexico rather than be taken advantage of by crooked army agents. The two former enemies join forces to fight off the soldiers of Emperor Maximilian and those of the rebel leader Juarez. When the rebels take the Confederate party prisoners, the Union men end up sacrificing their horses to free the Southerners.

This is a good, old-fashioned, leisurely John Wayne Western, filmed in Durango, Mexico. In addition to excellent production values, the film features Armendariz as a bandit, Rivas as an emissary of Maximilian and Aguilar as a no-nonsense rebel general.

Tony Aguilar (left) as a rebel general raises glasses with a Confederate colonel (Rock Hudson, right) and a Union colonel (John Wayne, center) who have fled the post-Civil War South, in an unlikely liaison in *The Undefeated*.

Under a Texas Moon (1930 Warner Bros.)

D: Michael Curtiz

S: Gordon Rigby, based on the story "Two Gun Man" by Stewart
  Edward White

P: Unknown

Cast: Frank Fay, Raquel Torres, Myrna Loy, Armida, Noah Beery,
  Inez Gomez, Mona Maris

This film is distinguished as the first sound Western shot in Technicolor. Director Curtiz juggled color, music, dialogue and a temperamental lead actor, Fay. Originally from vaudeville, Fay had played the master of ceremonies in the revue film *Show of Shows* (1929) and was not easy to work with. An atypical Western, *Under a Texas Moon* is set in Mexico and Texas, and is full of fiestas and beautiful ladies fighting over its singing desperado hero, Don Carlos (Fay), who renders the title song frequently.

Under Fire (1983 Orion)

D: Roger Spottiswoode

S: Ron Shelton and Clayton Frohman

P: Jonathan Taplin

Cast: Gene Hackman, Nick Nolte, Joanna Cassidy, Alma Martinez,
  Jean-Louis Trintignant, Rene Enriquez, Ed Harris

Three longtime journalist friends find themselves in Managua, Nicaragua, on the eve of the Sandinista Revolution in 1979. Russell Price (Nolte) is a photojournalist. Claire Snyder (Cassidy) is a radio correspondent who is about to split up with her husband, Alex (Hackman), a newspaper correspondent who decides to leave war-torn Nicaragua to work as a television reporter in the States. Perhaps Gene Hackman expressed it best in the movie: "Two guys in love with the same dame in an exotic country with bullets flying."

The film features a multidimensional, humanistic view of the events surrounding the fall of the Somoza regime and the struggle of the Sandinista rebels as seen through the eyes of American journalists.

The attractive translator at the hotel, Isela Cruz (Martinez), turns out to be a rebel. At one point, Russell, the photographer, cries out in anguish, "Christ, what are we doing here?" He meets up with an old acquaintance, Hobbs (Harris), an American mercenary who, in Africa, had confided to Russell that he couldn't stand "too many spooks," and now in Nicaragua, "a shit load of greasers." Hobbs is a cold-blooded killer who hires himself out to whichever side pays him the most, in this case the CIA and the Somoza regime.

Russell and Claire help the rebels convince the world that the charismatic leader Rafael is not dead, as had been announced by the government, by showing photos that make him appear to be still alive. This unethical act helps bring down the Somoza regime but also brings Alex back to Nicaragua and leads to his eventual death by Somoza soldiers at a roadblock. Hackman's casual, unprovoked murder in front of the journalists is one of the movie's most startling moments. Seeing Claire mourning over Alex, a Nicaraguan woman asks, "You knew the dead journalist?" She answers yes in a flood of tears. Unmoved, the woman says, "Fifty thousand Nicaraguans have died and now one Yankee. Perhaps now America will be afraid of what is happening here. We should have killed an American journalist fifty years ago."

A powerful, if flawed, movie that opts for perhaps too much sentimentality in its portrayal of a very unpopular left-wing revolution.

Under the Pampas Moon (1935 Fox Film Corporation)

D: James Tinling
S: Ernest Pascal, Bradley King, and Henry Jackson, based on the original story by Gordon Morris
P: B.G. De Sylva
Cast: Warner Baxter, Ketti Gallian, J. Carroll Naish, John Miljan, Soledad Jimenez, Armida

A passenger plane makes a forced landing, and Cesar Campo (Baxter) takes the passengers to a ranch where he is one of the gauchos. They stay overnight to see a race in which Campo's rival engages in blatant cheating, but even in the face of such unscrupulous tactics, Campo manages to win the race. Armida appears only in the beginning sequence, and Baxter offers a variation of his Cisco Kid portrayal. Tito Guizar is seen briefly as a singer in the café (he achieved international popularity two years later). Many Latin players and extras worked on this film, including Rita Cansino (who later became Rita Hayworth), the popular dance team of Veloz and Yolanda, Chris-Pin Martin, George J. Lewis, Paul Porcasi, Joe Dominguez and Martin Garralaga.

Under the Volcano (1984 Universal)

D: John Huston
S: Guy Gallo, based on the novel by Malcolm Lowry
P: Michael Fitzgerald
Cast: Albert Finney, Jacqueline Bisset, Katy Jurado, Emilio Fernandez

Directed by Huston and based on the celebrated novel by Malcolm Lowry, Under the Volcano is the story of an alcoholic British consul's last days at his post in Mexico at the beginning of World War II.

Albert Finney, in an extraordinary performance, plays the consul Fermin, who descends into hell against an exotic and primitive Mexican background, filled with the symbolism of death during the Day of the Dead religious festival in 1939. Finney's Fermin, like Bogart's Fred C. Dobbs in Huston's Treasure of the Sierra Madre (1948), virtually disintegrates on screen. The film was photographed in color on location in Cuernavaca, Mexico, by noted Mexican cinematographer Gabriel Figueroa, who had worked previously with Huston on The Night of the Iguana (1964). Acclaimed Mexican artist Gunther Gerzo was the art director. Fernandez as a cantina patron and Jurado as an old friend of Fermin's are also featured in the film.

The movie perpetuated the image of Mexican women as whores and Mexican men as violent and treacherous. The climactic sequences in the El Farolito brothel are harrowing.

Under the Volcano is an adult and dark work from a master film-maker. The $4 million production was co-produced by the Mexican government, along with Twentieth Century-Fox and Universal, in an attempt to break into the international filmmaking arena after years of artistic slump. Both Figueroa's cinematography and Finney's performance received Academy Award® nominations.

Underwater! (1955 RKO Radio Pictures)
D: John Sturges
S: Walter Newman
P: Harry Tatelman
Cast: Jane Russell, Gilbert Roland, Richard Egan, Joseph Calleia, Eugene Iglesias

Theresa (Russell) is a shapely Cuban treasure hunter who is joined by her husband, Johnny (Egan), and an adventurer, Dominic (Roland), in a search for a long-lost Spanish galleon. The ship sank while en route from the Caribbean to the Old World and laden with gold and silver bullion. Accompanied on screen by Perez Prado and his Orchestra, Russell dances the mambo.

Up in Smoke (1978 Paramount)
D: Lou Adler
S: Cheech Marin and Tommy Chong
P: Lou Adler and Lou Lombardo
Cast: Cheech Marin, Tommy Chong

This crude and funny drug-counterculture-inspired comedy stars Cheech and Chong, the Mexican/Chinese American comedy team who achieved great success with their recordings and concert appearances. The film casts Marin as a character of his own creation, a low-riding, dope-smoking, ignorant Mexican American from East Los Angeles. This is one of the first film appearances of the low-rider car associated with the contemporary urban Mexican American culture. The enormous $28 million gross of this low budget entry spawned four more films starring the comedy team: *Cheech and Chong's Next Movie* (1980); *Cheech and Chong's Nice Dreams* (1981); *Things Are Tough All Over* (1982); and *Cheech and Chong: Still Smoking* (1983).

Up the Down Staircase (1967 Warner Bros.)
D: Robert Mulligan
S: Tad Mosel, based on the novel by Bel Kaufman
P: Alan J. Pakula
Cast: Sandy Dennis, Patrick Bedford, Eileen Heckart

Based on the best-selling novel by Bel Kaufman, the film dramatizes the first year frustrations of metropolitan high school teacher Sylvia Barrett (Dennis).

The story is set in a rundown school in the fictional Calvin Coolidge High School in New York's Spanish Harlem. Many of the students are hostile African Americans and Puerto Ricans with no inclination toward the joys of English literature, and Barrett is discouraged by her inability to get through to them. It was actually filmed at several high schools in New York, and many ethnic teenagers without prior acting experience were cast to play variations of their peers for the film.

José Rodriguez, from the New York School of Printing, was cast as a withdrawn Puerto Rican student who bursts to life as a tough-minded judge in a classroom trial. In this film, it is the Italian student who is the knife wielding gang tough.

In the tradition of *Blackboard Jungle* (1955), but with a female educator, this film is a deeply moving exposé of the deficiencies of the urban public school system. The film touches on the problems of delinquency, racial discrimination and drug addiction present in many inner-city American schools.

Valdez Is Coming (1971 United Artists)
D: Edwin Sherin
S: Roland Kibbee and David Rayfiel, based on the novel by
    Elmore Leonard
P: Ira Steiner
Cast: Burt Lancaster, Frank Silvera, Jon Cypher, Susan Clark,
    Hector Elizondo

Valdez Is Coming is a hard, violent Western about a solitary ex-cavalry man of Mexican heritage, Bob Valdez (Lancaster), who wages a private war to raise $200 for a widowed Apache woman. The woman is the squaw of an African American man, also a former soldier, whom Valdez helped to kill.

The film speaks out against racial prejudice and the oppression of the weak by the strong. Lancaster acquits himself well in a believable portrayal as the Mexican American constable Valdez. Silvera in his last film appearance gives a gritty performance as Valdez's Mexican campadre, Diego. Elizondo plays one of the bandidos. Filmed in Spain, it owes much in style to the "spaghetti Westerns" of the time.

Vera Cruz (1954 United Artists)
D: Robert Aldrich
S: James R. Webb and Roland Kibbee, based on the story by
    Borden Chase
P: James Hill
Cast: Burt Lancaster, Gary Cooper, Sarita Montiel, Cesar Romero

Devastated by the South's defeat in the Civil War and shunning his previous idealism, Colonel Ben Trane (Cooper) travels to Mexico as a soldier of fortune. While there, he meets a flamboyant and unscrupulous associate, Joe Erin (Lancaster). The two professionally hire out their guns to Emperor Maximilian, are courted by the Juaristas, and make plans to double-cross each other as they escort, through rebel territory, a countess who is making a trip to Vera Cruz. The trip is a cover-up for the shipment of a fortune in gold.

This is a fast-moving, colorful, action-filled and often humorous Western, with Cooper and Lancaster at their best in roles suited to their screen personas. This was Cooper's third film in Mexico, following *Blowing Wild* (1953) and *Garden of Evil* (1954). The supporting cast includes Romero as the military Marquis de Labordere, Denise Darcel as the unprincipled Countess Marie Duvarre, and Montiel as the young Mexican Nina, with whom Trane is smitten. George Macready appears as Emperor Maximilian, Ernest Borgnine is Donnegan, Morris Ankrum is the Juarista general and a young actor named Charles Buchinsky, later to be better known as Charles Bronson, is Pittsburgh.

Mexico is shown as a last untamed refuge for those seeking new adventures, beautiful señoritas and gold. In this fantasy Mexico, men could be spiritually renewed by upholding American values, such as the pursuit of happiness, through fighting for freedom or lusting after gold. In fact, Mexico attracted many Americans after the Civil War to fight for either Maximilian or the Juaristas. Others came as businessmen and opportunists or to establish religious communities.

It was filmed in Mexico utilizing such national landmarks as Chapultepec Castle, the Pyramids outside of Mexico City, Cuernavaca and at Churubusco Studios for some interiors.

Vibes (1988 Columbia)
D: Ken Kwapis
S: Lowell Ganz and Babaloo Mandel, based on a story by
    Deborah Blum, Ganz, and Mandel
P: Deborah Blum and Tony Ganz
Cast: Jeff Goldblum, Peter Falk, Cyndi Lauper, Elizabeth Peña,
    Ramon Bieri

Sylvia (Lauper) and Nick (Goldblum) help Harry (Falk) by using their extraordinary psychic powers to find a room of gold hidden in a lost Ecuadorian city. Peña plays Consuelo, a spitfire who tries to seduce and kill Nick. Overall, this is an extraordinarily weak film.

Victory (1981 Paramount)
D: John Huston
S: Evan Jones and Yabo Yablonsky, based on a story by Yablonsky,
    Djordje Milicevic, and Jeff Maguire
P: Freddie Fields
Cast: Sylvester Stallone, Michael Caine, Max von Sydow, Pelé

A group of Allied prisoners of war are forced to form a soccer team and play a life or death match against a well-trained Nazi team. Pelé, the world-renowned Brazilian soccer star, is featured as, Luis Hernandez, a soldier from British Trinidad who joins the Allied prisoner team.

Villa! (1958 Twentieth Century Fox)

D: James B. Clark
S: Louis Vittes
P: Plato A. Skouras
Cast: Rudolfo Hoyos, Jr., Brian Keith, Cesar Romero

Villa! is somewhat episodic, and the motivations for actions are not clear in the script. The Villa character begins as a small-time bandit, and the film follows his rise to national prominence when he meets Madera and is inspired to fight for the revolution.

Hayos is adequate as Villa but fails to infuse the character with the larger-than-life fire needed; though he is certainly not helped by the weakness of the script. The film is similar in concept in many ways *to Villa Rides* (1968) except the latter has a grounded performance by the charismatic Yul Brynner and a sweeping historical atmosphere that *Villa!* totally lacks. Keith is the Yankee adventurer who asks Villa to let him join his army, just as Mitchum does in *Villa Rides*. Romero and Carlos Musquiz are Villa's aides. Mexican actress Rosenda Monteros has a small role. Well photographed by Mexican cinematographer Alex Phillips on location in Mexico, the movie looks and plays like an above average B Western, which, in truth, it is.

Bewigged Yul Brynner (right) as Pancho Villa and Charles Bronson (left) as cold-blooded killer and Villa aide Fierro in *Villa Rides*.

Villa Rides (1968 Paramount)

D: Buzz Kulik
S: Sam Peckinpah and Robert Towne, based on the book *Pancho Villa* by William Douglas Lansford
P: Ted Richmond
Cast: Yul Brynner, Robert Mitchum, Charles Bronson, Grazia Buccella, Robert Viharo, Robert Carricart, Fernando Rey

This routine film, with grand and sweeping action sequences, is sadly lacking in impact considering its subject matter, though Yul Brynner's charismatic presence does manage to imbue his bewigged Villa star quality. Robert Mitchum plays Lee, an American soldier of fortune. Charles Bronson plays the cold-blooded killer Fierro, aide to Villa.

As directed by Kulik, in Panavision and Technicolor, the film begins with Villa and his cohorts attacking the city of Parral. Parral is captured by a ruse and without a shot. We see Villa's subordination to the power-hungry General Huerta and Villa's subsequent arrest. The film ends with Villa's final escape from prison and his quest to raise a new army.

The picture took some fourteen weeks to film and involved thousands of horses and extras, trains, three antique aircraft, more than ten different locations and a crew of 150 persons behind the camera. The film was shot in Spain for two primary reasons: the Spanish countryside offers much of the same terrain, architecture and backgrounds as the real Mexico; and the producers doubted that the Mexican government would have given approval for *Villa Rides* to film in Mexico.

Viva Max! (1969 Commonwealth United Release)
D: Jerry Paris
S: Elliot Baker, based on the novel by James Lehrer
P: Mark Carliner
Cast: Peter Ustinov, Jonathan Winters, John Astin, Keenan Wynn

This film is a contemporary comedy about Mexican soldiers taking back the Alamo. A present day second-rate general in the Mexican Army, General Maximilian (Ustinov), leads eighty-seven soldiers across the border to Laredo and on to San Antonio. Maximilian's occupation of the Alamo brings out the National Guard and an uptight conservative militia faction.

This uneven, spirited comedy features a buffoonish yet dignified portrayal by Ustinov, whose accent sounds more Spanish than Mexican. There are a few zany and comic bits, including some by John Astin as Sergeant Valdez, who is forever protecting his commanding officer.

The film elicited complaints from Mexican American civil rights groups regarding the Mexican portrayals by non-Mexicans, and from the Daughters of the Republic of Texas, who felt the film was insulting to the memory of those who died at the Alamo and would not allow the company to film there. After several weeks of location filming in San Antonio and just outside the Alamo shrine, the production left for Italy, where the interiors of the Alamo were built on a soundstage and the film was completed.

Viva Villa! (1934 Metro-Goldwyn-Mayer)
D: Jack Conway and (uncredited) Howard Hawks
S: Ben Hecht, based on the book by Edgecumb Pichon and O.B. Stade
P: David O. Selznick
Cast: Wallace Beery, Leo Carrillo, Stuart Erwin, Fay Wray, Frank Puglia, Katherine DeMille, Pedro Regas, George Regas

Wallace Beery plays the historical Mexican figure as a likable overgrown child who has great difficulty understanding why people try to dissuade him from slaughtering his defeated adversaries. Carrillo is excellent as his aide Fierro, as is Stuart Erwin as the newspaper reporter who follows Villa's campaign. Providing feminine interest are Fay Wray and Katherine DeMille. Julian Rivero and Chris-Pin Martin are featured in minor roles.

Filmed largely in Mexico, near San Marcos, and frequently despite obstacles that seemed insurmountable; director Howard Hawks walked off the picture and Jack Conway took over halfway through filming in Mexico. The Hollywood troupe was thrown out of Mexico when, in a state of intoxication, actor Lee Tracy urinated from his hotel balcony on a passing parade of Mexican soldiers. Louis B. Mayer, then president of MGM Studios, sent a telegram to Mexican president Abelardo Rodriguez apologizing for Tracy's deplorable conduct, which, he said, "shocked his company as deeply as it did Mexico." As a result, MGM dismissed Tracy and canceled his contract, and he was replaced in the film by Erwin.

The film was completed at MGM Studios and at a San Fernando Valley ranch location in California. *Viva Villa!* is presented as a fictional recording of Villa's achievements in freeing the poor, dethroning the tyrants and restoring peace to Mexico. Thousands of extras were used in the battle scenes. Beery's performance and the powerful visuals are among the reasons this version of the story is remembered better than any other.

Viva Zapata! (1952 Twentieth Century Fox)
D: Elia Kazan
S: John Steinbeck, based on the novel *Zapata the Unconquered* by Edgcumb Pichon
P: Darryl F. Zanuck
Cast: Marlon Brando, Anthony Quinn, Jean Peters, Joseph Wiseman, Alan Reed, Frank Silvera, Margo, Henry Silva

With the success of *The Pearl* (1948) and *The Red Pony* (1949), both adapted from his novels, Steinbeck began working on a script about the legendary Mexican Indian revolutionary leader Emiliano Zapata, spending considerable time in Mexico over the years gathering much information.

Director Elia Kazan had also been making notes for a possible film about Zapata, and his success with several films at Twentieth Century-Fox, including an Academy Award® for *Gentlemen's Agreement* (1947), made *Viva Zapata!* possible. Kazan claims that he and Steinbeck collaborated on the final script, though Steinbeck received sole screen credit.

Kazan and Steinbeck had hoped to film in Mexico, but the head of the Mexican film industry did not approve of the script or the idea of gringos making a film about their revolutionary hero.

Kazan and cinematographer Joe MacDonald tried to re-create the Mexican Revolution by poring through hundreds of photographs of the revolution and capturing the look and feel of the towns and terrain they were working in as well as the faces of the Mexican populace. Several moments in the film are almost exact reproductions of some of those photographs.

The film was shot in 1951 along the Texas-Mexico border near Del Rio, McAllen and Roma. Some scenes were shot at the Fox ranch near Malibu, just outside of Los Angeles. Interiors at the studio ranged from squalid mud huts to a re-creation of the ornate national palace in Mexico City. Kazan used Mexican American locals as extras wherever he could.

The story follows Zapata's life, beginning with his early years as the leader of a delegation to Mexico City to protest the stealing of land

Marlon Brando (seated)
portrays the legendary
Mexican Indian revolu-
tionary leader Emiliano
Zapata, and Anthony
Quinn (left) portrays
Zapata's brother in
Viva Zapata!

from his people. It follows his banishment, his leading role in the revolution that overthrew the Diaz regime and his assassination by political rivals.

Brando was cast as Emiliano Zapata over the protest of Fox chief
Darryl F. Zanuck, who favored Tyrone Power or Anthony Quinn. Zanuck
was quoted as saying of Brando, "How are you going to make that
Illinois farm boy a Mexican?" For the role, Brando studied every book
written on Zapata and the Mexican Revolution. He lived among
Mexicans for weeks at a time. It was Brando who suggested to the
makeup artists that they flare out his nostrils with plastic rings or
bands and glue up his eyelids to enhance his resemblance to Zapata.

Quinn was cast as his troubled brother, Eufemio. Kazan had directed both Brando and Quinn in the stage production of *A Streetcar Named Desire* (the film version had not been released at the time of *Viva Zapata!*). Quinn reprised Brando's star-making turn as Stanley Kowalski on Broadway in a national tour.

Kazan used his stage rehearsal techniques during location filming. While technicians lit the set, he rehearsed his actors. This allowed the actors to contribute more fully to each scene, such as the sequence when Emiliano (Brando) is captured by Federales troops. Eufemio (Quinn), while observing the capture, begins to tap two small rocks together and is joined by the townspeople, who mimic his action in a show of solidarity.

Quinn's surly portrayal of a man who has both an attractive appetite for life and a violent destructiveness had an inspired credibility. Quinn had only to look to his own origins, for he was born in Mexico at the height of the revolution and his parents fought for Villa before they immigrated to the United States. Quinn credited Kazan's intense direction for much of his successful performance: "I learned a lot from Kazan . . . a whole new style of acting. Kazan was able to create the atmosphere for you. Kazan works from a terribly personal point of view . . . sometimes so personal it's painful."

Quinn referred to the explosive confrontation scene between the brothers in which Quinn shows his disgust for Emiliano's selfishness, defies his authority and tells him he will take what he wants: "It took Brando and me three days to recover from that confrontation scene. Kazan had really worked us up, making us hate and love each other. Kazan insults you, tells you Brando hates your guts, anything!"

The cast included many of Kazan's Group Theater actors, among them Harold Gordon, Lou Gilbert, Joseph Wiseman and Alan Reid (as Pancho Villa). Among the Hispanic actors cast are Frank Silvera, Nina Varela, Margo and Henry Silva in his film debut. Nestor Paiva also has a small role.

The events of this complicated revolution are simplified for easier storytelling. In fact, Chicano activists of the 1960s criticized the film for casting Anglos in Mexican roles and questioned whether Kazan had a basic psychological understanding of the Latin male because of a scene in which, on the wedding night, Zapata perfers to learn to read than make love to his bride, Josefa (Peters). But before *Viva Zapata!*, very few Hollywood movies had told a story totally from a Mexican character's perspective. There is no gringo lead, nor are there any gringo supporting characters, as in other Hollywood Latin films. For example, in *Viva Villa!* (1934), the story is told through the eyes of a gringo reporter.

The studio was unsure how to market this story about an unknown-to-most-Americans Mexican hero and his country's struggle. Zanuck thought of the film as a Western. Zanuck insisted that Zapata ride a white horse and suggested the final fadeout, where the horse symbolically runs free in the mountains after Zapata's death. Kazan thought the idea clichéd, but it worked surprisingly well in the final film.

Though the film garnered several Academy Award® nominations and received generally good reviews, it became a victim of the

McCarthy era. In 1952, Kazan freely discussed his brief association with the Communist Party in the 1930s and named several Hollywood colleagues, which caused dissension among his Hollywood and New York associates. Given the pervasive political climate, the studio gave up on the film after its initial openings.

This remains Kazan's most visual movie, with striking black-and-white photography, while the editing helps the film's sweeping episodic structure, cutting on sound and image transitions. An example: Tricked into entering a deserted fort in search of munitions, Zapata finds himself alone but for his old white horse, which he had thought lost. An entire Mexican regiment encircles him from the battlements above and opens fire, emptying round after round of ammunition into his bleeding and mutilated body. A very similar ending was used over twenty years later by George Roy Hill in *Butch Cassidy and the Sundance Kid* (1969). Kazan went even further than Hill, however. Zapata's body is flung down with a dull thud in the plaza of a tiny village and is administered to by silent, shrouded Mexican women.

Brando was nominated for Best Actor for his brooding, passionate portrayal. Quinn won the Best Supporting Actor Oscar® for his work as the lustful, swaggering, weak-willed Eufemio.

Voyage of the Damned (1976 Avco Embassy)

D: Stuart Rosenberg
S: Steve Shagan and David Butler, based on the book by
   Max Morgan-Witts and Gordon Thomas
P: Robert Fryer
Cast: James Mason, Faye Dunaway, Max von Sydow, Oskar Werner,
   Malcolm McDowell, Orson Welles, José Ferrer, Fernando Rey

This is the shameful true story of 900 German Jewish refugees trapped on an ocean liner on the high seas. In 1939, the Nazis allowed a select group of German Jews of every social class and background to leave Europe aboard the German ocean liner *St. Louis*, bound for Cuba. The Nazis then conspired with the Cuban government to have the Jews' entry permits to Cuba canceled. The entry permits were invalidated eight days before the ship sailed, but no one on board ship knew this. The ship sat in Havana harbor for five days and then set sail toward the United States, where it was denied entry.

The Nazis allowed the ship to leave in response to worldwide pressure over their treatment of the Jews, using the incident as a propaganda tool to test the willingness of other countries to receive them. Not even the United States would allow the refugees entry.

James Mason plays the Cuban minister of state, Dr. Juan Remos, who unsuccessfully tries to persuade President Bru (Rey) to accept the large group of immigrants. Orson Welles plays Raul Estedes, an aristocratic Cuban industrialist. Ferrer plays the corrupt official Manuel Benitez. It was filmed in Barcelona, Spain, near the waterfront, which was transformed into Havana harbor and its environs.

A Walk in the Clouds (1995 Twentieth Century Fox)
D: Alfonso Arau
S: Robert Mark Kamen and Mark Miller & Harvey Weitzman, based on
  the film *Quattro Passi fra le Nuvole*
P: Gil Netter, David Zucker, Jerry Zucker
Cast: Keanu Reeves, Aitana Sanchez Gijon, Giancarlo Giannini,
  Anthony Quinn, Angelica Aragon, Evangelina Elizondo

The subject of this film is the 1940s romance between a candy sales-man and the daughter of an aristocratic Mexican-American vintner. Paul Sutton (Reeves) returns home to San Francisco after four years of World War II combat. Disenchanted with his wife and en route to Sacramento he encounters the lovely but distressed Victoria Aragon. She is on her way home to her family's Napa Valley vineyard, and is ter-rified her father will kill her when he finds out she is pregnant. The father of the child has abandoned her, and Paul gallantly offers to pose as Victoria's new husband thereby legitimizing the child in the family's eyes. After one night he will abandon his "bride" and leave, but things do not turn out as planned. Quinn gives an excellent performance as the shrewd and generous Don Pedro, the family patriarch.

The film is a fable, bathed in gold and tinged with magical realism. Bringing *A Walk in the Clouds* to the screen had been a seven year dream for its producers, who, in 1987, purchased the rights to the Italian neoclassic film *Quattro Passi fra le nuvole* (Four Steps in the Clouds), upon which this film is based. Impressed with Alfonso Arau's mix of sensuality, history and romance in *Like Water for Chocolate*, Producer Gil Netter approached Arau to direct. An admirer of the original film, Arau nonetheless wanted to tell a story closer to his own experience and suggested changing the family's origin from Italian to Mexican. The director hired Robert Mark Kamen to write the screenplay, and to ensure that the script had an authentic Mexican flavor, Arau invited Kamen to Mexico City to experience upper class Mexican culture through the director's eyes. Arau felt a personal responsibility to cast as many Latin actors as possible in the casting of the Aragon family. The grape crushing ritual was filmed high at Los Chamizal Vineyards, part of the Haywood winery in Napa Valley, California.

Walk Proud [aka: *Gang*] (1979 Universal)
D: Robert Collins
S: Evan Hunter
P: Lawrence Turman and David Foster
Cast: Robby Benson, Sarah Holcomb, Pepe Serna, Trinidad Silva,
  Domingo Ambriz, Henry Darrow

The story of youth gang rivalry in the barrio, set against the backdrop of Venice, California. Robby Benson stars as Emilio Mendez, a young Chicano gang member who wants to leave the gang life behind him when he finds true love at school with an Anglo girl from the ritzy side of town.

The movie resembles the 1950s gang movies in spirit, style, and execution and was scripted by Evan Hunter, who wrote the original novel on which the film *Blackboard Jungle* (1955) was based.

This well-acted drama, directed by Robert Collins, is a bit conventional and formulaic. It features a number of talented young Hispanic actors in major supporting roles, including Pepe Serna, Trinidad Silva, Domingo Ambriz, Irene Du Bari, Rose Portillo, Gary Cervantes, Angel Salazar, Panchito Gomez, Luis Reyes and Tony Alvaranga. Darrow plays a youth gang counselor. Felipe Turich plays a priest.

The Mexican American community protested the casting of Robby Benson (of Jewish American ancestry) as a Chicano youth and offered alternatives, such as A Martinez, who already had several respectable credits at the time. The studio's argument was that the film needed a recognizable name for the film to be a successful commercial venture at the box office, but there were no Hispanic leading actors. A star in a film did not always ensure financial success, as was proven with *Rocky* (1976) and other low-budget films that had gone on to enormous success. *Rocky* starred the then-unknown Sylvester Stallone in a role that catapulted him to stardom.

With a wave of films and television shows focusing on youth gangs, the Screen Extras Guild in 1978 found itself with few or no Hispanic teenagers in its ranks. The production of *Walk Proud* made it possible for a dozen young adults to enter the guild, making them eligible to be cast in other films.

Chicano youth gang members show their solidarity in *Walk Proud*. In back are (left to right) Gary Cervantes, Pepe Serna, Robby Benson as Emilio Mendez, Luis Reyes and Tony Alvaranga. In front are Trinidad Silva and Angel Salazar.

Walker (1987 Universal)

D: Alex Cox
S: Rudy Wurlitzer
P: Lorenzo O'Brien and Angel Flores Marini
Cast: Ed Harris, Marlee Matlin, Blanca Guerra, Alfonso Arau, Pedro Armendariz, Jr.

Alex Cox's (*Repo Man* [1984], *Sid and Nancy* [1986]) black, broad, comic approach can be an alienating, crazy, unsettling film experience. This film is ultimately a failed attempt at re-creating South American literature's Magical Realism and the surrealism of Buñuel by juxtaposing a historical story with modern artifacts on the screen.

Walker is the incredible saga of William Walker (Harris), an American freebooter who invaded Nicaragua in 1855 with fifty-six men, became president of the country and died in front of a Honduran firing squad in 1860 at age thirty-six.

Cox fills the movie with anachronisms that are as funny as they are glaring. The characters read about Walker in *People* magazine, for example. Walker sees himself on the cover of *Time*, and modern vehicles swoop across the screen. At the climax, the United States State Department sends a helicopter equipped with artillery to evacuate American citizens as the country teeters on the edge of collapse. As president of Nicaragua, Walker doesn't qualify for the airlift and is left behind to be executed. Ed Harris turns in a fine portrayal of the deranged Yankee imperialist. Asked about the turmoil he's inflicted on Nicaragua, he replies, "The ends justify the means." "What are the ends?" someone asks. "I forget," he replies.

Filmed on location in Nicaragua with the financial cooperation of the Sandinista government, the film paralleled and attacked the history of American involvement in Nicaragua from Walker to the present. The film engendered controversy because of its style and its statement against United States policy in Central America, which supported the Nicaraguan rebels, the Contras.

The Warriors (1979 Paramount)

D: Walter Hill
S: David Shaber and Walter Hill, based on the novel by Sol Yurick
P: Lawrence Gordon
Cast: Michael Beck, Deborah Van Valkenburgh, Marcelino Sanchez

A multiethnic urban gang, the Warriors, fights its way through the dark urban landscape of enemy gang territory back home to Coney Island from a Manhattan gang conference, where they had been falsely accused of slaying a gang leader. This fantasy about urban street gangs with outlandish wardrobes and stylized violence was shot in a cartoonish, pop art manner. This visually exciting film makes great use of color and has a very real sense of the bleak urban landscape. Deborah Van Valkenburgh plays a supposed Hispanic street girl named Mercy. Marcelino Sanchez, a young Puerto Rico-born actor raised in the Williamsburg section of Brooklyn, is featured as a quick-witted graffiti artist named Rembrandt.

The Waterdance (1992 Samuel Goldwyn)

D: Neal Jimenez and Michael Steinberg
S: Neal Jimenez
P: Gale Ann Hurd and Marie Cantin
Cast: Eric Stoltz, Wesley Snipes, William Forsythe, Helen Hunt,
    Elizabeth Peña

This film was inspired by the personal experience of screenwriter and co-director Neal Jimenez, who drew upon his rehabilitation after a paralyzing accident left him a wheelchair-bound paraplegic.

Writer Joel Garcia (Stoltz) falls off of a cliff while hiking and breaks his neck. When he awakens he is rolling on a hospital gurney and is told he will be paralyzed for life. Later he learns to deal with the tough world of the rehabilitation facility through his wardmates, who face the same challenges and fears, though they are from disparate backgrounds. The task at hand is to work through the conflicts, jealousies and prejudices that divide them, to find their personal roads to survival. This is an unflinching, straightforward, honest film, told with humor, compassion and humanity.

Way of a Gaucho (1952 Twentieth Century Fox)
D: Jacques Tourneur
S: Philip Dunne, based on the novel by Herbert Childs
P: Philip Dunne
Cast: Rory Calhoun, Gene Tierney, Richard Boone, Hugh Marlowe

This formula Western's unusual Argentine background is just different enough to make it interesting.

The soap opera-style story concerns one of the wild horsemen who once roamed the plains of Argentina. A sometime worker and full-time bandit before law and order fenced him in, the Gaucho (Calhoun) meets a girl (Tierney) and tries to make a go of a legitimate life.

The film crew traveled over 1,800 miles of Argentine plains and mountains from Mendoza in the Andean foothills and through San Luis, Cordova and Entre Rios. Some delays occurred before shooting could begin. The ship carrying the camera and other equipment arrived on the morning of the short-lived September 28 Revolution. The equipment was not unloaded, nor could it go through customs for over a week. There were a few delays with the clearing of the script by the Argentine government, but Raul Apold, head of the Secretariat of Information, gave his wholehearted approval. Most enthusiastic of all were the members of the Sixteenth Mountain Brigade, who not only acted as extras but helped as prop men and laborers when needed.

Argentine actors including Mario Abdah, Douglas Poole, C. Spindola, Claudio Torres and Lia Centeno were hired to play small roles. When actress Gene Tierney became ill and the company was forced to shoot around her for a week, President Juan Peron offered assistance, sending his personal physician to treat the actress.

Writer and producer Philip Dunne said in a *New York Times* interview (1/13/52), "We believe we've got a good picture. The scenery has been magnificent and Darryl F. Zanuck gave me some of his best people to work with. We've made everything authentic for the period. Whenever our Argentine technical advisor told us something wasn't right, we changed it."

Star Rory Calhoun recalled in a *Saturday Evening Post* interview (10/10/53), "I still rate this experience and my role as Martin, the Gaucho, as tops." *Way of a Gaucho* was really a Latin film, and although it did moderately well in the United States, it hit its peak of popularity South of the border.

We Were Strangers (1949 Columbia)

D: John Huston

S: John Huston and Peter Viertel, based on the novel *Rough Sketch* by Robert Sylvester

P: Sam Spiegel

Cast: John Garfield, Jennifer Jones, Pedro Armendariz, Gilbert Roland, Ramon Novarro, José Perez

The story of a Cuban-born American (Garfield) who returns to Cuba during the 1933 Machado Revolution. He gets involved in a plot to dig a tunnel underneath a cemetery in order to plant and explode a bomb where a state funeral will take place. The plan goes wrong when the family of the dead official makes a last-minute change in the arrangements. Garfield dies, but the revolution continues.

Though the film is slow-moving, ponderous and talky, Armendariz as a police captain, Roland as a Cuban revolutionary, and Novarro as a rebel chief all come off well. Argentina Brunetti, Felipe Turich, Julian Rivero and Tina Menard have minor roles in the film.

Weekend in Havana (1941 Twentieth Century Fox)

D: Walter Lang

S: Karl Tunberg and Darrell Ware

P: William LeBaron

Cast: Alice Faye, Carmen Miranda, Cesar Romero, John Payne, Billy Gilbert, Sheldon Leonard, Cobina Wright, Jr.

Nan Spencer (Faye), a salesgirl at Macy's New York department store, refuses to sign a waiver when the boat on which she is sailing to Havana hits a reef, but later agrees to do so if her trip to Havana is satisfactory.

Jay Williams (Payne), company vice president, who is engaged to Terry (Wright), is assigned to accompany Spencer and assure that her trip is a good one. Spencer craves romance and finally finds it with Monte Bianca (Romero), the manager of entertainer Rosita Rivas (Miranda). Bianca, however, turns out to be a heel who is after the money he thinks Spencer has.

Williams pays Bianca to make love to Spencer, and he takes over the management of Rosita to keep her away from Bianca. But the plan doesn't succeed. Williams discovers he loves Spencer, and vice versa. Terry, however, arrives and gets Spencer to sign the waiver through trickery. Williams learns the truth, ditches Terry and returns to Spencer.

This pleasant and colorful musical comedy is similar in content to other musicals set in South America, and showcases Miranda at her best.

Swank hotels, beautiful nightclubs and a spectacular gambling casino in Havana were all designed by Richard Day and Joseph Wright. Before Romero began work on the picture in Hollywood, Twentieth Century-Fox sent a Technicolor crew to Havana to film backgrounds for the picture. Romero's debutante cousins appeared as background models but did not learn that he was to star in the picture until after they wrote his mother in New York, mentioning that they had appeared in an American film called *Weekend in Havana*.

One of the musical high points is a production number with 200 gorgeous female zombies and Carmen Miranda in a voodoo jive called "Nango." Chris-Pin Martin and Alberto Marin are featured.

"A Technicolor Havana that the Cubans would be last to recognize," was the verdict from Nelson B. Bell, *Washington Post* (11/7/41).

West Side Story (1961 United Artists)

D: Robert Wise and Jerome Robbins
S: Ernest Lehman, based on the stage play by Arthur Laurents, Leonard Bernstein, and Stephen Sondheim
P: Robert Wise
Cast: Richard Beymer, Natalie Wood, George Chakiris, Rita Moreno

The winner of ten Academy Awards, *West Side Story*, based loosely on Shakespeare's *Romeo and Juliet*, is one of the most popular films of all

Rita Moreno (forefront) won an Academy Award® for her portrayal of the strong and fiery Anita in *West Side Story*. George Chakiris (left), who portrays Bernardo, and Yvonne Othon (right) are also pictured here.

time. Rival teenage gangs, one Puerto Rican, the other a mixture of Italian, Irish and Polish American youths, fight in the streets of New York. The story centers around Maria (Wood), a Puerto Rican girl, who falls in love with an Italian boy, Tony (Beymer), and the tragic consequences of their love for each other.

West Side Story depicted the very real problem of juvenile delinquency and gang warfare in New York City. It was filmed partly on the Upper West Side of Manhattan (the site where Lincoln Center for the Performing Arts stands today), where actual gangs roamed. The film exposed the plight and concerns of Puerto Ricans to a worldwide audience, although in a superficial way.

West Side Story was first presented as a hit Broadway stage musical in 1959 with landmark choreography by Jerome Robbins and a timeless musical score by Leonard Bernstein. For the motion picture version, Robbins' choreography and the direction by Robbins and Robert Wise achieved a delicate balance in their integration of the musical numbers within the story.

Moreno won an Academy Award® for Best Supporting Actress for her role as the strong and fiery Anita. The award cemented her image as a Latin spitfire, and for years all the roles offered to her were in that vein. However, she refused to accept roles that she felt limited her and that were demeaning, so she chose not to work in films for over seven years. She appeared instead in several stage productions in roles that she felt were challenging.

Among the Puerto Rican actors in the cast are Jaime Rogers, Rudy Del Campo, Yvonne Othon and José De Vega, who is part Filipino. George Chakiris, a Greek American, won an Oscar® as Best Supporting Actor for the role of the tough Puerto Rican gang leader, Bernardo.

The film's social commentary is particularly well expressed in Stephen Sondheim's lyrics for the song "America." It talks about how much easier it is for the women to adapt to life in the United States because of the various conveniences, whereas the men point out the realities of not being white in America.

In addition to Academy Awards® for Moreno and Chakiris, the film won for Best Picture and Best Director (Robbins and Wise).

What Happened to Santiago (1989 Manley Prod.)

D: Jacobo Morales
S: Jacobo Morales
P: Pedro Muniz
Cast: Tommy Muniz, Gladys Rodriguez, Johanna Rosaly,
      Rene Monclova

A charming love story about a retired accountant, Santiago Rodriguez (Muniz), and a mysterious younger woman in modern-day Puerto Rico.

Made on a budget of $480,000, the film was nominated for an Academy Award® for Best Foreign Language Film (Puerto Rico). Filmmaker Morales is a forty-year veteran of the Puerto Rican entertainment industry and has appeared in such American films as *Bananas* (1971) *and Up the Sandbox* (1972) and directed *Dias los Cria* (1980) and *Nicolas y los Demas* (1985).

Which Way Is Up? (1977 Universal)

D: Michael Schultz
S: Carl Gottlieb and Cecil Brown, based on the film script
   The Seduction of Mimi by Lina Wertmüller
P: Steve Krantz
Cast: Richard Pryor, Lonette McKee, Luis Valdez, Daniel Valdez

This is an unsuccessful reworking of Wertmüller's 1974 Italian comedy *The Seduction of Mimi*, in an American setting. Driven out of the groves by the boss when he accidentally becomes a union hero, an orange picker (Pryor) eventually goes to work for the company, turning his back on friends and family.

This was the first feature film appearance of actor/director/writer Luis Valdez and his brother, actor/composer/singer Daniel Valdez, and other members of the internationally acclaimed El Teatro Campesino (Farm Workers Theater). The Teatro's main contribution, aside from providing actors for the film, was in reshaping portions of the script dealing with the Chicano characters. Daniel plays Chuy Estrada, an energetic, fun-loving fruit picker with a serious streak, and Luis plays Ramon Juarez, a Cesar Chavez-like labor organizer. Director Michael Schultz had seen several of their stage presentations and sought out Luis and Daniel to work in the film.

White Men Can't Jump (1992 Twentieth Century Fox)

D: Ran Shelton
S: Ran Shelton
P: Dan Miller and David Lester
Cast: Woody Harrelson, Wesley Snipes, Rosie Perez

Two street basketball hustlers, one African American, Sid (Snipes), the other white, Billy (Harrelson), outwit each other and then decide to join forces and become partners in order to pull off a series of scams.

Billy shares a cramped motel room with his Puerto Rican girlfriend, Gloria (Perez), in this, the first Hollywood film to have a Puerto Rican female lead actually played by a Puerto Rican actress. Perez's eccentric portrayal is cute, comical, sexy and endearing. The Puerto Rican-Anglo American Gloria-Billy love relationship is another breakthrough in American cinema, as the characters are on equal standing in their sexual and psychological relationships. Gloria is obviously a "New Yorican" (a Puerto Rican born and raised in New York), so even though she is Latin she has a Brooklyn accent and is fully American, not a stereotyped Spanish-accented "Rosita" character.

Though the story takes place in an inner-city Los Angeles environment, it is free from the typical barrio trappings. Gloria sings a Puerto Rican song, "Que Bonita Bandera" (What a Beautiful Flag), while in the shower with Billy, indicating her cultural roots. She spends her days accumulating useless information, for she dreams of going on the popular television game show *Jeopardy* and winning a fortune, which she eventually does.

Why Worry? (1923 Pathé)
D: Fred Neumeyer and Sam Taylor
S: Sam Taylor
P: Hal Roach
Cast: Harold Lloyd

Silent. This Harold Lloyd comedy has the popular comedian caught in a South American revolution. It turns into a burlesque comedy filled with hilarious sight gags but with shallow stereotypes.

Harold Van Pelham (Lloyd) is a rich young man who is mistaken for a world banking executive when he arrives in Paradiso, a tiny island country off the west coast of Chile in which an American renegade has gathered together a band of outlaws who intend to overthrow the government.

The Wild Bunch (1969 Warner Bros.)
D: Sam Peckinpah
S: Walon Green and Sam Peckinpah, based on a story by Green and
    Roy N. Sickner
P: Phil Feldman
Cast: William Holden, Robert Ryan, Ernest Borgnine, Edmond O'Brien,
    Warren Oates, Ben Johnson, Jaime Sanchez, Emilio Fernandez,
    Alfonso Arau

A classic Western remembered more for its choreographed, balletic, slow-motion bloodbaths and less for its textured acting and feeling of authenticity. *The Wild Bunch* best illustrates the quintessential American view of Mexico as a place where gringos can play out their fantasies in a never-never land of sex, violence and ultra machismo.

In this brutal drama of violent men who have outlived their times, Holden as Pike, Borgnine as Dutch, Oates as Lyle Gorch, and Johnson as Tector Gorch fully realize the conflicting strains of their harsh yet humane characters.

After a violent bank robbery in a United States bordertown, the Bunch cross the Rio Grande into Mexico, where they are cleansed and given a rebirth. The film then takes on a sudden tranquility in a brief pastoral interlude when they enter the village of the Bunch's only Mexican member, Angel (Sanchez).

In 1913 Mexico, Pancho Villa is fighting a repressive Huerta government. Mexican women are seen slung with bandoleers, breast-feeding their babies and making tacos in General Mapache's (Fernandez) encampment while German military advisers stand by and watch. To Pike, Mexico is a last frontier, but the reality is that it has always been in a state of upheaval, exemplified by the contrast between Angel's village and Mapache's encampment.

Where the others in the Bunch are indifferent (a condition of their situation as well as the Western tradition), one part of Angel at least is committed to the still unsettled cause of his people. The others do not understand it but are affected by Angel's positive force. In the end, Pike urges the others to protect Angel from General Mapache, and even

Ernest Borgnine as Dutch and William Holden as Pike depart a Mexican village in a scene from *The Wild Bunch*, a classic Western directed by Sam Peckinpah.

Dutch sympathizes as far as he can with Angel's cause. It is Angel's inability to accept the brotherhood ethic in an American context that propels the Bunch into their final conflict. It is his sense of Latin machismo that leads him to shoot his former girlfriend, who has become one of Mapache's whores, an act that introduces a deadly imbalance into the relations of the Bunch and the Mexicans with whom they have managed to achieve a fragile détente. Mapache treats Angel like a peon. After this, a confrontation can be postponed but not avoided. The Bunch never kill or commit a crime in Mexico except for the final showdown. Instead, they cross back north of the border to rob a train.

Peckinpah does not portray Mexico as a complete paradise for the Bunch. Mapache represents an early form of twentieth-century petty tyrant. He is evil incarnate, possessed of the negative trappings of the industrial world. Before meeting Mapache, the Bunch has never seen an automobile. Later, that car will be used to drag around the body of the tortured Angel. The machine gun, which becomes the chief instrument of the Bunch's and Mapache's demise, is another modern-day weapon. Surrounded by adoring children, German military advisers, whores and sadistic killers, Mapache delights in the destructive power of a machine gun. Four Americans, killing hundreds of Mexicans before meeting their own demise, could be interpreted as a symbol of American superiority, a remnant of the Alamo ethic and the white man saving-the-poor-"little brown brothers"-from-themselves attitude of the Teddy Roosevelt era. The introduction of the machine gun, however, makes that an uncomfortable interpretation to maintain. Peckinpah's vision of a whole Mexican village lining up to bid farewell to the Americanos can be regarded as a projection of white benign imperialism. The villagers, as it turns out, do not need the protection of the Bunch; they are using the Americanos to preserve their revolution but are perfectly capable of careful planning and execution. This is illustrated by their swift action in retrieving the rifles promised to them by Angel. The villagers do not ask the Bunch (as in *The Magnificent Seven*) to do their fighting for them; all they want is guns. The elder says, "In Mexico, Señor, these are the years of sadness, but if we had rifles like these . . . ?!"

Poor Mexican women in the film are seen exclusively as whores. Angel screams "puta" (whore) and shoots his former girlfriend in the heart when he sees her with General Mapache, the man responsible for his parents' death. Mapache quickly replaces her with another woman. The Bunch seek comfort with the whores, and sex and death are irretrievably linked for the Bunch. Pike is shot dead in the back by a whore in the finale. The women in Angel's village, though not whores, seem to be easily available to the Americanos. Since Angel's girlfriend came from that village, the implication is clear, especially when she tells Angel it is better to have status as Mapache's woman than to starve to death in her own village. It is ironic that Emilio Fernandez, who as a director contributed—with cameraman Gabriel Figueroa—some of the most beautiful images of Mexico and its people and a national identity through its cinema, would in later life play some of the most despicable and memorable Mexican bandido characters in American films. Fernandez's larger-than-life off-screen personality, forged on drunken brawls, shoot-outs and run-ins with Mexican government officials, eventually became a caricature both on screen and off.

The movie was filmed in Parras, Coahuila, Mexico. The final shootout was filmed at La Cieniga de San Carmen, a 300-year-old winery that served as the set for Mapache's military headquarters. The screenplay, by director Peckinpah and Walon Green, is based on an original story by Green and Roy Sickner inspired by an actual border incident in 1913 when a gang of American outlaws posing as United States soldiers hijacked a munitions train on its way to Pancho Villa. *The Wild Bunch* touches on one of Peckinpah's favorite themes: the changing West and its impact on the unchanging loner in a frontier being replaced by civilization.

Jaime Sanchez, a Puerto Rican-born actor, plays Angel, the only Mexican member of the outlaw gang. The Mexican performers constitute a gathering of some of Mexico's most talented actors. They include Chano Urrueta as the village headman, Sonia Amalio as William Holden's lover, Alfonso Arau as one of Mapache's military aides (he played a comic version of this character in the later movie spoof ¡*Three Amigos!*), Fernando Wagner as a German military aide and Jorge Russek as Lieutenant Zamora, a military aide and bodyguard.

Charles Champlin in the *Los Angeles Times* (6/15/69) said, "It is all framed within the comfortably familiar conventions of the classic Western, including, I would say, the characterizing of Mexicans as childlike and simple, whether good (poor exploited but rebellious), bad (bandidos or army), or indifferent (fun loving señoritas)."

The Wild Wild West (1999 Warner Bros.)

D: Barry Sonnenfeld
S: Jeffrey Price and Peter S. Seaman
P: Jon Peters and Barry Sonnenfeld
Cast: Will Smith, Kevin Kline, Salma Hayek, Kenneth Branagh,
    Gary Cervantes

In the Old West, special government agent James West (Smith), long on charm and wit, and special government agent Artemus Gordon (Kline), a master of disguise and a brilliant inventor of gadgets large and small, are each sent to track down the diabolical genius Dr. Arliss Loveless (Branagh). Loveless is plotting to assassinate the President of the United States. The beautiful and mysterious entertainer Rita Escobar (Hayek) complicates matters for the duo as she insinuates herself into their plans to capture Loveless.

Loosely based on the television series of the late '60s.

The Winged Serpent

See *Q*.

Wings of the Hawk (1953 Universal)

D: Budd Boetticher
S: James E. Moser and Kay Leonard, based on the novel by
    Gerald Drayson Adams
P: Aaron Rosenberg
Cast: Van Heflin, Julia Adams, Rodolfo Acosta, Abbe Lane,
    Antonio Moreno, Pedro Gonzalez-Gonzalez

Heflin plays Irish Gallager, a Yankee prospector in Mexico, who finds himself at odds with government troops under the command of Colonel Ruiz (George Dolenz) and sides with a revolutionary army led by the beautiful Lieutenant Raquel (Adams) and Arturo (Acosta). Raquel's parents have been killed by Presidente Diaz's troops, and her sister Elena (Lane) is in league with the colonel. Gallager becomes the insurrectionist leader after deposing Arturo, who later betrays the insurrectionists. Gallager's feats range from slaughtering endless numbers of Presidente Diaz's troops to blowing up a gold mine.

This "gringo in Mexico" action adventure yarn is well directed with strong character flair by Boetticher in Technicolor. Gonzalez-Gonzalez scores in a comedic role. Also in the cast are Paul Fierro, Felipe Turich, Joe Dominguez, Rocky Ybarra and Ruben Padilla.

Woman on Top (2000 Fox Searchlight)
D: Fina Torres
S: Vera Blasi
P: Alan Poul
Cast: Penelope Cruz, Murilio Benicio, Mark Feuerstein,
    Harold Perrineau, Jr.

Set in Brazil, this film is a spicy, sexy comedy about the magic of food, love and relationships. Penelope Cruz, hugely popular in her native Spain and now an emerging star in Hollywood, stars as Isabella, a talented chef. Directed by Venezuela's Fina Torres, the film was shot in Brazil and San Francisco.

The Wonderful Country (1959 United Artists)
D: Robert Parrish
S: Robert Ardrey, based on the novel by Tom Lea
P: Charles Erskine
Cast: Robert Mitchum, Pedro Armendariz, Victor Mendoza

"Half-breed" Martin Brady (Mitchum) is a Mexican hired gun for the powerful Castro brothers (Armendariz and Mendoza), one a petty dictator and the other an army leader. "Why don't you start your life all over again this side of the border?" suggests an American to Brady. The prejudice he faces is not from the Anglos who resent his Mexican ancestry but from the Castro brothers, who label him a gringo because "it is not easy to wipe out the heritage in the blood."

Brady symbolically lays down his gun by his dead horse Lagrimas (Tears), crosses the Rio Grande and returns to his lover, reclaiming his heritage.

Mitchum, who also functioned as a producer, works somewhat uncharacteristically with a Mexican accent and the mannerisms of a Mexican peon. The movie was shot on location in Mexico.

The Wonderful Ice Cream Suit (1999 Buena Vista)
D: Stuart Gordon
S: Ray Bradbury
P: Roy Edward Disney and Stuart Gordon
Cast: Joe Mantegna, Esai Morales, Edward James Olmos,
    Clifton Gonzalez Gonzalez, Gregory Sierra, Liz Torres,
    Mike Moroff, Lisa Vidal

Five young men, down on their luck and with only $100 between them, buy one magical white suit that will transform their lives. Gomez (Mantegna) the fast talker, Vamenos (Olmos) the tramp, Martinez (Gonzalez Gonzalez) the innocent, Villanazul (Sierra) the intellectual and Dominguez (Morales) the romantic, are an eclectic bunch of characters living in a contemporary Los Angeles neighborhood. The suit brings out their innermost desires and makes their dream come true. They plan to wear it one night a week each, but are so restless with anticipation that they decide each will wear it for one hour that very evening. Their adventures on that wonderful, magical night change their lives in hilarious and meaningful ways.

Based on an original story by eminent American writer Ray Bradbury, *The Wonderful Ice Cream Suit* is a stylized, sweet, funny and touching film that plays much like a live action cartoon. The wonderful ensemble of actors features Edward James Olmos in an unusual comic role as the tramp Vamenos.

The Wrath of God
(1972 Metro-Goldwyn-Mayer)
D: Ralph Nelson
S: Ralph Nelson, based on the novel by
   James Graham
P: Ralph Nelson
Cast: Robert Mitchum, Rita Hayworth,
   Frank Langella, Victor Buono

Mitchum is a drunken American priest running guns in a fictional South American country. Hayworth, in her last film appearance, plays the mother of a deranged counter-revolutionary (Langella). Gregory Sierra plays Jurado, a one-eyed rebel. It was filmed in Mexico and includes the usual assortment of stereotypes.

Wrestling Ernest Hemingway (1993 Warner Bros.)
D: Randa Haines
S: Steve Conrad
P: Todd Block and Joe Wizan
Cast: Robert Duvall, Richard Harris, Shirley MacLaine, Piper Laurie, Sandra Bullock

Walter (Duvall), a circumspect Cuban immigrant always practicing for tomorrow's triumphs, and Frank (Harris), a salty Irish ex-sea captain, are two very different seventy-five-year-old men who meet in the park of a sleepy southern Florida town. They begin a shaky relationship that breathes new life into each of them.

Ray Bradbury's *The Wonderful Ice Cream Suit* stars (left to right) Joe Mantegna, Edward James Olmos, Gregory Sierra, Clifton Gonzalez Gonzalez and Esai Morales in a film directed by Stuart Gordon.

You Were Never Lovelier (1942 Columbia)

D: William A. Seiter

S: Michael Fessier, Ernest Pagano, and Delmer Daves, based on the story and screenplay "The Gay Señorita" by Carlos Olivari and Sixto Pondal Rios

P: Louis F. Edelman

Cast: Fred Astaire, Rita Hayworth, Adolphe Menjou, Adele Mara, Leslie Brooks, Xavier Cugat, Lina Romay

Set in Buenos Aires, *You Were Never Lovelier* is an enchanting musical bringing together Hayworth and Astaire at the top of their form for the second and last time. They were previously teamed in *You'll Never Get Rich* (1941).

A New York nightclub dancer (Astaire) with a passion for horse racing meets the daughter (Hayworth) of a wealthy Latin American hotelier (Menjou).

Xavier Cugat and his Orchestra, accompanied by singer/actress Romay, are on hand to provide the Latin flavor in a film shot entirely in Hollywood.

Young Guns (1988 Twentieth Century Fox)

D: Christopher Cain

S: John Fusco

P: Joe Roth and Christopher Cain

Cast: Emilio Estevez, Kiefer Sutherland, Lou Diamond Phillips, Charlie Sheen, Casey Siemaszko, Dermot Mulroney, Jack Palance, Terence Stamp

The year is 1878; the place is Lincoln County, New Mexico. John Tunstall (Stamp), a British rancher, hires six rebellious boys as "regulators" (gunfighters) to protect his ranch against a ring of ruthless cattle ranchers. When Tunstall is killed in an ambush, the regulators, led by Billy the Kid (Estevez), declare war on the cattle ranchers, and their vendetta turns into a bloody rampage. Lou Diamond Phillips plays a knife-wielding gunslinger called Chavez y Chavez, referred to as a "half-breed," who is part of Billy's gang.

Young Guns II (1990 Twentieth Century Fox)

D: Geoff Murphy

S: John Fusco

P: Paul Schiff and Irby Smith

Cast: Emilio Estevez, Kiefer Sutherland, Christian Slater, William Petersen, Lou Diamond Phillips, James Coburn

An old man on a deserted New Mexico highway circa 1940 agrees to meet a journalist and tell him the true story of Billy the Kid (Estevez) and Pat Garrett (Petersen). As he tells the story, the events unfold in flashback. The viewer comes to the slow realization that Billy did not meet his end at the hands of Garrett, as was documented, but that Garrett helped stage Billy's death so he could get on with his life and turn over a new leaf. The old man turns out to be Billy the Kid.

This effective, action-filled Western stars many of the young stars of the day. It is one of the few sequels that is as good as, if not better than, its original, *Young Guns* (1988). Lou Diamond Phillips reprised his role as Chavez y Chavez.

The Young Land (1959 Columbia)
D: Ted Tetzlaff
S: Norman Shannon Hall, based on the story "Frontier Frenzy" by
   John Reese
P: Patrick Ford
Cast: Patrick Wayne, Yvonne Craig, Dennis Hopper

The story of a town in post-Mexican War 1848 California that is acquired by the United States, and of the town's sheriff, Jim Ellison (Wayne).

A reckless Anglo gunman, Hatfield Carnes (Hopper), goads a respected Mexican into an obviously one-sided gun duel. This leads to the first murder trial involving an American accused of killing a Mexican, and in the eyes of the Mexicans, "American justice is on trial." Following the jury's verdict of guilty, the federal judge on the case faces the difficult task of sentencing the criminal, whose henchmen are preparing to save him while a group of Mexican vaqueros are planning to lynch him. The judge, stating that the laws of California have not been established, sets aside a twenty-years-to-life sentence and sentences Carnes, instead, to a life without the privilege of carrying a gun. This infuriates Carnes to the point of snatching a gun from a deputy's holster and inviting Ellison (Wayne) to a duel outside the courtroom. Ellison kills Carnes in the showdown. The film ends with Ellison's betrothal to Elena de la Madrid (Craig), the daughter of a wealthy Mexican patron of the region.

The cast also includes Roberto de la Madrid, Pedro Gonzalez-Gonzalez, John Quijada, Miguel Camacho, Carlos Romero, and the mariachi band Los Reyes de Chapala.

The Young Savages (1961 United Artists)
D: John Frankenheimer
S: Edward Anhalt and J.P. Miller, based on the novel *A Matter of
   Conviction* by Evan Hunter
P: Pat Duggan
Cast: Burt Lancaster, Dina Merrill, Edward Andrews, Shelley Winters,
   José Perez

An American social melodrama that addresses several important issues of the time: juvenile delinquency, racial prejudice, the death penalty, drugs and gangs.

It is the late 1950s and the Spanish Harlem section of New York is controlled by teenage gangs. Two such gangs are the Thunderbirds, from an Italian neighborhood, and the Horsemen, from a Puerto Rican neighborhood. Three members of the Thunderbirds stab and kill a blind Puerto Rican boy. The three youths are caught by the police, and the case is turned over to Hank Bell (Lancaster) of the District Attorney's office.

Bell's investigation takes him to the two neighborhoods, where he talks to the witnesses and the various gang members. It is revealed that the "innocent" Puerto Rican boy was, in fact, a gang member and a pimp for his sister. The boys are convicted of murder in varying degrees and are sentenced.

The film, based on a book by Evan Hunter, of *Blackboard Jungle* fame, has the familiar ring of the white-man-saving-the-poor-minorities-from-themselves theme, except that the "white man" in this film is a minority himself.

Hank Bell is actually Italian American Henry Bellini, who is trying to move up the social scale and forget his past, which he can never really escape. This well-intentioned film unfortunately further embellishes the stereotypes of Puerto Rican city dwellers as gang members, suffering mothers and easy women. Vivian Nathan plays Mrs. Escalante, the suffering mother of the blind boy (Rafael Lopez) and his sister Louisa (Pilar Seurat). Luis Arroyo plays the gang leader Zorro, and Perez plays Roberto Escalante. The movie was filmed on location in Spanish Harlem in New York City, where Lancaster grew up. It was a predominantly Italian area during Lancaster's youth, but by the time of the film, the area around First and Pleasant avenues was all that was left of the Italian area, and Puerto Ricans inhabited the area from Second to Fifth avenues.

Zandy's Bride (1974 Warner Bros.)
D: Jan Troell
S: Marc Norman, based on the novel *The Stranger* by Lillian Bos Ross
P: Harvey Matofsky
Cast: Gene Hackman, Liv Ullmann, Susan Tyrrell, Joe Santos,
    Fabian Gregory Cordova

Zandy (Hackman) is a frontiersman who sends for a mail-order bride, Hannah (Ullmann). The movie is the story of two very different people struggling to make a life together in the harsh Western environment of Monterey, California, in the 1860s. Zandy has a fling at a barbecue when he is seduced by the jealous, hot-blooded Maria Cordova (Tyrrell). Santos plays a Spanish cattle rancher named Frank Gallo. The film was directed by Swedish filmmaker Jan Troell, who won acclaim for The Emigrant Saga, including *The Emigrants* (1971) and its sequel, *The New Land* (1972).

"Susan Tyrrell makes a fiery Maria Cordova, an aggressive girl spurned by Zandy, but one can't help but wonder why [Maria] wasn't played by a Chicana actress," Kevin Thomas, *Los Angeles Times* (6/26/74).

Zoot Suit (1981 Universal)
D: Luis Valdez
S: Luis Valdez, based on his play
P: Peter Burrell, Kenneth Brecher, and
    William P. Wingate
Cast: Edward James Olmos, Daniel Valdez, Rose Portillo,
    Lupe Ontiveros, Abel Franco, Tyne Daly, Charles Aidman,
    John Anderson, Mike Gomez, Alma Beltran, Sal Lopez,
    Robert Beltran, Alma Rosa Martinez, Tony Plana

Luis Valdez became the first Mexican American or Chicano to write and direct a major studio-backed feature film with the screen adaptation of his hit play *Zoot Suit*.

The dramatic musical opened in 1978 at the Mark Taper Forum in Los Angeles to overwhelming critical and audience reception, breaking box office records. The run was extended and the production moved to the Aquarius Theatre in Hollywood, where it continued to break attendance records. With *Zoot Suit*, Valdez became the first Chicano playwright to have his work performed on the Broadway stage when the production opened at New York City's Winter Garden Theatre.

Set in the 1940s, *Zoot Suit* is the story of a group of Mexican American boys who are falsely accused of murdering another boy at a party in Los Angeles. Based on fact, it retells the events of the Sleepy Lagoon murder and the Zoot Suit riots that took place in 1942 and 1943 (Zoot Suits were a style of clothing popularized stateside by Mexican American and African American youths during World War II). The Sleepy Lagoon murder case is a landmark in American legal annals, for it established a precedent against mass trials. The trial was a mockery of justice, presided over by a biased judge who sentenced twelve of the defendants to San Quentin Prison for life, despite the fact that there was no hard evidence and there were no eyewitnesses to the killing. Fueled by racism, yellow journalism and wartime hysteria, Anglo G.I.'s stationed in Los Angeles invaded the downtown barrios, beating up any Mexican wearing a Zoot Suit. Police were either unable or unwilling to stop the rioting, which spread to other communities and lasted five days.

Edward James Olmos as the Zoot-Suited El Pachuco in Luis Valdez's *Zoot Suit*, the first major studio-backed feature film written and directed by a Mexican American.

In 1981, Universal Pictures agreed to film the play over a period of fourteen days on the stage of the Aquarius Theatre, using most of the original stage cast. The budget was $2.5 million.

Edward James Olmos re-created his award-winning (Los Angeles Drama Critics Circle Award and a Tony Award nomination), critically acclaimed portrayal the character El Pachuco for the screen. El Pachuco, giant switchblade in hand, cuts through blown-up newspaper headlines, in effect cutting through the stereotype by using one of its more potent images. Olmos swaggers and struts with an economical grace as the ultimate Zoot Suiter who symbolizes Chicano pride as well as a darker foreboding element. With the snap of his fingers, El Pachuco moves the film from one event to another, offering sly, witty and insightful commentary on the plight of the Mexican American.

The action centers around Henry Reyna (played by Daniel Valdez), the leader of the youths, his family, his followers and their girls, and the people they come into contact with during their arrest and trial. The drama is bathed in the sights and sounds of World War II Americana, such as the big band sounds of Glenn Miller and Harry James, patriotic flag waving, jitterbug and swing dancing and men in uniforms.

Zoot Suit skillfully combines cinematic theatrical techniques, cutting on movement and sound, making a radical and innovative film record of the stage play that sometimes works well and sometimes doesn't. Through the story of the four Chicano boys, it recounts the racial tension and rioting that plagued Los Angeles during World War II. Being a musical, however, it mixes these somber events with an uplifting and celebratory spirit. It was during the Zoot Suit era that Mexican Americans first recognized their cultural heritage and established a pride in their identity. Some of the music and songs in the play and film were contributed by Valdez and Lalo Guerrero.

Valdez explained the development of *Zoot Suit* thusly: "*Zoot Suit* is [an] extremely spiritual, political play and it was never understood. People thought it was about juvenile delinquents and that I was putting the Pachuco on the stage just to be snide. But the young man, Henry Reyna, achieves his liberation by coming into contact with this internal authority. The Pachuco is the Jungian self-image, the superego if you will, the power inside every individual greater than any institution. The Pachuco says, 'It'll take more than the United States Navy to beat me down [referring to the sailors and Marines stripping Zoot Suiters in the 1940s], I don't give a [damn] what you do to me, you . . . take [that] . . . guise from me, and I reassert myself in this guise.'

"The fact that the critics couldn't accept that guise was too bad, but it doesn't change the nature of what the play is about. It deals with self-salvation. And you can follow the playwright through the story. I was also those two dudes. With *Zoot Suit* I was finally able to transcend social conditions and the way I did it on stage was to give the Pachuco absolute power, as the master of ceremonies. He could snap his fingers and stop the action. It was a Brechtian device that allowed the plot to move forward, but psychically and symbolically, in the right way. Chicanos got off on it. That's why half a million people came to see it in Los Angeles, because I had given a disenfranchised people their religion back. I dressed the Pachuco in the colors of Testatipoka, the Aztec god of education, the dean of the school of hard knocks. There's another god of culture, Quetzalcoatl, the leathered serpent, who's much kinder. He surfaces in *La Bamba* as the figure of Ritchie Valens. He's an artist and poet and is gentle and not at all fearful. When audiences see *La Bamba*, they like the positive spirit. The Pachuco's a little harder to take. But these are evolutions."

"Enlightening and challenging musical drama that runs the gamut from Greek Tragedy to *West Side Story*," Mark Kane, *Film Journal* (1/16/82).

Television / Introduction

At first glance it seems that Hispanics have been as under-represented as African Americans and other minorities on network television. Character names like Ricky Ricardo, the Cisco Kid, Zorro, and Jose Jimenez come easily to mind, but it is difficult to come up with other names or role models. This is a deceptive conclusion, though, because more Hispanics have entered our homes and lives through our television sets than perhaps we realize.

For example, there were Henry Darrow and Linda Cristal on *The High Chaparral* (1967-71), and Elena Verdugo on *Marcus Welby, M.D.* (1969-76) in the late 1960s and early 1970s, and, though not an overwhelmingly positive Hispanic image, Freddie Prinze on *Chico and the Man* (1974-78). More recently, gifted actor John Leguizamo has had tremendous success with his three HBO specials, each adapted from his one-man shows on Broadway.

As is the case with many successful African American series, numerous early Hispanic television achievements focused on comedic images within an American framework. Only in the 1980s and early '90s—with shows such as *Miami Vice* (1984-89), *L.A. Law* (1986-94), and later *NYPD Blue* (1993-) and *Chicago Hope* (1994-2000) in particular—has there been any success within the dramatic format, and then only in supporting roles such as Edward James Olmos' Lieutenant Castillo; Jimmy Smits' high-powered Los Angeles lawyer Victor Sifuentes, and later, *NYPD Blue* Detective Bobby Simone. Hector Elizondo's beleaguered hospital Chief-of-Staff Dr. Philip Watters in *Chicago Hope* is another such example, as is, to a lesser degree, Rene Enriquez's beleaguered second-in-command station cop Lieutenant Ray Calletano on the gritty inner-city cop show *Hill Street Blues* (1981-87).

CHiPs (1978-83), starring Erik Estrada as a California Highway Patrol officer, was an exception in that, with its breezy Southern California action style, it fit neither the comedy nor the drama category comfortably.

On close inspection, one finds that a surprising amount of Hispanic American talent has been working constantly in American television, both in front of and behind the camera. Yet, although Hispanics have been featured on various series since television began, there have been few Hispanic star- or character-driven vehicles. Many of the shows that featured Hispanic characters were short-lived and the character portrayals were limited or simply unpopular with the public.

The first important Hispanic presence, of course, was Desi Arnaz as Ricky Ricardo on *I Love Lucy* (1951-57). Though *The Cisco Kid* (1950-55) was on the air prior to *I Love Lucy*, it came to television via its film success as one of the first Saturday matinee Westerns to be transferred to the new medium. *I Love Lucy*, with Arnaz as Lucy's husband, was a unique, contemporary and untried concept. Arnaz was not only a performer but also a producer, and his influence is still felt almost fifty years later. For example, he pioneered a three-camera technique for filming situation comedies that is still in use today. By filming *I Love Lucy* and retaining ownership of the filmed shows, he created the industry standard for syndicated reruns. Through the Desilu production company, owned by himself and his then-wife, Lucille Ball, he oversaw the development of such memorable television series as *The Untouchables* (1959-63), *Star Trek* (1966-69), *Lou Grant* (1977-82), and many others, while a number of shows of the time used the Desilu Studios facility.

The musician with the "funny accent," known rather patronizingly as "Cuban Pete," proved to be not only a capable performer but also a shrewd businessman. Arnaz followed the original *I Love Lucy* series with *The Lucy-Desi Comedy Hour* (1957-60), which ceased production the year Castro came to power in Cuba and the year Lucy and Desi, America's favorite comedy couple, filed for divorce. Two years later, Castro declared his Communist ties. Suddenly the image of the funny, friendly, romantic Cuban turned into the fierce, bearded, cigar-chomping Communist revolutionary Fidel Castro. Almost overnight, the image of the Hispanic on television was transformed by the evening news.

The American media bombarded the airwaves with images of Castro and his armed America-hating revolutionaries and the debacle of the Bay of Pigs affair. The public became terrified by the prospect of a nuclear World War III during the Cuban Missile Crisis.

Latin banana republics with revolutionaries or military dictators, most sporting Castro-like beards and military fatigues or spit-and-polish generalisimo images, became a staple of episodic action shows. From *The Twilight Zone* (1959-65) to *I Spy* (1965-68), and *Hart to Hart* (1979-84) to *The A-Team* (1983-87) to *MacGyver* (1985-92), the amusing, accented, South-of-the-Border clown had turned deadly.

During the 1950s, Duncan Renaldo as the Cisco Kid and Leo Carrillo as his sidekick Pancho, followed the pattern of the traditional Western hero. Some 156 half-hour episodes were filmed in color between 1950 and 1955. Making thousands of personal appearances in costume, Renaldo and Carrillo brought the magic of the Latin cowboy hero to small-town and big-city America alike. By the late 1960s, Chicano activists found fault with Carrillo's buffoonish portrayal of Pancho on the show, and the series was pulled from syndication for many years, primarily in the Southwestern United States.

In the late 1950s, when there was a preponderance of Western cowboy series like *Wagon Train* (1957-65), *Gunsmoke* (1955-75), *Maverick* (1957-62), *Cheyenne* (1955-63) and *Bonanza* (1959-73), Hispanics were portrayed in stock bandido, spitfire, or peon roles whether they were played by Hispanic actors or not. When the major movie studios began to let go of many of their stars and contract players in the 1950s, television was a way of escaping the rigid typecasting they had been subject to while under contract.

Ricardo Montalban, Fernando Lamas and Rita Moreno all worked regularly in television during the 1950s in a wider variety of roles than they had found in films. In a *TV Guide* interview (January 24, 1970), Montalban said, "It is to television that I owe my freedom from the bondage of the Latin Lover image. Television came along and gave me parts to chew on. It gave me wings as an actor." His television credits include varied parts in such vintage series as *Playhouse 90* (1956-61), *Climax!* (1954-58), *Wagon Train*, *Ben Casey* (1961-66), *Star Trek* and *Fantasy Island* (1978-84).

Hispanic women have usually been relegated to some version of the stout mamacita, the sexy spitfire, and the suffering mother or girlfriend. The image of the strong, self-reliant, attractive Latin woman was first memorably portrayed in two television series, by Linda Cristal as Victoria Cannon in *The High Chaparral* and then by Elena Verdugo as Nurse Consuelo in *Marcus Welby, M.D.*

Lucille Ball and Desi Arnaz in *I Love Lucy*.

Though both these characters were subservient to Anglo men (Victoria was married to John Cannon and Nurse Consuelo worked for Dr. Welby), this had as much to do with the portrayal of women on television in general as it did with what television producers thought the public would "accept." These two female characters were sufficiently developed through the course of the series to give them dimension and control over events in many of the storylines. One might laugh at their fiery tempers on occasion as they broke into frustrated rapid-fire Spanish (pretty much as Ricky Ricardo used to do when exasperated by Lucy's antics a decade earlier), but they were also portrayed with dignity and a generally implied acceptance of equality, in terms of both their gender and racial origin, which was refreshing. They were, in other words, as good as the Anglo males featured in the shows, and this was a reflection of the successful impact of the civil rights and women's rights movements of the 1960s and 1970s.

Beginning with the police series *Dragnet* (1952-59), Hispanics came to be recognized as part of the modern urban population. One of Sergeant Joe Friday's (as played by Jack Webb) detective partners was a Mexican American. *Naked City* (1958-63), a police series filmed on location in New York City, and *East Side/West Side* (1963-64), about social workers and also filmed in New York, featured a few episodes that dealt with Puerto Ricans.

However, another image was beginning to take shape in 1970s shows like *Baretta* (1975-78), *Kojak* (1973-78), *Starsky and Hutch* (1975-79), *Police Story* (1973-77), and 1980s shows such as *Hill Street Blues* (1981-87), *T.J. Hooker* (1982-86) and *Hunter* (1984-91). This image of Hispanics was as lower class, poverty-stricken ghetto dwellers, unable and unwilling to communicate in proper English, whose lives are filled with drugs, gang violence and extreme family crisis. A virtual parade of maids, hookers, hoods, gang members, and their suffering mamacitas and girlfriends has been the overriding contemporary image of Hispanics as presented on American television.

In 1969, Nosotros, a Hispanic American actors organization dedicated to improving the image of Hispanic Americans and Spanish-speaking peoples in the media, was formed (Nosotros is discussed further in the introduction to the "Movie" section of this book). The outcry from the community put national focus on the preponderance of negative stereotypical images of Hispanics in the media, and small but significant changes began to take place.

Movies made for television that deal with Hispanic characters have been relatively few compared with the total number made each year. Now, after nearly thirty years, the television movie has become a staple of network programming. All three networks and several cable networks such as Lifetime, USA, Showtime and HBO produce an average of 150 made-for-television movies a year.

Probably the most noteworthy television movies featuring Hispanics are those that have been produced by Hispanic producer Antonio Calderon for NBC, including *The Deadly Tower* (1975) and *Three Hundred Miles for Stephanie* (1981). Except for the two *Drug Wars* miniseries (1990 and 1992), there still has not been even one miniseries devoted exclusively to the Hispanic American experience. Meanwhile, there have been several African American-oriented miniseries (e.g., *Roots* [1977], *The Autobiography of Miss Jane Pittman* [1974], etc.,) and a number of movies-of-the-week about the Asian American experience (e.g., *Farewell to Manzanar* [1976], *Kung Fu* [1972], *Kung Fu: The Legend Continues* [1992]).

Hispanics continue to work in roles not perceived to be Hispanic, such as Joe Santos as Private Investigator Jim Rockford's cop buddy in *The Rockford Files* (1974-80) opposite James Garner; Lynda Carter in *Wonder Woman* (1976-79); Catherine Bach as Daisy on *The Dukes of Hazzard* (1979-85); and, most noticeably, Martin Sheen as the President of the United States in *The West Wing* (1999-). Ricardo Montalban played a man of unspecified origin, the mysterious Mr. Roarke, on *Fantasy Island* (1978-84). Montalban has contributed to the television image of Hispanics as glamorous with his panache, style and demeanor which contributed to such roles as multimillionaire playboy Zach Powers on *The Colbys* (1985-87), a spin-off of *Dynasty* (1981-89).

He won an Emmy Award for his portrayal of a Native American Cheyenne chief in the miniseries *How the West Was Won* (1978) and found lasting against-type fame towards the end of his career as the genius arch-villain Khan in the movie *Star Trek: The Wrath of Khan* (1982), reprising a role he had originally created on television in the 1960s for the original *Star Trek* series.

Rita Moreno won an Emmy Award for her portrayal of a Polish hooker on an episode of *The Rockford Files*. Child actor Brandon Cruz played the role of Eddie in the popular but short-lived series *The Courtship of Eddie's Father* (1969-72), opposite Bill Bixby as a single father. Alfonso Ribeiro, who came to television from Broadway as a child dance star, is a Dominican American and has played African American characters in such series as *Silver Spoons* (1982-87) and *The Fresh Prince of Bel Air* (1990-96).

Enrique Castillo, a young Mexican American actor, guest starred on an episode of *The Waltons* (1972-81) as World War II hero Sergeant Eddie Ramirez, who has a brief affair with Mary Ellen when he brings home her deceased husband's Medal of Valor.

Tour of Duty (1987-90) was the only show to consistently recognize Hispanic American involvement in the nation's armed conflicts—in this case, Vietnam—through the character of New York Puerto Rican Ruiz.

Ricardo Montalban as the elusive Mr. Roarke on *Fantasy Island*.

As mentioned earlier, Hispanic actors had guest spots on shows that briefly mentioned Hispanic American participation, from the World War II shows *Combat!* (1962-67) and *The Gallant Men* (1962-63), to the Korean War setting of *M*A*S*H* (1972-83), to the Vietnam-era *China Beach* (1966-91).

On daytime television, A Martinez drew a huge following as Cruz Castillo on the soap opera *Santa Barbara* (1984-92). He won a 1990 Daytime Emmy Award as Best Actor in a Drama Series, and Henry Darrow won a Daytime Emmy Award for Best Supporting Actor in his role as Castillo's father.

Geraldo Rivera, an award-winning, high-profile broadcast journalist, national television talk show host and producer, has contributed to a positive image of Hispanics in the United States media for nearly thirty years.

Notable behind-the-scenes people who are Hispanic American include Claudio Guzman, best known as the producer and director of the *I Dream of Jeannie* (1965-70) comedy series; Lalo Schifrin, the jazz pianist and composer of, among many others, the theme for the *Mission: Impossible* (1966-73) series; Jaime Rogers, choreographer and director of many musical specials and episodes of the series *Fame* (1982-87); and Vincent Gutierrez, a writer on Michael Landon's *Little House on the Prairie* (1974-83) and *Highway to Heaven* (1984-89) series.

One of the most interesting episodes of *Highway to Heaven*, titled "The People Next Door," was written by Gutierrez. It centered around a Hispanic doctor who passes himself off as an Anglo in order to get ahead, and the consequences of his living a lie for those closest to him.

The Cosby Show (1984-92) introduced many Hispanic characters in a variety of roles including doctors, nurses, social service assistants, students and even an estranged father. These characters were played by such well-known actors as Sonia Braga, Tony Orlando and Anthony Quinn. An episode with Tony Orlando as a community worker was intended as a series pilot, but the series was not picked up by the network. Tito Puente is heard on the soundtrack of the first several seasons, playing the show's opening theme music.

The sitcom series *227* (1985-90) and the hour family drama *Life Goes On* (1989-93) tried unsuccessfully to introduce Hispanic families to their established series formats. Playwright Jose Rivera co-created the one-season series *Eerie, Indiana* (1991-92) and managed to get it on the air, but it was not picked up for a second season.

Tony Orlando starred in a musical variety show on CBS in the 1970s, and Jose Feliciano starred in several musical specials on NBC at the height of his popularity in the late 1960s and early 1970s. Feliciano also performed the theme song for the series *Chico and the Man* (1974-78).

Dolores Del Rio and Cesar Romero co-hosted a special on Mexico in the mid-1960s, as did Ricardo Montalban, Gilbert Roland, and Janet Blair on the "Mexican Fiesta" special on *The Chevy Show* in 1960. Episodes of the popular series *Madigan* (1972-73) and many of the *Columbo* movies-of-the-week were filmed in Mexico City in the early 1970s with predominantly Latin casts.

For years, episodic television series always seemed to have at least one episode that featured the Anglo series protagonists in a Latin environment, either in the United States or outside of it. *The Fugitive* (1963-67) had Dr. Kimble hide out with some Mexican farm workers; in an episode of the Western series *The Rifleman* (1958-63), a Mexican gunman and his gang took over a town. An episode of *Ironside* (1967-75) reflected 1970s Chicano student activist unrest in the barrios; Buddy Ebsen in *Barnaby Jones* (1973-80) helped an aging Chicano cop involved in illegal activities who is determined to seek revenge on his son's murderer. On *Medical Center* (1969-76), the doctors faced a Mexican medicine man played by Gilbert Roland. Most recently, *Beverly Hills, 90210* (1990-2000) featured an episode in which a Mexican American teenager shows up at Beverly Hills High. As it turns out, she has left the confines of her Pomona home for East Los Angeles because she is in a witness protection program. She attracts the amorous attention of one of the Anglo boys in a mature and sensitively written cross-cultural love affair.

By the 1980s and into the 1990s, while the number of Hispanic characters seemed to diminish (with a few notable exceptions), Hispanic actors are paradoxically being seen in more mainstream and positive leading roles. Ironically, at the same time the number of Latino actors and actresses in supporting roles has diminished. Good examples of Hispanic actors in leading roles, as mentioned earlier, are Jimmy Smits in his Emmy Award-winning portrayals of lawyer Victor Sifuentes on *L.A. Law* and later *NYPD Blue* Detective Bobby Simone; Edward James Olmos, who also won an Emmy Award for his portrayal of the sullen no-nonsense Lieutenant Castillo on the trend setting *Miami Vice* (1984-89); Jon Seda, as a detective in the highly praised *Homicide: Life on the Street* (1993-99); Hector Elizondo as hospital Chief-of-Staff Dr. Phillip Watters in *Chicago Hope*; Martin Sheen as the President of the United States in *The West Wing*; and Cheech Marin in *Nash Bridges* (1996-). Meanwhile, Robert Beltran and Roxann Dawson became the first Latinos to go where no one has gone before, on the science fiction series *Star Trek: Voyager* (1995-99). Leonor Varela played one of the most powerful and beautiful women in history as *Cleopatra* (1999) in the ABC miniseries and John Leguizamo won an Emmy Award when HBO aired his one man show, *Freak* (1999).

Perhaps most cutting edge of all, although not particularly noticed by the critics, was *Law & Order* (1990-) creator Dick Wolf's hip-hop police drama *New York Undercover* (1994-98) on the fledgling Fox network, which featured Latino Michael DeLorenzo as Eddie Torres and African American Malik Yoba as his partner. The show also featured Lauren Velez as Latina detective Nina Morena, and Jose Perez as Torres' estranged formerly drug-addicted musician father, now suffering from AIDS. The show made an impact with the urban youth culture it sought to portray, and brought strong, well realized Puerto Rican characters to television.

When ABC, CBS, NBC and Fox announced their Fall 1999 lineup there were no minorities in leading roles in their new programs, and organizations representing Latinos, Asian Americans, African Americans and Native Americans united. In response, in September, 1999 sixteen minority civil rights and arts groups became united under an umbrella organization, and called for a "Brownout" of the four major networks.

The combined effects of a new umbrella lobby group and sympathetic news reports caused the networks to respond by adding minority characters in many of the new fall series, though in minor roles. It at least created a presence and work for a number of artists.

Desi Arnaz hit the airwaves in 1951, and over fifty years later, there is still not one regular network series featuring a Hispanic American leading character or one revolving around a Hispanic family, despite the fact that the Hispanic population in the United states is estimated to be over 30 million (a population equal to that of the whole of Canada) and growing.

In the following section, entries are listed alphabetically, with general credits and information for that could be considered major Hispanic oriented prime time network and cable television series. Also included are comments, credits and information on prime time network and cable miniseries, made-for-television movies and specials that reflect the Hispanic experience. Hispanic performers have played non-Hispanic roles on episodic series television, but they are not listed. Some have been mentioned already in this introduction (e.g., Lynda Carter in *Wonder Woman*, Martin Sheen's several portrayals of John F. Kennedy and other roles, and Catherine Bach on *The Dukes of Hazzard* as Daisy) There are also no listings for individual episodes of series that from time to time featured Hispanic themed story lines or guest characters.

Hispanic Americans on American Network Television

This section focuses on Hispanic American images and talent as presented on the American television networks from 1951 through 2000: the American Broadcasting Company (ABC), the Columbia Broadcasting System (CBS), the National Broadcasting Company (NBC), Fox Broadcasting Company (FOX), The Warner Bros. Channel (WB) and the United Paramount Network (UPN). From 1949 to 1956 there was a fourth, small-scale national television network in operation called the Dumont Network. Programming from cable television is also presented, including HBO, TNT and Showtime, as well as from the non-commercial Public Broadcasting System (PBS).

TV Series

Air America (1998 Syndicated)
Cast: Lorenzo Lamas

Lorenzo Lamas plays a government agent who runs a private air service in a Central American country similar to Costa Rica.

A.E.S. Hudson Street (1978 ABC)
Cast: Gregory Sierra, Rosana De Soto

In this short-lived half-hour situation comedy, Sierra plays Dr. Ralph Menzies, who works in an emergency ward in a New York hospital on Lower East Side.

A.K.A. Pablo (1984 ABC)
Cast: Paul Rodriguez, Katy Jurado, Hector Elizondo, Maria Richwine

A struggling young comedian's chance to star in his own television series thrills his large Mexican American family but provokes a dramatic confrontation with his proud father, who disapproves of his son's lifestyle.

This half-hour situation comedy, created by Norman Lear and Rick Mitz, reflected every stereotype in the book with its story of a thirteen-member Hispanic family in a single household. The show was created to showcase stand-up comedian Paul Rodriguez, who was discovered by Lear. It was not on the air long, but did mange to introduce many Hispanic performers. Actor Hector Elizondo made his television directorial debut with an episode of the series.

Acapulco (1961 NBC)
Cast: Ralph Taeger, James Coburn, Telly Savalas

This half-hour show was broadcast for only four weeks. Two veterans of the Korean War take on the job of protecting a crime-busting attorney, now residing in sunny Acapulco. This is very similar to the later hit, *Magnum P.I.* (1980-88).

The Addams Family (1964-66 ABC)
Cast: Carolyn Jones, John Astin, Jackie Coogan

Based on the wickedly dark-humored Charles Addams cartoons that have been published by *The New Yorker* magazine since the 1930s. The show was fashioned by creator and executive producer David Levy into a bizarre and outlandish but lovable family sitcom. John Astin plays Gomez Addams, the darkly romantic swashbuckler with a Hispanic name. In 1991, the characters were reworked into a hit theatrical movie, *The Addams Family*, with Raul Julia as Gomez (*see* Movie listings).

The Adventures of Kit Carson (1951-55 syndicated)
Cast: Bill Williams, Don "El Toro" ("The Bull") Diamond

The Brooklyn-born Don Diamond played Kit's Mexican sidekick.

All in the Family (1971-70 CBS)
Cast: Carroll O'Connor, Jean Stapleton, Rob Reiner, Sally Struthers

All in the Family, developed by Norman Lear from scriptwriter Johnny Speight's successful British comedy *Till Death Do Us Part* (1966-74), changed the course of television history with its harsh and merciless look at a working-class bigot named Archie Bunker (O'Connor). Archie derides every minority group and says aloud what most other bigots only thought about negative ethnic stereotypes. In the 1976-1977 season Archie was temporarily laid off from his job, and the Bunkers are forced to take in a Puerto Rican boarder, Teresa Betancourt, played by Liz Torres. When the show changed format to *Archie Bunker's Place* (1979-1980), following the departure of Archie's long-suffering wife, Edith (Stapleton), Abraham Alvarez joined the cast as the Puerto Rican busboy, Jose.

America's Funniest Home Videos (1990- ABC)
In 1998, Daisy Fuentes became the host of the popular series which features home videos sent in by viewers across the country.

Amigo (1959 MGM-TV)
Cast: Gilbert Roland

This pilot film stars Gilbert Roland as police detective Johnny Domingo, who fights crime in the El Paso-Juarez border area.

The A-Team (1983-87 NBC)
Cast: George Peppard, Dirk Benedict, Mr. T., Dwight Schultz

A one-hour adventure series, created by Frank Lupo and Stephen J. Cannell, and filled with action, explosions and near-death escapes. Hannibal Smith and three of his buddies have all escaped from a military prison shortly before the end of the Vietnam War. Now back in the United States under assumed identities, they have formed the A-Team and will take on any mission, anywhere, for a price. In its last season, Eddie Velez joined the cast as Frankie Santana, a demolitions expert.

At Ease (1983 ABC)
Cast: David Naughton, Jimmie Walker, John Vargas

This peacetime Army service comedy in which John Vargas plays Cardinel, was on for only a few months.

Baywatch (1987- syndicated)

Cast: David Hasselhoff, Pamela Anderson, Yasmine Bleeth

The most popular syndicated show in the world, the stories revolve around the lives, loves and adventures of a group of lifeguards in Santa Monica, California. Jose Solano joined the cast of the series as lifeguard Manny Gutierrez for two seasons in 1996.

B.L. Stryker (1989-90 ABC)

Cast: Burt Reynolds, Rita Moreno, Ossie Davis

This two-hour-per-episode series features a private eye, now retired from the New Orleans Police Department, who lives on a houseboat in Palm Beach, Florida. Rita Moreno appears as Stryker's outrageous ex-wife, Kimberly Baskin.

Bakersfield P.D. (1993 FOX)

Cast: Giancarlo Esposito, Brian Doyle-Murray, Tony Plana, Jack Hallet, Chris Mulkey, Ron Eldard

This series revolves around the members of the Bakersfield, California, Police Department and features Tony Plana as Officer Luke Ramirez.

Barney Miller (1975-82 ABC)

Cast: Hal Linden, Jack Soo, Ron Glass, Abe Vigoda

Linden plays Barney Miller, the precinct captain, in this long-running half-hour ensemble comedy set in a New York City police station. Gregory Sierra is featured as Chamo, a Puerto Rican detective. The series was created by Danny Arnold and Theodore J. Flicker.

Bay City Blues (1983 NBC)

Cast: Michael Nouri, Bernie Casey, Dennis Franz

This one-hour series from Steven Bochco, the creator of *Hill Street Blues* (1981-87), is about the ups and downs of a minor league baseball team. It aired for only two months (October and November) before being canceled by the network. Marco Rodriguez and Eddie Velez are featured as members of the team.

Berenger's (1985 NBC)

Cast: Sam Wanamaker, Ben Murphy

This ensemble comedy is set in a big-city department store. Eddie Velez plays Julio Morales, a clothing designer.

The Bill Dana Show (1963-65 NBC)

Cast: Bill Dana

Bill Dana's comedic characterization of Jose Jimenez was a cross between Chaplin and Cantinflas, an immigrant in search of the American Dream. In this series he was a bellhop at a luxury hotel.

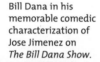

Bill Dana in his memorable comedic characterization of Jose Jimenez on *The Bill Dana Show.*

Jose Jimenez was born out of a joke on a skit Bill Dana wrote for *The Steve Allen Show* (1956-61). He chose the name Jose Jimenez because the "J" sound would emphasize a joke in the skit, in which a Latin American is teaching a class at a Santa Claus school for and mistakes the "Ho, Ho, Ho," for "Jo, Jo, Jo," as it would be said in Spanish. Dana had a good ear for dialect and was asked to play the character himself. The reaction to the character as played by Dana was phenomenal. Because Dana was a writer, and had not been previously seen on television, many thought he really was Jose Jimenez.

According to Bill Dana, "There were two Jose Jimenez characterizations that evolved. The first one is the Walter Mitty-like character who was the astronaut in the album recordings that sold over a million copies, both album and single. The second is the character on *The Danny Thomas Show* (1957-63) who was the bumbling doorman and elevator operator who was more a real person. A sweet guy trying to assimilate into American society. He was a unique non-stereotypical Latin portrayal, for up to that time Hispanics were portrayed as a Cha Cha, a bandido, or a switchblade-wielding youth."

Jose Jimenez is a Latin American, but he was purposely never identified with a particular nationality. Hispanic Americans assumed he was Puerto Rican, Cuban, or Mexican American and everyone thought of him as one of their own.

After *The Danny Thomas Show*, Jose Jimenez was given his own show, called *The Bill Dana Show*, of which forty-two episodes were produced. The series ran for a year and a half beginning in the fall of 1963. Jose Jimenez also headlined several television specials. The character was caught in the political crossfire of the civil rights movement in the mid-1960s, during which Latino political activists found the character offensive in light of the political realities of the times and the more positive assimilated vein in which they wished to be perceived. Advertisers shied away from Dana's Jose Jimenez character, and Dana went on to write and produce the television series *Get Smart* (1965-70). The character still remains a favorite of audiences to this day, and Dana occasionally brings him back for nightclub engagements and on award and variety shows.

The Brothers Garcia (2000 Nickelodeon)
Cast: Ada Maris, Jeffrey Licon, Alvin Alvarez, Carlos LaCamara, Bobby Gonzalez, Vanesa Leza Pitynski

The Brothers Garcia follows the lives of three energetic young brothers who joke and quarrel their way through adventure and mishap, as they grow up in a Latino household in San Antonio, Texas. John Leguizamo provides the voice of the narrator. Jeff Valdez is the executive producer.

The cast of *The Brothers Garcia* includes Ada Maris and Carlos La Camara as the parents, and Jeffrey Licon, Alvin Alvarez, Bobby Gonzalez and Veneza Leza Pitynski as their children.

Cade's County (1971-72 CBS)

Cast: Glenn Ford, Victor Campos

This series features Ford as contemporary New Mexico sheriff Sam Cade and Victor Campos as his deputy, Rudy Davillo.

Carrascolendas (1972-77 PBS)

Cast: Mike Gomez, Pete Leal

This bilingual series was aimed at Spanish-speaking children, grades K-2, to help them develop an increased pride in their Spanish heritage and foster a better understanding of the English language.

Cassie and Company (1982 NBC)

Cast: Angie Dickinson

Angie Dickinson stars as Cassie Holland, a private investigator who takes over an existing detective agency. A Martinez played Benny Silva, a streetwise fellow who runs a nearby gym. The series ran from January until August.

Hector Elizondo (second from right) is part of the ensemble cast of the TV series *Chicago Hope*.

Checking In (1981 CBS)

Cast: Marla Gibbs, Liz Torres

In this half-hour situation comedy, Marla Gibbs reprises her popular role as Florence Johnston. In this spin-off from *The Jeffersons* (1975-85), itself a spin-off from *All in the Family* (1971-79), Gibbs plays the executive house-keeper at a posh New York hotel. Liz Torres plays her efficient assistant Elena, who is happy to remain an assistant as long as the job leaves her free to attend to the needs of her young son. The show aired only three weeks before being canceled.

The Cheech Show (1988 NBC)

Cast: Cheech Marin, Jackée

Marin developed and stars in this pilot, which did not make it to series but aired as a one-time comedy/variety special.

Chicago Hope (1994-2000 CBS)

Cast: Hector Elizondo, Christine Lahti, Mandy Patinkin, Rocky Carroll

Hector Elizondo won an Emmy Award for Outstanding Supporting Actor in a Drama Series for his role as Dr. Phillip Watters, the hospital's Chief-of-Staff. As such, he is blessed with a talented but troubled team of medical professionals. This is a one-hour drama from David E. Kelley Productions.

Chico and the Man (1974-78 NBC)

Cast: Freddie Prinze, Jack Albertson, Scatman Crothers

This half-hour situation comedy, created by James Komack and starring Freddie Prinze and Jack Albertson, was really another variation of the Archie Bunker-type sitcom. A Chicano street kid in East Los Angeles finds employment working in a garage run by a bigoted old Anglo man. The comedy revolved around the stereotyped impressions of the many ethnic groups that make up the United States. Being half-Puerto Rican and half-Hungarian, Prinze made his ethnicity a focus of his routines. Albertson, a well-known stage actor and vaudevillian, made a perfect match for the spunky streetwise kid as Ed, the salty old garage owner. The mixing of the old and the new comedy styles proved so popular that the show was an immediate hit.

Prinze was most definitely a Hispanic American figure. He was not an immigrant and did not speak English with an accent, except as an exaggeration to make a point. He was an American, and he made Americans laugh at themselves.

There was a small backlash to the series when Chicano and Mexican American groups protested Prinze's portrayal of a Chicano. Prinze's character was that of a Mexican American raised in Los Angeles, but he came across as a New York Puerto Rican, which in fact he was. He was not yet a skilled enough actor or performer to put over the subtleties of characterization needed to make Chico a believable, ethnically correct portrayal. Audiences never seemed to mind or know any better, but the Chicano groups felt they were being misrepresented.

Prinze's meteoric rise as a superstar ended tragically in suicide in 1977. The show continued after his death with a young street urchin, played by Gabriel Melgar, replacing Prinze's Chico character. But the memory of Prinze was too big a void to fill. Several Hispanic American character actors were featured on the show, including Danny Nunez, Alma Beltran, Danny Mora and Tina Menard, with Charo in the final season.

CHiPs (1977-83 NBC)

Cast: Erik Estrada, Larry Wilcox

This series followed the adventures of two young California Highway Patrol motorcycle officers who patrol the speeding highways. Estrada's cocky streetwise portrayal of Frank "Ponch" Poncherello is one of the best and most positive portrayals of Hispanic Americans on television to that time.

Ponch is in the mainstream of American society and life. He is young, good-looking and very American. Very little mention is made of his Hispanic heritage. He is a fantasy character surrounded by fast vehicles, adventure and beautiful women. He is also a law enforcement officer dedicated to helping people and as such a positive role model.

On August 6, 1979, Estrada was injured in a motorcycle accident during the filming of the show's third season premiere episode. His injury was used on the show, and a stuntman re-created the motorcycle accident for the cameras. Rick Rosner created the popular MGM-TV series.

The Cisco Kid (1950-56 syndicated)
See "Zorro & The Cisco Kid" listings.

City (1990 CBS)
Cast: Valerie Harper

In this short-lived half-hour situation comedy, an energetic city manager (Harper) juggles the chaos of City Hall with her life as a single mother. Liz Torres and LuAnne Ponce appear as series regulars.

Common Law (ABC 1997)
Cast: Greg Giraldo, Gregory Sierra

A half-hour situation comedy about a Harvard Law school graduate who works at a prestigious New York law firm.

Condo (1983 ABC)
Cast: Luis Avalos, McLean Stevenson, Yvonne Wilder, Julie Carmen, James Victor

This half-hour situation comedy focuses on an upwardly mobile Hispanic American family living next door to a WASP family in a new condominium complex. There are constant comedic clashes based on racial prejudice and cultural differences between the two families. The head of the Hispanic family is Jesse Rodriguez (Avalos) and the head of the WASP family is James Kirkridge (Stevenson). Yvonne Wilder, who plays Mrs. Rodriguez, was one of the dancers in the film version of *West Side Story* (1961), under the name Yvonne Othon. With the aid of make-up, forty-three-year-old actor James Victor memorably and effectively plays a seventy-year-old grandfather. John Rich directed the original teleplay, which was created and written by Sheldon Bull.

The Cowboys (1974 ABC)
Cast: Jim Davis, Diana Douglas

Based on the hit John Wayne film of the same name, seven homeless boys go to work on a ranch run by a widower. This show features many of the film's young actors, including Clay O'Brian, Robert Carradine and A Martinez as Cimarron, a Mexican American youth.

CPO Sharkey (1976-78 NBC)
Cast: Don Rickles, Harrison Page

This half-hour comedy series stars Don Rickles as Naval Chief Petty Officer Sharkey, and Richard Beauchamp plays Rodriguez.

Crime and Punishment (1993 NBC)

Cast: Rachel Ticotin, Jon Tenney

A one-hour limited-run series focusing on the professional and personal lives of Los Angeles Police Detectives Ken O'Donnell (Tenney) and Annette Rey (Ticotin). Rey is a single parent raising a teenage daughter. This pairing of an Anglo man and a Hispanic woman on a series as equals, and showing them as positive members of law enforcement, was a major step toward more varied and rounded portrayals of Hispanics on television.

Crisis Center (1997 NBC)

Cast: Kellie Martin, Matt Roth, Nia Peeples, Dana Ashbrook,
Clifton Gonzalez Gonzalez

A riveting one-hour drama set in a San Francisco Assistance Center features Clifton Gonzalez Gonzalez as Counselor Nando Taylor. This was a short-lived mid-season replacement series.

The D.A. (1971-72 NBC)

Cast: Robert Conrad, Harry Morgan, Ned Romero

This short-lived half-hour courtroom drama series features Ned Romero as investigator Bob Ramirez.

Dangerous Minds (1997 ABC)

Cast: Annie Potts, Tamal Jones, Michael Jace, Jenny Gago,
Greg Serrano, Maria Costa

A one-hour drama series based on the hit 1995 feature film of the same name, written by Ron Bass. *Dangerous Minds* is the story of Louanne Johnson (Potts) an ex-marine who comes to teach English to the tough and troubled students in a special high school program. Jenny Gago is featured as the school's principal, Mrs. Bardales, and among the students are Gusmaro Lopez (Serano), who fancies himself a Casanova, and Blanca Guerrero (Costa), a student more interested in her wardrobe than what is going on in the classroom.

Dallas (1978-91 CBS)

Cast: Larry Hagman, Patrick Duffy, Victoria Principal, Linda Gray,
Barbara Bel Geddes, Charlene Tilton, Jim Davis

Dallas premiered on April 2, 1978, and evolved into an American institution, chronicling the personal and professional lives of the wealthy Ewing family and the South Fork ranch in Texas, centering on the battles between the ruthless J.R. Ewing (Hagman) and his brother, the beloved Bobby Ewing (Duffy). Victoria Principal, in a non-Hispanic role, plays Pamela Ewing, an outsider and the straight-laced, loving wife of Bobby. The popularity of *Dallas* transcended domestic appeal; the show was an international sensation in the more than fifty-six countries in which it aired. The show brought international recognition, fame and wealth to all the regular cast members. After thirteen seasons and a total of 356 filmed episodes, its run ended in 1991. Well-known Hispanic guest stars who appeared on the show over the course of its run include Barbara Carrera, Mel Ferrer and Henry Darrow.

Dan August (1970-71 ABC)

Cast: Burt Reynolds, Ned Romero

Produced by Quinn Martin, this hour-long police action show stars Burt Reynolds as Police Detective Dan August. Ned Romero appears as his partner, Detective Sergeant Joe Rivera. The show is set in the fictional city of Santa Luisa, California,

The Danny Thomas Show (1953-57 ABC; 1957-64 CBS)

Cast: Danny Thomas, Marjorie Lord

In 1960, Bill Dana's character Jose Jimenez, introduced in 1959 on *The Steve Allen Show* (1956-61), was further expanded and joined the cast of *The Danny Thomas Show* (originally known as *Make Room for Daddy*) as a bumbling doorman and elevator operator. Jimenez is a Latin American who speaks very little English and meets any situation coolly and with the now legendary line, "My name, Jose Jimenez." The Jose Jimenez character was so popular that he was spun off into his own series (*The Bill Dana Show* [1963-65]) and television specials.

DEA—Drug Enforcement Agency (1991 FOX)

Cast: Jenny Gago, Tom Mason, Byron Keith Minns, Chris Stanley, David Wohl

Jenny Gago plays Teresa Robles—one of five United States Drug Enforcement Agency officers in the war against drugs—in this violent, reality-inspired and short-lived one-hour action series. Pepe Serna has a recurring role as a bodyguard to the daughter of a drug kingpin. John Vargas, Miguel Sandoval and Ron Henriquez are also featured. . Set in the United States and South America, the show was created by Richard Dilello.

Disney Presents the 100 Lives of Black Jack Savage (1991 NBC)

Cast: Daniel Hugh-Kelly, Steven Williams, Bert Rosario

In this hour-long fantasy/adventure/comedy series, Wall Street wizard Barry Tarberry (Hugh-Kelly), a fugitive billionaire, flees to the Caribbean island of San Pietro, where he sublets an ancient castle. He gets a ghostly roommate in the bargain: Black Jack Savage, a dastardly seventeenth-century pirate who haunts the castle. Bert Rosario played the corrupt island governor General Abe Vasquez.

Doctors' Hospital (1975-76 NBC)
Cast: George Peppard

In this hour-long medical series, George Peppard stars a neurosurgeon and Victor Campos is featured as one of the doctors.

Dr. Quinn: Medicine Woman (1991-1998 CBS)
Cast: Jane Seymour, Joe Lando, Chad Allen, Orson Bean, Jonelle Allen

Dr. Michaela Quinn (Seymour), a physician from Boston, faces the personal and professional trials of being a female doctor in the Colorado Springs of the 1870s.

In the sixth season, Alex Meneses joined the cast as schoolteacher Teresa Morales. When she agrees to marry an Anglo barber. The idea of intermarriage between a Mexican-American and an Anglo brings about much discussion and dissension among the townspeople.

Dudley (1993 CBS)
Cast: Dudley Moore, Lupe Ontiveros

This six-episode half-hour situation comedy series starred Dudley Moore as a much sought-after piano-playing composer in New York City. Lupe Ontiveros plays Marta, his Spanish-speaking housekeeper.

E/R (1984-85 CBS)
Cast: Elliott Gould

This half-hour sitcom about the staff and patients of a Chicago hospital emergency room featured Luis Avalos as Dr. Thomas Esquivel.

Eisenhower and Lutz (1988 CBS)
Cast: Scott Bakula, Henderson Forsythe, DeLane Matthews

An ambitious young attorney runs a law firm in Palm Springs. Rose Portillo plays Millie Zamora, a harried secretary, in this short-lived half-hour situation comedy series created by eight-time Emmy Award-winner Allan Burns.

The Electric Company (1971-85 PBS)
Cast: Bill Cosby, Rita Moreno, Irene Cara, Morgan Freeman

The Children's Television Workshop designed this series to teach reading skills to children seven to ten years old. It included fast-moving comedy, song and animation sequences, many involving state-of-the-art means of putting print on the screen. Original shows were aired from 1971 through 1977; for the following eight seasons it was seen in repeats. It won six Emmys and a Grammy as well as other major awards.

Empire (1962-63 NBC; 1964 ABC)
Cast: Richard Egan

This modern Western series stars Richard Egan as Jim Redigo, the foreman of a huge cattle ranch in New Mexico. During the 1963 run of the show, Charles Bronson joined the cast as Paul Moreno, a Mexican American ranch hand.

Falcon Crest (1981-90 CBS)
Cast: Jane Wyman, Lorenzo Lamas, Ana Alicia

Created by Earl Hamner, who also created *The Waltons* (1972-81), *Falcon Crest* was the story of a wealthy vineyard family headed by matriarch Angela Channing (Wyman) in the fictional Tuscany Valley of California. A Hispanic family of caretakers, headed by Gus Nunouz, played by Nick Ramus, was dropped after the first season. Through the years the show featured Hispanic performers in both Hispanic and non-Hispanic roles. The show made stars out of series regulars Lorenzo Lamas (son of movie star Fernando Lamas) as Lance Cumson, Angela's grandson; and Ana Alicia as Melissa Agretti, the daughter of a rival vineyard family. Victoria Racimo plays Corene Powers; Apollonia Kotero plays a character called Apollonia; Cesar Romero plays Greek tycoon Peter Stavros; and Julie Carmen plays Romero's daughter Sofia.

During the 1988-1989 season a Hispanic vineyard foreman and his family were reintroduced into the storyline. Pilar Ortega (Kristian Alfonso), the foreman's daughter, and a powerful bank executive, returns home after many years away and finds herself in direct conflict with Angela Channing. Castulo Guerra is Cesar, the patriarch of the Hispanic family; Don Ferro is featured as his son Tommy, and Danny Nucci as his other son, Gabriel.

Fame (1982-83 NBC; 1983-87 syndicated)
Cast: Debbie Allen, Gene Anthony Ray

Based on the hit movie of the some name, the series first aired for one season on NBC and then was picked up for advertiser-supported first-run syndication in 1983. The hour-long dramatic musical series revolves around multi-ethnic students at New York City's High School of the Performing Arts. Coco Hernandez, a talented dance student, is played by Erica Gimpel. From 1984 to 1987, Jesse Borrego appeared as the Mexican American dancer Jesse Velasquez. These characters are an integral part of the storylines, which tried, though sometimes rather unsuccessfully, to reflect their ethnicity. Jaime Rogers choreographed and directed a few episodes.

Family Law (1999- CBS)
Cast: Kathleen Quinlan, Dixie Carter, Julie Warner,
    Christopher McDonald

A one-hour drama series stars Dixie Carter as Randi King, a successful family law attorney who finds herself starting over after a devastating divorce and the hijacking of her practice by her ex-husband.

Cristian de la Fuente portrays Andres Diaz, the handsome young law clerk in Randi's office.

The Family Martinez (1986 CBS)
Cast: Robert Beltran, Daniel Faraldo, Anne Betancourt, Karla Montana

This domestic half-hour comedy show, directed by Oz Scott and produced and written by Tommy Chong (of Cheech and Chong fame), about a contemporary Hispanic family, did not make it onto the network schedule as a series, but its pilot was broadcast as a special. The story involves Hector Martinez (Beltran), a former gang member, now a law school graduate, who moves back home to live with his family.

Fantasy Island (1978-83 ABC)
Cast: Ricardo Montalban, Herve Villechaize

In this one-hour anthology drama series, guests arrived at the tropical island paradise of the mysterious Mr. Roarke (Montalban) and his associate Tattoo (Villechaize) seeking to realize their fantasies.

The series began as a two-hour television movie that drew incredibly high viewer ratings in 1977. Then, another two-hour movie, *Return to Fantasy Island*, earned high ratings as well in January 1978. The series began its very successful run on January 28, 1978.

In an immaculate pressed white suit, Roarke ushers the guests in and out of Fantasy Island, delivering expository speeches between the stories. Many times the fantasies did not quite turn out as expected, but guests always gained valuable insight while on the island, usually helped by Montalban's counsel. Montalban as Roarke embodied elegance and class, playing a man of unspecified origin. The formal figure of Roarke and the lusty, outspoken Tattoo were an odd team that nevertheless worked within the concept of the series.

The network originally wanted Orson Welles for the Mr. Roarke role, but when he was reluctant or unable to commit, producer Aaron Spelling called on Montalban, who was perfectly suited to play the enigmatic Roarke.

Father Knows Best (1954-55 CBS; 1955-58 NBC; 1958-62 CBS; 1962-63 ABC)
Cast: Robert Young, Jane Wyatt

Natividad Vacio occasionally appears as Frank Smith, the Mexican gardener, on this family show in which Young played insurance salesman Jim Anderson.

Flamingo Road (1981-82 NBC)

Cast: Howard Duff, Morgan Fairchild, Mark Harmon

Loosely based on the 1949 Joan Crawford movie of the same name, this one-hour prime time soap opera took place in the steamy fictional Florida city of Truro. The series concerns the pursuit of power and pleasure among wealthy and working class citizens. There are subsidiary Hispanic characters in the form of Cuban refugees. Fernando Allende plays Julio Sanchez and Gina Gallego appears as his sister, Alicia, in plotlines that deal with the Cuban barrio of the city.

The Flying Nun (1967-70 ABC)

Cast: Sally Field, Alejandro Rey

This comedy series, starring Sally Field as Sister Bertrille, takes place in the fictional Convent San Tanco in the hills above San Juan, Puerto Rico. Alejandro Rey stars as swinging playboy Carlos Ramirez, who is constantly befuddled by Bertrille's antics. It was based on the book *The Fifteenth Pelican* by Tere Rios. Shelley Morrison plays Sister Sixto, a nun who mangles the English language to comic effect.

Foley Square (1986 CBS)

Cast: Hector Elizondo

Elizondo, in a refreshing bit of casting in a non-Hispanic role, plays a Jewish deputy district attorney in New York City.

For Love and Honor (1983 NBC)

Cast: Cliff Potts, Yaphet Kotto

This hour-long drama series focuses on the personal and professional lives of Naval Air recruits. Rachel Ticotin portrays Corporal Grace Pavlik.

Fort Figueroa (1988 CBS)

Cast: Pepe Serna, Charly Heard, Evelyn Guerrero

Luis Valdez directed this hour-long pilot for Warner Bros. Television. An Anglo family from the Midwest lose their farm and move to Los Angeles to live in a building that has been left to them by a deceased relative. When they arrive in Los Angeles, they discover that the building is a dilapidated apartment building in the heart of the inner city. Among the building's tenants are a Hispanic family and a Vietnamese family. The Midwestern family moves into the empty apartment and must face the trials and tribulations of learning to live in a multiethnic inner-city community.

Four Corners (1997 CBS)

Cast: Ann-Margret, Sonia Braga,
Kamar de los Reyes

A sweeping saga of two Southwestern ranching families at a crossroads, starring Ann-Margret as Amanda Wyatt and Sonia Braga as her friend Carlota Alvarez. The ambitious series started as a two-hour movie premiere and aired two episodes before being canceled due to low ratings.

Frannie's Turn (1992 CBS)

Cast: Miriam Margolyes, Tomas Milian

This short-lived half-hour situation comedy centers on a middle-aged Brooklyn woman. Tomas Milian plays her Cuban-born husband, Joseph Escobar.

Freak (1998 HBO)

D: Spike Lee
S: John Leguizamo
P: Denis Biggs, David Bar Katz,
John Leguizamo, Robert Morton
Cast: John Leguizamo

This Emmy Award-winning one-man show is a television adaptation of Leguizamo's acclaimed Broadway show. HBO has aired two previous Leguizamo shows: *Mambo Mouth* (1991) and *Spic-O-Rama* (1993), both to tremendous audience and critical acclaim.

Ann-Margret (left) and
Sonia Braga (right) in the
short-lived CBS series
Four Corners.

Freebie and the Bean (1980-81 CBS)

Cast: Hector Elizondo, Tom Mason

This one-hour crime/comedy/drama is based on the motion picture of the same name. The series starred Elizondo as Dan "The Bean" Delgado and Mason as Tim "Freebie" Walker.

From Here to Eternity (1979-80 NBC)

Cast: Barbara Hershey, William Devane, Will Sampson

This hour-long short-lived series began as a successful television miniseries, which was based on the classic 1953 Columbia Pictures movie, which was in turn adapted from the James Jones novel of the same name. The storyline follows the lives of several members of the armed forces in Hawaii in the days before the attack on Pearl Harbor. Rocky Echevarria, who later changed his name to Steven Bauer, plays Private First Class Ignacio Carmona.

FX: The Series (1996-1998 Syndicated)
Cast: Cameron Daddo, Christina Cox, Jacqueline Torres

The show, which offers viewers an inside look at the high-tech world of motion picture special effects combined with compelling characters and intriguing storylines. Cox plays Angie Ramirez, Rollie's cyber savvy assistant. In the second season, Jacqueline Torres joined the cast as Mira Sanchez, a hard-edged and streetwise detective who gets results.

Gavilan (1982-83 NBC)
Cast: Robert Urich, Fernando Lamas

This hour-long action adventure series features Fernando Lamas in the role of Caesar de Portago in the first episodes. Lamas became ill and passed away soon after the series began, and Patrick Macnee took over in a similar role.

Going to Extremes (1992-93 ABC)
Cast: Erika Alexander, June Chadwick, Roy Dotrice, Camilo Gallardo

This one-hour drama series about young Americans attending medical school on a fictional West Indian island. Camilo Gallardo plays medical student Kim Selby, from an old and prominent Chilean family, though Gallardo was born in Miami.

The Golden Palace (1992-93 CBS)
Cast: Betty White, Rue McClanahan, Estelle Getty, Cheech Marin

America's favorite Golden Girls—Rose Nylund (White), Blanche Devereaux (McClanahan) and Sophia Petrillo (Getty)—purchase an Art Deco-style Miami hotel and set up housekeeping. The three continue the characters they portrayed on the seven-year hit *The Golden Girls* (1985-92), and for which they each won Emmy Awards. Cheech Marin plays Chuy Castillos, a recently divorced chef from East Los Angeles who finds his kitchen at the mercy of the tyrannical Sophia.

Grand Slam (1990 CBS)
Cast: John Schneider, Paul Rodriguez

An hour-long action adventure series about two rival bounty hunters in San Diego who decide to make a go of it together. The series premiered after the 1990 Super Bowl, but the ratings never lived up to its promise and it was quickly canceled.

Hangin' with Mr. Cooper (1992- ABC)
Cast: Mark Curry, Dawnn Lewis, Holly Robinson

Mark Cooper (Curry) is a teacher at a local high school who shares a house with two young women in this half-hour situation comedy created by Jeff Franklin. Luis Avalos has a recurring role as Rivera, the school principal.

Harry O (1974-76 ABC)

Cast: David Janssen, Henry Darrow

This hour-long detective series, created by Howard Rodman and executive produced by Jerry Thorpe, stars David Janssen as a former police detective who has left the force to become a private eye. Henry Darrow co-stars as Lieutenant Manny Quinlan for the show's first season. For the second season, the show switched locales from San Diego to Los Angeles, and his character was killed off.

Harts of the West (1993 CBS)

Cast: Beau Bridges, Lloyd Bridges

A contemporary hour-long series about a man with a mid-life crisis who moves his family from the East to settle on a ranch near a small town in Nevada. Talisa Soto is a series regular as a Native American girl.

The Hat Squad (1992 ABC)

Cast: Nestor Serrano

In this series Nestor Serrano plays Rafael Martinez, the Latino member of a special crime unit consisting of three young men and their foster father, who is also their commanding officer. All the boys have lost their parents to violence and have vowed to fight crime.

Hawkeye (1997 Syndicated)

Cast: Lee Horsley, Lynda Carter,
   Rodney A. Grant

A one-hour series set against the backdrop of the French and Indian Wars. Legendary woodsman Hawkeye (Horsley) and Virginia gentlewoman Elizabeth Shields (Carter) face the adventure, hardship and beauty of frontier life together as they search for Elizabeth's kidnapped husband.

Head of the Class (1986-91 ABC)

Cast: Howard Hesseman

In this half-hour situation comedy, created by Michael Elias and Rich Eustis, Charlie Moore (Hesseman) is a substitute teacher at a New York City high school who has to deal with and motivate bright but unmotivated students. Leslie Bega played the grade-obsessed student Maria Borges from 1986 through 1989, and Michael DeLorenzo played student Alex Torres from 1989 through 1991.

Lynda Carter and Lee Horsley in the historical adventure series *Hawkeye*.

Hernandez, Houston P.D. (1973 NBC)
Cast: Henry Darrow

Darrow starred in this one-hour pilot episode for a possible series. He played Juan Hernandez, a detective with the Houston Police Department.

The High Chaparral (1967-71 NBC)
Cast: Leif Ericson, Cameron Mitchell, Linda Cristal, Frank Silvera, Henry Darrow

This Western adventure series, set in the Arizona Territory of the 1870s, prominently features a Hispanic family alongside an Anglo family. It was created by David Dortort, who also created *Bonanza* (1959-73). Frank Silvera plays the Mexican cattle baron Don Sebastian Montoya with grace, dignity and a ruthlessness that is every bit the equal of his Anglo counterpart, John Cannon (Ericson). Henry Darrow, as Montoya's son, Manolito, is a slightly soiled, less-than-heroic dashing caballero. He captured the television public's imagination with his spirited portrayal that brought him stardom and international recognition. Linda Cristal, already an established film actress, plays Victoria Cannon, Montoya's daughter, who becomes the young wife of John Cannon. The uneasy alliance of the two families seemed symbolically to characterize United States-Mexican relations. Several Hispanic actors are featured on the show in regular roles including Rodolfo Acosta and Roberto Contreras. In its final year Rudy Ramos joined the show as a half-breed, and Gilbert Roland took the role of Montoya's brother when Frank Silvera unexpectedly passed away.

High Incident (1996 ABC)
Cast: David Keith, Cole Hauser, Catherine Kellner, Julio Oscar Mechoso

A one-hour action filled drama series about patrol officers in the suburbs of a California metropolis.

High Mountain Rangers (1988 CBS)
Cast: Robert Conrad

An hour-long action adventure series that focuses on an elite rescue squad in California's High Sierras. Veteran ranger Jesse Hawks (Conrad) leads the young men and women of the rescue squad. Tony Acierto played Ranger Frank Avila.

High Sierra Search and Rescue (1995 NBC)
Cast: Robert Conrad, Dee Wallace Stone

A one-hour adventure series about a civilian mountain rescue team. Ramon Franco plays Enrique Cruz, the town's only schoolteacher, who stands ready at a moment's notice to pack up his gear and respond to the call for trained and dedicated rescuers.

Highcliffe Manor (1979 NBC)

Cast: Shelley Fabares

This comic horror movie spoof show features Luis Avalos as Dr. Sanchez, an evil scientist.

Hill Street Blues (1981-87 NBC)

Cast: Daniel J. Travanti, Bruce Weitz, Michael Conrad, Veronica Hamel, Michael Warren, Betty Thomas, Rene Enriquez, Kiel Martin, Barbara Bosson

Steven Bochco and Michael Kozoll created this much-acclaimed, Emmy Award-winning, long-running, hour-long drama series about the practical, sometimes brutal, and occasionally humorous sides of police work. Set in a decaying section of a large American city, the precinct had one Hispanic officer, Lieutenant Ray Calletano, played by Rene Enriquez, among its large ensemble cast of regulars. His importance as a major character in the show was diffused by the tepid storylines written for him, which gave him little to do and often played off the image of Hispanics as the victims or perpetrators of many crimes.

Through the seven-year run of the series there is a recurring character of a gang leader named Jesus, played by Trinidad Silva, who becomes a social worker and a lawyer by the end of the seventh season. Another recurring character is a troubled youth, Hector Ruiz, played by Panchito Gomez, who is finally jailed after a robbery turns into a hostage situation. Future star Andy Garcia played a small role in the series' premiere episode.

Rene Enriquez (left) as Lt. Calletano and Daniel J. Travanti (right) as Captain Frank Furillo in *Hill Street Blues*.

Home Free (1988 NBC)

Cast: Michael Warren, Trinidad Silva

This hour-long dramatic pilot features a social worker who runs a home for troubled youths. He is assisted by his Mexican American cook, Benny, played by Trinidad Silva.

Homicide: Life on the Streets (1991-1999 NBC)

Cast: Yaphet Kotto, Andre Braugher, Kyle Secor, Reed Diamond

Hailed by television critics across the country, the series recounts the brutality faced daily by detectives on the homicide squad of the Baltimore Police Department. Jon Seda joined the talented cast in the fall of 1997, as Detective Paul Falsone.

Hotel Baltimore (1975 NBC)

Cast: James Cromwell, Richard Masur, Al Freeman, Jr.

This half-hour comedy series is based on the hit off-Broadway play of the 1970s. Jeannie Linero is featured in the cast.

Hotel Malibu (1994 CBS)

Cast: Joanna Cassidy, Cheryl Pollak, John Dye, Pepe Serna,
   Jennifer Lopez

A short-lived series that was a spin-off of another short-lived series, *Second Chances* (1993-94), produced by Lynn Marie Latham and Bernard Lechowick. A contemporary ensemble drama depicting the upstairs/downstairs intrigues of a family-owned luxury hotel on the Southern California coast. Jennifer Lopez plays Melinda Lopez, a young co-ed who works at the hotel. Pepe Serna plays her father, Sal Lopez.

John Leguizamo (center) was both creator and star of Fox's Emmy Award-winning urban comedy/variety sketch series *House of Buggin'*.

House of Buggin' (1994 FOX)

Cast: John Leguizamo, Tami Cubilette,
   Jorje Luis Abreu, Luis Guzman, Yelba Osorio

A half-hour comedy show that is a mix of satirical humor and outrageous sketches featuring characters created by Leguizamo and based on his own experiences. The show has a strong Latino contemporary inner city slant.

Houston Knights (1987-88 CBS)

Cast: Michael Pare, Michael Beck

This hour-long crime drama concerned two police detectives, one from Texas and one from Chicago, who are partnered in Houston, Texas. Efrain Figueroa plays Lieutenant Esteban Gutierrez. The series lasted for only one season.

Hunter (1984-91 NBC)

Cast: Fred Dryer, Stepfanie Kramer

In the 1987 season of this police action drama, created by Frank Lupo, Erik Estrada guest starred on a three-part episode, "City of Passion." His character is Detective Brad Navarro, who joins series lead characters Hunter and McCall in tracking down a serial rapist. Also in the 1987-1988 season, Rudy Ramos appears as a recurring character named Reuben Garcia.

I Had Three Wives (1985 CBS)
Cast: Victor Garber

This hour-long comedy adventure features a charming private detective who is aided by his three ex-wives. Luis Avalos stars as Lieutenant Gomez.

I Love Lucy (1951-57 CBS)
Cast: Lucille Ball, Desi Arnaz, William Frawley, Vivian Vance

This long-running series introduced Ricky Ricardo to the world. As Ricky, Desi Arnaz was the first Hispanic presence to be accepted by mainstream American audiences and networks. The classic series was initially turned down by CBS, even though Lucille Ball had been successful in both movies and radio. She had a hit CBS Radio series called *My Favorite Husband*, which the network wanted to transfer to television. But Ball was interested in starting a family and wanted her real-life husband, Desi Arnaz, to star in the series with her. CBS felt the concept of a redheaded, all-American housewife married to an excitable Cuban bandleader was not one that would appeal to a broad enough segment of the American public. So Desi and Lucy took their series concept and worked out a stage act with the help of comedian Buster Keaton and clown Pepito Perez. The couple performed before live audiences all around the country, and the enthusiastic response proved they were accepted as a show-business husband-and-wife team. Arnaz and Ball financed the pilot episode of the television show themselves. It was produced in March 1951, with Lucy and Desi playing the characters named Lucy and Desi Lopez.

Later, their neighbors, Ethel and Fred Mertz, were added to the show, and the characters were renamed Lucy and Ricky Ricardo. The network and sponsors approved the show, and the first episode aired on October 15, 1951. It was filmed before a live studio audience with three 35mm film cameras capturing the action simultaneously from different angles. The show was then edited together like a film. *I Love Lucy* was an immediate hit and turned television watching into a pop cultural event. Over the course of its six years of original episodes, the show rarely ranked lower than third in the ratings. Arnaz's portrayal of the good-looking, excitable, short-tempered Cuban bandleader who spoke with an accent and rattled off exclamations in Spanish was so well etched that he created an image of the Hispanic American that could almost be regarded as archetypal. The character of Ricky was an exaggerated comedic characterization that grew to a certain extent over the life of the series. In comparison to similar shows and formats of the same era, *I Love Lucy* was somewhat realistic. (On *The Adventures of Ozzie and Harriet* (1952-66), for example, Ozzie was never seen going to work, and the family never had trouble making financial ends meet.) During a 1990 television interview, Lucille Ball said, "We wanted to focus on all the trials and tribulations that most people experience. We didn't want to be a Hollywood couple no one could relate to."

Lucille Ball and Desi Arnaz

Television audiences of the 1950s readily related to the Ricardos' all-too-human circumstances. Hispanics saw a bit of themselves in Arnaz's portrayal of the hardworking husband and father trying to make it in American society. The Spanish and Cuban music that alternated with American popular music on the show gave an understanding and cultural awareness, no matter how superficial, to millions of television viewers. Ricky's difficulty with the English language and his speaking Spanish on the show were for many a source of amusement, but Hispanic Americans well appreciated what became a real, honest and personal bond to them. From time to time, relatives from Cuba and other Spanish-speaking characters appeared on the show.

When the Ricardos were first introduced to the public, they were living in a New York apartment. They then had a baby and moved to the suburbs, and Ricky eventually came to own the nightclub at which he worked. The couple became the incarnation of the 1950s post-World War II American Dream for millions of television viewers.

Behind the scenes, Arnaz was responsible for the development of the multicamera techniques still used today in most filmed or taped situation comedies. Because *I Love Lucy* was filmed, and Arnaz and Ball retained ownership of the programs after the initial CBS runs, they created an industry standard for syndicated reruns. The couple purchased RKO Studios and re-named it Desilu Studios. It was turned into a rental facility and also produced many filmed television series including *The Untouchables* (1959-63) and the original *Star Trek* (1966-69) series. In a 1984 television interview Arnaz said, "*I Love Lucy* is something that happens only once in a lifetime, if you're lucky enough to have it happen at all."

Lucy and Desi are part of American popular culture and a part of our lives, and more than forty years later these shows are still being seen in reruns worldwide and have become fodder for fiction in such books and movies as *The Mambo Kings* (1992).

I Married Dora (1987-88 ABC)
Cast: Elizabeth Peña, Daniel Hugh-Kelly

This half-hour sitcom is about a widowed architect with two children who marries his Central American housekeeper so she will not be deported as an illegal alien.

The Jackie Guerra Show/First Time Out (1995 WB)

Cast: Jackie Guerra, Tracy Vilar, Mia Cottet, Leah Remini, Craig Anton

A half-hour comedy series built around the life of a single Latina and her two roommates as they cope with life in Los Angeles in the '90s.

Jesse (1998-1999 NBC)

Cast: Christina Applegate, Bruno Campos

Bruno Campos plays Diego Vasquez, boyfriend to Christina Applegate's Jesse in this half-hour situation comedy.

The John Larroquette Show (1993-97 NBC)

Cast: John Larroquette, Liz Torres

Torres portrays Mahalia Sanchez, urban bus station manager John Hemingway's (Larroquette's) closest ally. As his streetwise, no-nonsense assistant, she's tough and sarcastic, but her years of experience at the station make her invaluable to Hemingway. In 1995, she was nominated for an Outstanding Actress in a Comedy Series Emmy for her work on the show.

Juarez (1987 ABC)

Cast: Benjamin Bratt, Ada Maris

This one-hour pilot for a series about an El Paso police detective stars Benjamin Bratt. The stories were to concern the border area around El Paso and Juarez, Mexico. The series had an initial six-episode order as a mid-season replacement, but only two episodes were shot. *Juarez* was canceled before it was aired due to creative differences between the producers and the network. No Hispanic writers, producers, or directors were part of the show's creative team, and the scripts prominently featured border stereotypes. The pilot did eventually air as a one-hour special.

Kay O'Brien (1986 CBS)

Cast: Patricia Kalember, Lane Smith

This hour-long hospital drama focuses on a twenty-eight-year-old female second-year surgical resident at a New York City hospital as she strives to excel in the male-dominated world of surgery. Priscilla Lopez plays nurse Rosa Villanueva.

Knight & Daye (1989 NBC)

Cast: Jack Warden

This half-hour four-week summer replacement series features a Hispanic family, the Escobars, most of whom are played by non-Hispanic actors.

Knightwatch (1988-89 ABC)

Cast: Benjamin Bratt, Don Franklin, Ava Haddad, Joshua Cadman

An hour-long series about a dedicated group of young inner-city people—men and women, Hispanic, African American and Anglo—who voluntarily band together to battle the crime sweeping over their city. They are called the Knights, and are led by the founder of Knightwatch, Tony Maldonado (Bratt).

L.A. Law (1986-94 NBC)

Cast: Corbin Bernsen, Jill Eikenberry, Richard Dysart, Susan Dey,
   Susan Ruttan, Michael Tucker, Larry Drake, Jimmy Smits,
   Blair Underwood, Harry Hamlin

This hour-long drama series about a law firm, created by Steven Bochco and Terry Louise Fisher, won fourteen Emmy Awards in its first five years, including Outstanding Drama Series in 1987, 1989, 1990 and 1991. Located in a downtown Los Angeles high-rise building, the partners and associates of McKenzie, Brackman, Chaney and Kuzak constitute a full-service, if chaotic, law firm that wrangles with the mounting contradictions of the contemporary legal system.

The series features an important Hispanic American character in lawyer Victor Sifuentes, played by Jimmy Smits. Sifuentes is a Mexican American who is every bit an equal of the Anglo members of the law firm. He is part of the American mainstream of good education, hard work and perseverance and he is socially responsible. Many of the episodes center around Sifuentes, his court battles and his personal life.

Tomas Milian and Miriam Colon play Sifuentes' parents in one episode; actors such as Tony Plana and Joaquin Martinez appear as guest stars on the show. Jimmy Smits left the series in May 1991 to pursue a career in motion pictures following his leading role in *Old Gringo*, which gave him the chance to work opposite Jane Fonda. Smits had a grueling schedule, working simultaneously on *L.A. Law* and *Old Gringo*, flying back and forth every three weeks between Los Angeles and Mexico to complete production.

Smits won an Emmy Award as Outstanding Supporting Actor in a Continuing Series in 1990 for his work on the series during the 1989-1990 season.

In 1992, A Martinez joined the cast as the eagle-eyed single-parent litigator David Morales.

Law and Order (1989- NBC)

Cast: Jerry Orbach, Benjamin Bratt, S. Epatha Merkerson, Carey Lowell,
   Sam Waterston, Steven Hill

Filmed entirely on location in New York City, this realistic program looks at law and order from a dual perspective. In the first half hour, Detectives Lennie Briscoe (Orbach) and Reynaldo "Rey" Curtis (Bratt) investigate crimes and apprehend law breakers, in the second half hour, the focus shifts to the criminal courts.

Live Shot (1995 UPN)

Cast: Sam Anderson, David Birney, Wanda de Jesus, Hill Harper, Eddie Velez

A fast-paced one-hour ensemble drama focusing on the people and personalities inside and out of the most frenzied dog-eat-dog work environment of all: the television newsroom. Wanda de Jesus portrays investigative reporter and anchor Liz Vega with intelligence and determination. Eddie Velez plays Ricardo Sandoval, an anchor and reporter who has been known to focus more attention on the creases in his expensive trousers than the story he has been assigned to cover.

In a special episode of TV's *Law and Order*, cast members Jerry Orbach (left) and Benjamin Bratt (right) are joined by Richard Belzer and Michael Michele (center), guest starring as their characters on *Homicide: Life on the Streets*.

Love Boat: The Next Wave (1998 UPN)

Cast: Robert Urich, Phil Morris, Joan Severance, Heidi Mark, Corey Parker

Randy Vasquez plays the irrepressible bar manager Paolo Kaire, who can mix a drink to cure just about anything. In one episode, Ricardo Montalban guest stars as Paolo's estranged father.

The Lucie Arnaz Show (1985 CBS)

Cast: Lucie Arnaz

Arnaz (daughter of Desi Arnaz and Lucille Ball) stars in her own half-hour sitcom as Jane Lucas, a psychologist who co-hosts a popular radio talk show in New York.

The Lucille Ball-Desi Arnaz Show [aka: The Lucy-Desi Comedy Hour] (1957-60 CBS)

Cast: Lucille Ball, Desi Arnaz

Thirteen one-hour episodes were produced for this series, which was a continuation of their Lucy and Desi characterizations. Desi Arnaz directed several of the episodes.

Mama Malone (1984 CBS)

Cast: Lila Kaye

This offbeat half-hour comedy series about a cooking show host features Richard Yniguez as Father Jose Silva, a regular character.

The Man and the City (1971-72 ABC)

Cast: Anthony Quinn

In his first foray into series television, Anthony Quinn stars as Thomas Jefferson Alcala, the socially conscious Mexican American mayor of a Southwestern metropolis. The hour-long drama series lasted for only half a season after the initial television movie presentation.

Marblehead Manor (1987-88 syndicated)

Cast: Paxton Whitehead, Linda Thorson, Phillip Morris, Dyana Ortelli

Dyana Ortelli plays the wacky maid, Lupe, in this syndicated situation comedy series, which also features her son Humberto Ortiz as Elvis. It was syndicated in the United States and also aired in England, France, Israel and Spain, where it was known as Casa de Locos. Rob Dames and Bob Fraser were the creators, writers and producers of the series.

Marcus Welby, M.D. (1969-76 ABC)

Cast: Robert Young, James Brolin, Elena Verdugo

In this medical series Elena Verdugo is the all-knowing, wisecracking Nurse Consuelo Lopez who works for Dr. Welby (Young). Entire scripts were written to match Verdugo's comedic and dramatic talent. Dolores Del Rio plays her mother in an episode in which Del Rio was dying of cancer. A love story features Verdugo and guest actor Joseph Campanella, who was suffering from a back ailment. She was twice nominated for an Emmy as Best Supporting Actress in a Continuing Drama Series.

Meet Millie (1952-56 CBS)
Cast: Elena Verdugo

In this half-hour comedy series, Elena Verdugo stars as an all-American girl, Millie Branson, who lives and works as a secretary in Manhattan.

Michael Hayes (1997- CBS)
Cast: David Caruso, Ruben Santiago Hudson

Caruso stars in the title role as the newly appointed acting United States Attorney in New York City. Santiago-Hudson portrays Eddie Diaz, Hayes' dedicated chief investigator.

Miami Vice (1984-89 NBC)
Cast: Don Johnson, Phillip Michael Thomas, Edward James Olmos, Saundra Santiago

Created by Anthony Yerkovich and a creative team headed by executive producer Michael Mann, this was an innovative police drama set in Miami with a 1980s art deco style, integrating MTV-like visuals, editing and music, and a multiracial cast.

Detective Sonny Crockett (Johnson) and Detective Ricardo Tubbs (Thomas) are two flashy vice cops who work in bustling Miami, battling drug dealers from the city's fast-paced boulevards and dimly lit back alleys to Art Deco hotels, mansions and open waterways. The show won four Emmys in 1984-1985, its first season. *Miami Vice* was characterized by the *New York Times* as "aggressively contemporary," hailed by *Newsweek* for its "visual style and audio tone" and "impressionistic fast cut cinematography," and by *USA Today* as a "pop palette, full of visions lovely, complex, surreal."

While the show had some positive role models, it overwhelmingly paraded African Americans and Hispanics as drug dealers, pimps and prostitutes in an exotic, crime-filled city. Many Hispanic actors appear over the length of the show's five-year run, including Tito Goya, Miguel Pinera, Esai Morales, Pepe Serna, Luis Guzman, Rosana De Soto, Lou Diamond Phillips, Daniel Lugo, Francesca Quinn and Alfonso Arau.

Edward James Olmos created the role of the sullen, no-nonsense Lieutenant Martin Castillo. He won an Emmy Award as Best Supporting Actor in a Drama Series as well as a Hollywood Foreign Press Association Golden Globe Award. Olmos also directed an episode of the series called "Bushida," which was one of the highest rated episodes of the series. Saundra Santiago appears as Detective Gina Calabrese, an undercover police officer. Gregory Sierra portrayed Lieutenant Lou

Robert Young (left), Elena Verdugo (center) as Nurse Consuelo and James Brolin (right) in the TV series *Marcus Welby, M.D.*

Rodriguez in the pilot and initial episodes, but his character was killed off and replaced by Olmos' Lieutenant Castillo.

My So Called Life (1994 ABC)
Cast: Bess Armstrong, Claire Danes, Wilson Cruz

Wilson Cruz plays Rickie Vasquez, a sensitive homosexual teen, in this series about the different sides of adolescence in high school.

Nash Bridges (1996- CBS)
Cast: Don Johnson, Cheech Marin, Jaime P. Gomez

Don Johnson stars as Nash Bridges, a San Francisco police inspector and Cheech Marin stars as his wise cracking ex-partner Joe Dominguez. Jaime P. Gomez plays Evan Cortez.

This one-hour police series is filmed entirely on location in San Francisco.

Nasty Boys (1990 NBC)
Cast: Dennis Franz, Benjamin Bratt, Don Franklin

This hour-long action adventure series was inspired by the real-life North Las Vegas "Nasty Boys," a crime-fighting unit whose members protect their anonymity by wearing black ninja-style hoods. Bratt plays Cruz, a maverick undercover cop.

The New Dick Van Dyke Show (1971-74 CBS)
Cast: Dick Van Dyke

In its third and final season the show changed its locale to Los Angeles from Phoenix, Arizona. The season co-starred Chita Rivera as next-door neighbor Connie Richards, Henry Darrow as Alex the stage manager and Carmen Zapata as the maid.

The New Odd Couple (1982-83 ABC)
Cast: Ron Glass, Demond Wilson

In this African American version of the popular Neil Simon play, film and series *The Odd Couple*, Liz Torres plays the role of Maria.

New York Undercover (1994-1997)
Cast: Malik Yoba, Michael DeLorenzo, Patti D'Arbanville, Lauren Velez

A one-hour drama about a squad of young New York City police detectives struggling to clean the streets of criminals while attempting to make sense of their own lives. Set to a contemporary musical beat and filmed in a driving visual style, the series offers a close up look at the lives of many of America's urban youth, dealing with complex issues such as racism, family conflicts, drugs and guns. Coping with the senseless murder of his fiancée, Detective J.C. Williams (Yoba) is an African-

American cop whose faith in people and his job has been pushed to its limits. His partner, Eddie Torres, is a risk-taking Puerto Rican whose emotions sometime cloud his pursuit of justice. Together they've busted deadly drug rings, exposed corruption and gone undercover as garbage men, homeboys, lawyers and drag queens. They were joined in the second season by Detective Nina Moreno (Velez), a street-smart female detective out to prove herself to Torres and Williams. Filmed on location in the streets of New York City, The show has an authentic feel and brings strong Puerto Rican characterizations to television. Jose Perez plays Torres' estranged father who is an ex-drug addict stricken with AIDS.

Nick Freno: Licensed Teacher (1997 WB)
Cast: Mitch Mullany, Stuart Pankin, Charles Cypher, Jonathan Hernandez

Jonathan Hernandez plays a student, Orlando, in this situation comedy set in an elementary school.

Nightingales (1989 NBC)
Cast: Suzanne Pleshette

Roxann Biggs plays a Hispanic nurse, Yolanda Puente, in this short-lived, controversial series about the professional and personal lives of young student nurses.

The Nine Lives of Elfeco Baca (1958-60 NBC)
Cast: Robert Loggia, Robert F. Simon, Nestor Paiva, Rico Alaniz

Walt Disney produced a series of ten color episodes detailing the story of Elfeco Baca, a Spanish American sheriff turned lawyer in the New Mexico Territory of the Old West. Robert Loggia plays Elfeco Baca; the series was directed by Norman Foster and based on his teleplay. James Pratt was the producer.

The show relies on formula Western adventures and is condescending toward its protagonist, with Anglo characters spouting lines like, "You're not going to like this job; you're going after one of your own countrymen," to which Elfeco responds, "A man like that gives our people a bad name."

9 to 5 (1982-83 ABC)
Cast: Rita Moreno, Valerie Curtin, Rachel Dennison

Rita Moreno co-stars as Violet, an office worker, in this half-hour comedy series. She represents a modern Hispanic woman without an accent, a positive role model who is part of the mainstream. Violet is an integral part of the storylines, which revolve around herself and her two co-workers in and out of the office. She is also a single mother with a young son. The series presented a refreshing image change. The show was based on the hit movie of the same name, in which Violet's character was originally non-Hispanic and played by Lily Tomlin. Moreno asked that the character Violet use the maiden name of Fernandez instead of Newstead, given that Violet's husband was deceased.

Nothing Sacred (1997 ABC)

Cast: Devin Anderson, Jose Zuniga

This one-hour long series focuses on the daily activities of an unconventional young priest who is constantly struggling to balance his faith in God with the temptations and troubles of modern day life. Jose Zuniga dons the cloth in his role as J.A. Ortiz.

Jimmy Smits as Bobby Simone and Dennis Franz as Andy Sipowitz in *NYPD Blue*.

Nurses (1991-94 NBC)

Cast: Stephanie Hodge, Arnetia Walker, Mary Jo Keenen, Markus Flanagan, Ada Maris

Susan Harris (*Soap* [1977-81]) created this ensemble situation comedy, which features five nurses—four women and a man—who face their professional lives with lighthearted camaraderie, despite being overworked, underpaid and often unappreciated. It features Gina Cuevas (Maris), the ethical young Central American immigrant who is zealously studying to become an American citizen, and Paco Ortiz (Carlos LaCamara), the orderly with his finger on the pulse of life at the hospital.

NYPD Blue (1993- ABC)

Cast: Dennis Franz, Jimmy Smits, Nick Turturro, James McDaniel, Kim Delaney

A groundbreaking one-hour dramatic series revolving around the professional and personal lives of the men and women of the detective squad of the 15th precinct in New York City.

Jimmy Smits joined the cast of the series in its second season as Detective Bobby Simone. He and his new partner, Andy Sipowicz (Franz) do not always see eye to eye on cases, largely because of their conflicting personalities—Andy is loud and coarse while Bobby is quiet and often introverted—but Simone manages to show Andy what a dogged investigator he is. Simone had an off again, on again affair with fellow Detective Diane Russell (Delaney), but, because she is a recovering alcoholic, the relationship was unstable. Nicholas Turturro plays Puerto Rican detective James Martinez.

Smits remained on the show for four seasons until his character died of a heart ailment at the beginning of the fifth season. The episode in which Bobby Simone died was one of the highest rated episodes of the series.

Ohara (1987-88 ABC)
Cast: Pat Morita, Kevin Conroy, Madge Sinclair

Pat Morita stars in this one-hour crime series as an offbeat Asian American police detective in Los Angeles. The first season features Richard Yniguez as police detective Jesse Guerrera in a regular supporting role. In its second season, Rachel Ticotin is featured as Assistant District Attorney Teresa Storm.

On the Rocks (1975-76 ABC)
Cast: Jose Perez, Buddy Sandler, Hal Williams

This half-hour situation comedy is set in a Southwest prison and aired for one season.

100 Centre Street (1984 ABC)
Cast: Len Cariou, Dee Wallace, J.A. Preston, Lela Ivey, Henry Darrow

This half-hour comedy pilot about life in the judge's chambers shows that it isn't all law and order: Supervising Judge Charles Felt wishes his colleagues would stick to the law and stop complaining about their assignments. His own life becomes disordered when his wife files for divorce. Henry Darrow stars as Judge Ramon Robledo.

One of the Boys (1989 NBC)
Cast: Maria Conchita Alonso, Robert Clohessy

Alonso made her American television debut in this half-hour situation comedy. She stars as Maria, a vivacious Venezuelan immigrant who hopes to gain her share of the American Dream by working as a bookkeeper in an otherwise all-male construction firm. The series lasted for only a few episodes.

Oye Willie (1979 PBS)
Cast: Fernando Lopez, Alfonso Ribeiro

This seven-part half-hour dramatic series is about a twelve-year-old Puerto Rican boy, Willie, and his adventures growing up in New York's Spanish Harlem. The series was filmed on location, and offered the largest concentration, up to that time, of Hispanics in front of and behind the camera. Olivia Perez directed three segments, as did Luis Soto. The executive producer and creator was Lou de Lemos.

Oz (1997- HBO)
Cast: Ernie Hudson, Terry Kinney, Tony Musante, Rita Moreno, Lauren Velez, Kirk Acevedo

The fictional Oswald Maximum Security Prison is the setting for this dramatic series which examines the relationships among the facility's administrators and inmates. Rita Moreno plays nun and counselor Sister Peter Marie, Lauren Velez is the resident doctor and Kirk Acevedo plays an inmate whose father and grandfather also are in Oz.

Passport to Danger (1954-1956 syndicated)
Cast: Cesar Romero

Romero starred in thirty-nine episodes of this weekly half-hour adventure series in which he played Steve McQuinn, a diplomatic courier sent on assignment to different countries.

Phyllis (1975-77 CBS)
Cast: Cloris Leachman

Leachman plays Phyllis and Liz Torres plays Julie Erskine, a photographer, on this series spin-off from *The Mary Tyler Moore Show* (1970-77).

The PJs (1999- Fox)
Cast: Eddie Murphy, Pepe Serna

In this claymation half-hour comedy series set in a Chicago low-income housing project, Pepe Serna provides the voice to the character of Sanchez, one of the residents.

Popi (1976 CBS)
Cast: Hector Elizondo, Edith Diaz, Anthony Perez, Dennis Vasquez

This short-lived series about a Puerto Rican widower (Elizondo) and his two sons living in New York's Spanish Harlem is based on the 1969 motion picture of the same name (*see* Movie listings). The pilot episode was shown on CBS in May 1975, but the series did not air until January 1976.

Profiler (1996-2000 NBC)
Cast: Ally Walker, A Martinez

In February 1997, A Martinez became a series regular on *Profiler* as Cooper, a take-charge, gum-chewing expert in terrorism and explosives who thrives on danger. After having guest starred in two previous episodes as the intense Cooper, his character formed a romantic bond with Dr. Sam Waters (Walker), a gifted forensic psychologist.

Que Pasa, U.S.A.? (1978 PBS)

Cast: Velia Martinez, Luis Oquendo, Ana Margarita Menendez,
Rocky Echevarria [Steven Bauer], Manolo Villaverde

Set in Miami's Cuban exile community of Little Havana, this series traces the lives of Cuban Americans trying to make it in their new homeland. Three generations—grandparents, parents and teenagers—each with their own special needs and desires, form the central core of the storyline. A host of supporting characters of various races and nationalities blend to create unique situations fraught with both comic and serious consequences.

The show was the first national Hispanic situation comedy/drama series written, directed, produced by and starring Cuban Americans. It originated and was taped at WPBT, the Miami public television station. Rocky Echevarria went on to achieve stardom when he landed the role of Manny in *Scarface* (1983) opposite Al Pacino. He later changed his name to Steven Bauer.

Rawhide (1959-66 CBS)

Cast: Eric Fleming, Clint Eastwood

This Western series was created by Charles Marquis Warren and dealt with the adventures of cowboys on the long cattle drives between Texas and Kansas. One of the cowboys is a Mexican called Hey Soos, more than likely a supposed comic takeoff on the Spanish name Jesus. He was played by Robert Cabal from 1961 through 1964.

The Real McCoys (1957-62 ABC; 1962-63 CBS)

Cast: Walter Brennan, Richard Crenna

This half-hour rural comedy series about a contemporary California farm family stars Walter Brennan and Richard Crenna. It features the supporting character Pepino Garcia, a musically inclined farmhand, memorably played by Tony Martinez. A largely one-dimensional character, Pepino is a live-in Mexican farmworker who speaks broken English in an exaggerated manner.

Realidades (1975-76 PBS)

This magazine format show was produced locally at WNET-TV 13 in New York. In its first year, it had a predominantly Puerto Rican focus, which broadened to a focus on Hispanic issues and culture in the United States when it began broadcasting nationally in 1975 and 1976. It was the first national Hispanic bilingual show in the history of American television, a breakthrough for American Hispanics in the media. *Realidades* featured everything from drama (film and videotaped segments and entire shows) to documentary to news features. It was one of the first shows to present Luis Valdez's El Teatro Campesino and many other prominent Hispanic arts groups and performing artists. Jesus Trevino and Jose Luis Ruiz were segment producers for a number of episodes concerning Chicanos in the Southwest. Willie Colon was musical director for the series. The executive producer was Humberto Cintron and the series producer was Lou de Lemos.

The Redd Foxx Show (1986 ABC)
Cast: Redd Foxx, Rosana De Soto, Pamela Segall

In this half-hour comedy created by Rick Kellard and Bob Comfort, Foxx plays Al Hughes, owner of a combination newsstand and coffee shop in the heart of New York City. The comedy was accented by Diana Olmos (De Soto), Al's flippant and sexy Puerto Rican cook-waitress, who served up as many wisecracks as she did lunch specials.

Resurrection Blvd. (2000 Showtime)
Cast: Michael DeLorenzo, Elizabeth Peña,
       Tony Plana, Nicholas Gonzalez, Ruth Livier,
       Mauricio Mendoza, Marisol Nichols,
       Daniel Zacapa

This is a one-hour ensemble drama about the Santiago family and their struggles to catch the American Dream. Set in contemporary East Los Angeles, their stories intertwine as the demands of family traditions affect their careers, friendships and the family itself.

This is the first drama series on American television to prominently feature Hispanics both in front of and behind the camera. Dennis E. Leoni created the show; he also serves as an executive producer, along with Robert Eisele. Jesus Trevino directed the two-hour series pilot and serves as the supervising producer.

The cast of Showtime's landmark series *Resurrection Blvd.*, the first dramatic series on television to feature Latinos prominently, both in front of and behind the camera. (Back row, left to right) Elizabeth Peña, Mauricio Mendoza, Tony Plana, Nicholas Gonzalez, Daniel Zacapa; (front row, left to right) Ruth Livier, Michael DeLorenzo and Marisol Nichols.

Rhoda (1974-78 CBS)
Cast: Valerie Harper

Rhoda was a spin-off of *The Mary Tyler Moore Show* (1970-77), where Rhoda was first introduced as a supporting character. Now in her own series, Rhoda returns from Minnesota to live in New York. One of the regulars during 1977-78 season was Ramon Diaz, played by Rafael Campos, a happy-go-lucky Hispanic worker. The half-hour comedy series was created by James L. Brooks and Allan Burns.

The Rita Moreno Show (1976 ABC)
Cast: Rita Moreno

This half-hour comedy pilot film starred Rita Moreno as Googie Gomez, the zany character she created in the Broadway play and feature film *The Ritz* (*see* Movie listings), and for which she won a Tony Award.

Roseanne (1988-97 ABC)

Cast: Roseanne Arnold, John Goodman

Evelina Fernandez played a small role as Juanita Herrera, a factory co-worker of Roseanne's in the first season of this half-hour situation comedy about a blue-collar family barely making ends meet.

Ryan Caufield: Year One (1999 Fox)

Cast: Sean Maher, Michael Ripsoli, Roselyn Sanchez

A one-hour drama focusing on the life of Ryan Caufield, a nineteen-year-old who decides to join the police force instead of going to college. The series was cancelled after airing only three episodes. Roselyn Sanchez played Officer Kim Veras.

Sabrina: The Teenage Witch (1996- ABC)

Cast: Melissa Joan Hart, Caroline Rhea

A half-hour situation comedy about a young teenage girl with supernatural powers.

Jon Huertas joined the cast in 1999 as Brad, the best friend who comes between Sabrina and her boyfriend.

Sanchez of Bel Air (1986 USA Cable)

Cast: Reni Santoni, Marcia Del Mar, Richard Coca, Alitzah Wiener, Alma Beltran

This thirteen-episode situation comedy series was executive produced and created by April Kelly and Dave Hackel. Ricardo Sanchez's (Santoni's) clothing business has finally taken off after twenty years of struggling, and the family is able to move to Beverly Hills from their East Los Angeles barrio. However, the move causes crises for all members of the family as they adapt to life in well-to-do Beverly Hills.

This series was essentially The Beverly Hillbillies (1962-71) and The Jeffersons (1975-85) by another name, and reworked for Latinos. The two non-Hispanic writers, who had limited knowledge of American Latino life and culture, were never able to convey a comedic cultural identity; thus the show rang false with audiences. Latino actors played all three generations of the Sanchez family; the only non-Hispanic regular character on the series was next-door neighbor Frankie Rondell, played by Bobby Sherman.

Sanford and Son (1972-77 NBC)

Cast: Redd Foxx, Demond Wilson

This half-hour situation comedy was developed from a successful British comedy series (Steptoe and Son, [1962-74] by Ray Galton and Alan Simpson). Sanford and Son starred Redd Foxx as the cantankerous old Fred Sanford and Demond Wilson as his thirty-year-old bachelor son, Lamont. The two run a junk business out of their home in South Central Los Angeles. Gregory Sierra became a semiregular in the role of

Julio Fuentes, the Puerto Rican next-door neighbor whose ethnicity was the brunt of many jokes, exposing the ugly face of prejudice among minorities themselves. Sierra created a very human and charismatic character.

Santa Barbara (1984-93 NBC)

Cast: Dame Judith Anderson, Marcy Walker, Lane Davies, Todd McKee, A Martinez

The lush, progressive beach community of Santa Barbara, California, was the setting for this NBC-TV continuing daytime drama, created by Jerome and Bridget Dobson, focusing on the lives and loves of four resident families—the Lockridges, Perkinses, Andrades and Capwells.

The Andrades are a Mexican American family struggling to attain the American Dream. Strong-willed daughter Santana (Ava Lazar) is determined to rise above her parents' lot and find the baby she was forced to give up for adoption years before. The family members are played by Ismael "East" Carlo, Margarita Cordova and Rupert Ravens.

Santa Barbara was the first daytime drama series to prominently feature a Mexican American family and major Hispanic characters and the first to feature a relationship between a Mexican American and an Anglo.

Over the course of the first five seasons, the series focused almost exclusively on the lives and loves of the Capwell family. A Martinez was one of the original cast members. His character, Cruz Castillo, is a strong leading man who interactes with nearly all the show's other characters. Cruz went on to marry the series' heroine, Eden Capwell, culminating a four-year romance; their wedding was one of daytime television's most eagerly anticipated events.

Due to the show's syndication outside the United States, Martinez developed passionately devoted fans in over thirty countries. When Santa Barbara went on location to Paris, France, to shoot a few segments, Martinez and other cast members were mobbed wherever they went. Martinez won a Daytime Emmy as Outstanding Lead Actor in a Drama Series for his role as Castillo. Henry Darrow played Cruz Castillo's father, Rafael, on the series and won a Daytime Emmy for Outstanding Supporting Actor in a Drama Series. The series ended its run on January 15, 1993.

Saved by the Bell (1989-93 NBC)

Cast: Mario Lopez, Mark-Paul Gosselaar, Tiffani-Amber Thiessen

Mario Lopez, born in California of Mexican descent, is featured as muscleman Slater in this Saturday morning situation comedy series about a group of high school students. The series was produced by Peter Engel.

Saved by the Bell: The College Years (1993 NBC)

Cast: Mario Lopez, Mark-Paul Gosselaar, Tiffani-Amber Thiessen

Mario Lopez reprises his role of Slater from the highly successful Saturday morning series *Saved by the Bell* (1989-93). In this prime-time series, Slater is stuck being a freshman all over again—this time at California University. Despite his wrestling scholarship, he discovers that life away from home isn't as easy as he had anticipated.

Saved by the Bell: The New Class (1993-2000 NBC)

Cast: Jonathan Angel

This Saturday morning continuation of *Saved by the Bell* (1989-93) with a new class of students features Hispanic student Tommy DeLucca (Angel).

seaQuest DSV (1993-95 NBC)

Cast: Roy Scheider, Stephanie Beacham, Don Franklin, Marco Sanchez

This futuristic action adventure series set in the year 2018 is about a spectacular submarine and its multinational crew, who serve to explore and oversee the expanding oceanic frontier. Marco Sanchez plays Mundo Ortiz, a naval crewman responsible for the submarine's high-tech information systems—an exemplary role model as a responsible, respected and intelligent Hispanic man.

Second Chances (1993-94 CBS)

Cast: Connie Sellecca, Matt Salinger, Jennifer Lopez, Ronnie Cox,
    Megan Follows, Michelle Phillips, Pepe Serna

This hour-long drama series follows a group of characters whose lives are tied together by a murder investigation. Pepe Serna plays Sal Lopez, a proud, middle class Chicano parole officer whose daughter Melinda (Lopez), a beautiful co-ed, is to be wed to the son of a blue-blood Anglo family.

The Second Half (1993-94 NBC)

Cast: John Mendoza, Wayne Knight

This situation comedy stars stand-up comedian John Mendoza as a recently divorced sportswriter who is raising two young daughters and facing a mid-life crisis.

Sesame Street (1969- PBS)

A creation of the Children's Television Workshop, *Sesame Street* has been on the air for over thirty seasons and has won more than fifty Emmy Awards. For over two decades Maria (Sonia Manzano) and Luis (Emilio Delgado) have been a vital Latino (Puerto Rican and Mexican) presence on the national children's show, which features an array of live performers, music, song and dance, filmed segments, animation and puppets to teach young children. Many of the segments are bilingual and bicultural, introducing children to Spanish culture in the United States. It also introduced Big Bird and Jim Henson's world famous Muppet characters, including Kermit the Frog. Manzano is a Puerto Rican who grew up in the South Bronx section of New York City. Delgado was born in Calexico, California, and studied in Los Angeles before moving to New York.

Shannon's Deal (1990-91 NBC)

Cast: Jamey Sheridan, Elizabeth Peña

This hour-long drama series was created by independent filmmaker, writer and director John Sayles. It centers on a Philadelphia lawyer with heavy gambling debts whose gaming habits have cost him his family and a lucrative partnership in a prestigious corporate law firm. Returning to his roots to start over, Shannon is eking out a living in solo practice. Elizabeth Peña co-stars as his loyal secretary, Lucy Acosta, in a non-stereotypical portrayal. Jazz trumpeter Wynton Marsalis performs the theme music.

TV's *Star Trek: Voyager* series features Robert Beltran as Chakotay and Roxann Dawson as Torres.

Slattery's People (1964-65 CBS)

Cast: Richard Crenna, Ed Asner

This series focuses on the professional and personal conflicts of an idealistic state representative (Crenna). In the first season, Paul Geary played the politician's aide, Johnny Ramos. Alejandro Rey, who played Mike Valera, replaced Geary in the second season.

StarTrek: Voyager (1994- UPN)

Cast: Kate Mulgrew, Robert Beltran,
    Roxann Dawson

Robert Beltran plays First Officer Chakotay, the fearless former Maquis Captain. When the Maquis rebels united with the Federation crew of the Starship *U.S.S. Voyager*, Chakotay agreed to become Captain Janeway's first officer. Roxann Dawson is Chief Engineer B'Elanna Torres, a beautiful young woman who is half human, half Klingon.

The Steve Allen Show (1956-60 NBC; 1961 ABC)

Cast: Steve Allen

In 1959, this variety show introduced Bill Dana as the character of Mexican immigrant Jose Jimenez.

Suddenly Susan (1996-2000 NBC)

Cast: Brooke Shields, Nestor Carbonell, Judd Nelson, David Strickland

Ensemble comedy set at a hip San Francisco magazine. The show focuses on Susan (Shields) a beautiful, but somewhat sheltered magazine writer, who forfeited the opportunity to marry rich for the chance to discover more about life and herself. Nestor Carbonell portrays Luis Rivera, a suave photographer for *The Gate* magazine.

Sword of Justice (1978-79 NBC)

Cast: Dack Rainbo, Bert Rosario

An ex-con goes after lawbreakers with the help of his former cellmate, Hector Ramirez (Rosario), in this hour-long adventure series.

T.H.E. Cat (1966-67 NBC)

Cast: Robert Loggia, Robert Carricart

This half-hour series is about a former circus aerialist and cat burglar who now fights crime as a personal bodyguard. He is aided by his friend Pepe (Carricart), a Spanish Gypsy who runs a nightclub, the Casa Del Gato, where The Cat maintains an office.

Tarzan (1966-69 NBC)

Cast: Ron Ely, Manuel Padilla, Jr.

This hour-long *Tarzan* series was filmed entirely in Mexico though it was purportedly set in Africa. It had a decidedly Latin flavor in its atmosphere, and featured Manuel Padilla, Jr., as Jai, Tarzan's young native companion.

That '70s Show (1998- FOX)

Cast: Topher Grace, Mila Kunis, Ashton Kutcher, Danny Masterson, Laura Prepon and Wilmer Valderrama.

A half-hour comedy about teenagers and their parents in late 1970s suburban Wisconsin. Valderrama plays Fez, an exchange student.

Third Watch (1999 NBC)

Cast: Bobby Cannavale, Kim Raver, Eddie Cibrian

A one-hour series about New York firefighters, police and paramedics who staff the "Third Watch," the relentless twilight shift from 3 to 11 p.m.

Time of Your Life (1999 Fox)

Cast: Jennifer Love Hewitt, Pauley Perette, Diego Serrano

Diego Serrano plays J.B.on this series that follows Sarah's adventures in the Big Apple. This is a spin-off from the hugely popular *Party of Five* (1994-2000).

Maria Canals (center back) with fellow cast members of *The Tony Danza Show*.

The Tony Danza Show (1997 NBC)

Cast: Tony Danza, Maria Canals, Majandra Delfino

Maria Canals portrays witty, beautiful computer whiz and editorial assistant, Carmen Cruz, who revels in bantering with her boss (Danza), a computerphobic sportswriter and single dad.

Tony Orlando and Dawn (1974-76 CBS)

Cast: Tony Orlando

This one-hour musical variety show started as a four-week summer replacement and was continued when it met with good audience response and ratings.

Total Security (1997 ABC)

Cast: Jim Belushi, Tony Plana

Tony Plana plays the manager of the hotel where Total Security has its base of operations.

Touched by an Angel (1994- CBS)

Cast: Della Reese, Roma Downey

During the fourth season Alexis Cruz was introduced in a recurring role as Rafael, a streetwise angel who helps out young people in need.

Tough Cookies (1986 CBS)

Cast: Robby Benson, Lainie Kazan

In this half-hour police drama Robby Benson stars as Cliff Brady, a young Chicago police detective who lives and works in the tough Chicago neighborhood where he grew up. Elizabeth Peña, in her first television series, is featured as Connie Rivera, a young undercover policewoman.

Tour of Duty (1987-90 CBS)

Cast: Terence Knox, Stephen Caffrey, Joshua Maurer, Ramon Franco

This story of the American soldiers at Firebase Ladybird, who forged friendships under fire in Vietnam in 1967, was created by L. Travis Clark and Steve Duncan. Ruiz, played by Ramon Franco, is a Puerto Rican recruit from the streets of New York. The subtleties of the character's New York Puerto Rican background are successfully conveyed by the writers and by actor Franco. *Tour of Duty* is the only television show to recognize Hispanic American involvement in the nation's armed conflicts, through the character of Ruiz. From *Combat* through *M*A*S*H* to *China Beach*, Hispanics had never before been acknowledged in the form of leading characters. Miguel Nunez also plays a recruit, but not a specifically Hispanic one.

Trial and Error (1988 CBS)

Cast: Eddie Velez, Paul Rodriguez

A young lawyer, John Hernandez (Velez), and a T-shirt seller, Tony Rivera (Rodriguez), are roommates in Los Angeles in this short-lived half-hour situation comedy.

Union Square (1997 NBC)

Cast: Michael Landes, Harriet Sansom Harris, Jim Pirri, Constance Marie

A half-hour situation comedy in which Marie plays Gabriella Valdez, a struggling Tejana actress from El Paso, Texas who moves to New York in hopes of being discovered.

The Untouchables (1959-63 ABC)

Cast: Robert Stack, Paul Picerni, Nicholas Georgiade, Abel Fernandez

In 1959, this show originally aired as a two-part *Desilu Playhouse* (1958-60) drama with a strong cinematic style. It was such a ratings hit that ABC and Desilu Productions developed it into a weekly series. Abel Fernandez played Bill Youngfellow, one of *The Untouchables* on the popular series, which was based on the real-life exploits of Eliot Ness and his squad of incorruptible Treasury agents who fought Al Capone and other gangland figures during Prohibition in 1920s Chicago.

Robert Stack (left) and Abel Fernandez (right) on *The Untouchables* TV series.

Villa Alegre (1974-81 PBS)

Cast: Gilbert Duron, Julio Medina, Carmen Zapata

This bilingual (Spanish/English) series was geared toward 4- to 10-year-olds to teach them about human relations, the natural environment, communication, energy and man-made objects. Claudio Guzman was the executive producer.

Viva Valdez! (1976 ABC)

Cast: Carmen Zapata, Rodalfa Hayos, James Victor, Jorge Cervera, Jr.

This series about a Mexican American family in Los Angeles was neither well received nor well conceived. It ran from May until September of 1976. The show is only noteworthy in that it was an attempt to produce a Hispanic family series and in that it showcased a number of talented Hispanic performers.

The West Wing (1999 NBC)

Cast: Martin Sheen, Rob Lowe, Moira Kelly, Bradley Whitford.

A one-hour drama series that offers a behind-the-scenes glimpse into the inner-workings of the Oval Office as seen through the eyes of its eclectic group of frenzied staffers. Sheen plays President Josiah Bartlet, who from his office in the White House, leads the most powerful nation on earth.

Welcome Back, Kotter (1975-79 ABC)

Cast: Gabriel Kaplan, Marcia Strassman, John Sylvester White, John Travolta, Robert Hegyes, Lawrence-Hilton Jacobs

This half-hour comedy revolves around a young teacher, Gabe Kotter (Kaplan), who returns to the city high school from which he graduated and attempts to teach unmotivated remedial students. The class members, reluctantly enrolled in school, were affectionately known as "The Sweathogs." Robert Hegyes played Juan Epstein, a half-Hispanic, half-Jewish student. The series was created by Gabriel Kaplan and Alan Sacks.

What a Country (1986-87 syndicated)

Cast: Garrett M. Brown, Yakov Smirnoff, Gall Strickland, George Murdock, Ada Maris, Julian Reyes, Leila Hee Olsen

This was a first-run syndicated comedy series about the humorous adventures of an American citizenship class taught by a rather reluctant but dedicated night school teacher. Ada Maris portrays Maria Conchita Lopez, a sexy Mexican girl working as a maid for a wealthy Beverly Hills couple. Maria thinks she has found the Promised Land on Rodeo Drive. Julian Reyes plays Victor Ortega, a macho street kid who has the same dreams and insecurities as many immigrants.

The White Shadow (1978-81 CBS)

Cast: Ken Howard, Kevin Hooks, Thomas Carter

This hour-long series about a Anglo basketball coach in a racially mixed Los Angeles high school features Ira Angustain as Hispanic team member Ricardo Gomez. Several episodes revolve around his character.

Wichita Town (1959-60 NBC)

Cast: Joel McCrea, Jody McCrea, Carlos Romero

Marshall Mike Dunbar (Joel McCrea) maintains law and order in Wichita, Kansas, in the years following the Civil War in this twenty-six-episode, half-hour Western series. Carlos Romero plays a regular supporting role as Rico Rodriguez.

Wiseguy (1986-90 CBS)
Cast: Steven Bauer

In its fourth and last season, this critically acclaimed one-hour drama series from Stephen J. Cannell introduced a new leading actor, Steven Bauer, following the departure of its original star, Ken Wahl. Bauer plays disbarred federal prosecutor Michael Santana, who joins forces with the FBI's Organized Crime Bureau in order to infiltrate the ranks of powerful criminal organizations. This six-hour (five-episode) first arc of the 1990-1991 season was filmed on location in Miami. It involved an investigation by Santana into the murder of undercover agent Vinnie Terranova (Wahl's character) by a Latin American death squad.

The story guest starred Academy Award® winner Maximilian Schell as Cuban Areado Guzman, and Manolo Villaverde. This reincarnated *Wiseguy* gives us a Miami where two of the main characters are veterans of the Bay of Pigs invasion; where the hero's father was a prisoner in a Castro jail; and where the love interest is a Cuban American singer. It brought recognition to the contributions made by Cuban Americans over the last thirty years to American culture, history, politics and crime, particularly in Miami and southern Florida, in a realistic manner with Cuban-born, Miami-reared central characters. The Nielsen viewers did not accept this new incarnation of *Wiseguy*, and the series ended its run after the Miami episodes.

The Xavier Cugat Show (1957 NBC)
Cast: Xavier Cugat

This musical variety show, only fifteen minutes long, was paired with the fifteen-minute NBC Nightly News. The show lasted from February to May of 1957 and starred Cugat and his then-wife, singer Abbe Lane.

The Yellow Rose (1983-84 NBC)
Cast: Sam Elliott, Cybill Shepherd, Susan Anspach, David Soul

This hour-long drama series is centered on a contemporary Anglo ranch family in Texas as they struggled to maintain values and traditions established a century earlier. One of the sons, a half-Mexican lawyer named Quisto Champion, is played by Edward Albert, who is half-Hispanic himself. Several of the storylines deal with border smuggling and exploitation of Latino undocumented workers.

You Again (1986-87 NBC)
Cast: Jack Klugman

A middle-aged divorcé is surprised when his seventeen-year-old son enters his life again. Luis Avalos plays the character of Luis Robles.

Zorro (1957-59 ABC)
See Zorro & The Cisco Kid" listings.

Zorro and Son (1983 CBS)
See "Zorro & The Cisco Kid" listings.

TV Movies and Miniseries

Alambrista! (1977 PBS)
See Film listings.

The Alamo: Thirteen Days to Glory (1987 NBC)
D: Burt Kennedy
S: Clyde Ware and Norman Mcleod Morrill
P: Bill Finnegan, Pat Finnegan, and Sheldon Pinchuk
Cast: James Arness, Brian Keith, Raul Julia, Alec Baldwin, Isela Vega, Fernando Allende

This is a routine version of the Alamo story, which tried minimally to show the participation of the Mexican defenders at the Battle of the Alamo, including Juan Seguin and Gregorio Esparza as well as the Hispanic women. It does delve into the character of General Santa Anna, as played by Raul Julia. Among the other Hispanic actors featured are Eloy Casados, Laura Martinez Herring, Loyda Ramos, Laura Fabian, Sol Castillo and Bel Sandre.

All Star Fiesta at Ford's (1992 ABC)
Cast: Ricardo Montalban

This two-hour taped gala evening at Ford's Theater in Washington, D.C., featured President and Mrs. George Bush in a salute to Hispanic heritage and the achievements of the National Hispanic Scholarship Fund. It also starred Paul Rodriguez, Rita Moreno, Tito Puente, Vikki Carr and many other celebrities.

Antonio and the Mayor (1976 CBS)
D: Jerry Thorpe
S: Howard Rodman
P: Jerry Thorpe
Cast: Gregory Sierra

This story of a young Mexican boy who defies the authority of the town's mayor was filmed in Mexico.

Asteroid (1998 NBC)

D: Bradford May
S: Robbyn Burger, Scott Sturgeon
P: John Davis, Merrill H. Karpf, Phil Margo, Christopher Morgan
Cast: Annabella Sciorra, Michael Biehn, Carlos Gomez, Don Franklin

A Colorado astronomer discovers a huge fragment of a disintergrating comet on an collision course with Earth. Gomez stars as Adam Marquez, assistant director of FEMA who is a dedicated disaster relief administrator in this big event four-hour miniseries

Atomic Train (1999 NBC)

D: Dick Lowery and David Jackson
S: D. Brent Mote and Phil Penningroth
P: Mike Joyce and Dennis Hammer
Cast: Rob Lowe, Esai Morales

Morales plays Mac, an overzealous Denver police captain who sacrifices himself to save his son in this four-hour miniseries about an out-of-control train carrying nuclear warheads headed for a huge population center and the efforts to stop it.

The Ballad of Gregorio Cortez (1983 PBS)

See Movie listings.

The Boy and the Turtle (1971 PBS)

S: Eugene Poinc
P: Earl Miller
Cast: Gilbert Roland, Katy Jurado, Henry Calvin, Enrique Lucero, Manuel Padilla, Jr.

This drama, written especially for WNET's Childrens Special and filmed on the Yucatan Peninsula, concerns a twelve-year-old Mexican youth who discovers a Mayan relic and an enormous friendly turtle.

Brotherhood of the Gun (1992 CBS)

D: Vern Gillum
S: Robert Ward
P: Robert Ward
Cast: Brian Blessed, Jorge Cervera, Jr.

Jorge Cervera, Jr., plays Sheriff Charlie Sanchez, who may look like a stereotype, but who is also tough, smart and self-sufficient. Sanchez is overweight, wears a large, wide-brimmed Mexican hat and eats tamales as he chases bad guys. He also helps the film's hero out of a tough situation.

Burden of Proof (1992 ABC)
D: Mike Robe
S: John Gay
P: John Pertin Flynn
Cast: Hector Elizondo, Brian Dennehy, Stephanie Powers,
    Victoria Principal, Mel Harris

Elizondo plays Sandy Stern (the character Raul Julia played in the 1990 theatrical feature *Presumed Innocent*), a middle-aged Jewish criminal attorney of Argentine and German descent who finds his ordered world turned upside down after his wife commits suicide. Elizondo is the best thing about this otherwise overlong, rather weak mystery, which aired in two parts.

The Burning Season: The Chico Mendes Story (1994 HBO)
D: John Frankeheimer
S: Ron Hutchinson
P: David Puttnam, Thomas M. Hammel,
    John Frankenheimer
Cast: Raul Julia, Edward James Olmos, Sonia
    Braga, Esai Morales, Kamala Dawason, Luis
    Guzman, Nigel Havers, Tomas Milian, Tony
    Plana, Carlos Carrasco, Marco Rodriquez

The true story of Chico Mendes, who was assassinated while he fought to protect his home and his people in the rain forest of the Brazilian Amazon. Raul Julia won a posthumous Emmy Award as Best Actor in a Miniseries for his performance as the slain environmentalist.

Filmed in Comoapan in the state of Veracruz, Mexico, by noted director John Frankenheimer.

Edward James Olmos (left) and Raul Julia (right) in his Emmy Award-winning role as Chico Mendes in HBO's *The Burning Season: The Chico Mendes Story*, directed by John Frankenheimer.

Can You Hear the Laughter? The Story of Freddie Prinze (1979 CBS)
D: Burt Brinckerhoff
S: Dalene Young
P: Roger Gimbel
Cast: Ira Angustain, Kevin Hooks, Julie Carmen

Ira Angustain was selected to portray the brilliant but tragic young comedian Freddie Prinze in this television movie dealing with Prinze's life and death by suicide in 1977.

Centennial (1978-79 NBC)

D: Paul Krasny, Virgil W. Vogel, Harry Falk, and
   Bernard McEveety

S: John Wilder

P: John Wilder

Cast: Robert Conrad, Richard Chamberlain,
   Barbara Carrera, Dennis Weaver, David
   Janssen, Karmin Murcelo, A Martinez,
   Rafael Campos

The Mexican American cultural influence in the winning of the American West is significantly portrayed in this epic twenty-six-hour miniseries Centennial, based on the novel by James A. Michener. It traces the lives of founders the fictional town of Centennial, Colorado, and their descendants from their Native American beginnings to the present.

The miniseries features a number of Hispanic actors in important roles. In the early episodes involving the trappers and Indians, beautiful Barbara Carrera portrays the Native American woman Clay Basket. Trail cook Nacho Gomez, who helped on the great cattle drives from Texas to Colorado during the 1870s, is played by Rafael Campos. The political unrest of turn-of-the-century Mexico, along with the beginnings of the exploitation of migrant workers, is brought into play in the story of Tranquilino Marquez, played by A Martinez. The racism and injustice that Tranquilino's descendants encounter and their struggle to make a life for themselves as Americans is touched upon. An Anglo-Chicano marriage in the contemporary final episode between Flor Marquez (Murcelo) and Paul Garrett (Janssen) represents a further bridging of peoples. Julio Medina, Silvana Gallardo, Henry Darrow, Rene Enriquez, Alex Colon and David Yanez are also in the cast.

A Martinez holds a
wounded Rafael Campos
in the miniseries
Centennial.

CHiPs '99 (1999 TNT)

D: Jon Cassar

S: Morgan Gendel

P: Erik Estrada, Larry Wilcox

Cast: Erik Estrada, Larry Wilcox

After fifteen years of self-imposed retirement from the CHP, Ponch (Estrada) reunites with his partner Jon (Wilcox) to break up a car theft ring. The duo are soon back in action, this time navigating California's highways on sleek new BMW motorcycles. *CHiPs '99* is a blast from the past with a '90s sensibility, built on the same can't-miss combination of cool bikes, tight pants and widespread disregard for the California traffic code that marked the original series.

Choices of the Heart [aka: *In December the Roses Will Bloom Again*] (1983 NBC)

D: Joseph Sargent
S: John Pielmeier
P: Joseph Sargent and David W. Rintels
Cast: Melissa Gilbert, Martin Sheen, Mike Farrell, Rene Enriquez, Pamela Bellwood

This fact-based movie concerns the life of Jean Donovan, the twenty-seven-year-old missionary, who was slain with three American nuns in El Salvador in 1980. Gilbert plays Donovan and Sheen plays Father Corcoran, an Irish priest who was an inspiration to Donovan. Enriquez portrays Archbishop Romero, the martyred Salvadoran church leader.

Copacabana (1986 ABC)

D: Waris Hussein
S: James Lipton
P: Dick Clark
Cast: Barry Manflow, Annette O'Toole, Joseph Bologna

A musical drama based on the popular hit song by Barry Manilow, this film focuses on the characters who work and inhabit the legendary Copacabana Latin nightclub in 1940s New York. All the lead characters are Anglo or Italian, and the Latin characters are minor. Silvana Gallardo plays an aging nightclub headliner and Dyana Ortelli plays a showgirl.

Corridos! Tales of Passion and Revolution (1987 PBS)

D: Luis Valdez
S: Luis Valdez
P: Janis Blackschleger
Cast: Clancy Brown, Evelyn Cisneros, George Galvan, Sal Lopez, Alma Martinez, Linda Ronstadt, Daniel Valdez, Luis Valdez (as El Maestro)

KQED San Francisco, in association with El Teatro Campesino, produced this one-hour videotaped entertainment special. Written, directed and starring El Teatro Campesino founder Luis Valdez, the production realizes the dramatic potential of the most famous and tuneful Mexican American folk ballads, or *corridos*. Brought to life through a rich combination of drama, music, dance and imaginative art direction, these ballads carry the viewer from Mexico in the late 1800s to 1920s America. It was adapted for television from the acclaimed El Teatro Campesino stage production featuring members of the original cast. A bilingual production with songs in Spanish and dialogue in English, the special featured the talents of fifteen musicians, including Los Camperos, America's premier Mariachi group, all under the musical direction of Daniel Valdez.

Crazy from the Heart (1991 TNT)

D: Thomas Schlamme
S: Linda Voorhees
P: R.J. Louis
Cast: Christine Lahti, Rubén Blades, William Russ, Tommy Muniz, Kamala Lopez

In this charming tale of unexpected love that defies logic and small-town prejudice, an uptight southern Texas high school principal falls in love with a Mexican American janitor.

For seven years, Charlotte Bain (Lahti) has been content with her career and the noncommittal relationship she has with Coach Dewey Whitcomb. The bubble bursts when she learns that her childhood best friend is going to be a grandmother, a revelation that reminds Charlotte of her own ticking biological clock.

Wanting more from her life, she gives Dewey a wedding ultimatum, and their relationship buckles under the pressure. On the rebound, she meets Ernesto Ontiveros (Blades), a down-on-his-luck Mexican American farmer who is working as a janitor at her high school to save his ranch from foreclosure. Ernesto asks Charlotte for a date, and, despite herself, she accepts. Love is not far behind.

Tommy Muniz plays Tomas, Ernesto's father, and Kamala Lopez portrays Ernesto's strong-willed daughter, Alcira, who is a lawyer determined to carve her own niche in town. Rubén Blades was nominated for an Emmy in 1992 for his role in this dramatic comedy.

Curacao (1993 Showtime)

D: Carl Schultz
S: James David Buchanan
P: Art Levinson
Cast: George C. Scott, William Petersen, Julie Carmen

Two loners are washed up on Curacao, a Caribbean island located in the Netherland Antilles, off the coast of Venezuela, during Carnival time. Julia Fernandez (Carmen), the Caribbean station chief for an American intelligence agency, adds an element of intrigue and romance to the mix when she is sent to Curacao from Puerto Rico to investigate the two men.

Dead Man Out (1989 HBO)

D: Richard Pearce
S: Ran Hutchinson
P: Forrest Murray
Cast: Danny Glover, Rubén Blades, Tom Atkins

Psychiatrist Alex Marsh (Glover) is hired to "cure" an insane convict, Ben (Blades), so the state can execute him. This is a gritty drama about the battle of wits that erupts between the psychiatrist and the death-row inmate when they confront each other without the protection of prison bars.

Larry McMurtry's Dead Man's Walk (1996 ABC)
D: Yves Simoneu
S: Larry McMurtry and Diana Ossana
P: Robert Halmi Jr., Larry Levinson, Larry McMurtry, Diana Ossana, Suzanne De Passe
Cast: F. Murray Abraham, Keith Carradine, Edward James Olmos

Edward James Olmos plays Captain Salazar, a Mexican Army officer who attempts to lead Woodrow, Gus, and the rest of the cowboys across a daunting desert known as the "Jornado del Muerto" (Dead Man's Walk) in this miniseries which tells the early story of *The Lonesome Dove* characters.

The Deadly Tower (1975 NBC)
D: Jerry Jameson
S: William D. Lansford
P: Antonio Calderon
Cast: Kurt Russell, Richard Yniguez

This film re-creates the Texas tower massacre of August 4, 1966, during which disturbed student Charles Whitman (Russell), at the University of Texas began firing on students. A Texas officer, Ramiro Martinez (Yniguez), brought him down.

The Desperate Mission (1971 NBC)
D: Earl Bellamy
S: Jack Guss
P: David Silver
Cast: Ricardo Montalban, Roosevelt Grier, Slim Pickens, Ina Balin, Miriam Colon

This is a fictionalized story of the legendary bandit Joaquin Murieta (Montalban) and how he aids a group of pioneers.

Double Crossed (1991 HBO)
D: Roger Young
S: Roger Young
P: Albert J. Salzer
Cast: Dennis Hopper, Robert Carradine, Adrienne Barbeau

This film is loosely based on the real-life story of drug dealer Barry Seal (Hopper). When Seal piloted his plane to deliver illicit cargo from South America into eager American hands, he flew with a sense of adventure. However, when Seal switched allegiances, identifying the pivotal drug kingpins and at the same time accumulating evidence for the federal government while continuing his smuggling operation, this new twist made the game even more tantalizing.

But then the government double-crossed him, leaving him out in the cold, and Barry Seal became easy prey for the drug dealers he had betrayed. He was gunned down in Baton Rouge, Louisiana, on February 19,

1986, after the IRS had confiscated his assets for back taxes owed on the money he had made smuggling. His widow and children were left homeless and penniless. It was filmed partly in Louisiana and Puerto Rico.

Drug Wars: The Camarena Story (1989 NBC)
D: Brian Gibson
S: Christopher Canaan, Mel Frohman, Ann Powell, and Rose Schacht
P: Branko Lustig
Cast: Steven Bauer, Elizabeth Peña, Craig T. Nelson, Treat Williams, Miguel Ferrer

This is a powerful miniseries about United States Drug Enforcement Administration agent "Kiki" Camarena, who in 1985 was tortured and killed in Mexico because his investigations threatened major drug lords allegedly connected to senior members of the Mexican government. His fellow agents and his wife, Mika, are determined to identify and expose the murderers. To do so, they fight corrupt Mexican officials, American diplomatic inaction and personal frustration in their struggle to bring those responsible to justice. This straightforward drama is based on *Desperados*, a book by *Time* reporter Elaine Shannon, which exposes the greed and corruption extending from those behind the drug cartels to high government officials. Michael Mann ("Miami Vice") executive produced the miniseries. It also features Hispanic actors Pepe Serna, Tony Plana, Benicio Del Toro, Tomas Goros, Eddie Velez, Mike Moroff, Jacob Vargas, Joaquin Martinez, Geoffrey Rivas and Tomas Milian. It was filmed in Los Angeles and in Spain because the Mexican government would not allow the company to film in Mexico, as the movie put the Mexican government in an unfavorable light due to the political controversy that still lingers over Camarena's murder.

Drug Wars: The Cocaine Cartel (1992 NBC)
D: Paul Krasny
S: Gordon Greisman and Gail Morgan Hickman
P: Richard Brams and Gordon Greisman
Cast: Alex McArthur, Dennis Farina, Julie Carmen, John Glover

This is a dramatic retelling of the fight to bring down two powerful drug lords in Medellin, Colombia, and the inside story of the Drug Enforcement Agency's courageous infiltration into an empire of billionaire narco-terrorists. It was filmed in Miami and Spain.

Dying to be Perfect: The Ellen Hart Peña Story (1996 ABC)
D: Jan Egleson
S: Susan Arnout Smith
P: Karen Shapiro
Cast: Crystal Bernard, Esai Morales, Casey Sander, Shirley Knight

Crystal Bernard portrays Hart, a world class runner with Olympic aspirations who kept her condition (Bulimia) a secret until she became pregnant. Esai Morales co-stars as her husband, Federico Peña.

El Baquine de Angelitos Negros (1977 PBS)
D: Mike Cuesta
S: Lou de Lemos
P: Lou de Lemos and Livia Perez
Cast: Brunilda Ruiz, Hector Mercado, Beatriz Rodriguez

The first all-Latino dance production ever to be produced exclusively for national television distribution, this was part of the *Realidades* (1975-76) television series. Salsa bandleader Willie Colon composed an entire musical ballet expressly for this film program. It is a modern-day version of Latin American folklore set in New York's Puerto Rican community of Spanish Harlem.

When a black Puerto Rican child dies on the island, a festival was held to celebrate the passage of the innocent child's soul to heaven, where it was welcomed by God and immediately transformed into an angel. Friends and family danced late into the night to assure the ascent of the child's spirit. This joyous celebration is called a Baquine. Brunilda Ruiz was a principal dancer with the Harkness Ballet. Hector Mercado was a dancer with the Alvin Ailey company and went on to perform on Broadway and in feature films.

El Corrido: La Gran Carpa de los Rasquachis (1976 PBS)
D: Kirk Browning
S: Luis Valdez
P: Barbara Schultz
Cast: Felix Alvarez, Lily Alvarez, Socorro Cruz, Jose Delgado,
  Phil Esparza, Andres Gutierrez, Diane Rodriguez, Daniel Valdez

This seventy-minute videotaped broadcast production was presented as part of the "Visions" series. Written and staged by Luis Valdez, it evolved out of the skits performed by members of the theater group El Teatro Campesino during the early days of the farmworkers' strikes. This work centers on the adventures of a fictional farm laborer, Kose Pelado Rasguachi, a character in the tradition of Mexican comedic actor Cantinflas.

El Diablo (1990 HBO)
D: Peter Markle
S: Tommy Lee Wallace, John Carpenter, and Bill Phillips
P: Mickey Borofsky and Todd Black
Cast: Anthony Edwards, Robert Beltran, Lou Gossett, Jr.

A comic Western with a twist. When a Mexican bandit, El Diablo (Beltran), rides into town with his band of armed men, he robs the bank and kidnaps a sweet-faced frontier student. A mild-mannered tenderfoot schoolteacher, Billy Ray (Edwards), takes a crash course in Wild West gunslinging from the grizzled veteran Van Leek (Gossett, Jr.) in order to rescue the girl.

Evita Peron (1981 NBC)

D: Marvin J. Chomsky
S: Ronald Harwood
P: Marvin J. Chomsky
Cast: Faye Dunaway, James Farentino, Rita Moreno, Jose Ferrer,
    Michael Constantine, Katy Jurado, Pedro Armendariz, Jr.

Argentina's charismatic famed First Lady, Evita Peron (Dunaway), rises from the slums of Buenos Aires to become a film actress and win the heart of Dictator Juan Peron and the people of the country. This miniseries was filmed in Mexico.

Finding the Way Home (1991 ABC)

D: Rod Halcomb
S: Scott Swanton
P: Peter K. Duchow and Rob Halcomb
Cast: George C. Scott, Hector Elizondo, Julie Carmen, Beverly Garland

An elderly hardware store owner finds himself and redemption among some Latino farmworkers in the Southwest.

Florida Straits (1986 HBO)

D: Mike Hodges
S: Roderick Taylor
P: Stuart B. Rekant
Cast: Raul Julia, Fred Ward, Daniel Jenkins

A trio of adventurers brave the treacherous Cuban jungle to search for a fortune in buried gold.

Carlos (Julio) has just been released after twenty years in a Cuban jail for the part he played in the Bay of Pigs invasion. During the invasion, Carlos piloted a plane loaded with $2 million in gold for the United States government. When the plane crashed in the Cuban jungle, Carlos went to jail and the gold stayed in the wilderness. Now he wants to go back and get it. Carlos hires the boat *White Witch* and fast-talks its crew, Lucky (Ward) and Mac (Jenkins), into joining him in his quest to retrieve the $2 million treasure.

For the Love of My Child: The Anissa Ayala Story (1993 NBC)

D: Waris Hussein
S: Anna Sandor
P: Michelle Maxwell MacLoren
Cast: Priscilla Lopez, Teresa DiSpina, Tony Perez, Danny Nucci

In 1990, leukemia patient Anissa Ayala made national headlines when her parents conceived a child in the hope of achieving a successful bone marrow match and saving Anissa's life. The events that led up to that decision and the national controversy that followed are dramatized in this telefilm. Miraculously, the Ayalas' new daughter turns out to be a perfect bone marrow match, and Anissa courageously triumphs over leukemia. Tony Award-winner Priscilla Lopez stars as the mother in a television movie that presents a middle-class Hispanic American family without stereotypical trappings. The cast was made up of experienced but not well known Hispanic actors, which contributed to the credibility of the film.

Gangs (1988 CBS)
D: Jesus Trevino
S: Paul Cooper
P: Howard Metzer and Eli Johnson
Cast: David Labiosa, Gabriel Gonzales, Raymond Cruz, Will Gotay, Kamala Lopez, Panchito Gomez

A former gang member returns to his East Los Angeles home from a stint in the Army to find his younger brother involved in his former gang. Director Jesus Trevino won a Directors Guild of America Award for Best Direction of a Daytime Television Drama for this movie. It is sensitively written and directed and offers no easy answers to the serious problems of drugs and gang violence that confront families in the barrio.

Panchito Gomez plays the lead in the ABC Afterschool Special *Gaucho.*

Gaucho (1978 ABC)
D: Rob Lieberman
S: Arthur Heinemann
P: Martin Tahse
Cast: Panchito Gomez, Alma Beltran

A fourteen-year-old Puerto Rican boy, Gaucho, moves to New York City with his mother and older brother and must deal with conflicting values in his new environment, His older brother, Angel, marries an Anglo girl and forgets his promise to take his mother back to Puerto Rico. Gaucho is determined to earn money any way he can to take his mother home. The movie is based on the book *Gaucho* by Gloria Gonzalez.

Glitz (1988 NBC)
D: Sandor Stern
S: Alan Trustman and Steve Zito
P: Steve McGlothen
Cast: Jimmy Smits, Markie Post, John Diehl, Geno Silva

In this adaptation of Elmore Leonard's best-selling detective novel about a Miami based police officer, Vincent Mora (Smits) tracks down a call girl's Killer. The chase takes him through the casinos of Atlantic City and Puerto Rico, unaware that he has been the killer's real target all along.

Gore Vidal's Billy the Kid (1989 TNT)

D: William A. Graham
S: Gore Vidal
P: Frank Von Zerneck and Robert M. Sertner
Cast: Val Kilmer, Duncan Regehr, Julie Carmen, Wilford Brimley

This two-hour film about Billy the Kid, the legendary outlaw of the New Mexico Territory of the 1870s, was scripted by Gore Vidal, one of America's most prolific and respected writers. Julie Carmen plays Celsa, Billy's romantic interest. An earlier Vidal teleplay, *The Death of Billy the Kid*, was adapted as a feature-length film in 1958, *The Left-Handed Gun* (*see* Movie listings).

Gryphon (1988 PBS)

D: Mark Cullingham
S: Manuel Arce and Carl Haber
P: Manuel Arce and Carl Haber
Cast: Amanda Plummer, Sully Diaz, Alexis Cruz

Based on a short story by Charles Baxter, this is a tale of a tough Hispanic boy whose life is changed by a magical substitute teacher. This was a presentation of the "WonderWorks" series.

Hollywood Confidential (1997 UPN)

D: Ray Villalobos
S: Anthony Yerkovich
P: Anthony Yerkovich
Cast: Edward James Olmos

This is a two-hour pilot for a series that never made it on the schedule. Edward James Olmos stars as Stan Navarro, a twenty-year veteran of the L.A.P.D., who heads an elite private detective agency staffed primarily with talented misfits who do not fit into the conventional world of law enforcement.

Honeyboy (1982 NBC)

D: John Berry
S: John Berry and Lee Gold
P: Erik Estrada and John Berry
Cast: Erik Estrada, Morgan Fairchild, Hector Elizondo

Erik Estrada produced this television film about the rise and fall of Rico "Honeyboy" Ramirez, a tough boxer from the streets of New York's Spanish Harlem, in the classic melodramatic John Garfield Warner Bros. tradition.

The House of Ramon Iglesias (1986 PBS)
D: Luis Soto
S: Jose Rivera
P: Laura Mola
Cast: Jaime Sanchez, Robert Badillo, Annie Golden, Nick Corri,
    Marina Durell

Adapted by Rivera from his own stage play, this is the story of a Puerto Rican family in New York who, after nineteen years, decides to move back to Puerto Rico. The oldest son objects to the move, and the resulting conflict highlights the themes of assimilation and returning to one's homeland. The movie aired on the *American Playhouse* series in April 1986.

Jacobo Timerman: Prisoner Without a Name, Cell Without a Number (1983 CBS)
D: Linda Yellen
S: Linda Yellen, Jonathan Platnick, and Oliver Drexell, Jr.
P: Terry Ellis and Richard Dorso
Cast: Roy Scheider, Liv Ullmann, Sam Robards

Set in Argentina, this political thriller is based on the true story of outspoken newspaper publisher Timerman (Scheider), who was imprisoned and tortured by a repressive political regime. No Latin actors are featured in leading roles in this film, shot in New Jersey.

La Carpa (1993 PBS)
D: Carlos Avila
S: Carlos Avila and Edit Villareal
P: Michael Zapanta and Carlos Villareal
Cast: Jaime Gomez, Nicolas Coster, E.J. Castillo, Bel Sandre,
    Karla Montana

In 1938 in Florencia, California, a farmworker witnesses the accidental shooting of his friend by the local sheriff in a dark alley. Disturbed by his friend's death and everyone's complacent attitude toward the shooting, he raises the ire of local authorities, both Mexican and Anglo, with his blatant outrage and constant questions. He finds employment and spiritual renewal with La Carpa, a traveling sideshow of performers that entertains Mexican farmworkers. Through a chance encounter in the same dark alley where his friend met his death, the farmworker and the sheriff find mutual understanding and truth. The film aired on the *American Playhouse* series in June 1993.

La Pastorela (1991 PBS)

D: Luis Valdez
S: Luis Valdez
P: Richard Soto
Cast: Paul Rodriguez, Cheech Marin, Linda Ronstadt, Karla Montana

Presented on the Public Broadcasting Service as part of the "Great Performances" series, this contemporary one-hour film adaptation of a traditional holiday play, performed by Luis Valdez's El Teatro Campesino at San Juan Bautista Mission, California, features music by Los Lobos and Lalo Guerrero. La Pastorela is a musical retelling of the shepherd's journey to Bethlehem to see the Christ child. Valdez opens up the pageant for television, taking it outdoors and adding more comedy, music and special effects. The play is seen through the eyes of a young Chicana accidentally knocked unconscious during a rather raucous performance. In her surrealistic dream, she repeats the shepherd's journey through her own contemporary frame of reference.

The Last Prostitute (1991 Lifetime)

D: Lou Antonio
S: Carmen Culver
P: Peter Bogart
Cast: Wil Wheaton, Sonia Braga, David Kaufman, Cotter Smith

Young boys leave home and go in search of an infamous prostitute they read about in their late grandfather's diary. Their goal is to lose their virginity. They find a not-so-beautiful middle-aged woman living alone on a ranch, and proceed to learn lessons about life.

Lifestories: Families In Crisis, P.O.W.E.R.: The Eddie Matos Story (1994 HBO)

D: Jesus Trevino
S: Jose Rivera
P: Howard Meltzer
Cast: Alexis Cruz, Socorro Santiago, Rafael Alvarez, Lydia Montes,
    Nestor Serrano

Matos' childhood was endlessly painful—his father abandoned the family when he was two, his mother, addicted to drugs and alcohol, left him with his grandmother, who soon died. At age fourteen, Matos began dealing drugs to provide for his aunt and himself.
He succumbed to the lure of big money on the streets, dealing drugs in his East New York neighborhood. A rival gang of drug pushers sought revenge for a killing of one of their men, and Matos was the unlucky recipient of a bullet in the back of the head that left him paralyzed from the neck down. Now a quadriplegic, he was inspired—along with other victims of youth violence—to address high school student assemblies not to use guns or drugs.

Lucy and Desi: Before the Laughter (1991 CBS)

D: Charles Jarrott
S: William Luce and Cynthia Cherback
P: John Lenox
Cast: Frances Fisher, Maurice Benard

This movie tells of the intimate, and often stormy, private life of Lucille Ball and Desi Arnaz. Beginning on the eve of their unprecedented career success, the night the first episode of *I Love Lucy* is to be filmed before a live audience, their story unfolds through a series of flashbacks and recounts their relationship from 1940 to 1951. Fisher and Benard turn in credible performances as Lucy and Desi.

Mambo Mouth (1991 HBO)

D: Thomas Schlamme
S: John Leguizamo
P: Jeff Ross
Cast: John Leguizamo

This is a stellar performance adapted from John Leguizamo's acclaimed Off-Broadway one-man show. *Mambo Mouth* was inspired by characters Leguizamo encountered growing up in Jackson Heights, Queens. A response to the media's negative image of Latinos, the show is Leguizamo's declaration that "Latinos can be funny and strong in the face of adversity." The original stage presentation at the American Place Theatre in New York in 1990 won an Obie and an Outer Critics Circle Award.

Manhunt: Search for the Night Stalker (1989 NBC)

D: Bruce Seth Green
S: Joe Gunn
P: Ron Gilbert
Cast: A Martinez, Richard Jordan, Julie Carmen

In this fact-based drama, Los Angeles detectives Gil Carrillo (Martinez) and Frank Salerno (Jordan) are assigned to head the investigation into a string of brutal murders. Their work leads to the arrest of Richard Ramirez, a serial killer who terrorized the state of California during the summer of 1985.

Maricela (1984 PBS)

D: Christine Burrell
S: Nancy Audley
P: Richard Soto
Cast: Linda Lavin, Carlina Cruz, Irene Du Bari

A young El Salvadoran girl struggles to find her place in America when she and her mother come to work for a wealthy Malibu, California, family. This presentation was part of the "WonderWorks" series.

Menendez: A Killing in Beverly Hills (1994 CBS)

D: Larry Ellikan
S: Philip Rosenberg
P: Zev Braun and Vahan Moosekian
Cast: Edward James Olmos, Beverly D'Angelo

The story of Lyle and Erik Menendez, who committed the sensational murder of their wealthy parents, and the media circus that surrounded their trial.

Mrs. Cage (1992 PBS)

D: Robert Allan Ackerman
S: Nancy Barr
P: Dan Lupovitz
Cast: Anne Bancroft, Hector Elizondo

This powerful, essentially two-character drama was adapted from Barr's stage play about the interrogation of a housewife who, for unknown reasons, has murdered a woman in the parking lot of a local supermarket. She is interrogated by Police Lieutenant Ruben Angel, played by Elizondo. The movie aired on the *American Playhouse* series in May 1992.

Ned Blessing: The Story of My Life and Times (1993 CBS)

D: Jack Bender
S: William D. Wittliff
P: William D. Wittliff
Cast: Brad Johnson, Wes Studi, Luis Avalos

This two-hour movie and four-episode limited series about a Western outlaw turned sheriff, Ned Blessing (Johnson), and his sidekick, Crecencio (Avalos), in Plum Creek, Texas. It was created and written by William D. Wittliff.

Nostromo 1996 PBS

D: Alastair Reid
S: John Hale
P: Fernado Ghia
Cast: Claudio Amendola, Colin Firth, Albert Finney,
    Claudia Cardinale Joaquim de Almeida, Ismael E; Carlo,
    Emiliano Diez, Nelson E. Guerrero, Mario E. Sanchez

A lavish international production capturing the love, honor, obsession and greed of a mythical South American country in the 1890s in Joseph Conrad's *Nostromo*, one of the greatest novels of our time becomes a six-hour miniseries. Shot entirely on location in Cartegena de Indias, Colombia, for Mobil Masterpiece Theatre

The Old Man and the Sea (1990 NBC)

D: Jud Taylor
S: Roger O. Hirson
P: Bill Storke and Robert Fuisz
Cast: Anthony Quinn, Gary Cole, Patricia Clarkson, Francesca Quinn, Valentina Quinn

Anthony Quinn gives a powerful performance as Santiago in Ernest Hemingway's *The Old Man and the Sea*, based on the classic novella about on old Cuban fisherman's battle with a giant marlin in the Gulf Stream. It was filmed on Tortola in the Virgin Islands and is the second version of the Pulitzer Prize-winning book to be produced, following the 1958 theatrical original, in which Spencer Tracy played Santiago.

One Man's War (1991 HBO)

D: Sergio Toledo
S: Mike Carter and Sergio Toledo
P: Ann Skinner
Cast: Anthony Hopkins, Norma Aleandro, Rubén Blades

When the authorities brutalize Dr. Joel Filartaga's (Hopkins) fellow citizens, he courageously speaks out against the injustice of repression. But when the secret police kidnap, torture and murder his teenage son, he declares his own war.

Based on a real-life case, *One Man's War* is the shocking story of a South American family resisting a brutal dictatorship in Paraguay. The Filartagas' enlisted a celebrated criminal lawyer, Perrone (Blades), to aid them. The family subsequently carried their struggle to the United States, where, working with the Center for Constitutional Rights, they filed a civil suit in federal court. The result was a landmark victory for international human rights which set a legal precedent that continues to this day.

Prison Stories: Women on the Inside—"Esperanza" (1991 HBO)

D: Donna Deitch
S: Martin Jones
P: Gerald T. Olson
Cast: Rachel Ticotin, Talisa Soto, Francesca Roberts

Prison Stories is a feature-length dramatic trilogy that takes a gritty look at the struggles of women in prison, portraying the family tragedy when a mother is jailed. "Esperanza" is the story of a child who follows in his mother's criminal footsteps. Iris Martinez (Ticotin), sentenced to hard time for a drug deal engineered by her husband, must leave her son Mico in the care of her sister Rosina (Soto) for the duration of her prison term. Despite his aunt's efforts, Mico continues his family's crime cycle by selling crack and ends up being arrested and sentenced to juvenile detention.

Return of the Gunfighter (1967 ABC)

D: James Neilson
S: Robert Buckner
P: Frank King and Maurice King
Cast: Robert Taylor, Chad Everett, Ana Martin, Rudolfo Hayos, Jr.

An aging gunfighter and a wounded saddle tramp team up to help a Mexican girl avenge the deaths of her parents, murdered for their land.

Rita Hayworth: The Love Goddess (1983 CBS)

D: James Goldstone
S: E. Arthur Kean
P: Andrew Susskind
Cast: Lynda Carter, Michael Lerner, Alejandro Rey

This television movie dramatizes the remarkable story of the legendary actress from her early career as a dancer through her evolution into one of Hollywood's most glamorous and popular stars.

River of Promises (1977 NBC)

D: Lee Katzin
S: Michael Mann
P: David Gerber
Cast: Richard Yniguez, Joe Santos, Julio Medina, Jaime Sanchez,
    Rose Portillo, Gregory Sierra, Edward James Olmos

This two-hour special "Police Show" episode stars Richard Yniguez as Ratazza, a policeman who goes undercover to expose a ring smuggling illegal aliens into East Los Angeles. This sensitively written drama is acted by a top-notch, predominantly Hispanic cast.

The Sacketts (1979 CBS)

D: Robert Totten
S: Jim Byrnes, based on the novels *The Day Breakers* and *Sackett* by
    Louis L'Amour
P: Douglas Netter and Jim Byrnes
Cast: Sam Elliott, Tom Selleck, Jeff Osterhage, Glenn Ford,
    Ben Johnson, Gilbert Roland, Ana Alicia

This four-hour, two-part miniseries is based on a story by famed Western writer Louis L'Amour about the adventures of the three Sackett brothers in the New Mexico Territory after the Civil War. Gilbert Roland plays Don Luis Alvarado, a terminally ill rancher who is anxious to preserve the lands of the New Mexico Territory from the marauding Anglos. His granddaughter, Drusilla Alvarado, played by Ana Alicia, falls in love with the youngest of the Sackett brothers, Tyrell (Osterhage), who is recruited to the Alvarado cause by Don Luis.

Santiago's America (1973 ABC)
D: Albert Waller
S: Albert Waller
P: Albert Waller
Cast: Ruben Figueroa, Alex Colon, Rene Enriquez, Miriam Colon

This one-hour color film, a sequel to the highly successful *Santiago's Ark* (see below), was designed as a series pilot but was never picked up. It concerned the further adventures of young Santiago, who, with a New York City junk man, sets off in a battered taxicab to discover America.

Writer/producer/director Albert Waller packaged both *Santiago's Ark* and *Santiago's America*, and based on original story ideas by Waller, who saw Santiago as "a modern-day Hispanic Huckleberry Finn." Waller went on to write, direct and produce "La Raza," a series of three one-hour documentaries that were broadcast on television nationwide. Narrated by Ricardo Montalban, they traced the history of Mexican Americans in the United States.

Santiago's Ark (1972 ABC)
D: Albert Waller
S: Albert Waller
P: Albert Waller
Cast: Ruben Figueroa, Alex Colon, Rene Enriquez

Santiago's Ark was the one-hour color dramatic film that launched the "ABC Afterschool Specials," under the auspices of executive producers Michael Eisner and Brandon Stoddard.

It is the story of a boy from Spanish Harlem in New York who dreams of building a boat out of scraps of lumber on the roof of his East Side tenement building. The ark becomes a symbol of the hopes and dreams of the entire neighborhood.

The film stars Ruben Figueroa, who was known for his work in the film *Popi* (1969) starring Alan Arkin, and his father was played by Rene Enriquez, who a decade later became famous as Lieutenant Calletano on *Hill Street Blues* (1974-80).

The *New York Times* listed *Santiago's Ark* as one of the ten best television shows of the year. It won numerous awards including the Gabriel Award, the Christopher Award, the Peabody Award, and a Golden Gate Award from the San Francisco International Film Festival.

Seguin (1982 PBS)
D: Jesus Trevino
S: Jesus Trevino
P: Severo Perez
Cast: A Martinez, Henry Darrow, Rose Portillo, Pepe Serna, Danny De La Paz, Enrique Castillo, Lupe Ontiveros, Edward James Olmos

Seguin is the story of Juan Seguin, an unsung hero of the Texas Wars for Independence and one of the Mexican defenders of the Alamo. Don Erasmo Seguin, along with Stephen Austin, brought the first Anglo settlers to help develop the Mexican state of Texas. His son Juan came into conflict with his father because he sympathized with both Mexico and the American colonists' struggle for possession of Texas.

This sensitive film features evocative color cinematography, a good central performance by A Martinez and a cast that includes many of the most prominent young Hispanic American actors of their generation. Edward James Olmos plays a snarling and vicious General Santa Anna.

Filmed as part of a proposed PBS series called "La Historia," which never received additional funding, *Seguin* was shown at film festivals around the United States and in Spain. It was broadcast as part of the PBS *American Playhouse* series. It was filmed in 16mm on a twenty-one-day schedule and at a cost of $500,000. Shot in Brackettville, Texas, the production used many of the sets John Wayne had used to film *The Alamo* (1960).

Spic-O-Rama (1993 HBO)
D: Peter Askin
S: John Leguizamo
P: Jeff Ross
Cast: John Leguizamo

In his second HBO Comedy Hour special based on his own stage production, acclaimed talent John Leguizamo portrays all five members of a dysfunctional New York Latino family. He ranges from a nine-year-old self-proclaimed genius to a troubled Desert Storm vet to a cynical mom; all in a one-man tour-de-force performance filmed in front of a live audience at New York's American Place Theatre. *Spic-O-Rama* premiered at the Goodman Theatre in Chicago, moving to the West Side Arts Theatre in New York for a sold-out three-month run. *Time* magazine called it one of the best plays of 1992, hailing Leguizamo for "hilarious monologues that moved beyond performance art to become a true and deeply moving play."

Steambath (1973 PBS)
D: Burt Brinckerhoff
S: Bruce Jay Friedman, based on his play
P: Norman Lloyd
Cast: Bill Bixby, Jose Perez, Valerie Perrine

A videotaped production aired on KCET's "Hollywood Television Playhouse" series, this show was controversial due to its language and partial nudity. Bruce Jay Friedman adapted his bizarre and inventive off-Broadway play about recently deceased people who find themselves in a steambath, only to discover it to be a purgatory. Only later do they discover that the Puerto Rican steambath attendant is God.

Stones for Ibarra (1988 NBC)
D: Jack Gold
S: Emest Kinoy
P: Bruce Pustin
Cast: Glenn Close, Keith Carradine, Alfonso Arau, Jorge Cervera, Jr.,
Ron Joseph, Lupe Ontiveros, Trinidad Silva

This "Hallmark Hall of Fame" contemporary drama concerns an American couple who move to a small Mexican village and adapt to the different values and perceptions of life and death. The film portrays Mexicans as simple, superstitious and emotionally volatile. Except for the two leads, nearly the entire cast is Hispanic.

The Streets of L.A. (1979 CBS)
D: Jerrold Freedman
S: Marvin A. Gluck
P: George Englund
Cast: Joanne Woodward, Fernando Allende, Pepe Serna, Isela Vega

A middle-class Anglo woman (Woodward) goes off in lone pursuit of three teenage hoods in the Los Angeles barrio after becoming incensed by their malicious mayhem. Spanish-language film star Fernando Allende made his American television debut as the lead thug. Mexican actress Isela Vega joins him with a fine performance as his mother. The film shows stereotypical images of urban violence, Mexicans and Mexican Americans.

Streets of Laredo (1995 CBS)
D: Joseph Sargent
S: Larry McMurtry based on his novel
P: Robert Halmi Jr., Larry Levinson, Suzanne De Passe,
James Lee Barrett
Cast: James Garner, Sissy Spacek, Sam Shepard, Sonia Braga,
Alexis Cruz, James Victor

This is a four-hour miniseries that is shown in two parts. Captain Woodrow Call (Garner), now retired from the Rangers, is a bounty hunter who goes down to Mexico to search for cold-blooded killer Joey Garza (Cruz). Sonia Braga plays Joey's mother, Maria Garza.

Sudden Terror: The Hijacking of School Bus #17 (1996 ABC)
D: Paul Schneider
S: Jonathan Rintels
P: S. Bryan Hickox, Jonathan Rintels, Diane Jacques,
Laurie Hannan-Anton
Cast: Maria Conchita Alonso, Marcy Walker, Michael Paul Chan,
Bruce Weitz

A courageous female school bus driver, Marta Caldwell (Alonzo), confronts a deranged hijacker, who seizes command of her bus filled mentally challenged youngsters and leads police on a twenty-five mile chase. The two-hour drama is a fictionalized account inspired by an actual event.

Sweet 15 (1990 PBS)

D: Victoria Hochberg
S: Sharon Weil
P: Richard Soto
Cast: Karla Montana, Jenny Gago, Susan Ruttan, Tony Plana, Panchito Gomez, Liz Torres

Marta, a fourteen-year-old Mexican American, has never taken the plight of undocumented immigrants seriously. She selfishly looks forward to her *Quinceanera* celebration. In preparation, she must perform some kind of community service, which consequently finds her working at the church's amnesty office, leading her to the shocking discovery that her own father is an illegal immigrant. Another presentation from the "WonderWorks" series, *Sweet 15* was an Emmy Award winner.

Swing Vote (1999 ABC)

D: David Anspaugh
S: Ron Bass and Jean Rusconi
P: Chad Oman and Jonathan Littman
Cast: Andy Garcia, Ray Walston, James Whitmore, Robert Prosky, Harry Belafonte

When a successful African-American woman is convicted of murder after she terminates her pregnancy, it is the vote from the newest and youngest Supreme Court Justice, Joseph Kirkland (Garcia) that will decide her case. While he and the other Supreme Court Justices grapple with the controversial case that has polarized the nation, Kirkland must also come to terms with a personal interest he has in the matter.

Texas (1995 ABC)

D: Richard Lang
S: Sean Meredith
P: Aaron Spelling, E. Duke Vincent and John Wilder
Cast: Maria Conchita Alonso, Benjamin Bratt, Patrick Duffy, Chelsea Field, Anthony Michael Hall, Stacy Keach, John Schneider

Based on the James A. Michener's novel, *Texas*, the miniseries begins in 1821, and tells how a small group of Anglos ("Texicans") traveled West to settle in a harsh land that had been inhabited for thousands of years by Indians and claimed by Spanish explorers for Mexico only two centuries earlier. Led by the impresario Stephen F. Austin, whose father had received a royal commission to colonize the land, the settlers co-existed peacefully with the Mexican government until the military, under the command of General Santa Anna, began seizing their freedoms. The resulting struggle to settle the land and achieve freedom—including the defense of the Alamo and the Battle of San Jacinto—became legendary. Alonzo portrays Lucha Lopez Garza, a bandita, and the wife of Benito Garza. Bratt stars as Benito Garza, a proud and heroic vaquero descended from Spanish royalty.

Texas debuted first as a video release in 1994 and premiered as a two-part miniseries on ABC television in 1995. Filmed on location in South Texas in and around Brackettville, Texas.

Things You Can Tell Just by Looking at Her (2000 Showtime)

D: Rodrigo Garcia
S: Rodrigo Garcia
P: John Avnet, Lisa Lindstrom, Marsha Oglesby
Cast: Kathy Baker, Glenn Close, Cameron Diaz, Calista Flockhart, Gergory Hines, Holly Hunter

A romantic comedy about the physical and emotional intricacies affecting the everyday lives of a very diverse group of women, and the strategies they adopt in coping with events, large and small, overt and hidden, which shape the way they live. The directorial debut of cinematographer Rodrigo Garcia, based on his own screenplay.

(Left to right) Edward James Olmos, Tony Orlando and Pepe Serna in the TV movie *Three Hundred Miles for Stephanie.*

Three Hundred Miles for Stephanie (1981 NBC)

D: Clyde Ware
S: Clyde Ware
P: Antonio Calderon
Cast: Tony Orlando, Julie Carmen, Edward James Olmos, Pepe Serna, Gregory Sierra

This film was based on the true story of a San Antonio, Texas, police officer (Orlando) who vowed to run more than 300 miles as a grueling act of faith for his critically ill and brain-damaged daughter. This film showed sensitivity in portraying Mexican Americans in the mainstream of society with the subtleties of their Latin backgrounds. This was Orlando's dramatic acting debut.

Victims for Victims: The Theresa Saldana Story (1984 NBC)

D: Karen Arthur
S: Arthur Heinemann
P: Harry R. Sherman
Cast: Theresa Saldana, Adrian Zmed

This is a fact-based account of one woman's struggle to survive both physically and mentally after a near-fatal attack on her life. Once attacked by a deranged fan who stabbed her repeatedly, actress Theresa Saldana played herself in this television movie. In the aftermath of her long, painful recovery, she went on to form an organization (Victims for Victims) devoted to helping victims of violent crime deal with their pain and anger.

The Wall (1998 Showtime)

D: Joseph Sargent
S: Scott Abbott, Patrick Sheane Duncan, Charles Fuller
P: Edgar J. Scherick, Lynn Raynor
Cast: Edward James Olmos, Michael DeLorenzo, Ruby Dee, Savion Glover

Three stories about the Vietnam war and its effects on those who survived it.

Olmos plays a high ranking United States Army Colonel in one story and Michael DeLorenzo plays a brilliant guitar playing grunt in another. The film recognizes the participation of Latinos in the Vietnam war.

Wanted: The Sundance Woman (1976 ABC)

D: Lee Philips
S: Richard Fielder
P: Stan Hough
Cast: Katharine Ross, Steve Forrest, Hector Elizondo

After Butch Cassidy and the Sundance Kid are reportedly killed in Bolivia, Etta Place (Ross) roams around the Southwest pursued by Charlie Siringo (Forrest). She winds up in Mexico with Pancho Villa, played by Hector Elizondo.

The Young Indiana Jones Chronicles: Young Indiana Jones and the Curse of the Jackal (1992 ABC)
D: Carl Schultz
S: Jonathan Hale
P: Rick McCallum
Cast: Sean Patrick Flanery, Mike Moroff, Francesco Quinn

The second half of this two-hour movie, which begins in Egypt on an archeological dig for Tutankhamen's tomb, takes sixteen-year-old Indiana Jones to 1916 Mexico, where he meets and joins Pancho Villa. The General and his men are on the run from General John Pershing and his American troops, led by young George Patton, who is already displaying his rugged individualistic command style. This is a well-done, nicely balanced, insightful and stereotype-free episode, with a strong performance from Moroff as Villa and featuring Quinn as one of his men. Filmed in Spain, the movie was executive produced by George Lucas, who was responsible for the theatrical *Indiana Jones* trilogy starring Harrison Ford.

Zorro and The Cisco Kid

Despite the overwhelmingly negative images and stereotypes presented by mainstream American media, two positive Hispanic American heroes have managed to make it into popular American culture—Zorro and the Cisco Kid.

Antonio Banderas as Zorro in *The Mask of Zorro*.

Duncan Renaldo (left) as Cisco and Leo Carillo (right) as his sidekick, Pancho.

Zorro

Zorro means "fox" in Spanish and first appeared in an original story "The Curse of Capistrano" by Johnston McCulley, published in 1919 in the pulp magazine *All Story*. Though based on California history and the romanticism surrounding the Spanish/Mexican period, Zorro is a purely fictional character. His story is the amalgam of two different historical periods (the apex of the Mission and the Rancho periods were many years apart) and facts set around the period of 1820 when California was still a borderland territorial possession of Spain.

Though the story takes place in the pueblo of Los Angeles, McCulley used the Capistrano title solely for its alliterative appeal and had only a cursory knowledge of California history. He may also have been influenced by another literary work with a heroic leading man, *The Scarlet Pimpernel*, written in 1905.

Zorro and his alter ego, Don Diego de la Vega, the seemingly spoiled son of Spanish aristocrats, is one of the best-known characters of popular fiction. When confronted with injustice, Don Diego transforms himself into Zorro, a Robin Hood defender of his countrymen. Zorro identifies himself to villains with his bullwhip, black mask, cape and his signature: using his foil to make a figure of a "Z" at the site of the deed. Zorro's popularity, fed by a continuous stream of magazine stories, books, comic books, motion pictures and television, has remained high through the years. Zorro stories have been published in twenty-six languages. He remains the most popular fictional character in many of the Spanish-speaking countries. During the 1960s and 1970s, a number of low-budget Zorro adventure films were made by Italian, Spanish and Mexican production companies; most bear little resemblance to the original concept or character except for the black outfit and mask. Frank Latimore, an American-born actor, plays Zorro in several Italian movies; Sean Flynn (Errol Flynn's son, who became a war photographer in Vietnam and who is still among the missing in action) plays Zorro in *Mark of Zorro* (1963). Gordon Scott (a former Tarzan) became Zorro in *Zorro and The Three Musketeers* (1963), set in seventeenth-century Spain and France, where Zorro and The Three Musketeers fight the men of Cardinal Richelieu and defend Isabella, Duchess of Seville. In 1990, on a nationally syndicated talk show, cartoonist Bob Kane revealed that Zorro had been the inspiration for Kane's modern-day crime-fighting hero, Batman.

On April 23, 1991, a story in the *Hollywood Reporter* announced that Steven Spielberg would produce and direct a big-budget feature version of Zorro for TriStar pictures. In 1994, Speilbeg relinquished the directing reins to Mikael Salomon but remained as executive producer with Andy Garcia slated to star as Zorro and Sean Connery as the elder Don Diego. The premise was now somewhat based on *Pygmalion*; a common thief is transformed into a freedom fighter and justice seeker as Zorro by an elder Zorro—Don Diego past his prime. Salomon dropped out of the project and in 1995 it was announced that Robert Rodriguez would direct a Zorro film with Antonio Banderas playing the title character. Banderas was attracted to the role of Zorro because it was a chance to play the only real Spanish hero Hollywood has ever created. "I knew the character because the Disney television series starring Guy Williams aired during the 1960s in Spain," he remarked in a press interview. "I loved watching the show when I was a kid and pretending I was Zorro. When the chance came to play the role, I didn't hesitate to say yes." Later that year, Rodriguez left the project after budgetary and creative differences with the producers. After many script versions and rewrites, Banderas remained attached as star and Martin Campbell, who had just scored a big success with the James Bond thriller *GoldenEye* (1995) with Pierce Brosnan, was selected to direct the film now called *The Mask of Zorro*. It went on to become an international box office sensation upon its release in 1998.

Zorro Movies

The movies and television listings below appear in chronological order, tracing the development of the character's popularity.

The Mark of Zorro (1920 United Artists)

D: Fred Niblo
S: Elton Thomas [Douglas Fairbanks], based on the story "The Curse of Capistrano" by Johnston McCulley
P: Douglas Fairbanks
Cast: Douglas Fairbanks

Silent. Douglas Fairbanks was the first to recognize the cinematic potential in Zorro. He purchased the screen rights in 1920 and promptly made the film.

One of United Artists' (the company Fairbanks founded in 1919 with Mary Pickford, Charlie Chaplin and D.W. Griffith) first feature films, *The Mark of Zorro* provided Fairbanks with a new type of role, The overwhelming success of the movie launched his career as a swashbuckling screen hero in adventure dramas. He continued in this vein until 1934, when the aging star was no longer accepted as a vigorous, virile hero by the public. He was succeeded in these roles by Errol Flynn, Tyrone Power and his own son, Douglas Fairbanks, Jr.

Fairbanks brought his athletic ability to the part of Zorro and his well-known comic skill to the role of the fop Don Diego. All of the props and sets were made to glorify Fairbanks's athletic abilities. The emphasis of the film is on action: There are several exciting duel sequences and a chase in which Zorro eludes his pursuers through an amazing series of acrobatic stunts. Fairbanks established the classic model after which all later interpretations of Zorro would be patterned. The film's story, too, set the style for most of the screenplays to follow.

Many of the characters in the photoplay are stereotypes, present merely to move the action along.

The aristocratic Don Diego, returning from Spain, where he has been educated, is horrified at the tyranny prevailing in Spanish California. As El Zorro, Diego wages a one-man war against the villainous Captain

Douglas Fairbanks in
The Mark of Zorro.

*Photo courtesy of The Museum of
Modern Art/Film Stills Archive.*

Ramon (Robert McKim), who is in cahoots with the corrupt governor. In order to divert suspicions from himself, Diego assumes the guise of an empty-headed, handkerchief-flourishing dandy, fooling everyone—including his ladylove, Lolita, and his own father. The basic plot is the same as that of any number of nineteenth-century American morality plays in which the hero saves a family from ruination and thereby wins the daughter. Both Fairbanks and his director, Fred Niblo (a former actor) came to films from the stage.

The Mark of Zorro inaugurated a series of historical costume dramas that Fairbanks would star in and produce for United Artists.

Don Q, Son of Zorro (1925 United Artists)

D: Donald Crisp
S: Jack Cunningham, based on "Don Q's Love Story" by
    Hesketh Prichard and Kate Prichard
P: Douglas Fairbanks
Cast: Douglas Fairbanks, Mary Astor, Jack MacDonald, Enrique Acosta

Silent. This sequel to The Mark of Zorro (1920) repeats the success of the original. As Valentino did in Son of the Sheik (1926), Fairbanks plays a dual role as the son as well as the father, who comes to the aid of his offspring in Spain. Enrique Acosta plays the villain, Captain Ramon.

Bold Caballero (1936 Republic Pictures)

D: Wells Root
S: Wells Root
P: Nat Levine
Cast: Robert Livingston, Heather Angel, Ferdinand Munier,
    Chris-Pin Martin, Carlos de Valdez

After Don Q, Son of Zorro (1925), Zorro did not appear again on screen again until this 1936 Republic feature film. The star was Robert Livingston, a popular Western serial star at Republic.

The storyline is that Diego, incensed by the cruelty and taxation being imposed upon the Indians of Santa Cruz by the commandante of the local garrison, decides to correct the situation. When a governor appointed by the King of Spain arrives in California to take over the province, the commandante kills him and accuses Zorro of the murder.

The Phantom of Santa Fe (1937 Burroughs-Tarzan Pictures)

D: Jacques Jaccard
S: Charles Royal
P: Ashton Dearholt
Cast: Norman Kerry, Frank Mayo

This pseudo-Zorro movie was actually filmed six years previously, in 1931, as The Hawk.

This feature was originally put on the shelf due to technical difficulties, not the least of which was star Norman Kerry's poor speaking voice. A leading man in silent films, Kerry found his inferior vocal abilities to be his downfall in the talkies.

Ashton Dearholt, a former actor-turned-producer and one of the partners in the Burroughs-Tarzan Company, became interested in the footage of *The Hawk* in 1936 and managed to turn it into a salable property.

Reedited and with a completely new dubbed voice track as well as a musical score, the resulting effort was titled *The Phantom of Santa Fe* and was sold as a brand new film. While not an exact imitation of Zorro, in that the hero did not wear a mask, the screenplay did follow the classic storyline laid down by McCulley. Kerry employed the lazy, sleepy fop persona as a disguise and became the mysterious Hawk to avenge the wrongs perpetrated by the villain (Mayo) and his band of renegades.

Zorro Rides Again (1937 Republic Pictures)

D: William Witney and John English
S: Barry Shipman, John Rathmell, Franklyn Adreon [alternate spelling: Franklin], Ronald Davidson, and Morgan Cox
P: Sol C. Siegel
Cast: John Carroll, Duncan Renaldo, Noah Beery, Dick Alexander

Republic Pictures followed *Bold Caballero* (1936) with a twelve-chapter serial. These serials were thirty-minute or so shorts that played in theaters as an accompaniment to the main film. Directed to appeal to younger audiences, they were usually full of action and cliffhanger endings to keep the audience returning week after week.

Zorro Rides Again was a contemporary Western in which Zorro was no longer Don Diego but was instead his great-grandson, James Vega (Carroll). The plot revolves around attempts to sabotage the building of the California-Yucatan Railroad. Yakima Canutt did all the double and stunt work for Carroll.

Zorro's Fighting Legion (1939 Republic Pictures)

D: William Withey and John English
S: Ronald Davidson, Franklyn Adreon [alternate spelling: Franklin], Morgan Cox, Sol Shor, and Barney A. Sarecky
P: Hiram S. Brown, Jr.
Cast: Reed Hadley

This next twelve-chapter serial was the first of the Zorro adventures to take place in Mexico rather than California. The story was also set almost forty years after the original. In the film, the Legion is organized to combat the activities of a false Yaqui Indian idol who is stealing much-needed gold that was to be used to help Benito Juarez.

Tyrone Power in the
classic *The Mark of Zorro*.

The Mark of Zorro (1940 Twentieth Century-Fox)

D: Rouben Mamoulian
S: John Taintor Foote, Garrett Fort, and Bess Meredyth
P: Raymond Griffith
Cast: Tyrone Power, Basil Rathbone, Linda Darnell, Gale Sondergaard,
   Eugene Pallette, Chris-Pin Martin, George Regas, Frank Puglia,
   Pedro de Cordoba

In November of 1940, Twentieth Century-Fox released the first official *Zorro* remake bearing the original title. Directed by noted stylist Rouben Mamoulian, the film stars Tyrone Power, Basil Rathbone and Linda Darnell.

Power's performance as Zorro was thought by many critics to suffer in comparison to that of Fairbanks. While a capable actor, Power was not an athlete in the fashion of Fairbanks and Flynn; he was, however, handsome, romantic and dashing. The new film proved successful and popular with audiences, and it made Power a star in South America. A rousing finale in the form of an action-filled duel between the unmasked Zorro (Power) and the villainous Captain Esteban (Rathbone) remains one of the memorable examples of swordplay on screen. In addition to the Hispanics in the cast list above, Fortunio Bonanova has a small role in the film.

Rathbone was a classically trained British actor and an accomplished fencer and athlete. He also played the villainous Sir Guy of Gisbourne in *The Adventures of Robin Hood* (1938), in which he gave another memorable screen display of swordplay, this time against Errol Flynn. The dueling scenes were created by Albert Cavens, who also instructed Douglas Fairbanks.

Mamoulian chose his extras as if they were playing leads. He insisted that all extras be either Spaniards or Mexicans. When Mamoulian started drawing up plans for the film, he discovered through the studio's research department that the Los Angeles of 1820 was a hot and dusty place, a squat adobe settlement inhabited by Indians, Spaniards and only one American. Street brawls were an everyday affair, and the people mostly used hides as a medium of exchange. The director decided that such a primitive, dirty outpost would never do.

At the Fox Ranch in Agoura, California, he had a town constructed that glistened in its whiteness, pleased the eye with its greenness, and boasted a preponderance of dashing caballeros, gentlemen adventurers and beautiful señoritas—a classic example of Hollywood never letting the facts interfere with a good story. History was followed closely, though, in re-creating the town plaza and church.

A Franciscan monk donated original music from the period to be used in the film, which was scored by Alfred Newman. Power and Darnell practiced a dance sequence for weeks. Ernesto A. Romero, former vice consul of Mexico in Los Angeles, was the technical adviser, hired at the insistence of Fox chief Darryl F. Zanuck.

Zorro's Black Whip (1944 Republic Pictures)
D: Spencer Bennet and Wallace Grisell
S: Basil Dickey, Jesse Duffey, Grant Nelson, and Joseph Poland
P: Ronald Davidson
Cast: George J. Lewis, Linda Sterling

This twelve-chapter serial has a female lead, clad in black leather, who uses a whip. It utilizes the name Zorro but has no other connection to the character.

Son of Zorro (1947 Republic Pictures)
D: Spencer Bennet and Fred C. Bannon
S: Franklyn Adreon [alternate spelling: Franklin], Basil Dickey, Jesse Duffy, and Sol Shor
P: Ronald Davidson
Cast: George Turner, Peggy Stewart

Turner is a descendant of Zorro, assuming the name to fight injustice in the West following the Civil War.

Ghost of Zorro (1949 Republic Pictures)
D: Fred C. Bannon
S: Royal Cole, William Lively, and Sol Shor
P: Franklyn Adreon [alternate spelling: Franklin]
Cast: Clayton Moore, Pamela Blake

A twelve-chapter serial starring Clayton Moore, who became famous as the Lone Ranger on television a few years later. A reedited version of this serial was released in 1959.

Moore plays the grandson of the original Zorro, who fights a gang out to stop the extension of telegraph lines from St. Joseph to Twin Bluffs, California. Alex Montoya has a small role as Yellow Hawk.

Don Daredevil Rides Again (1951 Republic Pictures)
D: Fred C. Bannon
S: Royal Davidson
AP: Franklyn Adreon [alternate spelling: Franklin]
Cast: Ken Curtis

In this twelve-chapter serial, Ken Curtis plays the masked hero, who is dressed to utilize stock film footage from the old *Zorro* serials.

Curtis had a long association with director John Ford, appearing in several of his Westerns; he is best known as the character of Festus on the long-running *Gunsmoke* (1955-75) television series in the 1960s and 1970s.

The Man with a Steel Whip (1954 Republic Pictures)
D: Franklin Adreon
S: Donald Davidson
AP: Franklin Adreon [alternate spelling: Franklyn]
Cast: Richard Simmons

Dressed in a costume identical to that worn by Zorro, Simmons was called El Latigo. Old film footage was again utilized in this last Western serial to be produced by Republic Pictures.

The Sign of Zorro (1960 Buena Vista)
D: Norman Foster and Lewis R. Foster
S: Norman Foster, Lowell S. Hawley, Bob Wehling, and
   John Meredyth Lucas
P: Walt Disney and William H. Anderson
Cast: Guy Williams, Henry Calvin, Gene Sheldon, Britt Lomond,
   George J. Lewis, Romney Brent

Two theatrical feature films were released that drew heavily from footage from the first year of the Walt Disney *Zorro* television series. *The Sign of Zorro*, from episodes 1 through 13, was released worldwide in June 1960.

Don Diego returns home from his schooling in Spain to find injustices being inflicted on the people of the pueblo of Los Angeles. As Zorro, he fights to defeat the corrupt rule of Captain Monastario (Lomond). Aided by his mute manservant (Sheldon) and astride his remarkable horse, Tornado, Zorro thwarts and finally defeats the evil official and his men in a series of escapades complete with thrilling encounters of swordplay and feats of horsemanship.

Zorro, the Avenger (1961 Buena Vista)
D: Charles Barton
S: Lowell S. Hawley and Bob Wehling
P: William H. Anderson
Cast: Guy Williams

Culled from the Walt Disney television series *Zorro*, episodes 27 through 39, *Zorro, the Avenger* was released worldwide in April 1961. The story pits Zorro against The Eagle, portrayed by Charles Korvin. The Eagle is a Spanish renegade of the 1820s who plots to overthrow Spanish rule and turn California over to the highest bidder.

Zorro (1975)
D: Duccio Tessari
S: Giorgio Arlorio
P: Luciano Martino
Cast: Alain Delon, Stanley Baker

This film was never released in American theaters but is shown quite often on American television, primarily because it was shot in color. Alain Delon, a leading French actor and international star, plays Zorro in a story curiously set in Latin America. This "spaghetti Zorro" from Spain is fun on its own terms.

Zorro, the Gay Blade (1981 Twentieth Century Fox)

D: Peter Medak
S: Hal Dresner
P: George Hamilton and C.O. Erickson
Cast: George Hamilton, Brenda Vaccaro, Ron Leibman

Zorro's son, Don Diego, returns to California only to find his father mysteriously dead and his one-time friend Esteban (Leibman) the ruthless new alcalde (mayor). The father had one last wish—that the legend of Zorro be carried on by either Don Diego or his long-lost twin brother, Ramon. Diego accepts his calling and assumes his father's trademark cape and mask.

George Hamilton stars in the swashbuckling adventure/comedy *Zorro, the Gay Blade* as the son of the legendary hero of Old California who crosses swords with the enemies of the oppressed.

All goes well for the new Zorro until he breaks his foot in a fall and is forced to retire. In his absence the peasants suffer, but just as the outlook becomes hopelessly grim, his brother Ramon shows up. During his absence, he has become a prissy aesthete, very much the stereotypical flamboyant homosexual. Diego tells Ramon (who has changed his name to Bunny Wigglesworth) that he must fulfill their father's wish and take over the job of Zorro, an idea that fails to thrill Bunny. However, he sees it as a chance to spruce up Zorro's rustic image. Dressed in mauve silk and with bullwhip, Bunny goes out into the night and fights for the people. Two women who had been vying for Zorro's attention get the two Zorros confused, with predictable humorous results.

George Hamilton plays Zorro in this spoof, which was not popular with audiences. It is debatable who overacted more, Leibman or Hamilton. Hamilton's portrayal of a "gay" caballero is sophomoric and offensive, and he was not as successful spoofing Zorro and the swashbuckling genre as he was spoofing Dracula in *Love at First Bite* (1979). *Zorro, the Gay Blade* was handsomely produced and filmed on location with Cuernavaca, Mexico, doubling for early Los Angeles, California. The cinematographer was John Alonzo. The film was affectionately dedicated to the director of the 1940 *The Mark of Zorro*, Rouben Mamoulian.

The Mask of Zorro (1998 TriStar)

D: Martin Campbell
S: John Eskow and Ted Elliott & Terry Rossio
P: Doug Claybourne David Foster
Cast: Antonio Banderas, Anthony Hopkins, Catherine Zeta-Jones,
　　　Stuart Wilson, Matt Letscher, Maury Chaykin, Tony Amendola,
　　　Pedro Armendariz, L.Q. Jones, William Marquez, Jose Perez,
　　　Victor Rivers, Julieta Rosen

The Mask of Zorro is a sweeping romantic adventure of love and honor, of tragedy and triumph set against Mexico's fight for independence from the iron fist of Spain. It is also a rousing and often hilarious

Anthony Hopkins (left),
Catherine Zeta-Jones
(center) and Antonio
Banderas (right) in
The Mask of Zorro.

swashbuckling fable about a roguish outlaw whose only knowledge of a sword is that "the pointy end goes into the other man" is transformed into an elegant hero.

It has been twenty years since Don Diego de la Vega (Hopkins) successfully fought Spanish oppression in Alta California as the legendary romantic hero, Zorro. Imprisoned for two decades, he now must find a successor to stop Don Rafael Montero (Wilson), the powerful, former Spanish governor of Alta California who cost de la Vega his freedom, his wife, Esperanza (Rosen) and his daughter Elena (Zeta-Jones). Montero is now making plans to purchase California from Mexico's president, General Santa Anna. Alejandro Murieta (Banderas), a bandit with a troubled past, is transformed by Don Diego into a new Zorro who he hopes will help him foil Montero's schemes once and for all. Tracing the heroic story of these highly charged relationships, the film follows the new Zorro as he assumes de la Vega's mantle and enters into a romantic relationship with a woman close to his predecessor's heart.

The Mask of Zorro marked the first major Hollywood theatrical feature film production of *Zorro* in over forty years and was a rousing romantic swashbuckling entertainment. Banderas was the perfect actor to embody the dashing Zorro. Hopkins brought dignity and strength to the aging Zorro/Don Diego. Catherine Zeta-Jones was exactly right in the role of the beautiful Elena. It is a beautifully realized film that incorporates a jigsaw puzzle of many historical elements.

Filmed entirely on location in Central Mexico. Production began at Churubusco Studios in Mexico City. Filming continued at the San Blas Hacienda outside the city of Tlaxcala: the Telapayac hacienda outside Pachuca and Santa Maria Regla, both in the state of Hildalgo; and along the beaches of Guaymas.

Zorro Television Series

Zorro (1957-1959 ABC)
Cast: Guy Williams

The *Zorro* television series premiered on ABC in the fall of 1957 and ran for two seasons of thirty-nine episodes each. It completed the second season with a 26.6 average Nielsen rating. It proved so popular that Walt Disney produced four one-hour specials—"Adios El Cuchillo," "Auld Acquaintances," "El Bandido" and "The Postponed Wedding"— after the series run for the Walt Disney program. A legal battle arose when Walt Disney wanted to move the show from ABC to NBC. The dispute was not settled for two years, which put an end to the show.

Guy Williams, a handsome six-foot, three-inch Italian American actor from New York, whose real name was Armando Catalano, achieved a personal triumph with the role of Zorro. His magnetic personality, good looks, acting and physical abilities all made him an instant star. He was still closely associated with the role when he died at age sixty-five in 1989.

Williams was a struggling New York actor when he made a screen test at Walt Disney Studios in April 1957. A few months later he debuted on television as Zorro, the legendary masked hero of Spanish California. Henry Calvin co-starred as Sergeant Garcia, the robust, bumbling comic villain, and Gene Sheldon co-starred as Bernardo, Zorro's mute servant and sidekick. George J. Lewis played Zorro's father, Don Alejandro de la Vega and Britt Lomond played Monastario, the arch villain governor of El Pueblo de Los Angeles. Many Hispanic actors found work on the series, and both Gilbert Roland and Cesar Romero guest starred on the show. As a television series, *Zorro* went far beyond the story confines of the earlier motion pictures, though it continued to follow the classic formula.

Three horses portrayed Tornado, Zorro's talented black stallion, because no single horse could perform all the feats required. One reared magnificently before the cameras, another worked uninhibitedly with other horses during fight sequences and a third was used for the long, treacherous runs over hills.

Zorro became a phenomenon that was accorded one of the largest merchandising campaigns of its time. The series spawned a Zorro craze among the youth of the nation. Kids wrote Z's on their homework assignments and carried Zorro lunchboxes to school. Toy stores sold

Guy Williams as the swashbuckling swordsman Zorro, in Walt Disney's *The Sign of Zorro*, a 1960 feature that drew heavily from the opening episodes of the acclaimed TV series.

Zorro capes, hats, masks and swords. Twentieth Century-Fox re-released the Tyrone Power version of *The Mark of Zorro* (1925) and Republic Pictures re-released its *Zorro* serials to cash in on the tremendous interest the television show created.

The Disney story begins with Don Diego de la Vega (Williams) en route from Spain to his home in the pueblo of Los Angeles. He learns of the unjust military dictatorship imposed on the city by the villainous Monastario (Lomond) and vows to fight this evil regime.

Posing as a foppish intellectual, Don Diego and his manservant Bernardo (Sheldon) arrive in time to witness Monastario's hatred for the de la Vega family when Monastario's men unjustly accuse a neighbor, Torres, of treason and throw him into jail. Convinced that open resistance to the tyranny would be fatal, Diego transforms himself into El Zorro, "The Fox," a black-clad, masked avenger who will fight tyranny with a flashing sword, superior horsemanship and daring bravery. Bernardo, who is mute—and also often pretends to be deaf—serves as Diego's listening post.

Don Diego is careful to keep his identity secret from his father and constructs a secret passageway at the rancho that leads from the main house to an underground cavern where he keeps his horse, Tornado, and his Zorro disguise. This cavern leads out to a brush-covered hillside cave entrance not far from the main road into and out of Los Angeles.

Norman Foster, who had directed Disney's phenomenally successful *Davy Crockett* television films starring Fess Parker, directed the *Zorro* series. A former actor, Foster first made a name for himself directing the Charlie Chan and Mr. Moto film series for Twentieth Century-Fox. He then joined Orson Welles' Mercury Theater and co-directed and co-wrote *Journey into Fear* (1942) for RKO. He went to Mexico for several years, where he directed a number of Mexican films before returning to the States, where he directed films until assignments at Disney Studios, beginning with *Davy Crockett*, brought him into the forefront of television film directors. Having lived and worked in Mexico, Foster had an understanding of Latin culture and style that served the *Zorro* series well.

The main exterior *Zorro* set covered several acres of the Disney backlot in Burbank, California. It included the governor's fortress, the barracks, an inner courtyard, stables, Don Diego's hacienda, the plaza and the church. Considerable attention was given to authenticity and detail in the set design and construction to give the entire pueblo an aged and weathered adobe and wood appearance. Location scenes were shot at the Disney Ranch and at Mission San Luis Rey near Oceanside, California, where a special archway was constructed and added to the existing historical structure, which is still standing over thirty years later.

Albert Cavens, the fencing master who had coached both Douglas Fairbanks and Tyrone Power, was brought in to work with Williams, who was an accomplished fencer. Dave Sharpe, who had worked as a stuntman in Republic serials, was also brought in to choreograph the exciting screen swordplay. William Lava provided the music and director Foster provided the lyrics to the *Zorro* theme song, which became a best-selling record.

The Mark of Zorro (1974 Twentieth Century Fox)

D: Don McDougall
S: Brian Taggert
P: Robert C. Thompson and Rodrick Paul
Cast: Frank Langella, Ricardo Montalban, Gilbert Roland

Frank Langella took up the Zorro mantle in this inferior Twentieth Century-Fox television film remake, which went so far as to borrow the stirring music score by Alfred Newman from the 1940 version by the same name. Ricardo Montalban plays the evil Captain Esteban and Gilbert Roland plays Zorro's father.

Zorro and Son (1983 CBS)

D: Various
Cast: Henry Darrow, Paul Regina, Bill Dana, Gregory Sierra

Henry Darrow of television's *The High Chaparral* (1967-71) fame became the first Hispanic American or Latino to play Zorro in this short-lived comedy series produced by Walt Disney Studios. Paul Regina plays the youthful son who wants to follow in his father's footsteps.

Zorro, the Legend Continues (1990 New World Television)

D: Various
Cast: Duncan Regehr, Henry Darrow,
       Patrice Camhi [aka: Patrice Martinez]

In Spain in 1990, New World Television began production on twenty-two episodes of a *Zorro* series for international syndication. The first major *Zorro* television series commitment in over thirty years and the first *Zorro* television production to be filmed in color, the series brought the classic spirit of the masked crusader to a new generation. Don Diego is portrayed not as a fop or a dandy but as an educated man, well versed in the arts as well as the sciences, who uses his knowledge to solve the problems he faces in his adventures.

The series stars Duncan Regehr (who had previously portrayed another swashbuckler, Errol Flynn, in a television movie based on his life), whose distinctive style and personality enhanced the role. Regehr is a native of Canada and was once an Olympic boxing contender and a champion figure skater; in addition, he has classical Shakespearean stage training. Veteran stunt coordinator and fencing master Peter Diamond tutored Regehr and handled the exciting swordplay, the chases on

Duncan Regehr as Zorro, the swashbuckling defender of Old Spanish California, brandishes his sword to defend his beauteous señorita, Victoria Escalante (Patrice Camhi) in the *Zorro* TV series.

horseback and leaps from balconies and garrison walls. Diamond, who made his name as a stunt director for British television, lists among his credits the spectacular laser lightsaber battles in the *Star Wars* trilogy and the more traditional swashbuckling of *The Princess Bride* (1987).

In contrast to the Walt Disney series, this Zorro character was given a continuing love interest, Victoria Escalante (portrayed by Patrice Camhi), a beautiful señorita. She is attracted to the dashing Zorro but not to Don Diego in a variation of the Lois Lane and Superman/Clark Kent affair. Also in the cast are James Victor, as the bumbling Sergeant Mendoza, and Efrem Zimbalist, Jr., as Zorro's father. In the second season, Henry Darrow replaced Zimbalist. Darrow, coincidentally, was the only Hispanic to date to have played Zorro (in the short-lived *Zorro and Son* [1983] series), and he also provided the voice of Zorro for a syndicated thirteen-episode animated series.

Zorro, the Legend Continues was produced over a four-year period for a total of eighty-eight episodes, four of which were culled into a two-hour television movie. It is shown on the cable Family Channel in the States and is in syndication throughout the world.

The Cisco Kid

O. Henry's Robin Hood of the Old West first came to life in a short story called "The Caballero's Way," originally published in the collection *Heart of the West* in 1904, and then three years later in *Everybody's* magazine.

O. Henry's character is a rather unlovable Anglo gunfighter who kills "for the love of it—because he was quick tempered, to ovoid arrest, for his own amusement, any reason that came to mind would suffice." In the story, the Cisco Kid tricks a Texas Ranger into shooting the Kid's unfaithful girlfriend and then disappears into the chaparral.

No one is quite sure where O. Henry discovered the Cisco Kid. O. Henry (William Sidney Porter) had spent much of his life as a gambler, working odd jobs and wandering around New Orleans, Texas and Central America. He began writing short stories while serving time in prison near Cisco, Texas. The character is thought to be a combination of the legend of Billy the Kid and the Mexican gunfighter Blas. The development of the Cisco Kid into the character we know today is largely the work of many different people over nearly a century of film, comics, radio and television.

Again, we list the screen career in chronological order.

The Cisco Kid Movies

The Cisco Kid (1914-16 Eclair Films)
Cast: Herbert Stanley Dunn

Silent. When the Cisco Kid was first brought to the screen, the O. Henry image remained intact. Eclair Films, a French company, produced numerous one-reel films during the silent era that portray a bittersweet individual who was neither all bad nor all good. Stan Dunn was the first actor to play the Cisco Kid.

In Old Arizona (1929 Fox Film Corporation)
D: Raoul Walsh and Irving Cummings
S: Tom Barry, based on O. Henry's short story
P: William Fox
Cast: Warner Baxter, Edmund Lowe, Dorothy Burgess

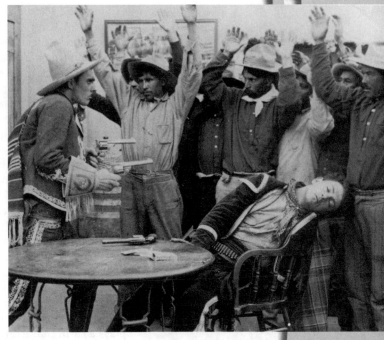

A landmark 1929 film, shot near Zion National Park in Utah, this was the first outdoor talkie Western. As such, it made an impact on the public, as did Warner Baxter's Academy Award®-winning performance as the Cisco Kid.

Baxter and director Raoul Walsh took liberties with O. Henry's character, in particular removing much of the viciousness from Henry's original character. Baxter immersed himself in Latin culture. (This was the era of Latin leading actors in Hollywood.)

Walsh, a former cowboy, had wanted to play the role himself, but he lost an eye in an accident on location when a jackrabbit jumped through the windshield of his car and shattered the glass. During Walsh's absence from the film, Irving Cummings took over as director and Warner Baxter signed on to play the Cisco Kid. Duncan Renaldo, a later Cisco, was also considered for the role, but he was in Africa filming *Trader Horn* (1931).

A great deal of the early footage was still usable, and Walsh returned in time to complete the picture. Microphones were concealed under prairie shrub, hung from foliage and hidden behind rocks. The sounds of bacon sizzling, six-guns shooting, horses' hooves and cowboy ballads made the difference for audiences.

The time of the film is the late 1890s, and the beautiful half-breed girl Tonia Maria (Burgess), a temperamental flirt, lives in a little adobe house in a Mexican settlement near Wolf Crossing, a town close to the Grand Canyon. She is adored by the notorious Cisco Kid (Baxter), a charming, daring and often eccentric bandit. He is a murderer but also a lover, and he has a $5,000 price on his head. The Cisco Kid has such a reputation that, in order to illegally obtain a Wells Fargo strongbox, he merely fires two warning shots and the stagecoach drivers readily hand it over.

Herbert Stanley Dunn (left), the original Cisco Kid, subdues his adversaries in this scene from *The Caballero's Way*, the first Cisco Kid movie, filmed in 1914 by Eclair Film Co. in Tucson, Arizona. It has been claimed that Dunn was the first Western film star to feature two six-guns, as evidenced here. The heavy leather gloves were cumbersome and Dunn couldn't fire the trigger until he cut a hole for his index finger. The tight leather costume was ordered from El Paso, Texas. Dunn once remarked that it was so tight "I had to get into it with a shoehorn."

Photo courtesy of Gene Autry Western Heritage Museum.

Warner Baxter (left) as the Cisco Kid, Dorothy Burgess (center) and Edmund Lowe (right) in *In Old Arizona*.

Sergeant Mickey Dunn (Lowe), an Irishman from Brooklyn and a member of the 17th Cavalry, is dispatched to capture the Cisco Kid. Dunn is no less a ladies' man than the Kid, and he also romances Tonia Maria, offering her a cash reward for her betrayal of the Kid, then waiting in her home to take in the outlaw.

The Cisco Kid, meanwhile, has been involved with cattle rustlers in Guadalupe. When he returns to Wolf Crossing, he finds Tonia Maria in the arms of Dunn. The Kid then sings a song, which begins: "Don't you monkey with my lulu girl, or I'll tell you what I'll do."

He overhears the two plotting to kill him and determines to settle matters with his faithless lover and the man who stole her from him. Tonia Maria sends Dunn a note asking him to go back to her shack; the Kid gets hold of it and forges an addition to it, saying that the outlaw will be there dressed as a woman. Dunn arrives and accidentally kills Tonia Maria. The Kid then escapes.

Unlike most cinematic lawbreakers, he is neither caught nor killed at the finale. It is generally thought that Warner Baxter made five Cisco Kid films, though, in fact, he made only four theatrical features and a short subject in which he appeared as a character similar to Cisco. *Romance of the Rio Grande* (1929) is mistakenly listed as a Cisco Kid film and appears in many books and film listings as such because Baxter plays a Latin character and it was made during the same period as the other films. *Romance of the Rio Grande* was directed by Alfred Santell, who directed the Baxter Cisco feature *The Arizona Kid* (1930). *Romance of the Rio Grande* was also used as the title of a Cesar Romero Cisco Kid film in 1941, so many film historians supposed that it was a remake of the 1929 film.

Baxter recalled in a 1948 *Saturday Evening Post* article, "I must admit that I rate the Kid's first film, *In Old Arizona*, as my top favorite. I like the role because of its warmth and color. I enjoyed trying out the lingo of a Mexican and I thought the mixture of comedy and drama in the story was fine... Then, too, the fact that I got an Oscar® for the job caused me no pain."

Soledad Jimenez appears as the cook.

The Arizona Kid (1930 Fox Film Corporation)
D: Alfred Santell
S: Ralph Block
Cast: Warner Baxter, Mona Maris, Carole Lombard

The Cisco Kid has a secret gold mine in Utah that is his main source of revenue. Nick Hoyt (Theodore Von Eltz) robs the gold mine and attempts to turn the Kid in to the local sheriff.

Cisco Kid (1931 Fox Film Corporation)
D: Irving Cummings
S: Alfred Cohn, based on a story by O. Henry
Cast: Warner Baxter, Edmund Lowe, Conchira Montenegro, Nora Lane

The Cisco Kid robs a bank for the money to save a widow's ranch from foreclosure, which sends Sergeant Mickey Dunn (Lowe), in pursuit. This film reunited Baxter and Lowe in a rather poor sequel of sorts to *In Old Arizona* (1929).

The Stolen Jools (1931 Fox Film Corporation)
D: Victor Heerrnan, William McGann, and others
S: Unknown
P: National Variety Artists
Cast: Warner Baxter, Edmund Lowe, Richard Barthelmess,
    Wallace Beery, Gary Cooper, Fay Wray, Joan Crawford

Warner Baxter appeared as the Cisco Kid and Edmund Lowe was Sergeant Dunn in this two-reel short subject, which was produced for the National Vaudeville Association's benevolent fund. Fifty-five major stars of the era, representing every film studio, made cameo appearances.

The film is an amusing piece in which actress Norma Shearer's jewels are supposed to have been stolen and a police inspector in various disguises visits the different screen players, who are supposed to have been at a dance where the jewels were last seen.

The Return of the Cisco Kid (1939 Twentieth Century Fox)
D: Herbert I. Leeds
S: Milton Sperling
P: Kenneth MacGowan
Cast: Warner Baxter, Lynn Bari, Cesar Romero, Chris-Pin Martin

The Cisco Kid (Baxter) helps a young woman hold onto her ranch in this, Baxter's final Cisco role. The next actor to play Cisco, Cesar Romero, has a supporting role in this film as Lopez.

The Cisco Kid and the Lady (1939 Twentieth Century Fox)
D: Herbert I. Leeds
S: Frances Hyland
P: John Stone
Cast: Cesar Romero, Marjorie Weaver, Chris-Pin Martin

This is Cesar Romero's first film as the Cisco Kid. With Chris-Pin Martin as his sidekick, Gordito. Cisco battles bandits out to steal a gold mine owned by an orphan whose father has been shot by the bandit leader.

When Romero, a Twentieth Century-Fox contract player, replaced Warner Baxter in the role, the Cisco Kid became decidedly more Latin. A Cuban American with a Broadway stage background, Romero added his own debonair flair to the role.

The State Department asked Darryl F. Zanuck, the head of Twentieth Century Fox, to either change the format or stop production on the pictures because some Latin countries were having problems with the "greaser" portrayal of Gordito by Chris-Pin Martin. Zanuck decided to abandon the films (which were shot near Lone Pine, California) and sold the rights to Monogram Studios.

Cesar Romero as the Cisco Kid in the Twentieth Century Fox film series.

The Gay Caballero (1940 Twentieth Century Fox)

D: Otto Brower

S: Albert Duffy and John Larkin, based on a story by Walter Bullock, Duffy, and characters created by O. Henry

P: Walter Morosco and Ralph Dietrich

Cast: Cesar Romero, Chris-Pin Martin

Cisco seeks to clear himself after a series of crimes are committed using his name.

Lucky Cisco Kid (1940 Twentieth Century Fox)

D: H. Bruce Humberstone

S: Robert Ellis and Helen Logan, based on a story by Julian Johnson

P: Sol M. Wurtzel

Cast: Cesar Romero, Chris-Pin Martin

The Cisco Kid fights a gang of crooks led by a dishonest judge.

Viva Cisco Kid (1940 Twentieth Century Fox)

D: Norman Foster

S: Samuel G. Engel and Hal Long

P: Sol M. Wurtzel

Cast: Cesar Romero, Jean Rogers, Chris-Pin Martin

The Cisco Kid rescues a stagecoach from a robbery attempt and falls for one of the lovely passengers, only to discover her father is involved in crimes with a vicious partner.

Ride On, Vaquero (1941 Twentieth Century Fox)

D: Herbert I. Leeds

S: Samuel G. Engel

P: Sol M. Wurtzel

Cast: Cesar Romero, Mary Beth Hughes, Chris-Pin Martin

The Cisco Kid works with the law in order to trap a gang of kidnappers.

Romance of the Rio Grande (1941 Twentieth Century Fox)

D: Herbert I. Leeds

S: Harold Buchman and Samuel G. Engel, based on the novel *Conquistador* by Katherine Fullerton Gerould

P: Sol M. Wurtzel

Cast: Cesar Romero, Patricia Morison, Ricardo Cortez, Chris-Pin Martin, Pedro de Cordoba, Inez Palange

An aging cattle baron sends for his grandson to help him with the ranch. The grandson is shot en route, and the Cisco Kid takes his place so he can apprehend the culprit.

The Cisco Kid Returns (1945 Monogram)

D: John P. McCarthy
S: Betty Burbridge
P: Philip N. Krasne
Cast: Duncan Renaldo, Martin Garralaga

The Cisco Kid finds himself a guardian to a four-year-old girl whose father has been shot to death.

While the *Cisco Kid* film rights were changing hands from Fox to Monogram, there was a rising consciousness in Latin America over the portrayal of Latinos in Hollywood films. The Cisco Kid films were not offenders in this regard (having made Cisco a hero and using many Latin supporting actors in the features), but the new producer and star, Duncan Renaldo, wanted to make sure that his portrayal was fair and acceptable.

After many meetings and discussions in Washington, D.C., Mexico City and Hollywood, Renaldo hit upon the idea of adapting O. Henry's original character by basing him more on Cervantes' classic Spanish hero Don Quixote. He therefore created the character of Pancho from Sancho Panza, and the Mexican opera singer Martin Garralaga was chosen for this supporting role. Their first three films were immensely successful in the States and Latin America, and were shot with the kind of speed we associate with television shows today.

In Old New Mexico (1945 Monogram)

D: Phil Rosen
S: Betty Burbridge
P: Philip N. Krasne
Cast: Duncan Renaldo, Martin Garralaga, Pedro de Cordoba

The Cisco Kid comes to the aid of a pretty young nurse who has been falsely accused of murder.

South of the Rio Grande (1945 Monogram)

D: Lambert Hillyer
S: Victor Hammond and Ralph Bettinson
P: Philip N. Krasne
Cast: Duncan Renaldo, Martin Garralaga, George J. Lewis, Armida,
   Lillian Molieri, Pedro Regas, Soledad Jimenez, Tito Renaldo

The Cisco Kid goes after a dishonest Mexican official.

Beauty and the Bandit (1946 Monogram)

D: William Nigh
S: Charles S. Belden
P: Scott R. Dunlap
Cast: Gilbert Roland, Martin Garralaga, Ramsay Ames, Felipe Turich,
   Alex Montoya, Frank Yaconelli

The Cisco Kid meets a female bandit (Ames) and brings out the best in her.

Gilbert Roland as the Cisco Kid.

The Gay Cavalier (1946 Monogram)

D: William Nigh
S: Charles S. Belden
P: Scott R. Dunlap
Cast: Gilbert Roland, Martin Garralaga

The Cisco Kid has two prime goals: to rescue a maiden who is about to marry a supposedly wealthy suitor in order to save the family hacienda, and to capture the outlaws who held up a stagecoach bearing gold for a mission.

Gilbert Roland took over the role temporarily when Duncan Renaldo went back to work for the war effort, which was just winding down. Roland, a Mexican American who was raised in El Paso, Texas, had his own ideas about the character of the Cisco Kid and freely incorporated them in his portrayal. Over the course of the next few films, he downplayed Pancho. Martin Garralaga soon left the role after his first picture with Roland, because of an allergy to horses. But Garralaga managed to stay in the series, usually playing an assortment of Spanish aristocrats usually in interior scenes away from horses. Then Frank Yaconelli replaced him as a Pancho-like character called Baby, followed by the return of Chris-Pin Martin as Pancho.

There was no Pancho in the original O. Henry short story; Cisco was alone. Drawing upon the standard Hollywood convention that every Western hero needed a sidekick, a saddle partner named "Gordito" was introduced in the earlier Cesar Romero series.

Roland's interpretation also heightened the Robin Hood aspect and made his more Cisco Casanova-like with the ladies.

Gilbert Roland said, "My Cisco Kid may have been a bandit, but he fought for the poor and was a civilized man in the true sense of the word." He also described an instance on the set: "Once I insisted on a piece of dialogue which as a result showed Cisco reading Shakespeare by a river bank. I wanted to be sure the Mexicano was not portrayed as an unwashed, uneducated, savage clown."

Riding the California Trail (1947 Monogram)

D: William Nigh
S: Clarence Upton Young
P: Scott R. Dunlap
Cast: Gilbert Roland, Martin Garralaga, Inez Cooper, Alex Montoya,
    Rosa Turich, Gerald Echeverria, Frank Yaconelli

The Cisco Kid aids a young woman who is tricked out of an inheritance by a scheming uncle.

Robin Hood of Monterey (1947 Monogram)

D: Christy Cabanne
S: Bennett Cohen
P: Jeffrey Bernerd
Cast: Gilbert Roland, Chris-Pin Martin, Pedro de Cordoba,
    Nestor Paiva, Julian Rivero

The Cisco Kid steps in when a woman kills her husband and frames her stepson for the crime.

South of Monterey (1947 Monogram)

D: William Nigh
S: Charles S. Belden
P: Scott R. Dunlap
Cast: Gilbert Roland, Martin Garralaga, Frank Yaconelli

The Cisco Kid sets out to stop a land-swindling scheme involving a police captain and a tax collector in a small Western town.

King of the Bandits (1948 Monogram)

D: Christy Cabanne
S: Bennett R. Cohen, based on an original story by Cabanne.
    Additional dialogue by Gilbert Roland
P: Jeffrey Bernerd
Cast: Gilbert Roland, Chris-Pin Martin

The Cisco Kid pursues a stagecoach robber who has been impersonating him.

The Valiant Hombre (1948 United Artists)

D: Wallace Fox
S: Adele Buffington
AP: Duncan Renaldo
P: Philip N. Krasne
Cast: Duncan Renaldo, Leo Carrillo

When John James, who has just discovered gold, disappears and his partners are murdered, Cisco and Pancho set out to right things.

Barbara Billingsley, who plays the damsel in distress, went on to find success as June Cleaver, mother of the Beaver, on the *Leave It to Beaver* (1957-63) television series in the late 1950s and the early 1960s.

In 1948, Duncan Renaldo returned to the role and, in a brief period of time, became the most famous Cisco Kid of them all. With his friend Leo Carrillo as Pancho, he did five feature films between 1948 and 1950 for United Artists and producer Philip Krasne. Renaldo took an active part as associate producer and in the further development of the character.

The Cisco Kid changed dramatically when Renaldo returned to the role. "I came up with the idea of making Cisco a Don Quixote, only more reasonable and fighting the windmills of the troubles of humanity: also making Pancho a real compassionate, kind-hearted human being who thus inadvertently gets his partner into trouble."

Cisco's costume changed too, and Renaldo lost the mustache. The new costume reflected something from several Latin countries in style and dress. Cisco's hat is from early California, the boots and belt are from the Argentinean gaucho and the shirt is from Mexico with a French-influenced fleur-de-lis design. The Cisco Kid's new horse was named Diablo.

Garralaga did not return to the role of Pancho. Veteran character actor Leo Carrillo better complemented Renaldo as Pancho, in that he was not merely a sidekick but was a strong personality himself. Renaldo claims to have cautioned Carrillo about his comedic overplaying of Pancho with the accent, but Carrillo just went with the characterization, and children loved it.

The Daring Caballero (1949 United Artists)
D: Wallace Fox
S: Betty Burbridge
P: Philip N. Krasne
Cast: Duncan Renaldo, Leo Carrillo, Kipper Valez, Pedro de Cordoba

When a little boy's father is wrongly accused of murder and embezzlement, Cisco and Pancho must clear his name.

The Gay Amigo (1949 United Artists)
D: Wallace Fox
S: Doris Schroeder
P: Philip N. Krasne
Cast: Duncan Renaldo, Leo Carrillo, Armida

A series of stagecoach holdups, ranch raids and murders are terrorizing a western community. The commander of an Army post suspects Cisco and Pancho of the banditry, and they go about clearing their names by capturing the real outlaws.

Satan's Cradle (1949 United Artists)
D: Ford Beebe
S: Jack Benton
P: Philip N. Krasne
Cast: Duncan Renaldo, Leo Carrillo

Cisco and Pancho come to the defense of a preacher who has been roughed up by a gang of crooks running the town.

The Girl from San Lorenzo (1950 United Artists)
D: Derwin Abrahams
S: Ford Beebe
P: Philip N. Krasne
Cast: Duncan Renaldo, Leo Carrillo

Cisco and Pancho are accused of various crimes, which are being committed by a duo impersonating them.

The Cisco Kid (1994 TNT)
D: Luis Valdez
S: Michael Kane and Luis Valdez
P: Moctesuma Esparza and Robert Katz
Cast: Jimmy Smits, Cheech Marin, Sadie Frost, Bruce Payne, Ron
    Perlman, Tim Thomerson, Yareli Arizmendi, Pedro Armendariz, Jr.

A reinterpretation of the classic Hollywood film hero, filmed on actual locations in Mexico, starring Jimmy Smits (*L.A. Law* [1986-94]) as Cisco and Cheech Marin (*Born in East L.A.* [1987]) as Pancho. Directed and co-scripted by Luis Valdez (*La Bamba* [1987], *Zoot Suit* [1981]), the story takes place during the French occupation of Mexico in 1867. Cisco smuggles guns across the border to help the Juaristas and finds a cause and a friend to believe in.

The Cisco Kid is a tongue-in-cheek Western filled with fast gunplay, narrow escapes, wild rides, battling armies and romance. It is also a funny and offbeat character study of the beginnings of the remarkable friendship that develops between Cisco and Pancho in this two-hour television film, the first Cisco Kid film to be produced in thirty-eight years.

In this version Cisco is a Californian, born in Los Angeles in 1836 when it was still a part of Mexico. He lives through California's struggles with statehood in 1850 and all the dramatic, sweeping changes that occur.

Cisco is a man in search of his own identity. Pancho is a Juarista and a family man whose cause is to free Mexico from the French. Cisco and Pancho are equal partners in this adventure, unlike previous portrayals of the duo.

Director Luis Valdez remarked in an interview, "I wanted to get away from the bandido stereotype, so I made Cisco independently wealthy, like Batman, so he could be free to roam the western landscape in search of his own identity and help fight injustice wherever he encountered it." The director added, "I've also tried to ground the characters in a historical setting without losing the fun, romance and appeal of what audiences expect from a Cisco Kid adventure."

Jimmy Smits (left) as the Cisco Kid and Cheech Marin (right) as Pancho in the 1994 TNT production.

The Cisco Kid Television Series

The Cisco Kid was transferred to television in 1950, and 156 episodes were produced in color until 1955. The shows were originally shown in black and white, in part because color broadcasting and color televisions did not become widely available until the end of the decade. Seemingly overnight, the Cisco Kid became a major pop figure alongside such other popular film and television heroes as the Lone Ranger, Roy Rogers, Hopalong Cassidy and Gene Autry, all of whom made the jump to television in its formative years.

Renaldo and Carrillo made over 100 personal appearances a year at rodeos, county fairs, hospitals and market openings. While the television program was being shown around the world, a radio program was

Duncan Renaldo (left) as the Cisco Kid and Leo Carrillo (right) as his sidekick Pancho in the TV series *The Cisco Kid*.

running weekly. A series of Dell comics appeared; a superbly drawn comic strip by Jose Luis Salinas was widely featured in the daily newspapers. Children carried Cisco Kid lunchboxes and coloring books to school and wore Cisco Kid gun belts. Renaldo, who felt that television played an important role in forming character, was an early opponent of unnecessary violence on television, and campaigned against it. Renaldo's popularity was such that he still toured actively until 1965, ten years after the last television episode was filmed.

Set in the Old West, the Cisco Kid represents the epic qualities of the classic hero combined with Latin gentility. Duncan Renaldo, an orphan who had no country but his adopted one, saw Cisco as a modern knight, "a man of generosity and a friend to a better world." Gilbert Roland's Cisco was a "friend to the poor" and a dashing lover, while Warner Baxter and Cesar Romero gave him his devil-may-care attitude and his debonair suavity.

The television show has never really gone away. Through cable channels and videos, the Cisco Kid is still breaking señoritas' hearts, fighting injustice, laughing in the face of danger and riding off into endless sunsets.

In the late 1970s, MGM announced a new Cisco Kid feature film to star then-popular television actor Erik Estrada, but the film was never produced.

Biographies

T he following is a listing of Hispanic American actors, actresses and behind-the-camera professionals. Biographies are also
included for a number of non-Hispanic individuals who are
nevertheless identified in the public mind as Hispanic, on the
basis of the roles they played or their Hispanic-sounding
names. Birth and death dates are given when available, followed by a brief biography and, in some cases, selected film
and television credits. Information has been difficult to
obtain on less prominent artists. If there are no birth and
death dates, it is because they were not available despite
research in the *Motion Picture and Television Almanac*, the
Daily Variety obituaries, *Theater World*, *Screen World*, several
screen *Who's Who's*, newspaper and magazine articles and
studio biographies or through personal interviews with the
subjects whenever possible. The Screen Actors Guild, agents
and personal managers were also contacted for information
on their clients' histories.

Enrique Acosta

B: 1870

D: 5/1949

Born in Mexico City, he left Mexico for the United States at the time of the revolution. He drifted to Los Angeles and found work as a bit player in Hollywood silent films such as *Don Q, Son of Zorro* (1925).

With the advent of talking pictures he began getting work in Spanish-language versions of Hollywood films as well as in original Hollywood Spanish-language productions of the early 1930s. With Laurel and Hardy, Acosta's credits include *Ladrones* (Night Owls) (1929), *Tiembla y Titubea* (Below Zero) (1930), *De Bote en Bote* (Pardon Us) (1931) and *Politiquerias* (Chickens Come Home) (1931).

Rodolfo Acosta
[alternate spellings: Rodolpho, Rudolpho, Rodolfa]

B: 7/29/1921

D: 11/7/1974

Acosta was a character actor with Mexican Indian features, a burly frame and lightning quick changes of expression that usually condemned him almost exclusively to playing bandidos and Indians in American Western dramas. He was born near El Paso, Texas, in the then-American community of Chamizac, midway between El Paso and Juarez, Mexico, which has since been ceded back to Mexico. When he was three years old, his family moved to California, where he attended Los Angeles City College and UCLA. He was fascinated by acting, studying it at school as well as at the Pasadena Playhouse. His success in dramatic studies reached a peak at age nineteen, when he accepted a prize scholarship from the Palacio de Bellas Artes in Mexico City, where he stayed for three years. With the advent of World War II, Acosta joined the United States Navy, where he was assigned to Naval Intelligence. Following the war, director John Ford saw him in a stage production and offered him a featured role in *The Fugitive* (1947). Following this, in 1948, the famous Mexican actor/director Emilio Fernandez wrote for him the role of Paco, a gigolo, in the Mexican film classic *Salón México* (1948). The part won Acosta Mexico's highest acting award, the Ariel. He was immediately signed by Hugo Fregonese to co-star with James Mason in the 1950 production of *One Way Street*, which led to a Universal contract. He acted with a gallery of top box office stars, including John Wayne, Robert Mitchum, Marlon Brando and Dean Martin. He also appeared periodically on many Western television series, including *Have Gun Will Travel* (1957-63), *The Big Valley* (1965-69) and *The High Chaparral* (1967-71). Other credits include *Pancho Villa Returns* (1950), *Hondo* (1953), *Wings of the Hawk* (1953), *A Life in the Balance* (1955), *The Littlest Outlaw* (1955), *Bandido* (1956), *The Proud Ones* (1956), *The Tijuana Story* (1957), *One-Eyed Jacks* (1961), *How the West Was Won* (1962), *The Sons of Katie Elder* (1965), *Return of the Seven* (1966) and *Pat Garrett and Billy the Kid* (1973).

Tony Aguilar

B: 6/13/1922

A popular charro (Mexican cowboy) singing film star, Aguilar's only Hollywood film appearance was as the Juarista General Rojas in *The Undefeated* (1969), starring John Wayne.

Carlos Alazraqui

Alazraqui was born and raised in Northern California of Argentinean parents. As a voice-over artist, he has worked on Nickelodeon's *Rocko's Modern Life* (1993-96) as the title character, in the feature film *A Bug's Life* (1998) and has made several guest appearances on *The Family Guy* (1999-). His voice is probably most recognized from the popular "talking Chihuahua" ads for Taco Bell.

    As an actor, he has made guest appearances on such shows as *That '70s Show* (1999-) and in the feature film *The Dirt Merchant* (1999).

Jessica Alba

B: 1982

Alba played Kirsten in the teen comedy *Never Been Kissed* (1998) opposite Drew Barrymore. Other feature film credits include *Idle Hands* (1999) and *Paranoid* (2000). Alba made her feature film debut at the age of twelve with a small part in *Camp Nowhere* (1994).

Edward Albert

B: 2/20/1951

The son of Margo and Eddie Albert, Edward Albert made his motion picture debut in *Butterflies Are Free* (1972). A consistently working actor, his career has spanned television, movies-of-the-week and large studio feature films.

Felix Enriquez Alcala

A director of photography, Alcala made his feature motion picture directing debut with *Fire Down Below* (1998) starring Steven Seagal, after two decades as a cinematographer and director in television, documentaries and commercials. Born in Bakersfield, California, and raised in Christoval, Texas, Alcala graduated from the film school of Southern Methodist Univeristy in Dallas. Alcala won an ASC nomincation for his cinematography on the Amblin/NBC pilot *Earth II* (1994). Alcala has also worked on such recent critically acclaimed television drama series as *I'll Fly Away* (1991-93), *Going to Extremes* (1992), *Homefront* (1991) and *Equal Justice* (1992). He has directed episodes of *I'll Fly Away*, *Homefront*, *South Beach* (1993) and *ER* (1994-). He won a Directors Guild nomination for his work on the Emmy-winning *ER*.

Norma Aleandro

B: 1941

An Argentine actress, Aleandro won critical plaudits, including a New York Film Critics Award for Best Actress, for her role in the Argentinean film *The Official Story*, which won the Best Foreign Language Film Oscar® in 1985. She played a Mexican Indian maid in *Gaby—A True*

Norma Aleandro as Edie Costello in the romantic comedy *Cousins*.

Story (1987), for which she was nominated for an Academy Award® for Best Supporting Actress. She co-starred as Edie Costello in *Cousins* (1989) and in *Vital Signs* (1990).

Ana Alicia
B: 1957
Born in Mexico City, Alicia attended high school in El Paso, Texas, and graduated with a degree in Drama from the University of Texas. She moved to New York and landed a role on a soap opera and then went to Los Angeles, where she was signed as a contract player for Universal Television, appearing on many shows. In 1980 she landed the role of Melissa Cureson, starring with Jane Wyman and Lorenzo Lamas, among others, on the hit television series *Falcon Crest* (1981-90). Her only feature film appearance to date is 1989's *Romero*, in which she played the wife of an aristocrat opposite Raul Julia.

Fernando Allende
B: 11/10/1954
A Cuban-born, Mexican-raised leading man, Allende had a strong run of successful films in Mexico in the late 1970s and 1980s. He made an unsuccessful bid for stardom in the United States in the independent feature film *Heartbreaker* (1983), after having played opposite Joanne Woodward as a young gang tough in the television film *The Streets of L.A.* (1979). He has continued to work, guest starring in American television and international productions.

Laurindo Almeida
B: 1917
D: 8/1/1995
A Brazilian-born master guitarist and composer, Almeida immigrated to the United States in 1947 after achieving tremendous success in his native country. With a recording career of fifty years, five Grammy Awards, sixteen Grammy nominations and several hundred films on his resume, Almeida has contributed to the scores of many motion pictures, including *A Song Is Born* (1948), *The Old Man and the Sea* (1958), *Camelot* (1967), *The Adventurers* (1970) and the 1992 Academy Award®-winning Best Picture, *Unforgiven*, in which his solo guitar work is prominently featured.

Nestor Almendros
B: 10/30/1930
D: 3/4/1992
A Spanish-born, Cuban-raised cinematographer, Almendros won an Academy Award® for Best Cinematography for *Days of Heaven* (1978). He was nominated four more times for Best Cinematography, for the films *Kramer vs. Kramer* (1979), *The Blue Lagoon* (1980), *Sophie's Choice* (1982) and *Places in the Heart* (1984). *Madame Rosa* (1977), for which he was the director of photography, won the Academy Award® as Best Foreign Language Film. Almendros served as director of photography on eight films for French director Francois Truffaut. His other films

include *Goin' South* (1978), *Nadine* (1987) and *Billy Bathgate* (1991). He died of lymphoma in 1992.

Chelo Alonso

B: 1938

A Cuban-born actress, Alonso went to Italy and starred in a number of Italian sand-and-spear spectacles of the 1960s that were dubbed into English and released in the States. Her credits include *Goliath and the Barbarians* (1960) opposite Steve Reeves, *Sign of the Gladiators* (1960) and a small part in Sergio Leone's "spaghetti Western" *The Good, the Bad, and the Ugly* (1967).

John Alonzo

B: 1/3/1934

Cinematographer Alonzo was nominated for an Academy Award® for his work on *Chinatown* (1974). He began his career as an actor in *The Magnificent Seven* (1960), in which he plays one of Calvera's bandidos.

Alonzo was born to Mexican parents in Dallas, Texas. He worked as a cameraman at a local television station before moving to Los Angeles in 1957. There he found work doing bit parts in movies and television, usually as a Mexican bandido. Alonzo worked with some of the great old cameramen, including Joe MacDonald, who shot *Invitation to a Gunfighter* (1964), in which Alonzo worked as an actor. It was MacDonald who encouraged the young Alonzo to pursue a career as a cinematographer. Alonzo shot a few short subjects and documentaries, but his big break came when he assisted cameraman James Wong Howe and director John Frankenheimer on the film *Seconds* (1966). Impressed with his work, Howe and Frankenheimer made it possible for Alonzo to join the cameramen's union. Frankenheimer later hired Alonzo to be his cameraman on *Black Sunday* (1977). His other films include *Harold and Maude* (1971), *Lady Sings the Blues* (1972), *Sounder* (1972), *Norma Rae* (1979), *Blue Thunder* (1983), *Scarface* (1983), *Runaway Train* (1985) and *Steel Magnolias* (1989).

Maria Conchita Alonso in *Moscow on the Hudson*.

Maria Conchita Alonso

B: 5/13/1957

The strikingly beautiful Alonso made a memorable film debut as the Italian immigrant salesgirl who gives sanctuary to, and then falls in love with, a Russian defector (played by Robin Williams) in Paul Mazursky's *Moscow on the Hudson* (1984). She has since appeared in *Touch and Go* (1986), in which she plays the mother of an eleven-year-old who involves her with a hockey player; *A Fine Mess* (1986), as the Chilean wife of a gangster; and the Arnold Schwarzenegger thriller *The Running Man* (1987), as a girl on the run with him. She plays a Mexican cantina singer in *Extreme Prejudice* (1987), a Chicana in *Colors* (1988) and a Latina cop in *Predator 2* (1990). Her most recent feature film credits are *Roosters* (1995) and *Caught* (1996). Alonso has the distinction of having worked opposite some of the world's most recognized stars, including Robin Williams, Robert Duvall, Sean Penn, Michael Keaton, Danny Glover and Gary Busey.

Born in Havana shortly before Castro came to power, Alonso immigrated with her family to Venezuela at age five and settled in the capital city of Caracas. At fifteen, she won the title of Miss Teenager of the World; she was later crowned Miss Venezuela and began a modeling career that led to television commercials, frequent appearances on variety shows, a two-year stint as the star of a soap opera and a singing career that produced several albums.

Although successful in South America, Alonso was not fully satisfied in her career. She was fascinated with the idea of returning to the States (she had spent a year at a Catholic high school in Spokane, Washington, years earlier), even though it would mean starting all over again. In 1982 she settled in Miami and later moved to New York City. By the end of her first year there, after enduring a seemingly endless string of auditions, she began landing the small television roles that led to her cinematic bow in *Moscow on the Hudson*. Other films to her credit include *Vampire's Kiss* (1989) and *McBain* (1991).

Carlos Alvarado
[born: Carlos Page]
B: 6/22/1901
D: 6/22/1983
The brother of actor Don Alvarado, Carlos became a noted agent of Latino talent in Hollywood, founding his own agency in 1943. He was born and raised in New Mexico under his real name of Page.

Don Alvarado
[born: Don Page]
B: 1905
D: 1967
A native of Albuquerque, New Mexico, Alvarado came to Hollywood as a youngster. He began his career as an extra in 1924 and became a leading man in the early 1930s, appearing in such films as *The Loves of Carmen* (1927) with Dolores Del Rio, *Breakfast at Sunrise* (1927) with Constance Talmadge, *The Bridge of San Luis Rey* (1929), *Captain Thunder* (1931) and *Black Beauty* (1933). He changed his name from Page to Alvarado (taken from a street in Los Angeles) when Latin leading men were in vogue.

He survived the transition from silent to sound movies, but his career never gained momentum. Alvarado appeared as a gigolo opposite Katharine Hepburn in *Morning Glory* (1933) and had a role in *La Cucaracha* (1934), the first Technicolor short subject. In the 1940s he appeared in films intermittently and became an assistant director at Warner Bros., managing a ranch for the Warner family under his real name.

His credits as an assistant director under the name Don Page include *Rebel Without a Cause* (1955), *The Old Man and the Sea* (1958) and *Auntie Mame* (1958). His ex-wife, Ann Page, later married studio chief Jack L. Warner. With Ann, Alvarado had a daughter, Joy, who also became an actress. Alvarado's brother, Carlos, became the first talent agent in Hollywood to handle Hispanic talent exclusively.

Don Alvarado.

Fernando Alvarado

A Mexican American child actor, Alvarado appeared in a number of films during the mid-1940s in a variety of ethnic roles. His credits include *A Medal for Benny* (1945), *Without Reservations* (1946), *Tycoon* (1947) and *Wake of the Red Witch* (1948).

Magali Alvarado

Born in Puerto Rico and raised in New Jersey, Alvarado made her motion picture debut in *Salsa* (1988), followed by Allison Anders' *Mi Vida Loca (1993)*.

Trini Alvarado

B: 1967

Alvarado co-starred with Bette Midler and John Goodman in *Stella* (1989) and co-starred with Goodman in *The Babe* (1991), as Ruth's first wife.

A professional actress and dancer since childhood, she had early starring roles in Joseph Papp's Broadway production of *Runaways* (1978) and the part of Anne Frank in *Yours, Anne* (1989).

Born into a show business family in New York, Alvarado began performing at age seven as a flamenco dancer with her parents' dance troupe. After graduating from the Professional Children's School in New York, she enrolled at Fordham University.

Alvarado made her film debut at age eleven in Robert M. Young's *Rich Kids* (1979) and subsequently played Diane Keaton's daughter in *Mrs. Soffel* (1984). She later had leading roles in *Times Square* (1980), *Sweet Lorraine* (1987), *The Chair* (1987), *Satisfaction* (1989) and *American Blue Note* (1991).

Domingo Ambriz

B: 2/29/1948

A Texas-born Mexican American actor, Ambriz starred as the illegal Mexican immigrant in the film *Alambrista!* (1978). *Walk Proud* (1979), *Green Ice* (1981), *Young Guns II* (1990) and *American Me* (1992) are among his other motion picture credits.

Ramsay Ames
[born: Rosemary Phillips]

B: 3/30/1924

D: 3/30/1998

Born in New York of a Spanish mother and an English father, Ames came to Hollywood's attention as a nightclub entertainer with her hazel-blue eyes, auburn hair and tawny complexion. She was a singer and the leader of her own rumba orchestra and made her film debut in a small role in *Two Señoritas from Chicago* (1943). She also appeared as a harem beauty in *Ali Baba and the Forty Thieves* (1944) and in three serials, *Black Widow* (1954) and *G-Men Never Forget* (1948) at Republic and *The Vigilante* (1947) at Columbia. Ames also appeared in Monogram's *Beauty and the Bandit* (1946) and, much later, *Alexander the Great* (1956). She passed away in 1998, in Santa Monica, California.

Ramsay Ames.

Ira Angustain

B: 8/6/1958

Born in Glendale, California, Angustain is best known for his portrayal of Gomez on the CBS television series *The White Shadow* (1978-81). He also portrayed comedian Freddie Prinze in the telefilm *Can You Hear the Laughter? The Story of Freddie Prinze* (1979). His acting career began at age three with an appearance in the television series *Pete and Gladys* (1960-62). He was an active child actor, appearing in such shows as *Dan August* (1970-71), *Ironside* (1967-75) and *Lancer* (1968-70).

Marc Anthony

B: 1969

Anthony is a talented and diversified entertainer who is making break-throughs as both a singer and actor.

As an actor, Anthony most recently was seen as Noel in Scorsese's *Bringing Out the Dead* (1999) and earned critical praise for his role as the silent waiter representing the soul of the movie in the 1996 *Big Night*. He also co-starred in the 1996 film *The Substitute* with Tom Berenger. He has also appeared on Broadway. In addition, Anthony recorded the theme song to *The Mask of Zorro* (1998), co-wrote and composed "You Sang to Me," a song on the number one soundtrack to the film *Runaway Bride* (1999) and has released four albums. The most recent, the self-titled *Marc Anthony*, successfully crossed over to the American pop market and became a multi-platinum success.

Apollonia

See Apollonia Kotero.

Alfonso Arau

B: 1932

A Cuban-born actor and director whose professional life was developed in Mexican cinema, Arau played a South American drug dealer in *Romancing the Stone* (1984), a Mexican army officer in *The Wild Bunch* (1969), a maniacal used car salesman in *Used Cars* (1980), a bandido in *El Topo* (1971) and the bandit chieftain El Guapo in *¡Three Amigos!* (1986). His other films include *Posse* (1975), *Scandalous John* (1971) and over twenty-five Mexican films. Arau also directed the highly acclaimed Mexican art film *Like Water for Chocolate*, which was released in the States in 1993 and won more than forty international awards. Arau's American directorial debut was the critically acclaimed *A Walk in the Clouds* (1995).

Yareli Arizmendi

The co-star of the hit *Like Water for Chocolate* (1993), Arizmendi plays the gaseous older sister Rosaura. In the Turner Network Television film *The Cisco Kid* (1994), she plays Rosa, Pancho's independent, strong-willed and loving wife. Arizmendi has a role as a Latin mother in *Beverly Hills Cop III* (1994) opposite Eddie Murphy. Born in Mexico, she attended schools in the States and now resides near San Diego, where she teaches drama at San Marcos College.

Pedro Armendariz

B: 5/12/1912

D: 6/18/1963

One of Mexico's most popular dramatic film stars, Armendariz came to symbolize the heart and soul of the Mexican nation and its manhood in much the same way his good friend John Wayne symbolized America. Like Wayne, Armendariz made some of his best-known American films under the direction of John Ford. These included his roles as the police lieutenant who stalks Henry Fonda in *The Fugitive* (1947), a Mexican bandit in *Three Godfathers* (1948) and a Southern-born cavalry sergeant in *Fort Apache* (1948). Armendariz was able to escape the rigid typecasting of the period and played a diverse selection of roles because he did not possess classic Latin Lover good looks and spoke English without an accent. However, in American films, he was relegated to supporting actor roles and was never the star he was in Mexican films.

Pedro Armendariz.

He was a descendant, through his father, Pedro Armendariz, Sr., of one of Mexico City's oldest families, though his mother, Della Hastings, was an American. Armendariz was born in Mexico City and was educated in San Antonio, Texas, and at California Polytechnic, where he majored in engineering.

The young actor began his career on the stage in Mexico City, entering films in 1935. Armendariz was an immediate success and rose from obscurity to stardom within the space of a few pictures. From *Maria Lena* in 1935 to *Maria Candelaria* in 1946, he made forty-two Spanish-language films, establishing himself as one of Latin America's greatest actors and a leading figure in the development of the Mexican film industry. Director Emilio Fernandez and Cinematographer Gabriel Figueroa worked with co-stars Armendariz and Dolores Del Rio in a series of films that were instrumental in creating a national cinema that came to be recognized on an international level.

He ventured to Hollywood in 1947 under contract to Argosy Pictures and made his Hollywood debut in John Ford's *The Fugitive* for RKO. In 1948, Armendariz starred as a peasant fisherman in John Steinbeck's *The Pearl*, directed by Emilio Fernandez and brilliantly photographed by Gabriel Figueroa on location in Mexico. The actor played a Cuban police officer in *We Were Strangers* (1949), an American Indian in *Tulsa* (1949), a Mexican general in *Border River* (1954) and a Mongol warrior in *The Conqueror* (1956).

An international star, Armendariz worked in films all over the world. His final film was the James Bond thriller *From Russia with Love* (1963), in which he portrayed agent Kerim Bey opposite Sean Connery. While shooting the film, he was seriously ill with advanced cancer of the lymph glands. Upon receiving the news that he had only a year to live, Armendariz shot and killed himself in his hospital room in Los Angeles.

Some of his other English-language films include *The Torch* (1950), *Lucrece Borgia* (1953), *Diane* (1955), *The Littlest Outlaw* (1955), *The Big Boodle* (1957), *Stowaway Girl* (1957), *The Little Savage* (1959), *The Wonderful Country* (1959), *Francis of Assisi* (1961), *Captain Sinbad* (1963) and *My Son, the Hero* (1963).

Pedro Armendariz, Jr.

B: 1941

Son of the late international Mexican screen idol, Armendariz, Jr., has forged a career for himself in over 130 Mexican and Hollywood films. Among his many motion picture credits are *The Undefeated* (1969), *Earthquake* (1974), *Walker* (1987), *Licence to Kill* (1989) and *Old Gringo* (1989). In addition, Armendariz has appeared as a guest star on many television programs, including *The High Chaparral* (1967-71), *Knight Rider* (1982-86), *The Love Boat* (1977-86) and *Murder, She Wrote* (1984-96).

Armida

B: 5/29/1913

Armida in *Always in My Heart* (1942).

Born in Sonora, Mexico, Armida moved to and was raised in Arizona. She is the daughter of Joaquin Venrell, a well-known stage actor of the early 1920s. At age sixteen, while performing in a dance act with her two sisters, she was seen by vaudeville producer/songwriter Gus Edwards, who put her on the Orpheum circuit. She appeared in several short films before coming to the attention of actor/director/producer John Barrymore, who signed her for a part in his picture *General Crack* in 1929. She appeared in many films throughout the 1930s, usually as a jungle princess, an island beauty, or a cantina girl. Her credits include RKO's *Border Romance* (1930), *On the Border* (1930), *Under a Texas Moon* (1930), *Border Cafe* (1937), *La Conga Nights* (1940), *Always in My Heart* (1942), *The Girl from Monterey* (1943), *Machine Gun Mama* (1944), *Jungle Goddess* (1948) and *Rhythm Inn* (1951).

Desi Arnaz

B: 5/17/1912
D: 12/2/1986

He was called "Cuban Pete" and "Mr. Babalu," but Desi Arnaz will always be best remembered as Ricky Ricardo, the excitable Cuban bandleader husband of the crazy American redhead, Lucille Ball, on the popular television series *I Love Lucy* (1951-57).

The multi talented Arnaz assumed many roles in his show business career, including musician, singer, actor, bandleader, showman, producer, director and studio chief. During the late 1930s and 1940s, along with Xavier Cugat and other musicians, he popularized Latin American and Afro-Caribbean music in the United States. On the *I Love Lucy* show he pioneered the use of three-cameras to film situation comedy performed in front of a live audience, a technique that set the standard still in use today. By producing the shows on film for a licensing fee from the networks and retaining ownership, he led the way for the syndicated rerun. As producer and studio head of Desilu (which occupied the former RKO Studios), he was responsible for the development and production of numerous filmed television shows including *The Untouchables* (1959-63), *Make Room for Daddy* (1953-1965), *Star Trek* (1966-1969) and *The Mothers-in-Law* (1967-69).

Born in Santiago, Cuba, where his father was the town mayor, Desi and his family fled the 1933 Cuban revolution and settled in Miami. Desi worked at odd jobs until his musical training landed him a job as a guitarist in a rumba band; eventually he went to New York and joined Xavier Cugat's band.

Arnaz started the first conga dance line in America, taken from dances performed at Afro-Cuban religious festivals. The conga dance craze soon swept through the States. His popularity led him to Broadway, where he had a featured role in George Abbott's *Too Many Girls* (1940) as Manuelito, a South American football player. Arnaz was brought to Hollywood in 1940 to re-create the role for the film version of the musical. He met Lucille Ball at RKO, where *Too Many Girls* was being filmed, and they married in November of that year. He then landed a role in *Father Takes a Wife* (1941), and at MGM he portrayed one of the Mexican American defenders in *Bataan* (1943) with Robert Taylor. Road tours with his orchestra, movie roles and family life kept him busy throughout the 1940s.

Arnaz was the first Hispanic American presence on network television. When CBS proposed bringing Lucille Ball's popular radio series, *My Favorite Husband*, to television, Ball requested that Arnaz be cast as her husband. CBS doubted that viewers would accept Arnaz as the mate of an average American female. But after the two performed together on a band tour across the country to enthusiastic audience response, proving that they would be accepted publicly as a couple, CBS finally agreed. Arnaz and Ball formed Desilu Productions and *I Love Lucy* debuted on October 15, 1951 and ran through the 1956-1957 season.

Desi, in his Ricky Ricardo character, drew on his Latin background, making Ricky a struggling, not yet successful bandleader. Arnaz and Ball capitalized on their television success in two theatrical features, *The Long, Long Trailer* (1954) and *Forever Darling* (1956).

With the success of *I Love Lucy*, Desi and Lucy created their own production company and purchased the facilities of the bankrupt RKO Studios. Desilu soon became one of the most important suppliers of filmed television programs.

Arnaz and Ball divorced in 1960. In 1962, Arnaz sold his holdings in Desilu to Ball. He appeared as a guest star on several television series through the years and was a producer of *The Mothers-in-Law* series. His last film appearance was in Francis Ford Coppola's *The Escape Artist* (1982). Arnaz died of cancer in December 1986 at his home in Del Mar, California. His other film credits include *Four Jacks and a Jill* (1941), *The Navy Comes Through* (1942) and *Cuban Pete* (1946).

Desi Arnaz.

Desi Arnaz, Jr.

B: 1/19/1953

The son of Lucille Ball and Desi Arnaz, Desi Jr., first made appearances on the *Here's Lucy* (1968-74) series with his mother and sister, Lucie. He formed a rock 'n' roll band called Dino, Desi and Billy in the late 1960s. He made his motion picture debut in *Red Sky at Morning* (1971), for which he received wide critical acclaim, and followed it with a starring role in a Western filmed in Israel, *Billy Two Hats* (1973), which starred Gregory Peck. He starred in the stage musical *Marco Polo* with Zero Mostel. On television in 1983-1984, he starred in his own series, *Automan*. Alcohol- and drug-related problems kept him off the screen for many years, but after making a complete recovery, he entered a Christian ministry. He has starred in summer stock productions of *Sunday in New York*, *Grease* and *Promises, Promises* at the Melody Top Theatre and at the Sacramento Music Circus. He made a cameo appearance playing his father, Desi Arnaz, in the feature film *The Mambo Kings* in 1992.

Lucie Arnaz
B: 7/17/1951
The daughter of Lucille Ball and Desi Arnaz, Lucie began her show business career on the *Here's Lucy* (1968-74) television show. Among her film credits are *The Jazz Singer* (1980), a remake with Neil Diamond, and *Second Thoughts* (1983). She was featured in a short-lived television series in 1985, *The Lucie Arnaz Show* and in *Sons and Daughters* (1991). On Broadway, she starred in the Neil Simon-Marvin Hamlisch-Carole Bayer Sager musical *They're Playing Our Song* and took over the leading role during the run of Simon's *Lost in Yonkers*.

Isaac Artenstein
B: 12/5/1954
Artenstein served as a director, writer and producer on the independent feature dramatic film *Break of Dawn* (1989), which was based on the television documentary *Ballad of an Unsung Hero* (1983). Artenstein directed and edited *Ballad*, which was based on the life of Pedro J. Gonzalez, the first Spanish-language radio personality in southern California. *Ballad of an Unsung Hero* aired nationally in 1983 on PBS and won numerous awards and honors including an Emmy. Artenstein was born in San Diego and grew up in Tijuana. He studied in the Fine Arts Department at UCLA and received his BFA in film/video from the California Institute of the Arts in 1977.

Miguel Arteta
B: 1965
Born In Puerto Rico of a Peruvian father and Spanish mother, Arteta is the writer and director of the independent feature film, *Star Maps* (1997). He has also directed episodes of *Homicide: Life on the Street* (1993-99), the critically acclaimed *Freak and Geeks* (1999) and the feature film *Chuck & Buck* (2000).

Joe Aubel
B: 11/10/1939
The art director on *Dead and Buried* (1981) and *The Milagro Beanfield War* (1988) and production designer on *American Me* (1992), Aubel was born in East Los Angeles. He grew up speaking Spanish and claims to have learned English watching Hollywood movies. Attempting to link his artistic leanings with a practical career, Aubel set out to be an architect, studying at a local junior college and interning at an architectural firm. One of his employers there suggested that his talents could be better utilized in movies and television. In 1964, he got his first television work as a junior set designer on *The Adventures of Ozzie and*

Harriet (1952-66). Over the next six years, he worked as an assistant set designer on such television programs as *The Danny Thomas Hour* (1967-68), *The Fugitive* (1963-67), *The Mod Squad* (1968-73), and on such prestigious feature films as *The Chase* (1966), *Camelot* (1967), *Cool Hand Luke* (1967) and *The Wild Bunch* (1969). His other film credits include *Viva Max!* (1969), *Close Encounters of the Third Kind* (1977) and *Star Trek IV: The Voyage Home* (1986).

Luis Avalos
B: 9/2/1946

A Cuban-born character actor, Avalos has appeared in numerous films and television shows. His first film role was as a junkie in *Badge 373* (1973), followed by a major role in the comedy caper *Hot Stuff* (1979). His other film credits include *Love Child* (1982), *The Hunter* (1980), *The Butcher's Wife* (1991) and *Fires Within* (1991).

He directed two films in Mexico and a television pilot in Venezuela. On television he has guest starred on many episodic series and starred in the short-lived series *Condo* (1983). He has appeared as a regular on *Hangin' with Mr. Cooper* (1992-97) and a featured player in the CBS series *Ned Blessing* (1993).

Elizabeth Avellan

Avellan is the co-producer of Robert Rodriguez's *Desperado* (1995), *From Dusk Till Dawn* (1996) and *The Faculty* (1998). She has also co-produced *From Dusk Till Dawn 2: Texas Blood Money* (1999) and *From Dusk Till Dawn 3: The Hangman's Daughter* (2000), both for video release. She was the associate producer of Rodriguez's feature directorial debut *El Mariachi* (1992). Avellan was born in Caracas, Venezuela and moved with her family to Houston, where she graduated from Rice University.

Carlos Avila
B: 6/26/1961

The award-winning writer/director of the 1993 PBS *American Playhouse* television presentation *La Carpa*, Avila was born in Lima, Peru, but moved to the Echo Park area of Los Angeles at an early age. His work has been presented internationally at film festivals and museums. His short film, *Distant Water,* won the Grand Prize at the first Film Festival of International Cinema Students in Tokyo, Japan. He holds a master of fine arts degree from UCLA's School of Film and Television.

Angel Aviles

Among the young actress's film credits are Alan Rudolph's *Equinox* (1993) and the critically acclaimed *Mi Vida Loca (1993)*.

Rick Aviles
B: 1954
D: 4/17/1995

An actor/comedian, Aviles was featured in the film *Ghost* (1990) as Patrick Swayze's murderer and in *The Saint of Fort Washington* (1993), *Carlito's Way* (1993) and *Waterworld* (1995). Aviles made his screen debut in *The Cannonball Run* in 1981.

Luis Avalos (center front) with (left to right) *Condo* cast members Julie Carmen, James Victor and Yvonne Othon.

Hank Azaria

B: 4/25/1964

Queens, New York-born Azaria made an indelible impression on audiences and critics for his role as Agador Spartacus, the scene stealing Guatemalan houseboy in *The Birdcage* (1995). His additional film credits include *Pretty Woman* (1990), *Quiz Show* (1994), *Heat* (1995), *Grosse Pointe Blank* (1997), *Godzilla* (1998) and *Mystery Men* (1999). He was one of the actors who participated in the performance of *Fail Safe* (2000) for live television. The multi-faceted actor is also the voice of several key characters on Fox Television's long running comedy series *The Simpsons* (1989-).

Hector Babenco

B: 2/7/1946

An acclaimed director, Babenco gained the attention of international audiences in 1981 with his film *Pixote*, in which an abandoned young boy is forced into a life of crime in the slums of São Paulo. In *Kiss of the Spider Woman* (1985), Babenco told the story of an emerging friendship between a political revolutionary and a homosexual child molester imprisoned in a South American jail. In *Ironweed* (1987), Babenco's first major Hollywood production, he directed Jack Nicholson and Meryl Streep in the screen version of William Kennedy's Pulitzer-Prize-winning novel set in Depression-era America about a man who spends twenty-two years of his life as an alcoholic street bum. In 1991, Babenco directed *At Play in the Fields of the Lord*, the story of a group of missionaries in the Amazon jungle, which featured an all-star cast.

Babenco was born in Buenos Aires, Argentina. His father was a tailor and embroiderer for the opera; he died when his son was only a year old. Babenco's mother, who had a classical education, taught him the appreciation of music and literature and as a youth he read all the classics, both Latin and American. Buenos Aires, one of South America's most European cities, also provided Babenco with the opportunity to see the films of all the great filmmakers of the period.

As he grew older, Babenco became aware of the immense threat that the military posed to democracy in his native country. At age eighteen, he refused army service and spent five years in Spain, working at various menial jobs before taking work in low-budget "spaghetti Westerns." Facing a long prison sentence because he avoided army service, Babenco was unable to return to Argentina, and finally settled in Brazil in the early 1970s.

Babenco's first film was a documentary made in 1972 with money borrowed from friends. *The King of the Night* (1975) was his first feature. *Lucia Flavia* (1977), Babenco's next feature, was extremely well received. Based on actual evidence, this was the first film in Brazil to expose the full apparatus of death squads and the relationship between paramilitary and official police involved in drug dealing and prostitution. His next film, *Pixote* (1981), grew out of Babenco's deep involvement with juvenile delinquents. He worked with nearly 500 street youths, none of whom were professional actors, shooting over a period of five difficult months during 1979 and 1980. Critics have named *Pixote*, Buñuel's *Los Olvidados* (1950) and Truffaut's *The 400 Blows* (1959) as the three most important movies ever made about dispossessed children. *Pixote* was chosen by the New York and Los Angeles film critics societies as the best foreign film of the year.

Unable to raise money for it in the United States, he made *Kiss of the Spider Woman* (1985), his first film in English, on a $1.2 million budget with funds raised in Brazil. The film, starring William Hurt and Raul Julia, received four Academy Award® nominations: Best Director, Best Film, Best Screenplay and Best Actor for William Hurt, who won the Oscar®.

Catherine Bach

B: 3/1/1954

An actress of German-Mexican heritage, Bach co-starred as Daisy Duke on the popular television series *The Dukes of Hazzard* (1979-85). Among her film credits are *The Midnight Man* (1974), *Thunderbolt and Lightfoot* (1974), *Hustle* (1975) and *Cannonball Run II* (1984).

Antonio Banderas

B: 10/10/1960

A Spanish born leading actor and international star, Banderas first came to the public's attention in 1982 in a series of films with eccentric Spanish writer/director Pedro Almodovar including *Tie Me Up, Tie Me Down* (1990), *Women on the Verge of a Nervous Breakdown* (1988), *Law of Desire* (1987), *Matador* (1986) and *Labyrinth of Passion* (1982). The international success of these films brought Banderas to the attention of American audiences. He made his American film debut in Madonna's documentary *Truth Or Dare* (1991), followed by leading role as a young Cuban musician in *The Mambo Kings* (1992). He went on to significant supporting roles in four major films *Philadelphia* (1993), *Interview with a Vampire* (1994), *Miami Rhapsody* (1995) and *The House of Spirits* (1994). His first starring role in an American film came in Robert Rodriguez's *Desperado* (1995) which he followed up with *Four Rooms* (1995), *Never Talk to Strangers* (1995), *Two Much* (1996) and *Assassins* (1997). Banderas then earned critical praise for his acting and vocal talents playing the role of Che Guevara opposite Madonna in Alan Parker's big screen adaptation of the musical *Evita* (1996). His international stardom was solidified when he took on the role of Zorro/Don Diego in the 1998 box office hit, *The Mask of Zorro*. He followed this with *The 13th Warrior* (1999), *Play It to the Bone* (1999) and made his feature film directing debut with *Crazy in Alabama* (1999). His most recent project is *Spy Kids* (2001), directed by Robert Rodriguez.

Antonio Banderas.

Norberto Barba

Barba directed the feature film *Solo* (1996) starring Mario Van Peebles and *Blue Tiger* starring Harry Dean Stanton. For television, he directed an episode of the limited run series *Vanishing Son* (1995), a telefilm for the Family Channel, *Apollo 11* (1996) based on the Apollo 11 landing and the telefilm *Terror in the Mall* (1998). Barba is a native of the Bronx. and was awarded a directing fellowship at the American Film Institute. He directed *Chavez Ravine* (1992) for Universal Television's Hispanic Film Program.

Lita Baron
[aka: Isabelita; born: Isabel Beth Castro]
B: 8/11/1929

Born in Almaria, Spain, Baron came to the United States with her family when she was four years old. At first she adopted a single name, following a precedent set by the Mexican actress Margo. It was while singing with Xavier Cugat's band at the Trocadero in Hollywood that she was signed for her first film, an RKO musical titled *Pan-Americana* (1945). She appeared in a number of Paramount Technicolor musical short subjects, one of which, *Champagne for Two* (1947), was nominated for an Academy Award®. She also appeared in six features, *That's My Baby* (1944), *A Medal for Benny* (1945), *Club Havana* (1946), *The Gay Señorita* (1946), *Slightly Scandalous* (1946) and *Border Incident* (1949).

Steven Bauer
[born: Rocky Echevarria]
B: 12/2/1956

A Havana-born leading man, Bauer's big-screen break came when director Brian De Palma cast him as Al Pacino's Cuban gangster buddy, Manny Rivera, in the remake of *Scarface* (1983). He followed with the lead role in *Thief of Hearts* (1984) and appeared in *Running Scared* (1986), *Two Moon Junction* (1988) and the telefilm *Drug Wars: The Camarena Story* (1989).

Steven Bauer and
Elizabeth Peña in *Drug
Wars: The Camerena Story.*

Bauer's family fled Castro's regime in 1959, moving to Miami, where he was raised. He attended the University of Miami for two years before moving to Los Angeles. Bauer made his acting debut on the Miami-based PBS -television series *Que Pasa, U.S.A.?* under his real name of Rocky Echevarria. He changed his name to Steven Bauer just before starring in *Scarface.* In Los Angeles he signed a short-term contract with Columbia Television and appeared on several series such as *The Rockford Files* (1974-80), *Hill Street Blues* (1981-87), *From Here to Eternity* (1980) and *Wiseguy* (1987-90). Bauer portrayed an Afghan rebel chief in *The Beast* (1988) and a detective in *Gleaming the Cube* (1989).

Alfonso Bedoya
B: 1904
D: 1957

Bedoya established a permanent niche in American movie history when he spoke the memorable line to Bogart, "Badges? We don't need no stinkin' badges," in *The Treasure of the Sierra Madre* (1948). With just that line, his portrayal of Gold Hat, the absurdly menacing bandit, became a moment of film history.

Director John Huston met Bedoya and cast him in the film while on location in Mexico. Bedoya appeared in many American films over the next decade, mostly Westerns, usually as a Mexican bandit. Bedoya had no formal training as an actor but appeared in seventy Mexican films, most notably in a comedic characterization in *Las Abandonados* (1944). His other films include *The Pearl* (1948), *Streets of Laredo* (1949), *The Black Rose* (1950), *California Conquest* (1952), *Border River* (1954), *Ten Wanted Men* (1955) and *The Big Country* (1958).

Alma Beltran

B: 1927

A veteran character actress, Beltran is best known for her role as the maid in the 1980 film *Oh God/Book II*, starring George Burns. She has also appeared in such films as *Red Sky at Morning* (1971), *The Marathon Man* (1976), *Zoot Suit* (1981), *Nobody's Fool* (1986), *Ghost* (1990) and *Luminarias* (2000), as well as several telefilms. She has worked extensively in Los Angeles theater and in Spanish-language radio. She co-starred in the cable television series *Sanchez of Bel Air* (1986), and played Freddie Prinze's aunt on *Chico and the Man* (1974-78) and Julio Fuentes' mother on *Sanford and Son* (1972-77). Beltran was born in Mexico and raised in California and Arizona.

Robert Beltran

B: 11/19/1953

Best known for his role as first officer Chakotay, the fearless Maquis Captain on the syndicated *Star Trek: Voyager* (1995-99) television series. Born and raised in Bakersfield, California, Beltran graduated from Fresno State University with a degree in Theater Arts. His love for acting began in elementary school and his passion has flourished throughout the years into an impressive list of credits.

He made his film debut with a small role in *Zoot Suit* (1981), and his feature film credits include a critically-acclaimed performance as Raoul in the 1982 cult film *Eating Raoul*, plus leading roles in *Gaby* (1987) and *Kiss Me a Killer* (1991). He has also co-starred in such films as *Lone Wolf McQuade* (1983), *Latino* (1985), *Scenes from the Class Struggle in Beverly Hills* (1989), *Nixon* (1996) and *Luminarias* (2000).

Maurice Benard

Benard's film credits include roles in Allison Anders' *Mi Vida Loca (1993)* and *Ruby* (1992) directed by John MacKenzie. He played Desi Arnaz in the telefilm *Lucy and Desi: Before The Laughter* (1991). He is perhaps best known for his role as Sonny on the long running daytime drama *General Hospital* (1963-).

Jellybean Benitez

Benitez began his career as a disc jockey for the famed Studio 54 nightclub in Manhattan. It was as a young DJ that Benitez discovered Madonna and went on to produce her first chart-topping album. He has produced for numerous major recording artists since then and currently has his own recording label.

In the early nineties, Benitez began branching out and working as a music supervisor for film and packaging soundtrack albums. As a music supervisor, his credits include *Mi Vida Loca* (1993), *The Perez Family* (1995), *2 Days in the Valley* (1996); and *Table One* (1999) and *Havana Nocturne* (2000) as executive music supervisor.

He has also composed theme songs for several television shows, such as the critically acclaimed *House of Buggin'* (1995). and *The Ricki Lake Show* (1930).

Currently, Benitez has moved into the producers' arena, serving as the executive producer on several feature films, among them the documentary *Nuyorican Dream* (2000); *Angel Eyes* (2000), with Jennifer Lopez; and *Get Carter* (2000) with Sylvester Stallone.

Gabriel Beristain

Honored with the Silver Bear for Cinematography at the 1987 Berlin Film Festival for his work in *Caravaggio*, directed by Derek Jarman, Beristain has numerous other film credits in Latin America, Europe and the United States. Born in Mexico, he grew up in a theatrical family; his father, Luis Beristain, was a successful Mexican actor (his last film was *The Exterminating Angel* (1962), Luis Buñuel's masterpiece). Beristain's American films are *Waiting for the Light* (1990), starring Shirley MacLaine; Jonathan Lynn's *The Distinguished Gentleman* (1992), with Eddie Murphy; and Taylor Hackford's *Bound by Honor* (1993).

Anne Betancourt
(aka: Yolanda Marquez)

Born in Los Angeles, Anne has appeared on television in guest star roles in such series as *The Rockford Files* (1974-80), *Lou Grant* (1977-82), *Fantasy Island* (1978-84), *Babylon 5* (1994-98), *Seventh Heaven* (1996-), *Cagney and Lacey* (1982-88) and *NYPD Blue* (1993). She played Salma Hayek's mother, Amalia, in the romantic comedy *Fools Rush In* (1997) and recently completed a co-starring role opposite Kim Basinger and Jimmy Smits in *Bless the Child* (2000). Betancourt hosted the national Emmy Award-winning PBS childrens reading program, *Storytime*, for five years.

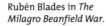
Rubén Blades in *The Milagro Beanfield War.*

Rubén Blades

B: 7/6/1948

Born and raised in Panama City, Panama, Blades grew up listening to a melange of Latin music, American rock and calypso from the West Indies. While performing with a number of Latin bands, he studied law at the University of Panama. He lived in New York City for a brief time and then returned to Panama, got his law degree, and then went back to New York, where he began performing with various salsa bands.

Salsa music singer/songwriter turned actor, Blades made his starring film debut in Leon Ichaso's *Crossover Dreams* (1985) as a Latin star who abandons his salsa roots in an ill-fated bid for pop stardom. Vincent Canby in his *New York Times* review called Blades "a fine new film performer who's also a screen natural."

Blades went on to appear in such films as *The Milagro Beanfield War* (1988), *The Two Jakes* (1990), *The Super* (1991), *A Million to Juan* (1994), *The Devil's Own* (1997), *Cradle Will Rock* (1999) and *All the Pretty Horses* (2000). He also wrote and performed the music score for the film *Q & A* (1990).

For television, Blades won a CableAce Award as Best Actor for his portrayal of a death row inmate in HBO's *Dead Man Out* (1989) and played an Italian count in *The Josephine Baker Story* (1990), also for HBO. He was nominated for an Emmy Award for his role as a janitor in the Turner Network Television film *Crazy from the Heart* (1991).

Vicente Blasco Ibanez

B: 1867

D: 1928

The novels of this Spanish writer were very much in vogue during the 1920s, and inevitably several of them found their way to the screen, including *The Four Horsemen of the Apocalypse*, *Blood and Sand* and *Mare Nostrum*. Greta Garbo's first two American films, *The Torrent* (1926) and *The Temptress* (1926), were also adapted from Blasco Ibanez novels. He had been writing since early in the century, but his international reputation began with *The Four Horsemen of the Apocalypse* (originally published in 1916; published in English in 1918), which became a record-breaking best-seller. *Sangre y Arena* (1908) had been published in English in 1911 as *Blood in the Arena*, but was reissued in 1919 as *Blood and Sand*.

Fortunio Bonanova

B: 1895

D: 1969

A character actor in American films, Bonanova is best known for his roles in *Citizen Kane* (1941), as the singing teacher who tries to teach Kane's talentless wife; *For Whom the Bell Tolls* (1943), as the Spanish mountain guerrilla fighter; and *Kiss Me Deadly* (1955), as an opera lover whose rare, vintage record is snapped in two before his eyes by private eye Mike Hammer.

The actor and opera star was born in Palma de Mallorca, Spain, the son of Nicolas Bonanova, an attorney. Bonanova studied at the Barcelona Institute, the University of Madrid Law School, the Real Conservatory of Madrid, with private music teachers in Milan, Italy, and at the Paris Conservatoire. At age seventeen, the young baritone was singing solo with the Royal Chapel group in Madrid when the great Feodor Chaliapin heard him and encouraged him in his musical ambitions. Bonanova made his operatic debut in Paris as the toreador in *Carmen* and later sang in opera companies internationally.

At age nineteen he wrote, produced, directed and starred in the first screen version of *Don Juan* in his native Spain. He wrote plays, operettas and novels and toured with his own repertory company throughout Latin America. He performed in the American theater opposite actress Katharine Cornell on Broadway. In 1927 he made his American film debut in *The Love of Sunya* with Gloria Swanson. He was the star, writer, producer and director of twelve Spanish-language shorts made at the Fort Lee Studios in New Jersey.

From 1932 to 1935 Bonanova starred in many Spanish-language films made in Spain, Mexico and South America. In 1935, he began appearing in Hollywood films, starring in numerous Spanish versions of English films and playing roles in many English-language Hollywood productions as well. When *La Immaculada* was made in 1939, Bonanova adapted the story, wrote the music, produced, directed and starred. His other films include *Bulldog Drummond in Africa* (1938), *Romance in the Dark* (1938), *Tropic Holiday* (1938), *Blood and Sand* (1941), *Down Argentine Way* (1940), *I Was an Adventuress* (1940), *The Mark of Zorro* (1940), *That Night in Rio* (1941), *Double Indemnity* (1944) and *Going My Way* (1944).

Arturo Bonilla

Bonilla's film credits as an actor include *Salvador* (1986), *Bestseller* (1987); the telefilm *Drug Wars: The Camarena Story* (1990); *American Me* (1992) and *The Coneheads* (1993).

Jesse Borrego

B: 1962

A San Antonio, Texas, native, Borrego can be found in feature roles in *Bound by Honor* (1993), *Mi Vida Loca (1993)*; Martin Scorsese's segment of *New York Stories* (1989); *I Like It Like That* (1994), *Lone Star* (1997) and *Con Air* (1997). He played the Mexican American dancer, Jesse, for four years on the syndicated *Fame* (1982-87) television series; he also appeared in the telefilms *Tecumseh: The Last Warrior* (1995) and *Hell Swarm* (2000).

Sonia Braga

B: 6/16/1950

A Brazilian-born actress, Braga has gained attention in several American films for her dark beauty, screen sensuality and acting talent. Her full talent has never been utilized as effectively in her American films as in her Brazilian films. Her Brazilian films have capitalized on her flair for comedy juxtaposed with her smoldering sexuality. *Kiss of the Spider Woman* (1985) was her first English-language film and the one that brought her the greatest international recognition. "When I made the film I still couldn't speak the language well. Sometimes I would say a line and wonder what it meant," the actress admitted during an interview. In the film she essayed three roles, Raul Julia's girlfriend, a French chanteuse who falls in love with a Nazi officer in one of the films within the film, and the mysterious Spider Woman in another of the film's fantasy sequences.

American audiences first became aware of her in the 1977 Brazilian movie *Dona Flor and Her Two Husbands*, directed by Bruno Barreto. She followed this with Arnaldo Jabor's *I Love You* (1981), and Barreto's *Gabriela* (1983), based on Jorje Amado's best-seller, in which she starred opposite Marcello Mastroianni.

In the States, she co-starred in *The Milagro Beanfield War* (1988), directed by Robert Redford, in which she played Ruby Archuleta; and in *Moon over Parador* (1988), directed by Paul Mazursky, in which she co-starred opposite Raul Julia and Richard Dreyfuss as the sensuous mistress of a dictator. Her other films include *Lady on the Bus* (1978) and *The Rookie* (1990).

Braga's rise to international fame began in Marinaga, Paran, in the south of Brazil, where her childhood was shaken by her father's death when she was eight years old. She quit school at fourteen and took a series of clerical jobs. A walk-on part as a little princess in a children's television program began her acting career. By eighteen, Braga was working in theater and created a minor sensation by taking her clothes off on stage in a production of *Hair*.

In 1968, Braga starred in a television soap opera, *The Girl of the Blue Sailboat*. She followed with a series of soaps for TV Globo, the leading

Sonia Braga stars as Madonna, the mistress of the dictator of Parador, in *Moon over Parador*.

Brazilian network. Two of these, *Gabriela* and *Dancin' Days*, made her a star.

Benjamin Bratt
(born: Benjamin Bratt Banda)
B: 12/16/1963

One of five children, Bratt grew up in San Francisco, California and graduated from Lowell High School. His mother is a Peruvian Indian who immigrated to the States when she was fourteen.

Bratt developed his acting skills as an undergraduate at the University of California at Santa Barbara, continuing in the master's program at San Francisco's prestigious American Conservatory Theater. He is best known for his role as Detective Reynaldo "Rey" Curtis on the Emmy Award-winning television series *Law & Order* (1995-), which he joined as a regular cast member from 1995-1999. Bratt's feature film credits include appearances in *One Good Cop* (1991), *Bound by Honor* (1993), *Demolition Man* (1993), *Clear and Present Danger* (1994) and *Follow Me Home* (1997). In 2000, he made the leap to big screen stardom with starring roles in *The Next Best Thing* (2000), *Red Planet* (2000) and *Miss Congeniality* (2000).

Peter Bratt
The writer, director and producer of *Follow Me Home* (1997), he is also the brother of Benjamin Bratt.

J. Robert Bren
B: 1903

A film producer and writer, Bren made his film writing debut in 1934 with *Looking for Trouble*. He wrote the screenplays for such films as *In Old California* (1942), *The Great Sioux Uprising* (1953) and *The Siege at Red River* (1954). Bren was born in Guanajuato, Mexico.

Romney Brent
[born: Romulo Larralde]
B: 1/26/1902
D: 9/24/1976

An actor and writer born in Saltillo, Mexico, Brent was a stage actor in London and New York. He made his screen debut in the British production *East Meets West* in 1936. Other screen credits include *Dreaming Lips* (1937), *The Dominant Sex* (1937), *Under the Red Robe* (1937) and *The Adventures of Don Juan* (1949).

Ruth Britt
An actress of Puerto Rican descent, Britt was one of the last Universal contract players in the late 1970s. She appeared in *The Nude Bomb* (1980) and *Night School* (1981). Britt was a regular on the *Operation Petticoat* (1977-79) television series, playing a native island girl and has made numerous guest appearances on episodic series and in television movies. Recently, she has appeared as a voice-over artist in such films as *Reality Bites* (1994) and *Dead Badge* (1995).

Benjamin Bratt.

Georg Stanford Brown

B: 1944

An actor and director born in Havana, Cuba, and raised in New York's Harlem, Brown is perhaps best known for his role as a tough cop on *The Rookies* (1972-76) television series and as the staunch Tom in the history-making telefilms *Roots* (1977) and *Roots: The Next Generation* (1979) miniseries. His film credits include *The Comedians* (1967), *Bullitt* (1968), *The Man* (1972) and *Stir Crazy* (1980). Brown has devoted most of his creative energies to directing for television, where his credits include *Starsky and Hutch* (1975-79), *Charlie's Angels* (1976-81), *Hill Street Blues* (1981-87) and *Cagney & Lacey* (1982-88).

Argentina Brunetti

B: 8/31/1907

This Argentine-born veteran character actress has over sixty motion picture credits. She usually plays dignified Latin donas or mothers. Her credits include such classic motion pictures as *California* (1946); *Miracle on 34th Street* (1947); *Broken Arrow* (1950), in which she played Cochise's (Jeff Chandler's) Indian squaw; *The Lawless* (1950), as the mother of a Mexican youth on the run from the law; *The Caddy* (1953), in which she played Dean Martin's Italian mother (and to whom he sang the famous "That's Amore"); *King of the Khyber Rifles* (1953), as a Hindu woman; *Three Violent People* (1956); *The Brothers Rico* (1957); and *The Appaloosa* (1966), with Marlon Brando. Brunetti also appeared on the popular daytime television soap opera *General Hospital* (1963-) for three years in the late 1980s. Brunetti's mother was the internationally renowned stage actress Mimi Aguglia, who in the 1930s, late in her career, appeared in several Spanish-language films made in Hollywood.

Luis Buñuel

B: 2/22/1900

D: 7/29/1983

A Spanish filmmaker, Luis Buñuel was a giant of world cinema. In 1929 he collaborated with artist Salvador Dali to make *Un Chien Andalou*, one of the most scandalous films of its time. The movie, which is about dreams, contains unexplained images such as a dead donkey on a grand piano and a scene in which an eyeball is sliced by a razor. In 1940 Buñuel worked as a technical adviser for an uncompleted pro-Spanish Loyalist film at MGM Studios in Hollywood. From 1941 to 1944, he worked in the film department at the Museum of Modern Art in New York City. He was scheduled to direct *The Beast with Five Fingers* (1946), starring Peter Lorre, but the job went to Robert Florey. He returned to France after the war for a short time but then moved to Mexico.

Buñuel's Mexican period, which lasted until 1961, was one of his most prolific. He worked regularly for the first time and directed some twenty productions including *Los Olvidados* (1950), *Robinson Crusoe* (1952) and *El Bruto* (1952), a melodrama about a butcher who falls in love with a rich man's daughter, starring Pedro Armendariz and Katy Jurado. He returned to Spain and made *Viridiana* (1961), which Franco promptly banned. From then on Buñuel worked in France, where he made such films as *Belle de Jour* (1967) and *Tristana* (1970). His final film was *That Obscure Object of Desire* (1977).

Robert Cabal
An actor of Filipino descent, Cabal appeared in such films as *Crisis* (1950), *Mara Maru* (1952) with Errol Flynn, and *The Man behind the Gun* (1952) with Randolph Scott. He played Hey Soos for two years on the television series *Rawhide* (1959-66).

David Cadiente
An actor/stuntman, Cadiente has been featured in such films as *Donovan's Reef* (1963), *Ride the Wild Surf* (1964), *The Sting II* (1983) and *Stick* (1985). His numerous television credits include *Adventures in Paradise* (1959-62), *The Gallant Men* (1962-63) and *The A-Team* (1983-87).

Paul Calderon
Calderon's film credits include Quentin Tarantino's *Pulp Fiction* (1994), Spike Lee's *Clockers* (1995), Abel Ferrara's *The Addiction* (1995), James Mangold's *Cop Land* (1997) and Steven Soderbergh's *Out of Sight* (1998). He has also appeared on numerous episodic series and in several telefilms.

Joseph Calleia
B: 8/4/1897
D: 10/31/1975
Born on the island of Malta, the son of English and Spanish parents, Calleia was a character actor of extraordinary range, best known for his sadistic gun-toting gangster or villain portrayals. He is also closely identified with his many Latin roles in such films as *Juarez* (1939), *For Whom the Bell Tolls* (1943), *Gilda* (1946), *Branded* (1950), *The Treasure of Pancho Villa* (1955), *The Littlest Outlaw* (1955), *Serenade* (1956), *Touch of Evil* (1958), *Cry Tough* (1959) and *The Alamo* (1960). In 1936 he wrote a film script for MGM called *The Robin Hood of El Dorado*, which starred Warner Baxter.

Jacqueline Cambas
This film editor has collaborated with director Richard Benjamin on *City Heat* (1984), *Racing with the Moon* (1984), *The Money Pit* (1986), *Little Nikita* (1988), *My Stepmother Is an Alien* (1988), *Downtown* (1990), *Mermaids* (1990) and *Made in America* (1993). Cambas was born in New York. She originally was a teacher but left the profession to enroll in UCLA's Film School. Her first film job was as an apprentice editor on *Billy Jack* (1971). Her other film credits include *School Ties* (1992), *Zoot Suit* (1981) and *Cat People* (1982) as co-editor.

Bruno Campos
Campos, of German-Portuguese descent was born in Rio de Janeiro, Brazil and is best known as the Chilean character Diego Vasquez on the television series *Jesse* (1998-2000) opposite Christina Applegate. He guest starred on such series as *Suddenly Susan* (1996-2000), *Chicago Sons* (1997), *Cybill* (1995-98) and the miniseries *The Last Don* (1997).

Rafael Campos

B: 5/13/1936

D: 7/9/1985

A smiling and ebullient actor, Campos is best known for his role as the young Puerto Rican boy, Pete Morales, in the classic 1955 MGM film *Blackboard Jungle*, starring Glenn Ford as a besieged inner-city school-teacher. He followed this with the role of a Mexican American boy accused of murder in MGM's *Trial* (1955), with Ford and Katy Jurado. Campos played Native American youths in Disney's *The Light in the Forest* and *Tonka* (both 1958). Later in his career, he played character roles in such films as *The Appaloosa* (1966) with Marlon Brando and *Oklahoma Crude* (1973) with George C. Scott. His other films include *The Sharkfighters* (1956) and *This Could Be the Night* (1957).

Campos worked consistently on television in such distinguished early series as *Studio One* (1948-58), *Playhouse 90* (1956-61) and *Alcoa Theatre* (1957-60). He was a regular as Ramon Diaz on *Rhoda* (1974-78), starring Valerie Harper. The epic miniseries *Centennial* (1978) provided Campos an important role as Nacho Gomez, a trail cook.

A native of the Dominican Republic, Campos came to the States in 1949 with his family. He attended the High School for the Performing Arts in New York City where he was spotted by film writer and director Richard Brooks, who cast him—along with such other then-little-known actors as Vic Morrow, Paul Mazursky, Jamie Farr and Sidney Poitier—in *Blackboard Jungle*. Campos was reunited with Brooks for his last film, *Fever Pitch* (1985). Campos died of cancer at age forty-nine.

Victor Campos

An actor who co-starred in *Newman's Law* (1974) and *Five Days from Home* (1978), opposite George Peppard, and *The Master Gunfighter* (1975) with Tom Laughlin, Campos also co-starred in the television series *Doctors' Hospital* (1975-76) and *Cade's County* (1971-72).

Maria Canals

A Cuban-American actress, born and raised in Miami, Canals made her film debut in *Cop and a Half* (1993) starring Burt Reynolds. Canals then co-starred as the young Irene in *My Family* (1995). On television she has co-starred opposite Tony Danza in *The Tony Danza Show* (1997) and in *Beggars and Choosers* (1999).

Larry Cano

Cano was the executive producer of the 1983 feature film *Silkwood*.

Cantinflas

[born: Mario Moreno]

B: 8/12/1911

D: 4/20/1993

Charlie Chaplin once said, "Cantinflas is the world's greatest comedian." Cantinflas made people laugh throughout the Spanish-speaking world for over fifty years and at times held the position of number-one box office star. He became a hero figure for the common man, a symbol and idol for the people of Mexico and Latin America.

Maria Canals.

He appeared in only two English-language motion pictures, *Around the World in Eighty Days* (1956) as Passepartout, Phileas Fogg's (David Niven's) valet and traveling companion in the Academy Award®-winning film, and *Pepe* (1960), in which he portrays a peon ranch hand whose love for his horse involves him with many celebrities. Cantinflas had first come to Hollywood in 1944 under an arrangement with RKO Studios for a series of pictures, but the details were never worked out to the satisfaction of Cantinflas or the studio.

Michael Todd, the producer of *Around the World in Eighty Days*, said in an interview at the time, "I picked him for the part because he is an expert in pantomime. This picture will be as international as we can possibly make it and therefore securing players from different countries, if they fit into the screenplay, will be the thing to do." He also said, "The fact that Cantinflas always liked the Passepartout character makes him doubly desirable. It is easy to change Phileas Fogg's servant into a Mexican in this modern time, and thus the character can be perfectly tailored to his needs."

Cantinflas stated, "Mr. Todd demonstrated his excellent intentions about the Jules Verne story when he permitted me to see a treatment. He also permitted me to portray the character as a Mexican rather than a French character. So I was still Cantinflas to my audiences in Latin America." In a *Los Angeles Times* interview many years later, Cantinflas pointed out that it took some convincing on his part to make Todd see the role the way he expressed it in those interviews.

Cantinflas was born Mario Moreno in 1911, in a poverty-ridden district of Mexico City called Tenampa. He ran away from home as a young man in order to join a *carpas*, a traveling circus. To avoid bringing shame on his family, he adopted the name Cantinflas.

Over the years the name has come to mean "the little guy with the funny two-piece mustache and the baggy pants, barely held up by a length rope." The character always wants to help his fellow man, even though he himself can use some help.

The Cantinflas character represents the common man who battles hunger, suffering, sickness and injustice—while still finding goodness, love and hope in mankind and life. Cantinflas, like Chaplin, is a comedian who represents the underdog. Cantinflas once remarked that a crucial difference between his tramp and Chaplin's is that Chaplin's tramp stood helpless before the blows of fate—while Cantinflas' tramp, with luck, wit and unparalleled flexibility of character, can and does do something about those blows. Chaplin's tramp is a figure of semi-tragedy, while Cantinflas plays a figure of hope.

Cantinflas the artist always conveyed a social and humanistic message. He showed a positive road for people in all his films. Cantinflas made such inroads in the affection of all Spanish-speaking peoples that his name has become part of the Spanish language, meaning "to talk much, say little and indulge in frenetic speech."

Cantinflas made his motion picture debut in 1936 and starred in forty-nine Mexican films. Two years after he began making films, he established his own production company, which gave him complete ownership of most of his films and made him a multimillionaire.

Cantinflas.

Nestor Carbonell.

Irene Cara
B: 3/18/1959

A versatile actress, singer and dancer, Cara co-starred in *Aaron Loves Angela* (1975), *Sparkle* (1976), *Fame* (1980), *City Heat* (1984) and *Certain Fury* (1985). In 1984 she won an Academy Award® for co-writing the Best Original Song, "Flashdance . . . What a Feeling," the title song to the film *Flashdance* (1983). Cara also recorded the song, which became a Top 40 hit. Born of Cuban and Puerto Rican parents Cara has been performing since the age of seven on the Broadway stage and in television and films.

Nestor Carbonell

Born in New York City, Carbonell found success as the suave photographer Luis Rivera on the NBC television series *Suddenly Susan* (1996-2000), after previously appearing in the telefilm *Ray Alexander: A Taste for Justice* (1994) and in the short-lived series *Muscle* (1995).

Annette Cardona
[aka: Annette Charles)

A multitalented actress, Cardona was featured as Cha Cha in the film *Grease* (1978). She also co-starred in Haskell Wexler's *Latino* (1985).

Elsa Cardenas
B: 8/3/1935

Born in Tijuana, Mexico, and raised in Mexico City, Cardenas made her Mexican film debut in March 1954 in *Magdalena*. Her first American film was *The Brave One* in 1956. She followed this with a role in *Giant* (1956), in which she played Juana Benedict, the wife an oil rancher's son. Cardenas was off the American screen for six years until 1963 when she played opposite Elvis Presley in *Fun in Acapulco* as a lady bullfighter. In 1964 the actress was cast in a minor Western for Universal called *Taggart*, and later won the role of Elsa in *The Wild Bunch* (1969).

Silvia Cardenas
B: 1972

Graduated from Loyola Marymount College in 1992. She caught the writing bug as a stage manager on Univision's *El Show de Paul Rodriguez*, and went on to assist writers on such television comedies as *The Sinbad Show* (1993-94), *The Wayans Brothers* (1995-99) and *The Nanny* (1993-99). Cardenas is a producer on the series *Moesha* (1996-).

Ismael ("East") Carlo
B: 1/19/1942

A Puerto Rican-born, New York-raised character actor, Carlo usually plays corrupt officials, drug kingpins and concerned fathers or merchants on television and in feature films. His credits include the films *A Piece of the Action* (1977) and *Defiance* (1980) and his credits in episodic television include *The A-Team* (1983-87); *Murder, She Wrote* (1984-96); and *Crime Story* (1986-88).

Julie Carmen

B: 4/4/1960

Carmen won the Best Supporting Actress prize at the Venice Film Festival for her role as the young mother in John Cassavetes' *Gloria* (1980). She starred opposite Raul Julia and Armand Assante in *The Penitent* (1988) and played the strong-willed wife of a New Mexico farmer in *The Milagro Beanfield War* (1988). Carmen played a beautiful and outlandish vampire in *Fright Night II* (1988).

Born in New York City, she graduated from the State University of New York and studied acting with Uta Hagen, Sanford Meisner and Jose Quintera. Soon she was playing leading roles on stage and in television movies like *Can You Hear the Laughter? The Story of Freddie Prinze* (1979) and *Fire on the Mountain* (1981), opposite Ron Howard. She made her film debut in Robert Butler's *Night of the Juggler* (1980). Her other film credits include *Blue City* (1986) and *Last Plane Out* (1983).

Carlos Carrasco

A native of Panama, Carrasco has appeared in feature films including *Crocodile Dundee II* (1988), *The Fisher King* (1991) and *Bound by Honor* (1993).

Barbara Carrera

B: 12/31/1945

A Nicaraguan-born fashion model turned actress, Carrera has put her exotic look to good use in a variety of leading roles in several major film and television productions, usually playing strong-willed women.

Carrera came to the States at age ten and attended the St. Joseph Academy in Memphis, Tennessee. At fifteen she moved to New York City and just a few months later was spotted on Fifth Avenue by designer Lily Daché, who suggested that Carrera had a fresh face and an ideal figure for modeling. She signed with the Eileen Ford Agency, but after several attempts to conform to the requisite fashion, she decided to go with her own unique, indigenous look; within a year she had her first magazine cover on Harper's Bazaar and within four years, she was one of the highest-paid models in the world.

She made her major motion picture debut in 1975 as a Spanish señorita in *The Master Gunfighter* opposite Tom Laughlin, who spotted her picture on a magazine cover and arranged a screen test for her.

Carrera was soon cast in another film, *Embryo* (1976), which starred Rock Hudson. Next followed roles as a mysterious island woman opposite Burt Lancaster in *The Island of Dr. Moreau* (1977), a Hawaiian in the all-star *When Time Ran Out* (1980), followed by the female lead in *I, the Jury* (1982), starring Armand Assante as Mickey Spillane's Mike Hammer.

She received praise from critics and the public for her role as Fatima Bush, the villainess and assassin in the James Bond adventure *Never Say Never Again* (1983), starring Sean Connery.

On television she portrayed the Indian woman Clay Basket in the epic 24-hour miniseries *Centennial* (1978-1979), starring opposite Robert Conrad and Richard Chamberlain. She portrayed a beautiful Jewish woman in the miniseries *Masada* (1981), starring Peter O'Toole.

Edward Carrere

B: 1905

D: 1979

An art director/production designer born in Mexico City of a Spanish mother and a French father, Carrere won an Academy Award® for his work on *Camelot* (1967), and worked on a number of films during his long tenure at Warner Bros., including *The Adventures of Don Juan* (1949), *The Fountainhead* (1949), *White Heat* (1949), *Sunrise at Campobello* (1960) and *The Wild Bunch* (1969). He worked with Hecht-Hill-Lancaster on *Separate Tables* (1958) and *Run Silent, Run Deep* (1958). He was the brother of Fernando Carrere and the father of Leon Carrere.

Fernando Carrere

B: 12/31/1910

An art director and production designer, Carrere was born in Mexico City of a Spanish mother and a French father. He designed sets for such Hollywood productions as *The Pride and the Passion* (1957), *Birdman of Alcatraz* (1962), *The Great Escape* (1963) and several of the Pink Panther films. In 1961, he was nominated for an Academy Award® for William Wyler's *The Children's Hour*. He is the brother of Edward Carrere.

Leon Carrere

B: 2/26/1935

The son of Edward Carrere, Leon Carrere is a television film editor and director who has worked on such shows as *Charlie's Angels* (1976-81) *The Rookies* (1972-76) and *In the Heat of the Night* (1988-94).

Robert Carricart

B: 1/18/1917

A veteran character actor featured in such films as *Black Orchid* (1959), *Follow that Dream* (1962), *Fun in Acapulco* (1963), *Robin and the Seven Hoods* (1964), *Villa Rides* (1968) and *The Milagro Beanfield War* (1988). Carricart was born in Bordeaux, France, of a Spanish mother and a French father. He worked consistently on the Broadway stage in such major productions as *Antony and Cleopatra* with Katherine Cornell, *Detective Story* with Ralph Bellamy, *The Rose Tattoo* and *Annie Get Your Gun*, until 1957 when he turned to film acting and moved to Hollywood. He co-starred in the television series *T.H.E. Cat* (1966-67).

Elpidia Carrillo
[alternate spelling: Elpedia]

B: 8/16/1961

A Mexican actress, Carrillo has become Hollywood's favorite all-purpose natives since 1981. She made her film debut opposite Jack Nicholson in *The Border* (1982) as a Guatemalan immigrant whose baby is stolen on the United States-Mexico border. She played the love interest of Michael Caine and Richard Gere in *Beyond the Limit* (1983), and a captured Central American rebel in *Predator* (1987), starring Arnold Schwarzenegger. In Oliver Stone's *Salvador* (1986), she was the Salvadoran girlfriend of an American photographer, played by James

Woods. In 1995, she was cast in *My Family*; and in 1997, starred in *The Brave*, with Johnny Depp.

Leo Carrillo

B: 8/6/1881

D: 9/11/1961

A versatile character actor who had a long career in stage, films and television, Carrillo is best known for his role as the loyal and trustworthy sidekick Pancho in a series of Cisco Kid films and television programs. His buffoonish interpretation of Pancho, who was overweight and spoke an accented English full of malapropisms, was so well etched that it endeared him to audiences worldwide and overshadowed his other film and theatrical work.

Leo Carillo, "Mr. California."

He was called "Mr. California" because of his deep pride in California's Spanish-Mexican history, and the prominent part his family had played in it. Leo Antonio Carrillo was born in an adobe building in Los Angeles, the fifth of eight children in a family that could trace its lineage back to the colonization of California by Spanish conquistadors. His great-great-grandfather, Joe Reimundo Carrillo, accompanied Father Junipero Serra and explorer Gaspar De Portola on the expedition north from Baja California in 1769 to settle San Diego. His great-grandfather, Carlos Antonio Carrillo, was in 1837 appointed in Mexico as provisional governor of California. Carlos Antonio once controlled a tract of 70,000 acres in what is now West Los Angeles. Carlos Antonio's brother, Jose Antonio Esquivel, was a signer of the Treaty of Cahuenga, in which the Mexican forces capitulated to the Americans in 1847. Leo's grandfather, Pedro C. Carrillo, was an early Los Angeles judge and the actor's father, Juan Jose, was once mayor of Santa Monica.

Leo Carrillo recalled in a newspaper interview, "In my family, I never needed *The Arabian Nights*, we had our own. It was compounded of the mighty saga of priests, leather jacketed soldiers, grizzly bear hunters, bagueros who rode horses as swift as the wind, ropers who flung a reata with the precision of rifle fire, grandees of the rancheros and dancing girls with castanets who sang the siren song of California to the tune of a Spanish guitar in a jasmine scented patio" (*Los Angeles Times* Calendar, 10/29/61).

The future actor received his early education at Santa Monica High School and at St. Vincent's (now Loyola Marymount University). Carrillo decided to pursue a career as an artist. To earn money for additional studies, he took a job in the engineering department of the Southern Pacific Railroad. He was assigned to construction along California's coast. He worked with men of many nationalities and learned dialects that he later used on stage. Carrillo was next hired by the *San Francisco Examiner* as a cartoonist. He made his first stage appearance at an amateur benefit. Then, when an act on the Orpheum circuit didn't show up, Carrillo filled in and was a hit. He remained in vaudeville for several years as a headliner, but his career as a legitimate actor began when, while playing polo at a fashionable Long Island club, he ad-libbed a comic Italian, was overheard by a theatrical producer, and was given the part of an Italian in the Broadway production *Twin Beds* (1914).

This led to his appearance in a number of Broadway hits after World War I. His greatest success in the theater was in *Lombardi, LTD.*, written especially for him by Frederic and Fanny Hatton, in which he starred in 1917.

Carrillo made his screen debut in *Mr. Antonio* in 1929. He appeared in over 100 motion pictures, the most notable being *Girl of the Rio* (1932), *Viva Villa!* (1933), *Love Me Forever* (1935), *The Gay Desperado* (1936), *Twenty-Mule Team* (1940), *Crazy House* (1943), *Follow the Band* (1943), *Frontier Badmen* (1943), *Phantom of the Opera* (1943), *Bowery to Broadway* (1944), *Gypsy Wildcat* (1944), *Moonlight and Cactus* (1944); *Crime, Inc.* (1945); *The Girl from San Lorenzo* (1950) and *Pancho Villa Returns* (1950).

Lynda Carter
B: 7/24/1951
Born in Phoenix, Arizona of English-Mexican heritage, Carter is best known for the title role of the television series *Wonder Woman* (1976-79). Carter evolved from a comic book champion to a leading actress with such television movies as *Born to Be Sold* (1981), the coveted title role of *Rita Hayworth: The Love Goddess* (1983); *Mike Hammer: Murder Takes All* (1989), *When Friendship Kills* (1996), *Jack Reed: Death and Vengeance* (1996), *Someone to Love Me* (1998) and *Family Blessings* (1999). She also starred in the short-lived series *Partners in Crime* (1984) with Loni Anderson, and *Hawkeye* (1994).

Movita Castenada
See Movita.

Antonio Castillo
A Spanish-born Parisian fashion and theatrical costume designer, Castillo won an Academy Award® for his work on *Nicholas and Alexandra* (1971).

Enrique Castillo
[aka: E.J. Castillo]
B: 12/10/1949
A Mexican American actor, Castillo was featured in *Borderline* (1980), *Losin' It* (1983), *Bound by Honor* (1993) and *The Hi-Lo Country* (1998). His television credits include *The Waltons* (1972-81) and the telefilm *Fighting Back: The Rocky Bleier Story* (1980) with Robert Urich.

Eduardo Castro
A film and stage costume designer, Castro designed the period costumes for the film *Shout* (1991) and was co-designer on *Bird on a Wire* (1990). In 1987, he designed a full season of the television series *Miami Vice* (1984-89). His other credits include *The Perez Family* (1995), *A Thin Line Between Love and Hate* (1996), *A Fare to Remember* (1998), *Jazz Night* (1999), *Till the End of Time* (2000) and *What's Cookin'* (2000). Castro a master of fine arts in scenic and costume design from

Carnegie-Mellon University and was an in-house assistant at the Western Costume Company in Hollywood, working with major film costume designers.

Lumi Cavazos
B: 1968

A native of Monterey, Mexico, Cavazos gained international attention for her spirited portrayal of Tita, a woman who was born in the kitchen and whose ability to transmit her passion through her cooking transforms a family destiny in Alfonso Arau's award-winning film *Like Water for Chocolate* (1992). Cavazos began her acting career at age fifteen, working with an avant-garde theater company. Her film credits include Wes Anderson's *Bottle Rocket* (1996), *Sugar Town* (1999) and *Bless the Child* (2000).

Larry Ceballos
B: 10/21/1887
D: 9/12/1978

One of Hollywood's foremost dance directors during the late 1920s and early 1930s, the Chilean-born-and-raised Ceballos worked on numerous Vitaphone shorts and feature films at Warner Bros. and RKO. The dance sequences that he choreographed were typical 1920s stage dance arrangements adapted directly to the screen. Some of his credits include *Gold Diggers of Broadway* (1929), *On with the Show* (1929), *Show of Shows* (1929), *Hold Everything* (1930); *No, No Nanette* (1930); and *Sally* (1930).

Ara Celi
(born Araceli Valdez)
B: 5/31/1974

A former Miss Texas (1994), Araceli made her acting debut in Televisa's soap opera *Valentina*. Soon after, she guest starred on the American prime time television hit *Buffy the Vampire Slayer* (1997-). She next joined the cast of the soap opera *All My Children* (1970-) and starred in *Macarena* (1998) for Showtime, and in the direct to video release *From Dusk Till Dawn 3: The Hangman's Daughter* (2000).

Gary Cervantes

A Mexican American character actor, Cervantes usually plays heavies and criminal felons. He holds the distinction of having been killed on screen by such stars as Al Pacino in *Scarface* (1983), Arnold Schwarzenegger in *Commando* (1985), Burt Reynolds in *Stick* (1985), Nick Nolte in *Extreme Prejudice* (1987) and Whoopi Goldberg in *Fatal Beauty* (1987). His other film credits include *Colors* (1988), *Grand Canyon* (1991), *Bound by Honor* (1993), *A Low Down Dirty Shame* (1994), *Under the Hula Moon* (1995) and *Last Chance* (1999). Cervantes also has many episodic television credits.

Jorge Cervera, Jr.

This actor has appeared in *Papillon* (1973), *The Big Fix* (1978), *Black Marble* (1979), *True Confessions* (1981) and *¡Three Amigos!* (1986). His extensive television work includes thirteen episodes as a co-star of *Viva Valdez* (1976).

Damian Chapa

A young actor of Mexican American and German heritage, Chapa's first leading role was as Miklo in *Bound by Honor* (1993). He has appeared in feature films such as *Money Talks* (1997), *Kill You Twice* (1998) and *Hitman's Run* (1999); the telefilms *Menendez: A Killing in Beverly Hills* (1994), *Rockford Files: Godfather Knows Best* (1996) and the popular series *Melrose Place* (1992-99).

Charo

B: 1/15/1951

This vivacious Spanish-born singer, actress and comedienne has appeared in the films *Airport '79* (1979) and *Moon over Parador* (1988). She received her professional start in the States with Xavier Cugat, to whom she was married. Charo has guest starred in numerous television variety shows and on many situation comedies. She also guest starred in a somewhat serious dramatic role on an episode of the television series *Fantasy Island* (1978-84), starring Ricardo Montalban.

Richard Chaves

An actor whose Vietnam War experience has been catalytic, Chaves co-wrote the highly successful stageplay *Tracers*. He co-stars in the film *Predator* (1987) as Poncho and was also in *Cease Fire* (1985) opposite Don Johnson. He co-starred in the television film *Fire on the Mountain* (1981) with Buddy Ebsen and has guest starred on numerous popular series.

Linda Christian
[born: Bianca Rosa Welter]

B: 11/13/1924

Born in Mexico of Dutch parents, Christian was signed by an MGM talent scout in 1945 for *Holiday in Mexico* (1946) and *Green Dolphin Street* (1947). Afterward, she decided to freelance and appeared in the made-in-Mexico *Tarzan and the Mermaids* (1948) and *The Happy Time* (1952), with Louis Jourdan. Christian became best known when she married actor Tyrone Power in 1949. After her marriage to Power ended in divorce in 1955, she resumed her film acting career in Europe.

Cynthia Cidre

B: 1957

A Cuban-born screenwriter, Cidre's credits include *Fires Within* (1991) and *The Mambo Kings* (1992). She also co-scripted *In Country* (1989), starring Bruce Willis and directed by Norman Jewison.

Alex Colon

B: 1/26/1941
D: 1/6/1995

A Puerto Rican-born actor, Colon was raised in New York. He has worked extensively in theater, television and film. Colon appeared on Broadway in Neil Simon's *The Gingerbread Lady* (1970) with Maureen Stapleton.

He can be seen in such films as *Invasion, U.S.A.* (1952), *The Cross and the Switchblade* (1970), *The Hospital* (1971), *Harry and Tonto* (1974), *The Super Cops* (1974), *The Taking of Pelham 1,2,3* (1974), *The Ultimate Warrior* (1975) with Yul Brynner, *Special Delivery* (1976), *When You Comin' Back, Red Ryder?* (1979), *Back Roads* (1981), *Deal of the Century* (1983), *Death of an Angel* (1985), *Deep Cover* (1988), *The Mighty Quinn* (1989) and *Red Scorpion* (1989). His television films include *The Law* (1974), *Hustling* (1975) with Jill Clayburgh, *Raid on Entebbe* (1977), *Women of San Quentin* (1983) and the 24-hour epic miniseries *Centennial* (1978-1979).

Miriam Colon

B: 1925

A Puerto Rican-born actress, Colon has appeared as a Mexican in such films as *One-Eyed Jacks* (1961) and *The Appaloosa* (1966), both starring Marlon Brando. She had an important and strong role as Tony Montana's (Al Pacino's) mother in Brian De Palma's *Scarface* (1983). Her other films include *The Possession of Joel Delaney* (1972), *Back Roads* (1981) and *The House of the Spirits* (1994).

Spotted as a serious talent while she was a drama student at the University of Puerto Rico, Colon was admitted to New York's prestigious Actors Studio on her first audition. After studying under Lee Strasberg and Elia Kazan, she appeared on the New York Stage in *In the Summer House, The Innkeepers, The Wrong Way Light Bulb* and *The Oxcart*.

Colon has guest starred in more than 100 television shows and is the founder and artistic director of New York's Puerto Rican Traveling Theatre, which she established over twenty years ago.

Anjanette Comer

A talented actress, Comer has co-starred in such films as *Quick, Before It Melts* (1964), *The Loved One* (1965), *The Appaloosa* (1966), *Banning* (1967), *Guns for San Sebastian* (1968), *Lepke* (1975) and *Fire Sale* (1978).

James Contreras

B: 1923
D: 1990

A film sound man for over forty years, Contreras' credits include *Easy Rider* (1969) and *The Night of the Iguana* (1964). In television, he worked on such series as *Kung Fu* (1972-75) and *The Streets of San Francisco* (1972-77). He was the brother of actor Roberto Contreras and the son of Director Jamie Contreras.

Luis Contreras

B: 9/18/1950

A Mexican American character actor, Contreras usually plays unsavory characters and heavies in films and episodic television shows. Among his multitude of film credits are *Coming Home* (1978), *Borderline* (1980), *The Long Riders* (1980), *Barbarosa* (1982), *Pee-Wee's Big Adventure* (1985), *Red Heat* (1985), *Blues City* (1986), *Extreme Prejudice* (1987), *Walker* (1987) and *Bound by Honor* (1993). His television work includes such shows as *Gunsmoke* (1955-75) (his first appearance in 1969), the original *Mission: Impossible* (1966-73), *Hill Street Blues* (1981-87), *Dallas* (1978-91), the new *Adam-12* (1989-90) and *MacGyver* (1985-92). He is the son of actor Roberto Contreras, and the nephew of James Contreras.

Roberto Contreras

Born in St. Louis and raised in Mexico City, Contreras, son of Director Jaime Contreras and brother of James Contreras, began his acting career at age eight, appearing in Mexican films and television productions. His film credits include *The Sun Also Rises* (1957), *The Magnificent Seven* (1960), *Ship of Fools* (1965), *The Appaloosa* (1966), *The Professionals* (1966), *Topaz* (1969), *Barbarosa* (1982), *Scarface* (1983) and *Streets of Fire* (1984). Among his numerous television credits was a regular role as a ranch hand on *The High Chaparral* (1967-71) series. His son, Luis Contreras, is also an actor.

Caesar Cordova

B: 5/16/1936

A Puerto Rican-born character actor, Cordova's film credits include *Shark's Treasure* (1975), starring and directed by Cornel Wilde, *Where the Buffalo Roam* (1980), *Nighthawks* (1981) and *Scarface* (1983) opposite Al Pacino. His television credits include *East Side/West Side* (1963-64) and *Kojak* (1973-78).

Mapy Cortes
[born: Maria del Pilar; aka: Mapy Cortez]

B: 3/1/1919

D: 8/2/1998

Born in Puerto Rico, Cortes entered musical comedy in Spanish theater, performing throughout Latin America and Spain. She made films in Spain and Mexico, where she was enormously popular. The Latin star came to Hollywood in 1942, where at RKO she made *Seven Days Leave* (1942), on entertaining all-star musical extravaganza with Victor Mature and Lucille Ball. She essentially played herself, a Puerto Rican singing and dancing star, with Les Brown and his Band of Renown.

Ricardo Cortez
[born: Jacob Krantz]

B: 9/19/1899

D: 4/28/1977

Born in Vienna, Cortez immigrated to New York City with his family at age three. He started as on extra in movies when he was seventeen in

New York. In 1922, Jesse Lasky, head of Paramount Studios, spotted him because of his dark good looks, and Lasky's secretary picked the name Ricardo Cortez when it was decided he needed a Latin name. Ricardo was on his way to stardom as a screen Latin Lover and successor to Valentino, who was Lasky's big star then. Valentino was threatening to leave the studio, and Lasky cast Cortez in the next movie intended for him and let Valentino go his own way, allowing Ricardo to achieve prominence. He stayed with Lasky for six more years and then moved to MGM, where he was the only star billed above Garbo in her first American motion picture, *The Torrent* (1926, silent). Cortez's career waned with the coming of sound.

Cortez is included here because, though not Latin, he was closely identified as one and had adopted a Latin name.

Stanley Cortez
[born: Stanley Krantz]
B: 11/4/1908
D: 12/23/1998
Stanley Cortez adopted the stage surname of his actor brother, Ricardo Cortez. As a cinematographer he created powerful images in *The Magnificent Ambersons* (1942) for Orson Welles, for which he received an Oscar® nomination; *Since You Went Away* (1944), *The Night of the Hunter* (1955) and *The Three Faces of Eve* (1957).

He worked as a young portrait photographer in New York City in the 1920s and entered motion pictures as a camera assistant to D.W. Griffith on two of his last films. He is recognized as having played a key role in defining cinematography as an art form by the powerful example of his body of work.

Maria Costa
Costa starred in the short-lived television series *Dangerous Minds* (1996) based on the hit feature film of the same name. Of Cuban and Hungarian parentage, the Detroit native at the age of nineteen produced an MTV-style series *Club Connect* for PBS.

Oscar L. Costo
B: 1954
Costo has held positions as producer, director and production manager in television . He co-produced series *Sins of the City* (1998), and produced the series *Vanishing Son* (1994) and *Hitz* (1996). He directed episodes of *SeaQuest DSV* (1993-95), *New York Undercover* (1994-98), *Sliders* (1995-2000), *Dark Skies* (1996-97) and *Soldier Of Fortune, Inc.* (1997).

Manny Cota
A writer and director, Cato directed the 1992 theatrical feature film *Dr. Giggles*. For television he has directed episodes of HBO's *Tales from the Crypt* (1989) and the syndicated series *Monsters* (1988-90). Cota was born in Havana, Cuba, and was raised in Orlando, Florida.

Linda Cristal.

Linda Cristal
[born: Marta Luis Maya Burgess]
B: 2/24/1935

An Argentine-born actress, Cristal achieved popularity in the States during the late 1950s and early 1960s. Her most important film role was in *The Alamo* (1960), starring John Wayne (however, in theatrical reissues and on television her part has been considerably edited), and she later starred in the NBC television series *The High Chaparral* (1967-71) as the strong-willed and beautiful Victoria Cannon.

The actress was born in Buenos Aires, Argentina. She was orphaned at age thirteen, and at age seventeen, while vacationing in Mexico, she was noticed by Mexican film producer/director Raul de Anda during a concert. He persuaded her to do a screen test. Upon seeing the results he put her under contract and gave her a leading role in his next production, *Genio y Figure*. She starred for six years in Spanish-language films and was then signed to a Hollywood contract by Universal-International, which exploited her Latin background, as this press release indicates: "Universal-International's best bet for stardom is an Argentinean beauty with more zing than a chili pepper, more beauty than a Buenos Aires sunset and more curves than a roadmap of the Andes."

Cristal began the American phase of her career playing virginal señoritas and Indian maidens in a number of films. She played a Mexican girl in *The Last of the Fast Guns* (1958), an Italian movie star in *The Perfect Furlough* (1958) with Tony Curtis, a Cuban dance hall hostess in *Cry Tough* (1959) and a Mexican woman captured by Indians in John Ford's *Two Rode Together* (1961). Her last major motion picture role to date was in *Mr. Majestyk* (1974), starring Charles Bronson, as a socially concerned Chicana activist. Her other films include *Comanche* (1956) and *The Fiend Who Walked the West* (1958).

Her role as Victoria Cannon on the long-running television series *The High Chaparral* (1967-71) demonstrated acting ability and a maturity that brought her great popularity. She received two Emmy Award nominations as Best Actress in a Drama Series.

Alexis Cruz
B: 1974

Cruz has been featured in a regular role on the series *Touched by an Angel* (1994-), guest starred on numerous episodic television series and appeared in several telefilms. His feature film credits include *The Pick-Up Artist* (1992), *Stargate* (1994), *Why Do Fools Fall In Love?* (1998), *Learning to Swim* (1999) and *Tortilla Heaven* (2000).

Penelope Cruz
B: 1974

Penelope Cruz made her American film debut as the intuitive Josepha O'Neil in *The Hi-Lo Country* (1998). The Madrid born actress is considered one of Spain's brightest young stars. Already a veteran of over a dozen feature films, the actress starred in Pedro Almodovar's Academy Award®-winning *All About My Mother* (1999) and in Almodovar's *Live*

Flesh (1997). Her other film credits include Bigas Luna's *Jamon, Jamon* (1992), Fernando Trueba's *Belle Époque* (1992), Alejandro Amenabar's *Open Your Eyes* (1997), Trueba's *The Girl of Your Dreams* (1998), as well as Maria Ripoll's *Twice Upon a Yesterday* (1998). Most recently, she has appeared in *Blow* (2000) and *All the Pretty Horses* (2000).

Raymond Cruz

Cruz has played featured roles in *Out for Justice* (1991), *Under Siege* (1992), *Clear and Present Danger* (1994), *Up Close and Personal* (1996), *The Substitute* (1996), *Alien: Resurrection* (1997) and the video release *From Dusk Till Dawn: Texas Blood Money* (2000). Cruz began his career with guest appearances on such television series as *Cc:gney & Lacey* (1982-88), *Hill Street Blues* (1981-87) and *Beauty and the Beast* (1987-90).

Wilson Cruz

B: 12/27/1973

Cruz's credits include a recurring role on the series *Party of Five* (1994-2000) and a featured role in *Supernova* (2000). His first series regular role was on the critically acclaimed *My So-Called Life* (1994-95) as a troubled homosexual teen. He has also starred in the theatrical production of *Rent*.

Alfonso Cuaron

Cuaron made his American film directorial debut with the critically acclaimed film *A Little Princess* (1995) which won him the Los Angeles Film Critics New Generation Award. He followed this with *Great Expectations* (1998) starring Gwyneth Paltrow. Born and reared in Mexico City, Cuaron studied filmmaking and philosophy at the National University of Mexico. He worked as an assistant director on many American films shot in Mexico and directed Mexican television before helming his first feature, *Solo Con Tu Pareja* (Love in the Time of Hysteria) (1991). The unusual comedy about AIDS was made on a budget of only half a million dollars and became the highest grossing film in Mexico in 1992. Cuaron shared an Ariel (the Mexican Academy Award) for screenwriting. The film garnered a great deal of attention for Cuaron in Hollywood. Cuaron's direction of "Murder Obliquely," an episode of the Showtime series *Fallen Angels* (1993) starring Laura Dern and Alan Rickman, earned him a CableAce Award for Best direction in 1995.

Xavier Cugat

B: 1/1/1900

D: 10/27/1990

A Spanish-born orchestra leader, Cugat was instrumental in popularizing Latin American music in the United States during the 1930s and 1940s. Through nightclub performances, radio, recordings, motion pictures and television, Cugat became a household name in America. More than any other person, he is credited with starting the rumba craze in the States. His flair for featuring beautiful singers with his band helped launch the careers of Lina Romay, Margo, Abbe Lane and Charo.

Xavier Cugat and
Carmen Miranda supply
the chili-flavored romantic
doings in the musical
A Date with Judy.

While under contract to MGM, Cugat was featured in several musicals of the late 1930s and the 1940s in sumptuous production numbers that spotlighted him and his band. *Go West, Young Man* (1936); *Bathing Beauty* (1944), *Two Girls and a Sailor* (1944), *Holiday in Mexico* (1946); *No Leave, No Love* (1946); *This Time for Keeps* (1947), *A Date with Judy* (1948), *Luxury Liner* (1948), *On an Island with You* (1948) and *Neptune's Daughter* (1949).

Born in Barcelona, Spain, on New Year's Day, Cugat discovered at an early age that all the members of his artistic family were expected to help to support the group. His three brothers were struggling artists, his parents, musicians. His father became a political refugee from Spain, and the family moved to Cuba when Cugat was three years old. They lived across the street from a violin maker, and when Cugat was given one as a gift, he quickly mastered the instrument. At age twelve, Cugat's violin playing with a symphony orchestra in Havana earned enough to support his entire family. Eventually, the talents of his brothers were recognized also, and all achieved success.

Later, back in Spain, Cugat studied under Tullio Serafin. He then came to America and enrolled at the Frank Damrosch School, studying under Frank Kneisel. In Italy he became acquainted with Enrico Caruso, who engaged him to play his violin between Caruso's numbers on concert tours. It was Caruso who started Cugat drawing, an endeavor that brought the bandmaster as much fame as his music.

Returning to America, Cugat found the concert field far from lucrative. Stowing his fiddle in its case, he went to California, where he became a cartoonist on the staff of the *Los Angeles Times* from 1924 to 1925. Music was his first love, however, and he soon found work as a composer for a motion picture studio. He also found six other musicians to play commercial music with him. "Well, almost commercial," remarked Cugat in an interview quoted in the *Los Angeles Times* obituary (10/28/90), "They were a Latin Music combo, and in the 1920s (Rudolph Valentino notwithstanding) such rhythms were considered 'gigolo music' and demand was limited."

This led to the organization of a small band, with which he made a short subject with Rita Cansino (later to become Rita Hayworth). He took the same band to Hollywood's Montmartre Cafe, and they caused a sensation whenever they played. His big break came when he was booked into the Starlight Roof of New York City's famed Waldorf-Astoria Hotel. There followed long engagements at the Waldorf-Astoria for almost a decade. In 1941, Louis B. Mayer's limousine drew up in front of Hollywood's Palladium, a famous dance palace frequented by the younger generation. He took notice of Cugat's name on the marquee and the excitement of the crowd and signed Cugat to a contract. Hayworth and Cugat were reunited in 1942 for his appearance in the musical *You Were Never Lovelier* (1942), in which Hayworth co-starred with Fred Astaire. Cugat usually played himself, along with his band, in these film appearances.

Bertila Damas

A Cuban-Puerto Rican actress, Damas co-starred opposite Jimmy Smits in *Fires Within* (1991) and was featured in *Nothing But Trouble* (1991) with Chevy Chase and in *Stop! Or My More Will Shoot* (1992). Since then, she has appeared in several television movies, including *Dean Koontz's Mr. Murder* (1998).

Henry Darrow
[born: Henry Delgado]
B: 1931

A New York-born Puerto Rican actor, Henry Delgado grew up in the Washington Heights area of Manhattan. He decided to seek opportunities in California and studied at the Pasadena Playhouse. Producer David Dortort saw him in a production of Ray Bradbury's *The Wonderful Ice Cream Suit* at the Coronet Theatre; a year later Dortort remembered the young actor's spirited performance and felt he might be right for the role of Manolito on a television show he was creating called *The High Chaparral* (1967-71). A casting call for Delgado went out, but he could not be found, for Delgado had changed his name to Darrow to further his acting opportunities. He finally got word that Dortort was looking for him, and he landed the role that would lead him to television stardom as the rascally son of a wealthy Mexican cattle baron. He later co-starred with David Janssen on the *Harry-O* (1974-76) series and on *The New Dick Van Dyke Show* (1971-74). He made his feature film debut in a small role in *Holiday for Lovers* (1959) starring Clifton Webb. Darrow has had co-starring roles in such films as *Badge 373* (1973), *Walk Proud* (1979) and *Losin' It* (1983).

Henry Darrow.

Howard da Silva

B: 5/4/1909
D: 2/16/1986

Often cast as a heavy, da Silva, born in Cleveland, Ohio, the son of Benjamin and Bertha da Silva, was of Russian-Portuguese descent. He made his motion picture debut in 1940 in *I'm Still Alive*, and gained recognition as the bartender in Billy Wilder's *The Lost Weekend* (1945) and as the sadistic captain in *Two Years Before the Mast* (1946). His more than forty motion picture credits include *Duffy's Tavern* (1945), *Unconquered* (1947), *David and Lisa* (1962), *Topkapi* (1964) and *Nevada Smith* (1966). He created the role of Jud in the original Broadway stage production of *Oklahoma!,* and starred in both the stage and film (1972) versions of the musical *1776* as Ben Franklin. He won an Emmy Award for Outstanding Performance by a Supporting Actor in the television special *Verna, USO Girl* (1978). He also directed the original Broadway production of *Purlie Victorious* (1961) starring Ruby Dee and Ossie Davis.

Rosario Dawson

Born in Coney Island and raised in New York, Dawson played Lala Bonilla in Spike Lee's *He Got Game* (1998). She has also starred in *Light It Up* (1999) and *Down to You* (2000). She made her feature film debut in the controversial semi-documentary cult hit *Kids* (1995) and lived in

Texas until she returned to New York to study acting at the Lee Strasberg Institute.

Roxann Dawson
B: 9/11/1964
Roxann Dawson is best known as Chief Engineer B'Elanna Torres, a beautiful young woman who is half human, half-Klingon, on the syndicated *Star Trek: Voyager* (1995-99). Born and raised in Los Angeles, California, Dawson was a theater arts major at the University of California at Berkeley. The actress soon found her first acting stint nothing short of remarkable as he landed the role of Diana Morales in the Broadway production of *A Chorus Line*. Her feature film credits include *Guilty by Suspicion* (1991) and *Darkman III: Die Darkman Die* (1995).

Francisco ("Chico") Day
[born: Francisco Alonso]
B: 1907
D: 4/11/1995
Born in Juarez, Mexico, and raised in El Paso and Los Angeles, Day was the first Hispanic American assistant director in Hollywood. He worked for over thirty years at Paramount Studios on such films as *The Big Broadcast of 1938* (1938), *Lady in the Dark* (1944), *Whispering Smith* (1948), *Streets of Laredo* (1949), *Samson and Delilah* (1949), *The Ten Commandments* (1956), *Teacher's Pet* (1958) and *One-Eyed Jacks* (1961). He later became a unit production manager on such noted films as *The Magnificent Seven* (1960), *Hello, Dolly!* (1969) and *Patton* (1970).

Joaquim de Almeida
Born in Portugal, de Almeida is a very well-known international star. Some of his American film credits include *The Soldier* (1982), *Beyond the Limit* (1983), *Good Morning Babylon* (1987), *Only You* (1994), *Clear and Present Danger* (1994), *Desperado* (1995), *Vendetta* (1999) and *No Vacancy* (1999). He won the Best Actor Award at the Cairo Film Festival for his 1992 performance in *Portrait de Famille*. On television, he has been seen in the miniseries *Nostromo* (1996) and the telefilm *Dead Man's Walk* (1996).

Pedro De Cordoba
B: 9/28/1881
D: 1950
A tall, gaunt-looking character actor who appeared in numerous silent and sound films, De Cordoba was born in New York City to Cuban-French parents. His credits include the silent 1915 version of *Carmen* as Escamillo, *Temptation* (1915, silent), *Ramona* (1936), *The Garden of Allah* (1936), *The Sea Hawk* (1940), *The Mark of Zorro* (1940), *Aloma of the South Seas* (1941), *The Song of Bernadette* (1943), *The Keys of the Kingdom* (1944), *Samson and Delilah* (1949) and *Crisis* (1950).

Assistant director Francisco "Chico" Day (left) with Cecil B. DeMille (right) on the set of *The Ten Commandments*.

Arturo De Cordova
[born: Arturo Garcia Rodriguez]

B: 1908

D: 11/3/1973

Arturo De Cordova had a likable, pleasant manner on screen, but he never quite clicked with American audiences. After starring in a number of films at Paramount, he decided to return to Mexico and South America, where he began his career and became a screen idol, consistently starring in leading roles until his death.

Born in Merida, Mexico, he initially worked as a sports writer for UPI and as a radio announcer. While working in Argentina as a sports writer, he met Russian stage director Aready Boytler, who suggested that De Cordova become an actor. De Cordova did not take him seriously until the two met again years later in Mexico City, where Boytler was about to produce a film with Fernando Soler. Boytler asked De Cordova to play the romantic lead. He took the job, thinking that it might help his radio announcing career. In 1935 he starred in the hit film *Cielito Lindo*, at which time he formally adopted the screen name of De Cordova.

In 1938, De Cordova made his first Hollywood film, the Spanish language *Son's Command*, followed by *The Miracle of Main Street*, with Margo, in 1939. De Cordova's first big break in American films came with the role of Augustin in Paramount's adaptation of Ernest Hemingway's *For Whom the Bell Tolls* (1943), with Gary Cooper and Ingrid Bergman.

Under contract to Paramount Pictures, he had important roles in such films as *Duffy's Tavern* (1945), *A Medal for Benny* (1945), *Incendiary Blonde* (1945) and *Masquerade in Mexico* (1945). Paramount gambled and assigned him the leading role opposite Joan Fontaine in the important and expensive film *Frenchman's Creek* (1944). Although it was not a hit, De Cordova turned in an impressive performance as the French pirate. He left Paramount for Mexico, where he starred in a version of *The Count of Monte Cristo* (1934), which became a smash hit and made him the idol of millions of women in seventeen Latin countries. De Cordova became one of the stars of Mexico's Golden Age of Cinema (1942-1952) as a romantic leading man in a wide variety of roles. His other United States films include *New Orleans* (1947) and *The Adventures of Casanova* (1948).

Frederick De Cordova

B: 10/27/1910

De Cordova was born in New York City and came to films from the stage in 1944 as a dialogue director at Warner Bros. He directed many routine medium-budget entertainment features through the mid-1960s but has been active mainly in television since the mid-1950s. From 1971 until his retirement in May 1992, he was the producer of NBC's *The Tonight Show Starring Johnny Carson*.

Wanda de Jesus.

Josie De Guzman

A Puerto Rican Broadway stage actress, De Guzman was featured in the film *F/X* (1986) starring Bryan Brown, and then again in *F/X 2* (1991). Her stage credits include her Tony-nominated starring role in the 1992 revival of *Guys and Dolls*.

Wanda de Jesus

De Jesus has co-starred in the feature films *Flawless* (1999) opposite Robert De Niro, as Karen, his sultry dancer girlfriend, *The Insider* (1999) opposite Al Pacino, and *Once in the Life* (1999) starring and directed by Laurence Fishburne. Other film credits include *Executive Decision* (1996), Charles Burnett's *Glass Shield* (1995), *Robocop 2* (1990) and *Downtown* (1989) .

De Jesus' impressive television credits include starring as investigative reporter Liz Vega in the series *Live Shot* (1995) for UPN and the miniseries *Lucky/Chances* (1990). Her many guest appearances include such shows as *Civil Wars* (1991-93), *Equal Justice* (1990-91), *L.A. Law* (1986-94), *Diagnosis Murder* (1993-), *Babylon 5* (1995-98), *NYPD Blue* (1993-), *Nash Bridges* (1996-) and *Promised Land* (1996-99). She appeared in a featured role opposite David Caruso in Elmore Leonard's *Gold Coast* (1997) for Showtime.

Joe (Jose) de la Cruz

B: 3/19/1892
D: 12/14/1965

A Mexican-born Western film supporting player from the 1920s through the 1940s, de la Cruz usually played a Mexican bandit or vaquero. His films include *The Bearcat* (1922, silent) with Hoot Gibson, *A Devil with Women* (1930) with Victor McLaglen and Mona Maris, *The Cactus Kid* (1935) with Jack Perin, *Zorro's Fighting Legion* (1939, 12-chapter serial) with Reed Hadley and *Oklahoma Frontier* (1939) with Johnny Mack Brown. De la Cruz's final film was *The Black Scorpion* (1957).

Cristian de la Fuente

B: 1974

Born and raised in Chile, the young actor's rise to fame has been rapid with his role as Andres Diaz, the law clerk on the CBS series *Family Law* (1999-).

Danny de la Paz

B: 4/13/1957

An intense actor, de la Paz has played starring roles in such films as *Boulevard Nights* (1979) as Chuco, a young and troubled gang member; *Cuba* (1979), as a Cuban rebel; *Barbarosa* (1982), as the Mexican American son who sacrifices himself to the wishes of his father; and *American Me* (1992), as Puppet, a prison gang member who is forced to kill his own brother in order to uphold a deadly code. He was also featured in *Miracle Mile* (1989) and *Freejack* (1992). He then took a four year hiatus from films, returning in 2000 with roles in *Gabriela*, *Two Coyotes*, *Road Dogz* and *Picking Up the Pieces*.

George de la Peña

B: 1958

Born in New York of mixed Russian-Argentinean parentage, de la Peña, a remarkable young dancer from the American Ballet Theatre, portrayed the legendary Russian dancer who electrified the world in the 1980 film *Nijinsky*, directed by Herbert Ross.

Marcus De Leon

The director/writer of the independent feature *Kiss Me a Killer* (1991), De Leon is the son of a prominent Mexican American artist and a German-born educator. A native of Los Angeles, he attended UCLA Film School and wrote and directed a short film, *Xavier*, that went on to win the school's prestigious Best Film Award. De Leon and several of his UCLA classmates made a film called *Border Radio* (1988).

Marcel Delgado

B: 1900

D: 1976

With special effects genius Willis O'Brien, Delgado worked on many films, most notably as chief model maker and sculptor on the 1933 RKO production of *King Kong*. Born in La Parrita, Mexico, he moved with his family to California in 1909. A self-educated sculptor, he worked on such films as *The Lost World* (1925, silent), *Son of Kong* (1934), *Mighty Joe Young* (1949), *Jack the Giant Killer* (1962), *It's a Mad Mad Mad Mad World* (1963) and *Fantastic Voyage* (1966).

Marcia del Mar

Del Mar's feature film credits include roles in *Under Fire* (1983) and *Body Double* (1984). She also co-starred on the USA cable television series *Sanchez of Bel Air* (1986).

Maria del Mar

A versatile film and television actress, del Mar was born in Madrid, Spain, the daughter of a diplomat and grew up in Ottawa, Canada. Del Mar co-stars as Rita opposite Jimmy Smits in Carlos Avila's *Price of Glory* (2000). She was a regular on the UPN television series *Mercy Point* (1998-99) and has guest starred on such series as *Frasier* (1993-), *The Practice* (1997-) and *The Outer Limits* (1995). Del Mar has numerous Canadian film and television credits.

Michael DeLorenzo

In addition to his starring role as Police Detective Eddie Torres in the Fox Network television series *New York Undercover* (1994-98), DeLorenzo is currently starring in the Showtime series *Resurrection Blvd.* (2000-), and was a member of the cast for the series *Head of the Class* (1986-91). He has appeared in episodes of *A Different World* (1987-93), *Miami Vice* (1984-89), *Crime Story* (1986-88), *Bronx Zoo* (1987-88) and *Fame* (1982-87). His feature film debut was in the feature film *Fame* (1980); credits since then include *A Few Good Men* (1992) *Judgment Night* (1993), *Alive* (1993), *My Family* (1995), *Phantoms* (1998) and *Gun Shy* (2000). Born and

Michael DeLorenzo in *New York Undercover*.

raised in the Bronx, DeLorenzo is a graduate of New York's famed High School of the Performing Arts.

Kamar de los Reyes
He is probably most recognized for his role of Antonio Vega on the ABC daytime television drama *One Life to Live* (1968-). A native of Puerto Rico, he came to the continental United States at the age of two and grew up in Las Vegas. His feature film credits include *Nixon* (1995) and *Mambo Cafe* (1999). He has starred in off-Broadway stage productions as well as having guest starred on such television series as *E.R.* (1994-), *New York Undercover* (1994-98) and *Promised Land* (1996-99).

Nancy de los Santos
Born and raised in Chicago, de los Santos was associate producer of *Selena* (1997) and *My Family* (1995). Previously, she worked as an associate producer, then later as a producer, of the *Siskel and Ebert at the Movies* (1986-) syndicated television show.

Pilar Del Rey
An actress, Del Rey made her film debut as a young girl in *The Miracle of Our Lady of Fatima*, starring Gilbert Roland, in 1952. She went on to appear on early dramatic television shows and in such films as *Black Horse Canyon* (1954) with Joel McCrea, *Mark of the Renegade* (1951) with Ricardo Montalban and *And Now Miguel* (1966) with Michael Ansara. Del Rey played the mother of Sal Mineo and the wife of Victor Millan in George Stevens' *Giant* (1956). Her other film credits include *The Naked Jungle* (1953) and *Lonely Are the Brave* (1962).

Dolores Del Rio
[born: Lolita Dolores Martinez Ansunsolo Lopez Negrette]
B: 8/3/1905
D: 3/11/1983
Dolores Del Rio was one of the legendary beauties of the silver screen, and her fifty-year career spanned the transition from silent to sound movies and television. Though she starred in a number of silent and early talkie Hollywood film classics, such as *What Price Glory?* (1926, silent), *Resurrection* (1927, silent), *The Loves of Carmen* (1927, silent), *Ramona* (1928, silent), *Flying Down to Rio* (1933) and *Bird of Paradise* (1932), the greater part of her career from 1943 was spent in her native Mexico, where she became a top star after filming *Maria Candelaria* (1943). Her luminous beauty and natural dignity combined with her acting ability gained her a wide range of starring roles in Mexican films.

She was born in Durango, Mexico, where her father was a banker. At age four, Dolores and her family were forced to leave Durango for Mexico City when Pancho Villa threatened them. At fifteen she married Jaime Martinez del Rio and took his name, capitalizing the "D" on the "del" for her career, which began quite casually after she studied dancing and began to perform at various society galas and festivals.

American film director Edwin Carewe, honeymooning in Mexico in the early 1920s, saw Del Rio dancing a tango at a party in his honor and was immediately struck by her beauty and dancing ability. The Del Rios and the Carewes became friends, and eventually Dolores acceded to his request to come to Hollywood in 1925. "He told me I was the female Valentino," said Del Rio in a 1981 interview. "He kept sending me wires and eventually my husband and I decided to go. I didn't know what would happen but I thought it would be fun to meet all the people I idolized—like Chaplin and Valentino." Bridget Byrne, *San Francisco Chronicle* (11/20-27/81).

Del Rio played her first small part, as a vamp society girl, in Carewe's minor jazz tale *Joanna* (1925, silent). She followed this with a second film for Carewe, *High Steppers* (1926, silent), in which her role was subordinate to star Mary Astor. Her first lead was in *Pals First* (1926, silent), and then she filmed *The Whole Town Is Talking* (1926, silent). Her first real success, however, was as the provocative French flirt Charmaine in Raoul Walsh's *What Price Glory?* that same year. The film brought her wide praise and immediate fame. It also proved not only that she was beautiful but that she could handle comedy as well, especially opposite two scene-stealing leading men like Edmund Lowe and Victor McLaglen.

Del Rio's next film was *Resurrection* (1927, silent) from the novel by Tolstoy, directed by Carewe and with Rod La Rocque as her leading man. She portrayed Katusha, who is forced into prostitution after an unhappy affair with a married man. That same year she starred in *The Loves of Carmen* for Raoul Walsh, and the following year she played the first in a series of native roles as a half-caste girl in love with a tough railroad manager (Walter Pidgeon) in *The Gateway of the Moon* (1928, silent). In 1928 she was also directed by Carewe in *Ramona*, the famous love story of an Indian girl and a Spaniard, which became one of her most successful films. Her leading man was Warner Baxter. With her great success, a studio released a quickie she had made two years before with Don Alvarado called *No Other Woman* (1926, silent), and she followed her success with *Revenge* (1928, silent) also for Carewe. Raoul Walsh directed her again in *The Red Dance* (1928), in which she played the role of the Red Dancer of the Russian Revolution. She played the part of a dance hall girl in *The Trail of '98* (1928, silent) opposite Harry Carey. *Evangeline* in 1929 with Roland Drew was a tearjerker, the story of youthful lovers who are reunited in old age. Del Rio sang two songs and spoke one line of dialogue at the end of this otherwise silent film.

Her first all-talking picture was *The Bad One* (1930) with Don Alvarado and Edmund Lowe, with Del Rio as an inmate of a brothel. After the film she broke her contract with Carewe and signed with Joseph Schenck of United Artists. Following the signing she suffered a nervous breakdown, which kept her away from the cameras for almost two years. She returned in 1931 to RKO with a new contract and filmed *Girl of the Rio* (1932), in which she played a cantina performer opposite Leo Carrillo and Norman Foster. The film was later banned in Mexico for its unflattering portrayals of Mexican and Latin characters.

She played Luana, a native girl of the Hawaiian Islands, in *Bird of Paradise* (1932), directed by King Vidor mostly on location in Hawaii. Producer David O. Selznick later reportedly told Vidor: "I don't care what story you use as long as we call it *Bird of Paradise* and Del Rio jumps

Dolores Del Rio.

into a flaming volcano at the finish." Her leading man was Joel McCrea, at the time the epitome of the new athletic leading man and much in demand. The film was a tremendous hit with the public—the photography was outstanding, and Vidor's direction kept a strong hand on the flimsy plot contrivances of love and uprising in the South Seas.

In 1933 she accepted a role in the musical *Flying Down to Rio*. On paper she had the lead opposite Gene Raymond, but Fred Astaire and Ginger Rogers danced away with the film. Her tango to "Orchids in the Moonlight" with Astaire was seen in the picture before his now more famous dances with Ginger Rogers in the landmark musical. In an interview many years later she said, "For the first time I was to play the part of a smart modern woman with plenty of music and comedy around me. I knew it was a sign that I could play a sophisticated role. I was no longer little Luana or Ramona. The picture was a great success. The credit mainly belonged to others, but my private battle was partly won," *Film Weekly* (July 1972).

In 1934 she made three pictures for Warner Bros. that, according to her contract (located at the Warner Bros. Archives at the University of Southern California Library), earned her a total of $100,000—not a bad sum for the middle of the Depression, when the average worker, if lucky enough to have a job, was earning only $12 a week. In *Wonder Bar* (1934) she was the dance partner of Ricardo Cortez. She starred in *Madame du Barry* (1934) with Reginald Owen and Anita Louise. This bedroom comedy proved a disappointment to the star, who considered it her best work of that period. The film suffered at the hands of the censors and the public was uninterested in the result. *In Caliente* and *I Live for Love* (both 1935) marked the change in image that she had been striving for, but she was used more for decorative purposes in these musical fantasies. Del Rio continued working in such films as *The Widow from Monte Carlo* (1936), *Accused* (1936), *Ali Baba Goes to Town* (1937), *Devil's Playground* (1937), *Lancer Spy* (1937), *International Settlement* (1938) and *The Man from Dakota* (1940).

By the early 1940s, between program pictures and marital difficulties, both her career and her personal life were in distress. She had already divorced her first husband, and her marriage to famed MGM art director Cedric Gibbons was now on the rocks. Meanwhile, she was engaged in a close relationship with Orson Welles and appeared as a nightclub dancer in the first two reels of his *Journey into Fear* (1942), an espionage thriller starring Joseph Cotten. Dissatisfied with her work and life in Hollywood, Del Rio returned to Mexico. She recalled in a 1981 interview, "I didn't want to be a star anymore, I wanted to be an actress and with all of those gowns they put on me, all of those millions of feathers, I couldn't be. I chose instead the chance to be a pioneer in the movie industry of my country, an exciting new challenge," Herb Michelson, *Variety* (10/15/81).

The Mexican film industry had developed tremendously since she had left in 1926 and was technically as proficient and accomplished as Hollywood. In Mexico, Del Rio found a director, Emilio Fernandez, who realized her full potential as an actress and star. *Flor Silvestre*, her first film for him in 1943, established her as Mexico's top star and gained her the first of the four Ariels (Mexico's Oscar®) she was to receive as Best

Actress. Pedro Armendariz, Director Fernandez, Cinematographer Gabriel Figueroa and Del Rio became known as "The Team" of the Mexican film industry. *Maria Candelaria*, directed by Emilio Fernandez, showcased Del Rio at her finest, as a peasant girl of simplicity and deep spirituality who is stoned to death by her fellow villagers, who mistrust and fear her. As a result of its showing at the Cannes Film Festival, it was the first Mexican film to make an impact on the international film community following World War II. In a folkloric style enhanced by Gabriel Figueroa's brilliant black-and-white photography, the film reflected a national identity rooted in the Mexican culture. The team stayed together for several more films, including *Bugambilia* (1944), *Las Abandonadas* (1944) and *La Malquerida* (1949).

John Ford's *The Fugitive* (1947), though an American film, was shot largely in Mexico by Figueroa and starred Henry Fonda as an alcoholic priest on the run; it featured Pedro Armendariz, Del Rio and Leo Carrillo. She continued starring in Mexican films as a top star during and beyond the so-called Golden Age of Mexican Cinema (1942-1952).

In 1960 she returned to Hollywood to play Elvis Presley's Indian mother in Don Siegel's *Flaming Star*. Critics noted her moving performance and her enduring beauty. She had planned an earlier return to Hollywood to act with Spencer Tracy in *Broken Lance* (1954), but the State Department delayed her visa until they were satisfied that she had not been affected by her association with communists in the Mexican film industry, and by that time production had gone ahead with Mexican actress Katy Jurado, who was fresh from her success with *High Noon*.

In 1964 she played an Indian woman in John Ford's *Cheyenne Autumn*. As the character called Spanish Woman, Del Rio with little dialogue stood out in a cast that included Gilbert Roland, Richard Widmark, Sal Mineo and James Stewart. While in the States she made several television guest appearances on such shows as *I Spy* (1965-68), *Marcus Welby, M.D.* (1969-76), *Schlitz Playhouse of Stars* (1951-59), *U.S. Steel Hour* (1953-63) and her own special *Dolores Del Rio's Mexico* (1968). She also followed her aspirations for the stage, where she received more accolades as the "First Lady of the Mexican Theater," having appeared in numerous stage productions in Mexico City. Her last film appearance was in a brief role as the grandmother in Hall Bartlett's little-seen *The Children of Sanchez* (1978), in which the essence of Del Rio's dignity and beauty were captured by her longtime cinematographer and collaborator Gabriel Figueroa. At a tribute in her honor at the San Francisco Film Festival in 1981, she remarked, "I gave fifty years to my career. It was number one, two and three in my life, the thing I lived for. Everything I did was with my career in mind. I was very honest with my career but there was a lot of personal sacrifice which I had to undergo." She died at her Newport Beach, California, home of natural causes in 1983.

Benicio Del Toro

B: 1967

Born and raised in San Turce, Puerto Rico, Del Toro's film acting credits include *Christopher Columbus: The Discovery* (1992), *The Usual Suspects* (1995), *Basquiat* (1996); *Fear and Loathing in Las Vegas* (1998) as Dr. Gonzo; *The Pledge* (2000) and *Snatch'd* (2000). He also wrote, directed and produced the film *Submission* (1995), and his television credits include *Miami Vice* (1984-89) and the miniseries *Drug Wars: The Camarena Story* (1989).

Nick De Ruiz
De Ruiz appeared in twenty-seven feature films from 1920 to 1930 in a variety of roles ranging from Mexican bandits to sultans. Some of his better-known credits are *The Hunchback of Notre Dame* (1923) with Lon Chaney, *Old Ironsides* (1926), and *The Unknown* (1927) with Lon Chaney, all of which are silent.

Rosana De Soto
B: 1947
Born in San Jose, California, De Soto studied drama at San Jose University and joined the Northern California Light Opera Company. Having made the transition from repertory theater to television to feature films, De Soto received critical acclaim for her role as Ritchie Valens' mother in the hit film *La Bamba* (1987). She co-starred in *Stand and Deliver* (1988) as Fabiola Escalante and had the pivotal role of the translator in *The Ballad of Gregorio Cortez* (1983). Her feature film credits include *Family Business* (1989), *Star Trek VI: The Undiscovered Country* (1991), *Mambo Cafe* (1999) and *The 24 Hour Woman* (1999). On television she has guest starred in many series and appeared in many telefilms, such as *Child of Rage* (1992), *Kissing Miranda* (1995); the miniseries *Invasion* (1997) and *Thicker than Blood* (1998).

Steven E. De Souza
De Souza is a writer of Spanish and Portuguese background whose screenplays include *48 HRS.* (1982), *Die Hard* (1988), *Die Hard 2* (1990), *Ricochet* (1991), *The Flintstones* (1994), *Judge Dredd* (1995) and *Knock Off* (1998). He spent years at Universal Studios as a contract writer on many television series.

Carlos J. de Valdez
B: 3/19/1894
D: 10/30/1939
A Peruvian-born stage and screen actor, de Valdez was featured in such films as *The Robin Hood of El Dorado* (1936), *Conquest* (1937), *Lancer Spy* (1937), *Suez* (1938), *The Girl from Mexico* (1939), *Juarez* (1939) and *The Llano Kid* (1940).

Jose De Vega, Jr.
B: 1935
D: 1991
Jose De Vega, Jr., played Chino in the Broadway and film versions of *West Side Story* (1961). He also appeared as one of Elvis Presley's Hawaiian backup singers in *Blue Hawaii* (1962). His other films include *The Spiral Road* (1962), *A Covenant with Death* (1966) and *Ash Wednesday* (1973). He was born in San Diego to a Filipino father and a Colombian mother.

Rosana De Soto as Ritchie Valens's mother in *La Bamba*.

Don Diamond

B: 1917

Brooklyn-born Don Diamond played El Toro, Bill Williams' Mexican side-kick, on the television series *The Adventures of Kit Carson* (1951-55). He also portrayed Corporal Reyes on Walt Disney's *Zorro* (1958-59) and Crazy Cat on *F Troop* (1965-67).

Cameron Diaz

B: 1972

Diaz made her feature film debut at age twenty-one in the Jim Carrey film, *The Mask* (1994), though she had virtually no acting experience. She followed the advice of her modeling agent and went to audition for a small role in the motion picture, and, as fate would have it, director Chuck Russell saw something special in her and asked her to read for the female lead, which she won. In *The Mask*, Cameron played Tina Carlyle, a floozy who dumps her gangster boyfriend for geek-turned-wisecracking-superhero, Stanley Ipkiss (Carrey). The film became one of Jim Carrey's biggest hits and became known as the film that launched Diaz's career in motion pictures. Diaz scored another triumph in 1998 with the hit comedy *There's Something About Mary* (1998) and has worked non-stop ever since, displaying a unique versatility in front of the camera in numerous diverse roles. She played a liberal college student in the art house hit *The Last Supper* (1996); a betrothed debutante in *My Best Friend's Wedding* (1997), with Julia Roberts and Rupert Everett; the manipulative ex-hooker in Edward Burns' *She's the One* (1996); the white trash bride who falls for her brother-in-law in *Feeling Minnesota* (1996); and the victim of an unusual kidnapping in Danny Boyle's romantic comedy, *A Life Less Ordinary* (1997). Diaz's film credits also include the Academy Award® nominated *Being John Malkovich* (1999), *Any Given Sunday* (1999) opposite Al Pacino and *Charlie's Angels* (2000) with Lisa Liu and Drew Barrymore. She was born in Long Beach, California. Her father is of Cuban extraction and her mother's heritage is German, English and American Indian.

Cameron Diaz as Tina Carlyle in *The Mask*.

Edith Diaz

A Puerto Rican-born actress, Diaz was featured as one of the singing nuns in *Sister Act* (1992). Her other film credits include *Scenes from the Class Struggle in Beverly Hills* (1989) and *Born on the Fourth of July* (1989). She starred on the *Popi* (1976) and played Desi Arnaz's mother in the telefilm *Lucy and Desi: Before the Laughter* (1991).

Ken Diaz

A makeup artist, Diaz was nominated for an Academy Award® for his work on *Dad* (1989), which starred Jack Lemmon. Through makeup, Diaz turned Lemmon into an aged and terminally ill man. The 1990s proved to be busy, with Diaz working on such projects as *My Family* (1995)—for which he was nominated for an Academy Award®, along with Mark Sanchez—*Heat* (1995), with Al Pacino and Robert De Niro; *Anaconda* (1997), with Jennifer Lopez; *The Mask of Zorro* (1998), with Antonio Banderas, and featuring Catherine Zeta-Jones in her breakout role;

Why Do Fools Fall in Love? (1998); culminating with *Luminarias* and *The Perfect Storm* in 2000.

Placido Domingo
B: 1/21/1941
A Spanish-born, Mexican-raised international opera and recording star, Domingo was encouraged in his youthful interest in music by his parents, as other family members were professional practitioners of the Zarzuela, a three-century-old operatic form from Spain. He starred in Franco Zeffirelli's 1982 film production of *La Traviata* as Alfredo, and in 1986 as Verdi's tragic Moor in *Otello*. He also starred in Bizet's *Carmen* (1984) as Don Jose opposite Julia Migenes Johnson, directed by Francisco Rosi.

Joe Dominguez
B:3/19/1894
D:4/11/1970
A Mexican-born character actor, Dominguez was featured in countless films over his fifty year film career that began in the twenties. He played a Mexican bandido so often, he owned his own bandido costume because the film studio would pay actors more if they brought their own wardrobe. Dominguez's many feature film credits include *Suicide Fleet* (1930), *The Broken Wing* (1932), *Viva Villa* (1933), *Under the Pampas Moon* (1935), *Stagecoach* (1939), *Northwest Passage* (1940), *A Medal for Benny* (1945), *Red River* (1948), *The Furies* (1950), *Ride Vaquero* (1953), *The Hitch Hiker* (1953), *Man of the West* (1958), *One Eyed Jacks* (1961); and *I Love You, Alice B. Toklas* (1968).

Marta Du Bois
An actress of French and Panamanian heritage who grew up in the United States, DuBois made her feature film debut as Shady in *Boulevard Nights* (1979) and has appeared in numerous telefilms, including *Tales of the Gold Monkey* (1982), *Grace Kelly* (1983), *Johhnie Mae Gibson: FBI* (19986), *Deadline Madrid* (1988), *Fear* (1990) and *Trials of Life* (1997). Recent film credits include *Dead Badge* (1995), *Black Out* (1996) and *Luminarias* (2000).

Larry Duran
B: 7/26/1925
A Mexican American actor and stuntman born in Los Angeles, Duran had featured roles in *Viva Zapata!* (1952), *The Magnificent Seven* (1960) and *One-Eyed Jacks* (1961). His father worked as an extra and as a runner (a person who recruited extras) for the studios and Duran worked occasionally as an extra as a young man before he entered the military, where he became an amateur boxer. After military service he continued to box and met Marlon Brando at a bout. They took an immediate liking to each other, and Brando offered him a job as his stand-in. Soon Duran began doing bit parts, and with his athletic and boxing abilities, he learned to do stunt work. He learned movie fisticuffs, horsefalls, car crashes and explosions, doubling for Brando on the motorcycle fall in *The Young Lions* (1958). After that, he did most of Brando's film stunt

Joe Dominguez (right) with Rosita Ballestero (left) and Juan Verona (center) in *El Hombre Malo.*

work. Duran was even employed as one of the background dancers on *Guys and Dolls* (1955), which starred Brando. As he met producers and other stuntmen, he began to work on films not associated with Brando. His son, Larry Duran, Jr., has followed in his father's footsteps and is currently a stuntman.

"I wasn't looking to be a movie star," remarked Duran during a 1992 interview. "Not bad for a guy who only completed junior high school with no skills. I was able to travel the world and now I'm retired and own my own home but I owe everything to Marlon Brando."

Chuy Elizondo
B: 12/25/1942

This renowned American television and film cinematographer was born in Torreon, Mexico, and was brought to the States at age twelve. He learned about photography at a commercial production house and started as a camera assistant at Universal Studios. He developed an association with cinematographer John Alonzo, with whom he worked as a camera operator on such films as *Chinatown* (1974), *Conrack* (1974), *Farewell, My Lovely* (1975) and *The Bad News Bears* (1976). Elizondo became a director of photography on the feature *Shadow of Kilimanjaro* (1987). His extensive television credits include *La Pastorela* (1991), *Bodies of Evidence* (1992) and *Terror in the Towers* (1993).

Hector Elizondo
B: 12/22/1936

Well known for his supporting character portrayals in both films and television, the Puerto Rican-born Elizondo was raised in New York City. Elizondo's memorable portrayal of the hotel manager in *Pretty Woman* (1990) earned him a Golden Globe Nomination. More recent film credits include *Turbulence* (1996), *The Other Sister* (1999), *Entropy* (1999) and the cable feature *Picking up the Pieces* (2000).

Elizondo received an Emmy Award for Outstanding Supporting Actor in a Drama Series for his portrayal of Dr. Phillip Watters in the critically acclaimed CBS television drama *Chicago Hope* (1994-2000); Elizondo has earned five nominations to date for his role in the series. His other television credits include the miniseries *The Burden of Proof* (1992) and the telefilm *Borrowed Hearts* (1997).

A native New Yorker, Elizondo is Puerto Rican of Basque parentage and began his career on stage. He won an Obie Award for his portrayal of God in *Steambath* and a Drama Desk Award nomination for *Sly Fox*. He also starred on Broadway in *The Prisoner of Second Avenue*, *The Great White Hope* and the 1992 revival of Arthur Miller's *The Price*.

Rene Enriquez
B: 11/25/1933
D: 3/23/1990

An actor, born in San Francisco and raised in Nicaragua, Enriquez is best known for his role as Lt. Ray Calletano on the long-running *Hill Street Blues* (1981-87) television series. His film credits include *Bananas* (1971), *Under Fire* (1973) and *The Evil That Men Do* (1984).

Hector Elizondo as
Dr. Phillip Watters on
Chicago Hope.

Moctesuma Esparza

B: 3/12/1947

An award-winning film and television producer, Esparza produced *The Milagro Beanfield War* (1988) and *Only Once in a Lifetime* (1979). Esparza has an impressive record of achievement as both a filmmaker and a political activist.

Born in Los Angeles, he attended public schools and UCLA, where he received his BA and MFA in film. During his college years, Esparza became involved in many antiwar and civil rights groups and was a founder of the Chicano Research Center at UCLA. While still a graduate student, he produced bilingual films for *Sesame Street* (1969-). His master's thesis took the form of a 1973 documentary film for NBC entitled *Cinco Vidas (Five Lives)*, a poignant look at five people living in the barrio of East Los Angeles. *Cinco Vidas* won Esparza an Emmy in 1973. After that, Esparza was hired as producer for a PBS children's series called *Villa Alegre* (1970) and did a series of documentaries for the McGraw-Hill broadcasting series *La Raza*, for which he won the John F. Kennedy Journalism Award. Forming Moctesuma Esparza Productions in 1974, he continued to work in the documentary and children's film fields. In 1977, he produced his first feature, Alejandro Grattan's *Only Once in a Lifetime*, the story of a down-on-his-luck Chicano painter. That same year, Esparza was nominated for an Academy Award® in the Best Documentary Short category for *Agueda Martinez*, a portrait of an old woman from northern New Mexico.

Deciding to focus his energies on feature films, Esparza teamed up with the National Council of La Raza, a civil rights group, to develop a series of films exploring the literature and history of Chicanos in the United States. The first was Robert M. Young's *The Ballad of Gregorio Cortez* (1983), the true story of a young Chicano cowhand (Edward James Olmos) who kills a Texas sheriff in self-defense and is pursued by the Texas Rangers. The film was released theatrically by Embassy Pictures in 1983 and aired on PBS's *American Playhouse* series. The second was *The Milagro Beanfield War* (1988), to which Esparza had optioned the film rights in 1979. Through Esparza/Katz Productions, has produced such popular and critical successes as *Lorca* (1997), starring Edward James Olmos, Andy Garcia and Esai Morales; the Warner Bros. hit *Selena* (1997), starring Jennifer Lopez; and *Price of Glory* (2000), with Jimmy Smits. For television, Esparza/Katz has produced the theatrically released TNT miniseries *Gettysburg* (1994); *The Cisco Kid* (1994), starring Jimmy Smits; TNT's *Rough Riders* (1997), starring Tom Berenger (1997); and most recently, HBO's *Introducing Dorothy Dandridge* (1999), starring Halle Berry.

Richard Espinoza

B: 4/4/1948

A Texas-born assistant director, Espinoza rose through the ranks of the Directors Guild of America Training Program and has worked on such films as *North Dallas Forty* (1979), *The Border* (1982), *Remo Williams* (1985), *American Me* (1992) and *Dr. Giggles* (1992). His television credits include *Jake and the Fatman* (1987-92), *Baywatch* (1989-), *Beauty and the Beast* (1987-90) and four seasons on *Dr. Quinn, Medicine Woman* (1993-98).

Emilio Estevez

B: 5/12/1962

The son of actor Martin Sheen (whose real name is Ramon Estevez), Emilio chose to use the family's original surname, and quickly established himself as a young star. Upon graduation from Santa Monica High School, Estevez made his professional acting debut in an after school television special and was soon featured in several television film dramas, including *In the Custody of Strangers* (1982), in which he worked opposite his father.

Estevez made his feature film debut in *Tex* (1982), based on the novel by S.E. Hinton, starring Matt Dillon. The film adaptation of Hinton's *The Outsiders* (1983), directed by Francis Ford Coppola, provided him with a second screen role as Two Bit Matthews. He then played a young punker who becomes involved with automobile repossessors and alien beings in the cult film *Repo Man* (1984).

His additional acting credits include a driven video-game champion in *Nightmares* (1983), a high school jock in John Hughes's *The Breakfast Club* (1985) and a law student obsessed with an older woman in *St. Elmo's Fire* (1985).

Emilio Estevez.

Estevez wrote the screenplay and starred in *That Was Then . . . This Is Now* (1985), which he adapted from an S.E. Hinton story, and *Wisdom* (1987), in which he also starred and made his directorial debut, becoming, at age twenty-three the youngest person ever to write, direct and star in a major motion picture.

Estevez co-starred in the enormously successful comedy *Stakeout* (1987) with Richard Dreyfuss, and its far less successful sequel, *Another Stakeout* (1993), and in the Westerns *Young Guns* (1988) and *Young Guns II* (1990) as Billy the Kid. *Young Guns* also provided the actor his first opportunity to star alongside his brother, actor Charlie Sheen. They followed this by starring together in *Men at Work* (1990), which Estevez also directed. In 1992, he starred in *The Mighty Ducks*; a sequel, *D2: The Mighty Ducks*, was released in 1994. Rounding out the trilogy in 1996, Estevez starred in *D3: The Mighty Ducks*.

Returning to directing, he lens *The War at Home* (1996), *The Bang Bang Club* (1998) and the Showtime telefilm *Rated X* (2000), in which he co-starred again with Sheen.

Angelina Estrada

B: 2/28/1932

A veteran character actress, Estrada started her career as a small child working as an extra in films. She had her first line in *Only Angels Have Wings* (1939), as a child tortilla vendor who says, "Tortillas," to Cary Grant. Estrada is an accomplished Hawaiian dancer, and she danced with Elvis Presley in *Blue Hawaii* (1961). Her film credits include *Aloma of the South Seas* (1941), The *Jungle Book* (1942) with Sabu, *Tortilla Flat* (1942), *A Medal for Benny* (1945), *One-Eyed Jacks* (1961), *Paint Your Wagon* (1969), *Ghost* (1990), with Patrick Swayze; *My Family* (1995); *The Big Sqeeze* (1996) and *Luminarias* (2000), in which she appears as Tia Concha.

Erik Estrada (right) and
Larry Wilcox (left) in *CHiPs*.

Erik Estrada

B: 3/16/1949

Born in Spanish Harlem, New York, of Puerto Rican parents, Estrada was catapulted to television stardom with his role as Ponch Poncherello, an extroverted motorcycle officer, during the six-year run, from 1978 to 1983, of the successful and popular series *CHiPs*.

Estrada's first break came when actor/director Don Murray was looking for a new face to co-star opposite Pat Boone in *The Cross and the Switchblade* (1970), in which he landed the co-starring role of a gang leader.

When Estrada heard that director Richard Fleischer was in New York to cast his new film, *The New Centurions* (1972), he knew, having read the book, that the important co-starring role of the Mexican American rookie policeman was exactly right for him and that a film credit opposite George C. Scott and Stacy Keach would be extremely beneficial to his career. The director did not agree and told him he was much too young for the part. Undaunted, Estrada pursued the director to Hollywood and landed the role.

Estrada has kept busy with numerous film and television projects, such as *Airport 1975* (1974), *Trackdown* (1976), in which he starred opposite James Mitchum. He was cast in the lead role in *Honeyboy* (1982) and *A Show of Force* in 1990 with Robert Duvall. He appeared as himself in *Loaded Weapon I* (1993) and as Joe in *Tom Sawyer* (1998).

Antonio Fargas

Flashy nightclub owner, malicious villain, pathetic barfly, powerful witch doctor—all these characters are within the creative province of Antonio Fargas, who has appeared in such films as *Shaft* (1971), *Across 110th Street* (1972), *Conrack* (1974), *Car Wash* (1976), *Next Stop, Greenwich Village* (1976), *Pretty Baby* (1978), *I'm Gonna Get You Sucka* (1989) and *Whore* (1991).

Born and raised in New York's Spanish Harlem, Fargas was first drawn to an acting career during his days at Fashion Industries High School, which led to study with several New York theater groups. His big break came when he landed a role as a witch doctor in the Broadway production of *The Great White Hope*, starring James Earl Jones.

Joao Fernandes

A Brazilian-born cinematographer, Fernandes has photographed a number of international Hollywood productions, including *Invasion, U.S.A.* (1952), *Missing in Action* (1984), *Red Scorpion* (1989), *Hellbound* (1993), *Sprung* (1997) and *Gideon* (1999). He has also worked on numerous telefilms, including *Love Kills* (1991), *Deconstructing Sarah* (1994), *Road to Galveston* (1996) and *Silencing Mary* (1998).

Abel Fernandez

B: 7/14/1930

Fernandez is best known for his portrayal of American Indian Treasury Agent Youngfellow on *The Untouchables* television series from 1959 to 1963. Born and raised in East Los Angeles of Mexican American ancestry,

Fernandez appeared on many classic television series of the 1950s including *Rin-Tin-Tin* (1954-59) and *Lassie* (1954-74), usually as an Indian or a Mexican.

Benjamin Fernandez

A native of Spain, Fernandez is equally at home as a production designer for futuristic action films as he is working on epic period dramas. He began his career as a draftsman on such classic as producer Samuel Bronston's *King of Kings* (1961) and *El Cid* (1961); and Sam Spiegel's monumental production of *Lawrence of Arabia* (1962), directed by David Lean. In 1964, he moved to the position of assistant art director on David Lean's *Doctor Zhivago* (1965), followed by such films as *Patton* (1970) and *Nicholas and Alexandra* (1971), Richard Lester's *The Three Musketeers* (1973) and Ridley Scott's *Alien* (1979). Moving to the position of art director, Fernandez worked on *Revenge of the Pink Panther* (1978), *Conan the Barbarian* (1982), *Indiana Jones and the Last Crusade* (1989) and *Gladiator* (2000). He served as production designer on *Revenge* (1990), *True Romance* (1993) and *Dragonheart* (1996).

Emilio "El Indio" Fernandez

B: 3/26/1904
D: 8/6/1986

The single most important Mexican director of the 1940s, Emilio "El Indio" Fernandez's cinematic vision of Mexico forged a national identity for its people, folklore and country. In later years his work became a caricature of itself, with his larger-than-life portrayals of stereotypical Mexican bandidos or generals in American films, in which he worked as an actor from the early 1960s.

Emilio Fernandez, director/actor/screenwriter, was born in a mining town called El Hondo in the Sabinas area of Coahuila, Mexico, the son of a Spanish-Mexican father and an Indian mother (hence the nickname "El Indio"). When his father left to join one of the revolutionary armies, Emilio, at age nine, became head of the family. Almost immediately he shot and killed a man for assaulting his mother. Placed in a reform school, he escaped and joined the revolution. He fought under General Carranza against Pancho Villa, was captured, was sentenced to die at dawn, but escaped from a drunken guard. Later, he fought with Obregon against Carranza, then against Obregon for General de la Huerta. Jailed again, he blew up his cell with smuggled dynamite, appropriated a horse, and galloped north to the border.

In San Antonio he worked by day and studied English at night school. He picked cotton, herded sheep, stuck pigs, whatever he could to make a living. One day, the sharp-eyed Emilio saved a girl from drowning off a Chicago

John Huston (right) directs Emilio Fernandez (left) in *Under the Volcano.*

beach. She turned out to be an Earl Carroll dancer. Indio was picked up by the Edgewater Beach theatrical crowd, where his proficiency at Latin dancing attracted the attention of Rudolph Valentino, who became his friend. After Valentino's death, El Indio rode the funeral train to Los Angeles, where he arrived broke and jobless. He got a job at United Artists Studios as a busboy, worked occasionally as an extra, and did bit parts as a heavy in Westerns. He returned to Mexico with the desire to make films and found work as an actor.

He made his film debut in *Janitzio* (1934) as an Indian who loses his lady love to a Spaniard. The film served as a major influence for two films he later directed. His directing career began in 1943 with *Isla de la Pasion* (Of Passion Island*)*. He quickly became the single most important Mexican film director of Mexico's Golden Age (1942-1952).

The Mexican film industry had been established as both a creative and commercial force since the late 1920s and, along with Argentina and Cuba, it was one of the three predominant motion picture producers of the Spanish-speaking world.

Maria Candelaria (1943) won the Grand Prize at the Cannes Film Festival in 1947, *Flor Silvestre* (1943) won at Locarno that same year, and *La Perla* (1945) won at San Sebastian in 1946. He recalled at a University of California symposium, "I worked with John Steinbeck on the screenplay for *The Pearl*, which I directed in Spanish. It was released in an English version as well with the same actors' voices dubbed in."

Fernandez's films were immediately seen as uniquely Mexican, both in style and subject matter. Although Fernandez and his ever-present cameraman, Gabriel Figueroa, had both worked on American films while in Hollywood for a time early in their careers, El Indio resolved to divorce himself from their influence and to bring a sense of Mexican social consciousness, nationalism and a glorification of poetic populism to his films. Mexico's colorful folklore, expansive landscapes, coastlines, dramatic skies, vibrant cloud patterns, and, most importantly, the ethereal presence and passionate indigenous beauty of the actors—most notably Dolores Del Rio, Pedro Armendariz, Maria Felix and Maria Elena Marques—were captured by Gabriel Figueroa's stunning photography. Fernandez and co-writer Mauricio Magdaleno synthesized and depicted a unique and identifiable Mexican cinematic vision.

He assisted Director John Ford, whom he greatly admired, on the production of *The Fugitive* (1947), which was shot in Mexico.

It is ironic that Emilio Fernandez, who as a director gave the Mexican cinema an identity forged on images of its people and its past, as an actor in his later career in American films usually played despicable Mexican generals or bandidos. He will perhaps remain best known for his role as the drunken, excessive and vicious General Mapache in Sam Peckinpah's *The Wild Bunch* (1969). His other American film credits include *The Reward* (1965), *A Covenant with Death* (1966), *Return of the Seven* (1966), *Pat Garrett and Billy the Kid* (1973), *Bring Me the Head of Alfredo Garcia* (1974) and *Under the Volcano* (1984).

In later years, alcoholism, violent, irrational behavior, poor health, political disagreements, and an alleged murder charge hindered his ability to direct films in Mexico. The last film he wrote and directed in Mexico was *La Choca*, made in 1973. Fernandez died in 1986.

Esther Fernandez

B: 4/23/1920

Born in Mexico City, where she achieved tremendous success in films, Fernandez was brought to the States under contract to Paramount Studios in 1941. In a year and a half, no suitable roles were found, due largely to her poor English. She went over to RKO for six months, but nothing happened. She then left for Mexico but returned to the States a year later, after her success in the Mexican film *Santa* (1943), which was directed by Norman Foster and which co-starred Ricardo Montalban. Paramount quickly found her a role as Maria Dominguez y Peralta, the Spanish beauty who becomes a passenger on the hellship Pilgrim in *Two Years Before the Mast* (1946), in which she falls in love with star Alan Ladd. She returned to Mexico after the film and never made another Hollywood film.

Evelina Fernandez

B: 4/28/1954

With Edward James Olmos, Fernandez co-starred as Julie in *American Me* (1992). Fernandez has been featured in such films as *Downtown* (1989), *Flatliners* (1990) and *Postcards from the Edge* (1990). On television she had a recurring role as Juanita Herrera, a factory co-worker, on the first season of the long-running series *Roseanne* (1988-97).

Juan Fernandez

Fernandez has played sinister character roles in such films as *Kinjite: Forbidden Subjects* (1989) with Charles Bronson and Oliver Stone's *Salvador* (1986) opposite James Woods. He had featured roles in *Uncommon Valor* (1983), *Fear City* (1984), *Crocodile Dundee* (1986) and *Cat Chaser* (1990) with Kelly McGillis.

Jose Ferrer

B: 1/8/1912

D: 1/26/1992

Jose Ferrer in his tripartite career as actor, director and writer received three New York Drama Critics Circle Awards, five Tony Awards, two Oscar® nominations for Best Actor and one for Best Supporting Actor, and one Academy Award® as Best Actor for *Cyrano de Bergerac* (1950). He was the first Hispanic American actor to receive an Academy Award®.

Ferrer was born in Puerto Rico in 1912. His father was an attorney, his mother's family owned sugar cane land. Ferrer said of his father, "Perhaps the most important influence in my life. He and his friends inculcated a thirst for knowledge, inquisitiveness, the desire to grow and develop to the utmost, to be as good as you can be."

All three children were taught French and English, as well as Spanish, and were educated in private schools in the United States. Ferrer attended Princeton University, majoring in architecture and graduating in 1933. In his last year at Princeton, however, Ferrer was asked to be in a play. "I began to hang around with some theater people. Eventually I realized that the only thing that made any sense to me was to be an actor. It really was an obsession. Sure, my parents took me to the theater from early on, six or seven, and I still remember those

What's in a nose? Jose Ferrer turns on an impish grin as the lead character in *Cyrano de Bergerac* (1950) for which he won the Academy Award® for Best Actor.

Photo by Acme Photo.

first shows. But without the play at Princeton, I'd never have focused on a theatrical career."

Ferrer is reported to have said that he would not have been any good as an architect, and so he went on to Columbia University to study modern languages, intending to become a college professor instead.

However, for Ferrer, there were no fledgling actor's struggles. "I couldn't believe it. In the beginning I was getting jobs right and left. It got tougher when I was successful. Then I had to be more careful. I had to select; when you're young, you just want to be seen and to learn, you know."

Although *Brother Rat* (1936) was Ferrer's first critical success, his professional stage debut had actually come one year earlier (the same year he joined Actors' Equity) with *A Slight Case of Murder* (1935), in which he had one line. He had his first major role in a revival of *Charley's Aunt* (1940). In 1941, he made his directorial debut with *The Admiral Had a Wife*, but it was his portrayal of Iago opposite Paul Robeson's *Othello* in 1942 that first brought him wide public attention.

Jose Ferrer's other theater credits included *Cyrano de Bergerac* (1947), *The Silver Whistle* (1948) and *Man of La Mancha* (1970).

He produced, directed and starred in a revival of *Twentieth Century* (1951) and directed *The Four Poster* (1952), for each of which he won a Tony Award. He produced, directed and starred in *The Shrike* (1955), Joseph Kramm's Pulitzer Prize-winning play, for which he received three New York Drama Critics Circle Awards and two Tony Awards. He also directed *My Three Angels* (1952), *Stalag 17* (1952) and *The Andersonville Trial* (1959).

Joan of Arc (1948), in which he played the Dauphin to Ingrid Bergman's Joan of Arc, marked his first screen appearance as well as his first Oscar® nomination. He next played a con man and killer in *Whirlpool* (1949) with Gene Tierney and a small part in *The Secret Fury* (1950). Ferrer then played a Latin American dictator, Raoul Farrargo, in *Crisis* (1950), written and directed by Richard Brooks.

For the film version of *Cyrano de Bergerac*, Ferrer won an Academy Award® for Best Actor of 1950. "My life was changed by that. We did [the movie] with very little money in four six-day weeks. Michael Gordon directed it. I think it was done for something like $400,000," Ferrer said in an interview. He received another Oscar® nomination for Best Actor for the role of the famed diminutive French painter Toulouse Lautrec in *Moulin Rouge* (1952), directed by John Huston.

Additional films through the years included *Miss Sadie Thompson* (1953), *The Caine Mutiny* (1954), *Deep in My Heart* (1954), *Lawrence of Arabia* (1962), *Nine Hours to Rama* (1963), *The Greatest Story Ever Told* (1965), *Ship of Fools* (1965), *Enter Laughing* (1967), *Behind the Iron Mask* (1977), *Fedora* (1978) and *The Big Brawl* (1980).

He entered the ranks of film directors by directing such films as *Cockleshell Heroes* (1955), *Return to Peyton Place* (1961) and *State Fair* (1962). He served as both director and star of *The Shrike* (1955), *The Great Man* (1957), *The High Cost of Loving* (1958) and *I Accuse* (1958).

Among his many television credits are the original *Kojak* pilot: *The Marcus Nelson Murders* (1973), *Kismet* (1967), *A Case of Libel* (1968), *The*

Amazing Captain Nemo (1978), *The Dream Merchants* (1980), *Evita Peron* (1981) and the miniseries *Blood & Orchids* (1986).

Directing remained Ferrer's preferred craft and theater his preferred form. Despite the range of his work and despite those honors accorded him, Ferrer viewed the things he hadn't yet done ruefully in an interview several years before his death. "Really, in twenty years or more, I haven't played so many of the roles I think I should have played. In a sense, it was a series of bad judgments. I went to California with my wife, Rosemary Clooney, who was successful in films and recordings and I stayed there about fifteen years. My agent told me I'd have a career there too, but my kind of actor didn't suit the studio casting system as it was then. I either did not deliver the goods or I made bad choices. When I finally returned to New York, I found I'd lost the position I'd had there. My career went downhill and has remained fairly downhill for a long time," David Galligan, *Drama Logue* (10/8/87).

Ferrer's later film credits include Woody Allen's *A Midsummer Night's Sex Comedy* (1982), *To Be or Not to Be* (1983) and *Dune* (1984).

"I'm grateful for the work I have received in the last twenty or thirty years, I appreciate the fact that I've been able to survive and live very well," said the actor. Ferrer has six children, one of whom, Miguel, is an actor. Jose Ferrer directed a national tour of a production of *The Best Man* (1987) starring his friend and colleague Mel Ferrer. Jose Ferrer died on January 26, 1992, after a short illness.

Mel Ferrer
[born: Melchior Gaston Ferrer]
B: 8/25/1917

Director/actor/producer Mel Ferrer has displayed his talents in such diverse theatrical mediums as screen, stage, radio and television.

He was born and raised in New York City of Spanish-Cuban parents and attended Princeton University. A writing award led to a trip to Mexico. Ferrer began his career as an actor on Broadway and in radio, where he later became a producer. In 1945 Ferrer was signed as a dialogue supervisor and director at RKO. His first directorial effort was *The Girl of the Limberlost* (1945). Ferrer also co-founded the La Jolla Playhouse near San Diego.

After two years he returned to Broadway and landed the lead in *Strange Fruit* (1947) and directed Jose Ferrer in the stage production of *Cyrano de Bergerac* (1947).

Ferrer went to Mexico as John Ford's assistant on *The Fugitive* (1947). He directed two plays in Mexico with Margo and Eddie Albert. As an actor he has starred in such films as *The Brave Bulls* (1951), in which he was quite effective as a Mexican peasant who rises to eminence and idol status in the bullring as a matador; *Scaramouche* (1952); *Lili* (1953), as a lame puppeteer; *Knights of the Round Table* (1953); and *War and Peace* (1956), with Henry Fonda and Audrey Hepburn. He has directed such films as *The Secret Fury* (1950), *Vendetta* (1950) and *Green Mansions* (1959), starring Audrey Hepburn. He also produced the hit thriller *Wait Until Dark* (1967), starring Audrey Hepburn and Alan Arkin. On television, Ferrer had a recurring role as Phillip Erikson on the series *Falcon Crest* (1981-90) and directed a number of episodes.

Miguel Ferrer

The son of Jose Ferrer and singer Rosemary Clooney, Miguel Ferrer has been featured in such films as *Heartbreaker* (1983), *RoboCop* (1987), *Valentino Returns* (1987) and *Revenge* (1990). On television he starred in two short-lived series, *Broken Badges* (1990) and *UnSub* (1989) and made an impression with his occasional role on the series *Twin Peaks* (1990-91), as the quirky FBI agent Albert Rosenfield. He has been active in television movies and miniseries, appearing in over a dozen in the last decade, including *The Stand* (1994) and *The Shining* (1997). Recently, he has added voice over work to his repertoire, providing the voice of Shan-Yu for Disney's *Mulan* (1998).

Pablo Ferro

B: 1/15/1935

Born in Havana, Cuba, and raised in New York City, Ferro is a leading optical special effects director for films and television commercials. His special visual optical effects have been seen in *The Thomas Crown Affair* (1968), in which Ferro pioneered split-screen images; *A Clockwork Orange* (1971), in which Ferro used split second intercutting; and *Midnight Cowboy* (1969). More recent credits include *Darkman* (1990) and *Mobsters* (1991). In 1992 he directed his first film, the intimate comedy *Me, Myself, and I,* starring George Segal. Since then, he has designed titles credits for such acclaimed films as *Philadelphia* (1993), *That Thing You Do!* (1996), *L.A. Confidential* (1997), *Good Will Hunting* (1997), *Beloved* (1998), Gus Van Sant's *Psycho* (1998) and *For Love of the Game* (1999).

Efrain Figueroa

An actor, Figueroa has appeared in *Tequila Sunrise* (1988), *Pretty Woman* (1990), *Drug Wars: The Cocaine Cartel* (1992); the critically acclaimed *Star Maps* (1997) and *Desperate Measures* (1998), with Andy Garcia and Michael Keaton.

Gabriel Figueroa

B: 4/24/1907

D: 4/27/1997

A world-renowned master Mexican cinematographer, Figueroa studied for a short time under Gregg Toland at RKO Studios. He photographed John Ford's *The Fugitive* (1947), John Huston's *The Night of the Iguana* (1964), and *Under the Volcano* (1984), for which he was nominated for an Academy Award®. He also photographed *Two Mules for Sister Sara* (1970) in Mexico for director Don Siegel and *Kelly's Heroes* (1971) in Yugoslavia.

He started in the film business in 1932 as an assistant to Alex Phillips, the leading Mexican cameraman. A few years later he went to RKO Studios in Hollywood to be a pupil of the American cinematographer Gregg Toland for four months. He returned to Mexico and began a prolific career as a cameraman on over one hundred films. His first film as director of photography, *Alla en Rancho Grande* (1936), was also the first Mexican film to become an international hit.

Figueroa ranked among the leading directors of photography in the world and was considered one of the greatest interpreters of black-and-white photography.

He is noted for his unforgettable images of indigenous Mexican landscapes highlighted against white cloud-filled skies, men in big sombreros and women in black shawls. He made his reputation with a remarkable series of films he collaborated on with Mexican director Emilio Fernandez beginning with *Flor Silvestre* in 1943 and including such classics as *Maria Candelaria* (1943) and *The Pearl* (1945). These films gave Mexican cinema a national identity and raised it to an unprecedented level of aesthetic sophistication and international acclaim.

William Fraker

B: 1923

A six-time Academy Award®-nominated cinematographer, William Fraker was born in Los Angeles of a Mexican mother and an American father.

He is a graduate of the University of Southern California Film School. Following extensive work in television, Fraker entered feature films as a camera operator and an assistant to the famed Cinematographer Conrad Hall.

Fraker is one of the few cinematographers who has also directed films. He made his directorial debut with *Monte Walsh* (1970), and followed that with *A Reflection of Fear* (1973) and later with *The Legend of the Lone Ranger* (1981). He has worked as a director of photography on such films as *Rosemary's Baby* (1968), *Bullitt* (1968), *Paint Your Wagon* (1969), *Looking for Mr. Goodbar* (1977) and *Heaven Can Wait* (1978).

Abel Franco

B: 1922

A Pasadena, California, schoolteacher and an actor, Franco has credits on such films as *The Searchers* (1956), *Zoot Suit* (1981), *El Norte* (1984), *The Falcon and the Showman* (1985) and *¡Three Amigos!* (1986). He won an Emmy Award for writing the PBS daytime drama *Cancion de la Raza*.

Ramon Franco

B: 1963

Born in Caguas, Puerto Rico, Franco began his acting career at age fourteen. His films include *Boardwalk* (1979), *Heartbreak Ridge* (1986), *Bulletproof* (1988), *Kiss Me a Killer* (1991) and *Street Knight* (1993). He has also appeared in several telefilms, among which are *Chains of Gold* (1991), *Shattered Image* (1994), *Search and Rescue* (1994) and *Justice* (2000). He is best known for his role as Private Ruiz on the Vietnam War television series *Tour of Duty* (1987-90).

Ramon Franco in
Tour of Duty.

Director Hugo Fregonese (left) discusses a love scene between co-stars Cyd Charisse and Ricardo Montalban during the filming of *Mark of the Renegade*, a story of adventurous early California.

Hugo Fregonese

B: 4/8/1909
D: 1/25/1987

An Argentine-born director of international thrillers and Westerns, Fregonese worked in Hollywood in the late 1940s and throughout the 1950s.

The son of a winemaker from Venice who settled in Mendoza near Buenos Aires, Fregonese studied economics in college. He became a sportswriter for an Argentine magazine, and shortly thereafter moved to New York City to become a press agent.

While in New York he acted as a technical adviser for a producer on a movie script with a South American background. He came to Hollywood, but the film was never made, and Fregonese then worked as an extra in movies. That career was short-lived because he kept getting fired, as he could never keep the place the assistant director assigned him. Instead, he was always near the camera, trying to find out how movies were made. As an extra he worked as a prisoner in *The Hurricane* (1937) and as a pirate in *The Buccaneer* (1938) with Fredric March.

In Los Angeles he went to a film trade school to learn the craft of editing. Fregonese returned to Argentina, where he began a career as an assistant director in the film industry there. He got the opportunity to co-direct a film called *Pampa Barbara* in 1943. He then directed *Hardly a Criminal* (1949), the story of a clerk's attempt to hide and hold a half-million dollars he has stolen. The film was purchased for release in the States with dubbed English dialogue. Fregonese made another film, *Where Words Fail* (1948), entirely on location and then had the actors' voices and sound effects "looped in," or added, during post-production. On the strength of this he was signed at MGM. They kept him around for a year but gave him nothing to do. Universal International signed him to a contract to direct the thriller *One Way Street* (1950), starring James Mason. He followed by directing several Westerns, including *Saddle Tramp* (1950) with Joel McCrea, *Apache Drums* (1951), *Mark of the Renegade* (1951) with Ricardo Montalban and Gilbert Roland, and *Untamed Frontier* (1952).

He moved to Columbia Pictures and directed the prison comedy *My Six Convicts* (1952), produced by Stanley Kramer and starring Gilbert Roland. Though mainly known for his B pictures, Fregonese also made some films with top stars, among them *Blowing Wild* with Barbara Stanwyck, Gory Cooper and Anthony Quinn in 1953.

During the remainder of the 1950s he made several pictures for Twentieth Century-Fox, including *Man in the Attic* (1953), starring Jack Palance, a well-regarded version of the Jack the Ripper tale.

Fregonese's career became international at this time and included all-star projects such as *Decameron Nights* (1953) for RKO, the Italian epic *The Beast of Marseilles* (1957) and the Italian *Marco Polo* (1962) with Rory Calhoun. During the 1960s he directed the European Western *Old Shatterhand* (1964) with Lex Barker, *Secrets of Dr. Mabuse* (1964), and *Savage Pampas* (1966), a remake of his debut *Pampa Barbara*, with Robert Taylor, filmed on location in Argentina.

In the 1970s he directed *La Mala Vida* (1973) and *Mas Alla del Sol* (1975). Fregonese married actress Faith Domergue. He died of a heart attack at age seventy-seven in Buenos Aires.

Julie Friedgen

Born Julietta Martha Maria del Pilar Francesconi-Sanchez, writer Julie Friedgen was raised in East Los Angeles. She has written multiple episodes of such televison shows as *In the Heat of the Night* (1988-94), *Walker, Texas Ranger* (1990-), *21 Jump Street* (1987-92), *Magnum P.I.* (1980-88) and *Knight Rider* (1982-86).

Daisy Fuentes

B: 11/17/1966

Born in Havana, Cuba, Fuentes first found fame as a VJ on MTV where she was wildly popular. She went on to host MTV's *House of Style* (1989-) in 1997 and then became a host for *America's Funniest Home Videos* (1990-). She has made numerous guest appearances on episodic television and is slated to star in the show *Shutterspeed* (2000).

Jenny Gago

Gago's film credits include *Under Fire* (1983), *No Man's Land* (1987), *Irreconcilable Differences* (1984), *Innerspace* (1987), *Best Seller* (1987), *Old Gringo* (1989) and *My Family* (1994). She has guest starred on such shows as *Cagney & Lacey* (1982-88) and *Falcon Crest* (1981-90) and earned recurring roles on *Dallas* (1978-91) and *Knots Landing* (1979-93), in which she played the character Maria for three years.

Nacho Galindo

D: 6/22/1973

A character actor, Galindo appeared in films from the 1940s through the 1960s, including *Tycoon* (1946), *South of St. Louis* (1949), *Borderline* (1950), *Border River* (1954), *Broken Lance* (1954), *One-Eyed Jacks* (1961) and *El Dorado* (1967).

Silvana Gallardo

B: 1/13/1953

An actress born in New York City of Venezuelan-Cuban parents, Gallardo was featured in *Windwalker* (1980), *Death Wish II* (1982) and *Solar Crisis* (1993). Her television credits include the telefilms *Copacabana* (1986), *The Calendar Girl Murders* (1984), *Prison Stories: Women on the Inside* (1991) and *The Corpse Had a Familiar Face* (1994). and guest appearances on numerous episodic series.

Gina Gallego

B: 10/30/1959

An actress of Mexican heritage, born and raised in Los Angeles, Gallego's feature film credits include *The Men's Club* (1986) with Treat Williams, *My Demon Lover* (1987) with Scott Valentine and *Lust in the Dust* (1985) with Cesar Romero. She is perhaps best known for her two years as a regular on the daytime soap opera *Santa Barbara* (1984-92)

Jimmy Smits and Daisy Fuentes co-host the Alma Awards.

as Santana and for her work on the soap opera *Rituals* (1984-85). Gallego was also a regular on the television series *Flamingo Road* (1981-82) and co-starred in the Showtime movie *Keeper of the City* (1991).

Joaquin Garay II

B: 1911

D: 1990

A veteran vaudeville song and dance man, Garay shared the bill with such performers as Jack Benny and later Martin and Lewis and provided the voice of Panchito (the pistol-packin' parrot) for Walt Disney's *The Three Caballeros* (1944). He was also one of the featured singers on the bus in *It Happened One Night* (1934). His son, Joaquin Garay III, starred as an eleven-year-old street urchin in the Disney feature film *Herbie Goes Bananas* in 1980.

Allan Garcia

B: 3/18/1887

D: 9/4/1938

Credited with working as a casting director at Chaplin Studios, Garcia had his first major role in Chaplin's *The Circus* (1923, silent) as the circus proprietor. He played the butler in Chaplin's *City Lights* (1931, silent) and appeared in Chaplin's *Modern Times* (1936, silent) as the factory boss. His other film credits include *The Idle Class* (1921, silent), *Pay Day* (1922, silent), *Morgan's Last Raid* (1929), *Under the Tonto Rim* (1933), *The California Trail* (1933) at Columbia, and *The Gay Desperado* (1936).

Andy Garcia.

Andy Garcia

B: 4/12/1956

Born in Cuba, Garcia came to the United States with his parents when he was five years old. He grew up in Miami Beach, Florida, where he began his acting career performing in regional theater productions. After moving to Los Angeles, Garcia made his television acting debut in the pilot for the television series *Hill Street Blues* (1981-87) and made guest appearances in other series and telefilms. Garcia made his film debut as a police detective in the Phillip Borsos film *The Mean Season* (1985) opposite Kurt Russell and Mariel Hemingway.

He became an international star with the role of Italian American rookie cop George Stone in Brian De Palma's hit film *The Untouchables* (1987), which followed Garcia's noted performance as the treacherous but suave cocaine kingpin Angel Maldonado in Hal Ashby's *8 Million Ways to Die* (1986). De Palma had wanted Garcia to play Capone's murderous sidekick Frank Nitti, but Garcia persuaded the director to let him play Stone, against type. His star continued to ascend with his roles as Michael Douglas's detective partner in *Black Rain* (1989) and as police investigator Ray Avila opposite Richard Gere in *Internal Affairs* (1990). Full-fledged stardom was reached in Francis Ford Coppola's epic *The Godfather, Part III* (1990), in which his portrayal of Sonny Corleone's illegitimate son Vincent Mancini earned him Best Supporting Actor nominations for the Golden Globe Award and the Academy Award®. He went on to star in *Hero* (1993) opposite Dustin Hoffman and *When a*

Man Loves a Woman (1994) with Meg Ryan. In recent years, he has appeared in the title role of *The Disappearance of Garcia Lorca* (1997), then in *Desperate Measures* (1998) opposite Michael Keaton. He also produced the romantic comedy *Just the Ticket* (1999), in which he starred with Andie MacDowell.

Rick Garcia

An American-born actor with numerous screen and television credits, Garcia is best known for uttering Alfonso Bedoya's immortal line from *The Treasure of the Sierra Madre* (1948), "Badges? We don't need no stinkin' badges," as a Mexican bandit in Mel Brooks' spoof *Blazing Saddles* (1974), and as the Mexican border official who gets kicked in the crotch by Kirk Douglas in *Tough Guys* (1986), also starring Burt Lancaster.

Rodrigo Garcia

Garcia is a Mexican director of photography who attended Harvard University and the American Film Institute. Garcia's credits as a cinematographer include Maria Novaro's *Danzon* (1991), Robert Spera's *The Minister's Wife* (1992), Allison Anders' *Mi Vida Loca* (1994), the acclaimed telefilm *Gia* (1998) and *Body Shots* (1999). He made his debut as a director and screenwriter with the film *Things You Can Tell Just by Looking at Her* (2000), which debuted on the film festival circuit and was then picked up for distribution by the Showtime cable network.

Ron Garcia

This noted cinematographer's feature film credits include *Disorganized Crime* (1989), *Side Out* (1990), *Twin Peaks: Fire Walk with Me* (1992) and *The Great White Hype* (1996). In television, Garcia's credits include the series *Crime Story* (1986-88) *Hunter* (1984-91), and numerous television movies. He was nominated for an Emmy Award for his work on the television miniseries *Murder in the Heartland* (1993) and garnered another nomination for *The Day Lincoln Was Shot* (1998).

Stella Garcia

An actress, Garcia co-starred in the films *The Last Movie* (1971) with Dennis Hopper and *Joe Kidd* (1972) with Clint Eastwood.

Carlos Gardel

B: 12/11/1890
D: 6/24/1935

Argentinian singer, composer and movie star, Gardel had an immense reputation in the Spanish speaking world and in France, and he popularized the tango. He was actually born in France but was raised in Argentina from the age of one, where he was exposed to the musical form that he would make world famous. He made four Spanish language films in New York for Paramount in 1934 and 1935—*Tango en Broadway* (1934), *Cuesta Abajo* (1934), *Tango Bar* (1935), *El Dia Que Me Quieras* (1935*)*. Prior to that he made several films at Paramount's studios in Joinville, France. His meteoric career was cut short when he was killed in a plane crash in Colombia in 1935.

Martin Garralaga

B: 11/10/1898

D: 6/12/1981

A Spanish-born singer and actor, Garralaga portrayed many Spanish and Mexican characters in films. He began his career in Barcelona as a singer, and this talent carried him to the concert and opera stages of South and North America and eventually to the motion picture studios of Hollywood.

He made his motion picture debut in the Spanish version of *The King of Jazz* (1930), in which he played the master of ceremonies, and thereafter appeared in many Spanish-language films, both in heavy and comedic parts. Garralaga had his first important English-speaking role in 1936 in *A Message to Garcia*. His other films include *Rose of the Rio Grande* (1938), *Starlight over Texas* (1938), *The Fighting Gringo* (1939), *Juarez* (1940), *Rhythm of the Rio Grande* (1940), *Stage to Chino* (1940), *In Old California* (1942), *The Lady Has Plans* (1942), *For Whom the Bell Tolls* (1943), *Man in the Shadow* (1957), *The Left-Handed Gun* (1958) and *The Last Angry Man* (1959). He played the Cisco Kid's sidekick, Pancho, in several films with Duncan Renaldo.

John Gavin
[born: John Anthony Golenar]

B: 4/8/1931

Born in Los Angeles, Gavin is the Stanford University-educated son of a Mexican mother and an American father. He joined the Navy and became interested in acting through a friend while he was on leave. Soon under contract to Universal Pictures, the young actor made his motion picture debut in *Behind the High Wall* (1956) with Sylvia Sidney. Two of his most important film credits are Alfred Hitchcock's *Psycho* (1960) and as Julius Caesar in *Spartacus* (1960) opposite Charles Laughton and Sir Laurence Olivier. Gavin's Ivy League good looks made him a leading man in the Cary Grant tradition. His other films include *Back Street* (1961), *Tammy, Tell Me True* (1961) and *The Madwoman of Chaillot* (1969).

In the late 1970s he left films for politics and was appointed the United States Ambassador to Mexico.

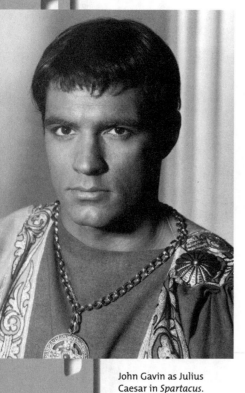

John Gavin as Julius Caesar in *Spartacus*.

Tony Genaro

A supporting actor, Genaro's credits include *The Milagro Beanfield War* (1988), *Tremors* (1989), *Bound by Honor* (1993), *Speechless* (1994), *Phenomenon* (1996), *The Mask of Zorro* (1998) and *Mighty Joe Young* (1998).

Carlos Gomez

B: 1957

Born in New York and raised in Miami of Cuban immigrant parents, Gomez's has appeared in over twenty telefilms and feature projects. His feature film credits include *The Mambo Kings* (1992), *Desperado* (1995), *Fools Rush In* (1997), *The Peacemaker* (1997), *The Replacement Killers* (1998), *Enemy of the State* (1998) and *That Summer in L.A.* (1999). On television he has appeared on *Friends* (1994-), *New York Undercover* (1994-98), *E.R.* (1994-) and the miniseries *Asteroid* (1997).

Ian Gomez

B: 1965

Gomez has appeared in such feature films as *Rookie of the Year* (1993), *'Til There Was You* (1997), *Edtv* (1999) and *The Big Tease* (2000). His television credits include *The Drew Carey Show* (1995-), *Felicity* (1998-) and *The Norm Show* (1999).

Jaime Gomez

Gomez is best known for his portrayal of Evan Cortez on the television series *Nash Bridges* (1996-). The young actor made his feature film debut in *Clear and Present Danger* (1994), with Harrison Ford; followed by a role in *Crimson Tide* (1995), opposite Gene Hackman and Denzel Washington. On television he has made guest appearances on *21 Jump Street* (1987-92), (1995-96) and *Picket Fences* (1992-97). He also starred in the PBS *American Playhouse* presentation of *La Carpa* (1992).

Mike Gomez

B: 4/18/1951

A Dallas-born and -raised character actor, Gomez has appeared in such films as *The Border* (1982) as a greaser Mexican type, opposite Jack Nicholson; *Heartbreak Ridge* (1986) as a Marine recruit, opposite Clint Eastwood; and *Zoot Suit* (1981) as Joey, one of the pivotal Pachuco characters.

Panchito Gomez

B: 1964

A New York-born actor, Gomez has been acting since age four. For over twenty-five years he has played a tough-talking urban or rural Latino youth on many network television shows, dramatic and comedic. He received attention for his role as the teenage Santana in Edward James Olmos' 1992 Universal film *American Me*, and went on to do *Mi Vida Loca* (1993) and *Selena* (1997), with Jennifer Lopez. His television credits include *Barney Miller* (1975-82), *CHiPs* (1978-83), *Simon & Simon* (1981-88) and *Baretta* (1975-78). His film credits include *Uncle Joe Shannon* (1978), *Run for the Roses* (1978), *Walk Proud* (1979), *Borderline* (1980).

Thomas Gomez
[born: Sabina Thomas Gomez]

B: 7/10/1905

D: 6/20/1971

A versatile character actor, Gomez was adept at playing every type of character role, from assorted urban types to period and classical types. In 1942 the actor signed with Universal International following a notable stage career highlighted by seven years with Alfred Lunt and Lynn Fontanne. In addition, Gomez opened the Guild Theater in 1925, with Helen Hayes.

　　Gomez's paternal grandfather came to the States from Santander, Spain, in 1842 to run a coffeehouse and an oyster boat fleet in New Orleans. His paternal grandmother was born in Gibraltar and came to New Orleans about the same time as her future husband. Gomez's

Thomas Gomez as Louvain, chief of the French police, in *Casbah*.

maternal grandfather, Frank Thomas, commanded a ship under Admiral David Farragut when the famed naval officer captured New Orleans for the Union in the American Civil War.

Born in New York City, he attended Public School 77, and later went to Jamaica High School on Long Island. There, he won a citywide speech contest. Gomez went on to study acting and joined a theater troupe, making his professional debut in *Cyrano de Bergerac* in 1924. After playing a variety of roles over the next seven years, Gomez joined a stock company in Cleveland, Ohio. In three years there he did forty leading character roles. He then went on the road, and the following year, 1934, he joined the Lunts.

The actor's cumulative performances on the stage attracted attention from studio scouts. His screen bow came in Sherlock Holmes and the *Voice of Terror* in 1942. He then turned in some of his finest character portrayals in such films as *Ride the Pink Horse*, which earned him an Oscar® nomination in 1947 for Best Supporting Actor; *Pittsburgh* (1942), *White Savage* (1943), *Captain from Castile* (1947) and *Casbah* (1948), to name just a few.

Gomez's other film credits include *Phantom Lady* (1944), *Key Largo* (1948), *Kim* (1950), *The Magnificent Matador* (1955), *Summer and Smoke* (1961); *Stay Away, Joe* (1968); and *Beneath the Planet of the Apes* (1970).

Vicente Gomez

B: 1915

Gomez, who was strumming flamenco melodies in his father's cafe in Madrid when he was only ten years old, is one of the few composers of Spanish Gypsy music. In 1941, at age twenty-six, after touring Europe and South and Central America as a soloist and with symphony orchestras, he was brought to Hollywood by director Rouben Mamoulian to compose Gypsy music and play guitar for motion pictures.

Myrtle Gonzales

B: 9/23/1891
D: 10/22/1918

Gonzales grew up in Los Angeles and was a rapidly rising player at Vitagraph Studios in 1913. She co-starred with William Duncan in many Westerns and appeared also in other types of films. Her career was cut short when she died unexpectedly at age twenty-seven.

Nicholas Gonzalez

A native of San Antonio, Texas, Gonzalez has appeared on television's *Dharma and Greg* (1997-), been featured on MTV's *Undressed* (1999) and starred in the telefilm *My Little Assassin* (1999). He is one of the original cast members on Showtime's *Resurrection Blvd.* (2000-), the first dramatic cable series to feature predominantly Hispanic characters.

Peter Gonzales
[born: Peter Gonzales Falcon]

A Texas-born actor, Gonzales played the Young Fellini in Fellini's *Roma* (1972). He also appeared in Burt Reynolds's *The End* (1973).

Clifton Gonzalez Gonzalez
(aka: Clifton Collins, Jr.)
The grandson of veteran character actor Pedro Gonzale-Gonzalez, this young actor received critical acclaim for his role as the young gang member Cesar in Kevin Reynold's controversial film *187* (1997). From there, his career has taken off, with more than ten projects in the last two years. His other film credits include *Menace II Society* (1993), *Dead Presidents* (1995), *The Replacement Killers* (1998), *The Wonderful Ice Cream Suit* (1998), *Light It Up* (1999), *Price Of Glory* (2000) and *Traffic* (2000).

Jose Gonzalez-Gonzalez
B: 5/25/1925
The identical twin brother of Pedro, Jose followed his brother to Hollywood and pursued a successful acting career by assuming his brather's characterization of the short, comical Mexican. His credits include *Cha-Cha-Cha Boom* (1956), *Panama Sal* (1957) and television appearances.

Pedro Gonzalez-Gonzalez
B: 5/25/1925
A San Antonio comic, Gonzalez-Gonzalez was propelled by his appearance on the 1950s television game show *You Bet Your Life* (1950-61) with Groucho Marx into a film and nightclub career. On the half-hour show, Pedro hilariously topped every line that expert funnyman Groucho said to him, with his exaggerated comedic stereotypical "Si, Senor" dumb Mexican characterization. After the original telecast, young Pedro was flooded with offers from nightclubs and film studios. He finally settled on a personal contract with John Wayne. Pedro made his screen debut as a comic revolutionary in *Wings of the Hawk* (1953). There then followed *The High and the Mighty* (1954), *I Died a Thousand Times* (1955), *Strange Lady in Town* (1955), *The Sheepman* (1958), *Rio Bravo* (1959) and *Hostile Guns* (1967). Gonzalez-Gonzalez also made numerous television and nightclub appearances.

Jose Greco
B: 1919
The Italian-born, Brooklyn-raised master of Spanish dance, Greco made film appearances as a Spanish Gypsy pimp in *Ship of Fools* (1965) and in a Spanish dance sequence in *Around the World in Eighty Days* (1956) and a dance sequence in *Sombrero* (1953).

Pedro Gonzalez-Gonzalez (right) with John Wayne (left) in *Rio Bravo*.

He was brought to the United States at age eight and began learning Spanish dance steps at age ten. "My neighborhood had ethnic diversity, and from the beginning I was drawn to things Spanish," he recalled in an interview (Walter Price, *Los Angeles Times* [10/19/86]). Performing in nightclubs in New York, he was noticed and was asked to be the touring partner of "La Argentinita," the greatest female Spanish dancer of modern times, from 1941 until her untimely death in 1945. He later went to Spain, where he became a sensation, and formed his own dance troupe. In the same interview, Greco recounted, "They couldn't believe I wasn't Spanish, they just dismissed the idea that an Italian from Brooklyn could master this Spanish art form. No one had ever done it before and they thought I was lying."

In 1946 Greco was invited to choreograph and lead a Spanish dance sequence in a Spanish film called *Manolete*, based on the life of Spain's greatest bullfighter. Every time the film was shown, the theater patrons stopped the show and asked the manager to rerun the reel with the dance sequence. Greco toured throughout Europe and returned triumphantly to the States in 1948.

Castulo Guerra

A professional actor in Argentina until 1971, Guerra came to the United States on a Fulbright scholarship to do theater research in New York City. He has appeared as an underworld kingpin in *Stick* (1985), as a desert inhabitant in *Terminator 2: Judgment Day* (1991), in the critically acclaimed *The Usual Suspects* (1995) and in Spielberg's *Amistad* (1997), as well as numerous telefilms. He has guest starred on a number of weekly television series and was a regular for a season on *Falcon Crest* (1981-90).

Dan Guererro

Guerrero is a veteran television producer with extensive credits and experience in both the Spanish and English language media in the United States and Latin America. He produced a PBS music special with Vikki Carr and was the Executive Producer of Telemundo's talk variety show with actress Maria Conchita Alonso. At Guber-Peters Television, Guerrero became head writer and co-producer of *The Paul Rodriquez Show*, a landmark bilingual talk program on the Univision network. Guerrero has also worked as a theatrical agent and casting director in New York.

Jackie Guerra

A stand up comedian who starred in her own short-lived television series *First Time Out* (1995) for the WB network, Guerra has also appeared in the feature film *Selena* (1997) and the cable feature *Picking Up the Pieces* (2000).

Evelyn Guerrero

B: 2/24/1949

A Mexican American actress, Guerrero was featured as Cheech Marin's dream girl, the sexy, unpredictable and elusive Donna, in *Cheech and Chong's Next Movie* (1980), *Cheech and Chong's Nice Dreams* (1981) and *Things Are Tough All Over* (1982).

Born in East Los Angeles, Guerrero moved to Hollywood at age three, when her mother became a teacher at a Hollywood dancing school. She was motivated by her mother and her aunt, Sally Marr. She also appeared in *Lenny* (1974), in Ralph Waite's *On the Nickel* (1980) and in *Bound by Honor* (1993). She played Dora's sister Marisol on the television series *I Married Dora* (1987-88), and also starred as Lupe Cordera in the Luis Valdez-directed television series pilot *Fort Figueroa* (1988).

Tito Guizar

B: 4/8/1908
D: 12/24/1999

A Latin singer, songwriter and recording and film star, Guizar made a dozen American films in the 1930s and 1940s. He is best remembered for his colorful roles in numerous musicals at Paramount Pictures, where he was under contract, beginning with *The Big Broadcast of 1938* (1938) with Bob Hope and *Tropic Holiday* (1938). He is responsible for solidifying the romantic screen image of the Mexican vaquero or charro (cowboy) in both Mexican and American cinema.

Guizar was born in Mexico City of French and Italian ancestry. After training there, he studied voice in Milan, Italy, and later made his stage debut at the Hippodrome in New York City with the Chicago Opera Company. He performed at the Ritz Carlton and the Central Park Casino and become a popular radio soloist. When Guizar switched from classical to popular music, he made a number of musical short subjects. He later returned to his native Mexico and starred in the first successful musical motion picture in Mexican cinema, *Rancho Grande* (1936), creating a genre of musical that became closely identified with Mexican cinema for over fifty years.

His career received a brief boost at Paramount Pictures from 1938 through 1940. Besides *The Big Broadcast of 1938*, he also filmed a Western, *The Llano Kid* (1940). He later went to Republic, where he appeared in *Brazil* (1944), *On the Old Spanish Trail* (1947) and *The Gay Ranchera* (1948) with Roy Rogers. He appeared in American musical all-star extravaganzas throughout the 1940s, making guest appearances as himself.

Tito Guizar, Mexican tenor, guitarist and film star.

Vincent R. Gutierrez

A writer of television dramas, Gutierrez had a long association with Michael Landon Productions, for which he wrote a number of episodes for *Little House on the Prairie* (1974-83), as well as many of the episodes of Landon's subsequent series, *Highway to Heaven* (1984-89).

Claudio Guzman

B: 1931

Guzman produced and directed four years of the popular hit series *I Dream of Jeannie* (1965-70), starring Barbara Eden and Larry Hagman. He also directed episodes of *The Wackiest Ship in the Army* (1965-66), *Love on a Rooftop* (1966-67), *The Flying Nun* (1967-70) and *The Iron Horse* (1966-68).

Born in Santiago, Chile, he attended the University of Chile's school of architecture. He came to the United States in 1952 to continue his studies at the University of Southern California and later at the Chouinard Art Institute. An instructor at USC was so impressed with the Guzman's work that he suggested Claudio do work on film sets, and thus a new career was born. At Desilu Studios, Guzman acted as art director on *The Danny Thomas Show* (1957-65), *Official Detective* (1957), *The Life and Legend of Wyatt Earp* (1955-61), *December Bride* (1954-59), *I Love Lucy* (1951-57) and *Our Miss Brooks* (1952-56). During his Desilu tenure, he created, produced and directed *The Victor Borge Show* (1957). He also directed segments of *I Love Lucy*, *The Dick Van Dyke Show* (1961-66), *The Fugitive* (1963-67), *The Patty Duke Show* (1963-66) and *The Untouchables* (1959-63). He is the brother of Pato Guzman.

Luis Guzman

Guzman has had an extensive career as a working actor. He made his feature film debut in *Short Eyes* (1977), and has appeared in more than forty full-length film projects and has guest starred on numerous episodic series. Among his credits are *Crocodile Dundee II* (1988), *Rooftops* (1989), *Q&A* (1990), *McBain* (1991), *Innocent Blood* (1992), *Mr. Wonderful* (1993), *The Cowboy Way* (1994), *Boogie Nights* (1997), *Out of Sight* (1998), *The Limey* (1999), *Magnolia* (1999), *The Bone Collector* (1999) and *Traffic* (2000). In addition, he has been a series regular on television's *House of Buggin'* (1995) and *Oz* (1997-).

Pato Guzman

B: 1934
D: 1/2/1991

A producer and production designer on eleven films with Paul Mazursky, Guzman's association with the director began in 1967: "I was designing *I Love You, Alice B. Toklas*, which Paul wrote with Larry Tucker. Paul was on the set a lot, and we talked about what we'd do when we made a movie together. When *Bob & Carol & Ted & Alice* (1969) came along we hooked up," recalled Guzman during an interview with publicist Vic Heutschy while making *Enemies, a Love Story* (1989), on location in New York.

Born in Santiago, Chile, Guzman studied architecture and came to the United States in the late 1950s. After a summer of stock and a three-month stint with the MGM design department, he began to work in television. He worked happily for many years at Desilu, doing all its pilots as well as *The Danny Thomas Show* (1957-1965), *The Dick Van Dyke Show* (1961-66), and others, including *Star Trek* (1966-69), which inspired him and hinted at the design possibilities of the film medium.

He left television and traveled, later returning to Los Angeles to visit his brother Claudio and got a job on *The President's Analyst* (1967), directed by social satirist Ted Flicker. "I tend to be very serious," says Guzman. "The Weidman house in *Down and Out in Beverly Hills* (1986), for example, was so outsized it became monumental and funny." Guzman cited a special chemistry with Mazursky as the key to their twenty years of enormously successful collaboration. "We guide all our energy into the project," said Guzman. "There are no battling egos, and it's fun." Their other hits include *Blume in Love* (1973), *An Unmarried Woman* (1978), *Tempest* (1982) and *Moscow on the Hudson* (1984). Guzman also designed *The In-Laws* (1979) and *Hide in Plain Sight* (1990).

Daniel A. Haro

B: 5/27/1955

A Los Angeles-born actor, Haro has played a prison gang member in *American Me* (1992), a classroom teacher in *Stand and Deliver* (1988), and the baseball player Burns in *Talent for the Game* (1993).

Salma Hayek

B: 9/2/1966

Hayek gave up a successful career as a major television star in Mexico and Latin America and moved to the United States to start over, though at the time she spoke no English. Since then, the beautiful and talented Hayek has mastered the English language and accumulated an impressive list of film credits. Hayek made her feature film debut as an actress with a small role in Allison Anders' *Mi Vida Loca* (1994) and played her first starring role in Robert Rodriquez's *Desperado* (1995) opposite Antonio Banderas. Her other film credits include the award-winning *Midaq Alley* (1995); *From Dusk Till Dawn* (1996) in which she played the Queen of the Vampires; *Fools Rush In* (1997), a romantic comedy about a beautiful Mexican American woman and her unexpected involvement in a relationship with an East Coast yuppie played by Matthew Perry; *54* (1998); *Wild Wild West* (1999) as Rita Escobar opposite Will Smith and Kevin Kline; Mike Figgis' *Time Code* (2000); and is slated to play the title role in *Frida Khalo* (2000). Her telefilm credits include Rodriguez's *Roadracers* (1994) for Showtime and *The Hunchback* (1997) for TNT. Hayek has guest starred on the HBO series *Dream On* (1990-96), *Jack's Place* (1992-93), *Nurses* (1991-94) and had a regular series role on the short-lived show, *Sinbad* (1993).

Hayek was born and raised in Coatzacoalcos, a small town in Southeast Mexico and began acting in Children's theater. She was discovered by a television producer who cast her in her first television series, *Nuevo Amanecer*, for which she won the 1989 TV Novela Award as Best Newcomer. The young actress followed this with the title role in the prime time series *Teresa* (1989-91) which was an instant hit in Mexico and syndicated to over thirty countries, turning Hayek into an international star.

Salma Hayek in *From Dusk Till Dawn*.

Dick Haymes

B: 9/13/1916

D: 1980

Born in Buenos Aires, Argentina, of Scottish-English descent, he was educated in France and England before coming to the United States in 1936. Haymes began his show business career as a radio announcer, bond vocalist and occasional film extra and bit player. In the early 1940s he became a highly successful nightclub and recording artist and developed into one of the leading crooners of his time. In 1943, he was signed to a film contract by Twentieth Century-Fox and enjoyed great popularity during 1944-1947. His singing personality, however, didn't quite come across on the screen. In 1953, he married Rita Hayworth, but they divorced in 1955.

Among Haymes' film credits are *Four Jills in a Jeep* (1943), *State Fair* (1945), *Diamond Horseshoe* (1945), *Do You Love Me?* (1946), *The Shocking Miss Pilgrim* (1947), *Carnival in Costa Rica* (1947) and *One Touch of Venus* (1948).

Rita Hayworth
[born: Margarita Cansino]
B: 10/17/1918
D: 5/14/1987

Called "The Love Goddess," Rita Hayworth was one of the most beautiful and exciting talents ever to grace the Silver Screen.

Rita Hayworth is truly one of the first Hispanic American stars, having been able to transcend her ethnic origins and become the ethereal all American girl to a generation of moviegoers worldwide. Her popularity reached its zenith during the 1940s through a succession of roles that began with such films as *Only Angels Have Wings* (1939), *Blood and Sand* (1941), *The Strawberry Blonde* (1941), *You Were Never Lovelier* (1942), *Cover Girl* (1944) and was capped off by *Gilda* (1946).

She was born Margarita Cansino in Brooklyn, New York, to Eduardo Cansino, a noted Spanish dancer, and his Irish wife, Volga Haworth. Eduardo was one of seven children of famous Andalusian dance master Don Antonio Cansino. Eduardo was a vaudeville headliner in a Spanish dance act with his sister Elisa, and they performed throughout the United States and Europe. By the time Margarita was four years old, she was already learning dance steps from her father. The family performed and traveled as The Dancing Cansinos. Settling in California, Eduardo opened a dance school in Hollywood and picked up work from the film studios whenever they needed a Spanish or Mexican dance number.

He saw potential in his teenage daughter and teamed with her in a dance act that played in nightclubs south of the border in Tijuana and Agua Caliente. These bordertowns were filled with gaming, free-flowing liquor, loose women and drugs. The rich and powerful of Hollywood's elite would often cross the border for a weekend or a night of fun. The artistry of the father-and-daughter dance act immediately drew attention. Winfield S. Sheehan, vice president in charge of production at Fox Studios, was taken by Margarita's looks and dance movements and felt she had some qualities that might photograph well for the movies. She began taking acting and elocution lessons at the studio, and within a month she worked in her first film, a Spanish-language short subject.

She made her screen debut in *Dante's Inferno* (1935) in a dance sequence choreographed by her father. Of this period she recalled in an interview years later, "I developed a burning ambition, as only a too-fat seventeen-year-old can burn, to become a good actress." She followed her debut with *Under the Pampas Moon* (1935) and then began to work steadily in movies. She had parts in *Charlie Chan in Egypt* (1935), *Paddy O'Day* (1935) and *Human Cargo* (1936).

When Fox combined with Twentieth Century, Darryl Zanuck dropped her contract even though she was set to star in *Ramona* (1936). "I cried and screamed. I vowed that I would show those men. I would become famous and they would be sorry," she said in a 1940s magazine interview.

She got leading roles as Mexican señoritas in several B pictures and then was put under contract by Columbia Pictures. She toiled in run-of-the-mill films, but she was being groomed for stardom by the studio. She shortened her name to Rita and adopted a surname similar to her mother's, Hayworth. The actress underwent a weight-loss program and painful electrolysis treatments in order to broaden her forehead and to accentuate a widow's peak. Her raven hair was changed to auburn and still later to the famous coppery red.

She continued in undistinguished roles until she was loaned to Warner Bros., where she worked opposite James Cagney in the turn-of-the-century romance *The Strawberry Blonde* (1941).

Rita was catapulted to stardom as a result of her role as the temptress Dona Sol, opposite Tyrone Power, in *Blood and Sand* (1941), directed by Rouben Mamoulian. Twentieth Century-Fox paid Harry Cohn, the head of Columbia, five times the salary she was receiving from Columbia for her services. "You don't have to be a vengeful person to taste the sweetness of that," commented Rita, who, appearing for the Technicolor cameras for the first time, realized an ambition that had been thwarted by Fox years before. *The Hollywood Reporter*

Rita Hayworth (as Rita Cansino, 1935; 1944; 1964).

(5/20/41) commented in its review of the film, "To us there were two standouts, Rita Hayworth and Rouben Mamoulian. In her performance, Miss Hayworth, who has been widely cheered for her beauty, comes through with a well defined artistry that must win for her some of the top acting roles." *Daily Variety* (5/20/41) commented, "Miss Hayworth takes another stride toward her assured position among the stars in demand. Her unforgettable performance as the luscious but heartless Dona Sol is among her finest screen achievements."

It was impossible to pick up a magazine at that time without finding Hayworth either on the cover or featured in an article. Columbia, realizing what they had, teamed her with Fred Astaire for a Cole Porter musical, *You'll Never Get Rich* (1941), allowing her to showcase her dance talent with the supreme master of film dance. She was loaned to Twentieth Century-Fox again for *My Gal Sal* (1942) with Victor Mature. Hayworth couldn't sing, so her singing voice was dubbed; she could dance, however, and she was teamed with Fred Astaire again in *You Were Never Lovelier* (1942), and with Gene Kelly in *Cover Girl* (1944).

"Dancing," she once said, "is my natural heritage and I have always loved it, but I have also always hated to practice. When I was younger I used to study ballet, Spanish and tap dancing for four and five hours a day, and it was no cinch, especially having a father who was so strict. It was hard and tedious work and there were times when I didn't think I could go on. But I did and, of course, as it turned out, the effort was worth it."

In 1946 Hayworth attained her greatest success in the role with which she is now most identified, the beautiful adventuress *Gilda*, a woman lost in a Latin country who vies for the affections of Glenn Ford and George Macready. The ads for the film proclaimed: "There never was a woman like Gilda!" In a low-cut black satin dress with elbow-length gloves, she did a sensuous striptease number as she sang "Put the Blame on Mame."

She went to Acapulco with her then husband Orson Welles, to film *The Lady from Shanghai* (1948), which he directed and in which they co-starred. The film did not do well at the box office. Columbia then cast her as Carmen in *The Loves of Carmen* (1948), opposite Glenn Ford as Don Jose. Her father choreographed many of the dance sequences. She was next teamed with Glenn Ford in *Affair in Trinidad* (1952), an attempt to recapture the magic of *Gilda*. The film didn't work as well as the original, but was popular with audiences and a box office hit, taking in more money than *Gilda*. Some of the best of her later work includes the title role in *Miss Sadie Thompson* (1953), *Pal Joey* (1957) and *Separate Tables* (1958)

During the 1960s her career faltered, and sporadic appearances in second-rate films did little to revive it. There were reports of public drunkenness, and she often seemed lost and would turn down roles. Her behavior became erratic; no one knew what was wrong. Her daughter was surprised when her mother had memory lapses during which she could not recall the names of her closest friends. After visiting several doctors, she was diagnosed as having Alzheimer's disease. Her last film was *The Wrath of God* in 1972.

Hayworth died from complications arising from the disease on May 14, 1987, at her home in New York under the care of her daughter Yasmin (from her marriage to Prince Aly Khan). Her daughter said at a tribute to her mother at the Deauville Film Festival in France, "Had we known the early stages of Alzheimer's disease, we could have saved her notoriety and adverse publicity. But at least her suffering was a catalyst for more knowledge and research about the disease."

Ron Henriquez

Born in Panama, Henriquez started a boxing career at age fifteen becoming a welterweight contender and served in the United States Marine Corps before seeking an acting career. His film credits include *Hickey and Boggs* (1972), *The Main Event* (1979) and *Code of Silence* (1985). On television, Henriquez has guest starred in over 400 episodic series including *The High Chaparral* (1967-71), *Adam-12* (1968-75), *Falcon Crest* (1981-90) and the miniseries *Drug Wars: The Camarena Story* (1990).

Pepe Hern
[born: Pepe Hernandez]

Born in Spain, Hern came to the United States at an early age. He appeared in many films of the fifties including *Borderline* (1950), *The Ring* (1952), *The Magnificent Seven* (1960) and *Joe Kidd* (1972).

George F. Hernandez

B: 6/6/1863
D: 12/19/1922

A screen and stage actor from 1912 to 1922, Hernandez had major roles in such silent films as *When Helen Was Elected* (1912), *Arabia* (1922) and *Flaming Hearts* (1922). In 1917 he co-starred in five silent films at Universal: *Mutiny, God's Crucible, Southern Justice, The Showdown* and *The Greater Law*.

Juano Hernandez

B: 1898
D: 7/19/1970

A Puerto Rican actor, Juano Hernandez usually played African American or African characters in films. His deep, resonant voice and dignified presence were used effectively in his 1949 film debut in MGM's *Intruder in the Dust*.

Hernandez was born in Puerto Rico, the son of a Puerto Rican seaman, and orphaned as a small child. He went to live with his aunt in Rio de Janeiro, where he acquired his Portuguese first name. As a boy he joined a little troupe of street urchins who sang, danced and did acrobatics. He ran away with a carnival that toured Latin America and the Caribbean, and he wound up in New Orleans in 1915. Though lacking any formal education, Hernandez taught himself to read and write in several languages. "One thing I learned very soon," said the actor, "was that if you speak English with any kind of accent people are inclined to laugh at you." Gladwin Hill, *New York Times* (5/28/50).

Juano Hernandez as the Mau Mau leader Njogu in *Something of Value*.

As a result, he cultivated perfect diction and along the way acquired a knowledge of Shakespeare's works and other dramatic classics. He worked in carnivals, circuses and minstrel shows, appeared in vaudeville comedy sketches and performed dramatic readings. He settled in New York City and found work as an actor in the theater. He played his first Broadway role in *Show Boat*, followed by *Strange Fruit* and *Let My People Free*. A keen interest in exotic foreign chants, languages and customs developed into work on radio.

For his film debut as the poor Southern sharecropper in *Intruder in the Dust*, Hernandez won praise. He turned in a moving portrayal as an aging jazz musician in *Young Man with a Horn* (1950), starring Kirk Douglas. In *The Breaking Point* (1950), he was John Garfield's buddy, and in *Trial* (1955), he was an African American judge, while in *Something of Value* (1957), he portrayed an African Mau Mau leader.

He continued to work in featured roles in such films as *Stars in My Crown* (1950), *Kiss Me Deadly* (1955), *St. Louis Blues* (1958), *The Sins of Rachel Cade* (1960), *Sergeant Rutledge* (1960) and *Uptight* (1968).

Laura Martinez Herring
[alternate spelling: Harring]
B: 3/3/1967
A former Miss USA, Herring starred in the film *Lambada-The Forbidden Dance* (1990). She has guest starred on many episodic series including Baywatch (1989-) and the television films *The Alamo: Thirteen Days to Glory* (1987), *Desperado 2* (1991) and *Rio Diablo* (1993). Born in Los Mochis, Sinaloa, Mexico, she moved with her family to Texas when she was eleven.

Miguel Higuera
Higuera has directed exclusively for NBC studios through Peter Engel Productions since 1993 for their very popular Saturday morning shows *Saved by the Bell* (1989-93) and *Hang Time* (1995-). Upon the creation of Sony/Telemundo's situation comedy series *Solo en America* he directed fourteen episodes. Born in Mexico City, Higuera began his career in the United States in 1975 as a television cameraman. By 1984, he garnered two Emmy Awards and steadily moved up the ranks as technical director and associate director for such shows as *Punky Brewster* (1984-86) and *Days of Our Lives* (1965-).

Lance Hool
An independent producer for over two decades, Hool was born in Mexico City and educated in Mexico and the United States. Hool has produced, written, or directed a variety of feature films on location all over the world. His credits include *Missing in Action* (1984) and *Missing in Action II* (1985), both starring Chuck Norris; *The Evil That Men Do* (1984) and *10 to Midnight* (1983), both starring Charles Bronson; and *Steel Dawn* (1987), starring Patrick Swayze. He also produced the comedy *Pure Luck* (1991), starring Martin Short and Danny Glover.

Rodolfo Hoyos, Sr.
[alternate spelling: Rudolfo]
B: 1896
D: 5/24/1980
Long regarded as Mexico's best baritone, Hoyos first came to the States in the late 1920s to perform with New York's Metropolitan Opera. During the 1930s and 1940s, Hoyos both appeared in films and coached such actors as Nelson Eddy and Paul Lukas. Movies in which Hoyos sang include *A Night at the Opera* (1935), starring the Marx Brothers; and *One Night of Love* (1934), with Grace Moore. Fans of the Golden Age of television will remember Hoyos' portrayal of Ricky Ricardo's uncle in an episode of *I Love Lucy* (1951-57). His son, Rudolfo Hoyos, Jr., also became an actor.

Rudolfo Hoyos, Jr.
[alternate spelling: Rodolpho Hoyas, Jr.]
B: 3/14/1916
D: 4/15/1983
A Mexican character actor, Hoyos usually made his presence felt as a heavy or stern father in such films as *The Americano* (1955) and *The Brave One* (1956).

Rudolfo, Jr., was born in Mexico City and was brought to the States in the late 1920s. He made his film debut as a fourteen-year-old boy in Howard Hughes' *Hell's Angels* (1930) with Jean Harlow.

As an adult, Rudolfo could not get a role as a Mexican until he grew a mustache, because casting directors said he did not look the part. Hoyos played Pancho Villa in an undistinguished film called *Villa!* produced in 1958.

Among his many motion picture credits are *The Fighter* (1952), *Second Chance* (1953), *Timetable* (1956), *The First Texan* (1956), *The Three Outlaws* (1956), *Operation Eichmann* (1961) and *Return of the Gunfighter* (1967). Hoyos also appeared in over 300 television shows.

Jon Huertas
Huertas joined the cast of the ABC-television series *Sabrina, the Teenage Witch* (1996-) in 1999. His film credits include *Why Do Fools Fall In Love?* (1998), *Buddy Boy* (1999) and the cable feature *Picking Up the Pieces* (2000).

Leon Ichaso
B: 1949
The Cuban-born director of the award-winning independent films *El Super* (1979), *Crossover Dreams* (1985) and *Harlem* (1994). Ichaso's career began with commercials, documentaries and industrial film production. He was raised in the world of radio, television and cinema—his father, Justo Rodriguez Santos, having been a well-known television and film director and writer in Cuba. Leon left Cuba at age fourteen and finished his education in the States. He has since directed episodes of such television hits as *Miami Vice* (1984-89), *Crime Story* (1986-88), *The Equalizer* (1985-89) and over half a dozen television movies.

Eugene Iglesias
B: 12/3/1926

A character actor during the 1950s, Iglesias appeared as the lighthearted Pepe Bello in *The Brave Bulls* (1951) and in such films as *The Naked Dawn* (1955), *War Cry* [aka: *Indian Uprising*] (1952), *The Mask of the Avenger* (1951)with John Derek, and *East of Sumatra* (1953) in a Gilbert Roland-type role opposite Jeff Chandler.

He was born in San Juan, Puerto Rico, and at age seven he became a child actor in radio dramas. He left Puerto Rico and attended Columbia University. Iglesias acted with theater companies in Puerto Rico, New York and Mexico City before entering films.

Gloria Irrizary
A Puerto Rican character actress, Irrizary was featured as Maria Holly's Puerto Rican mother in *The Buddy Holly Story* (1978) and as another Puerto Rican mother in *Q & A* (1990). She has many other motion picture and television credits.

Isabelita
See Lita Baron.

Al Israel
An actor and musician, Israel was born in New York City. His film credits include *Scarface* (1983), *Body Double* (1984), *Carlito's Way* (1993) and *Dangerous Minds* (1995).

Jose Iturbi
[born: Jose De Iturbi]
B: 11/28/1895
D: 6/28/1980

A world-famous pianist and conductor, Iturbi appeared as himself in several MGM musical films during the 1940s, including *Thousands Cheer* (1943) and *Two Girls and a Sailor* (1944). He did all the piano playing for actor Cornel Wilde as Chopin on the soundtrack for the movie *A Song to Remember* (1945). His recording of Chopin's "A-flat Polonaise" from the movie was the first classical record to become a million-seller.

During the mid-1940s, Iturbi was one of the most famous pianists, rivaling Oscar Levant.

Born in Valencia, Spain, Iturbi was a child prodigy. By age seven, he was teaching piano and supporting his entire family. His first steady job was playing piano in the first movie theater in his native Valencia. He started at two in the afternoon and played until two in the morning, a steady 12-hour job. In the Basque language the name Iturbi means "twin fountains." His original name was De Iturbi, but he dropped the De. The people of Valencia took up a collection to send him to Barcelona to study under Joaquin Malats.

He played piano in cafes at night to earn room and board. Graduating with honors at age seventeen, he was eventually offered a post vacated by Liszt at the Zurich Conservatory. He stayed four years and then embarked on a career as a virtuoso. He performed in concert

Jose Iturbi in
That Midnight Kiss.

in all the leading world capitals and toured extensively throughout South America.

Later in his career, he was criticized for his work in movies. Some charged he had sold out to commercialism. Iturbi commented, "I would not go that way again if I had to do it over. My critics misunderstood. They thought I abandoned serious pursuits, but others thought it was good that I exposed a whole new audience to a music they would have been ignorant of."

At age eighty-three, a year before his death, Iturbi drew rave reviews for a packed concert at the Ambassador Auditorium in Pasadena, California.

Marabina Jaimes

Jaimes is the Emmy Award-winning host of PBS *Storytime*, a popular childrens series. She has guest starred on *Beverly Hills, 90210* (1990-2000); *Melrose Place* (1992-99), *Unhappily Ever After* (1995-99) and *Murder, She Wrote* (1984-96). Her feature film credits include *Mi Vida Loca* (1993), *High School High* (1996) with Jon Lovitz and *Steel* (1997) with Shaquile O'Neill.

Neal Jimenez

B: 5/22/1960

Scriptwriter Neal Jimenez launched himself as a director in 1992 with his autobiographical film *The Waterdance*, co-directed with Michael Steinberg. The film dealt with Jimenez's own experiences after a serious hiking accident in 1984 left him permanently paralyzed and confined to a wheelchair. He has also written the screenplay for *River's Edge* (1987) and co-scripted *For the Boys* (1991), starring Bette Midler and James Caan.

Soledad Jimenez

[aka: Solidad]

B: 1872

D: 10/17/1966

Soledad Jimenez was a character actress who appeared in many silent and sound films including In *Old Arizona* (1929) with Warner Baxter, the first outdoor sound Western, and *The Robin Hood of El Dorado* (1936) also with Warner Baxter.

Raul Julia

B: 3/9/1940

D: 10/24/1994

Julia will ultimately be best remembered on film for his memorable and exuberant portrayal of Gomez Addams in the enormously successful feature films *The Addams Family* (1991) and *Addams Family Values* (1993). He brought all his years of experience and love of acting and his own playfulness to the role of Gomez Addams. It brought him success and recognition in Hollywood and made him one of the most respected and sought after performers of both stage and screen. He first gained international recognition for his portrayal of a South American

Raul Julia in *Romero*.

political prisoner in the Oscar®-winning *Kiss of the Spider Woman* (1985). Other roles included a Hispanic detective in *Compromising Positions* (1985); the title role of the Salvadoran martyr in *Romero* (1989); and the attorney Sandy Stern in *Presumed Innocent* (1990).

After proving himself on stage in Shaw's *Arms and the Man*, Shakespeare's *Othello*, Coward's *Design for Living* and Pinter's *Betrayal*, as well as the title roles in *Dracula* and *Where's Charley?*, Raul Julia came full circle as an actor with his return to the Broadway stage portraying Cervantes and Don Quixote in the musical *Man of La Mancha* (1991) and with the enormous success of his film portrayal of Gomez Addams in *The Addams Family* and *Addams Family Values*.

A native of San Juan Puerto Rico, Julia was the oldest of four children of a prominent restauranteur. After graduating from high school, and at the behest of his parents, he enrolled at the University of Puerto Rico to study law. But after earning a bachelor's degree in liberal arts, he opted top work in several local theater troupes and in an ocasional nightclub revue.

He arrived in New York city from Puerto Rico in 1964. "I came to (to the United States) to be an actor," stated Julia at a press conference for the movie *Romero*. "I didn't come here to be a stereotype. So I always looked for the opportunity to do something that was challenging. I never wanted to take the easy route.

"An actor must be regarded as an actor and he must be given the opportunity to prove that he can play any role, whether it's part of his background or not. Unfortunately, many of the people in casting and producing and directing see actors only as types. So the actor must constantly fight the limitations others want to put on him."

After arriving in New York, he studied drama at the American Palace theatre and began a long and fruitful association with theatrical producer Joseph Papp and the New York Shakespeare festival in 1966. He made his Broadway debut in 1968 in a short-lived drama about the Castro revolution called *The Cuban Thing*. He was nominated for Broadway's Tony Award for his roles in *Two Gentlemen from Verona*, *Where's Charley?*, *The Threepenny Opera* and *Nine*.

Julia's motion picture career began in 1971 with roles in *The Organization* and *Panic in Needle Park*. Since then his films have included *Gumball Rally* (1976) *Eyes of Laura Mars* (1978), *The Escape Artist* (1982) Francis Ford Coppola's *One from the Heart* (1982), *The Morning After* (1986) and *The Penitent* (1988). For director Paul Mazursky, he starred in *Moon over Parador* (1988) and *Tempest* (1982). He also co-starred in *Tequila Sunrise* (1988), *The Rookie* (1990), *Havana* (1990) and his last theatrical feature film, *Streetfighter* (1994).

On television Julia's credits include the miniseries *Mussolini* (1985), the telefilm *Onassis: The Richest Man in the World* (1988) in which he played the title role; *The Alamo: Thirteen Days to Glory* (1987) in which he played General Santa Ana; and the HBO film *Florida Straits* (1986).

He won an Emmy Award for his role in another HBO film *The Burning Season: The Chico Mendes Story* (1994) in which he played the slain environmentalist. His last telefilm was Showtime's *Down Came a Blackbird* (1995). Julia died of heart failure following a short illness in 1994.

Katy Jurado
[born: Maria Cristina Estela Marcela Jurado Garcia]
B: 1/16/1927

A Mexican actress, Jurado is best known for her strikingly dark beauty and for her many strong roles in such classic Western dramas as *High Noon* (1952) and *Broken Lance* (1954).

Born in Mexico City, she was the daughter of a rancher and an opera singer. As a teenager, despite her parents' objections, Jurado became an actress and made her first film, *No Mataras*. Her friendship with famed Mexican director Emilio Fernandez helped her entry into the Mexican film industry, where she became an overnight sensation. For her third motion picture, *La Vida Inutil de Pito Perez* (1943), she was honored with many awards.

In Mexican films she was always cast as a glamour girl or wealthy socialite, and sometimes sang and danced. In American films she almost always played a sultry Mexican beauty, Indian squaw, or suffering mother.

Katy Jurado (left) and Rita Moreno (right) at a party given after Ed Sullivan's *Toast of the Town*. Jurado had recently won Mexico's Ariel Award, the equivalent of Hollywood's Oscar®.

Photo by Mel Traxel.

She made her American film debut in 1951 in *The Bullfighter and the Lady*, as the wife of an aging bullfighter played by Gilbert Roland. Later, Stanley Kramer hired her for the role of Helen Ramirez in *High Noon* (1952) opposite Gary Cooper, which brought her attention from critics and audiences alike. Knowing very little English, she learned her lines phonetically. She followed this with a role as a "halfbreed" Apache-Mexican squaw in *Arrowhead* (1953) starring Charlton Heston. Jurado played Spencer Tracy's Indian wife in *Broken Lance*, for which she was an Academy Award® nominee for Best Supporting Actress in 1954. Her many motion picture credits include *San Antone* (1953); *The Racers* (1955); *Trial* (1955); *The Man from Del Rio* (1956); *Trapeze* (1956); *The Badlanders* (1958); *One-Eyed Jacks* (1961), starring and directed by Marlon Brando; *Barabbas* (1962), *A Covenant with Death* (1966), *Stay Away, Joe* (1968*), Pat Garrett and Billy the Kid* (1973), *Under the Volcano* (1984) and *The Hi-Lo Country* (1998). She has made guest appearances on American television.

Tichi Wilkerson Kassel

An innovative businesswoman, Tichi Wilkerson Kassel was publisher emeritus of the trade newspaper *The Hollywood Reporter* until 1991.

She acquired the newspaper after her husband's death in 1963. Under her guidance and leadership, the newspaper expanded and became an internationally respected and read entertainment publication. Through the Wilkerson Foundation and her many civic efforts, she distinguished herself for her continuing devotion and service to the entertainment industry. She has a star on the Hollywood Walk of Fame.

Born in Los Angeles, California, a daughter of the Verdugo family, whose ancestors came to Latin America in 1520 with Cortes, Tichi was raised in Mexico City and returned to Los Angeles as a teenager.

Pancho Kohner

B: 1/7/1939

Son of agent Paul Kohner and Mexican actress Lupita Tovar, and brother of actress Susan Kohner, Pancho produced such films as *St. Ives* (1976), *The White Buffalo* (1977), *The Evil That Men Do* (1984), *Death Wish 4: The Crackdown* (1987), *Kinjite: Forbidden Subjects* (1989) and *Madeline* (1998).

Susan Kohner

B: 11/11/1936

As the daughter of Mexican actress Lupita Tovar and Hollywood agent Paul Kohner, it is not surprising that Susan Kohner became an actress. She was nominated for an Oscar® for Best Supporting Actress for her role as a young black woman who tries to pass for Anglo in Universal's 1959 remake of *Imitation of Life*.

She made her film debut as Maria in *To Hell and Back* starring Audie Murphy in 1955. Her other films include *Trooper Hook* (1957), *All the Fine Young Cannibals* (1960), *By Love Possessed* (1961) and *Freud* (1962). She semi-retired in 1964 when she married designer John Wurtz. The actress is a graduate of UCLA and has appeared on the Broadway stage.

Apollonia Kotero

A Mexican American actress/singer/dancer, Kotero co-starred with Prince in the hit film *Purple Rain* (1984) and played a character named Apollonia on *Falcon Crest* (1981-90) for a season.

Carlos LaCamara

B: 1957

Best known for his role of Paco, on the NBC-television series *Nurses* (1991-94), LaCamara went on to appear in *Independence Day* (1996) and *10 Things I Hate About You* (1999). Born in Havana, Cuba, LaCamara moved with his family to Washington, D.C., at age two, when Fidel Castro came to power. He credits his interest in theater, which he says began in elementary school, to the influence of his father, a graphic artist, and his mother, who was an opera singer in Cuba. At age seven, his family moved to Los Angeles. He attended the University of California at Los Angeles, where he earned a Bachelor of Arts degree.

Fernando Lamas

B: 1/9/1915

D: 10/8/1982

A handsome, virile, athletic MGM star of the 1950s, Lamas played opposite some of the most beautiful actresses in Hollywood, including Lana Turner, Elizabeth Taylor, Esther Williams, Arlene Dahl and Rhonda Fleming.

He was born in Buenos Aires, Argentina, the son of electrical engineer Emelio Lamas and his wife, Maria, who died when Fernando was

Smooth, suave, sophisticated Fernando Lamas starred as a smooth, suave, sophisticated French patriot seeking refuge from the Nazis during the 1940s in *The Cheap Detective* (1978).

only four years old. He was subsequently raised by an aunt and a grandmother. He joined the local theater group as a young boy, and became a major film star in Europe and in Argentina before coming to MGM in 1950.

In an interview with Burt Prelutsky in the *Los Angeles Times* (3/19/78), Lamas described his early years at MGM: "I couldn't break the Latin Lover image, hard as I tried. It was a great image to have off screen, but a pain in the ass in the movies." He spent ten years under contract to MGM, where he earned $2,500 a week and an occasional $25,000 bonus.

In another interview, with Paul Rosenfield, also of the *Los Angeles Times,* in 1977, Lamas remarked, "I was the Technicolor boy; get me the guitar, the horse, the girl and get it over with. We were bottled and sold as products. Audiences then were buying trips, not truth."

After his contract was up, Lamas starred in and directed a number of unsuccessful films in Europe. He directed more than sixty episodic television shows over the years, including several episodes of the popular series *Falcon Crest* (1981-90), which starred his son Lorenzo, born of his marriage to actress Arlene Dahl. Lamas later married Esther Williams. He died of cancer in 1982 shortly after beginning work as Robert Urich's co-star in a new television series called *Gavilan* (1982-83). A caricature of his personality was made famous for a new generation by comedian Billy Crystal on the television show *Saturday Night Live* (1975-) with a character whose catch phrase was "You look maaahvelous!"

His films include *The Law and the Lady* (1951), *Rich, Young and Pretty* (1951), *The Merry Widow* (1952), *Dangerous When Wet* (1953), *The Girl Who Had Everything* (1953), *Rose Marie* (1954), *The Girl Rush* (1955), *The Lost World* (1960), *100 Rifles* (1969) and *The Cheap Detective* (1978).

Lorenzo Lamas

B: 1/20/1958

Best known for his role as Lance Cumson on the long-running CBS-television series *Falcon Crest* (1981-90), Lamas has appeared in numerous television shows and feature films including *Grease* (1978), *Take Down* (1979), *Body Rock* (1984) and *Final Impact* (1991). In the 1990s he appeared in a host of action adventure films, as well as starring in the popular syndicated television series *Renegade* (1992-97). He also directed several episodes of *Renegade*.

Born in Santa Monica, California, he is the son of Fernando Lamas and Arlene Dahl.

Dorothy Lamour

B: 12/10/1914
D: 9/22/1996

The dark, alluring, blue-eyed beauty Lamour is of French, Scots-Irish and Spanish descent and was born in New Orleans. Indeed, she was crowned Miss New Orleans in 1931.

Her first picture was *The Jungle Princess* in 1936. She became an overnight star at Paramount Pictures when it was released, and the abbreviated costume she wore, a sarong, became her trademark as a native island siren and started an international fashion trend. She

Lorenzo Lamas.

played a Latin in *A Medal for Benny* (1945), *Masquerade in Mexico* (1945) and *The Road to Rio* (1947). She played a Spaniard in *The Last Train from Madrid* (1937). Lamour's first outstanding screen success was in Samuel Goldwyn's *The Hurricane* (1937). Her singing and comedic talents were put to good use as the female co-star in a series of successful *Road to...* pictures with Bob Hope and Bing Crosby. In some of her other fifty-two films, she co-starred with Ray Milland, Alan Ladd, Tyrone Power, William Holden and Fred MacMurray.

William Douglas Lansford

B: 7/13/1922

A film and television writer, Lansford was born and raised in East Los Angeles of a Mexican mother and an Anglo father. His credits include such series as *Bonanza* (1959-73), *The Virginian* (1962-71), *The High Chaparral* (1976-71), *Fantasy Island* (1978-84), *The Rookies* (1972-76), *Matt Houston* (1982-85) and *CHiPs* (1978-83). He wrote a best-selling book on Pancho Villa, for which he wrote a film treatment from which Sam Peckinpah wrote a script. Peckinpah was fired from the project, which he had planned to direct, and Robert Towne reworked the script. The film was eventually shot in Spain by producer Ted Richmond with Yul Brynner as Villa, and titled *Villa Rides* (1968). Lansford also wrote the television movies *The Deadly Tower* (1975) and *Don't Look Back: The Story of Leroy "Satchel" Paige* (1981).

Mario Larrinaga

A native Californian, Larrinaga was a background effects scenic artist. He worked at RKO and was a significant contributor to the classic 1933 production *King Kong*. He was also a noted painter and artist.

John Leguizamo

B: 7/22/1964

Leguizamo has established a career that defies categorization in film, theater, television and literature. As a rising young actor and writer, Leguizamo began his career in films such as *Casualties of War* (1989), *Regarding Henry* (1991), *Super Mario Bros.* (1993) and *Whispers in the Dark* (1993). But it was his role as a giggly transvestite beauty queen in *To Wong Foo, Thanks for Everything, Julie Newmar* (1995), that earned him a Golden Globe Award for Best Supporting Actor and widespread recognition. Since then, he has starred with Kurt Russell in the action film *Executive Decision* (1996), in Baz Luhrmann's *Romeo + Juliet* (1996) as Tybalt, as the title role in *The Pest* (1997) and in Spike Lee's *Summer of Sam* (1999). Recent projects include *Moulin Rouge* (2000) with Nicole Kidman and the voice of Gune in the animated *Titan A. E.* (2000).

In 1991, Lequizamo became an off-Broadway sensation as the writer and performer of his one man show, *Mambo Mouth*. He received an Obie, Outer Critics Circle and Vanguard Award for the play in which he portrayed seven different characters. The show later aired on the HBO cable network. His second one man show *Spic-O-Rama*, had an extended sold out run in Chicago before opening to rave reviews and sellout houses in New York. It was also taped for airing on HBO.

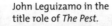

John Leguizamo in the title role of *The Pest*.

Leguizamo's latest one man show, the Tony Award nominated *Freak* had a successful run on Broadway. The critically lauded show was written by Lequizamo and won him The Drama Desk Award for Outstanding Solo Show and the Outer Critics Circle Award for Outstanding Solo Performance. Spike Lee directed the HBO cable television presentation of *Freak*, which won Lequizamo an Emmy Award in 1999.

Leguizamo set a precedent when he created and starred in the first ever Latin comedy/variety show, the Emmy Award-winning *House of Buggin'* (1995) for Fox Television network. Other television credits include the role of Calderone Jr. on *Miami Vice* (1984-89). Leguizamo was born in Bogota, Columbia and raised in New York.

Dennis E. Leoni

Born and raised in Tucson, Arizona, Leoni is the writer, creator and executive producer of the Showtime original series *Resurrection Blvd.* (2000), which is the first dramatic cable series to have a Hispanic focus. He started his entertainment career working as an actor and stuntman before turning to writing. He has written episodes of several television series including *The Commish* (1991-95) *Covington Cross* (1992), *Raven* (1992-93) and *McKenna* (1994).

George J. Lewis

B: 12/10/1904

A veteran character actor born in Guadalajara, Mexico, Lewis has over 250 American feature film credits, beginning in 1924 with *Captain Blood* for Vitagraph and ending with *The Comancheros* in 1961. He is perhaps best remembered as Zorro's father in the Walt Disney television series starring Guy Williams.

Lewis appeared in countless B Westerns and serials for such studios as Monogram, Republic and Columbia. He also appeared in many Spanish-language features produced in Hollywood in the 1930s. His better-known feature film credits include *Gilda* (1946), *Crisis* (1950), *Branded* (1951), *The Bad and the Beautiful* (1952), *The Iron Mistress* (1952), *Viva Zapata!* (1952), *Shane* (1953) and *Hell on Frisco Bay* (1956).

Ruth Livier

Born in Guadalajara, Mexico, Livier has guest starred on several episodic series, including *Weird Science* (1994-97), *Soldier of Fortune, Inc.* (1997) and the highly acclaimed *NYPD Blue* (1993-). She appeared as Joy Taylor on *Beverly Hills, 90210* (1990-2000) for the 1996-1997 season, and has a starring role on Showtime's *Resurrection Blvd.* (2000-).

Luis Llosa

A Peruvian filmmaker, Llosa started his career in Peru as a newspaper film critic and magazine writer. He then went on to direct documentaries and a popular weekly news magazine for Peruvian television. Hemade his American theatrical motion picture directing debut in 1993 with *Sniper*, starring Tom Berenger. He has since directed *The Specialist* (1994), with Sylvester Stallone and Sharon Stone; and *Anaconda* (1997), with Jennifer Lopez.

Gerry Lopez
B: 1948
A surfer, actor and entrepreneur, Lopez was featured in *Big Wednesday* (1978) as himself and co-starred in *Conan the Barbarian* (1982) as Subotai the Mongol, Conan's loyal partner. He was also featured in *North Shore* (1987), *Farewell to the King* (1989) and *The Endless Summer 2* (1994).

Lopez was born and raised in Honolulu. His father is a New Yorker of Cuban German descent who first went to Hawaii as a soldier in World War II. His mother is of Japanese descent.

Jennifer Lopez
B: 7/24/1970
In 1995, Lopez made her feature film debut in the highly acclaimed *My Family* (1995) winning an independent Spirit Award nomination for her role as the young mother Maria Sanchez. She followed with a starring role as Grace McKenna opposite Sean Penn and Nick Nolte in Oliver Stones' *U-Turn* (1997). Lopez then starred in the title role of *Selena* (1997) earning widespread acclaim for her performance as the tragically murdered Tejano singer. For the role she was paid one million dollars—to date, the largest sum ever paid to a Latina actress in Hollywood. She again won praise for her work as Federal Marshal Karen Sisco opposite George Clooney in *Out of Sight* (1998). In 1998, she also provided the voice of Azteca in the DreamWorks animated film *Antz*. For 2000, she starred in *The Cell* and the romantic comedy, *The Wedding Planner*.

Her other film credits include *Money Train* (1995) as Grace Santiago, a New York Transit cop caught between two jealous brothers Woody Harrelson and Wesley Snipes; Francis Ford Coppola's *Jack* (1996) as the teacher Ms. Marquez opposite Robin Williams; *Blood and Wine* (1996) as Gabriella, a maid involved in a jewel heist and love triangle opposite Jack Nicholson; and *Anaconda* (1997) as a documentary filmmaker, with Jon Voight and Eric Stoltz.

Lopez began her career in 1990 after winning a national competition for a position as a Fly Girl on the hit Fox television series *In Living Color* (1990-94). Soon thereafter, she landed roles in other television series, including a co-starring role as a regular on *Second Chances* (1993-94) and the subsequent spin-off *Hotel Malibu* (1994). The actress was born and raised in the Bronx and is of Puerto Rican parentage.

Jennifer Lopez in the starring role of *Selena*.

Kamala Lopez
[aka: Kamala Lopez Dawson]
B: 1965
An actress, Lopez made her feature film debut as Dolores, the female lead, in *Born in East L.A.* (1987). She was born in New York City of an Indian mother and a Venezuelan father. Before entering Yale University, she spent two seasons on television's *Sesame Street* (1969-). Her television credits include guest starring roles on *Spenser: For Hire* (1985-88), *Miami Vice* (1984-89) and *The Cosby Show* (1984-92).

Mario Lopez

Lopez portrayed muscleman A.C. Slater on the long running teen television series *Saved By the Bell* (1989-93). Lopez also starred in the telefilm *Breaking the Surface: The Greg Louganis Story* (1996) in the title role and has a regular role on the series *Pacific Blue* (1996-) for the USA Network. Lopez made his television debut as a youngster on the short-lived ABC series *A.K.A Pablo* (1984).

Perry Lopez
[born: Julius Caesar Lopez]
B: 7/31/1931

In a career that spans over forty years, Lopez has worked for such distinguished and legendary directors as Roman Polanski, who gave him his most notable role, as Detective Luis Escobar in the classic *Chinatown* (1974); John Ford in *Mister Roberts* (1955); and Raoul Walsh, who directed him in his film debut as Spanish Joe in *Battle Cry* (1954).

Warner Bros. put Lopez under term contract in 1953, and the actor subsequently appeared in *Drum Beat* (1954) and *The McConnell Story* (1955). He starred as a young ex-con in *The Steel Jungle* (1956), and he co-starred with Tony Curtis and Yul Brynner in *Taras Bulba* (1962).

The son of Puerto Rican parents, Esther and Alphonso Lopez, he was born in New York City and christened Julius Caesar. However, a few years later his parents relented and renamed him Perry. He was educated at Public Schools 57 and 172 and George Washington High School in New York, and then attended New York University. It was there that a chance meeting with director Joshua Logan in 1950 started him on an acting career. He stopped by the theater at which Logan was rehearsing the national company of *South Pacific* to pick up actress Diosa Costello for a lunch date. The director spotted Perry and asked him to read, and he got a role as a Seabee.

He left NYU and toured with *South Pacific* for three years. Lopez left the musical, returned to New York, and toured in summer stock productions. Then, in 1953, an automobile accident almost ended his life. While recuperating from his injuries with relatives in Los Angeles, an interview at Warner Bros. brought him a screen test that resulted in a contract, and the role in *Battle Cry*. More recently, he reprised the role of Detective Luis Escobar in *The Two Jakes* (1990), the sequel to Chinatown, and co-starred with Charles Bronson in *Kinjite: Forbidden Subjects* (1989). His other films include *I Died a Thousand Times* (1955), *Hell on Frisco Bay* (1956), *The Young Guns* (1956), *Omar Khayyam* (1957), *Cry Tough* (1959), *Flaming Star* (1960), *McLintock!* (1963), *Bandolero!* (1968), *Che!* (1969) and *Deadlock* (1969)

Priscilla Lopez

Born in the Bronx and raised in Brooklyn, Lopez is a dancer, singer and actress. She won an Obie Award and was nominated for a Tony for her performance on Broadway in *A Chorus Line*, and won the Tony for Featured Actress in a Musical in 1980 for *A Day in Hollywood, A Night in the Ukraine*. On television she was a regular on the series *In the*

Beginning (1978) as Sister Agnes and *Kay O'Brien* (1986) as nurse Rosa Villanueva. She has also guest starred on *All in the Family* (1971-79), *Trapper John, M.D.* (179-86) and *Family* (1976-80).

Rafael Lopez
[alternate spelling: Raphael]
B: 1948
Lopez was a juvenile actor in Hollywood films of the 1960s. His film credits include *The Young Savages* (1961), *Dime with a Halo* (1963) and *Trackdown* (1976).

Sal Lopez
B: 11/8/1954
A Mexican American actor, Lopez played a young recruit in Stanley Kubrick's *Full Metal Jacket* (1987) and appeared Edward James Olmos' *American Me* (1992). He made his feature film debut in the film version of Luis Valdez's *Zoot Suit* (1981). A busy working actor, Lopez has been featured in numerous television movies and feature film projects, most recently, *Selena* (1997), *Out to Sea* (1997), *Gabriela* (1999), *Luminarias* (2000) and *Price of Glory* (2000).

Sylvia Lopez
A Spanish-born actress, Lopez worked in Italian sand-and-spear epics of the 1960s that were dubbed into English and released in the States. Her credits include *Hercules* (1960) and *Herod the Great* (1961).

Trini Lopez
B: 5/15/1937
A Dallas-born Mexican American singer and recording artist, Lopez played a major role as Private Pedro Ramirez, one of the *Dirty Dozen* in the hit 1967 World War II action film of the same name. Lopez played himself in the films *Marriage on the Rocks* (1965) and *The Poppy Is Also a Flower* (1960). In 1964 he signed a five-picture contract with Twentieth Century-Fox, but no suitable film roles were found for him.

Lopez grew up in a Dallas ghetto in a one-room house with his parents, four sisters and a brother. He didn't finish high school, but his father taught him to play guitar and to sing. Lopez was discovered by Frank Sinatra, who signed him to his label, Reprise Records, for whom Lopez went on to record a number of top sellers. Lopez quickly became an international recording star with such hit records as "If I Had a Hammer" and "La Bamba."

Jose Lopez Rodero
B: 10/20/1937
Born in Madrid, Spain, the oldest of four children, Rodero entered films at age fifteen and since that time has worked on over 100 movies in a range of capacities, largely in Europe. Among the better known of the international films on which he served as either first or second assistant director are *Solomon and Sheba* (1959), *Spartacus* (1960), *King of*

Kings (1961), *55 Days at Peking* (1963), *Cleopatra* (1963), *Patton* (1970), *Papillon* (1973), *The Boys from Brazil* (1978) and *Conan the Barbarian* (1982). He was also associate producer of *Dune* (1984).

Eduardo Lopez Rojas
B: 1937
D: 8/1/99
Born in New York and raised in Mexico, Lopez Rojas appeared in almost two dozen feature films before his death in 1999. His credits include *Romero* (1989), *My Family* (1995) and *Herod's Law* (1999).

Linda Loredo
[born: Herlinda Loredo]
B: 1908
D: 8/11/1931
Born in Los Angeles to a prominent Mexican American family, Loredo did bit parts in silent films and appeared prominently in several Spanish-language Laurel and Hardy and Charley Chase comedy short subjects. Loredo appeared in the Spanish version of *The Shrimp* (1930) with Henry Langdon and in the English language version of *Come Clean* (1931), as Start Laurel's wife. She died at an early age after a long illness.

Jorje Luke
One of Mexico's leading film stars has appeared in such American films as *Outpost* (1944), *The Return of a Man Called Horse* (1976) *Ulzana'a Raid* (1972) and *The Evil That Men Do* (1984).

Barbara Luna
B: 1939
A beautiful, raven-haired actress, Luna has played a Latin in so many films and television shows throughout the 1950s, 1960s and 1970s that she has become closely identified with Mexican or Latin dancer, cantina girl, spitfire and señorita roles. Her father is Filipino-Spanish, her mother Hungarian-Italian and Jewish, and she was reared in a Puerto Rican neighborhood in New York City. Her father supported the family by working as a waiter at the Copacabana nightclub. She first came to public attention as a child actress in the original Broadway production of *South Pacific* (1949).

Her exotic good looks took her into an active film and television career in which she played Japanese Geisha girls, island girls, or Chinese and Mexican maidens. Luna made her television debut as a guest star on *Westinghouse Desilu Playhouse* (1958-60). As a young adult she scored as a blind nurse who helps Frank Sinatra in the film *The Devil at 4 O'Clock* (1961). She was also featured in *Ship of Fools* (1965) and *Dime with a Halo* (1963). Other credits include *Five Weeks in a Balloon* (1962), *Firecreek* (1968), *Che!* (1969), *Synanon* (1965) and *The Concrete Jungle* (1982). Her television credits include over 400 roles on episodic series and in movies-of-the-week.

Julio Macat

An Argentine-born cinematographer, Macat immigrated with his family to the United States at age fourteen. Macat shot the 1990 box office hit *Home Alone* for director Chris Columbus, and went on to such projects as *Ace Ventura: Pet Detective* (1994), *Moonlight and Valentino* (1995), *The Nutty Professor* (1996), *Home Alone 3* (1997), *Crazy in Alabama* (1999); and *The Wedding Planner* (2000), starring Jennifer Lopez.

Bill Maldonado

B: 5/25/1921

Maldonado was construction coordinator and supervisor on a number of films for the Mirisch brothers, including such large-scale international film productions as *Some Like It Hot* (1959), *The Great Escape* (1963), *Kings of the Sun* (1963, filmed in Mexico), *Hawaii* (1966), *Hour of the Gun* (1967, filmed in Mexico); *Gaily, Gaily* (1969); and *Fiddler on the Roof* (1971).

Maldonado served in the Armed Forces during World War II, and after his discharge went to work as a carpenter at one of the studios, where it was some time before he was admitted to the union. He landed work as a propmaker, which led to construction. His first film was a Gary Cooper Western called *Man of the West* (1958). He is now retired; his last film was *The Milagro Beanfield War* (1988).

Luis Mandoki

B: 8/17/1954

Raised in Mexico City, Mandoki attended college in San Francisco and London before making his international breakthrough with the drama *Gaby, A True Story* (1987). That film's success brought him to Hollywood where he made *White Palace* (1990) with Susan Sarandon and a remake of the comedy classic *Born Yesterday* (1993) with Melanie Griffith. He has also directed *When a Man Loves a Woman* (1994), starring Andy Garcia and Meg Ryan, *Message in a Bottle* (1999) starring Kevin Costner and Robin Wright Penn, and *Angel Eyes* (2000) starring Jennifer Lopez.

Adele Mara
[born: Adelaide Delgado]

B: 4/28/1923

Born in Dearborn, Michigan, Mara was a starlet at Republic Pictures and co-starred in two major hits with John Wayne in the late 1940s, *Wake of the Red Witch* (1949) and *Sands of Iwo Jima* (1949).

At the close of World War II, she was crowned Hollywood's new pinup girl over reigning Betty Grable by the service magazine *Yank*.

In 1941, Harry Cohn spotted her with Xavier Cugat's band at the Waldorf-Astoria in New York City and cast her as Rita Hayworth's younger sister in *You Were Never Lovelier* (1942). Later she was put under contract by Republic Pictures, where she appeared in many B Westerns such as *Bells of Rosarita* (1945) with Roy Rogers, *Girls of the Big House* (1945), *The Tiger Woman* (1945) and *Vampire's Ghost* (1945). She also starred for the studio in the big-budget *The Avengers* (1950) and *California Passage* (1950).

Margo
[born: Maria Margarita Guadalupe Teresa Estella Castilla Bolado y O'Donnell]

B: 5/10/1918

D: 7/17/1985

Margo will always be remembered as the girl in Frank Capra's *Lost Horizon* (1937) who withered and died a centuries-old woman as she fled the idyllic valley of Shangri-La.

Born in Mexico City and reared in the United States, Margo was taught dance by Eduardo Cansino, father of Rita Hayworth, and at age ten began her professional career dancing and singing at various community affairs.

Her aunt married Xavier Cugat, and Margo joined them in Cugat's band where, for a year and a half, they played at the Waldorf-Astoria in New York.

She was spotted by a talent scout in New York and made her film debut at age sixteen playing Carmen Brown, the discarded mistress of a middle-aged district attorney, in the Ben Hecht-Charles MacArthur production *Crime Without Passion* (1934). She went on to Hollywood and made *Rumba* (1935) with George Raft and Carole Lombard and *The Robin Hood of El Dorado* (1936) with Warner Baxter.

On Broadway she did *Winterset* (1935), a performance for which she received fantastic notices and which she repeated in the memorable 1936 film version.

She took a brief respite from acting and then appeared in films throughout the 1940s and early 1950s, most notably in *Cat People* (1942), *The Leopard Man* (1943), *A Bell for Adano* (1945) and *Viva Zapata!* (1952). She recalled in an interview, "I was exposed to a great amount of ignorant prejudice and it hurt me." She continued, "I was frightened by the whole situation at the studios. I didn't seem to fit in, in that environment. I was terribly young and inexperienced. People thought I was much older as I had registered on the screen as mature in my first picture but nobody realized I was then only eighteen."

Margo married actor Eddie Albert in 1945 and devoted herself largely to raising a family. She was deeply involved in Mexican American community affairs and founded Plaza De La Raza, a theater and cultural center in East Los Angeles. She was the mother of actor Edward Albert.

Constance Marie

A California native, Marie starred in Gregory Nava's multi-generational drama *My Family* (1995) as Toni Sanchez, an ex-nun and political activist. She worked with Nava two years later on *Selena* (1997) as Marcella Quintanilla, Selena's strong, supportive mother. Marie's additional feature film credits include *Body Rock* (1984) *Back to the Beach* (1987) and *Salsa* (1988). She has also worked on a number of telefilms and episodic series, such as *Union Square* (1997-98) and the hit comedy series *Spin City* (1996-).

Constance Marie.

Cheech Marin as Joe
Dominguez on the TV
series *Nash Bridges*.

Cheech Marin

B: 7/13/1946

Cheech Marin and his partner, Tommy Chong, as Cheech and Chong, were one of the most successful comedy duos of the 1970s with their drug and counterculture humor.

Cheech (short for "chicharron," a Mexican snack made of deep-fried pork skins) was born in Central Los Angeles. He was one of four children of a Los Angeles police officer and was raised in the San Fernando Valley.

A straight-A student in high school, Cheech also took the time to sing with neighborhood rock bands. After putting himself through college working as a dishwasher and janitor, he earned a bachelor of arts degree in English from the California State University at Northridge.

Cheech's break in comedy came when he drove to Vancouver, B.C., to audition for an improvisational comedy group called City Works, run by Tommy Chong. When the troupe broke up in 1970, Cheech and Chong formed their own comedy duo. Their first album, *Cheech and Chong*, went gold. Their second, *Big Bamboo*, was voted the number-one comedy album of 1972. Their third, *Los Cochinos*, brought them a Grammy Award.

Cheech and Chong teamed together in eight feature films. The first, *Cheech and Chong's Up in Smoke*, was the highest-grossing comedy of 1979, generating more than $100 million at the box office. Their other films are *Cheech and Chong's Next Movie* (1980), *Cheech and Chong's Nice Dreams* (1981), *Cheech and Chong: Things Are Tough All Over* (1982), *Cheech and Chong: Still Smokin'* (1983) and *Cheech and Chong' s The Corsican Brothers* (1984). They also made cameo appearances in *Yellowbeard* (1983) and in Martin Scorsese's *After Hours* (1985).

In 1985, after fifteen years together, Cheech and Chong decided to branch out into other projects and pursue their own creative ideas. Two years later Cheech wrote, directed and starred in *Born in East L.A.* (1987) for Universal Pictures. He did the voice of Tito the streetwise Chihuahua in Disney's animated film *Oliver and Company* (1988), and in 1994, he performed as the voice of Banzai the hyena in Disney's *The Lion King*. Marin hosted 1997 Latino Laugh Festival, and has appeared in *Desperado* (1995) with Antonio Banderas; *From Dusk Till Dawn* (1996) with George Clooney; and *Tin Cup* (1996) with Kevin Costner. Marin also portrayed Pancho in TNT's *The Cisco Kid* (1994) and Joe Dominguez in the series *Nash Bridges* (1996-).

Ada Maris

B: 6/13/1963

Maris starred for four seasons as Gina Cuevas, an immigrant nurse, on the NBC-television series *Nurses* (1991-94). Maris was born and raised in East Los Angeles, and began her performing career after attending Boston University and the University of California at Los Angeles. She co-starred with Tony Orlando in a series pilot that aired as an episode of *The Cosby Show* (1984-92).

Mona Maris

B: 11/8/1908

D: 3/22/1992

Born in Buenos Aires, Argentina, to a Spanish family, Maris made her screen debut in England in 1926. In Europe, she met Dolores Del Rio, who encouraged her to go to Hollywood. After a brief time at United Artists, she made *Romance of the Rio Grande* (1929) opposite Warner Baxter, followed by *Under the Texas Moon* (1930) and *The Arizona Kid* (1930), also with Baxter. She filmed *One Mad Kiss* (1930) simultaneously in English and Spanish, which marked the first screen appearance of Jose Mojica, lyric tenor for the Chicago Opera Company. Maris made many Spanish-language films, frequently appearing as a sophisticated woman. Her later films include *I Married an Angel* (1942), *The Falcon in Mexico* (1944), *Tampico* (1944), *Heartbeat* (1946), *Monsieur Beaucaire* (1946) and *The Avengers* (1950). She died in 1992, having retired from the screen many years earlier.

William Marquez

B: 3/14/1943

A Cuban Born actor, Marquez has appeared in over two dozen films to date. His feature film credits include *Deal of the Century* (1983), *8 Million Ways to Die* (1986), *Wrestling Ernest Hemingway* (1993); *Steal Big, Steal Little* (1994); *Dance with Me* (1998), *The Mask of Zorro* (1998) and *Forces of Nature* (1999). He has appeared in numerous episodic television series, such as *Quincy* (1963-83), *CHiPs* (1978-83) and *Hart to Hart* (1979-84).

Chris-Pin Martin

B: 11/19/1893

D: 6/27/1968

A famed character actor, Martin usually played lackadaisical Mexicans. He was best known for his role as Cisco's sidekick in a series of Cisco Kid films starring Cesar Romero.

Martin began in the motion picture business in 1911. For a time he was an extra, then he became what is known as a runner, recruiting Mexican and Indian extras. When a studio wanted any given number of these types rounded up, they'd call on Chris. When the formation of Central Casting ended this business, he turned to acting. His first part of any consequence was in *The Gay Desperado* in 1936. His other films include *Under the Pampas Moon* (1935), *The Cisco Kid and the Lady* (1939), *Frontier Marshall* (1939), *The Return of the Cisco Kid* (1939), *Stagecoach* (1939), *The Mark of Zorro* (1940), *Romance of the Rio Grande* (1941), *Robin Hood of Monterey* (1947) and *The Beautiful Blonde from Bashful Bend* (1949).

Martin was born in Tucson, Arizona, to Toro ("Bull") Martin, a Yaqui Indian, and his wife, Florence Morales Martin, a Mexican. His father rejoined his tribe during the Mexican-Yaqui troubles at the beginning of the century and is believed to have died in battle.

Possessing very little formal education, Martin early learned a lot about life while working at Silver Bell and other Arizona mining camps.

Somewhere along the line he picked up a knowledge of the barber's trade and served in the Army as a barber at Fort Snelling, Minnesota. In 1911 he returned to Arizona and joined a group of Indians whom Universal Studios was bringing to Hollywood for picture work. The wages were $5 a week and a ration of meat. Martin led an uprising when it was discovered that the meat was horsemeat. In 1912, he married Margaret Avell in Pomona, California, and he lived near Chavez Ravine in Los Angeles.

Richard Martin
[born: Herbert Pinney]
B: 12/12/1919
D: 9/13/1994
Born in Spokane, Washington, of Scots-Irish descent, Martin is best known for his role as Chito Jose Gonzales Bustamante Rafferty, Mexican-Irish sidekick to B Western hero Tim Holt in twenty-nine films at RKO in the late 1940s and early 1950s. Chito was tall, handsome, witty and could win any señorita's heart or beat any man in a fight. Martin actually created the role in the World War II film *Bombardier* (1943), with Randolph Scott and Pat O'Brien, as a character named simply Chito Rafferty. The character was transferred to an Old West setting for several Westerns that starred Robert Mitchum and James Warren, and then Chito was successfully paired up with Tim Holt.

He was typecast in the role, and when the film series ended in 1952, he decided to leave films. He went on to become a successful insurance agent.

Martin grew up in the predominantly Mexican American area of Los Angeles, where the family moved from Washington during the Great Depression. He picked up the accent he used so well in his film characterizations from the people in the neighborhood. Though not Latin, Martin is included here because he is so identified with the role of Chito and because he made Chito different from the stereotypical sidekick. In fact, Chito was taller and much better looking than his Western hero buddy, though perhaps not as smart.

Ricky Martin
B: 12/24/1971
A worldwide superstar, Martin burst upon the American music scene in 1999, with the smash hit "Livin' La Vida Loca." Prior to his musical success in the United States, he had already sold over 15 million albums throughout the world.

Born Enrique Martin Morales in Hato Rey, Puerto Rico, Martin in 1983 became a member of the teen group Menudo. In 1994 he landed a regular role on the television soap opera *General Hospital* (1963-) as Puerto Rican singer turned bartender, Miguel Moretz. Martin also provided one of the voices for the Spanish language version of Walt Disney's *Hercules* (1997). Martin starred in his own CBS musical television special in November 1999.

A Martinez
[born: Adolpho Martinez]
B: 9/27/1948

A native Californian, Martinez was age twelve when he made his professional singing debut at the Hollywood Bowl, where he won a talent competition. Later, while attending UCLA, he got his first feature film experience in *The Young Animals* (1968). He made his motion picture debut as the young Mexican American cowhand, Cimarron, in *The Cowboys* (1972), starring John Wayne.

He followed this in quick succession with *Once upon a Scoundrel* (1973), *Joe Panther* (1976), *Shoot the Sundown* (1981), *Beyond the Limit* (1983) starring Michael Caine and *Walking the Edge* (1983), among others. His extensive television credits include two daytime soap operas—*Santa Barbara* (1984-92), for which he won a Daytime Emmy Award in 1990; and most recently, *General Hospital* (1963-)—as well as numerous telefilms and a two year stint on the Emmy Award-winning *L. A. Law* (1986-94).

Among Martinez's feature film credits, he has starred as a Native American political activist in *Powwow Highway* (1989), which earned acclaim at several international film festivals; *One Night Stand* (1995), *Last Rites* (1998) and *What's Cookin'* (2000).

Alma Martinez
B: 3/18/1953

An actress, Martinez has appeared in such films as Luis Valdez's *Zoot Suit* (1981), as Della, the younger sister; Roger Spottiswoode's *Under Fire* (1983), as an unassuming secretary who is really a rebel; and Fred Schepisi's *Barbarosa* (1982), in the role of Willie Nelson's daughter. On television, Martinez was featured as a police sergeant in the syndicated series the new *Adam 12* (1989-90).

Carmen Martinez
B: 1933

Featured in *Heartbreaker* (1983) and *Fires Within* (1992), Martinez has also appeared in countless episodic television series.

Joaquin Martinez
B: 11/5/1932

A Mexican-born actor, Martinez left Mexico to work in American films. Martinez played the title role of the Indian renegade in *Ulzana's Raid* (1972), starring Burt Lancaster and directed by Robert Aldrich. He also appeared in *Joe Kidd* (1972), starring Clint Eastwood, and co-starred as the friendly Mexican peasant Mauro in *Revenge* (1990), starring Kevin Costner. His credits include guest appearances in dozens of television shows over the years.

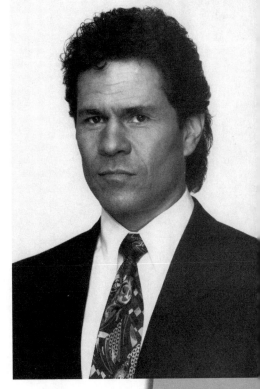

A Martinez on *L.A. Law.*

Patrice Martinez
[aka: Patrice Camhi]
B: 6/12/1963
Born in Albuquerque, New Mexico, Martinez is best known for her role as Carmen in *¡Three Amigos!* (1986). As Patrice Camhi, she starred for four seasons on the new *Zorro* (1990-93) television series starring Duncan Regehr. Her first film appearance was in *Convoy* (1978), directed by Sam Peckinpah, who encouraged her to study drama. Upon graduation from high school, she obtained a scholarship to study at the Royal Academy of Dramatic Art in London. Martinez guest starred twice on *Magnum, P.I.* (1980-88) opposite Tom Selleck and appeared in the film *Beetlejuice* (1988).

Ron Martinez
B: 11/17/1943
Born in Santa Ana, California, first assistant director Martinez worked his way up at Universal Studios, where he worked on such films as *Red Sky at Morning* (1971), *Dillinger* (1973), *Walk Proud* (1979), *Little Miss Marker* (1980) and *The Yakuza* (1975). His episodic television credits include *Quincy* (1976-83) and *Little House on the Prairie* (1974-83). He was an executive production manager and later a vice president of television production for Universal Television, where he was responsible for such shows as *Murder, She Wrote* (1984-96), *Major Dad* (1989-93), *Coach* (1989-97) and *Quantum Leap* (1989-93). This led to his association with Viacom Productions and projects such as *Diagnosis Murder* (1993-) and *Sabrina, the Teenage Witch* (1996-). He is currently working as a producer for Showtime's *Resurrection Blvd.* (2000-).

Tony Martinez
A comedic character actor of Puerto Rican decent, Martinez is best known for his portrayal of Pepino, the Mexican farmworker, on *The Real McCoys* (1957-63) television series. In the late seventies, he toured in the Broadway stage revivals of *Man of La Mancha* as Sancho Panza with Richard Kiley. He reprised his role in 1992, with Raul Julia in the lead.

Ricardo Mendez Matta
Born In Puerto Rico, Matta directed ten episodes of the USA Network series, *Weird Science* (1994-97) for producer John Landis. He has worked as 1st AD on such films as Ken Loach's *Bread and Roses* (2000), Stuart Gordon's *The Wonderful Ice Cream Suit* (1999), Carlos Avila's *Price of Glory* (2000) and the Fox telefilm *Ali* (2000). Matta is a graduate of USC and the Assistant Directors Training Program.

Graciela Mazon
Mazon has acted as costume designer on *Desperado* (1995), *From Dusk Till Dawn* (1996) *The Mask of Zorro* (1998), Antonio Banderas' directorial debut *Crazy in Alabama* (1999); *The Vertical Limit* (2000). A native of Mexico, Mazon is an accomplished artist whose paintings, drawings and sculptures have been exhibited in museums and galleries in Mexico, France and the United States. Mazon worked on several projects with

director Luis Valdez, including the TNT presentation of *The Cisco Kid* (1997) starring Jimmy Smits. Her Mexican film credits include *Miroslava* (1993) and *Queen of the Night* (1994).

Benny Medina

Medina was the co-producer of the hit NBC television series *The Fresh Prince of Bel Air* (1990-96) starring Will Smith. He has worked as the executive producer for the series *Getting Personal* (1998) and is credited as producer a and contributed the story for the feature film *Above the Rim* (1994).

Laura J. Medina

After working in a wide variety of capacities on features, documentaries and television, Medina began to specialize in the production aspects of independent feature films. A member of the Directors Guild of America, she has rapidly advanced from unit manager to production manager and later to line or co-producer on such films as *Frankenstein Unbound* (1990), *Born to be Wild* (1995), *Race the Sun* (Hawaii Unit, 1996) and *The Wonderful Ice Cream Suit* (1998).

Patricia Medina

B: 7/19/1920

The daughter of the Spanish-born English barrister Laureano Medina and Englishwoman Gouda Strode, Patricia attended school in England and France. This brunette beauty made her American film debut in MGM's *The Secret Heart* in 1946. She has more than forty film appearances to her credit, including *The Foxes of Harrow* (1947), *Fortunes of Captain Blood* (1950), *Valentino* (1951), *Desperate Search* (1952), *Botany Bay* (1953), *Snow White and the Three Stooges* (1961) and *The Killing of Sister George* (1968).

Bill Melendez

[born: Jose Cuauhtemoc (Bill) Melendez]

B: 1917

Animator Jose Cuauhtemoc (Bill) Melendez is best known as the producer of the "Peanuts" television specials. He has produced forty-nine specials and is considered one of the top independent animators in the industry.

A native of Mexico, Melendez started working for Walt Disney in 1938 during the production of the film *Fantasia* (1940) and has been in Hollywood ever since.

Tina Menard

A character actress and bit player for over fifty years, Menard is most noted for her participation in George Stevens' *Giant* (1956), in which she was responsible for the coordination of Mexican extras and bit players.

Sam Mendes
One of today's most celebrated theatre directors, Mendes made his feature film directorial debut with the Academy Award® winning *American Beauty* (1999). Born in England of Peruvian heritage and educated at Cambridge University, he directed the acclaimed Broadway revival of *Cabaret* and the recent production of *The Blue Room*, which starred Nicole Kidman.

John Mendoza
B: 1953
A half-Puerto Rican, half-Irish stand-up comedian, Mendoza was born in the Bronx, New York. He starred in the situation comedy *The Second Half* (1993).

Mauricio Mendoza
Born in Davis, California, Mendoza was raised in Colombia. He has been a series regular on *Angeles* (1999), a Sony/Tri-Star/Telemundo co-production, and has co-starred on the series *Babylon 5* (1994-98). Mendoza co-stars on the Showtime dramatic series *Resurrection Blvd.* (2000-) and has completed a role in the feature film *Blow* (2000), opposite Johnny Depp.

Ramon Menendez
The Cuban-born Menendez directed the celebrated 1988 film *Stand and Deliver*, his only major film to date. He studied at the American Film Institute, where he made several short films.

Alex Meneses
Born and raised in Chicago, Meneses is probably best known for her role as Teresa, the school teacher in *Dr. Quinn, Medicine Woman* (1993-98). She has also appeared in such feature films as *Kissing Miranda* (1995), *Selena* (1997), *My Father's Love* (1998) and *The Flintstones in Viva Rock Vegas* (2000).

Hector Mercado
B: 1953
A Puerto Rican actor, Mercado can be seen in *Slow Dancing in the Big City* (1978) and *Delta Force 2: Operation Stranglehold* (1990).

Ricardo Mestres
B: 1/23/1958
The former president of Disney's Hollywood Pictures, Mestres is a graduate of Harvard University. Mestres started as a production assistant and became a creative executive at Paramount Pictures in 1981. In 1982, he was promoted to executive director of production, Paramount; in 1984, vice president of production, Motion Picture Group; in 1985, vice president of production, Walt Disney Pictures; in 1986, senior vice president of motion picture production, Walt Disney Pictures; in 1988, head of Hollywood Pictures, a position he held until 1994.

As a producer, Mestres' credits include *Jack* (1996) with Robin Williams, *101 Dalmations* (1996) with Glenn Close, *Flubber* (1997) again with Robin Williams, and *Reach the Rock* (1998). As executive producer, he worked on *Home Alone 3* (1997).

Tomas Milian
B: 3/3/1937
A Cuban-born actor, Milian immigrated to the United States in the mid-1950s. He has appeared in such American films as *Cat Chaser* (1989), *Revenge* (1990) and *Havana* (1990). Milian has starred in over 100 Italian films and worked almost exclusively in Europe for almost two decades. He is the recipient of the Nostro d'Argento, Italy's equivalent to the Oscar®, for his role as the schoolteacher in Bernardo Bertolucci's *Luna* (1979). He co-starred with Rod Steiger and Shelley Winters in Francesca Maseli's *Time of Indifference* (1965) and starred in Michelangelo Antonioni's *Identification of a Woman* (1983).

Victor Millan
B: 8/1/1920
A Mexican American actor, Millan has given dignified portrayals in such classic films as Raoul Walsh's *Battle Cry* (1954), George Stevens' *Giant* (1956) and Orson Welles' *Touch of Evil* (1958). His other film credits include *Drum Beat* (1954), *Walk the Proud Land* (1956), *The Ride Back* (1957), in which he co-starred with Anthony Quinn, *The FBI Story* (1959) and *Boulevard Nights* (1979).

Born and raised in East Los Angeles, Millan served in World War II and always had the desire to be an actor. He used the G.I. Bill to study at the Pasadena Playhouse and at UCLA, where he attended classes with James Dean. He made his professional acting debut in 1951 co-starring in a Schlitz Playhouse production entitled *A Pair of Shoes*. For over forty years he has guest starred in most of the major television series. He was a series regular on the *Ramar of the Jungle* (1952-54) program and on the *Broken Arrow* (1956-60) series he played Taza, son of Cochise. He served for thirty years as a drama professor and department head at Santa Monica College.

Yvette Mimieux
B: 1/8/1939
A beautiful blonde actress, Mimieux specialized in ingenue roles under a long-term MGM contract in the early 1960s. Her father, Rene Mimieux, of French parentage, was born in London. Her mother, Carmen, was born in Mexico. She made her film debut in 1960 in the science fiction classic *The Time Machine* opposite Rod Taylor. Her other credits include *Where the Boys Are* (1960), *The Four Horsemen of the Apocalypse* (1962), *Light in the Piazza* (1962), *Diamond Head* (1962) and *Toys in the Attic* (1963).

Aurora Miranda
The younger sister of Carmen Miranda, Aurora appeared in the films *Phantom Lady* (1944), *Brazil* (1944) and *The Three Caballeros* (1945).

Carmen Miranda in
The Gang's All Here.

Carmen Miranda

B: 2/9/1909
D: 8/5/1955

"The Brazilian Bombshell," Miranda combined her radiant smile and personality with gyrating hips and samba rhythms to become one of the best-remembered performers of the 1940s. Her act was punctuated by extravagant fruit-topped headdresses, colorful skirts and platform shoes. Her success in Hollywood was instantaneous, and she was often imitated and parodied.

Miranda appeared in four Hollywood films, many of which were Technicolor musicals designed to encourage the Good Neighbor Policy between the United States and Latin America. She made many guest appearances on early television shows and was a top attraction at nightclubs throughout the States.

From 1932 to 1939, she was the most popular female performer in all of South America, where she sang on the radio, performed in nightclubs, made nine concert tours throughout the region, and starred in four movie musicals. She was brought to the United States by theatrical producer Lee Shubert and made her Broadway debut in 1939 with an appearance in the musical *The Streets of Paris*. She also performed a show at the Waldorf-Astoria Hotel and made her first American film appearance in *Down Argentine Way* in 1940. Although identified as a Brazilian, Miranda was actually born near Lisbon, Portugal. Her parents moved to Rio de Janeiro, Brazil, when she was a baby. The singer, actress and dancer died of a heart attack after taping a mambo dance number for American television's *The Jimmy Durante Show* in 1955. Her film credits include *That Night in Rio* (1941), *Weekend in Havana* (1941), *Springtime in the Rockies* (1942), *The Gang's All Here* (1943), *Doll Face* (1945), *If I'm Lucky* (1946), *Copacabana* (1947), *A Date with Judy* (1948), *Nancy Goes to Rio* (1950) and *Scared Stiff* (1953).

Robert Miranda

A former University of South Carolina student, Miranda began acting in college when a teacher prescribed it as a way of compensating for previously undiagnosed dyslexia. He then decided to move to New York to pursue an acting career. Miranda's feature film credits include *The Untouchables* (1987), *Midnight Run* (1988), *My Blue Heaven* (1990), *The Rocketeer* (1991), *Sister Act* (1992), *Lost in Yonkers* (1993), *Eraser* (1996), *Blue Streak* (1999) and the telefilm *The Rat Pack* (1998). He has garnered a sizable list of television credits, including a recurring role on the series *Roseanne* (1988-97).

Susan Miranda

B: 1949

Born in East Los Angeles, Miranda made her film debut at age twenty-one in *Flap* (1970), co-starring opposite Anthony Quinn. Miranda danced with the Jose Greco company and on the television series *Rowan & Martin's Laugh-In* (1968-73).

Miroslava
[born: Miroslava Stern]
B: 1928

D: 3/10/1955

Born in Prague, Czechoslovakia, Miroslava and her family immigrated to Mexico after escaping the Nazi occupation at the beginning of World War II. She learned to speak Spanish fluently, and after a beauty pageant victory she entered the Mexican film industry as an actress in 1946. She quickly ranked with Dolores Del Rio as one of the leading ladies of Mexican cinema. Miroslava co-starred in two Hollywood films, *The Brave Bulls* (1951), starring Mel Ferrer and Anthony Quinn and directed by Robert Rossen, and the adventure Western *Stranger on Horseback* (1955) opposite Joel McCrea. Miroslava committed suicide by taking poison after a disastrous affair with famed Spanish bullfighter Luis Miguel Dominguin.

Jose Mojica
B: 1896

D: 9/20/1974

An Argentine-born, internationally renowned opera singer, Mojica starred in Spanish-language film musicals in the 1930s produced in Hollywood, including the American film *One Mad Kiss* (1930).

Victor Mojica
B: 7/15/1940

A New York-born Puerto Rican actor, Mojica was featured in the films *The Final Countdown* (1980), *Ghost Dance* (1983) and *Bound by Honor* (1993). His television credits include guest starring roles on *Murder, She Wrote* (1984-96), *Hill Street Blues* (1981-87) and *The Streets of San Francisco* (1972-77).

Alfred Molina
The British-born Molina has an extensive resume in theatre and film, and was nominated for a Tony Award for his performance of *Art* on Broadway. His film credits include *Raiders of the Lost Ark* (1981), *Prick Up your Ears* (1987), *Enchanted April* (1992), *Maverick* (1994), *The Perez Family* (1995), *Boogie Nights* (1997), *The Imposters* (1998), *Magnolia* (1999) and *Choclat* (2000).

Carlos Montalban
B: 3/28/1904

D: 4/4/1991

The older brother of actor Ricardo Montalban, Carlos worked as an actor in the early 1930s in such films as *Flying Down to Rio* (1933). He later had a role in *The Harder They Fall* (1956), with Humphrey Bogart, and is perhaps best known as the general in Woody Allen's *Bananas* (1971). He did Spanish-language commercials and voice-overs for many years.

Ricardo Montalban.

Ricardo Montalban
B: 11/25/1920

Actor, caballero and star: these words aptly describe Ricardo Montalban, who has become a living symbol of the endurance and longevity of the Hispanic American artist in Hollywood. Few actors today can look back at a successful career during the heyday of MGM Studios as a contract player, through the exciting infancy of television, and on into the present.

Besides the success of his seven-year run as the mysterious Mr. Roarke on the television series *Fantasy Island* (1978-84), and his Emmy Award-winning portrayal of Chief Satangkai in the miniseries *How the West Was Won* (1977), Montalban enjoyed tremendous public and critical acclaim for his role as Khan in *Star Trek II: The Wrath of Khan* (1982) (a role he re-created from a previous appearance on the *Star Trek* (1966-69) series) and as the villain in *Naked Gun* (1988). Both films were box office smashes.

When asked to describe his most positive attribute, Montalban replied, "Tenacity." This, along with a devotion to his craft, his family and his Catholic faith, has been his touchstone. His steadfastness has allowed him to survive during the lean years when roles were scarce, which fostered his growth as a person and an actor. If film roles were not available, Montalban went to the stage, following the axiom: An actor is not an actor when he is not acting.

On stage, Montalban starred as Don Juan in George Bernard Shaw's *Don Juan in Hell*, a role he still considers the most challenging of his career. Top critics called him "superb," "awesome," "compelling," and "dashing." He went on the road with the production on three separate occasions from 1972 to 1976, on tours that lasted several months and visited over 150 cities, in collaboration with such talents as Agnes Moorehead and director John Houseman. He also won critical acclaim for his performance in the L.A. Music Center production of *The King and I* (1967) and the Broadway musical *Jamaica* (1957), which he starred in for two years with Lena Horne.

Born in Mexico City, the son of Jenaro and Ricarda Montalban, he is the youngest of four children. The family moved to Torreon in northern Mexico and away from the teeming city that had been Ricardo's early home. The young Ricardo learned to ride and swim, with the great outdoors as his playground.

After receiving his basic education in Mexico City, he was brought to the United States by his older brother Carlos. Ricardo finished his schooling at Fairfax High School in Hollywood, where he also made his theatrical debut in a number of school productions. It was there that he attracted the attention of studio talent scouts and was offered an MGM screen test after graduation. However, his brother convinced him to join him in New York to continue his studies. In New York, Ricardo was dazzled by the legitimate stage and talked his brother into letting him take a year's absence from college so that he might attempt to seek out acting opportunities.

He found himself among hundreds of aspiring young actors, ranking the rounds of talent agents, auditioning with dozens of others for the same role. But his break finally came when he was cast in a small part opposite Tallulah Bankhead in the stage play *Her Cardboard Lover*. From that point on, he became a much employed stage actor.

In 1941, he returned to his native Mexico and made thirteen Spanish-language films in four years. Montalban was nominated for the Ariel, the Mexican equivalent of the Academy Award®, for the film *Santa* (1943), in which he played a bullfighter. He was the most important leading man in Mexico at the time, and Louella Parsons, a noted columnist of the time, called him the "Tyrone Power of Mexico."

Montalban was then rediscovered by MGM through producer Jack Cummings, who went to Mexico looking for a young Mexican actor for a leading role opposite Esther Williams in *Fiesta* (1947). After the picture was released, Montalban was immediately put under contract for a ten-year period. He made three pictures with Esther Williams and danced with Cyd Charisse in several musicals.

In *Neptune's Daughter* (1949), he and Esther Williams introduced the hit song "Baby, It's Cold Outside." Several major dance numbers with Cyd Charisse in *On an Island with You* (1948) and *The Kissing Bandit* (1948) convinced audiences that Montalban was a dancer, when in actuality he had never before danced professionally.

Soon after, Montalban starred in another film, *Two Weeks with Love* (1950), with Jane Powell and the cover of *Life* magazine proclaimed him the "New Romantic Star!"

Montalban co-starred in three William Wellman films, *Battleground* (1949), *Across the Wide Missouri* (1951) with Clark Gable and *My Man and I* (1952) with Shelley Winters. While filming *Across the Wide Missouri*, he suffered a serious injury on location in the Colorado Rockies. A horse he was riding was spooked by the noise of a cannon firing and took off down a mountain trail. Montalban fell on some rocks, seriously injuring part of his spine. The injury left him in constant pain, with one leg partially paralyzed for many years, but through exercise, therapy and sheer willpower, he recovered the full use of his leg.

In his early MGM films, Montalban often portrayed the archetypal Latin Lover; he even starred in a film called *Latin Lovers* (1953) with Lana Turner. The actor also turned in some solid dramatic work in such films as *Border Incident* (1949), *Right Cross* (1950) with June Allyson and Dick Powell and *Mystery Street* (1950). He was released from his MGM contract (along with other big MGM stars) in 1953.

As a freelance star, Montalban appeared in *A Life in the Balance* (1955) with Anne Bancroft and Lee Marvin; as a Japanese Kabuki dancer in *Sayonara* (1957) with Marlon Brando; *Adventures of a Young Man* (1962) for director Martin Ritt; *The Money Trap* (1966) with Glenn Ford and Rita Hayworth; *The Singing Nun* (1966) with Debbie Reynolds; and *Sol Madrid* (1968).

His co-starring role with Shirley MacLaine as a Latin movie idol in *Sweet Charity* (1969), directed by Bob Fosse for Universal, was a great success. "It was really a satire on the Latin Lover," recalled Montalban. "The role was basically comedic and the circumstances that developed were quite hilarious."

Montalban had a co-starring role as Little Wolf in John Ford's Western epic *Cheyenne Autumn* (1964), in which he also worked for the first and only time with both Dolores Del Rio and Gilbert Roland.

His other English language films include *Mark of the Renegade* (1951), *Sombrero* (1953), *The Saracen Blade* (1954), *The Queen of Babylon* (1956), *Let No Man Write My Epitaph* (1960), *The Reluctant Saint* (1962), *Love Is a Ball* (1963), *The Longest Hundred Miles* (1967), *Blue* (1968), *The Deserter* (1971) and *The Train Robbers* (1973).

He has over 300 television credits, including many made-for-television films. Prior to the *Fantasy Island* series, Montalban attained new success after several years of film and television inactivity as a spokesperson for the Chrysler Cordova automobile in a series of national television commercials and print ads, making the car a top seller. After *Fantasy Island*, he co-starred as a Greek tycoon on *The Colbys* (1985-87) series, a spin-off of the popular nighttime soap *Dynasty* (1981-89).

Conchita Montenegro

B: 9/11/1912
An actress, Montenegro appeared in silent and sound films and in Spanish-language films produced in Hollywood in the 1930s. Her credits include *Caravan* (1934), *Grenadiers of Love* (1934), *Handy Andy* (1934), *Hell in the Heavens* (1934) with Warner Baxter and *Insure Your Wife* (1935) with Raul Roulien.

Maria Montez
[born: Maria Garcia Van Dahl de Santa Silas]
B: 6/6/1919
D: 9/7/1951
One of Universal's most beautiful and top money-making stars during the 1940s, Maria Montez is renowned for reducing the dance of the seven veils to one veil in *Arabian Nights* (1942), and she amused her public in *Ali Baba and the Forty Thieves* (1944) by her sinuous actions in a harem bubble bath. Montez made eighteen films for Universal, fourteen of them in color. Her name became synonymous with exotic adventures as Universal's "Queen of Technicolor Epics."

She was born in Ciudad Trujillo, Barahona, in the Dominican Republic. Her father was a Spanish consul, and she was educated in the Canary Islands, where she attended the Sacred Heart Convent. In her teens, Maria traveled in Europe. Her father held consular posts in South America, France, England and Ireland. After some minor stage experience in Ireland and a short-lived marriage, Montez come to New York. She was discovered in Manhattan in 1940 by a talent scout who had seen her picture in a magazine. Her progress in films was gradual. Universal offered her a movie contract at $150 a week, and the young actress began her Hollywood career with small roles in *The Invisible Woman* (1941) and in a Johnny Mack Brown Western, *Boss of Bullion City* (1941).

Her Spanish accent caused casting problems, and Universal loaned her to Fox for a small role as a Latin-spitfire type in *That Night in Rio* (1941), which was in color and featured Alice Faye, Don Ameche and Carmen Miranda.

The beautiful starlet captured public attention in *South of Tahiti* (1941), in which she played a jungle beauty, and *White Savage* (1943).

Maria Montez.

Universal soon discovered that, in a sarong, Montez could be serious competition for Paramount's Dorothy Lamour. Montez knew the value of publicity, and she was soon acting like a genuine movie star, receiving more publicity than better-established stars. She became a favorite pinup girl of servicemen during World War II. She was given a leading role in *Arabian Nights* (1942), an escapist exotic entertainment, and she looked stunning as Scheherazade. One critic's description of her role in the film applies to almost her entire career: "Maria Montez comes through ably in a role that consists chiefly of looking ravishing in scanty oriental costumes."

In *Cobra Woman* (1944), Montez had two roles as twin sisters, one good and one bad, involved in a snake cult. She followed with *Ali Baba and the Forty Thieves* and *Gypsy Wildcat* (1944). Her limitations as an actress became apparent when Universal cast her in *Bowery to Broadway* (1944) and *Tangier* (1946). Her last Universal film under contract was *Pirates of Monterey* in 1947, in which she was cast as a Spanish lady in an early California drama.

Her other films include *Moonlight in Hawaii* (1941), *Raiders of the Desert* (1941), *Bombay Clipper* (1942), *The Mystery of Marie Roger* (1942), *Follow the Boys* (1944), *Sudan* (1945), *The Exile* (1947) and *Siren of Atlantis* (1948).

She married French actor Jean-Pierre Aumont, and lived for several years in Europe, where she made a couple of French-Italian films. Montez died in September 1951 of an apparent heart attack.

Cecilia Montiel

Montiel her career as an architect in her native Peru. Working as a set designer on Alex Cox's film, *Walker* (1984), Montiel realized that she could apply all of her design abilities to the field of motion pictures. Since then she has become an internationally recognized production designer. Her film credits include *Desperado* (1995), *From Dusk Till Dawn* (1996), *The Mask of Zorro* (1999), *Crazy in Alabama* (1999).

Sarita Montiel
[born: Antonia Maria Abad]
B: 3/10/1928

Sarita Montiel was born in a small town near La Mancha, Spain, to a Spanish mother and a Moorish father. Early in her teens she won a beauty contest, which led to Madrid and work in films. Due to her success in Spanish films, she was signed for an American film, *That Man from Tangiers* (1953). In Mexico, she made fourteen films between 1951 and 1954.

Warner Bros. brought her to Hollywood for a co-starring role with Mario Lanza in *Serenade* in 1956. She was introduced to American film audiences in 1954 in *Vera Cruz*, opposite Gary Cooper and Burt Lancaster. She also starred as an Indian maiden opposite Rod Steiger in Sam Fuller's *Run of the Arrow* (1957).

Rod Steiger and Sarita Montiel on the set of *Run of the Arrow*.

Alex Montoya

B: 10/19/1907

D: 9/25/1970

A character actor, Montoya was featured in scores of films and television shows, usually as a heavy or bandit. He was born in El Paso, Texas, and among his feature film credits are *Conquest of Cochise* (1953), *Escape from Fort Bravo* (1953), *Apache Ambush* (1955), *Escape to Burma* (1955), *The Magnificent Seven* (1960) and *The Flight of the Phoenix* (1965) as Carlos Reyes, a Mexican oilfield worker.

Danny Mora

A stand-up comedian and comedy writer, Mora began his writing career on the *Laverne & Shirley* (1976-83) television series.

Esai Morales

B: 1963

Esai Morales is best known for his intense performance as Bob Morales, Ritchie Valens' half-brother, in *La Bamba* (1987) and as Sean Penn's Latin nemesis in *Bad Boys* (1983).

Born in Brooklyn, New York, Morales ran away from home at age fifteen because his mother would not let him study acting. He attended New York's prestigious High School of the Performing Arts while living in a group home as a voluntary ward of the state. He recalls, "I never graduated from school because I stopped going to any classes except my acting classes."

He appeared as a misfit in the stage production *Short Eyes* and in Paul Morrissey's *Forty Deuce* (1982), his first film. He was also seen on screen in *Rainy Day Friends* (1985) and *Bloodhounds of Broadway* (1989).

Among his proudest accomplishments is his role opposite Burt Lancaster in the television miniseries *On Wings of Eagles* (1986), in which he played an Iranian. In the 1990s, he appeared in more than half a dozen telefilms and more than fifteen feature films, including *Freejack* (1992), *Rapa Nui* (1994); *My Family* (1995); *The Disappearance of Garcia Lorca* (1997) and *The Wonderful Ice Cream Suit* (1998).

Jacobo Morales

A Puerto Rican-born actor, writer and director, Morales appeared in brief acting assignments in *Up the Sandbox* (1972) with Barbra Streisand and Woody Allen's *Bananas* (1971). More recent credits include *Linda Sara* (1994) and *Angelito Mio* (1998).

Morales starred in many television soap operas and theater productions in Puerto Rico. He directed his first film, *Dios los Cria*, a critical and satirical look at the new modern Puerto Rico, in 1980, and his second, *Nicolas y los Demas*, a romantic triangle involving two old friends, in 1985. *Whatever Happened to Santiago* (1989), the story of a widowed accountant whose life begins anew upon his retirement, was Morales' first feature in 35mm; it was nominated for the Best Foreign Language Film Oscar® in 1990. Since then he has directed *Linda Sara*, in which he also starred; and *Enredando Sombras* (1998).

Esai Morales.

Santos Morales

B: 6/1/1935

A Puerto Rican-born character actor, Morales is noted for his roles as the Marine drill instructor in the Vietnam War drama *The Boys in Company C* (1978) and as Joseph and Mary Rivas in *Cannery Row* (1982). He also has appeared in numerous television productions, including the nighttime soap *Santa Barbara* (1984-92).

Antonio Moreno
[born: Antonio Garcia Moreno Mantaugudo]

B: 9/27/1887

D: 2/15/1967

The first of Hollywood's suave Latin leading men of the silent movie era, Moreno had his greatest success in the 1920s, when he was ranked second only to Rudolph Valentino as the great lover of the screen.

Born in Madrid, Spain, he was destined to be a baker in the family business and began apprenticing at age nine. One day, two American tourists entered the bakery and were impressed with the boy. When they asked him his name, he replied, "Antonio Garcia Moreno Mantaugudo, at the service of you and God."

His mother permitted the two men to take the young Moreno to New York and place him in a school. Moreno began his acting career on the New York stage several years later but eventually gave up the New York stage for Hollywood. While playing bit parts on stage in Hollywood he was seen by D.W. Griffith, who launched him on his screen career.

Making his first screen appearance in 1914 in *The Voice of Millions*, the actor went on to star with Gloria Swanson in *My American Wife* (1923, silent), with Mary Miles Minter in *The Trail of the Lonesome Pine* (1923, silent), with Pauline Starke in *Love's Blindness* (1926, silent) and with Dorothy Gish in *Madame Pompadour* (1927, silent). Other movies included *Mare Nostrum* (1926, silent) with Alice Terry and directed by Rex Ingram, and *Romance of the Rio Grande* (1929). He starred with Greta Garbo in her second film, *The Temptress* (1926, silent).

Though Moreno made the transition to sound movies, he could not do it as a leading man and became a character actor in films such as *Rose of the Rio Grande* (1938), *Captain from Castile* (1947), *Thunder Bay* (1953), *Creature from the Black Lagoon* (1954) and *The Searchers* (1956). He directed some films in Mexico during the early 1930s and starred in that country's first sound film, *Santa* (1932). He died in 1967 at the age of seventy-nine.

Antonio Moreno and John Wayne in *The Searchers*.

Belita Moreno

And actress and on-set acting coach, Moreno's credits include *Mommie Dearest* (1981), *Swing Shift* (1984), *Nobody's Fool* (1986), *Men Don't Leave* (1990), *Clear and Present Danger* (1994) and the dark comedy *Grosse Pointe Blank* (1997). She has also guest starred on such episodic television shows as *Roseanne* (1988-97) and *Melrose Place* (1992-99).

Rita Moreno
[born: Rosa Dolores Alverio; aka: Rosita Moreno]
B: 12/11/1931

Her career as an actress, singer, dancer and comedienne has brought Rita Moreno the distinction of being one of only a few women to win an Oscar®, an Emmy, a Grammy *and* a Tony—the four most prestigious awards a performer can receive.

She was born in Humacao, Puerto Rico; after her parents divorced, she came to New York City with her mother at age five. Recognizing her daughter's talent, her mother held down two jobs in New York so that Rita could start dancing lessons. "Whenever I heard music," she recalls, "I used to dance around the room and show off for my grandmother." By age seven, she was performing professionally in local clubs. At thirteen, she made her Broadway debut in *Skydrift* (1945) with Eli Wallach, and by fifteen she had abandoned her formal education to work as a singer and dancer in Spanish Harlem and anywhere else that offered a booking.

It's a period of her life on which she still looks back with a shudder. "Often the only audience we had were the waiters. Even if there were no customers the management paid us and we had to give value for money," she recalled in a 1993 interview. Two days in a Broadway play and a handful of radio shows later, she was given the cinema seal of approval in the form of a contract with MGM from Louis B. Mayer, who saw her upon the insistence of an MGM talent scout who had discovered Moreno a few years earlier but felt her too young for movies at the time.

She made her film debut in an independent film called *So Young, So Bad* (1950), in which she was billed as Rosita Moreno. MGM changed her name, and her first film there was *The Toast of New Orleans* (1950), followed by *Pagan Love Song* (1950), and a bit part in the classic musical *Singin' in the Rain* (1952). After two years her contract was dropped. "I was shattered. I had visions of being the next Lana Turner. And then at nineteen, I was through. I couldn't go back to New York, I was ashamed. So I stayed on in Hollywood and did what every other actor did to survive. I worked in B movies and did television shows. I played all those roles the same way. Barefoot with my nostrils flaring."

She went to Twentieth Century-Fox where she became the resident "Latin Inferno." In eleven years she made fourteen films, among them, *Garden of Evil* (1954), *The Yellow Tomahawk* (1954), *Seven Cities of Gold* (1955) and *Untamed* (1955), in which she played mainly Indian squaws, Mexican dancers and handmaidens. "I did it because I needed the money for basics—like rent, food and analysis."

Rita began to be referred to in the press as "Rita the Cheetah." "One reporter claimed I had a necklace made from the teeth of my boyfriends. So with an image like that I wasn't offered many passive or interesting parts."

She won excellent notices for her performance as Tuptim in the film adaptation of *The King and I* (1956), and in 1960 Jerome Robbins cast her as Anita, the fiery Puerto Rican in *West Side Story* (1961). She auditioned for co-director/producer Robert Wise and screen tested and won approval from the Mirisch brothers, who were the producers. She gave a memorable performance that won her an Academy Award® in 1961 for Best Supporting Actress. "I couldn't believe it. I had just turned thirty and thought I had finally broken through as an actress. I was sure the Oscar® would change everything, but I soon found out that it made no difference." She did not work for seven years in films because all the roles offered her were the conventional Rosita and Pepita type roles and she refused to demean her talent any longer.

The following year she went to London. There she starred in *She Loves Me*, which led to her return to Broadway as the star of Lorraine Hansberry's last play, *The Sign in Sidney Brustein's Window* (1964).

In the 1960s and 1970s she was seen on Broadway as the female lead in the musical *Gantry* starring Robert Shaw, in Neil Simon's *The Last of the Red Hot Lovers* with James Coco, in *The National Health*, and in *The Ritz* as Googie Gomez, a role written especially for her by Terrence McNally. She won a Tony Award on Broadway for her Googie portrayal and re-created the role in Richard Lester's film version. "By playing Googie Gomez, I was thumbing my nose at all those Hollywood writers responsible for lines like, 'Ju Yankee Peeg, ju rape my seester. I keel ju!'" said Moreno.

Rita Moreno co-stars with Dennis Morgan in *Cattle Town* (1952).

Among her other films are *The Ring* (1952), *Latin Lovers* (1953), *Jivaro* (1954), *The Lieutenant Wore Skirts* (1956), *The Vagabond King* (1956), *The Deerslayer* (1957), *This Rebel Breed* (1960), *Summer and Smoke* (1961), *Marlowe* (1969); *The Night of the Following Day* (1969) with Marlon Brando; *Popi* (1969); *Carnal Knowledge* (1971) with Jack Nicholson; *The Boss' Son* (1978) and *The Four Seasons* (1981).

On television, Moreno won her Emmy for a performance in an episode of the series *The Rockford Files* starring James Garner, in which she played a free-spirited Polish hooker. Moreno starred for two seasons on *9 to 5* (1982-83) as Violet and had a recurring role as Burt Reynolds's estranged wife on the *B.L. Stryker* (1989-90). She won a Grammy Award for her contributions on the album recording of *The Electric Company* (1971-76), a popular children's educational television series in which she appeared regularly.

Her most recent credits are the feature film, *The Slums of Beverly Hills* (1999) and the role of Sister Peter Marie on the acclaimed HBO series *Oz* (1997-).

Rosita Moreno

B: 1904
D: 4/25/1993

A dancer from Buenos Aires, Moreno starred in many films during the late 1920s and 1930s, including *Her Wedding Night* (1930) with Richard Arlen and *Walls of Gold* (1933) with Norman Foster. In 1945, she returned to Paramount for a small part in *A Medal for Benny* (1945). She married a theatrical agent and remained in the States.

Ruben Moreno

A veteran character player, Moreno was usually cast as an Indian or a Mexican bandit in Westerns such as *El Dorado* (1967) and television shows including *Bonanza* (1959-73) and *The Big Valley* (1965-69).

Alberto Morin

B: 1903
D: 5/5/1989

A character actor, Morin portrayed many different nationalities during his fifty-five year career. Among his credits were *Gone with the Wind* (1939), *Casablanca* (1942), several John Ford films, *Two Mules for Sister Sara* (1970) and Robert Redford's *The Milagro Beanfield War* (1988).

A native of Puerto Rico, Morin moved to Europe at an early age and in the 1920s went to Mexico, where he studied acting. He moved to Hollywood in the 1930s to work in Spanish-language versions of films. Aside from acting, he was Errol Flynn's riding double in several films.

Morin appeared frequently in the theater and acted in many television shows, including *I Love Lucy* (1951-57), *Hopalong Cassidy* (1949-51) and *The Jack Benny Show* (1950-65). He also worked as a technical director and dialogue coach.

Michael Moroff

A towering Mexican American character actor, Moroff was featured in the film *La Bamba* (1987), and has appeared in several other feature films, including *Angel Town* (1990), *Desperado* (1995), *The Wonderful Ice Cream Suit* (1998); and the video release, *Candyman: Day of the Dead* (1999). In addition, he has many television credits and played Pancho Villa in an episode of *The Young Indiana Jones Chronicles* (1992-93).

Bob Morones

B: 1/6/1943

Morones was casting director and associate producer on Oliver Stone's *Salvador* (1986) and casting director on Stone's Academy Award®-winning *Platoon* (1986). He was also casting director on *Romero* (1989), starring Raul Julia; and Edward James Olmos' *American Me* (1992).

Movita
[born: Maria Luisa Castenada]

B: 4/12/1917

A Mexican actress, born in Nogales, Arizona, known simply as Movita. She costarred in MGM's classic 1935 production of *Mutiny on the Bounty* as the native girl who falls for Byam (Franchot Tone); the film also starred Clark Gable and Charles Laughton. She was also seen to good effect in John Ford's *The Hurricane* (1937), again as a native island girl.

While visiting friends in San Francisco, Movita attended a party where she was seen by Pandro S. Berman, who was then in charge of production at RKO Studios. He signed her to a contract, and she made her film debut in *Flying Down to Rio* (1933). Later, she made a film in Mexico and then appeared in *Mutiny on the Bounty*. In an interview, she reflected that, despite the attention she received for the film, MGM lost interest in promoting her after producer Irving Thalberg, who had been a supporter, died.

She went to Monogram Studios for a series of four Westerns in which she played the female lead. Movita later toured Europe in a musical/comedy review and made one film in England, *The Tower of Terror* (1942). Upon her return to the States in 1948, she appeared in minor roles in such films as *Fort Apache* (1948), *Red Light* (1949), *Kim* (1950), *Wagon Master* (1950), *Saddle Legion* (1951) and *Last of the Comanches* (1952). She has remained active in the film industry, doing both extra and featured work in recent years.

Movita in *Mutiny on the Bounty*.

Frankie Muniz

B: 1985

Though young, Muniz has already collected an impressive list of credits. He has guest starred on the popular *Spin City* (1996-), and is currently the star of the hit *Malcolm in the Middle* (2000-) and the telefilm *Miracle in Lane 2* (2000). He has also appeared in the feature films *It Had to be You* (1998), *Lost & Found* (1999) and the critically acclaimed *My Dog Skip* (2000).

Corrina Mura
[born: Corinna Wall]

Born in San Antonio, Texas, where she worked as a singer and an entertainer, Mura played Andrea, the French singer, at Rick's Cafe in the classic 1942 film *Casablanca*. She also appeared in *Call Out the Marines* (1942).

Karmin Murcelo

A Cuban-born actress, Murcelo co-starred with Charles Bronson in *Borderline* (1980). Her film credits include *Walk Proud* (1979), *Stir Crazy* (1980), *The Big Score* (1983), *Revenge* (1990) and *Bound by Honor* (1993). She has appeared in hundreds of television series episodes as well as the miniseries *Centennial* (1978) and *The Blue Knight* (1973). Most recently, she has played the role of Dr. Rodriguez on the soap opera *Port Charles* (1997-)

Daniel Nagrin

B: 1922

A Bronx-born Broadway dancer-choreographer, Nagrin was featured in a Mexican ballet sequence in *Just for You* (1952), starring Bing Crosby and Jane Wyman. He also choreographed the native Fijian dance sequences for *His Majesty O'Keefe* (1953), starring Burt Lancaster.

J. Carroll Naish

B: 1/21/1897

D: 1/31/1973

A consummate character actor, Naish portrayed every nationality and ethnic type over his long Hollywood career. With his dark complexion, black hair and mustache, he was closely identified with the many Latin roles he portrayed in films. He was nominated for an Academy Award® as Best Supporting Actor for his role as a Mexican American father in *A Medal for Benny* (1945).

Some of the other films in which he portrayed a Latin include *The Kid from Spain* (1932), *The Robin Hood of El Dorado* (1936), *Down Argentine Way* (1940), *Blood and Sand* (1941), *That Night in Rio* (1941), *The Fugitive* (1947) and *The Last Command* (1955).

In actuality Naish was an Irish American born in New York City, but as he explained in an *Los Angeles Herald Examiner* interview (1/27/73): "When the part of an Irishman comes along, nobody thinks of me, they call Barry Fitzgerald." Naish received two Oscar® nominations and amassed over 200 film credits.

Rick Najera

Najera has written for such episodic television series as *Dr. Quinn, Medicine Woman* (1993-98) and was a staff writer on the hit series *In Living Color* (1990-94).

Gregory Nava

B: 4/10/1949

A director and writer of Mexican and Basque heritage, Nava was born in San Diego and attended UCLA Film School, where his student film based on the life of Spanish poet Federico Garcia Lorca, entitled *The Journal of Diego Rodriguez Silva*, was named Best Dramatic Film at The National Student Film Festival. . In 1973, he wrote, produced and directed *The Confessions of Aman*, which won the 1976 Best Feature Award at the Chicago International Film Festival.

Nava was nominated for an Academy Award® along with Anna Thomas for their original screenplay for the film *El Norte* (1984), which Nava also directed. Shot on a limited budget, this moving and often harrowing film about two young Guatemalan refugees who endure numerous hardships in order to reach the American border was one of the first contemporary films to address honestly and compassionately the state of the immigrant experience in America today

Nava went on to direct *A Time of Destiny* (1988), starring William Hurt and Timothy Hutton; wrote and directed *My Family*, starring Jimmy Smits; *Selena* (1997), starring

Gregory Nava (right) with Edward James Olmos (left) on the set of *Selena*.

Jennifer Lopez; and *Why Do Fools Fall in Love?* (1998), starring Halle Berry, Lela Rochon and Vivica A. Fox.

Guillermo Navarro

Navarro's most recent film credits as director of photography *The Long Kiss Goodnight* (1995), directed by Renny Harlin; *From Dusk Till Dawn* (1996), his third collaboration with director Robert Rodriguez, Quentin Tarantino's *Jackie Brown* (1997) and Columbia Pictures' *Stuart Little* (1999). His other films with Rodriguez include *Desperado* (1995), starring Antonio Banderas; and Rodriguez's segment of the anthology film *Four Rooms* (1995). Navarro's additional film credits include TNT's *The Cisco Kid* (1994) starring Jimmy Smits; *Cronos* (1993), which won the Critics Award at the 1993 Cannes Film Festival and was the official Mexican entry for the Academy Awards®; and *Cabeza de Vaca* (1991), which was also an official Academy Award® entry from Mexico.

Taylor Negron

B: 1958

An actor/comedian of Puerto Rican-Italian heritage, born in Glendale, California, Negron is notable in several roles as an oversexed Latin party boy. He made his motion picture debut in 1982 as a love-struck, eye-popping intern in director Garry Marshall's *Young Doctors in Love*. He has since appeared as Rodney Dangerfield's Puerto Rican son-in-law, Julio, in *Easy Money* (1983), and in *Fast Times at Ridgemont High* (1982), *Bad Medicine* (1985), *Punchline* (1988), *Nothing But Trouble* (1991) and as a psychotic hitman in *The Last Boy Scout* (1992). Recent credits include *I Woke Up Early the Day I Died* (1998), *Civility* (1999), *Can't Stop Dancing* (1999) and *This Space Between Us* (1999).

Marisol Nichols

Nichols has appeared in a variety of television and feature film projects ranging from the telefilm *Friends 'Til the End* (1997), to feature films such as *Vegas Vacation* (1997), *Can't Hardly Wait* (1998) and *Bowfinger* (1999). Currently, she is starring in the Showtime series *Resurrection Blvd.* (2000-).

Barry Norton
[born: Alfredo Biraben]

B: 6/16/1905

D: 8/24/1956

A supporting actor, Norton worked in films from the 1920s until the mid-1950s. He was born in Buenos Aires, Argentina, and began his career in silent film productions like *The Lily* (1926) and *What Price Glory?* (1926). His ability to speak Spanish came in handy when sound films arrived, and he appeared alternately in many Hollywood-produced English- and Spanish-language productions.

(Left to right) Ramon Novarro, John Gilbert and Roy D'Arcy, on the set of *A Certain Young Man* (1928), pose for a publicity shot.

Ramon Novarro
[born: Jose Ramon Gil Samaniegos]

B: 2/6/1899

D: 10/31/1968

A leading man of silent films and early talkies, Mexican-born Novarro was one of Hollywood's first great Latin Lovers, a forerunner of a generation of darkly handsome young men with flashing eyes who were considered surefire box office successes during and after Valentino's reign as a popular sex symbol.

Novarro's fame crested in silent films and he never achieved the same heights of popularity in talking pictures; however, he did co-star with Greta Garbo in *Mata Hari* in 1931. In later years he continued his career as a character actor in films and television.

Novarro was born in Durango, Mexico, in 1899 into a well-to-do family. In 1913, his dentist father brought his wife, five sons and four daughters to California to escape from Pancho Villa and the Mexican Revolution.

When Ramon and his brother Mariano arrived in Los Angeles looking for work, they had just $100 between them. Young Ramon worked as a grocery clerk, theater usher, piano teacher, cafe singer and bit player until he was finally spotted by Marion Morgan, a dance instructor, who gave him a place in her vaudeville act. She sent him to New York, and Novarro's job for Miss Morgan led to a real break when Ferdinand Pinney Earle signed him to play the lead in *Omar Khayyam* on the West Coast. Rex Ingram, the famous silent screen director, heard about Novarro, saw him dance in a pantomime called *The Royal Fandango* at the Hollywood Community Theater, and engaged him to play Rupert of Hentzau in the 1922 version of *The Prisoner of Zenda*.

Novarro was an immediate hit. He followed this success with roles in *Trifling Women* (1922, silent), *Scaramouche* (1923, silent), *Where the Pavement Ends* (1923, silent), and *The Arab* (1924, silent), which ultimately rocketed him to stardom and international fame. However, it was as Ben-Hur in the classic 1926 epic of the same name that the actor's popularity reached its apex.

By 1934 Novarro had given up on Hollywood but kept busy with concert and theater performances. He made one film in Italy and another in his native Mexico. In 1948, he accepted a role in John Huston's *We Were Strangers* (1949) and followed this with an important part in *The Big Steal* (1949) at RKO. Next came *The Outriders* (1950) and *Crisis* (1950), both at MGM, the studio at which he gained his greatest fame. He received good reviews for his work in a small role in *Heller in Pink Tights* (1960) with Sophia Loren and Anthony Quinn, directed by George Cukor. His other films include *The Red Lily* (1924, silent), *Thy Name Is Woman* (1924, silent), *The Midshipman* (1925, silent), *Ben-Hur* (1926, silent), *Lovers?* (1927, silent), *The Road to Romance* (1927, silent), *The Student Prince in Old Heidelberg* (1927, silent), *A Certain Young Man* (1928, silent), *Devil May Care* (1929), *The Flying Fleet* (1929, silent), *The Pagan* (1929, silent), *Call of the Flesh* (1930), *In Gay Madrid* (1930), *Daybreak* (1931), *Son of India* (1931), *Huddle* (1932), *The Son-Daughter* (1932), *The Barbarian* (1933), *The Cat and the Fiddle* (1934), *Laughing Boy* (1934) and *The Night Is Young* (1935). Novarro also made occasional guest appearances on such television shows as *Bonanza* (1959-73).

He was found beaten to death after an apparent robbery at his Hollywood Hills home on October 31, 1968.

Danny Nunez

A veteran character actor and bit player, Nunez appeared in such films as *Viva Zapata!* (1952), *The Professionals* (1966), *Close Encounters of the Third Kind* (1977) and *The Legend of the Lone Ranger* (1981). His numerous television credits date back to the mid-1950s.

Miguel A. Nunez, Jr.

Raised in rural, North Carolina, Nunez headed to California at age seventeen on a Trailways bus with only one suitcase and three sandwiches. His acting career began when he used another aspiring thespian's resume at an audition and landed a lead role in a pizza commercial. His feature film credits include *Harlem Nights* (1989), *Lethal Weapon III* (1992), *Streetfighter* (1994), *A Thin Line Between Love and Hate* (1996), *Why Do Fools Fall in Love?* (1998) and *Flossin'* (2000).

Jacqueline Obradors

Obradors is of Argentine parentage and made her television debut guest starring in an episode of *Parker Lewis Can't Lose* (1990-93) followed by a guest starring role on the short-lived series *Vanishing Son* (1995). Her feature film credits include *Six Days Seven Nights* (1998), in which she plays Harrison Ford's girlfriend; and *Deuce Bigalow: Male Gigolo* (1999), with Rob Morrow.

Maria O'Brien

The daughter of actor Edmond O'Brien and actress Olga San Juan, Maria appeared in the 1975 film *Smile* as a pushy beauty pageant contestant who sells her Mexican American heritage for all it is worth.

Edward James Olmos
B: 2/21/1946

Edward James Olmos has become one of the most important Hispanic American actors of his generation with work in such films as *Zoot Suit* (1981), *The Ballad of Gregorio Cortez* (1983), and his Academy Award®-nominated role as the teacher Jaime Escalante in *Stand and Deliver* (1988). Olmos seeks out roles that both satisfy a performer's natural artistic desires and realistically dramatize socially relevant themes or incidents.

Olmos became a household name through his sullen, no-nonsense role as Lieutenant. Martin Castillo on the innovative police television series *Miami Vice* (1984-89), which ran for five years and won Olmos an Emmy Award and the Hollywood Foreign Press Association's Golden Globe Award for Best Supporting Actor in a Continuing Drama Series. Olmos made his directorial debut with a *Miami Vice* episode entitled "Bushido," which was the highest-rated show of the entire series according to the A.C. Nielsen ratings.

Olmos spent most of his youth in the Boyle Heights section of East Los Angeles, the son of a Mexican father and a mother born of three generations of Mexican American heritage.

Music had a profound effect upon him as a young man, and it was his immersion in the worlds of performers like James Brown and Little Richard that led him, at age thirteen, to announce to his parents that he wanted to pursue a career as a singer and dancer.

Following his graduation from Montebello High School, Olmos formed a band that he named Eddie and the Pacific Ocean. For several years, the group played various Sunset Strip clubs until, in 1968, it became the house band at the private club The Factory.

While music occupied Olmos' evenings, studies at East Los Angeles College and later California State University filled his daytime hours. Although he was initially interested in the social sciences of psychology and criminology, his later education leaned more toward dance and the theater.

In the early 1970s, he began acting in various small theater productions around Los Angeles and landed several bit parts in episodic television shows like *Kojak* (1973-78) and *Hawaii Five-O* (1968-80) while continuing to sing (and deliver antique furniture) to support himself and his family. He made his motion picture debut in a bit part in Floyd Mutrux's *Aloha, Bobby and Rose* (1975).

At age thirty-one, Olmos auditioned for and won the role that would alter his life, that of El Pachuco in Luis Valdez's *Zoot Suit*. The street theater musical, described by Olmos as "the first real play about Latinos," opened in 1978 for what was originally scheduled to be a mere ten-day run in Los Angeles. Instead, it ran a year and a half and then enjoyed a short but well-deserved run on Broadway, for which Olmos was nominated for a Tony and for which he won the prestigious Theatre World Award.

As a result of his work in the show, Olmos received accolades as a performer and became recognized as a positive role model for Latinos. He was honored by the American Theatre Wing for creating "one of three definitive performances in the history of the American Stage." He later reprised his stage role in the 1981 screen version of the successful musical for Universal Pictures.

When *Zoot Suit* closed on Broadway, Olmos was offered the role of an American Indian high beam steelworker in *Wolfen* (1981), starring Albert Finney, but he turned the part down, insisting that the producers cast a real Native American. When such efforts proved futile and the filmmaker returned to Olmos, he ultimately accepted the role, but only after securing the full approval and blessing of the American Indian Movement. Several years later, Olmos received a humanitarian award from the group.

He went on to play the title role in Robert M. Young's *The Ballad of Gregorio Cortez* (1983), a true turn-of-the-century story about a Mexican American farmhand unjustly accused of murder who became the object of the largest manhunt in Texas history.

The film debuted on the Public Broadcasting Service in the summer of 1982 and was then picked up for theatrical release by Embassy Pictures. For his work as an actor and associate producer on the film, Olmos was honored by the American Historical Association. Olmos and co-star Tom Bower devoted the next two years to promoting the film across the country. During this extensive national tour, Olmos coordinated his work on behalf of the film with personal appearances at public schools and prisons, enhancing Hispanic pride throughout the country.

Olmos appeared as a multiracial police detective in Ridley Scott's *Blade Runner* (1982) opposite Harrison Ford and in *Saving Grace* (1986) opposite Tom Conti.

In 1984, Olmos was invited by series creator Michael Mann to join the regular cast of *Miami Vice*. He declined the offer several times on the basis that he preferred to continue to seek out projects of a more personal nature, but eventually worked out an arrangement with Mann in which the actor would be allowed time off from the series if a project arose about which he felt strongly. Under those conditions, Olmos accepted the part of the austere, intense Lieutenant Castillo.

From the moment he first became aware of the project, Olmos' enthusiasm for *Stand and Deliver* extended well beyond playing the lead role; it resulted in his involvement as a member of the production team as well.

Edward James Olmos.

For his portrayal of the dynamic Bolivian-born teacher, Olmos was nominated for an Academy Award® as Best Actor. Olmos recalled his feelings when he heard he had been nominated: "It's like getting the best news and getting it thrown at your stomach. It's given to you at such a high dosage that it ends up making you queasy." He was in very good company that year, for his fellow nominees were Gene Hackman, Tom Hanks, Dustin Hoffman and Max von Sydow.

In 1992 Olmos made his theatrical feature film directorial debut with *American Me*, which he also starred in and produced. His other films include *Alambrista!* (1977), *Virus* (1980), *Triumph of the Spirit* (1989) and *Talent for the Game* (1991). He appeared as an angel in the Paul Rodriguez production of *A Million to Juan* (1994); as Pacos in *My Family* (1995); as Abraham Quintanilla in *Selena* (1997), and as Roberto Lozano in *The Disappearance of Garcia Lorca* (1997). Other recent credits include *The Wall* (1998), *Gossip* (2000) and the voice of Chief Tannabok in *The Road to El Dorado* (2000).

On television, Olmos has made guest appearances on such shows as *Touched by an Angel* (1994-) and *The West Wing* (1999-). His television include the miniseries *The Fortunate Pilgrim* 1988) and *Dead Man's Walk* (1996); the telefilms *Hollywood Confidential* (1997), *12 Angry Men* (1997), *The Taking of Pelham One, Two Three* (1998) and *Bonanno: A Godfather's Story* (1999).

Tony Orlando (left) and
Freddie Prinze (right).

Lupe Ontiveros

A versatile Mexican-American character actress, Ontiveros has been
featured in *My Family, Mi Familia* (1995), *Selena* (1997), the Oscar®-win-
ning *As Good As It Gets* (1997) opposite Jack Nicholson, *Gabriela* (1999),
Luminarias (2000) and the cable feature *Picking Up the Pieces* (2000).
Her other feature film credits include parts in *Zoot Suit* (1981), *The
Border* (1982), *El Norte* (1982), *The Goonies* (1985) and *Born in East L.A.*
*(*1987). She has numerous television and stage credits including a recurring role on the television series *Veronica's Closet* (1997-2000).

Tony Orlando

B: 4/12/1944

A Greek-Puerto Rican singer, songwriter and actor, Orlando hosted his
own musical variety television show on CBS, *Tony Orlando and Dawn*
(1974-76). He starred in the television film *Three Hundred Miles for
Stephanie* (1981) as a Mexican American police officer and made several guest appearances as a social worker on *The Cosby Show* (1984-92). In
1982, he appeared as Jose Ferrer in the telefilm *Rosie: The Rosemary
Clooney Story*.

Kenny Ortega

Considered the foremost choreographer for modern popular music,
Ortega is equally accomplished in film, stage and television work.
Ortega pioneered and set the standards of excellence for dance and
form in music videos. He has worked with Madonna, Cher, Diana Ross,
Billy Joel, Smokey Robinson, the Pointer Sisters and Miami Sound
Machine. Ortega is best known for his choreography for the 1987 smash
hit movie *Dirty Dancing*. For the movie *Salsa* (1989), he served as choreographer and as associate producer. Ortega's unique blend of dance
and film was developed through his association with the American
screen's living dance master, Gene Kelly, an association that began during the making of *Xanadu* (1980), starring Olivia Newton-John, for
Universal Pictures.

Ortega was born in Palo Alto, California, of Spanish parents. He grew
up in Redwood City California, and at an early age he developed an
interest in music and dance, earning scholarships to several dance
academies in the San Francisco area. As a teenager, his interest in the
arts expanded beyond dance and into theater.

At age thirteen, he began working as an actor in local repertory theater, which quickly became his passion. While still in high school, he
began associations with the Hyatt Music Theatre in Burlingame,
California, and the Circle Star Theatre in San Carlos, where as a company member he appeared in such shows as *Oliver!* with the late
Georgia Brown.

In 1968, he enrolled in Canada College, majoring in theater arts and
dance. The following year he landed the role of George Berger in the
San Francisco company of *Hair*. This was followed by a featured role in
The Last Sweet Days of Isaac for the American Conservatory Theatre. He
then played the role of Berger again in the national touring company
of *Hair*. After three years of touring, he returned to the San Francisco
area, where he began working with The Tubes, a multimedia recording

group. This began a new phase of his career; he staged and performed in five world tours with The Tubes.

At a Tubes performance at the Pantages Theater in Los Angeles, Cher approached Ortega to choreograph a television special. This marked the beginning of his successful choreography career and of a professional relationship with Cher that still continues. This association also led to his assisting Toni Basil on *The Rose* (1979), starring Bette Midler.

Following that film, Ortega served as co-choreographer on *Xanadu* and had the unforgettable experience of working with dancer/director/choreographer/actor Gene Kelly, who co-starred with Olivia Newton-John. Ortega credits Kelly with teaching him the art of choreographing for the camera. In the following years, he choreographed for television, stage shows, films and music videos.

Ortega's film credits as choreographer include *One from the Heart* (1982), *St. Elmo's Fire* (1985), *Ferris Bueller's Day Off* (1986) and *Pretty in Pink* (1986).

The choreographer's television directing debut came in 1988 with the short-lived series *Dirty Dancing* (1988-89). In 1990 he directed the pilot and several episodes of the series *Hull High* (1990), a program he also co-executive produced. He then choreographed *Newsies* (1992), a musical about turn-of-the-century newsboys in New York, which marked Ortega's feature film directorial debut, which he followed with *Hocus Pocus* (1993), starring Bette Midler.

Dyana Ortelli
B: 5/1/1961
Born in Nuevo Laredo, Mexico, and raised in California, Ortelli played a toughtalking Zoot Suiter in *American Me* (1992), a Tijuana beggar girl in *Born in East L.A.* (1987), a hooker in *La Bamba* (1987) and a Mexican village girl in *¡Three Amigos!* (1986). She co-starred as the wacky maid, Lupe Lopez, in the short-lived syndicated television series *Marblehead Manor* (1987-88). Recent credits include parts in *Luminarias* (2000) and *Picking Up the Pieces* (2000).

Humberto Ortiz
B: 10/12/1979
Born in Laredo, Texas, and raised in California, this child actor has been featured in such films as *¡Three Amigos!* (1986), *Salsa* (1989) and *Kickboxer II* (1991). Ortiz co-starred with his mother, Dyana Ortelli, on the syndicated series *Marblehead Manor* (1987-88).

Manuel Padilla, Jr.
B: 1956
A juvenile actor of the 1960s and 1970s, Padilla had important roles in *Dime with a Halo* (1963), *The Young and the Brave* (1963), *Robin and the Seven Hoods* (1964), *Tarzan and the Great River* (1967) and as a low-riding Mexican American teenager in *American Graffiti* (1973). He co-starred in the NBC-television series *Tarzan* (1966-68), starring Ron Ely, which was produced in Mexico. Padilla has been inactive in recent years, except for a small role in *Scarface* (1983).

Anita Page
[born: Anita Pomares]
B: 8/4/1910

An actress born of Spanish descent in Flushing, New York, the blonde and sexy Page was a leading lady of Hollywood silent films in the transition period from silent to sound. She began as an extra in 1924 and reached her peak in *The Broadway Melody* in 1929.

Joy Page
[born: Joanne Page]
B: 1921

The daughter of actor Don Alvarado and Ann Bayer (who later married Jack Warner), Page's best-known role is as the young Hungarian girl who offers herself to Colonel Renault in the 1942 Warner Bros. classic *Casablanca*. Her other film credits include *Kismet* (1944), *The Shrike* (1955) and *The Bullfighter and the Lady* (1951).

Nestor Paiva
B: 6/30/1905
D: 9/9/1966

A character actor born in Fresno, California, of Portuguese descent, Paiva appeared in 117 motion pictures, playing every type of role from comics to heavies. A flair for dialects and mimicry made him sought after to play characters of different nationalities. He became so skillful at these kinds of roles that he was often referred to as "that foreign actor."

Paiva decided from early boyhood that he wanted to become an actor. He attended St. John's School in Fresno, the University of San Francisco, and later the University of California at Berkeley, where he received his degree.

He made his stage debut at the Greek Theatre in Berkeley in *Antigone*. Following graduation, he did a series of plays in Oakland and San Francisco.

In 1934, he appeared in the L.A. Staging Company's production of *The Drunkard*, playing the role of Squire Cribbs, the villain. He continued in the role for eleven years and combined the work with film roles. Finally, Paiva's work load became so heavy that he was forced to resign from the production. Paiva made his film debut at Paramount in 1936. Among his many films are *Hold Back the Dawn* (1941), in which he played a hotel manager, *The Song of Bernadette* (1943), *Road to Utopia* (1945), *A Thousand and One Nights* (1945), *Badman's Territory* (1946), *Humoresque* (1946), *Carnival in Costa Rica* (1947), *Mighty Joe Young* (1949), *The Great Caruso* (1951), *Jim Thorpe—All American* (1951), *Comanche* (1956) and *Girls, Girls, Girls* (1962). His last film was *Caper of the Golden Bulls* in 1965.

His television credits include appearances on *I Love Lucy* (1951-57), *The Red Skelton Show* (1951-71), *The Loretta Young Show* (1953-55) and *Perry Mason* (1957-66).

Virginia Paris
Although best known for her role as Chairwoman Ortega, who opposes teacher Jaime Escalante in *Stand and Deliver* (1988), Paris has made over

100 appearances on such television shows as *Have Gun Will Travel* (1957-63), *Ironside* (1967-75), *Medical Center* (1969-76) and *Quincy* (1976-83).

Gil Parrondo

B: 1921

A two-time Academy Award®-winning Spanish production designer and art director, for his work on *Patton* (1970) and *Nicholas and Alexandra* (1971), Parrondo also received an Oscar® nomination for *Travels with My Aunt* (1972). His film credits as production designer include *The Wind and the Lion* (1975), *The Boys from Brazil* (1978), *Cuba* (1979), *Lionheart* (1987) and *Farewell to the King* (1989).

Born in Luarca, Spain, he began as an assistant director in 1945 in the Spanish film industry but quickly became more interested in using his architectural skills. He worked on many Spanish films, but his international film career as an art director began with *Mr. Arkadin* (1962) and such epic classics as *El Cid* (1961) and *Doctor Zhivago* (1965).

Pele

[born: Edison Arantes de Nascimento]

B: 1940

A popular, charismatic, internationally renowned Brazilian soccer star, Pele played Luis Hernandez, a British soldier from Trinidad who joins the Allied Paw soccer team, in John Huston's 1981 World War II drama *Victory* opposite Sylvester Stallone and Michael Caine. He has made other film appearances in European and Brazilian productions. In 1997, he was appointed as Minister of Sports by the Brazilian government.

Elizabeth Peña in *Jacob's Ladder.*

Pina Pellicer

B: 1940

D: 12/10/1964

A Mexican stage and screen actress, Pellicer starred as Luisa, opposite Marlon Brando, in the only film he directed as well as starred in, *One-Eyed Jacks* (1961). She won the Best Actress Award at the San Sebastian Film Festival for her work in the film.

She was discovered for the role while she was performing the lead in a Mexican stage production of *The Diary of Anne Frank*, which was later televised throughout Mexico. In 1963, she returned to the States, where she starred in "The Life Work of Juan Diaz" episode of Universal television's *The Alfred Hitchcock Hour* (1962-65). Suffering from depression, she committed suicide in her home in Mexico City in 1964.

Elizabeth Peña

B: 9/23/1959

This Cuban American actress was born in Elizabeth, New Jersey and spent her first eight years in her parent's native Cuba before emigrating to New York. Her father was an actor-writer-director and her mother is the creator and administrator of the Latin American Theatre ensemble. Before graduating from the High School of the Performing Arts, Peña had already appeared in over twenty off-Broadway plays.

Peña has contributed a gallery of vivid characterizations, including a tempestuous Latina in *Vibes* (1988) with Cyndi Lauper and Peter Falk; a murderously jealous ex-girlfriend in Peter Bogdanovich's *They All Laughed* (1981), starring Audrey Hepburn; Carmen, the sultry maid, in the hit *Down and Out in Beverly Hills* (1986); the jilted Rosie in Luis Valdez's *La Bamba* (1987); and Marissa in Steven Spielberg's **batteries not included* (1987). Peña also starred in the ABC series *I Married Dora* (1987-88) and the John Sayles series *Shannon's Deal* (1990-91) on NBC.

Her first major film role was in the highly acclaimed *El Super* (1979), followed by a co-starring role in *Crossover Dreams* (1985) with Rubén Blades. Since then, her credits include *Jacob's Ladder* (1990), *Free Willy 2: The Adventure Home* (1995), *Lone Star* (1996), *Rush Hour* (1998), *Seven Girlfriends* (1999), *On the Borderline* (2000) and the Showtime series *Resurrection Blvd.* (2000-).

Jose Perez
B: 1940
A diminutive Puerto Rican actor, Perez began as a child actor on the Broadway stage and has worked in motion pictures and television for over forty years. His film credits include *A Life in the Balance* (1955), in which he plays a young boy, and *The Sting II* (1983) and *Stick* (1985), in which he is featured as an adult.

Manuel Perez
An animator, Perez worked on over 200 projects for Warner Bros. in the course of a forty year career. Some films include *Baseball Bugs* (1946), *A Hare Grows in Manhattan* (1947), *I Taw a Putty Tat* (1948), *14 Carrot Rabbit* (1952), *Yankee Doodle Bugs* (1954), *Suppressed Duck* (1965), *Plastered in Paris* (1965), *Fritz the Cat* (172) and *The Lord of the Rings* (1978).

Pepito Perez
A famous clown, Pepito was born in Barcelona, Spain, and started his circus career with the Circa Parisch in Madrid, where he became a favorite of King Alfonso. He toured Europe and appeared in the United States at the New York Hippodrome and in vaudeville. He was also featured in the 1929 *Ziegfeld Follies*. Later, in Hollywood films, he performed in the circus sequence in *Lady in the Dark* (1944) and appeared in *A Medal for Benny* (1945). Perez coached Desi Arnaz and Lucille Ball in slapstick vaudeville routines for the pilot episode of *I Love Lucy* (1951-57), in which he also appeared.

Rosie Perez
B: 1966
Perez is the first Puerto Rican actress since Rita Moreno to make an impact in costarring roles in contemporary motion pictures that project her unique comic and ethnic personality as a sassy, smart-mouthed but vulnerable inner-city Hispanic American woman.

One of eleven children of Lydia and Ismael Perez, Rosie is a sixth-generation, 100 percent Puerto Rican native New Yorker. She made her motion picture debut and won recognition in the role of Tina in Spike Lee's controversial hit film *Do the Right Thing* (1989). She followed with a co-starring role as Gloria, an ex-disco queen from Brooklyn who aspires to become a contestant on the game show "Jeopardy" in

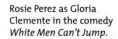

Rosie Perez as Gloria Clemente in the comedy *White Men Can't Jump*.

writer/director Ron Shelton's *White Men Can't Jump* (1992). In Tony Bill's *Untamed Heart* (1993) she plays a waitress, and in *Fearless* (1993) she plays a young mother who loses her baby. For her performance in *Fearless*, she was nominated for an Academy Award® as Best Supporting Actress. Recent film credits include *It Could Happen to You* (1994), with Nicolas Cage and Bridget Fonda; *Subway Stories: Tales from the Underground* (1997), for which she received executive producer credit; the title role in *Perdita Durango* (1997), *The 24 Hour Woman* (1999), which she also co-produced; and the voice of Chel in the animated DreamWorks feature *The Road to El Dorado* (2000).

She is also a noted choreographer and was nominated for an Emmy for her choreography of the Fox television series *In Living Color* (1990-94).

Severo Perez

Perez directed the *American Playhouse* presentation of *Tierra* (1994) and produced *Seguin* (1982), another *American Playhouse* presentation.

Alex Phillips, Jr.

Born in Mexico, the son of Hollywood cinematographer Alex Phillips, St., the younger Alex's fifty films as cinematographer are such Hollywood productions as *Buck and the Preacher* (1972), *Bring Me the Head of Alfredo Garcia* (1974), *The Savage Is Loose* (1974), *Caboblanco* (1980), *Fade to Black* (1980), *Little Treasure* (1985) and the television miniseries *Evita Peron* (1981).

Lou Diamond Phillips

B: 1962

This young actor rose to stardom in the role of the late rock 'n' roll legend Ritchie Valens in the hit film *La Bamba*, directed by Luis Valdez in 1987. Phillips has since starred in such films as *Stand and Deliver* (1988), *Young Guns* (1988), *The First Power* (1989), *Renegades* (1989), *A Show of Force* (1990), *Young Guns II* (1990) and *Ambition* (1991). His career seems to falter a bit in the early 90s, but regained force with such big budget projects as *Courage Under Fire* (1996) and *The Big Hit* (1998). Recent credits include *Brokedown Palace* (1999) and *Supernova* (2000). He is Dallas-born and -raised, and of Scots-Irish and Cherokee Indian background on his father's side and Filipino with Chinese and Spanish ancestry on his mother's side.

Miguel Pinero

B: 12/19/1946

D: 6/17/1988

A Puerto Rican-born playwright and actor, Pinero usually portrayed drug-addicted felons in films and television during the late 1970s and the 1980s. His award-winning play, *Short Eyes*, a searing portrayal of violent prison life, written while he was serving prison time in 1973 in Sing Sing, went on to win an Obie Award and the New York Drama Critics Circle Award as Best American Play in 1974. It was later made into a film, directed by Robert M. Young, for which he wrote the screenplay and in which he appeared. Pinero wrote scripts for the *Baretta* (1975-78) television series starring Robert Blake as well as several scripts for the *Kojak* (1973-78) and *Miami Vice* (1984-89) series. No one knew or wrote the terse, colorful and realistic language of the streets, drug dealers, pimps and prison inmates better than Pinero. Most of his writing was based on his own life experiences; this eventually hampered his creativity and productivity, and ultimately ended in his untimely death. His acting credits include *Times Square* (1980); *Fort Apache, The Bronx* (1981); *Breathless* (1983 Richard Gere version), *Deal of the Century* (1983), *Alphabet City* (1984) and *The Pick-up Artist* (1987).

Tony Plana
B: 4/19/1954
A Cuban-born actor, Plana has established himself as one of the most effective character actors in feature films. His varied film roles include the mohawked cadet Dellaserra in *An Officer and a Gentleman* (1982), Major Max in Oliver Stone's *Salvador* (1986), the bandido in *¡Three Amigos!* (1986) and the rat-like golden-toothed nemesis Feo in *Born in East L.A.* (1987). In addition, he starred as the gung ho Green Beret in Haskell Wexler's *Latino* (1985), the covetous waiter in the Oscar®-nominated *El Norte* (1984), the guerrilla priest in *Romero* (1989) and the journalist in *Havana* (1990). More recently, he has appeared in *Nixon* (1995), *Primal Fear* (1996), *Lone Star* (1996), *187* (1997), *The Disappearance of Garcia Lorca* (1997), the telefim *Noriega* (2000) and the Showtime series *Resurrection Blvd.* (2000-).

His television roles include three Emmy Award-winning special telecasts: the miniseries *Drug Wars: The Camarena Story* (1989), the PBS drama *Sweet 15* (1990), an episode of *L.A. Law* (1986-94) and appearances on *Murder One* (1995-97) and *The Drew Carey Show* (1995-).

Begonia Plaza
B: 1962
Plaza has worked with some of the film industry's most popular leading men, including Chuck Norris, Clint Eastwood, Nick Nolte, Eddie Murphy and Tom Cruise. Her feature films include *48 HRS.* (1982), *Heartbreak Ridge* (1986), *Maid to Order* (1987), *Born on the Fourth of July* (1989), *Delta Force 2: Operation Stranglehold* (1990) and *Heat* (1995). Born in Colombia, Plaza also lived in Spain before moving with her family at age nine to Los Angeles, where she developed an interest in acting.

Rose Portillo
B: 11/7/1953
A Mexican American actress, Portillo was featured in such films as *Walk Proud* (1979) and *Zoot Suit* (1981). On television, her credits include the series *Eisenhower and Lutz* (1988), the *American Playhouse* presentation of *Seguin* (1982) opposite A Martinez, and guest starring roles on *Party of Five* (1994-2000). She has appeared in the telefilms *Best Kept Secrets* (1984), *Palomino* (1991) and *Breaking Through* (1998).

The Los Angeles-born actress has also appeared in such films as *Exorcist II: The Heretic* (1977), *Where the Buffalo Roam* (1980), *The Mean Season* (1985) and *Love Always* (1997).

Jaime Prades

A native of Uruguay, Prades pioneered filmmaking in virtually every Spanish-speaking country, becoming an expert in production and global distribution. He served as vice president of Samuel Bronston Productions and was associate producer on such Bronston films as *El Cid* (1961) and *King of Kings* (1961).

Victoria Principal

B: 1/3/1950

An actress and television producer, Principal was born in Japan of an American career Army officer. She lived in many diverse places around the globe but began her dramatic studies with Max Croft in Springfield, Massachusetts, and in Miami. Principal went to New York to pursue an acting career and, earning her living as a model, decided to move to Hollywood. While studying with drama coach Estelle Harmons, Principal was picked by director John Huston for the role of Paul Newman's Mexican mistress in *The Life and Times of Judge Roy Bean* (1972). The films that followed were mostly forgettable, including *The Naked Ape* (1973), *Earthquake* (1974), *I Will, I Will . . . for Now* (1976) and *Vigilante Force* (1976).

In 1975, unhappy with her career, Principal quit for three years to become an agent. In a *TV Guide* interview (3/14/87), she recalled a producer candidly telling her, "You don't look American. Are you Latin or Eurasian?" Principal found that she did not fit the studio's image of a leading lady at that time.

In 1978, as a result of her successful work as an agent, she was asked to read for a part on a new television series called *Dallas* (1978-91). She won the role of Pamela Ewing on the hit long-running series, which brought her national and international fame. Principal played the role for nine years and left to pursue new career opportunities, forming her own television production company. Since then she has starred in the television films *Mistress* (1987), *Naked Lie* (1989), *Blind Rage* (1990), *Dancing in the Dark* (1995), *Love in Another Town* (1997).

Freddie Prinze

B: 6/22/1954
D: 1/29/1977

Prinze was born in New York City of Puerto Rican-Hungarian heritage. The comedian's brilliant career was cut short by his growing dependence on drugs and alcohol and his inability to cope with the pressures of Hollywood success. Prinze, a stand-up comedian who starred in major nightclubs as well as in the hit television series *Chico and the Man* (1974-78), died by his own hand, when, under the influence of drugs, he put a gun to his head and accidentally fired it.

Prinze's only dramatic role was in the telefilm *The Million Dollar Rip-Off* (1976), in which he starred as an ex-con electronics whiz who, with the aid of four females, attempts a robbery. He also made guest appearances on *Tony Orlando and Dawn* (1974-76). Prinze was the first Puerto Rican or Hispanic American comedian and television performer whose personality and special brand of street humor were able to cross over

Freddie Prinze, Jr.
in *She's All That*.

into mainstream America. Had he lived, it is possible that he would have had a career similar to that of black superstar comedian Eddie Murphy, who also came out of stand-up comedy and television.

Freddie Prinze, Jr.
B: 3/8/1976
The son of the late comedian, he was only a few months old when his father died.

Originally from Albuquerque, New Mexico, Freddie Prinze Jr. moved to Los Angeles in 1995 to focus on an acting career. He made his film debut in *To Gillian on Her 37th Birthday* (1996) and then appeared in the independent film *The House of Yes* (1997). These films led him to starring roles in *She's All That* (1999), *I Know What You Did Last Summer* (1997), *I Still Know What You Did Last Summer* (1998), *Wing Commander* (1999), *Down to You* (2000) and *Boys and Girls* (2000).

Tito Puente
B: 4/23/1920
D: 5/31/2000
Known as "The King of Latin Music," Tito Puente has contributed to the recognition and popularity of Latin music around the world. He was born in New York City of Puerto Rican parents and grew up in Spanish Harlem during the flowering of the big band era in the late 1930s, which led him to attend the New York School of Music. Puente was drafted into the Navy in 1942; after the war he expanded his knowledge of composition and arranging but got sidetracked into becoming a bandleader.

Prior to his screen appearance as himself in *The Mambo Kings* (1992), Puente appeared as a Xavier Cugat-like bandleader in Woody Allen's *Radio Days* (1987), in *Salsa* (1989) as himself, and *Armed and Dangerous* (1986) with John Candy. He also appeared in early soundies, the predecessors to today's music videos, with several Latin bands of the period. Puente also provided the opening theme music for several seasons of the long-running television series *The Cosby Show* (1984-92).

Luis Puenzo
B: 1946
An Argentinean, Puenzo directed and co-wrote *Old Gringo* (1989) for Columbia Pictures, starring Gregory Peck and Jane Fonda, following his Academy Award®-winning film *The Official Story* (1985). This acclaimed film, which Puenzo directed, produced and co-wrote, received more than thirty-five international awards, starting with the award for Best Actress and the Ecumenical Jury Award at the Cannes Film Festival in 1985 and culminating in the Academy Award® for Best Foreign-Language Film in 1985. *The Official Story* also received an Oscar® nomination for Best Original Screenplay.

Puenzo directed commercials from the age of nineteen in his native Argentina and has been awarded almost all the international prizes in this field. He had his own film production services company, Cinemania, in Buenos Aires for almost twenty years. In addition to *Old*

Gringo and *The Official Story*, Puenzo's feature credits include the 1973 film *Luces de Mis Zapatos* (Lights of My Shoes) and *Cinco Arias de Vida* (Five Years of Life), an episode of the 1975 film *Las Sorpresas* (Surprises).

Frank Puglia
B: 3/9/1892
D: 10/25/1975
A Sicilian-born actor, Puglia frequently played Latin types over a sixty-year career that included roles in a number of silent and sound films as well as stage and television productions. Among his many film credits are D.W. Griffith's silent masterpiece *Orphans of the Storm* (1922), *Viva Villa!* (1934), *The Gay Desperado* (1936), *For Whom the Bell Tolls* (1943), *The Road to Rio* (1947) and *Serenade* (1956).

John Quijada
Stuntman, stuntdouble and actor, Quijada has been featured in such films as *FBI Story* (1959), *The Alamo* (1960), *The Reward* (1965), *The Professionals* (1966) and *Joe Kidd* (1972). On television his work was featured on such series as *Gunsmoke* (1955-75), *Rawhide* (1959-66), *Bonanza* (1959-73), *The High Chaparral* (1967-71), and most recently in the miniseries *Lonesome Dove* (1989) as rancher Pedro Flores.

Anthony Quinn
B: 4/21/1916
Anthony Quinn's career spans more than sixty years, beginning with his first screen appearance in 1936 as a convict in *Parole* to his latest role as the patriarch Don Pedro in *A Walk in the Clouds* (1995). He co-starred opposite Kevin Costner as Tiburon Mendes, a charming but dangerous powerbroker in *Revenge* (1990); and assumed a trio of important character roles as an Italian don in *Mobsters* (1991), a domineering Italian father in Spike Lee's *Jungle Fever* (1991) and a romantic Greek widower in Chris Columbus's *Only the Lonely* (1991), opposite Maureen O'Hara.

Born during the Mexican Revolution in Chihuahua, Mexico, to an Irish-Mexican father and a Mexican mother, Quinn was raised in the slums of East Los Angeles, where his father found work at a film company. Though still young when his father died, he worked odd jobs to help support his mother, sister and grandmother.

Quinn has garnered two Academy Awards® for Best Supporting Actor, one in 1952 for his portrayal of Zapata's troubled brother Eufemio in Elia Kazan's *Viva Zapata!* opposite Marlon Brando, the other in 1956 for his interpretation of artist Paul Gauguin in Vincente Minnelli's *Lust for Life.* He also received Oscar® nominations as Best Actor for his portrayal of on Italian American rancher in George Cukor's *Wild Is the Wind* (1957) and for the role he has come to be so closely identified with, Zorba in *Zorba the Greek* (1964). He returned to that role in the musical stage version, *Zorba*, which ran for a year on Broadway and toured over seventy United States cities.

Quinn first appeared on a credit sheet when he was enrolled as a student at Polytechnic High School in Los Angeles. After nearly becoming a student of the great architect Frank Lloyd Wright, Quinn instead went to acting school to help correct a speech impediment and ended up playing stereotypical Hollywood roles as an Indian, a Mexican, a Pacific Islander, or a villain. In 1935 he gained his first professional acting job in the Los Angeles stage presentation of *Clean Beds*, which starred Mae West. It carried with it a weekly paycheck of $15. Quinn's big-screen break came in 1936 when he was signed to portray a Cheyenne Indian in Cecil B. DeMille's *The Plainsman* (1937), starring Gary Cooper. He vows he won his interview by claiming to be a member of the Blackfoot tribe and speaking the "doggannest Cheyenne gibberish you've ever heard." His early credits include such films as *Waikiki Wedding* (1937), *Blood and Sand* (1941), *They Died with Their Boots On* (1942), *Guadalcanal Diary* (1943), *The Ox-Bow Incident* (1943), *Buffalo Bill* (1944), *Black Gold* (1947) and *Tycoon* (1947).

In 1947 Quinn left Hollywood for the stage and appeared on Broadway in *The Gentleman from Athens*. Elia Kazan offered him the part of Stanley Kowalski in the road company of *A Streetcar Named Desire*, and he later followed Marlon Brando in the role in the Broadway production. In 1951, he returned to films in *The Brave Bulls*, as the manager of a gored toreador who fears a return to the bullring. Despite winning the Oscar® for Best Supporting Actor in *Viva Zapata!* he continued to be cast in the usual character parts: a Portuguese sailor in *The World in His Arms* (1952), a Madagascan pirate in *Against All Flags* (1952), a Seminole chief in *Seminole* (1953) and a Javanese despot in *East of Sumatra* (1953). He even played a Mexican bandit in *Ride, Vaquero!* (1953) to good reviews.

With no change in sight, Quinn left for Europe in search of better acting opportunities. Things did not fare well for him until he played the role of the brutish, gigantic circus strongman Zampano in Fellini's *La Strada* (1954). An internationally acclaimed film, it won the Best Foreign-Language Film Academy Award® in 1956. Quinn's performance was hailed by critics worldwide and established him as an international actor and star. Quinn said during a 1988 interview, "My life really started all over again when I did *La Strada*. I think *La Strada* really convinced people I was an actor."

In 1956, Quinn took on the challenge of directing the remake of the Cecil B. DeMille production of *The Buccaneer* (1958), at the request of his ailing father-in-law (Quinn had married DeMille's adopted daughter, Katherine DeMille, in 1938). Quinn had appeared in a small part in the original 1938 version. Featuring an all-star cast headed by Yul Brynner and Charlton Heston, the film did not measure up with critics or the public.

Back on Broadway, he and Laurence Olivier starred in the American production of *Becket* (1960), in which Quinn played King Henry II. About seven months after the opening, theatrical history was made when the two famous actors switched roles for the remainder of the play's year-long run, to the same high critical acclaim received on opening night. Shortly after that, Quinn co-starred with Margaret Leighton in *Tchin-Tchin* (1962) for nearly a year.

He entered into a period of rich characterizations in the 1960s with a series of roles beginning with *The Guns of Navarone* (1961) as a Greek resistance fighter, *Lawrence of Arabia* (1962) as an Arab leader, *Barabbas* (1962) in the title role in the biblical spectacle, and in two smaller dramas, *Requiem for a Heavyweight* (1962) as the washed-up fighter Mountain Rivera and *Zorba the Greek* (1964) as the uneducated, life-affirming Greek peasant.

In 1971 Quinn starred in the television series *The Man and the City* for ABC, in which he portrayed the Mexican American mayor of a southwestern city.

In 1972 he published his autobiography, *The Original Sin*, which became a best-seller.

Quinn's later films include *Guns for San Sebastian* (1968), *The Shoes of the Fisherman* (1968), *The Secret of Santa Vittoria* (1969), *The Don Is Dead* (1973), *The Greek Tycoon* (1978) and *The Lion of the Desert* (1981).

Acting and writing are not Quinn's only achievements. He is a recognized collector of paintings and sculptures and in 1982 his own talent as a sculptor and painter was publicly unveiled when the Center Art Galleries of Hawaii held an exhibition of his original artworks. The complete collection was sold out in three days, and enough back orders were on hand to occupy him full time as an artist for years.

However, in January 1983, he could not resist an offer to once again return to the stage to star in the musical version of *Zorba*, based on the Academy Award®-winning motion picture. Far surpassing everyone's expectations, the production ran on the road and in New York until August 1986. Quinn never missed even one of the 1,240 performances during the entire run of the play.

In 1986, the Hollywood Foreign Press Association gave Quinn one of its highest honors, the Cecil B. DeMille Award for Lifetime Achievement.

He was nominated for television's Emmy Award as Best Supporting Actor in a Miniseries for his portrayal of the father of Aristotle Onassis in *Onassis: The Richest Man in the World* (1988).

"Out of the 250 pictures I've done I've only worked with what I'd consider five or six great directors. I've had the joy of working with Kazan, Minnelli, Cukor and Fellini, who is one of the geniuses, and David Lean," remarked the actor in an interview. "I started working when I was a year and a half old and it's a way of life for me. I get bored doing nothing."

For television, in 1990 Quinn played the role of Santiago, the old Cuban fisherman, in an adaptation of Ernest Hemingway's *The Old Man and the Sea*. "I felt I was serving Santiago and not serving Anthony Quinn at any time in the picture. Each man, each actor has a soul, and he can only be guilty of what his soul wants to say. What my soul wanted to say about *The Old Man and the Sea* was very simple: You can be destroyed but not defeated."

Anthony Quinn as patriach Don Pedro in *A Walk in the Clouds.*

Ana Maria Quintana

Born in Chile, Quintana is a script supervisor on Hollywood films whose credits include *The Formula* (1980), *The Falcon and the Snowman* (1985), *Remo Williams: The Adventure Begins* (1985), *Jurassic Park* (1993), *Love Affair* (1994), the ill-fated *Waterworld* (1995), *Jurassic Park: The Lost World* (1997) and the award-winning *Saving Private Ryan* (1998) and *American Beauty* (1999).

Jose Quintero

B: 1925
D: 2/26/1999

An acclaimed Panamanian-born director, Quintero etched his career in the American theater interpreting the works of Tennessee Williams and Eugene O'Neill. He directed only one film, the 1961 Warner Bros. film *The Roman Spring of Mrs. Stone*, starring Vivien Leigh and Warren Beatty, based on a Tennessee Williams novel. Quintero has received two Tony Awards, two Drama Desk Awards, an Emmy and an Eugene O'Neill Gold Medal for his work in the theater and television direction.

Victoria Racimo

B: 12/26/1950

The dark-haired, dark-eyed Racimo has an extensive background in motion pictures, television and the theater and has portrayed a variety of ethnicities, including Vietnamese, Hawaiian, Mexican and Native American. Racimo is of Filipino, English, Irish and Native American descent. She began her career on the New York stage appearing in several award-winning productions at Joseph Papp's Public Theatre. The actress was featured in *Red Sky at Morning* (1971), *The Magic Garden of Stanley Sweetheart* (1971), *Prophecy* (1979) and *The Mountain Men* (1980). Her television credits include roles on *Falcon Crest* (1981-90) and in the telefilms *Green Eyes* (1973), *Brave New World* (1980) and *The Mystic Warrior* (1984).

Carlos Ramirez

B: 1915
D: 12/11/1988

A Colombian baritone, Ramirez appeared in various MGM musical films of the 1940s and 1950s in specialty musical numbers. He performed in *The Barber of Seville* at Carnegie Hall and at the Colon Theatre in Buenos Aires. He was discovered by MGM in 1943 during a successful singing engagement at New York's Waldorf-Astoria and was signed to a seven-year contract. His film credits include *Bathing Beauty* (1944), *Two Girls and a Sailor* (1944), *Anchors Aweigh* (1945), *Where Do We Go from Here?* (1945), *Easy to Wed* (1946), *Night and Day* (1946) and *Latin Lovers* (1953), for which he dubbed vocals for actor Ricardo Montalban.

Dan Ramirez

Ramirez has served as the casting director on such Columbia/TriStar television shows as *Solo en America* and *Los Beltran*. He also co-produced on the 1999 NCLR Alma Awards ABC special.

Loyda Ramos

B: 115/1958

A New York born Puerto Rican actress, Ramos has been featured in such films as *The Rich Man's Wife* (1996) and *Speed* (1994). Some of her other film credits include *Deal of the Century* (1983), *¡Three Amigos!* (1986), *Best Seller* (1987) and *Salsa* (1988).

Rudy Ramos

B: 1950

Born in Lawton, Oklahoma, Ramos was introduced as a regular cast member of the television series *The High Chaparral* (1967-71) during its last season. Among his credits are *Defiance* (1980), *Colors* (1988); and the telefilms *Everybody's Baby: The Rescue of Jessica McClure* (1989), *A Murderous Affairs: The Carolyn Warmus Story* (1992) and *Blindsided* (1993).

Vic Ramos

A longtime New York-based casting director, Ramos has been responsible for the casting of major television shows and feature films made in New York since the 1960s, including *The Godfather: Part II* (1974).

Donald Reed

B: 1905

D: 2/28/1973

Born in Mexico City, Reed was a leading man of a number of late Hollywood silent films. When sound was introduced, he turned to supporting actor roles. He usually played a Latin Lover or gigolo. His film credits include, *Naughty But Nice* (1927), *Showgirl* (1928) and *Evangeline* (1929).

George Regas

B: 1900

D: 12/13/1940

Born in Sparta, Greece, George Regas along with his brother, Pedro, came directly to America in a theatrical production of a Greek play that toured the United States. He appeared in the English-language plays *The Jade God* and *Zombie* on Broadway. In 1922 Mary Pickford brought him to Hollywood to play in *Lovelight*. His success was immediate. His brother, Pedro, followed with a role opposite Bebe Daniels in *Señorita* (1927). Among George Regas' many fine film credits are *Riptide* (1934), *Rose Marie* (1936), *Waikiki Wedding* (1937), *Beau Geste* (1939), *The Oklahoma Kid* (1939) and his last film, *The Mark of Zorro* (1940). He died on December 13, 1940, of throat cancer.

Pedro Regas

B: 1899

D: 8/10/1974

Pedro Regas carried on in many character roles. Five of his films were directed by Howard Hawks: *Scarface* (1932), *Tiger Shark* (1932), *Viva Villa!* (1934), *Only Angels Have Wings* (1939) and *To Have and Have Not* (1944). Among his other films are *Waikiki Wedding* (1937), *Juarez* (1939), *Viva Zapata!* (1952), *Lonely Are the Brave* (1962), *Flap* (1970) and *High Plains Drifter* (1973). He appeared in over a hundred episodic television shows over the years. He died at age seventy-four.

Duncan Renaldo.

Duncan Renaldo

B: 1904

D: 9/3/1980

Best known for his role as the Cisco Kid in films and on television during the late 1940s and throughout the 1950s, Renaldo was born in
Spain. He was orphaned and came to the United States in 1921 at age
seventeen. He landed in New York and worked in silent films as a studio artist, producer and assistant director. Soon, Renaldo became interested in acting and started securing parts in Hollywood films. In 1929,
he played the leading role of Esteban in the MGM classic *The Bridge of
San Luis Rey*. The picture was a success, and MGM decided to star
Renaldo with Harry Carey in *Trader Horn* (1931). Renaldo said, "I spent
two years in Africa making *Trader Horn*, 1929 and 1930. This was the
first time a Hollywood studio ever went on location in Africa. It was a
wonderful safari, and Africa was so much different than it is today. It
was still unspoiled. We shot over five million feet of exciting jungle
footage, with fantastic shots of the wild animals." *Trader Horn* was a
huge success, and Renaldo became one of the hottest stars in
Hollywood. Then the federal government prosecuted Renaldo for being
an illegal alien (he had claimed various citizenships). For the next four
years he was involved in difficult litigation and court trials, after which
he spent a year at McNeill Island detention center before being granted an unconditional presidential pardon in 1936 from Franklin
Roosevelt. Renaldo became a United States citizen in 1941.

Renaldo found it difficult to get work and finally landed a job as a
janitor at Republic Pictures. When studio president Herbert J. Yates, an
old friend, found out, he ordered that Renaldo be paid as an actor and
put him back in pictures. From 1936 until 1940, Renaldo played in a
number of Westerns and serials.

"I had an idea for a cowboy hero from Latin America. I told Mr. Yates
that if we did the character right, he would be able to sell his Westerns
all over Mexico and South America. We came up with the Three
Mesquiteers and I played the Latin member of the trio, named Rico. I
was right and those pictures were big hits in Latin America." John
Wayne was one of the trio in later films.

In 1941, when Fox dropped the Cisco Kid series, Renaldo, an associate
producer, bought the rights to the character from Doubleday and came
up with the idea of basing the Cisco Kid on Don Quixote and Pancho on
Sancho Panza. Renaldo subsequently starred in four Cisco Kid Westerns
with Martin Garralaga as Pancho, and the films were extremely popular. Renaldo entered the war effort and the series continued with
Gilbert Roland.

After the war, Renaldo continued the film series and decided that
the best man to play Pancho was Leo Carrillo, a top character actor who
had started out in silent films and had made over seventy-nine sound
features. Renaldo and Carrillo made six features as the Cisco Kid and
Pancho for United Artists. Carrillo was the perfect balance to Renaldo.
The Duncan Renaldo-Leo Carrillo team became the screen's most popular and best-known Cisco Kid and Pancho.

The movies were so successful that Renaldo and Carrillo decided to start the Cisco Kid television series in 1950. The television series was a great success and was the first Western to be produced especially for television in color. A total of 156 episodes were produced, the last filmed in 1955. Renaldo retired to a ranch in Santa Barbara and continued to make personal appearances until 1970.

Alejandro Rey

B: 2/8/1930
D: 5/21/1987

An Argentine-born actor, Rey appeared in American films and television shows. He was perhaps best known for his role as the swinging playboy Carlos Ramirez on the popular *The Flying Nun* (1967-70) television series from 1967 until 1970, opposite Sally Field.

Born in Buenos Aires, Rey appeared in such films as *Solomon and Sheba* (1959), *Fun in Acapulco* (1963), *Blindfold* (1966), *Mr. Majestyk* (1974), *Breakout* (1975), *Cuba* (1979) and *Moscow on the Hudson* (1984), in which he co-starred as a Cuban lawyer opposite Robin Williams.

His television work included guest appearances on such series as *Naked City* (1958-63), *Gunsmoke* (1955-75)," *Bob Hope Presents the Chrysler Theatre* (1963-67), *The High Chaparral* (1967-71), *Fantasy Island* (1978-84) and *The Love Boat* (1977-86). He played Rita Hayworth's father, Eduardo Cansino, in the television movie *Rita Hayworth: The Love Goddess* (1983).

Fernando Rey

B: 9/20/1918
D: 3/9/1994

An internationally recognized Spanish-born actor, Fernando Rey has appeared in over 150 films and is noted for his work with director Luis Buñuel yet is best known to American audiences for his role as the French drug dealer in the Academy Award®-winning *The French Connection* (1971) and its sequel, *The French Connection II* (1975).

Born in Galica, Spain, Rey had planned to be an architect until the Spanish Civil War interrupted his plans. He fought on the side of the Loyalists alongside his father, and the war brought them financial ruin. This led to work in the movies as an extra and later in bit parts. His knowledge of several languages soon gained him employment dubbing foreign films. Dubbing films proved to be good voice and acting training for the young Rey, who had never attended an acting school.

He has worked consistently in Spanish films over a fifty-year period in supporting roles and in American or international productions filmed in Spain.

His association with Luis Buñuel brought him worldwide critical acclaim, beginning with his role as Don Lope, the elderly guardian obsessed with his beautiful ward, in *Tristana* (1970). His other films for Buñuel include *Viridiana* (1961), *The Discreet Charm of the Bourgeoisie* (1972) and *That Obscure Object of Desire* (1977).

Alejandro Rey with Sally Field in the popular TV series *The Flying Nun*.

Ernie Reyes, Jr.
B: 1/15/1972
Born in San Jose, California, of Filipino heritage, Reyes has been competing in martial arts competitions under the tutelage of his father since the age of eight and has earned a black belt. He is the first child in the United States ever rated in the top ten in professional adult forms competition. The young actor starred in his own television series, *Sidekicks* (1986-87) and has appeared in six theatrical feature films, *The Last Dragon* (1985), *Red Sonja* (1985), *Teenage Mutant Ninja Turtles II: The Secret of the Ooze* (1991), *Surf Ninjas* (1993), *White Wolves II: Legend of the Wild* (1995) and *The Process* (1998).

Julian Reyes
A New York-born Puerto Rican actor, Reyes was featured in *Die Hard 2* (1990) and in *Point Break* (1991) as an FBI agent. On television he has guest starred on *Miami Vice* (1984-89) and was a regular on the syndicated series *What a Country* (1986-87).

Burt Reynolds
B: 1936
A popular leading man of part Native American heritage, Reynolds was born in Waycross, Georgia, and grew up in the area of Palm Beach, Florida. Because of his dark good looks, Reynolds began his career playing Indians and Mexican bandits in films and television shows, initially as a stuntman. Reynolds appeared on television in such series as *Riverboat* (1959-1960); *Gunsmoke* (1955-75), for three seasons as an Indian; *Hawk* (1966), as an Indian detective; and (1970-71). In the theatrical film *100 Rifles* (1969) he co-starred as Mexican bandit Yaqui Joe. His ascent to superstardom began with his performance in *Deliverance* (1972). The huge success of *Smokey and the Bandit* in 1977 took his career in new directions, and he has played a wide variety of roles. Reynolds has also directed a number of feature films and television shows, and, after a dip in popularity in the early 90s, roared back to prominence with roles in such films as *Striptease* (1996), with Demi Moore; and *Boogie Nights* (1997), which won him an Academy Award® nomination for Best Supporting Actor.

David Reynoso
A popular star in Mexico, Reynoso has worked in his native country for over three decades as an actor in 130 Mexican films. He has appeared in the American films *Rage* (1966), starring Glenn Ford and *Stick* (1985), starring Burt Reynolds.

Alfonso Ribeiro
B: 1968
A young actor, Ribeiro is best known for his role as Carlton Banks on the hit NBC-television series *Fresh Prince of Bel Air* (1990-96). More recently, he can be seen as Dr. Maxwell Stanton in the series *In the House* (1995-99). Ribeiro was also a regular as a teenager on the *Silver Spoons* (1982-87) series. He made his television debut at age eight on the PBS

series *Oye Willie*, and he created the leading role in the Broadway production of *The Tap Dance Kid*. His family is from the Dominican Republic.

Branscombe Richmond

B: 1955

A stuntman and actor, Richmond has appeared in more than 300 television shows and 100 feature films. His film credits include *Star Trek III: The Search for Spock* (1984), *Thief of Hearts* (1984), *Commando* (1985), *Licence to Kill* (1989), *Hard to Kill* (1990), *Grand Canyon* (1991), *Batman Returns* (1992) and *CIA II Target: Alexa* (1994). He also starred in the syndicated series *Renegade* (1992-97) with Lorenzo Lamas. He is part French, Hawaiian, Spanish and Aleutian Indian.

Maria Richwine

A Colombian-born, California-raised actress, Richwine co-starred as Maria Elena Holly, Buddy Holly's Puerto Rican wife, in the Academy Award®-nominated film *The Buddy Holly Story* (1978). She also co-starred on the short-lived television series *A.K.A. Pablo* (1984).

Lalo Rios

B: 2/7/1927
D: 3/14/1973

Rios played what could be considered the quintessential Mexican American or Chicano teenager of the 1950s in two films, *The Lawless* (1950) and *The Ring* (1952).

Rios was born in Sonora, Mexico, and moved to Los Angeles at an early age. While working as a carpenter, he was asked by some friends to play a role in a church drama. Director Joseph Losey discovered him on a construction job site in 1950, and he made his film debut in a major role in *The Lawless* as a Mexican youngster falsely accused of a crime in a small agricultural community in central California.

The following year he starred in the role of a young Mexican American boxer from East Los Angeles in *The Ring*, produced by the King Brothers.

Rios received good notices for his work from the critics, but was never able to land a leading role again due to the rigid Hollywood casting system of the time. (That he played those two leads had more to do with the director and the producers, who worked outside the established Hollywood mainstream.)

Rios played small roles in *Mark of the Renegade* (1951) and *City Beneath the Sea* (1970) for Universal and had a featured role in *Giant* (1956) for Warner Bros. and in Orson Welles' *Touch of Evil* (1958). After his small role in *City Beneath the Sea*, Rios never appeared in another film. He died of a liver ailment in 1973.

Carlos Rivas

B: 2/16/1925

A Mexican-born leading man and supporting actor, Rivas was popular during the mid-1950s and early 1960s. Rivas has appeared in numerous

American motion pictures, including *The King and I* (1956) as Tuptim's lover; *The Deerslayer* (1957) as an Indian; John Huston's *The Unforgiven* (1960) as an Indian chief; Alfred Hitchcock's *Topaz* (1969) as a Cuban; and *The Undefeated* (1969) and *True Grit* (1969), both with John Wayne. Rivas has guest starred on almost all the major television series of the past thirty-five years. He has starred in over twenty Mexican films. His other American film credits include *The Beast of Hollow Mountain* (1956) and *The Big Boodle* (1957).

Carlos Rivas
D: 1/15/1967
A sound technician who won three Academy Awards® for technical advancements in sound, Rivas worked for MGM from 1943 until his retirement in 1965.

Geoffrey Rivas
Actor Geoffrey Rivas' film credits include *La Bamba* (1987), *Born in East L.A.* (1987), *Bound by Honor* (1993), *Above Suspicion* (1995), *The Thirteenth Floor* (1999) and *Luminarias* (2000).

Chita Rivera
[born: Dolores Conchita del Rivera]
B: 1/23/1933
Broadway actress and dancer Chita Rivera made her motion picture debut in *Sweet Charity* (1969) as Shirley MacLaine's best friend. She created the role of Anita on Broadway in the original stage production of *West Side Story*, but the role in the film version went to Rita Moreno. Rivera also created the role of Dick Van Dyke's Latin secretary in the Broadway musical *Bye, Bye Birdie*. The film role went to Janet Leigh, but Rivera played the role in *The New Dick Van Dyke Show* (1971-74). A native of Washington, D.C., Rivera is of Puerto Rican descent.

Geraldo Rivera
B: 1943
A sometimes-controversial award-winning television broadcast journalist, television producer and syndicated talk show host for over twenty years, Rivera is half-Jewish and half-Puerto Rican. Though not an actor, he has played himself or a character like himself in several network television movies and specials.

Jorge Rivero
B: 1940
A popular Mexican leading man, Rivero has appeared opposite some of the American cinema's biggest stars in a number of American films shot in Mexico. Yet, despite his good looks, athletic physique and charming demeanor, the actor has never stirred much interest in the States.

He made his Hollywood film debut as an Indian chief in *Soldier Blue* (1970). He received co-star billing with John Wayne in *Rio Lobo* (1970), directed by Howard Hawks, in which he played a young cavalry officer. He also worked with Charlton Heston and James Coburn in *The Last Hard Men* (1976) and starred in *Fist Fighter* (1988).

Jose Rivera

B: 3/24/1955

A Puerto Rican-born screenwriter/playwright, Rivera has written mostly for television. He was a staff writer on the short-lived *A.K.A. Pablo* (1984) series. His play *The House of Ramon Iglesias* was filmed for the PBS *American Playhouse* series in 1986. He has written episodes of the situation comedy *Family Matters* (1989-98) and was co-creator and producer of the 1991-1992 series *Eerie, Indiana*.

Julian Rivero

B: 7/25/1891

D: 2/24/1976

A veteran character actor born in San Francisco, California, of Spanish-Mexican parents, Rivera left home at age sixteen to pursue a career as an actor in the theater in New York. He worked on the Broadway stage before arriving in Hollywood in 1920. He directed a few comedies and Westerns for World Film Co. and Canadian film companies. His first film appearance was in *The Bright Shawl* (1923, silent) for First National, which was filmed in Cuba.

Rivera appeared in dozens of B Westerns throughout the 1920s and 1930s with Harry Carey, Bob Steele, Tim McCoy, Gene Autry and Roy Rogers, usually as a Mexican bandit, a sidekick to the hero, or a don. His feature films include *The Night Rider* (1932) with Harry Carey, *The Westerner* (1940) with Gary Cooper, *The Outlaw* (1943), *The Treasure of the Sierra Madre* (1948) as the man who gives Bogart a haircut, *Broken Lance* (1954) with Spencer Tracy, *Don't Go Near the Water* (1957) with Glenn Ford and *The Reward* (1965) as El Viejo. On television he appeared on episodes of *The Cisco Kid* (1950-56), *Wyatt Earp* (1955-61), *Marcus Welby* (1969-76) and *The Bold Ones* (1969).

Miluka Rivera

The Puerto Rican born actress film credits include *Saturday Night Fever* (1977) as Maria's sister, *Taxi Driver* (1976) as a young hooker, *Fort Apache: The Bronx* (1981) and *Kramer vs. Kramer* (1979). In 1997 Rivera helped to establish a Screen Actors Guild branch office in Puerto Rico.

Victor Rivers
[born: Victor Rivas]

B: 1956

A Cuban-born actor, Rivers made his film debut in *8 Million Ways to Die* in 1986 playing a gang member. Rivers co-starred with Eddie Murphy and Sheryl Lee Ralph in *The Distinguished Gentleman* (1992) as Amanda, one of a trio of con artists who plot to get Murphy elected to Congress. He is also featured in *Bound by Honor* (1993), *Amistad* (1997), *The Mask of Zorro* (1998) and *What's Cookin'* (2000).

Estelita Rodriguez
[aka: Estelita]
B: 1930
D: 1966
Born in Juanara, Cuba, Rodriguez started her career at age nine singing on Cuban radio, where she was called "the Cuban Shirley Temple." While appearing at the National Theater in Havana at age fourteen, she was signed by an agent to appear at the famous Copacabana nightclub in New York City. She performed at the Copacabana for a season and was then signed by MGM. She lost the MGM contract when she had to return unexpectedly to Cuba and could not reenter the States for months.

She was put under contract by Herbert J. Yates, the head of Republic Studios, where she worked for almost ten years. She appeared in many Westerns and was a frequent co-star of Republic's singing cowboy star, Roy Rogers, in such films as *Along the Navajo Trail* (1945), On the *Old Spanish Trail* (1947), *Santa Susanna Pass* (1949) and *The Golden Stallion* (1949). She starred in *Belle of Old Mexico* (1950) and *Havana Rose* (1951). She was planning to star in a film about the life of actress Lupe Velez when she died in 1966 under mysterious circumstances.

Paul Rodriguez.

Marco Rodriguez
B: 7/10/1953
Rodriguez has played heavies in such feature films as *The Baltimore Bullet* (1980) and *The Rookie* (1990). He played Smiley in the film version of *Zoot Suit* (1981) and has appeared on many episodic television shows.

Paul Rodriguez
B: 1955
A stand-up Mexican American comedian, Rodriguez was born in Mexico and raised in California, the son of migrant workers. He came to the attention of producer Norman Lear while doing comedy warm-ups for Lear's show *Gloria* (1982-83). Lear ultimately wrote and developed a weekly series for him, *A.K.A. Pablo* (1984), focusing on the life of a Mexican American family in East Los Angeles. Although the ABC series was short-lived, it focused attention on Rodriguez's talents and was followed by series *Trial and Error* (1988) and *Grand Slam* (1990), in which he starred opposite John Schneider.

His feature film credits include *D.C. Cab* (1984), *The Whoopee Boys* (1986), *Quicksilver* (1986), *Born in East L.A.* (1987), *Made in America* (1993), *Rough Magic* (1995), *Mambo Cafe* (1999) and *The Price of Glory* (2000). Rodriguez's HBO and Fox comedy specials have attracted large viewing audiences. In 1994 he directed and starred in the comedy *A Million to Juan*, released by the Samuel Goldwyn Company.

Percy Rodriguez
Born in Montreal, Canada, the son of Maria and Juan Rodriguez, Percy plays dignified black American characters in films and episodic television programs in the United States. His film credits include *The Plainsman* (1966), *The Sweet Ride* (1968) and *The Heart Is a Lonely Hunter* (1968). His television work includes guest starring roles on such

series as *Naked City* (1958-63), *Peyton Place* (1964-69), *Route 66* (1960-64), *The Man from U.N.C.L.E.* (1964-68) and *Dynasty* (1981-89).

Robert Rodriguez
B: 1968

In 1991 Robert Rodriguez was a student at the University of Texas at Austin who had decided to make his first feature length film. The third of ten children born to Cecilio and Rebecca Rodriguez in San Antonio, Texas, he had prepared for film production classes by making his own home movies, recruiting family members as cast and crew. He wrote the script while sequestered at a drug research facility as a paid subject in a clinical experiment. That seven thousand dollar paycheck covered the cost of shooting the film. He planned to make the money back by selling the film to the Mexican home video market.

Robert Rodriguez.

The film was *El Mariachi* (1993) which Rodriguez wrote, directed, photographed, edited and sound recorded; and it gave him his big break into the American film industry. While shopping it to the video market, Rodriguez signed with a powerful agent at ICM. Columbia Pictures bought the distribution rights and signed Rodriguez to a two year writing and directing deal. *El Mariachi* then became the lowest budget movie ever released by a major studio and the first American film released in Spanish. *El Mariachi* won the coveted Audience Award for Best Dramatic film at the Sundance Film Festival and was also honored at the Berlin, Munich, Edinburgh, Deauville and Ubari (Japan) festivals. Rodriguez wrote about his experiences in *Rebel Without a Crew: Or, How a 23-year-old Filmmaker with $7000 Became a Hollywood Player* (1995) a diary of the making of *El Mariachi*. The book, published by Dutton/Signet, is currently in its third hardback printing.

He next wrote, directed and edited the film *Roadracers* (1994) starring David Arquette and Salma Hayek for Showtime's "Rebel Highway" series. His next feature was *Desperado* (1995) for Columbia, a sequel to *El Mariachi*, which Rodriguez wrote, directed produced and edited. The film introduced American audiences to Antonio Banderas as a leading man and also introduced the sexy and beautiful Salma Hayek. Next, Rodriguez wrote, directed and edited "The Misbehavers," one of the four segments of Miramax Films' *Four Rooms* (1995). He then teamed up with Quentin Tarantino on the outrageous *From Dusk Till Dawn* (1996) for Dimension films. Rodriguez directed a cast that included Tarantino, who wrote the script; George Clooney, Salma Hayek and Cheech Marin. He has also directed *The Faculty* (1998) and *Spy Kids*, slated for release in 2001.

Jaime Rogers
B: 1935

A Puerto Rican choreographer/director, Rogers was featured as an actor/dancer in the film *West Side Story* (1961). He has worked as a director/choreographer on many television shows with most of the top performing artists over the years. He directed episodes of the syndicated television series *Fame* (1982-87) and directed the musical numbers for the film *Breakin'* (1984).

Gilbert Roland
[born: Luis Antonio Damaso Alonso]

B: 12/11/1905

D: 5/15/1994

Gilbert Roland's career spanned over sixty years—from silent movies to his last screen role in the feature film *Barbarosa* (1982).

A resonant voice, athletic build, ever-present wristband, mustache and cigar or cigarette in hand are Roland's identifying on-screen trademarks. First as a romantic leading man, then later in supporting character roles, he became synonymous with action, adventure and romance as one of Hollywood's greatest stars. He has survived from silent films through the transition to sound, television, 3-D, CinemaScope and now video laser discs and cable television.

Roland was one of six children, born in Juarez, Mexico. His family moved to El Paso, Texas, during the Mexican Revolution when Pancho Villa threatened the lives of all Mexicans of Spanish ancestry (both his parents were Spanish-born.)

At an awards ceremony held by the organization Nosotros in his honor in 1980, Roland remarked, "As a child living near the Rio Grande, a great love came into my life. All my life I have loved all the people on the screen. It became an obsession."

He grew up in the barrios of El Paso, selling newspapers in 1913 in the plaza in front of Paso del Norte Hotel. He drifted to Hollywood during his teens with only $2.60 in his pocket, arriving in Los Angeles at age fourteen. Broke and desperate to get into the movies, he had to sleep on a park bench. A man who owned a shop near the park gave the boy $5, a lot of money in those days, to get something to eat. When Roland secured a job and was receiving a steady income, he returned and paid the man for his generosity.

After a few years of working at whatever jobs he could find, Roland found work as an extra in countless motion pictures, including *The Phantom of the Opera* (1925, silent) and *Blood and Sand* (1922, silent). "I worked as an extra for $2 a day and a box lunch alongside such would-be stars as Clark Gable," Roland recalled during an interview in 1982. "We all had something in common; we believed in ourselves while waiting for the chance to be discovered." He doubled for Ramon Navarro in *The Midshipman* (1925, silent). He remembers, "I was thrown into the icy waters of Chesapeake Bay at 2:00 a.m. for a scene."

Roland was discovered in a mob scene by agent Ivan Kahn, and was signed for the second lead in *The Plastic Age* (1925, silent), opposite Clara Bow. "An extra girl who was very beautiful asked if I would get a glass of water for her. In those days, things were so simple. The extra girls wanted only water. The set was a big Venetian square, and the water was on the other side of it. Ordinarily I would have walked around the set. But this time for some reason I took a shortcut. There I was in a fine costume all alone on the set, which was brilliantly lighted. When I reached the other side a man said, 'What is your name?' I said, 'Luis Antonio Damaso Alonso.' 'Well, come to my office tomorrow,' he said. He signed me to a contract and sold me to B.P. Schulberg for *The Plastic Age*."

At age nineteen, Roland chose his screen name by combining those of two of his favorites, John Gilbert and serial queen Ruth Roland. He attained stardom in 1927 with his next picture, *Camille* (silent), playing the young Frenchman Armand opposite Norma Talmadge. Now one of the most sought-after leading men, he starred opposite Mary Astor in *Rose of the Golden West* (1927, silent) and with Billie Dove in *The Love Mart* (1927, silent). He again starred opposite Norma Talmadge in *New York Nights* (1929). Other silent films include *The Blonde Saint* (1926, silent), *The Campus Flirt* (1926, silent), *The Dove* (1927, silent) and *The Woman Disputed* (1928, silent)

He had the looks associated with the fiery Latin Lover, and although he was cast in the role frequently, he also played a variety of international types. "If you seem to be a Latin Lover, they expect you'll be on screen a tough guy. But I am not a tough man. I have sentiment." Noting a difference between the private Roland and the public image he created in movies, he added, "My screen image never bothers me, but I have never tried to contradict it either."

Roland's career as a leading man waned during the early 1930s, although he was one of the few actors to survive the transition from silent to sound films. He went to Metro for both the English and Spanish versions of *Men of the North* (1930), and was cast opposite Clara Bow in *Call Her Savage* (1932) as a "half-breed." Roland starred in the English version of *Resurrection* (1931) opposite Lupe Velez. He was cast as a South American gigolo in Mae West's *She Done Him Wrong* (1933). Leading parts became fewer and far between for a while, though occasionally he made a few Spanish-language features.

Gilbert Roland.

Films he appeared in during the 1930s and 1940s include *Life Begins* (1932), *No Living Witness* (1932), *A Parisian Romance* (1932), *The Passionate Plumber* (1932), *The Woman in Room 13* (1932), *After Tonight* (1933), *Gigolettes of Paris* (1933), *Our Betters* (1933), *Elinor Norton* (1935), *Ladies Love Danger* (1935), *Mystery Woman* (1935), *Midnight Taxi* (1937), *Gambling on the High Seas* (1940), *Isle of Destiny* (1940), *Rangers of Fortune* (1940), *Angels with Broken Wings* (1941), *My Life with Caroline* (1941), *Enemy Agents Meet Ellery Queen* (1942), *Isle of Missing Men* (1942), *Captain Kidd* (1945), *Beauty and the Bandit* (1946), *The Gay Cavalier* (1946), *South of Monterey* (1946), *High Conquest* (1947), *The Other Love* (1947), *Pirates of Monterey* (1947), *Riding the California Trail* (1947), *Robin Hood of Monterey* (1947), *The Dude Goes West* (1948) and *King of the Bandits* (1949).

In 1937 he scored a good role in a Western at Paramount, *Thunder Trail*, and received good notices for his lead in *The Last Train from Madrid* (1937) opposite Lew Ayres, Dorothy Lamour and Anthony Quinn. A supporting role in *Gateway* (1938) was followed by the Columbia Pictures Spanish *La Vida Bohemia* (1937) then later, by roles in Warner Bros.' *Juarez* (1939) and *The Sea Hawk* (1940).

Roland enlisted in the United States Army during World War II. After the war, he starred in a series of popular Cisco Kid films at Monogram Studios.

In 1949 his career took an upward turn when director John Huston picked him to play a cynical guitar-plucking Cuban revolutionary in *We*

Were Strangers. "The producer said, 'not that so and so,' and Huston said 'that so and so is going to be in the picture,' and I was. The funny thing is that I scarcely knew Huston. Why he insisted on having me in the film, I don't know. The picture wasn't a success, but the critics, particularly in New York, gave me wonderful notices. Now I was back in business, after being buried in the Cisco Kid series for years."

This was the beginning of a new career period that was to see Roland successively appear in strong supporting character roles in above-average films throughout the 1950s. He appeared in Richard Brooks' *Crisis* (1950) opposite Cray Grant with several of his contemporaries, including Ramon Navaho and Antonio Moreno. He gave a moving and much-talked-about performance as an aging bull fighter in *The Bullfighter and the Lady* (1951), and played a Latin Lover opposite Lana Turner in Vincente Minnelli's *The Bad and the Beautiful* (1952). He also starred with James Stewart in *Thunder Bay* (1953), with Robert Wagner in *Beneath the 12-Mile Reef* (1953) and with Jane Russell in *Underwater* (1955). He played the role of the prison kingpin Punch Pinero in *My Six Convicts* (1952).

Roland's screen characters were always dashing, romantic and sly. No matter how roguish a character he played, however, audiences knew he would always do the fight thing by the last reel. Good examples of such portrayals are his role in *The Miracle of Our Lady of Fatima* (1952) and the role of the circus aerialist who walks a tightrope over Niagara Falls in *The Big Circus* (1959).

His other films of the period include *The Desert Hawk* (1950), *The Furies* (1950), *Malaya* (1950), *The Torch* (1950), *Mark of the Renegade* (1951), *Ten Tall Men* (1951), *Apache War Smoke* (1952), *Glory Alley* (1952), *The Diamond Queen* (1953), *The French Line* (1954), *The Racers* (1955), *That Lady* (1955), *The Treasure of Pancho Villa* (1955), *Bandido* (1956), *Three Violent People* (1956), *Around the World in Eighty Days* (1956), *The Midnight Story* (1957), *The Last of the Fast Guns* (1958), *Catch Me if You Can* (1959) and *The Wild and the Innocent* (1959).

Roland has worked occasionally on television on such shows as *Zorro* (1957-59); *Wagon Train* (1957-65), for which he wrote the script and guest starred in an episode titled "The Bernal Sierra Story"; *The High Chaparral* (1967-71); *Kung Fu* (1972-75); *Hart to Hart* (1979-84); and *The Sacketts* (1979). In 1959 he starred in a pilot program for MGM television called *Amigo* in which he played the title role of a police detective in the bordertowns of El Paso and Juarez.

In the 1960s he had a featured role as Chief Dull Knife in John Ford's *Cheyenne Autumn* (1964) with Dolores Del Rio, Ricardo Montalban and Sal Mineo. He went to Italy and made several "spaghetti Westerns" and also made a film in the Philippines. The films of this period include *Guns of the Timberland* (1960), *Samar* (1962), *The Reward* (1965), *The Poppy Is Also a Flower* (1966), *Any Gun Can Play* (1968), *The Christian Licorice Store* (1971), *Johnny Hamlet* (1972), *Running Wild* (1973) and *The Black Pearl* (1977).

In 1977 Roland played Captain Ralph in Ernest Hemingway's *Islands in the Stream*, starring George C. Scott. Unfortunately, the role was small and not sufficiently developed. He had a cameo role as a doctor in Charles Bronson's *Caboblanco* (1981). In 1980 Roland returned to the big screen in fine form to play a Mexican patriarch in the Western *Barbarosa* (1982), starring Willie Nelson.

Phil Roman
B: 12/21/1930

The farmlands of Fresno produced this gifted Mexican American artist whose fertile imagination drew his way from a comic strip in the high school paper to advance to one of the top positions in the colorful but highly competitive field of animation. A true success story, six time Emmy winner Phil Roman has produced and directed animated series, theatricals and commercials for four decades. At age eleven he saw Walt Disney's *Bambi* (1941) at the local cinema, and decided to devote himself to turning drawings into life on the screen. After completing high school, he boarded a bus for Los Angeles with only $60 in his pocket and a burning desire to be an animator. He entered Hollywood Art Center school then left to serve in the military during the Korean War and returned to the Art Center to continue his education on the G.I. Bill. In 1955 his dream to work at Disney came true when he was hired to work as an assistant animator on *Sleeping Beauty* (1955).

Through the years he worked for many of the top entertainment animation studios of the day. In the 1970s he began his association with Bill Melendez which lasted until 1983.

In 1984, Roman formed his own studio and the first production under his own banner was the Emmy Award-winning *Garfield in the Rough* (1984). His *Garfield and Friends*(1988-94) and *Bobby's World* (1990) series were nominated for Daytime Emmys in 1991. Roman personally directed and produced the animated theatrical *Tom and Jerry: The Movie* (1992). Under Phil's leadership, Film Roman also produces the popular series *The Simpsons* (1989-) and *King of the Hill* (1997-) for Fox network.

Lina Romay
[born: Elena Romay]
B: 1/16/1921

Born in Brooklyn, New York, Lina Romay was the daughter of Mexican diplomat Porfirio A. Romay and his wife, Lillian. She was the lead singer for Xavier Cugat before being signed to an MGM contract by producer Joe Pasternak. She was featured in a number of MGM musicals singing with Cugat's orchestra. She made her film debut in *You Were Never Lovelier* (1942), in which she appeared with Cugat and the film's stars, Fred Astaire and Rita Hayworth. Her initial dramatic role was in 1945s *Adventure* starring Clark Gable. In the small role of Gable's seaport girlfriend, Romay got to kiss Gable. Her other films include *The Heat's On* (1943), *Stage Door Canteen* (1943), *Bathing Beauty* (1944), *Two Girls and a Sailor* (1944), *Weekend at the Waldorf* (1945), *Honeymoon* (1947), *Embraceable You* (1948) and *The Lady Takes a Sailor* (1949).

Carlos Romero

B: 1927

A character actor born in Los Angeles to a vaudeville family, his credits include *They Came to Cordura* (1959) and *The Professionals* (1966). On television, he has guest starred in *Wagon Train* (1957-65), *Zorro* (1957-59) and *Rawhide* (1959-66). He was featured in a recurring role on the series *Falcon Crest* (1981-90) and *Wichita Town* (1959-60).

Cesar Romero

B: 2/15/1907
D: 1/1/1994

Tall, Dark and Handsome (1941) was the title of one of his early films and best describes the essential screen image of Cesar Romero.

Romero, in a career that spanned over sixty years as a leading man and supporting player, amassed on amazing array of screen portrayals. Whether playing a gangster, Latin Lover, rogue, Indian prince, or Frenchman, he had a sophisticated style, charm and manner that made him a favorite—especially with female moviegoers.

"I've had a long and fruitful career; who could ask for anything more?" Romero said during a 1990 interview. "I can't really complain. I was never a superstar in this business, I've always had a good steady position and that's a damn sight more than a lot of them have had that have come and gone."

Cesar Romero was born in New York City to an Italian-born sugar exporter and concert pianist Maria Mantilla. Cesar's grandfather was the great Cuban patriot and writer Jose Marti y Perez (1853-1895).

Romero started his career in show business in 1927 as a ballroom dancer in New York theaters and nightclubs, where he generated much attention with fancy footwork and dark good looks. He later began working as an actor in the legitimate theater and soon replaced an actor in a leading role in a touring production of *Strictly Dishonorable*, which led him to other stage work and inevitably to Hollywood.

In 1934, the young actor made his film debut with a small role in *The Thin Man*, with William Powell at MGM. He followed this with a leading role in *British Agent* (1934) at Warner Bros. and then *Clive of India* (1935) with Ronald Colman. At Universal, he did *Love Before Breakfast* (1936), opposite Carole Lombard.

He signed a long-term contract in 1937 with Twentieth Century-Fox and appeared in such films as *Wee Willie Winkie* (1937), *The Little Princess* (1939), *Frontier Marshall* (1939) and *Coney Island* (1943). During this time, Cesar became the first Hispanic American actor to portray the Cisco Kid in a series of popular films at Fox.

In the 1940s, he was cast in a series of musicals opposite such actresses as Betty Grable, Alice Faye and Carmen Miranda. These films included *The Great American Broadcast* (1941), *Dance Hall* (1941), *Weekend in Havana* (1941), *Springtime in the Rockies* (1942), *Wintertime* (1943) and *Tales of Manhattan* (1942).

World War II interrupted his career, and he joined the United States Coast Guard. He returned from the service in 1946 and made *Carnival in Costa Rica* (1947).

Cesar Romero.

In 1946, Fox sent Romero and Tyrone Power on a goodwill tour of South America. Romero's fluency in Spanish came in handy, and the tour was a resounding success. They were greeted officially in every Latin American country they visited and were mobbed by fans everywhere.

One of his best roles (his own personal favorite) came in 1947 in the film *Captain from Castile*, as the conquistador Hernando Cortez, a role that allowed Romero the rare opportunity to showcase his talent as a mature actor in a bravura performance that suggested the vigor, fire and complexity of the legendary Spanish conquistador.

Romero's Fox contract carne to an end in 1950, which coincided with the early clays of television. He immediately went to work in the new medium in a variety of roles in comedies, dramas and Westerns. He starred in his own television series, *Passport to Danger* (1954-56), and made guest appearances on most of the popular television series over the years, including *Bonanza* (1959-73) and *Zorro* (1957-59). The veteran actor's best-known and best-loved television role was as the comic villain the Joker on the *Batman* (1966-69) series. He appeared in a recurring role as Greek shipping magnate Nick Stavros in the long-running series *Falcon Crest* (1981-90) opposite Jane Wyman for several seasons, alternating easily between film and television.

During the 1950s as a freelance actor, Romero appeared in such films as *Vera Cruz* (1954) opposite Burt Lancaster and Gary Cooper, *The Americano* (1955) opposite Glenn Ford, *The Racers* (1955) opposite Kirk Douglas, and the all-star *Around the World in Eighty Days* (1956). His later film credits include *Ocean's Eleven* (1960), *Donovan's Reef* (1963), *The Castilian* (1963), *Two on a Guillotine* (1965), *Marriage on the Rocks* (1965), *Batman* (1966), *Skidoo* (1969), *The Computer Wore Tennis Shoes* (1969), *The Strongest Man in the World* (1975), *Won Ton Ton, the Dog Who Saved Hollywood* (1976) and *Lust in the Dust* (1985).

Romero was a romantic symbol to several generations of moviegoers and television watchers. In a business where long-lasting popularity is difficult to achieve, Romero continued working in films and television throughout his life. In 1992, Romero celebrated his eighty-fifth birthday and appeared as a guest star along with Mickey Rooney on an episode of the television series *Jack's Place* (1992) starring Hal Linden. Romero died on January 1, 1994.

George A. Romero
B: 1940

A screenwriter, director and producer, Romero has been one of America's most distinctive and original regional moviemakers since 1969, when he made his explosive debut with the low-budget horror classic *Night of the Living Dead*. From his adopted home base in Pittsburgh, Romero has consistently explored the dark underside of uniquely American subjects.

The most conspicuous example, before *The Dark Half* (1993), is probably *Dawn of the Dead*, the 1979 sequel in which the zombies of night gather for a flesh-eating orgy in an enormous suburban shopping center.

Raised in the Bronx, New York, Romero left home in the 1950s to enroll in the drama department of prestigious Carnegie-Mellon

University in Pittsburgh. After graduation, he founded a film production company and quickly became the leading local producer of commercials, reeling in high-profile Pittsburgh-based clients like Calgon, Alcoa and U.S. Steel.

His other films include *Martin* (1977), *Knightriders* (1981), *Creepshow* (1982), *Day of the Dead* (1985), *Monkey Shines: An Experiment in Fear* (1988), *Two Evil Eyes* (1991) and *Bruiser* (2000).

Ned Romero
A Louisiana-born actor, Romero is known for the many Native American roles he plays in films and television. He played Burt Reynolds's Hispanic detective partner in the television series *Dan August* (1970-71).

Thomas Rosales, Jr.
A stuntman and actor, Rosales has worked in countless motion pictures and television shows from 1977 until the present. His film credits include *Walk Proud* (1979), *Hunter* (1980), *Commando* (1985), *The Bedroom Window* (1987), *Extreme Prejudice* (1987), *Kindergarten Cop* (1990), *American Me* (1992), *Escape from L. A.* (1996), *Con Air* (1997), *The Lost World: Jurassic Park II* (1997), *Out of Sight* (1998) and *Lethal Weapon 4* (1998) to name just a few.

Bert Rosario
B: 11/7/1945
A Puerto Rican character actor, Rosario has a long list of television credits and feature films. His films include Blake Edwards' *S.O.B.* (1981), *Stick* (1985) and *Who's That Girl* (1987), with Madonna. Rosario co-starred in the television series *Sword of Justice* (1978-79), *A.K.A. Pablo* (1984) and *Disney Presents the 100 Lives of Black Jack Savage* (1991). Among his guest starring appearances are roles on such episodic series as *Baretta* (1975-78), *Murder, She Wrote* (1984-96), *Hill Street Blues* (1981-87) and *Knight Rider* (1982-86).

Raul Roulien
B: 10/8/1905
A Brazilian-born actor and singer, Roulien appeared in such films as *Delicious* (1931) with Janet Gaynor at Fox and *Flying Down to Rio* at RKO in 1933 with Dolores Del Rio. He also appeared in various Spanish-language productions at Fox during the 1930s and 1940s. Roulien was a popular entertainer who performed on the stage in his native Brazil and all over South America.

Daphne Rubin-Vega
The Panamanian born actress grew up in New York City and made her motion picture debut co-starring with Matt Dillon and Kevin Bacon in *Wild Things*. She went on appear as Tia in *Flawless* (1999) opposite Robert DeNiro. She has also appeared in the television series *New York Undercover* (1994-98) and *Trinity* (1998-99). Her portrayal of the tragic Mimi in the Tony Award-winning musical drama *Rent* earned her a Tony Award and Drama Desk nomination for Best Actress.

Mercedes Ruehl

An Academy Award®-winning actress in the supporting category for *The Fisher King* (1991), Ruehl first gained attention for her role as a Mafia wife in the film *Married to the Mob* (1988). She won a Tony Award on Broadway in 1991 for Neil Simon's *Lost in Yonkers* in the role of Aunt Bella, which she reprised in the 1993 film version. Her television roles include *Frasier* (1993-), HBO's *Subway Stories: Tales of the Underground* (1997) and *Gia* (1998) with Angelina Jolie. Among Ruehl's recent features films are *Roseanna's Grave* (1997), *The Minus Man* (1999) and *What's Cookin'* (2000). She is of Spanish-Irish descent.

Jose Luis Ruiz

A producer and director in the film and television industry since 1970, Ruiz's television programs have garnered eleven Emmy nominations and four Emmy Awards. He has been most recognized for his documentary films and his articulation of a vision for institutionalizing a Latino presence in television. Ruiz is formerly the director of the National Latino Communications Center, headquartered in Los Angeles.

Juan Ruiz Anchia

B: 1949

A Spanish-born cinematographer, Ruiz Anchia graduated from the Escuela Oficial Cinematografia in 1972 and from the American Film Institute in 1981. His credits as a cinematographer on America films include *Reborn* (1978), *That Was Then . . . This Is Now* (1985), *Glengarry Glen Ross* (1992), *The Jungle Book* (1994), *The Disappearance of Garcia Lorca* (1997) and *The Corruptor* (1999). Ruiz Anchia worked with writer/director David Mamet on two theatrical features, *House of Games* (1987) and *Things Change* (1988).

Andy Russell
[born: Andres Robago]

B: 9/16/1919
D: 4/16/1992

Born in East Los Angeles, Russell became a crooner of the 1940s and popularized such classic songs as "Besame Mucho" and "What a Difference a Day Makes." He made several musical film appearances as himself, in such films as *The Stork Club* (1945), *Breakfast in Hollywood* (1946) and *Copacabana* (1947).

Theresa Saldana

Of part Hispanic extraction, Saldana was adopted at five days old and raised by an Italian American couple in Brooklyn. Her feature film credits include *I Wanna Hold Your Hand* (1978), *Defiance* (1980), *Raging Bull* (1980), *The Evil That Men Do* (1984) and *Angel Town* (1989). She went on to win a co-starring role on television series *The Commish* (1991-95) and has made numerous episodic series guest appearances. Saldana starred as herself in the television movie *Victims for Victims: The Theresa Saldana Story* (1984); she also founded an organization called Victims for Victims after being brutally attacked by a crazed fan in 1980.

Jaime Sanchez plays Angel in *The Wild Bunch*.

Eduardo Sanchez

B: 1969

A native of Matanzas, Cuba, Sanchez and his partner, Daniel Myrick, wrote and directed the 1999 surprise sleeper hit *The Blair Witch Project* (1999). The $35,000 film has grossed more than $140 million to date, revolutionized the way films are marketed by the use of the Internet, and proven that audiences would pay to see a feature length video in theaters.

Jaime Sanchez

B: 12/19/1938

This Puerto Rican-born actor is best known for his portrayal of Angel, the idealistic Mexican member of the group known as the Wild Bunch in Sam Peckinpah's *The Wild Bunch* (1969). He made his film debut in *David and Lisa* (1963) and had an important co-starring role as Jesus Ortiz in Sidney Lumet's *The Pawnbroker* (1965), for which he won a Screen World Award and the Laurel Award. His other film credits include *Beach Red* (1967) and *Bobby Deerfield* (1977). Sanchez began his show business career in his native Puerto Rico at age fourteen as a radio actor on local island stations. He came to the States and got his first big break in the smash Broadway production of *West Side Story* in the role of Chino.

Mark Sanchez

B: 1955

A Los Angeles-born makeup artist, Sanchez began his career as an assistant on the television series *Sanford and Son* (1972-77) and on *Chico and the Man* (1974-78). He also worked on *The Tonight Show Starring Johnny Carson* (19962-92) for ten years, from 1976 to 1986. His feature film credits include *My Family* (1995) and *Why Do Fools Fall in Love?* (1998). With Ken Diaz, he earned an Academy Award® nomination for his work on *My Family*.

Roselyn Sanchez

Born and raised in Puerto Rico, Sanchez landed the role of dancer Lili Arguelo on the television series *Fame L.A.* (1997-98) and went on to star as Kim Veras on the short-lived series *Ryan Caulfield: Year One* (1999). Her feature film debut is *Held Up* (2000).

Miguel Sandoval

B: 1/16/1951

Born in New Mexico, Sandoval has appeared in *Repo Man* (1984), *Walker* (1987), *Ricochet* (1991), *Jurassic Park* (1993), *Clear and Present Danger* (1994), *Get Shorty* (1995) and *Things You Can Tell Just by Looking at Her* (2000).

Bel Sandre
[aka: Bel Hernandez]
B: 12/20/1956

A Mexican American actress, Sandre was featured in *Losin' It* (1983) and *Colors* (1988). On television she was featured in the PBS *American Playhouse* presentation *La Carpa* (1993) and in the miniseries *The Alamo: Thirteen Days to Glory* (1987).

Olga San Juan
B: 3/18/1927

A contract player for a short time at Paramount Pictures during the mid-1940s, San Juan, at age eighteen, co-starred in *Blue Skies* (1946) with Bing Crosby and Fred Astaire. In the film, she and Fred Astaire performed "Heat Wave," a torrid dance number that remains a classic.

She was born in Brooklyn, New York, the eldest daughter of Puerto Rican parents, Mercedes and Luis San Juan. The family moved to Puerto Rico when she was three years old and later returned to New York. There she started to establish a reputation as a teenage nightclub performer, appearing at many important clubs of the period, including El Morocco, the Copacabana and the Astor Hotel. While San Juan was featured on a radio show, a Paramount scout had her screen tested in New York. She flew to Hollywood, where, because of her age, she found herself attending school with such starlets as Mona Freeman and Gail Russell.

San Juan made her film debut in *Rainbow Island* (1944) opposite Dorothy Lamour and appeared as a blonde in Paramount's all-star *Variety Girl* (1947). She later went to Universal to star with Ava Gardner and Dick Haymes in *One Touch of Venus* (1948). She found success on Broadway in Lerner and Loewe's musical *Paint Your Wagon* (1951).

She retired from active involvement in the industry when she married actor Edmond O'Brien and raised three children.

Olga San Juan and Fred Astaire in *Blue Skies*.

Emily Santiago
[alternate spelling: Emile; born: Emily Richardson]
B: 1902

Santiago shared with Charles LeMaire an Academy Award® for costume design for the biblical motion picture *The Robe* (1953), starring Victor Mature and Richard Burton, the first movied filmed in CinemaScope. She specialized in period costumes for the stars. Beginning in 1928, she worked for 18 years at Hollywood's Western Costume house and then decided to go to work for various studios. Her film credits include *Wells Fargo* (1937), *The Prince and the Pauper* (1937), *The Adventures of Robin Hood* (1938), *One Million B.C.* (1940), *Quo Vadis* (1951) and *Strange Lady in Town* (1955). Santiago provided many costume sketches for Cecil B. DeMille. She was born in Bloomburg, Pennsylvania, and she married Santiago, a construction engineer, in 1923.

Ruben Santiago-Hudson
Santiago-Hudson won a Tony Award for Featured Actor in a Drama for his portrayal of Canewell in the Broadway theatrical production of *Seven*

Guitars. His feature film credits include *Coming to America* (1988), *Blown Away* (1994), *The Devil's Advocate* (1997) and *Shaft* (2000). He has also appeared in numerous televise films and episodic programs.

Reni Santoni
B: 4/21/1940

Born in New York of a Corsican father and a Spanish mother, Santoni was raised in a Puerto Rican neighborhood in the Bronx. He made his major film bow starring in *Enter Laughing* (1967). He has also appeared in *Anzio* (1968), *Dirty Harry* (1971), *I Never Promised You a Rose Garden* (1977), *Dead Men Don't Wear Plaid* (1982), *Brewster's Millions* (1985), *Howard Stern's Private Parts* (1997) and *28 Days* (2000). He has numerous television credits including guest star roles on *Seinfeld* (1990-98), *The Practice* (1997-) and *NYPD Blue* (1993-).

Joe Santos
B: 6/9/1933

Brooklyn-born of Italian and Puerto Rican parents, Santos began his acting career while in his mid-30s after years of odd jobs and traveling between the United States and the Caribbean. Accompanying a friend to an audition in Brooklyn, he was asked to read for the part of a boxer and was cast in the role.

Santos is a character actor best known for his work on television in the long-running series *The Rockford Files* (1974-80), as well as nine *Rockford* television movies, and his many guest appearances on such shows as *Hill Street Blues* (1981-87) and *Magnum P. I.* (1980-88). Among his many feature film credits are roles in *The Gang that Couldn't Shoot Straight* (1971), *Shamus* (1973), *Blue Thunder* (1983), *The Detective* (1985), *Revenge* (1990), *Mo' Money* (1992) and *The Postman* (1997).

John Saxon
[born: Carmen Orrico]
B: 11/5/1935

Born in Brooklyn, New York, the son of Italian immigrants, Saxon has endured as a successful and versatile film and television actor since the mid-1950s. He has played ethnics, "half-breeds," and Mexican bandits in a number of films including *Cry Tough* (1959), as Puerto Rican Miguel Estrada; *The Plunderers* (1960), as Rondo, a young Mexican vaquero; *The Unforgiven* (1960), as half-breed Johnny Portugal; *The Appaloosa* (1966), as Chuy, a Mexican bandit; and *Joe Kidd* (1972), as Luis Chama. His other film credits include *Enter the Dragon* (1973), *The Electric Horseman* (1979), *Wrong Is Right* (1982) and *Nightmare on Elm Street* (1984).

Lalo Schifrin
B: 6/21/1932

An outstanding Argentinean-born composer and jazz musician with more than sixty feature film scores and television series themes to his credit, Schifrin is also a six time Oscar®-nominated composer, for the films *Cool Hand Luke* (1967), *The Fox* (1968), *Voyage of the Damned* (1976), *The Amityville Horror* (1979), *The Competition* (1980) and *The Sting II*

(1983). He also scored such films as *The Cincinnati Kid* (1965), *Bullitt* (1968), *Dirty Harry* (1971), *Magnum Force* (1973), *The Mean Season* (1985), *The Beverly Hillbillies* (1993), *Money Talks* (1997) and *Rush Hour* (1998).

Schifrin was born in Buenos Aires, where his father was a concert master for the Buenos Aires Symphony. He developed a strong interest in American jazz, and he became a film buff at age sixteen. He studied at the Paris Conservatory of Music, where he met famed jazz musician Dizzy Gillespie, who was so impressed with the young man's talents that he helped Schifrin to enter the United States. He worked as a pianist for Gillespie for over two years, and then he secured a job at Universal Television. As a composer he is best known for his theme for the *Mission: Impossible* (1966-73) television series, among many other memorable scores.

Jon Seda
B: 10/14/1970

An actor of Puerto Rican Heritage, Seda was born in Manhattan and raised in New Jersey. Seda made his feature film debut in the role of the boxer, Romano, in *Gladiator* (1992). His other film credits include *Carlito's Way* (1993), *I Like It Like That* (1994), *12 Monkeys* (1995), *Primal Fear* (1996), the box office hit *Selena* (1997) opposite Jennifer Lopez, *Price of Glory* (2000), Seda joined the cast of the acclaimed television series *Homicide: Life on the Street* (1993-99) as Detective Paul Falsone in 1997. He has also appeared in the HBO films *Mistrial* (1996) opposite Bill Pullman and *Daybreak* (1993), starring Cuba Gooding Jr.

Pepe Serna
B: 7/23/1944

A talented supporting character actor, Serna usually portrays a sort of "modern Chicano everyman." His career encompasses the early prerequisite gang-tough roles to more recent diverse portrayals. Movie audiences will best remember Serna as Al Pacino's Cuban refugee buddy who meets an untimely demise from a chainsaw in Brian De Palma's *Scarface* (1983).

Born in Corpus Christi, Texas, Serna got his start in films at a casting audition, where the legendary producer Hal Wallis was so impressed with the young actor's talent that he offered him an important role in the film *Red Sky at Morning* (1971). Soon, Serna found himself acting opposite such stars as Gregory Peck in *Shootout* (1971) and Karen Black in *Day of the Locust* (1975).

His credits include *Deal of the Century* (1983), as an illegal arms dealer; *The Adventures of Buckaroo Banzai* (1984), a science fiction cult classic in which he portrayed Reno, a member of Buckaroo's elite squad; *Red Dawn* (1984), as the patriotic father of one of the rebellious boys; Lawrence Kasdan's Western spoof, *Silverado* (1985), as Scruffy, a hired gun; Clint Eastwood's *The Rookie* (1990), as Eastwood's police superior; and *Postcards from the Edge* (1990), as a revolutionary. The actor received critical acclaim for his portrayal of Atif, Egyptian president Anwar Sadat's brother, opposite Lou Gossett, Jr., in the television miniseries *Sadat* (1983). He has had the distinction of appearing in four PBS *American Playhouse* presentations: *Seguin* (1982), *The Ballad of Gregorio*

Jon Seda as Detective Paul Falsone in *Homicide: Life on the Streets*.

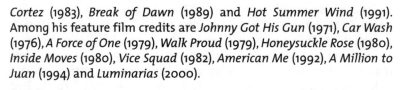

Cortez (1983), *Break of Dawn* (1989) and *Hot Summer Wind* (1991). Among his feature film credits are *Johnny Got His Gun* (1971), *Car Wash* (1976), *A Force of One* (1979), *Walk Proud* (1979), *Honeysuckle Rose* (1980), *Inside Moves* (1980), *Vice Squad* (1982), *American Me* (1992), *A Million to Juan* (1994) and *Luminarias* (2000).

Diego Serrano

Born and raised in Ecuador, Serrano left South America at age ten and emigrated to the United States with his family. He was a Star Search model and daytime television viewers will recognize Serrano as Tomas Rivera from the soap opera *Another World* (1964-). Serrano has appeared in two feature films, *Mixing Nina* (1998) and *The 24 Hour Woman* (1999) and has also been cast in *Time of Your Life* (1999-) with Jennifer Love Hewitt.

Carmen Sevilla

B: 1930

One of Spain's leading actresses of the 1960s, Sevilla was featured in Samuel Bronston's *King of Kings* (1961) as Mary Magdalene, and in *Spanish Affair* (1958).

Charlie Sheen
[born: Carlos Irwin Estevez]
B: 9/3/1966

Since his first starring role in 1984's *Red Dawn*, Charlie Sheen has seen his career skyrocket through a succession of motion pictures including *Lucas* (1986), *The Wraith* (1986), and the film that established him as a major talent, the Academy Award®-winning *Platoon* (1986), directed by Oliver Stone. His performance as the young soldier helped define the Vietnam War experience for the generation of the 1980s, as his father Martin Sheen previously had in the 1970s with his portrayal of Captain Willard in Francis Ford Coppola's *Apocalypse Now* (1979).

Born in New York and raised in California along the shores of Malibu, Charlie Sheen spent his childhood alternating between sports, making Super-8 movies, and going on location shoots with his father. He made his acting debut at age nine in the haunting television movie *The Execution of Private Slovik* (1974), which starred his father. But eight years passed before he played his second role, in the 1982 film *Grizzly II*.

Eight months in the Philippines with his father during the filming of *Apocalypse Now* provided a lasting impression that made him decide to pursue acting and working in films. After *Platoon*, Sheen starred as Bud Fox, a young stockbroker, in Oliver Stone's *Wall Street* (1987). Martin Sheen played his father in the movie, and they worked in several scenes together. His other feature film credits include *No Man's Land* (1987); *Three for the Road* (1987); *Young Guns* (1988), in which he played opposite his brother Emilio Estevez; *Eight Men Out* (1988), in which he played a young baseball player; *Major League* (1990), as another baseball player; *The Rookie* (1990) with Clint Eastwood; *Men at Work* (1990), which co-starred and was directed by Emilio Estevez; and *Cadence* (1991), which co-starred and was directed by Martin Sheen.

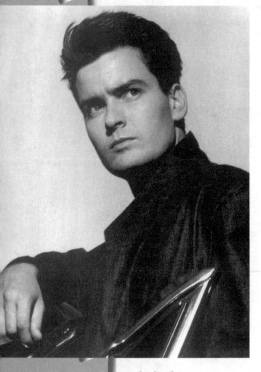

Charlie Sheen.

Despite being beset by drug and alcohol problems, Sheen managed to continue to work, appearing in such films as the spoofs *Major League* (1989) and *Major League II* (1994), *Hot Shots!* (1991) and *Hot Shots! Part Deux* (1993) and *Loaded Weapon 1* (1993). More recently, he has starred in such films as *Money Talks* (1997), *Being John Malkovich* (1999) and the HBO project *Rated X* (2000), directed by Emilio Estevez.

Martin Sheen
[born: Ramon Estevez]
B: 8/3/1941

A well-respected, critically acclaimed actor, Sheen has starred in such major motion pictures as *Apocalypse Now* (1979), *Badlands* (1974) and *Gandhi* (1982),without even achieving real "superstar" status.

Born in Dayton, Ohio, Sheen is the seventh son of ten children born to his Irish mother and Spanish father. As soon as he graduated from high school, he left for New York to begin his training at the off-off-Broadway Living Theater. He changed his given name at the beginning of his career when he discovered that New York casting directors had difficulty pronouncing it. "I looked Irish," he recollects, "so I thought of Bishop Sheen. Martin? It went with Sheen."

After making his off-Broadway debut in *The Connection* (1959) and his Broadway bow in the short-lived *Never Live Over a Pretzel Factory* (1964), Sheen starred as a returning Army veteran confronted by his parents' personal war in the Pulitzer Prize-winning play *The Subject Was Roses* (1964). That led to his film debut as one of a pair of punks terrorizing subway passengers in the 1967 film *The Incident*.

In 1968, he reprised his role in the film version of *The Subject Was Roses* opposite Patricia Neal and Jack Albertson for MGM. He went on to appear in such films as *Catch-22* (1970), *No Drums, No Bugles* (1971) and *Rage* (1972). He stunned critics and filmgoers with his work in Terrence Malick's *Badlands*, in which he performed opposite Sissy Spacek as a roving, youngster on a killing spree. Sheen was named Best Actor at the San Sebastian Film Festival for his work in the film.

He won the pivotal role of Captain Willard, an Army captain sent on a secret military operation at. the height of the Vietnam conflict, in Francis Ford Coppola's classic *Apocalypse Now*. Since then, Sheen has alternated between television and motion pictures, winning special praise for his moving work in the 1974 television movie *The Execution of Private Slovik*. He also scored on television as JFK in *Kennedy* (1983), as RFK in *Missiles of October* (1974), as John Dean in *Blind Ambition* (1979) and as the star of *The Atlanta Child Murders* (1985).

Sheen's other film credits include *Pickup on 101* (1972), *The Cassandra Crossing* (1977), *Eagle's Wing* (1979), *In the King of Prussia* (1982), *That Championship Season* (1982), *The Dead Zone* (1983), *Man, Woman and Child* (1983), *Firestarter* (1984), *A State of Emergency* (1986), *Wall Street* (1987), *Beyond the Stars* (1989), *Gettysburg* (1993), *The American President* (1995),and *Spawn* (1997). He made his motion picture directing debut with the film *Cadence* (1989), in which he and his son Charlie Sheen both appeared.

Recently, he has returned to television in the much acclaimed *The West Wing* (1999-) in the role of President of the United States.

Martin Sheen as Captain Hollister in *Firestarter*.

Gregory Sierra

B: 1/25/1937

Born and raised in New York City, Sierra began his career as a singer while in the Air Force. Sierra's first professional appearance was with the prestigious National Shakespeare Company, with whom he performed *Macbeth* and *The Taming of the Shrew*.

In 1969, after nearly ten years of working exclusively in New York theater, Sierra relocated to California to break into films and television. His transition to the West Coast proved beneficial, as he soon landed a role on *The Flying Nun* (1967-70) television series starring Sally Field. Sierra went on to appear in numerous television shows, including a recurring role as Julio Fuentes, Fred Sanford's Puerto Rican neighbor, on *Sanford and Son* (1972-77) and as a series regular on *Barney Miller* (1975-82) as Detective Chamo. He starred in his own short-lived series, *A.E.S. Hudson Street* (1978) and on *Miami Vice* (1984-89). He makes regular guest appearances on episodic television series. His feature film credits include *The Wrath of God* (1972), *The Towering Inferno* (1974); *The Prisoner of Zenda* (1979), with Peter Sellers; *The Trouble with Spies* (1987), *Deep Cover* (1992); *Hot Shots! Part Deux* (1993); *The Wonderful Ice Cream Suit* (1998) and *Vic* (1999).

Geno Silva

Silva is a New Mexico-born character actor seen in *The Cheyenne Social Club* (1970) with James Stewart and Henry Fonda, Steven Spielberg's *1941* (1979), Brian De Palma's *Scarface* (1983), Robert Towne's *Tequila Sunrise* (1988); and Spielberg's *The Lost World: Jurassic Park* and *Amistad,* both in 1997. He has appeared in over a dozen television movies and his many episodic television guest appearances include *Murder, She Wrote* (1984-96), *Miami Vice* (1984-89), *Hunter* (1984-91) and *Simon & Simon* (1981-88).

Henry Silva

B: 1927

Henry Silva has carved out a career playing a variety of villainous characters in a number of films, including *The Bravados* (1958), *Green Mansions* (1959), *The Manchurian Candidate* (1962) and *Sharkey's Machine* (1982). He has menaced such movie tough guys as Burt Reynolds, Gregory Peck, Chuck Norris and Frank Sinatra.

Born in Brooklyn, New York, of Italian-Puerto Rican parents, Silva left home at age thirteen to pursue his acting dreams. A variety of jobs eventually introduced Silva to a group of actors who sent him to study acting at the Harris and Lewis School. He auditioned for the Actors Studio, and when that company's production of *A Hatful of Rain* went to Broadway in 1956, Silva went with it and was nominated for a Tony Award for his role of Mother, a drug dealer.

He made his film debut in *Viva Zapata!* (1952) and has appeared in such films as *The Law and Jake Wade* (1958), *The Last of the Fast Guns* (1958), *Ocean's Eleven* (1960), *Sergeants 3* (1962), *A Gathering of Eagles* (1963), *The Hills Run Red* (1967), *The Italian Connection* (1973), *Buck Rogers in the 25th Century* (1979), *Wrong Is Right* (1982), *Megaforce* (1982), *Above*

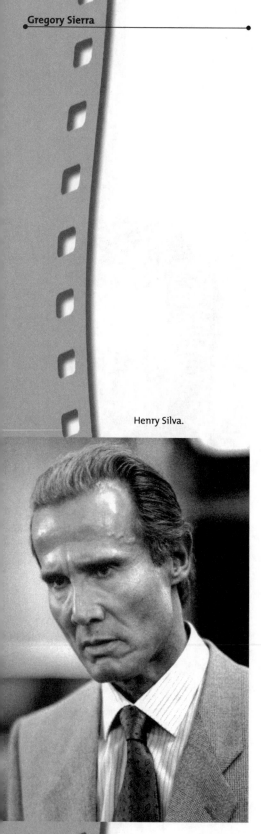

Henry Silva.

the Law (1989), *Dick Tracy* (1990), *Mad Dog Time* (1996), *The End of Violence* (1997) and most recently; Jim Jarmusch's, *Ghost Dog: The Way of the Samurai* (1999).

Silva starred in *Johnny Cool* (1963), a film about a young Sicilian mobster that has attained cult status through the years.

Trinidad Silva

B: 1950
D: 7/31/1988

A diminutive, charismatic character actor, Silva appeared in supporting roles in a number of films in the late 1970s and throughout the 1980s until his untimely death. He was born in Mission, Texas, and grew up in the Rio Grande valley. In his teens, Silva drifted to Los Angeles, where he met a hometown friend who was working as an actor. Silva visited him on the set of Tom Laughlin's *The Master Gunfighter* (1975) and was immediately hired as an extra. That marked the beginning of a promising career that was cut short by a drunk driver who killed Silva on impact.

Silva made his film debut in a major role in *Alambrista!* (1978), Robert M. Young's feature about the exploitation of illegal Mexican immigrants. He had roles in *Walk Proud* (1979), a story of urban youth gang rivalry, as Dagger; in *El Norte* (1983) as a friendly illegal; and in *Crackers* (1984), a caper film directed by Louis Malle and starring Donald Sutherland. He received good notices for his role as the older streetwise gang member Frog in *Colors* (1988), starring Robert Duvall and Sean Penn.

On television, Silva was featured in a recurring role as gang member Jesus Martinez on the critically acclaimed, Emmy Award-winning *Hill Street Blues* (1981-87).

Frank Silvera

B: 7/24/1917
D: 6/11/1970

A character player on stage, screen and television, Silvera worked for over two decades with scarcely anyone realizing he was a African American man. The actor recalled in an interview, "I didn't hide it, I simply made no point of it. I agreed with my agent that I wanted to realize myself as on actor, per se, not a Negro actor. In my profession, the word Negro meant death." Because of the lack of diverse roles available to African American actors, "unless one wanted to play servants or slaves for the rest of a career," he continued, "I was accepted as a Latin, [and] I let it go at that," Cecil Smith, *Los Angeles Times* (10/2/66).

He played a Mexican general in *Viva Zapata!* (1952), a Portuguese policeman in *The Miracle of Our Lady of Fatima* (1952), a Chinese general in *The Mountain Road* (1960), a Tahitian chieftain in the 1962 version of *Mutiny on the Bounty* and a Mexican outlaw with a surprising wit in *Hombre* (1967).

Silvera was born in Kingston, Jamaica, the son of a Spanish Jewish father and a Jamaican mother. He was raised in Boston and originally intended to become a lawyer, studying for two years at Northwestern University. But his secret desire to act took hold, and he eventually turned to drama studies at Boston University.

Frank Silvera as a Mexican bandit in a scene from *Hombre*.

Silvera appeared in the first two movies directed by Stanley Kubrick, *Fear and Desire* (1953) and *Killer's Kiss* (1955). Among his other film credits are *Heller in Pink Tights* (1960), *Key Witness* (1960), *The Appaloosa* (1966), *The St. Valentine's Day Massacre* (1967), *Uptight* (1968), *Guns of the Magnificent Seven* (1969) and *Valdez Is Coming* (1971). He achieved great success on television with his role of Don Sebastian Montoya in the popular Western series *The High Chaparral* (1967-71). With the success he achieved Silvera was able to organize a African American actors' workshop, a place where African American actors and writers were free to develop their talents. He died unexpectedly in Los Angeles in a freak electrical accident at his home.

Jimmy Smits
B: 7/9/1955

Smits has established himself as one of the most versatile actors working in television, films and stage. He is best known for his exemplary television career in which he played Bobby Simone for four years on the hit series *NYPD Blue* (1993-) and attorney Victor Sifuentes on the long running series *L.A. Law* (1986-74). Smits has received an Emmy nomination for every year he has been on a series: six nominations for *L.A. Law*, (receiving the Emmy in 1990) and five nominations for *NYPD Blue*.

"The role of Victor Sifuentes was so appealing to me as a chance to establish an alternative image of Hispanics in the United States," remarked Smits in a 1993 interview.

Smits made his major film debut as a crime czar in *Running Scared* (1986) opposite Billy Crystal and Gregory Hines. He was a police detective gripped with the fear of voodoo in John Schlesinger's *The Believers* (1987) with Martin Sheen. He followed with a bid for screen stardom in the role of the fiery young Mexican general in the epic *The Old Gringo* (1989) opposite Jane Fonda and Gregory Peck. He also starred in *Vital Signs* (1990), *Fires Within* (1991), Blake Edward's *Switch* (1991) and Gregory Nava's *My Family* (1995) in which he received critical acclaim for his performance as Jimmy Sanchez. His most recent film credits include *Price of Glory* (2000), *The Million Dollar Hotel* (2000) and *Bless the Child* (2000). He has guest starred on such television shows as *Spenser: For Hire* (1985-88) and *Miami Vice* (1984-89)—in which he played Don Johnson's initial partner in the pilot episode, and was killed in the first five minutes. The actor starred in the miniseries *Glitz* (1988), *The Tommyknockers* (1993) and *Solomon and Sheba* (1995). He played the title role in Luis Valdez's *The Cisco Kid* (1994) for TNT, and starred in the cable films *Marshal Law* (1996), and the award-winning *The Broken Chord* (1992).

An education major at Brooklyn College, Smits studied drama and the classics and went on to earn an MFA degree from Cornell University. He has appeared off-Broadway and with the New York Shakespeare Festival under the direction of Joseph Papp. In Los Angeles, he starred at the Mark Taper Forum in a production of Ariel Dorfman's *Death and the Maiden*. Smits was born in New York City; his mother is Puerto Rican and his father is from Surinam.

Jimmy Smits as Jimmy Sanchez in *My Family*.

Jose Solano

Solano played lifeguard Many Gutierrez on the international hit television show *Baywatch* (1989-) in 1997. becoming the first regular Hispanic cast member on the series. A California native, Solano is a former United States Navy medic and a Junior Olympic champion.

Luis Soto

A Puerto Rican-born, New York-raised television director, Soto has worked on such episodic series as *The Equalizer* (1985-89) and *Miami Vice* (1984-89).

Richard Soto

An award-winning producer with extensive credits in public television, Soto began his career as a documentary filmmaker. He produced two acclaimed episodes for the PBS "WonderWorks" series, *Maricela* (1986) and *Sweet 15* (1990), which won an Emmy Award. He was associate producer as well as supervising film editor of the film *The Ballad of Gregorio Cortez* (1983).

Talisa Soto

A Brooklyn-born Puerto Rican fashion model turned actress, Soto co-starred as Lupe Lamora, a James Bond girl in *Licence to Kill* (1989). She was also featured in *The Mambo Kings* (1992), *Don Juan de Marco* (1995), *Mortal Kombat* (1995) and *Mortal Kombat: Annihilation* (1997); *That Summer in L.A.* (1999) and *Flight of Fancy* (1999). She made her film debut in *Spike of Bensonhurst* (1988) as India, a Puerto Rican girl who falls in love with an aspiring Italian boxer.

Charles Stevens

B: 1893
D: 8/22/1964

A character actor who specialized in villainous roles, Stevens usually appeared as an Indian or a Latin. He worked on over 100 projects in Hollywood from the silent era through the talkies and television. His father was Welsh and served as a lawman; his mother, a Mexican-Indian named Eloisa, was a daughter of the Apache warrior Geronimo. Stevens was born in Arizona and was a great friend of Douglas Fairbanks, appearing in all of his films including *The Mark of Zorro* (1920). He played Warner Baxter's sidekick in the original series of Cisco Kid films, Spanish Ed in *The Virginian* (1929) opposite Gary Cooper, and Diabalito in *Ambush* (1949). His last film credit is *Sergeant's 3* (1962), opposite Frank Sinatra.

Madeleine Stowe

B: 1964

The daughter of a Costa Rican mother and an American father, Stowe was born in Los Angeles. She played the daughter of an English officer in Michael Mann's *The Last of the Mohicans* (1992) and a Latin American woman in *Revenge* (1990) opposite Kevin Costner. Stowe made her film debut as a Hispanic American woman, Maria McGuire, in *Stakeout*

(1987) starring Richard Dreyfuss and Emilio Estevez. She has also acted in *The Two Jakes* (1990) opposite Jack Nicholson; *Unlawful Entry* (1992), a thriller co-starring Kurt Russell; *Short Cuts* (1993), directed by Robert Altman; *Blink* (1994), a thriller co-starring Aidan Quinn; *China Moon* (1994), with Ed Harris; *Bad Girls* (1994) with Mary Stuart Masterson, Drew Barrymore and Andie MacDowell; *Twelve Monkeys* (1995), with Brad Pitt and Bruce Willis; *Playing by Heart* (1998); and starred in *The General's Daughter* (1999), with John Travolta.

Miguelangel Suarez

A Puerto Rican-born actor, Suarez co-starred as Jesus Ramirez, a prison convict, in the 1980 hit comedy *Stir Crazy*, opposite Richard Pryor and Gene Wilder. His other motion picture credits include featured roles in *Che!* (1969) and Woody Allen's *Bananas* (1971).

Carlos Thompson

B: 6/7/1923

D: 10/10/1990

A tall, green-eyed Argentine-born actor, Thompson starred in several major films during the 1950s. Born a blond, Thompson's hair was dyed dark for his American film roles, which were usually villains secondary romantic leads. He spent his formative years in New York, and his boyhood ambition was to become a novelist. His father was a newspaper editor and a Latin American correspondent for CBS Radio. He returned to Argentina to attend the University of Buenos Aires, and there he was introduced to a movie producer who urged him to try acting.

Thompson's acting studies led to a top role in an Argentine film, *Men of Tomorrow*, which resulted in his securing the role of Armand in the Argentine version of *Camille*. Both he and the film were popular successes throughout Latin America in 1952. That some year, he met American actress Yvonne De Carlo at the Uruguay Film Festival, and she convinced him to come to the United States, where he costarred with De Carlo in *Fort Algiers* (1953). MGM offered him a contract, and he co-starred with Lana Turner as a young Italian in *Flame and the Flesh* (1954) and with Robert Taylor in the dramatic adventure *Valley of the Kings* (1954). In 1958 he co-starred with Jeff Chandler and Esther Williams in *Raw Wind in Eden*.

Rachel Ticotin

B: 11/1/1958

Rachel Ticotin made her film debut in *Fort Apache, The Bronx* (1981), starring Paul Newman, in the role of a heroin-addicted nurse with whom Newman falls in love. She starred with Bryan Brown in *F/X 2: The Deadly Art of Illusion* (1991) and in *Critical Condition* (1986) with Richard Pryor; then she starred as Melina the mystery woman with Arnold Schwarzenegger in *Total Recall* (1990)—probably her best known role to date. Other credits include *Falling Down* (1993); *Steal Little, Steal Big* (1995); *Turbulence* (1997), *Civility* (1999) and *Can't Be Heaven* (1999).

Born in New York of Dominican parents, Ticotin is one of six children. She attended the High School of Music and Art and the Professional

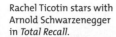

Rachel Ticotin stars with Arnold Schwarzenegger in *Total Recall.*

Children's School. As a teenager she joined the Ballet Hispanico of New York. She began to work in motion pictures as a production assistant on *The Wanderers* (1979), *Dressed to Kill* (1980) and *Raging Bull* (1980). On television she appeared as a regular on the series *For Love and Honor* (1983), *Ohara* (1987-88) and *Crime and Punishment* (1993).

Edwin Torres

B: 1930

New York State Supreme Court Justice Edwin Torres is the author of the novel *Carlito's Way* and its sequel, *After Hours*, both of which formed the basis for the feature film *Carlito's Way* (1993), starring Al Pacino. Another of his novels was adapted for Sidney Lumet's film *Q & A* (1990).

Born and raised in New York's Spanish Harlem, Torres studied for the bar at City College of New York and Brooklyn Law School, becoming the city's first assistant district attorney of Puerto Rican descent. From 1961 to 1977, he was in private practice, defending indigent clients without fee. He was elevated to the post of judge of the criminal court in 1977.

In 1979 he was named an acting justice of the New York State Supreme Court, becoming a fully elected justice the following year.

Jacqueline Torres

The actress co-starred as Mira Sanchez, a street-smart detective on the syndicated television program *FX: The Series* (1996-98). She has also appeared in the feature films *The Offering* (1996) and *Rum and Coke* (1997).

Liz Torres

A Puerto Rican actress/comedienne, Torres has been featured on *All in the Family* (1971-79) and co-starred on the popular television series *Phyllis* (1975-76) and on *The John Larroquette Show* (1993-95) Torres has guest starred on many episodic series and has appeared in such feature films as *Rescue Me* (1993), *A Million to Juan* (1994), *The Wonderful Ice Cream Suit* (1998), *The Odd Couple II* (1998).

Raquel Torres
[born: Paula Marie Osterman]

B: 11/11/1908

D: 8/10/1987

A dark-haired Mexican-born actress, Torres starred in a number of early sound films through the early 1930s.

She was born in Hermosillo, Mexico, and moved with her parents to Los Angeles and studied at a convent. At age nineteen she was chosen to co-star in W.S. Van Dyke's *White Shadows in the South Seas*, a 1928 MGM release that was the studio's first feature with fully synchronized dialogue, music and effects. She played Pepita in *The Bridge of San Luis Rey* (1929) and was in *The Desert Rider* (1929, silent). She also appeared in *The Sea Bat* (1930), *Under a Texas Moon* (1930), *Aloha* (1931), *Duck Soup* (1933), *So This Is Africa* (1933) and *The Woman I Stole* (1933). After a British feature, *The Red Wagon*, in 1934, she retired from the screen, but later made an occasional film appearance, as in *Tampico* (1944).

Raquel Torres.

Jose Torvay

B: 2/18/1910

A Mexican-born character actor, Torvay worked in both Mexican films and Hollywood films shot in Mexico. His credits include *The Fugitive* (1947), *The Treasure of the Sierra Madre* (1948), *Border Incident* (1949), *Borderline* (1950) and *Untamed* (1955).

Lupita Tovar

B: 1915

A Mexican-born actress, Tovar starred in the first Mexican sound film, *Santa* (1932). She came to Hollywood in 1931 and starred in many of the Spanish-language films produced in Hollywood, including the Universal Pictures Spanish version of *Dracula* (1931), *The Cat Creeps* (1930) and *The King of Jazz* (1930), produced by Paul Kohner, who at that time was a young, ambitious producer and later became a noted talent agent. He and Lupita were married a few years later. She appeared in numerous films throughout the 1930s and 1940s, including *East of Borneo* (1931), *Yankee Don* (1931), *Border Law* (1931), *Mr. Robinson Crusoe* (1932), *The Fighting Gringo* (1939), *South of the Border* (1939) and *The Westerner* (1940).

Bill Travilla

B: 1923

D: 11/2/1990

An Academy Award®-winning fashion designer, Travilla was under contract at Warner Bros. and then Twentieth Century-Fox, where he designed costumes for the studio's most important films. Travilla was born in Avalon, Santa Catalina, an island twenty-five miles off the Southern California coast. Travilla worked on eleven films with Marilyn Monroe; costumed *Viva Zapata!* (1952), with Marlon Brando; and worked on *The Loretta Young Show* (1953-55). With Leah Rhodes and Marjorie Best, he won the Academy Award® in 1949 for Best Costume Design for *The Adventures of Don Juan*, starring Errol Flynn. Travilla is known for his classic, glamorous, designs for men and women of the Hollywood period of the 1930s, 1940s and 1950s. His best-known creation is the white chiffon dress worn by Marilyn Monroe in *The Seven Year Itch* (1955).

In the 1980s Travilla worked for television, winning Emmy Awards for his costume designs for the series *Dallas* (1978-91) in 1985 and for the miniseries *Moviola* in 1980. He also designed costumes for such other miniseries as *The Thorn Birds* (1983), *Evita Peron* (1981), *Jacqueline Bouvier Kennedy* (1981) and *My Wicked, Wicked Ways* (1985).

Danny Trejo

A former boxing champion, Trejo first began working in films in 1984 while visiting a friend on the set of *Runaway Train* (1985) . Approached by screenwriter Eddie Brucker to choreograph fight sequences and train the film's star (Eric Roberts), he subsequently won a featured role in the film. Trejo went on to appear in such films as *Bound By Honor* (1993), *Desperado* (1995), *Heat* (1995), *From Dusk Till Dawn* (1996), *Anaconda*

(1997), *Con Air* (1997), *The Replacement Killers* (1998), *From Dusk Till Dawn 2: Texas Blood Money* (1999) and *Reindeer Games* (2000). He has also appeared in such episodic television programs as *NYPD Blue* (1993-).

Jesus Trevino

B: 3/26/1946

A Mexican American director, Trevino began in documentaries at public television station KCET in Los Angeles. He directed the feature film *Raices de Sangre* (Blood Roots) (1979) and the *American Playhouse* presentation of *Seguin* (1982). He won the Directors Guild of America Award for Best Daytime Drama Directing for the television film *Gangs* (1988). Trevino has directed episodes of the television series *Chicago Hope* (1994-), *Star Trek: Voyager* (1995-99), *The Practice* (1997-) and *Dawson's Creek* (1998-). Currently, he is directing the Showtime series *Resurrection Blvd.* (2000-), where is also a supervising producer.

Felipe Turich
[aka: Felipe Turriche]

B: 12/5/1898

D: 3/9/1992

A veteran character player, Turich's film career lasted from the 1930s till the late 1970s. Some of his film credits include *We Were Strangers* (1949), *Crisis* (1950), *The Lawless* (1950), *My Favorite Spy* (1951), *Giant* (1956), *One-Eyed Jacks* (1961), *Hook, Line and Sinker* (1969) and *Walk Proud* (1979).

Rosa Turich

B: 1903

D: 10/20/1998

A veteran character actress, Rosa Turich, along with her husband, Felipe, appeared in many Westerns at Republic Pictures from 1937 until 1965, usually as a Mexican mamacita or dona. Some of her film credits include *Starlight over Texas* (1938), *Rangers of Fortune* (1940), *Bowery Buckaroos* (1947), *The Loves of Carmen* (1948), *On the Isle of Samoa* (1950) and *Tripoli* (1950).

Natividad Vacio

B: 9/8/1912

D: 5/30/1996

Born in El Paso, Texas, Vacio started his career as a teacher and musician. He made his film debut in *The Loves of Carmen* (1948) at Columbia with Rita Hayworth. He has worked in countless motion pictures, including *Branded* (1951), *The Magnificent Seven* (1960) and *The Milagro Beanfield War* (1988).

Wilmer Valderrama

Best known for his work on *That '70s Show* (1998-), Valderrama plays Fez on the popular Fox Network series. He moved to Los Angeles from Venezuela with his family in 1995 and landed the role in 1998 after making his professional acting debut in a Spanish Pacific Bell commercial.

David Valdes

The executive producer of Clint Eastwood's *Bird* (1988), *White Hunter, Black Heart* (1990) and the Academy Award®-winning *Unforgiven* (1992). Valdes served as producer of *In the Line of Fire* (1993), *The Stars Fell on Henrietta* (1995), *Turbulence* (1997) and *The Green Mile* (1999). He served as an associate producer of *Pale Rider* (1985).

David Valdes (left) with Clint Eastwood (right).

Valdes rose through the ranks of film production, beginning his career with Francis Ford Coppola as an assistant director on *The Outsiders* (1983) and *Rumble Fish* (1983). He then moved to Clint Eastwood's Malpaso Productions and worked as first assistant director on *Any Which Way You Can* (1980), *Firefox* (1982), *Sudden Impact* (1983), *City Heat* (1984) and *Tightrope* (1984) before becoming a producer.

Valdes also worked with Brian Grazer, co-producing the feature *Like Father, Like Son* (1987), which followed a co-executive producer assignment with producer/director Francis Ford Coppola on *Gardens of Stone* (1987). He was also associate producer of *Ratboy* (1986), starring and directed by Sondra Locke.

Araceli Valdez

See Ara Celi

Daniel Valdez

B: 1949

The brother of Luis Valdez, Daniel is an actor, singer, songwriter and composer and starred as Henry Reyna in the 1981 film *Zoot Suit*. His other film credits include *Which Way Is Up?* (1971), *The China Syndrome* (1979), *La Bamba* (1987), *Born in East L.A.* (1987) and . . . *And the Earth Did Not Swallow Him* (1995). He was an associate producer on *La Bamba*.

Jeff Valdez

Raised in Pueblo, Colorado, Valdez is a writer/ producer who has created programs for NBC, Comedy Central, Showtime, Galavision and syndication including *Café Ole* and the Latino Laugh Festival. He is also co-chairman of Si TV and an executive producer of Nickoledeon's *The Brothers Garcia* (2000-).

Luis Valdez

B: 6/12/1940

Valdez founded El Teatro Campesino (The Farmworkers Theatre) on the strike lines in the fields of Delano, California, during its great grape strike of 1965. He created "actos"—short plays that were performed to dramatize the cause of the farmworkers and urban Chicanos. The Teatro toured these "actos" across the country, garnering for Valdez and the company national attention and acclaim with an off-Broadway Obie Award in 1969 and the Los Angeles Drama Critics Circle Award in

1969 and 1972. In the course of five major European tours, Valdez and ETC earned international plaudits from the World Theatre Festival in France, the Festival of Nations in Paris and numerous other prestigious European festivals.

Zoot Suit, the play that he wrote and directed, became one of the most critically acclaimed productions ever to originate in Los Angeles. Mounted on the New York stage by the Shubert Organization and the Mark Taper Forum, *Zoot Suit* became the first play by a Chicano playwright to be presented on Broadway.

In 1981 Valdez wrote and directed the motion picture version of his hit play *Zoot Suit*, garnering a Golden Globe nomination for Best Musical Picture.

Luis Valdez triumphed in Hollywood in 1987 with the motion picture *La Bamba*, which he wrote and directed for Columbia Pictures. The film was one of the biggest box office successes of that year and made its lead actor, Lou Diamond Phillips, a star. The main title song shot to the top of the charts and, thirty years after its original release, became an international hit once again.

For television, Valdez adapted his stage play (1987). It starred Linda Ronstadt and offered a striking visual history of Mexican folklore and songs, winning acclaim and a George Peabody Award. He went on to write and direct the Christmas fantasy *La Pastorela* (1991), starring Paul Rodriguez and Cheech Marin, for PBS's "Great Performances" series. Valdez directed an unsold series pilot for Warner Bros. Television, *Fort Figueroa*, starring Charles Haid.

His latest play, *I Don't Have to Show You No Stinking Badges*, completed a successful national tour that originated at the Los Angeles Theater Center. In the spring of 1994, a new musical melodrama, *Bandido*, written by Luis Valdez premiered at the Mark Taper Forum in Los Angeles. Also in 1994, Valdez directed a television version of *The Cisco Kid*, starring Jimmy Smits.

Harry Vallejo
[born: Enrique Juan Vallejo]
B: 1883
D: 1950
Born and raised in Mexico City in a well-to-do family, Vallejo left home at age nineteen and came to the United States, where he found work as a film cameraman for Charlie Chaplin, Mack Sennett, Douglas Fairbanks and Mary Pickford. In 1927 he returned to Mexico to make a series of promotional films for the oil industry.

Victor Vallejo
B: 1907
D: 1998
The son of Harry Vallejo, Victor worked as a costumer at Warner Bros. from 1937 to 1957. He became a second assistant director, then a first assistant and later unit manager at Warner Bros. For the next twenty years he was assigned to such episodic film television series as *Maverick* (1957-62), *Hawaiian Eye* (1959-63), *Mission Impossible* (1966-73) and *77 Sunset Strip* (1958-64).

Leonor Varela

Varela made her American feature film debut opposite Leonardo DiCaprio in *The Man in the Iron Mask* (1998). She has gone on to star in the title role of *Cleopatra* (1999) in the epic television miniseries, and in the feature film *Texas Rangers* (2000). Varela, who is of French and Chilean parentage, was born in Chile and raised in the United States, Costa Rica, Germany, Chile and Paris.

Nina Varela

B: 1908

D: 2/12/1982

A Mexican character actress, Varela appeared in numerous Westerns at Republic Pictures in the 1940s and 1950s, usually as a mamacita or dona. Some of her film credits include *Viva Zapata!* (1952), *Niagara* (1953), *Jubilee Trail* (1954) and *Madigan* (1968).

Jacob Vargas

B: 8/18/1970

Vargas' film credits include featured roles in *The Principal* (1987), *American Me* (1992); *Gas, Food, Lodging* (1992); *Mi Vida Loca (1993)*; *My Family* (1995); *Selena* (1997), *Romy and Michele's High School Reunion* (1997), *The Hi-Lo Country* (1998), *Next Friday* (2000), *Traffic* (2000).

John Vargas

B: 4/24/1955

A New York-born Puerto Rican actor, Vargas has been featured in such films as *Only When I Laugh* (1981), *Star Trek II: The Wrath of Khan* (1982), *Mass Appeal* (1984), *Hanoi Hilton* (1987), *Sunset Park* (1996), *Primary Colors* (1998) and *The Minus Man* (1999). He was a series regular on the soap opera *General Hospital* (1963-) and starred in the series *DEA* (1990-91).

Joseph B. Vasquez

B: 1963

D: 12/16/1995

From age twelve, when a family friend gave him an 8mm camera, writer/director Joseph B. Vasquez has been on a nonstop quest to make movies. Vasquez is both African American and Puerto Rican, and his low-budget films include *Street Story* (1989) and *Bronx War* (1991), in which he also acted. He directed the critically acclaimed film *Hangin' with the Homeboys* (1991), which helped to launch the careers of John Leguizamo, Mario Joyner, Doug E. Doug and Nestor Serrano. He has also directed *Street Hitz* (1992) and the video release *Manhattan Merengue!* (1996).

Randy Vasquez

Vasquez made his feature film debut in the Eddie Murphy classic, *Beverly Hills Cop* (1984). He has also appeared in the feature films *Fear City* (1985) and *The Demolitionist* (1995). On television, Randy joined the cast of *JAG* (1995-) in 1999. He previously starred as bar manager Paulo Kaire on UPN's *The Love Boat: The Next Wave* (1998-99) and had a leading role in the series *Acapulco H.E.A.T.* (1993) as well as a recurring role in the daytime drama, *Santa Barbara* (1984-92).

Isela Vega

B: 1940

The beautiful Isela Vega was a number-one film sex symbol and box office attraction in Mexico and Latin America. She capitalized on her beautifully sculptured face and body in revealing wardrobe and nude sequences in her films.

Born in Sonora, Mexico, Vega, by the late 1960s, began to be cast opposite such prominent Mexican leading men as Jorge Rivera, Mauricio Garces, Jorje Luke and even Cantinflas.

Vega made her American film debut in a small role in *The Deadly Trackers* (1973). She followed with a co-starring role as Elita, a burned-out, curvaceous, outspoken woman, in Sam Peckinpah's *Bring Me the Head of Alfredo Garcia* (1974). She proved herself a capable actress without the sexy glitter with co-starring roles in *Drum* (1976) and *Barbarosa* (1982). She has also appeared in the telefilms *The Rhineman Exchange* (1977), *The Streets of L. A.* (1979) and *The Alamo: Thirteen Days to Glory* (1987).

Sylvia Vega Vasquez

A costume designer, Vega Vasquez worked on such films as *La Bamba* (1987), *American Me* (1992), *Menace II Society* (1993), *Murder in the First* (1995), *Set It Off* (1996) and *Black & White* (1998).

Jerry Velasco

B: 1/31/1953

A Mexican-born actor, Velasco has appeared in such films as *The Jerk* (1979), *Boulevard Nights* (1979) and *Heartbreaker* (1983).

Anita Velasquez

Mexican American actress, Velasquez has been featured in such films as *Heartbreak Ridge* (1986), *Vibes* (1988), *In Harm's Way* (1965) and *Hawaii* (1966). Her television credits include *Hawaii Five-o* (1968-80), *Dallas* (1978-91), *The A-Team* (1983-87), *Amen* (1986-91), *L.A. Law* (1986-94).

Eddie Velez

A native of New York City, Velez attended the High School of Art and Design and served in the United States Air Force.

Velez had a major supporting role in the cult film *Repo Man* (1984). His other film credits include a role as a boxer in *Split Decisions* (1988), co-starring Gene Hackman, and *The Women's Club* (1987) with Michael Pare. Velez made his television debut in the NBC series pilot film *For Love and Honor* (1983) and appeared in the telefilms *Drug Wars: The Camarena Story* (1990), *Danger Island* (1992), *Body Bags* (1993), *Bitter Vengeance* (1994) and *A Father's Choice* (2000). He has also appeared on numerous television series, including *Live Shot* (1995) and his current role as Detective Alex Garcia on the soap opera *General Hospital* (1963-) and its spin-off, *Port Charles* (1997-).

Lauren Velez

Born in Puerto Rico, Velez appeared in a variety of Broadway, television and film roles including *I Like It Like That* (1994), *City Hall* (1995) and

Isela Vega starred as Elita, a Mexican girl who becomes involved in a headhunting search in *Bring Me the Head of Alfredo Garcia.*

I Think I Do (1997). On television she is best known for her role as Nina Moreno on the Fox series *New York Undercover* (1994-98). and a recurring role on the HBO series *Oz* (1997-). Velez's Broadway credits include *Into the Woods* and *Dreamgirls*.

Lupe Velez
[born: Guadalupe Villalobos Velez]
B: 1909
D: 12/14/1944

Born in the Mexican town of San Luis Potosi, the daughter of an opera singer and an army colonel, Velez received her formal education in a convent in San Antonio, Texas. The veteran stage actor Richard Bennett discovered Velez in Mexico City appearing in a musical. After a series of dancing jobs in Mexico and Hollywood, she landed her first motion picture assignment in a series of comedies for Hal Roach.

In 1927, at age eighteen, Velez got her start in films by accepting a role as a wild mountain girl opposite Douglas Fairbanks in the silent film *The Gaucho* after Dolores Del Rio turned it down. She received good notices and the film was a hit. Her next major role was as a girl of dubious morals in D.W. Griffith's *Lady of the Pavements* (1928, silent), set in 1868 Paris.

She co-starred in *Wolf Song* (1929) with a young Gary Cooper, who was smitten with Velez. They had an affair that lasted three years, until Cooper's family dissuaded him from marrying her because she was Mexican. In MGM's *Where East Is East* (1929), she played the half-caste daughter of Lon Chaney. In 1931 she did the talkie version of the Del Rio success *Resurrection* with John Boles. She appeared in DeMille's sound remake of *The Squaw Man* (1931), as an Indian maiden. After *Cuban Love Song* in 1931, she turned from heavy dramatics to comedic roles, for which she was better suited. Velez had a stormy five-year marriage to Johnny Weissmuller (the Olympic Gold Medal swimmer and a screen Tarzan), which ended in divorce. She gained new fame in 1939 when she returned in the B comedy *Mexican Spitfire* series for RKO, which proved successful. Her dynamic energy, coupled with rapid-fire line delivery and hot Latin temperament, led Velez to become known as the "Mexican Wildcat" or "Hot Tamale" as a result of these popular comedies. Despondent over a broken love affair that left her pregnant, Velez committed suicide in 1944.

Elena Verdugo
B: 4/20/1927

Elena Verdugo received two Emmy Award nominations as Best Supporting Actress while co-starring for seven years on the top-rated television series *Marcus Welby, M.D.* (1969-76) as Nurse Consuelo Lopez.

Born in Paso Robles, California, Elena was raised in Los Angeles. She is a fifth generation Californian and a direct descendant of Don Jose Maria Verdugo, to whom the King of Spain gave one of the first California land grants over 200 years ago.

As a child, Verdugo displayed a talent for dancing, so she was enrolled at a dance academy. Her first professional appearances were as a child dancer at several of the large downtown Los Angeles movie

Lupe Velez in the 1940s.

theaters. At seventeen she recorded "Tico Tico" with Xavier Cugat's Orchestra. Elena was spotted by a Twentieth Century-Fox talent scout and signed to a contract. She completed her schooling by attending classes with Anne Baxter, Roddy McDowall and Linda Darnell.

She made her film debut when she was only age thirteen, appearing in *Down Argentine Way* (1940) with Don Ameche and Betty Grable. This led to her first major role as a Tahitian beauty opposite George Sanders' Gauguin in the memorable *The Moon and Sixpence* (1942). She later appeared in *House of Frankenstein* (1944), the Abbott and Costello feature *Little Giant* (1946) and *Cyrano de Bergerac* (1950) with Jose Ferrer. In the early 1950s, Verdugo starred in one of CBS-television's biggest hit series, *Meet Millie* (1952-56), which firmly established her as a major talent. She played a secretary in New York with a very blonde, loud-mouthed mother. Following the series she became a popular guest star on numerous shows including *The Red Skelton Show* (1951-71) and *The Bob Cummings Show* (1961-62) and co-starred in *The New Phil Silvers Show* (1963-64).

Noah Verduzco

A child actor, Verduzco gained experience and exposure by appearing in commercials. His screen credits include *Radio Flyer* (1992), *Bound by Honor* (1993) and *D2: The Mighty Ducks* (1994).

James Victor

B: 7/27/1939

Born in the Dominican Republic, Victor immigrated with his family to New York City at age four. His feature film credits include *Rolling Thunder* (1977), as Lopez, a barroom brawler; *Boulevard Nights* (1979), as an auto shop owner; *Defiance* (1980), as a Puerto Rican priest; *Borderline* (1980), a Charles Bronson thriller in which he co-starred as Mirandez, the truck driver importing more than tomatoes across the border; and *Losin' It* (1983), in which he played a shady lawyer opposite Shelley Long. He went on to roles in *Stand and Deliver* (1987), *Executive Decision* (1996), with Kurt Russell.

In 1976, Victor starred in *Viva Valdez* (1976), the first prime-time network series to feature a Hispanic family. In 1982, he was signed for his second series, *Condo* (1983), an ABC situation comedy, as a seventy-five-year-old grandfather, a transformation which required forty-five-minute of makeup. He spent four seasons in Spain in the role of the bumbling Sergeant Garcia in New World Television's *Zorro* (1990-93) starring Duncan Regehr. He has appeared in the mini series *The Streets of Laredo* (1995) and the telefilm *The Second Civil War* (1997). Victor also has extensive theater credits in New York and Los Angeles.

Christina Vidal

B: 1982

A Puerto Rican child actress, Vidal starred in *Life with Mikey*, opposite Michael J. Fox, in 1993. She went on to star in Todd Solondz's critically acclaimed *Welcome to the Dollhouse* (1995) and *Nick Freno: Licensed Teacher* (1996-98) for the WB.

Elena Verdugo in her Emmy Award-winning role as Nurse Consuelo Lopez on *Marcus Welby, M.D.*

Lisa Vidal

Vidal's feature film credits include *Night and the City* (1992), *I Like It Like That* (1995), *The Wonderful Ice Cream Suit* (1998) and *Active Stealth* (1999). On television, she has appeared in the telefilms *The Third Twin* (1997), *The Taking of Pelham One, Two, Three* (1998) and *Naked City: A Killer Christmas* (1998). She has also starred in the series *High Incident* (1996-97), and guest starred on such shows as *Miami Vice* (1984-89), *New York Undercover* (1994-98) and *Law & Order* (1990-).

Reynaldo Villalobos

Villalobos has created memorable images for a remarkably diverse list of films, among them *9 to 5* (1980), *The Ballad of Gregorio Cortez* (1983), *Risky Business* (1983), *Punchline* (1988), *Major League* (1989), *Coupe de Ville* (1990), *American Me* (1992), *A Bronx Tale* (1993), *Romy and Michele's High School Reunion* (1997), *Return to Paradise* (1998) and *Love and Basketball* (2000).

Director of photography Reynaldo Villalobos (at camera) shooting a scene from *Punchline*, the bittersweet story about making it in the world of comedy.

He has also directed episodes of several television series, including *Tour of Duty* (1987-90), *Midnight Caller* (1988-91) and *L.A. Doctors* (1998-99). Villalobos directed *Conagher* (1991) for Turner Network Television and the Paramount Home Video release *Hollywood Confidential* (1997) starring Edward James Olmos.

The Los Angeles-born cinematographer was raised in Los Angeles, where his father was a standby painter on movie sets before running several studio paint departments. After high school, the younger Villalobos attended El Camino College and Dominican State College, majoring in art and design. He then enlisted in the Navy, where he worked as a photographer.

Returning to civilian life, Villalobos was employed as a studio laborer, painting and hauling equipment, before being hired as an assistant cameraman for *The Young Lawyers* in 1969.

After only eight months of camera crew experience, Villalobos was promoted to first assistant cameraman. He worked in that capacity for eight years before becoming an operator. He began his career as a cinematographer on *Urban Cowboy* (1980).

Carlos Villar
[born: Carlos Villarias]

Born in Cordoba, Spain, the actor Carlos Villor starred in the Spanish-language version of Universal's *Dracula* in 1931. He occasionally worked in English-language film roles throughout the 1930s and 1940s. He also appeared in the part of the head waiter in *Bordertown* (1935).

He lived in Cuba for many years and then went to Spain and was never heard of again. He is presumed to be deceased, for he could not be located in 1992 to be invited to attend a screening of the restored Spanish *Dracula* in Spain.

Daniel Villarreal

B: 11/19/1960

Villarreal played an unreachable gang tough in *Stand and Deliver* (1988), a young prison gang member in *American Me* (1992); and the role of Ray in the hit film, *Speed* (1994), with Keanu Reeves and Sandra Bullock.

Mike Vitar

B: 1979

A native of the Los Angeles area, Vitar played Benny Rodriguez in the film *The Sandlot* (1993) and Luis Mendoza in *D2: The Mighty Ducks* (1994) and *D3: The Mighty Ducks* (1996). On television he appeared on CBS's acclaimed series, *Brooklyn Bridge* (1991-94).

Sam Vlahos

B: 8/10/1935

Born in San Diego, California, of a Greek father and a Mexican mother, Vlahos has appeared in such feature films as *Summer and Smoke* (1961), *The Milagro Beanfield War* (1988), *Powwow Highway* (1989), *Kiss Me a Killer* (1991); *Steal Little, Steal Big* (1995); *Lone Star* (1996), *The Disappearance of Garcia Lorca* (1997), *American History X* (1998). He has made many episodic television appearances on such series from *Hawaiian Eye* (1959-63) in the early 1960s to *Hill Street Blues* (1981-87) in the 1980s and *General Hospital* (1963-) in the 1990s.

Raoul Walsh

B: 3/11/1887

D: 12/31/1980

Raoul Walsh was noted for his fast-moving direction of rugged and masculine action adventure films and roustabout comedies, where women fared well as strong, independent, pioneering types integral to his stories.

Born in New York City to a Spanish mother and Irish father, Walsh spent his late teens as a cowboy, traveling through Mexico and the American West. He later worked with his uncle as a seaman en route to Cuba. One of his first assignments as a filmmaker was working for D.W. Griffith, who sent him to Mexico to film the real-life exploits of Pancho Villa.

Walsh directed and shaped the exploits of the Cisco Kid in the early outdoor sound film *In Old Arizona* (1929). He had intended to play the leading role himself, but an unfortunate accident on location resulted in the loss of one eye, which ended his career as an actor. Walsh had already directed most of the outdoor action sequences, and director Irving Cummings guided actor Warner Baxter, who replaced Walsh, into an Academy Award®-winning role as the Cisco Kid.

Walsh also directed Dolores Del Rio in her first major screen role as the French farm maiden in the hit silent film *What Price Glory?* (1926), and as Carmen in *The Loves of Carmen* (1927). His critical acclaim now rests primarily with directorial work he did for Warner Bros. from 1939 through 1951.

Raoul Walsh.

He directed Cornel Wilde in a featured role as hotel clerk Victor Mendoza in the classic *High Sierra* (1941) starring Humphrey Bogart. He directed Anthony Quinn as Chief Crazy Horse in *They Died with Their Boots On* (1941) starring Errol Flynn, and fifteen years later in a starring role as a Portuguese sailor opposite Gregory Peck in the two-fisted nineteenth-century Barbary Coast drama *The World in His Arms* (1952). Walsh also directed Joel McCrea as a cowboy on the run and Virginia Mayo as a "half-breed" Mexican girl in *Colorado Territory* (1949). In *Distant Drums* (1951), he directed Gary Cooper in a tale of Yankee soldiers fighting Indians in the Everglades and Spanish soldiers along the Florida coast. In *Captain Horatio Hornblower* (1951), Walsh directed a romantic seafaring tale with Gregory Peck in the title role of a British naval captain at war with the French and the Spanish.

Ethan Wayne

B: 1962

The youngest son of actor John Wayne and his Peruvian-born wife, Pilar, Ethan was featured as the young boy who is kidnapped in *Big Jake* (1971), starring his father. He starred as an adult on the new *Adam 12* (1989-90) syndicated television series and on *The Bold and the Beautiful* (1987-). He has guest starred on several episodic series.

Raquel Welch in 1993.

Raquel Welch
[born: Raquel Tejada]
B: 9/5/1940

The last of the studio-manufactured screen sex goddesses, Raquel Welch reached the heights of popularity during the mid-1960s and early 1970s. She was born in Chicago, the daughter of Armand C. Tejada, a Bolivian-born engineer, and Josephine Sarah Hall. In over thirty-five films she has played opposite such leading actors as Richard Burton, Burt Reynolds, Dudley Moore, James Stewart, Frank Sinatra, Dean Martin, Vittorio De Sica, Jean-Paul Belmondo and Bill Cosby. She has worked with such directors as Stanley Donen, Richard Lester, Herbert Ross, Peter Yates and James Ivory.

Welch made her film debut in a small role as a college student in the Elvis Presley film *Roustabout* (1964) and soon after landed another small role, as a bordello girl in *A House Is Not a Home* (1964), starring Shelley Winters. A contract starlet at Twentieth Century-Fox, she was groomed for stardom after she gained attention as a beautiful bikini-clad prehistoric woman in *One Million Years B.C.* (1967). In 1965 *Time* magazine called her "The Nation's Number One Sex Symbol." In that one year, she was cast in four major productions, *The Biggest Bundle of Them All* (1968), *The Lovely Ladies* (1966), *Shoot Loud, Louder, I Don't Understand!* (1966) opposite Marcello Mastroianni, and the lead role in *Fathom* (1967). The response to her publicity photos and the attention drawn to her prompted the studio to cast her opposite important male stars in big-budget films such as *Fantastic Voyage* (1966) with Stephen Boyd, *Bandolero!* (1968) with Dean Martin and James Stewart, and *Lady in Cement* (1968) with Frank Sinatra.

Her roles in these films capitalized on her physical beauty and screen presence. She was cast as Maria, a Mexican woman, in

Bandolero!, and as Sarita, a Mexican Yaqui Indian, in *100 Rifles* (1969). Among her other film credits are *Bedazzled* (1967), *Kansas City Bomber* (1972), *The Last of Sheila* (1973), *The Wild Party* (1975) and *Mother, Jugs & Speed* (1976). As she matured, critics recognized her acting ability, beginning with Richard Lester's *The Three Musketeers* (1974). However, by this time her screen sex goddess image was so etched in the public mind that she could not escape it and the box office response to her films dipped. She did utilize her screen image to her advantage when she gambled and took over for Lauren Bacall in the Broadway musical *Woman of the Year* (1981). Audience curiosity over seeing the legendary body beautiful in person boosted ticket sales, and critics and audiences alike were surprisingly pleased with her live performing and acting abilities. Welch continued her live performing in Las Vegas and Atlantic City as well as in concert halls in London, Paris and Rio de Janeiro. On television she gave a critically acclaimed performance in the telefilm *Right to Die* (1987), as a victim of Lou Gehrig's disease, and followed that with *Scandal in a Small Town* (1988). In a *New York Times* interview on October 7, 1987, she remarked of her role in the television film, "I was letting go of everything I had ever used before in a part, everything that was the public Raquel Welch. It was a big relief. There was a great freedom in knowing for myself how much there was, without all that, and what a range of things I can look forward to personally, as well as for myself as an actress."

Recently, she had a starring role in the short-lived series, *Central Park West* (1995-96) and was featured in the telefilm *Chairman of the Board* (1998).

She is currently a woman's fitness guru, with herself as a stunning example.

Tahnee Welch

The daughter of Raquel Welch, Tahnee made her television debut on *Falcon Crest* (19981-90). Her feature film credits included *Cocoon* (1985) *Cocoon: The Return* (1988), *Improper Conduct* (1994), *I Shot Andy Warhol* (1996) and *Body and Soul* (1998).

Guy Williams
[born: Armando Catalano]
B: 1924
D: 5/8/1989

An actor whose name became a household word, Guy Williams became an overnight star with his role in the popular 1950s television series *Zorro* (1957-59) The 6'3" second-generation Italian American was born in New York City. He was chosen by Walt Disney to portray Zorro on television, the role having been made famous in motion pictures by Douglas Fairbanks, Sr. and later by Tyrone Power.

He could never quite equal the success of the *Zorro* films and was forever identified as the "Masked Avenger of Early California." He went on to guest star on a number of episodes of the television series *Bonanza* (1959-73) as a cousin to the Cartwright family. Williams starred in two theatrical films, *The Prince and the Pauper* (1962) and *Captain Sinbad* (1963).

Guy Williams, who starred in the Walt Disney TV series as Zorro.

From 1965 through 1968 Williams starred as Professor John Robinson in the television series *Lost in Space* (1965-68). He was offered the role of Zorro for the short-lived *Zorro and Son* comedy series for Disney, but he turned down the role. He remained inactive in films and television until his death of a heart attack in Buenos Aires, where he had resided off and on for several years.

David Wisnievitz

Born in Mexico City, Wisnievitz has worked as the co-executive producer of *Selena* (1997) and was production manager on the films *The Milagro Beanfield War* (1988) and *The Ballad of Gregorio Cortez* (1983). His other feature film credits include *Valentino Returns* (1988), *The Old Gringo* (1989), *Talent for the Game* (1991), *White Sands* (1992), *Searching for Bobby Fischer* (1993), *Marvin's Room* (1996), *Sliding Doors* (1998) and *A Civil Action* (1999).

David Yanez

A child actor, Yanez appeared in many episodic television series and films during the late 1970s and throughout the 1980s, usually as a Native American or Hispanic youth. His credits include the miniseries *Centennial* (1978) and the film *Born in East L.A.* (1987).

Alfred Ybarra

B: 1907
An art director, Ybarra has worked on such films as *The High and the Mighty* (1954) and the 1960 epic *The Alamo* for Batjac, John Wayne's production company.

A native-born Californian and a direct descendant of the original founding families of Los Angeles, Ybarra was an architect before entering the movie industry and spent two years on the plans for the Empire State Building in New York City. He entered the motion picture business as a set designer in 1935 at the Samuel Goldwyn Studios and became an art director in 1943. Ybarra worked for RKO Radio Pictures and oversaw the construction of their Churubusco Studios facility in Mexico City during the mid-1940s. He was production designer and art director on a number of films shot in Mexico during this period. Among his many credits as an art director are *The Fugitive* (1947), *The Bullfighter and the Lady* (1951), *Track of the Cat* (1954), *Blood Alley* (1955) and *The Comancheros* (1961). He retired in 1967.

Rocky Ybarra

B: 1900
D: 1965
A cowboy actor and stuntman, Ybarra worked in countless motion pictures, including *Viva Zapata!* (1952).

Richard Yniguez

B: 12/8/1946
A handsome Mexican American leading man, Yniguez starred in *Boulevard Nights* (1979) and *Raices de Sangre* (Blood Roots) (1979).

Yniguez has had major roles in such films as *Zandy's Bride* (1974) and *Cancel My Reservation* (1972). He has starred in the telefilms *Tribes* (1970), *The Deadly Tower* (1975), *River of Promises* (1977), *Memories Never Die* (1982), *The Dirty Dozen: The Fatal Mission* (1988), *Rio Diablo* (1993), *The Second Civil War* (1997) and the video release, *Judgment Day* (1999).

Born in Firebaugh, California, and raised in Sacramento, Yniguez moved with his family to Mexico, where he spent his early teenage years and considered a vocation in the priesthood. But at seventeen, he returned to California and served in the United States Navy for three years. Later, he attended East Los Angeles College, supporting himself as a night attendant in a mortuary. Considering his career options, he began writing songs and acting in local theater and aspired to start his own theater group. In 1968, Yniguez won his first daytime television role in *Cancion de la Raza* for PBS. It was the first Chicano-written and -produced series on television. Many guest appearances followed on such shows as *Marcus Welby, M.D.* (1969-76), *Bonanza* (1959-73), *Hawaii Five-O* (1968-80), *The Streets of San Francisco* (1972-77) and *Simon & Simon* (1981-88).

Joe Yrigoyen
B: 1910
D: 1/11/1998
A veteran Basque stuntman and actor, Yrigoyen was featured in numerous serials and films from the mid-1930s until 1965. Yrigoyen doubled for Roy Rogers in many Westerns and worked at Republic pictures from 1935 to 1958. His film credits include *Zorro's Fighting Legion* (1939), *Dark Command* (1940), *Saddle Pals* (1947), *Susanna Pass* (1949), *Ben Hur* (1959), *The Sons of Katie Elder* (1965).

Daniel Zacapa
His feature film credits include *Boulevard Nights* (1979) *Se7en* (1995), *Up Close & Personal* (1996), *The Odd Couple II* (1998), *The Mexican* (2001) and the telefilm *Witness Protection* (1999). He has appeared as a guest star on such television shows as *Beverly Hills, 90210* (1990-2000), *Diagnosis Murder* (1993-) and *The Practice* (1997-).

Del Zamora
Born in Roswell, New Mexico, Zamora was featured as one of the Castillo brothers in Repo Man (1984). Other film credits include *Sid and Nancy* (1986), *Born in East L.A.* (1987), *RoboCop* (1987), *Powwow Highway* (1998), *Man's Best Friend* (1993), *The Outfitters* (1999) and *Tortilla Heaven* (2000).

Carmen Zapata
B: 1927
During more than forty years in the industry, Zapata has enjoyed a highly diversified career as an actress, producer, translator, lecturer and narrator. Her career began in 1946 on the Broadway stage in the musical *Oklahoma!* She followed in other musicals such as *Bells Are Ringing* (1956), *Guys and Dolls* (1957) and many others. The Mexican American actress has been featured in many film roles including *Sol Madrid*

(1968), *Hail, Hero!* (1969), *Pete and Tillie* (1972), *Boulevard Nights* (1979) and as one of the nuns in the chorus in *Sister Act* (1992), starring Whoopi Goldberg. She has appeared in recurring roles on *Flamingo Road* (1981-82)" and *The Dick Van Dyke Show* (1971-74), and was seen for three years on the daytime soap *Santa Barbara* (1984-92) as Carmen Castillo. Zapata starred in a short-lived prime-time series, *Viva Valdez* (1976), and for nine seasons starred in PBS's bilingual children's series, *Villa Alegre*. She is a co-founder of the Bilingual Foundation of the Arts, a resident theater company in Los Angeles.

Zeppy Zepulveda

A longtime property master at Universal Studios, Zepulveda propped many movies during Universal's Golden Age from the late 1930s through the early 1970s.

Daphne Zuniga
B: 10/28/1962

Zuniga has co-starred in such films as Rob Reiner's comedy *The Sure Thing* (1985), as a traveling college student; Mel Brooks' *Spaceballs* (1987), as a Mercedes-riding space princess; and *The Fly II* (1989), as a computer programmer who falls in love with the ill-fated son of The Fly.

Born in San Francisco and raised in Berkeley, California, Zuniga lived briefly with her family in Vancouver, B.C. It was there at age twelve that she first appeared on stage, performing in a production of *H.M.S. Pinafore*. She performed in school and community stage productions and studied at the American Conservatory Theatre in San Francisco. Zuniga enrolled in UCLA's theater arts program, and in 1984, the actress made her professional debut in the thriller *The Initiation*. Among her other feature film credits are *Vision Quest* (1985) opposite Matthew Modine, *Modern Girls* (1986) and *Last Rites* (1988), as a Mexican temptress opposite Tom Berenger. Her television credits include the films *Stone Pillow* (1985) opposite Lucille Ball and *Quarterback Princess* (1983). She is best known for her role as Jo Reynolds, a beautiful strong-willed photographer in the Fox series *Melrose Place* (1992-99). Recent credits include the miniseries *Degree of Guilt* (1995), *Pandora's Clock* (1996) and the feature film *Artificial Lies* (2000).

Frank Zuniga
B: 3/20/1936

A film director, Zuniga's credits include the Goldwyn Company's *The Golden Seal* (1983), *Heartbreaker* (1983) and *Fist Fighter* (1988). Born in New Mexico, Zuniga began his career at Walt Disney Studios, where he was a cameraman and later a director on a number of wildlife films.

Jose Zuniga

His feature film credits include *Alive* (1993), *Crooklyn* (1994), *Smoke* (1995), *Striptease* (1996), Con Air (1997), *Hurricane Streets* (1998), *The Opportunists* (1999) and *Tortilla Heaven* (2000). Zuniga has also appeared on episodic television, in such shows as *Nothing Sacred* (1997), *Mad About You* (1992-99) and *NYPD Blue* (1993-).

Bibliography

Adams, Les, and Rainey, Buck—*Shoot Em Ups* (Arlington House:
New Rochelle, NY, 1978).

Agan, Patrick—*The Decline and Fall of The Love Goddesses* (Pinnacle
Books: Century City, CA, 1979).

Belafonte, Dennis, and Marill, Alvin H.—*The Films of Tyrone Power*
(Citadel Press: New York, 1979).

Bell, Geoffrey—*The Golden Gate and the Silver Screen*
(Cornwall Books: New York, 1984).

Boetticher, Budd—*When In Disgrace* (Neville Publishing:
Santa Barbara, CA, 1989).

Buscombe, Edward—*The BFI Companion To The Western*
(Atheneum: New York, 1988).

Cardoso, Abel, Jr.—*Carmen Miranda* (Simbolo S.A. Industria, Graficas:
São Paulo, Brasil, 1978).

Crowther, Bruce—*Charlton Heston: The Epic Presence* (Columbus
Books: London, England, 1986).

De Usabel, Gaizka—*The High Noon of American Film in Latin America*
(UMI Research Press: Ann Arbor, MI, 1982).

Eames, John Douglas—*The MGM Story* (Crown Publishers:
New York, NY, 1976).

Eames, John Douglas—*The Paramount Story* (Crown Publishers:
New York, NY, 1985).

Everson, William K.—*The Films of Laurel and Hardy* (Citadel Press:
New York, NY, 1967).

Gallagher, Tag—*John Ford: The Man and His Films* (University Of
California Press: Los Angeles, CA, 1986).

Gunning, Tom—*D.W. Griffith and the Origin of American Narrative
Film* (University of Illinois Press: Urbana and Chicago, 1991).

Haskell, Molly—*From Reverence To Rape* (Holt, Rinehart & Winston:
New York, NY, 1974).

Hirschhorn, Clive—*The Columbia Story* (Crown Publishers:
New York, NY, 1989).

Hirschhorn, Clive—*The Warner Bros, Story* (Crown Publishers:
New York, NY, 1979).

Hurst, Richard Maurice—*Republic Studios: Between Poverty Row and
The Majors* (Scarecrow Press: Metuchen, NJ, 1979).

Huston, John—*An Open Book* (Alfred A. Knopf: New York, NY, 1980).

Jewell, Richard B., and Harbin, Vernon—*The RKO Story* (Arlington House: New York, NY, 1982).

Koszarski, Diane Kaiser—*The Complete Films of William S. Hart* (Dover Publications: New York, NY, 1980).

Langman, Larry—*A Guide To Silent Westerns* (Greenwood Press: Westport, CT, 1992).

McCarty, John—*The Complete Films of John Huston* (Citadel Press: New York, NY,1990).

Miller, Frank—*Casablanca: As Time Goes By* (Turner Publishing: Atlanta, GA, 1992).

Mora, Carl J.—*Mexican Cinema: Reflections of a Society, 1896-1988* (University of California Press: Los Angeles, CA, 1989).

Nash, Jay R., and Ross, Stanley R.—*Motion Picture Guide,* 12 vols. (Bowker: New York, NY, 1986).

Newman, Kim—*Wild West Movies* (Bloombury Publishing Limited: London, England, 1990).

Noriega, Chon—*Chicanos and Film* (Garland Publishing: New York, NY, 1992).

Okuda, Ted—*The Monogram Checklist: The Films of Monogram Pictures Corporation, 1931-1958* (McFarland: Jefferson, NC, 1987).

Oshana, Maryann—*Women of Color: A Filmography of Minority and Third World Women* (Garland Publishing: New York, NY, 1985).

Parish, James Robert—*The Paramount Pretties* (Arlington House: New Rochelle, NY, 1972).

Parish, James Robert—*The RKO Gals* (Arlington House: New Rochelle, NY, 1974).

Parish, James Robert, and Bowers, Robert L.—*The MGM Stock Company* (Arlington House: New Rochelle, NY, 1973).

Sennett, Ted—*Warner Bros. Presents* (Arlington House: New Rochelle, NY, 1971).

Shipman, David—*The Great Movie Stars: The International Years* (Hill and Wang: New York, NY, 1980).

Vermilye, Jerry—*Burt Lancaster: A Pictorial Treasury* (Fallon Enterprises: New York, NY, 1971).

Walsh, Raoul—*Each Man in His Own Time* (Farrar, Strauss, & Giroux: New York, NY, 1974).

Wiley, Mason, and Bona, Damien—*Inside Oscar: The Unofficial History of the Academy Awards* (Ballantine Books: New York, NY, 1988).

Zmijewsky, Boris, and Pfeiffer, Lee—*The Films of Clint Eastwood* (Citadel Press: New York, NY, 1982, 1988).

Also from LONE EAGLE PUBLISHING . . .

1001: A VIDEO ODYSSEY
Movies To Watch For Your Every Mood!
by Steve Tatham

1001: A VIDEO ODYSSEY is the *must-have* video guide for every movie lover searching for the perfect video to rent (or buy). No more standing around the video store feeling foolish! This entertaining and often hilarious guide points you toward movies you absolutely need to see, movies you may have missed and movies you never even thought of watching, all cleverly organized and grouped by politically correct—and not so correct—feelings.

Written with wit, attitude and a touch of sarcasm, 1001: A VIDEO ODYSSEY contains capsule reviews and commentary of 1,001 movies in one hundred categories reflecting every mood, emotion, sentiment, attitude, and seasonal holiday. For each movie entry, author Steve Tatham lists the title, rating, cast members, availability on video/DVD, and commentary with a wicked sense of humor. Unlike many rival video guides, the book includes junk food suggestions that have been specifically selected for each category as well as a collection of off-beat quotes and dialogue.

Steve Tatham has performed stand-up comedy all over the world and has appeared numerous times in print, on the radio and on television. He is a writer at Walt Disney Imagineering, and he lives in Los Angeles.

$15.95 ISBN 1-58065-23-6, original trade paper, 8 x 10, 304 pp.

THE ULTIMATE FILM FESTIVAL SURVIVAL GUIDE
The Essential Companion for Filmmakers and Festival-Goers
by Chris Gore

Learn the secrets of successfully marketing and selling your film at over 500 film festivals worldwide. THE ULTIMATE FILM FESTIVAL SURVIVAL GUIDE reveals how to get a film accepted and what to do after acceptance, from putting together a press kit to putting on a great party to actually closing a deal. Easy to flip through, yet densely packed with information, this book will provide an inside perspective valuable to those who attend or enter festivals.

"Aspiring Todd Solondzes simply must pick up this treatise..."
—*Entertainment Weekly*

"Prospective filmmakers should purchase this title."
—*Library Journal*

Described as a "Roger Ebert of the people" and "the Gen-X Leonard Maltin," Chris Gore is the publisher of *Film Threat Weekly* and host of *The New Movie Show with Chris Gore* on FX Network.

$14.95 ISBN 1-58065-009-0, original trade paper, 6 x 9, 400 pp., over 25 celebrity pictures from film festivals

A CUT ABOVE: 50 FILM DIRECTORS
TALK ABOUT THEIR CRAFT
by Michael Singer, foreword by Leonard Maltin

Michael Singer takes the reader on an inside look at the craft, art, passion and vision of 50 great film directors. Candid, unrestrained conversations weave a personal, never-before-seen intimacy to each interview. This collection of elite artists from Hollywood and around the world elucidates significant developments in filmmaking and sheds a surprising new light on many familiar faces.

Michael Singer is an entertainment freelance journalist who has written many Making Of... books based upon studio film releases.

$19.95 ISBN 1-58065-000-7, original trade paper, 6 x 9, 224 pp.

To order or request a catalog, call 800-345-6257

Also from LONE EAGLE PUBLISHING . . .

FILMMAKER'S DICTIONARY, 2nd Edition

by Ralph S. Singleton and James A. Conrad

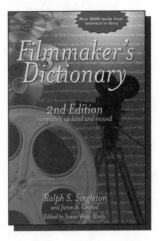

Hailed when it was first published as the "definitive film dictionary," FILMMAKER'S DICTIONARY has been completely updated and revised. This new edition covers all of the latest advances in filmmaking, including the huge impact of the digital and technology revolution, as well as the many changes that have taken place in the film business over the past few years. The new edition has been expanded to include over 5000 terms.

"So you don't know what pups, snoots, kooks, high hats, velocilators and wigwags are? Look them up in the Filmmaker's Dictionary, a marvelously comprehensive book that offers cincise nuts and bolts definitions of technical and legal terms used in scripts, contracts and every aspect of production and distribution. Also included are definitions for on-set slang and tradepaper jargon. Indispensable..."

—*Library Journal*

Ralph Singleton is an award-winning producer whose credits include *Taxi Driver, Another 48 Hrs* and *Clear and Present Danger* among many other distinguished movies. He has written four other film books on various aspects of film production, including *Film Scheduling* and *Film Budgeting.*

$22.95 ISBN 1-58065-022-8, original trade hardcover, 6 x 9, 360 pp.

TEN THOUSAND BULLETS

The Cinematic Journey of John Woo

by Christopher Heard

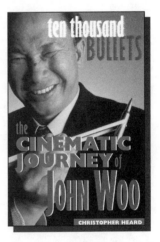

John Woo, Hollywood's hottest action film director, the man behind the scenes of *Face/Off, Broken Arrow, The Killer,* and the sequel to *Mission Impossible* starring Tom Cruise, has made a remarkable transition from his Hong Kong roots to his current American success. This sought-after director's cinematic history is the subject of this fascinating book, which opens on his early life in the violent slums of Hong Kong and follows Woo through his U.S. breakthrough.

Christopher Heard is a Canadian film critic who has interviewed hundreds of celebrities and reported on the Hollywood filmmaking scene for many years. He is the author of *Dreaming Aloud: The Life and Films of James Cameron* (Doubleday). He lives in Toronto.

$15.95 ISBN 1-58065-021-X, original trade paper, 6 x 9, 288 pp.

SILENT PICTURES

A Skewed Look at Showbiz

by Katie Maratta

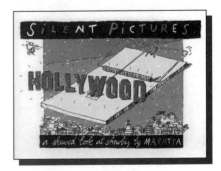

Maratta's incisive and often biting cartoons have given Hollywood something to laugh at, paste on bulletin boards, fax to others and generally wish they would have authored themselves. SILENT PICTURES gives readers an inside look at the "the biz."

$9.95 ISBN 0943728-49-5, original trade paper.

To order or request a catalog, call 800-345-6257

About the Author

Luis I. Reyes is a veteran film and television publicist whose credits include *The Lonely Guy, Zoot Suit, Stand and Deliver, American Me, Hoosiers* and New Line Cinema's *My Family*. He has also worked on HBO's *The Josephine Baker Story*, TNT's *The Cisco Kid*, the CBS-TV series *Dr. Quinn: Medicine Woman* and Showtime's *Resurrection Blvd.*

Reyes is an acknowledged authority on the history of Hispanics in the films of Hollywood and Hawaii and is generally credited with salvaging and chronicling Hollywood's Latino heritage. Reyes has been featured on CNN's *Showbiz Today*, the A&E *Biography* series and E! Entertainment Television, as well as in *USA Today*, the *Los Angeles Times*, the *San Francisco Chronicle*, and the *New York Daily News*. Reyes is also the author of *Made in Paradise: Hollywood's Films of Hawaii and the South Seas* (Honolulu, Mutual Publishing, 1995).

Reyes has lectured on film at UCLA and California State University, Northridge, and is a member of both the Director's Guild of America and The Publicists Guild. His articles on film have appeared in the *Los Angeles Times, The Oakland Tribune, Hemispheres* (United Airlines' in-flight magazine) and *Hawaii* magazine.

For three consecutive years, Reyes has curated his extensive photographic archives into an exhibit, "Latinos in Hollywood," for the City of Los Angeles' Latino Heritage month celebration and also an exhibit for the Autry Museum of Western Heritage in Los Angeles.

Reyes began his love affair with movies as a youngster growing up in a tenement apartment on New York's Upper West Side, where he frequently attended local cinemas and started collecting film still and movie posters.

He lives in Southern California with his family.